24 95

Programmer's Ref

D0599315

Microsoft® Open
Database Connectivity™
Software Development Kit
Version 2.0

For the Microsoft Windows™ and Windows NT™ Operating Systems

PUBLISHED BY
Microsoft Press
A Division of Microsoft Corporation
One Microsoft Way
Redmond, Washington 98052-6399

Library of Congress Cataloging-in-Publication Data
Microsoft ODBC 2.0 programmer's reference and SDK guide : for
  Microsoft Windows and Windows NT / Microsoft Corporation.
        p.   cm.
    Includes index.
    ISBN 1-55615-658-8
      1. Microsoft Windows (Computer file)   2. Windows NT.   3. ODBC.
  I. Microsoft Corporation.
  QA76.76.W56M56323   1994
  005.75'8--dc20   94-5039
                                                                CIP

Lucida Typeface Software. © 1985–1988 and 1990 by Bigelow & Holmes.
U.S. Patent Nos. D289420, D289421, D289422, D289773

U. S. Patent No. 4955066

Printed and bound in the United States of America.

  2 3 4 5 6 7 8 9 MLML 9 8 7 6 5 4

Contents

Part 2   Developing Applications

Part 5   API Reference

Appendixes

About This Manual

The Microsoft® Open Database Connectivity™ (ODBC) interface is a C programming language interface for database connectivity. This manual addresses the following questions:

- What is the ODBC interface?
- What features does ODBC offer?
- How do applications use the interface?

The following topics provide information about the organization of this manual, describe the knowledge necessary to use the ODBC interface effectively, set out the typographic conventions used, and give a listing of references that provide information about Structured Query Language (SQL) standards and SQL in conjunction with relational databases.

Organization of this Manual

This manual is organized into the following parts:

- Part 1 *Introduction to ODBC*, providing conceptual information about the ODBC interface and a brief history of Structured Query Language;
- Part 2 *Developing Applications,* containing information for developing applications using the ODBC interface;
- Part 3 *Developing Drivers*, containing information for developing drivers that support ODBC function calls;
- Part 4 *Installing and Configuring ODBC Software*, providing information about installation and a setup DLL function reference;
- Part 5 *API Reference*, containing syntax and semantic information for all ODBC functions.

Audience

The ODBC software development kit is available for use with the C programming language run with the Microsoft Windows™ operating system and the Microsoft Windows NT™ operating system. Use of the ODBC interface spans four areas: SQL statements, ODBC function calls, C programming, and Windows programming. For information about Windows programming, see the Microsoft Windows and Microsoft Windows NT Software Development Kit development tools for building Microsoft Windows applications. This manual assumes:

- A working knowledge of the C programming language.
- General DBMS knowledge and a familiarity with SQL.

Document Conventions

This manual uses the following typographic conventions.

Format	Used for
WIN.INI	Uppercase letters indicate filenames, SQL statements, macro names, and terms used at the operating-system command level.
RETCODE SQLFetch(hdbc)	This font is used for sample command lines and program code.
argument	Italicized words indicate information that the user or the application must provide, or word emphasis.
SQLTransact	Bold type indicates that syntax must be typed exactly as shown, including function names.
[ ]	Brackets indicate optional items; if in bold text, brackets must be included in the syntax.
|	A vertical bar separates two mutually exclusive choices in a syntax line.
{ }	Braces delimit a set of mutually exclusive choices in a syntax line; if in bold text, braces must be included in the syntax.
...	An ellipsis indicates that arguments can be repeated several times.
. . .	A column of three dots indicates continuation of previous lines of code.

Where to Find Additional Information

For more information about SQL, the following standards are available:

- Database Language—SQL with Integrity Enhancement, ANSI, 1989 ANSI X3.135-1989.
- X/Open and SQL Access Group SQL CAE specification (1992).
- Database Language—SQL: ANSI X3H2 and ISO/IEC JTC1/SC21/WG3 9075:1992 (SQL-92).

In addition to standards and vendor-specific SQL guides, there are many books that describe SQL, including:

- Date, C. J.: *A Guide to the SQL Standard* (Addison-Wesley, 1989).
- Emerson, Sandra L., Darnovsky, Marcy, and Bowman, Judith S.: *The Practical SQL Handbook* (Addison-Wesley, 1989).
- Groff, James R. and Weinberg, Paul N.: *Using SQL* (Osborne McGraw-Hill, 1990).
- Gruber, Martin: *Understanding SQL* (Sybex, 1990).
- Hursch, Jack L. and Carolyn J.: *SQL, The Structured Query Language* (TAB Books, 1988).
- Pascal, Fabian: *SQL and Relational Basics* (M & T Books, 1990).
- Trimble, J. Harvey, Jr. and Chappell, David: *A Visual Introduction to SQL* (Wiley, 1989).
- Van der Lans, Rick F.: *Introduction to SQL* (Addison-Wesley, 1988).
- Vang, Soren: *SQL and Relational Databases* (Microtrend Books, 1990).
- Viescas, John: *Quick Reference Guide to SQL* (Microsoft Corp., 1989).

PART 1

Introduction to ODBC

CHAPTER 1

ODBC Theory of Operation

The Open Database Connectivity (ODBC) interface allows applications to access data in database management systems (DBMS) using Structured Query Language (SQL) as a standard for accessing data.

The interface permits maximum *interoperability*—a single application can access different database management systems. This allows an application developer to develop, compile, and ship an application without targeting a specific DBMS. Users can then add modules called database *drivers* that link the application to their choice of database management systems.

ODBC History

In the traditional database world, *application* has usually meant a program that performed a specific database task with a specific DBMS in mind such as payroll, financial analysis, or inventory management. Such applications have typically been written using embedded SQL. While embedded SQL is efficient and is portable across different hardware and operating system environments, the source code must be recompiled for each new environment.

Embedded SQL is not optimal for applications that need to analyze data stored in databases such as DB2® and Oracle®, and prefer to do so from within a familiar application interface, such as a Microsoft Excel® spreadsheet. Under the traditional approach to database access, one version of Microsoft Excel would have to be precompiled with the IBM® precompiler and another with the Oracle precompiler, clearly a radical departure from simply buying a single packaged product.

ODBC offers a new approach: provide a separate program to extract the database information, and then have a way for applications to import the data. Since there are and probably always will be many viable communication methods, data protocols, and DBMS capabilities, the ODBC solution is to allow different technologies to be used by defining a standard interface. This solution leads to the idea of database drivers—dynamic-link libraries that an application can invoke on demand to gain access to a particular data source through a particular communications method, much like a printer driver running under Windows. ODBC provides the standard interface that allows both application writers and providers of libraries to shuttle data between applications and data sources.

ODBC Interface

The ODBC interface defines the following:

- A library of ODBC function calls that allow an application to connect to a DBMS, execute SQL statements, and retrieve results.
- SQL syntax based on the X/Open and SQL Access Group (SAG) SQL CAE specification (1992).
- A standard set of error codes.
- A standard way to connect and log on to a DBMS.
- A standard representation for data types.

The interface is flexible:

- Strings containing SQL statements can be explicitly included in source code or constructed on the fly at run time.
- The same object code can be used to access different DBMS products.
- An application can ignore underlying data communications protocols between it and a DBMS product.
- Data values can be sent and retrieved in a format convenient to the application.

The ODBC interface provides two types of function calls:

- Core functions are based on the X/Open and SQL Access Group Call Level Interface specification.
- Extended functions support additional functionality, including scrollable cursors and asynchronous processing.

To send an SQL statement, include the statement as an argument in an ODBC function call. The statement need not be customized for a specific DBMS. Appendix C, "SQL Grammar," contains an SQL syntax based on the X/Open and SQL Access Group SQL CAE specification (1992). We recommend that ODBC applications use only the SQL syntax defined in Appendix C to ensure maximum interoperability.

ODBC Components

The ODBC architecture has four components:

- **Application**   Performs processing and calls ODBC functions to submit SQL statements and retrieve results.

- **Driver Manager**   Loads drivers on behalf of an application.

- **Driver**   Processes ODBC function calls, submits SQL requests to a specific data source, and returns results to the application. If necessary, the driver modifies an application's request so that the request conforms to syntax supported by the associated DBMS.

- **Data source**   Consists of the data the user wants to access and its associated operating system, DBMS, and network platform (if any) used to access the DBMS.

The Driver Manager and driver appear to an application as one unit that processes ODBC function calls. The following diagram shows the relationship between the four components. The following paragraphs describe each component in more detail.

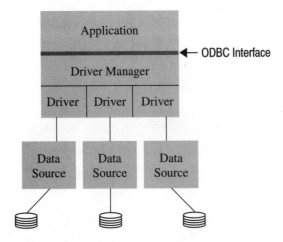

Application

An application using the ODBC interface performs the following tasks:

- Requests a connection, or session, with a data source.
- Sends SQL requests to the data source.
- Defines storage areas and data formats for the results of SQL requests.
- Requests results.

- Processes errors.
- Reports results back to a user, if necessary.
- Requests commit or rollback operations for transaction control.
- Terminates the connection to the data source.

An application can provide a variety of features external to the ODBC interface, including mail, spreadsheet capabilities, online transaction processing, and report generation; the application may or may not interact with users.

Driver Manager

The Driver Manager, provided by Microsoft, is a dynamic-link library (DLL) with an import library. The primary purpose of the Driver Manager is to load drivers. The Driver Manager also performs the following:

- Uses the ODBC.INI file or registry to map a data source name to a specific driver dynamic-link library (DLL).
- Processes several ODBC initialization calls.
- Provides entry points to ODBC functions for each driver.
- Provides parameter validation and sequence validation for ODBC calls.

Driver

A driver is a DLL that implements ODBC function calls and interacts with a data source.

The Driver Manager loads a driver when the application calls the **SQLBrowseConnect**, **SQLConnect**, or **SQLDriverConnect** function.

A driver performs the following tasks in response to ODBC function calls from an application:

- Establishes a connection to a data source.
- Submits requests to the data source.
- Translates data to or from other formats, if requested by the application.
- Returns results to the application.
- Formats errors into standard error codes and returns them to the application.
- Declares and manipulates cursors if necessary. (This operation is invisible to the application unless there is a request for access to a cursor name.)
- Initiates transactions if the data source requires explicit transaction initiation. (This operation is invisible to the application.)

Data Source

In this manual, *DBMS* refers to the general features and functionality provided by an SQL database management system. A *data source* is a specific instance of a combination of a DBMS product and any remote operating system and network necessary to access it.

An application establishes a connection with a particular vendor's DBMS product on a particular operating system, accessible by a particular network. For example, the application might establish connections to:

- An Oracle DBMS running on an OS/2® operating system, accessed by Novell® netware.

- A local Xbase file, in which case the network and remote operating system are not part of the communication path.

- A Tandem NonStop™ SQL DBMS running on the Guardian 90 operating system, accessed via a gateway.

Types of Drivers

ODBC defines two types of drivers:

- **Single-tier**   The driver processes both ODBC calls and SQL statements. (In this case, the driver performs part of the data source functionality.)

- **Multiple-tier**   The driver processes ODBC calls and passes SQL statements to the data source.

One system can contain both types of configurations.

The following paragraphs describe single-tier and multiple-tier configurations in more detail.

Single-Tier Configuration

In a single-tier implementation, the database file is processed directly by the driver. The driver processes SQL statements and retrieves information from the database. A driver that manipulates an Xbase file is an example of a single-tier implementation.

A single-tier driver may limit the set of SQL statements that may be submitted. The minimum set of SQL statements that must be supported by a single-tier driver is defined in Appendix C, "SQL Grammar."

The following diagram shows two types of single-tier configurations.

System A

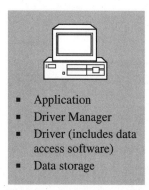

- Application
- Driver Manager
- Driver (includes data access software)
- Data storage

Client B   **Server B**

- Application   - Data storage
- Driver Manager
- Driver (includes data access software)

Multiple-Tier Configuration

In a multiple-tier configuration, the driver sends SQL requests to a server that processes SQL requests.

Although the entire installation may reside on a single system, it is more often divided across platforms. The application, driver, and Driver Manager reside on one system, called the client. The database and the software that controls access to the database typically reside on another system, called the server.

Another type of multiple-tier configuration is a gateway architecture. The driver passes SQL requests to a gateway process, which in turn sends the requests to the data source.

The following diagram shows three types of multiple-tier configurations. From an application's perspective, all three configurations are identical.

System C

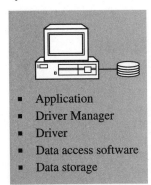

- Application
- Driver Manager
- Driver
- Data access software
- Data storage

Client D   **Server D**

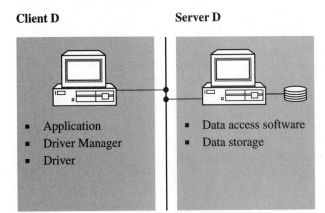

- Application   - Data access software
- Driver Manager   - Data storage
- Driver

Client E   **Server E1**   **Server E2**

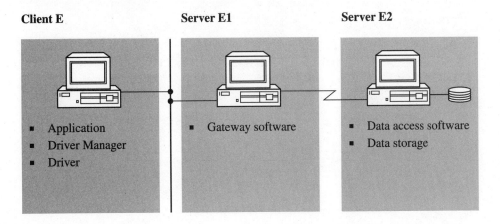

- Application   - Gateway software   - Data access software
- Driver Manager   - Data storage
- Driver

Network Example

The following diagram shows how each of the preceding configurations could appear in a single network. The diagram includes examples of the types of DBMS's that could reside in a network.

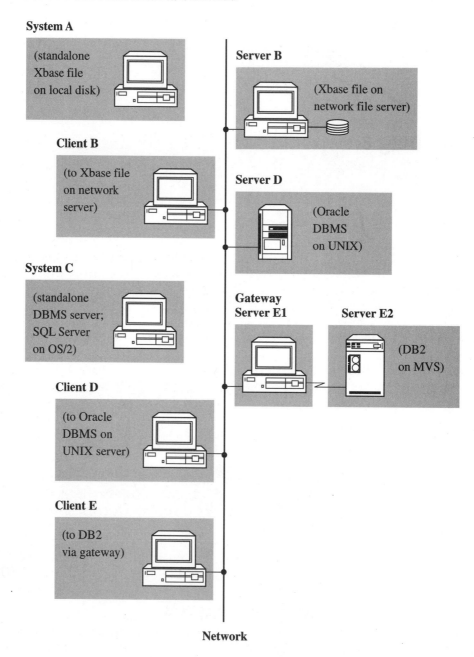

Applications can also communicate across wide area networks:

Client F   **Server F**

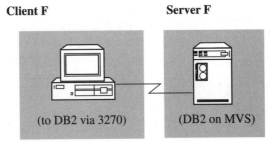

(to DB2 via 3270)   (DB2 on MVS)

Matching an Application to a Driver

One of the strengths of the ODBC interface is interoperability; a programmer can create an ODBC application without targeting a specific data source. Users can add drivers to the application after it is compiled and shipped.

From an application standpoint, it would be ideal if every driver and data source supported the same set of ODBC function calls and SQL statements. However, data sources and their associated drivers provide a varying range of functionality. Therefore, the ODBC interface defines conformance levels, which determine the ODBC procedures and SQL statements supported by a driver.

ODBC Conformance Levels

ODBC defines conformance levels for drivers in two areas: the ODBC API and the ODBC SQL grammar (which includes the ODBC SQL data types). Conformance levels help both application and driver developers by establishing standard sets of functionality. Applications can easily determine if a driver provides the functionality they need. Drivers can be developed to support a broad selection of applications without being concerned about the specific requirements of each application.

To claim that it conforms to a given API or SQL conformance level, a driver must support all the functionality in that conformance level, regardless of whether that functionality is supported by the DBMS associated with the driver. However, conformance levels do not restrict drivers to the functionality in the levels to which they conform. Driver developers are encouraged to support as much functionality as they can; applications can determine the functionality supported by a driver by calling **SQLGetInfo**, **SQLGetFunctions**, and **SQLGetTypeInfo**.

API Conformance Levels

The ODBC API defines a set of core functions that correspond to the functions in the X/Open and SQL Access Group Call Level Interface specification. ODBC also defines two extended sets of functionality, Level 1 and Level 2. The following list summarizes the functionality included in each conformance level.

Important Many ODBC applications require that drivers support all of the functions in the Level 1 API conformance level. To ensure that their driver works with most ODBC applications, driver developers should implement all Level 1 functions.

Core API

- Allocate and free environment, connection, and statement handles.
- Connect to data sources. Use multiple statements on a connection.
- Prepare and execute SQL statements. Execute SQL statements immediately.
- Assign storage for parameters in an SQL statement and result columns.
- Retrieve data from a result set. Retrieve information about a result set.
- Commit or roll back transactions.
- Retrieve error information.

Level 1 API

- Core API functionality.
- Connect to data sources with driver-specific dialog boxes.
- Set and inquire values of statement and connection options.
- Send part or all of a parameter value (useful for long data).
- Retrieve part or all of a result column value (useful for long data).
- Retrieve catalog information (columns, special columns, statistics, and tables).
- Retrieve information about driver and data source capabilities, such as supported data types, scalar functions, and ODBC functions.

Level 2 API

- Core and Level 1 API functionality.
- Browse connection information and list available data sources.
- Send arrays of parameter values. Retrieve arrays of result column values.
- Retrieve the number of parameters and describe individual parameters.
- Use a scrollable cursor.
- Retrieve the native form of an SQL statement.
- Retrieve catalog information (privileges, keys, and procedures).
- Call a translation DLL.

For a list of functions and their conformance levels, see Chapter 21, "Function Summary."

Note Each function description in this manual indicates whether the function is a core function or a level 1 or level 2 extension function.

SQL Conformance Levels

ODBC defines a core grammar that roughly corresponds to the X/Open and SQL Access Group SQL CAE specification (1992). ODBC also defines a minimum grammar, to meet a basic level of ODBC conformance, and an extended grammar, to provide for common DBMS extensions to SQL. The following list summarizes the grammar included in each conformance level.

Minimum SQL Grammar

- Data Definition Language (DDL): **CREATE TABLE** and **DROP TABLE**.
- Data Manipulation Language (DML): simple **SELECT**, **INSERT**, **UPDATE SEARCHED**, and **DELETE SEARCHED**.
- Expressions: simple (such as **A > B + C**).
- Data types: CHAR, VARCHAR, or LONG VARCHAR.

Core SQL Grammar

- Minimum SQL grammar and data types.
- DDL: **ALTER TABLE**, **CREATE INDEX**, **DROP INDEX**, **CREATE VIEW**, **DROP VIEW**, **GRANT,** and **REVOKE**.
- DML: full **SELECT**.
- Expressions: subquery, set functions such as **SUM** and **MIN**.
- Data types: DECIMAL, NUMERIC, SMALLINT, INTEGER, REAL, FLOAT, DOUBLE PRECISION.

Extended SQL Grammar

- Minimum and Core SQL grammar and data types.
- DML: outer joins, positioned **UPDATE**, positioned **DELETE**, **SELECT FOR UPDATE**, and unions.

Note In ODBC 1.0, positioned update, positioned delete, and **SELECT FOR UPDATE** statements and the **UNION** clause were part of the core SQL grammar; in ODBC 2.0, they are part of the extended grammar. Applications that use the SQL conformance level to determine whether these statements are supported also need to check the version number of the driver to correctly interpret the information. In particular, applications that use these features with ODBC 1.0 drivers need to explicitly check for these capabilities in ODBC 2.0 drivers.

- Expressions: scalar functions such as **SUBSTRING** and **ABS**, date, time, and timestamp literals.
- Data types: BIT, TINYINT, BIGINT, BINARY, VARBINARY, LONG VARBINARY, DATE, TIME, TIMESTAMP
- Batch SQL statements.
- Procedure calls.

For more information about SQL statements and conformance levels, see Appendix C, "SQL Grammar." The grammar listed in Appendix C is not intended to restrict the set of statements that an application can submit for execution. Drivers should support data source–specific extensions to the SQL language, although interoperable applications should not rely on those extensions.

For more information about data types, see Appendix D, "Data Types."

How to Select a Set of Functionality

The ODBC functions and SQL statements that a driver supports usually depend on the capabilities of its associated data source. Driver developers are encouraged, however, to implement as many ODBC functions as possible to ensure the widest possible use by applications.

The ODBC functions and SQL statements that an application uses depend on:

- The functionality needed by the application.
- The performance needed by the application.
- The data sources to be accessed by the application and the extent to which the application must be interoperable among these data sources.
- The functionality available in the drivers used by the application.

Because drivers support different levels of functionality, application developers may have to make trade-offs among the factors listed above. For example, an application might display the data in a table. It uses **SQLColumnPrivileges** to determine which columns a user can update and dims those columns the user cannot update. If some of the drivers available to the developer of this application do not support **SQLColumnPrivileges**, the developer can decide to:

- Use all the drivers and not dim any columns. The application behaves the same for all data sources, but has reduced functionality: the user might attempt to update data in a column for which they do not have update privileges. The application returns an error message only when the driver attempts to update the data in the data source.
- Use only those drivers that support **SQLColumnPrivileges**. The application behaves the same for all supported data sources, but has reduced functionality: the application does not support all the drivers.

- Use all the drivers and, for drivers that support **SQLColumnPrivileges**, dim columns the user cannot update. Otherwise, warn the user that they might not have update privileges on all columns. The application behaves differently for different data sources but has increased functionality: the application supports all drivers and sometimes dims columns the user cannot update.

- Use all the drivers and always dim columns the user cannot update; the application locally implements **SQLColumnPrivileges** for those drivers that do not support it. The application behaves the same for all data sources and has maximum functionality. However, the developer must know how to retrieve column privileges from some of the data sources, the application contains data source–specific code, and developement time is longer.

Developers of specialized applications may make different trade-offs than developers of generalized applications. For example, the developer of an application that only transfers data between two DBMS's (each from a different vendor) can safely exploit the full functionality of each of the drivers.

Connections and Transactions

Before an application can use ODBC, it must initialize ODBC and request an environment handle (*henv*). To communicate with a data source, the application must request a connection handle (*hdbc*) and connect to the data source. The application uses the environment and connection handles in subsequent ODBC calls to refer to the environment and specific connection.

An application may request multiple connections for one or more data sources. Each connection is considered a separate transaction space.

An active connection can have one or more statement processing streams.

A driver maintains a transaction for each active connection. The application can request that each SQL statement be automatically committed on completion; otherwise, the driver waits for an explicit commit or rollback request from the application. When the driver performs a commit or rollback operation, the driver resets all statement requests associated with the connection.

The Driver Manager manages the work of allowing an application to switch connections while transactions are in progress on the current connection.

CHAPTER 2

A Short History of SQL

This chapter provides a brief history of SQL and describes programmatic interfaces to SQL. For more information about SQL, see "Where to Find Additional Information" in "About This Manual."

SQL Background Information

SQL, or Structured Query Language, is a widely accepted industry standard for data definition, data manipulation, data management, access protection, and transaction control. SQL originated from the concept of relational databases. It uses tables, indexes, keys, rows, and columns to identify storage locations.

Many types of applications use SQL statements to access data. Examples include ad hoc query facilities, decision support applications, report generation utilities, and online transaction processing systems.

SQL is not a complete programming language in itself. For example, there are no provisions for flow control. SQL is normally used in conjunction with a traditional programming language.

ANSI 1989 Standard

SQL was first standardized by the American National Standards Institute (ANSI) in 1986. The first ANSI standard defined a language that was independent of any programming language.

The current standard is ANSI 1989, which defines three programmatic interfaces to SQL:

- **Module language**   Allows the definition of procedures within compiled programs (modules). These procedures are then called from traditional programming languages. The module language uses parameters to return values to the calling program.

- **Embedded SQL** Allows SQL statements to be embedded within a program. The specification defines embedded statements for COBOL, FORTRAN, Pascal, and PL/1.
- **Direct invocation** Access is implementation-defined.

The most popular programmatic interface has been embedded SQL.

Embedded SQL

Embedded SQL allows programmers to place SQL statements into programs written in a standard programming language (for example, COBOL or Pascal), which is termed the host language. SQL statements are delimited with specific starting and ending statements defined by the host language. The resulting program contains source code from two languages—SQL and the host language.

When compiling a program with embedded SQL statements, a precompiler translates the SQL statements into equivalent host language source code. After precompiling, the host language compiler compiles the resulting source code.

In the ANSI 1989 standard, the embedded SQL only supports *static* SQL. Static SQL has the following characteristics:

- To use static SQL, define each SQL statement within the program source code. Specify the number of result columns and their data types before compiling.

- Variables called *host variables* are accessible to both the host-language code and to SQL requests. However, host variables cannot be used for column names or table names. Host variables are fully defined (including length and data type) prior to compilation.

- If an SQL request is submitted that returns more than one row of data, define a *cursor* that points to one row of result data at a time.

- Each run of the associated program performs exactly the same SQL request, with possible variety in the values of host variables. All table names and column names must remain the same from one execution of the program to the next; otherwise, the program must be recompiled.

- Use standard data storage areas for status and error information.

Static SQL is efficient; SQL statements can be precompiled prior to execution and run multiple times without recompiling. The application is bound to a particular DBMS when it is compiled.

Static SQL cannot defer the definition of the SQL statement until run time. Therefore, static SQL is not the best option for client-server configurations or for ad hoc requests.

Current ANSI Specification

SQL-92 is the most recent ANSI specification, and is now an international standard. SQL-92 defines three levels of functionality: entry, intermediate, and full. SQL-92 contains many new features, including:

- Additional data types, including date and time.
- Connections to database environments, to address the needs of client-server architectures.
- Support for dynamic SQL.
- Scrollable cursors for access to result sets (full level).
- Outer joins (intermediate and full levels).

Dynamic SQL

Dynamic SQL, which is included in the most recent ANSI specification, allows an application to generate and execute SQL statements at run time.

Dynamic SQL statements can be prepared. When a statement is prepared, the database environment generates an access plan and a description of the result set. The statement can be executed multiple times with the previously generated access plan, which minimizes processing overhead.

Parameters can be included in dynamic SQL statements. Parameters function in much the same way as host variables in embedded SQL. Prior to execution, assign values to the place held by each parameter. Unlike static SQL, parameters do not require length or data type definition prior to program compilation.

Dynamic SQL is not as efficient as static SQL, but is very useful if an application requires:

- Flexibility to construct SQL statements at run time.
- Flexibility to defer an association with a database until run time.

Call Level Interface

A Call Level Interface (CLI) for SQL consists of a library of function calls that support SQL statements. The ODBC interface is a CLI.

A CLI is typically used for dynamic access. The CLI defined by the X/Open and SQL Access Group—and therefore the ODBC interface—is similar to the dynamic embedded version of SQL described in the X/Open and SQL Access Group SQL CAE specification (1992).

The ODBC interface is designed to be used directly by application programmers, not to be the target of a preprocessor for embedded SQL.

A CLI is very straightforward to programmers who are familiar with function libraries. The function call interface does not require host variables or other embedded SQL concepts.

A CLI does not require a precompiler. To submit an SQL request, place an SQL command into a text buffer and pass the buffer as a parameter in a function call. CLI functions provide declarative capabilities and request management. Obtain error information as for any function call—by return code or error function call, depending on the CLI.

A CLI allows for specification of result storage before or after the results are available. Results can be determined and appropriate action taken without being limited to a specific set of data structures that were defined prior to the request. Deferral of storage specification is called late binding of variables.

For a comparison between embedded SQL statements and the ODBC call level interface, see Appendix E, "Comparison Between Embedded SQL and ODBC."

Interoperability

Interoperability for call level interfaces can be addressed in the following ways:

- All clients and data sources adhere to a standard interface.
- All clients adhere to a standard interface; driver programs interpret the commands for a specific data source.

The second approach allows drivers to shield clients from database functionality differences, database protocol differences, and network differences. ODBC follows the second approach. ODBC can take advantage of standard database protocols and network protocols, but does not require the use of a standard database protocol or network protocol.

PART 2

Developing Applications

C H A P T E R   3

Guidelines for Calling ODBC Functions

This chapter describes the general characteristics of ODBC functions, determining driver conformance levels, the role of the Driver Manager, ODBC function arguments, and the values ODBC functions return.

General Information

Each ODBC function name starts with the prefix "SQL." Each function accepts one or more arguments. Arguments are defined as input (to the driver) or output (from the driver).

C programs that call ODBC functions must include the SQL.H, SQLEXT.H, and WINDOWS.H header files. These files define Windows and ODBC constants and types and provide function prototypes for all ODBC functions.

Determining Driver Conformance Levels

ODBC defines conformance levels for drivers in two areas: the ODBC API and the ODBC SQL grammar (which includes the ODBC SQL data types). These levels establish standard sets of functionality. By inquiring the conformance levels supported by a driver, an application can easily determine if the driver provides the necessary functionality. For a complete discussion of ODBC conformance levels, see "ODBC Conformance Levels" in Chapter 1, "ODBC Theory of Operation."

Note The following sections refer to **SQLGetInfo** and **SQLGetTypeInfo**, which are part of the Level 1 API conformance level. Although it is strongly recommended that drivers support this conformance level, drivers are not required to do so. If these functions are not supported, an application developer must consult the driver documentation to determine its conformance levels.

Determining API Conformance Levels

ODBC functions are divided into core functions, which are defined in the X/Open and SQL Access Group Call Level Interface specification, and two levels of extension functions, with which ODBC extends this specification. To determine the function conformance level of a driver, an application calls **SQLGetInfo** with the SQL_ODBC_SAG_CLI_CONFORMANCE and SQL_ODBC_API_CONFORMANCE flags. Note that a driver can support one or more extension functions but not conform to ODBC extension Level 1 or 2. To determine if a driver supports a particular function, an application calls **SQLGetFunctions**. Note that **SQLGetFunctions** is implemented by the Driver Manager and can be called for any driver, regardless of its level.

Determining SQL Conformance Levels

The ODBC SQL grammar, which includes SQL data types, is divided into a minimum grammar, a core grammar, which corresponds to the X/Open and SQL Access Group SQL CAE specification (1992), and an extended grammar, which provides common extensions to SQL. To determine the SQL conformance level of a driver, an application calls **SQLGetInfo** with the SQL_ODBC_SQL_CONFORMANCE flag. To determine whether a driver supports a specific SQL extension, an application calls **SQLGetInfo** with a flag for that extension. For more information, see Appendix C, "SQL Grammar." To determine whether a driver supports a specific SQL data type, an application calls **SQLGetTypeInfo**.

Using the Driver Manager

The Driver Manager is a DLL that provides access to ODBC drivers. An application typically links with the Driver Manager import library (ODBC.LIB) to gain access to the Driver Manager.

Whenever an application calls an ODBC function, the Driver Manager performs one of the following actions:

- For **SQLDataSources** and **SQLDrivers**, the Driver Manager processes the call. It does not pass the call to the driver.

- For **SQLGetFunctions**, the Driver Manager passes the call to the driver associated with the connection. If the driver does not support **SQLGetFunctions**, the Driver Manager processes the call.

- For **SQLAllocEnv**, **SQLAllocConnect**, **SQLSetConnectOption**, **SQLFreeConnect**, and **SQLFreeEnv**, the Driver Manager processes the call. The Driver Manager calls **SQLAllocEnv**, **SQLAllocConnect**, and **SQLSetConnectOption** in the driver when the application calls a function to

connect to the data source (**SQLConnect, SQLDriverConnect,** or
SQLBrowseConnect). The Driver Manager calls **SQLFreeConnect** and
SQLFreeEnv in the driver when the application calls **SQLDisconnect**.

- For **SQLConnect, SQLDriverConnect, SQLBrowseConnect,** and
  SQLError, the Driver Manager performs initial processing then passes the
  call to the driver associated with the connection.

- For any other ODBC function, the Driver Manager passes the call to the driver
  associated with the connection.

If requested, the Driver Manager records each called function in a trace file. The
name of each function is recorded, along with the values of the input arguments
and the names of the output arguments (as listed in the function definitions).

Calling ODBC Functions

The following paragraphs describe general characteristics of ODBC functions.

Buffers

An application passes data to a driver in an input buffer. The driver returns data to
an application in an output buffer. The application must allocate memory for both
input and output buffers. (If the application will use the buffer to retrieve string
data, the buffer must contain space for the null termination byte.)

Note that some functions accept pointers to buffers that are later used by other
functions. The application must ensure that these pointers remain valid until all
applicable functions have used them. For example, the argument *rgbValue* in
SQLBindCol points to an output buffer in which **SQLFetch** returns the data for a
column.

Caution ODBC does not require drivers to correctly manage buffers that cross
segment boundaries in Windows 3.1. The Driver Manager supports the use of
such buffers, since it passes buffer addresses to drivers and does not operate on
buffer contents. If a driver supports buffers that cross segment boundaries, the
documentation for the driver should clearly state this.

For maximum interoperability, applications that use buffers that cross segment
boundaries should pass them in pieces to ODBC functions. None of these pieces
can cross a segment boundary. For example, suppose a data source contains 100
kilobytes of bitmap data. A Windows 3.1 application can safely allocate 100K of
memory (beginning at a segment boundary) and retrieve the data in two pieces
(64K and 36K), each of which begins on a segment boundary.

Input Buffers

An application passes the address and length of an input buffer to a driver. The length of the buffer must be one of the following values:

- A length greater than or equal to zero. This is the actual length of the data in the input buffer. For character data, a length of zero indicates that the data is an empty (zero length) string. Note that this is different from a null pointer. If the application specifies the length of character data, the character data does not need to be null-terminated.

- SQL_NTS. This specifies that a character data value is null-terminated.

- SQL_NULL_DATA. This tells the driver to ignore the value in the input buffer and use a NULL data value instead. It is only valid when the input buffer is used to provide the value of a parameter in an SQL statement.

The operation of ODBC functions on character data containing embedded null characters is undefined, and is not recommended for maximum interoperability.

Unless it is specifically prohibited in a function description, the address of an input buffer may be a null pointer. When the address of an input buffer is a null pointer, the value of the corresponding buffer length argument is ignored.

For more information about input buffers, see "Converting Data from C to SQL Data Types" in Appendix D, "Data Types."

Output Buffers

An application passes the following arguments to a driver, so that it can return data in an output buffer:

- The address of the buffer in which the driver returns the data (the output buffer). Unless it is specifically prohibited in a function description, the address of an output buffer can be a null pointer. In this case, the driver does not return anything in the buffer and, in the absence of other errors, returns SQL_SUCCESS.

  If necessary, the driver converts data before returning it. The driver always null-terminates character data before returning it.

- The length of the buffer. This is ignored by the driver if the returned data has a fixed length in C, such as an integer, real number, or date structure.

- The address of a variable in which the driver returns the length of the data (the length buffer). The returned length of the data is SQL_NULL_DATA if the data is a NULL value in a result set. Otherwise, it is the number of bytes of data available to return. If the driver converts the data, it is the number of bytes after the conversion. For character data, it does not include the null termination byte added by the driver.

If the output buffer is too small, the driver attempts to truncate the data. If the truncation does not cause a loss of significant data, the driver returns the truncated data in the output buffer, returns the length of the available data (as opposed to the length of the truncated data) in the length buffer, and returns SQL_SUCCESS_WITH_INFO. If the truncation causes a loss of significant data, the driver leaves the output and length buffers untouched and returns SQL_ERROR. The application calls **SQLError** to retrieve information about the truncation or the error.

For more information about output buffers, see "Converting Data from SQL to C Data Types" in Appendix D, "Data Types."

Environment, Connection, and Statement Handles

When so requested by an application, the Driver Manager and each driver allocate storage for information about the ODBC environment, each connection, and each SQL statement. The handles to these storage areas are returned to the application. The application then uses one or more of them in each call to an ODBC function.

The ODBC interface defines three types of handles:

- The **environment handle** identifies memory storage for global information, including the valid connection handles and the current active connection handle. ODBC defines the environment handle as a variable of type HENV. An application uses a single environment handle; it must request this handle prior to connecting to a data source.

- **Connection handles** identify memory storage for information about a particular connection. ODBC defines connection handles as variables of type HDBC. An application must request a connection handle prior to connecting to a data source. Each connection handle is associated with the environment handle. The environment handle can, however, have multiple connection handles associated with it.

- **Statement handles** identify memory storage for information about an SQL statement. ODBC defines statement handles as variables of type HSTMT. An application must request a statement handle prior to submitting SQL requests. Each statement handle is associated with exactly one connection handle. Each connection handle can, however, have multiple statement handles associated with it.

For more information about requesting a connection handle, see Chapter 5, "Connecting to a Data Source." For more information about requesting a statement handle, see Chapter 6, "Executing SQL Statements."

Using Data Types

Data stored on a data source has an SQL data type, which may be specific to that data source. A driver maps data source–specific SQL data types to ODBC SQL data types, which are defined in the ODBC SQL grammar, and driver-specific SQL data types. (A driver returns these mappings through **SQLGetTypeInfo**. It also uses the ODBC SQL data types to describe the data types of columns and parameters in **SQLColAttributes**, **SQLDescribeCol**, and **SQLDescribeParam**.)

Each SQL data type corresponds to an ODBC C data type. By default, the driver assumes that the C data type of a storage location corresponds to the SQL data type of the column or parameter to which the location is bound. If the C data type of a storage location is not the *default* C data type, the application can specify the correct C data type with the *fCType* argument in **SQLBindCol**, **SQLGetData**, or **SQLBindParameter**. Before returning data from the data source, the driver converts it to the specified C data type. Before sending data to the data source, the driver converts it from the specified C data type.

For more information about data types, see Appendix D, "Data Types." The C data types are defined in SQL.H and SQLEXT.H.

ODBC Function Return Codes

When an application calls an ODBC function, the driver executes the function and returns a predefined code. These return codes indicate success, warning, or failure status. The return codes are:

SQL_SUCCESS	SQL_INVALID_HANDLE
SQL_SUCCESS_WITH_INFO	SQL_STILL_EXECUTING
SQL_NO_DATA_FOUND	SQL_NEED_DATA
SQL_ERROR	

If the function returns SQL_SUCCESS_WITH_INFO or SQL_ERROR, the application can call **SQLError** to retrieve additional information about the error. For a complete description of return codes and error handling, see Chapter 8, "Retrieving Status and Error Information."

CHAPTER 4

Basic Application Steps

To interact with a data source, a simple application:

1. Connects to the data source. It specifies the data source name and any additional information needed to complete the connection.

2. Processes one or more SQL statements:

   - The application places the SQL text string in a buffer. If the statement includes parameter markers, it sets the parameter values.

   - If the statement returns a result set, the application assigns a cursor name for the statement or allows the driver to do so.

   - The application submits the statement for prepared or immediate execution.

   - If the statement creates a result set, the application can inquire about the attributes of the result set, such as the number of columns and the name and type of a specific column. It assigns storage for each column in the result set and fetches the results.

   - If the statement causes an error, the application retrieves error information from the driver and takes appropriate action.

3. Ends each transaction by committing it or rolling it back.

4. Terminates the connection when it has finished interacting with the data source.

The following diagram lists the ODBC function calls that an application makes to connect to a data source, process SQL statements, and disconnect from the data source. Depending on its needs, an application may call other ODBC functions.

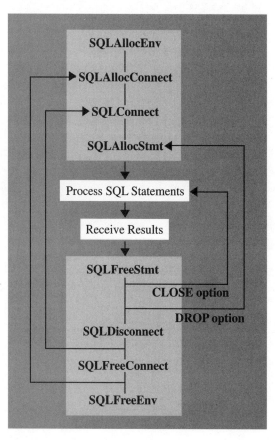

C H A P T E R   5

Connecting to a Data Source

This chapter briefly describes data sources. It then describes how to establish a connection to a data source.

About Data Sources

A data source consists of the data a user wants to access, its associated DBMS, the platform on which the DBMS resides, and the network (if any) used to access that platform. Each data source requires that a driver provide certain information in order to connect to it. At the core level, this is defined to be the name of the data source, a user ID, and a password. ODBC extensions allow drivers to specify additional information, such as a network address or additional passwords.

The connection information for each data source is stored in the ODBC.INI file or registry, which is created during installation and maintained with an administration program. A section in this file lists the available data sources. Additional sections describe each data source in detail, specifying the driver name, a description, and any additional information the driver needs to connect to the data source.

For example, suppose a user has three data sources: Personnel and Inventory, which use an Rdb DBMS, and Payroll, which uses an SQL Server DBMS. The section that lists the data sources might be:

```
[ODBC Data Sources]
Personnel=Rdb
Inventory=Rdb
Payroll=SQL Server
```

Suppose also that an Rdb driver needs the ID of the last user to log in, a server name, and a schema declaration statement. The section that describes the Personnel data source might be:

```
[Personnel]
Driver=c:\windows\system\rdb.dll
Description=Personnel database: CURLY
Lastuid=smithjo
Server=curly
Schema=declare schema personnel filename
➥ "sys$sysdevice:[corpdata]personnel.rdb"
```

For more information about data sources and how to configure them, see Chapter 20, "Configuring Data Sources."

Initializing the ODBC Environment

Before an application can use any other ODBC function, it must initialize the ODBC interface and associate an environment handle with the environment. To initialize the interface and allocate an environment handle, an application:

1. Declares a variable of type HENV. For example, the application could use the declaration:

   ```
   HENV henv1;
   ```

2. Calls **SQLAllocEnv** and passes it the address of the variable. The driver initializes the ODBC environment, allocates memory to store information about the environment, and returns the environment handle in the variable.

These steps should be performed only once by an application; **SQLAllocEnv** supports one or more connections to data sources.

Allocating a Connection Handle

Before an application can connect to a driver, it must allocate a connection handle for the connection. To allocate a connection handle, an application:

1. Declares a variable of type HDBC. For example, the application could use the declaration:

   ```
   HDBC hdbc1;
   ```

2. Calls **SQLAllocConnect** and passes it the address of the variable. The driver allocates memory to store information about the connection and returns the connection handle in the variable.

Connecting to a Data Source

Next, the application specifies a specific driver and data source. It passes the following information to the driver in a call to **SQLConnect**:

- **Data source name**   The name of the data source being requested by the application.

- **User ID**   The login ID or account name for access to the data source, if appropriate (optional).

- **Authentication string (password)**   A character string associated with the user ID that allows access to the data source (optional).

When an application calls **SQLConnect**, the Driver Manager uses the data source name to read the name of the driver DLL from the appropriate section of the ODBC.INI file or registry. It then loads the driver DLL and passes the **SQLConnect** arguments to it. If the driver needs additional information to connect to the data source, it reads this information from the same section of the ODBC.INI file.

If the application specifies a data source name that is not in the ODBC.INI file or registry, or if the application does not specify a data source name, the Driver Manager searches for the default data source specification. If it finds the default data source, it loads the default driver DLL and passes the application-specified data source name to it. If there is no default data source, the Driver Manager returns an error.

ODBC Extensions for Connections

ODBC extends the X/Open and SQL Access Group Call Level Interface to provide additional functions related to connections, drivers, and data sources. The remainder of this chapter describes these functions. To determine if a driver supports a specific function, an application calls **SQLGetFunctions**.

Connecting to a Data Source With SQLDriverConnect

SQLDriverConnect supports:

- Data sources that require more connection information than the three arguments in **SQLConnect**.

- Dialog boxes to prompt the user for all connection information.

- Data sources that are not defined in the ODBC.INI file or registry.

SQLDriverConnect uses a connection string to specify the information needed to connect to a driver and data source.

A connection string contains the following information:

- Data source name or driver description
- Zero or more user IDs
- Zero or more passwords
- Zero or more data source–specific parameter values

The connection string is a more flexible interface than the data source name, user ID, and password used by **SQLConnect**. The application can use the connection string for multiple levels of login authorization or to convey other data source–specific connection information.

An application calls **SQLDriverConnect** in one of three ways:

- Specifies a connection string that contains a data source name. The Driver Manager retrieves the full path of the driver DLL associated with the data source from the ODBC.INI file or registry. To retrieve a list of data source names, an application calls **SQLDataSources**.
- Specifies a connection string that contains a driver description. The Driver Manager retrieves the full path of the driver DLL. To retrieve a list of driver descriptions, an application calls **SQLDrivers**.
- Specifies a connection string that does not contain a data source name or a driver description. The Driver Manager displays a dialog box from which the user selects a data source name. The Driver Manager then retrieves the full path of the driver DLL associated with the data source.

The Driver Manager then loads the driver DLL and passes the **SQLDriverConnect** arguments to it.

The application may pass all the connection information the driver needs. It may also request that the driver always prompt the user for connection information or only prompt the user for information it needs. Finally, if a data source is specified, the driver may read connection information from the appropriate section of the ODBC.INI file or registry. (For information on the structure of the ODBC.INI file or the subkeys used in the registry, see "Structure of the ODBC.INI File" in Chapter 20, "Configuring Data Sources.")

After the driver connects to the data source, it returns the connection information to the application. The application may store this information for future use.

If the application specifies a data source name that is not in the ODBC.INI file or registry, the Driver Manager searches for the default data source specification. If it finds the default data source, it loads the default driver DLL and passes the application-specified data source name to it. If there is no default data source, the Driver Manager returns an error.

The Driver Manager displays the following dialog box if the application calls **SQLDriverConnect** and requests that the user be prompted for information.

On request from the application, the driver displays a dialog box similar to the following to retrieve login information.

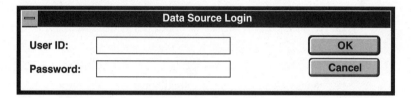

Connection Browsing With SQLBrowseConnect

SQLBrowseConnect supports an iterative method of listing and specifying the attributes and attribute values required to connect to a data source. For each level of a connection, an application calls **SQLBrowseConnect** and specifies the connection attributes and attribute values for that level. First level connection attributes always include the data source name or driver description; the connection attributes for later levels are data source–dependent, but might include the host, user name, and database.

Each time **SQLBrowseConnect** is called, it validates the current attributes, returns the next level of attributes, and returns a user-friendly name for each attribute. It may also return a list of valid values for those attributes. (Note, however, that for some drivers and attributes, this list may not be complete.) After an application has specified each level of attributes and values, **SQLBrowseConnect** connects to the data source and returns a complete connection string. This string can be used in conjunction with **SQLDriverConnect** to connect to the data source at a later time.

Connection Browsing Example for SQL Server

The following example shows how **SQLBrowseConnect** might be used to browse the connections available with a driver for Microsoft's SQL Server. Although other drivers may require different connection attributes, this example illustrates the connection browsing model. (For the syntax of browse request and result strings, see **SQLBrowseConnect** in Chapter 22, "ODBC Function Reference.")

First, the application requests a connection handle:

```
SQLAllocConnect(henv, &hdbc);
```

Next, the application calls **SQLBrowseConnect** and specifies a data source name:

```
SQLBrowseConnect(hdbc, "DSN=MySQLServer", SQL_NTS,
                 szBrowseResult, 100, &cb);
```

Because this is the first call to **SQLBrowseConnect**, the Driver Manager locates the data source name (MySQLServer) in the ODBC.INI file and loads the corresponding driver DLL (SQLSRVR.DLL). The Driver Manager then calls the driver's **SQLBrowseConnect** function with the same arguments it received from the application.

The driver determines that this is the first call to **SQLBrowseConnect** and returns the second level of connection attributes: server, user name, password, and application name. For the server attribute, it returns a list of valid server names. The return code from **SQLBrowseConnect** is SQL_NEED_DATA. The browse result string is:

```
"SERVER:Server={red,blue,green,yellow};UID:Login ID=?;PWD:Password=?;
➡ *APP:AppName=?;*WSID:WorkStation ID=?"
```

Note that each keyword in the browse result string is followed by a colon and one or more words before the equal sign. These words are the user-friendly name that an application can use as a prompt in a dialog box.

In its next call to **SQLBrowseConnect**, the application must supply a value for the **SERVER**, **UID**, and **PWD** keywords. Because they are prefixed by an asterisk, the **APP** and **WSID** keywords are optional and may be omitted. The value for the **SERVER** keyword may be one of the servers returned by **SQLBrowseConnect** or a user-supplied name.

The application calls **SQLBrowseConnect** again, specifying the green server and omitting the **APP** and **WSID** keywords and the user-friendly names after each keyword:

```
SQLBrowseConnect(hdbc, "SERVER=green;UID=Smith;PWD=Sesame", SQL_NTS,
                 szBrowseResult, 100, &cb);
```

The driver attempts to connect to the green server. If there are any nonfatal errors, such as a missing keyword-value pair, **SQLBrowseConnect** returns SQL_NEED_DATA and remains in the same state as prior to the error. The application can call **SQLError** to determine the error. If the connection is successful, the driver returns SQL_NEED_DATA and returns the browse result string:

```
"*DATABASE:Database={master,model,pubs,tempdb};
➡ *LANGUAGE:Language={us_english,Français}"
```

Since the attributes in this string are optional, the application can omit them. However, the application must call **SQLBrowseConnect** again. If the application chooses to omit the database name and language, it specifies an empty browse request string. In this example, the application chooses the pubs database and calls **SQLBrowseConnect** a final time, omitting the **LANGUAGE** keyword and the asterisk before the **DATABASE** keyword:

```
SQLBrowseConnect(hdbc, "DATABASE=pubs", SQL_NTS,
                szBrowseResult, 100, &cb);
```

Since the **DATABASE** attribute is the final connection attribute of the data source, the browsing process is complete, the application is connected to the data source, and **SQLBrowseConnect** returns SQL_SUCCESS. **SQLBrowseConnect** also returns the complete connection string as the browse result string:

```
"DSN=MySQLServer;SERVER=green;UID=Smith;PWD=Sesame;DATABASE=pubs"
```

The final connection string returned by the driver does not contain the user-friendly names after each keyword, nor does it contain optional keywords not specified by the application. The application can use this string with **SQLDriverConnect** to reconnect to the data source on the current *hdbc* (after disconnecting) or to connect to the data source on a different *hdbc*:

```
SQLDriverConnect(hdbc, szBrowseResult, SQL_NTS, szConnStrOut, 100, &cb,
                 SQL_DRIVER_NOPROMPT);
```

Connection Browsing Example for DAL

The following example shows how **SQLBrowseConnect** might be used in conjunction with a driver that uses Apple's Data Access Language (DAL) to access an Oracle host. To browse the available connections, an application repeatedly calls **SQLBrowseConnect**:

```
retcode = SQLBrowseConnect(hdbc, szConnStrIn, SQL_NTS,
                           szConnStrOut, 200, &cb);
```

In the first call, the application specifies a data source name in *szConnStrIn*. In each subsequent call, the application bases the value of *szConnStrIn* on the value of *szConnStrOut* returned by the previous call. The application continues to call

SQLBrowseConnect as long as the function returns SQL_NEED_DATA. The following list shows, for each call to **SQLBrowseConnect**, the value that the application specifies for *szConnStrIn* and the values that the driver returns for *retcode* and *szConnStrOut*. (For the syntax of the strings used in *szConnStrIn* and *szConnStrOut*, see **SQLBrowseConnect** in Chapter 22, "ODBC Function Reference.")

```
szConnStrIn  : "DSN=DAL"
szConnStrOut : "HOST:Host={MyVax,Direct,Unix};UID1:Host User Name=?;
               ➥ PWD1:Password=?"
retcode      : SQL_NEED_DATA

szConnStrIn  : "HOST=MyVax;UID1=Smith;PWD1=Sesame"
szConnStrOut : "DBMS:DBMS={Oracle,Informix,Sybase};UID2:DBMS User Name=?;
               ➥ PWD2:Password=?"
retcode      : SQL_NEED_DATA

szConnStrIn  : "DBMS=Oracle;UID2=John;PWD2=Lion"
szConnStrOut : "DATABASE:Database={DalDemo,Personnel,Production};
               ➥ *ALIAS:Alias=?;*UID3:User Name=?;*PWD3:Password=?"
retcode      : SQL_NEED_DATA

szConnStrIn  : "DATABASE=DalDemo;ALIAS=Demo"
szConnStrOut : "DSN=DAL;HOST=MyVax;UID1=Smith;PWD1=Sesame;DBMS=Oracle;
               ➥ UID2=John;PWD2=Lion;DATABASE=DalDemo;ALIAS=Demo"
retcode      : SQL_SUCCESS
```

Note that the database alias, database user name, and database password are optional, as indicated by the asterisk before those attribute names. The application chooses not to specify the user name and password.

Translating Data

An application and a data source can store data in different formats. For example, the application might use a different character set than the data source. ODBC provides a mechanism by which a driver can translate all data (data values, SQL statements, table names, row counts, and so on) that passes between the driver and the data source.

The driver translates data by calling functions in a translation DLL. A default translation DLL can be specified for the data source in the ODBC.INI file or registry; the application can override this by calling **SQLSetConnectOption**. When the driver connects to the data source, it loads the translation DLL (if one has been specified). After the driver has connected to the data source, the application may specify a new translation DLL by calling **SQLSetConnectOption**. For more information about specifying a default translation DLL, see "Specifying a Default Translator" in Chapter 20, "Configuring Data Sources."

Translation functions may support several different types of translation. For example, a function that translates data from one character set to another might support a variety of character sets. To specify a particular type of translation, an application can pass an option flag to the translation functions with **SQLSetConnectOption**.

Additional Extension Functions

ODBC also provides the following functions related to connections, drivers, and data sources. For more information about these functions, see Chapter 22, "ODBC Function Reference."

Function	Description
SQLDataSources	Retrieves a list of available data sources. The Driver Manager retrieves this information from the ODBC.INI file or registry. An application can present this information to a user or automatically select a data source.
SQLDrivers	Retrieves a list of installed drivers and their attributes. The Driver Manager retrieves this information from the ODBCINST.INI file or registry. An application can present this information to a user or automatically select a driver.
SQLGetFunctions	Retrieves functions supported by a driver. This function allows an application to determine at run time whether a particular function is supported by a driver.
SQLGetInfo	Retrieves general information about a driver and data source, including filenames, versions, conformance levels, and capabilities.
SQLGetTypeInfo	Retrieves the SQL data types supported by a driver and data source.
SQLSetConnectOption **SQLGetConnectOption**	These functions set or retrieve connection options, such as the data source access mode, automatic transaction commitment, timeout values, function tracing, data translation options, and transaction isolation.

C H A P T E R   6

Executing SQL Statements

An application can submit any SQL statement supported by a data source. ODBC defines a standard syntax for SQL statements (listed in Appendix C, "SQL Grammar"). For maximum interoperability, an application should only submit SQL statements that use this syntax; the driver will translate these statements to the syntax used by the data source. If an application submits an SQL statement that does not use the ODBC syntax, the driver passes it directly to the data source.

Note For **CREATE TABLE** and **ALTER TABLE** statements, applications should use the data type name returned by **SQLGetTypeInfo** in the TYPE_NAME column, rather than the data type name defined in the SQL grammar.

The following diagram shows a simple sequence of ODBC function calls to execute SQL statements. Note that statements can be executed a single time with **SQLExecDirect** or prepared with **SQLPrepare** and executed multiple times with **SQLExecute**. Note also that an application calls **SQLTransact** to commit or roll back a transaction.

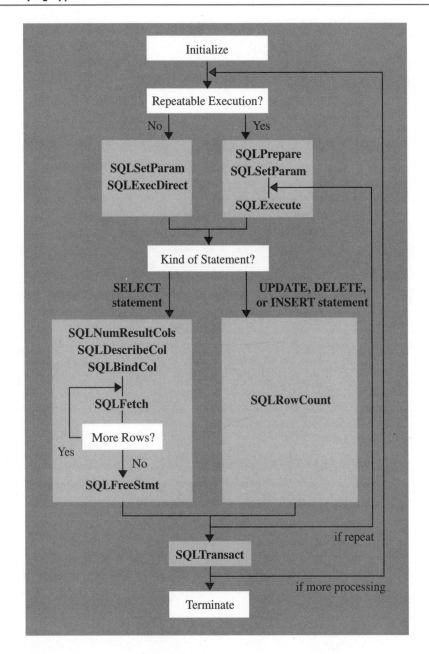

Allocating a Statement Handle

Before an application can submit an SQL statement, it must allocate a statement handle for the statement. To allocate a statement handle, an application:

1. Declares a variable of type HSTMT. For example, the application could use the declaration:

   ```
   HSTMT hstmt1;
   ```

2. Calls **SQLAllocStmt** and passes it the address of the variable and the connected *hdbc* with which to associate the statement. The driver allocates memory to store information about the statement, associates the statement handle with the *hdbc*, and returns the statement handle in the variable.

Executing an SQL Statement

An application can submit an SQL statement for execution in two ways:

- **Prepared**   Call **SQLPrepare** and then call **SQLExecute**.
- **Direct**   Call **SQLExecDirect**.

These options are similar, though not identical to, the prepared and immediate options in embedded SQL. For a comparison of the ODBC functions and embedded SQL, see Appendix E, "Comparison Between Embedded SQL and ODBC."

Prepared Execution

An application should prepare a statement before executing it if either of the following is true:

- The application will execute the statement more than once, possibly with intermediate changes to parameter values.
- The application needs information about the result set prior to execution.

A prepared statement executes faster than an unprepared statement because the data source compiles the statement, produces an access plan, and returns an access plan identifier to the driver. The data source minimizes processing time as it does not have to produce an access plan each time it executes the statement. Network traffic is minimized because the driver sends the access plan identifier to the data source instead of the entire statement.

Important Committing or rolling back a transaction, either by calling **SQLTransact** or by using the SQL_AUTOCOMMIT connection option, can cause the data source to delete the access plans for all *hstmts* on an *hdbc*. For more information, see the SQL_CURSOR_COMMIT_BEHAVIOR and SQL_CURSOR_ROLLBACK_BEHAVIOR information types in **SQLGetInfo**.

To prepare and execute an SQL statement, an application:

1. Calls **SQLPrepare** to prepare the statement.

2. Sets the values of any statement parameters. For more information, see "Setting Parameter Values" later in this chapter.

3. Retrieves information about the result set, if necessary. For more information, see "Determining the Characteristics of a Result Set" in Chapter 7, "Retrieving Results."

4. Calls **SQLExecute** to execute the statement.

5. Repeats steps 2 through 4 as necessary.

Direct Execution

An application should execute a statement directly if both of the following are true:

- The application will execute the statement only once.

- The application does not need information about the result set prior to execution.

To execute an SQL statement directly, an application:

1. Sets the values of any statement parameters. For more information, see "Setting Parameter Values" later in this chapter.

2. Calls **SQLExecDirect** to execute the statement.

Setting Parameter Values

An SQL statement can contain parameter markers that indicate values that the driver retrieves from the application at execution time. For example, an application might use the following statement to insert a row of data into the EMPLOYEE table:

```
INSERT INTO EMPLOYEE (NAME, AGE, HIREDATE) VALUES (?, ?, ?)
```

An application uses parameter markers instead of literal values if:

- It needs to execute the same prepared statement several times with different parameter values.

- The parameter values are not known when the statement is prepared.

- The parameter values need to be converted from one data type to another.

To set a parameter value, an application performs the following steps in any order:

- Calls **SQLBindParameter** to bind a storage location to a parameter marker and specify the data types of the storage location and the column associated with the parameter, as well as the precision and scale of the parameter.
- Places the parameter's value in the storage location.

These steps can be performed before or after a statement is prepared, but must be performed before a statement is executed.

Parameter values must be placed in storage locations in the C data types specified in **SQLBindParameter**. For example:

Parameter Value	SQL Data Type	C Data Type	Stored Value
ABC	SQL_CHAR	SQL_C_CHAR	ABC\0 [a]
10	SQL_INTEGER	SQL_C_SLONG	10
10	SQL_INTEGER	SQL_C_CHAR	10\0 [a]
1 P.M.	SQL_TIME	SQL_C_TIME	13,0,0 [b]
1 P.M.	SQL_TIME	SQL_C_CHAR	{t '13:00:00'}\0[a,c]

[a] "\0" represents a null-termination byte; the null termination byte is required only if the parameter length is SQL_NTS.

[b] The numbers in this list are the numbers stored in the fields of the TIME_STRUCT structure.

[c] The string uses the ODBC date escape clause. For more information, see "Date, Time, and Timestamp Data" later in this chapter.

Storage locations remain bound to parameter markers until the application calls **SQLFreeStmt** with the SQL_RESET_PARAMS option or the SQL_DROP option. An application can bind a different storage area to a parameter marker at any time by calling **SQLBindParameter**. An application can also change the value in a storage location at any time. When a statement is executed, the driver uses the current values in the most recently defined storage locations.

Performing Transactions

In *auto-commit* mode, every SQL statement is a complete transaction, which is automatically committed. In *manual-commit* mode, a transaction consists of one or more statements. In manual-commit mode, when an application submits an SQL statement and no transaction is open, the driver implicitly begins a transaction. The transaction remains open until the application commits or rolls back the transaction with **SQLTransact**.

If a driver supports the SQL_AUTOCOMMIT connection option, the default transaction mode is auto-commit; otherwise, it is manual-commit. An application calls **SQLSetConnectOption** to switch between manual-commit and autocommit mode. Note that if an application switches from manual-commit to auto-commit mode, the driver commits any open transactions on the connection.

Applications should call **SQLTransact**, rather than submitting a **COMMIT** or **ROLLBACK** statement, to commit or roll back a transaction. The result of a **COMMIT** or **ROLLBACK** statement depends on the driver and its associated data source.

Important   Committing or rolling back a transaction, either by calling **SQLTransact** or by using the SQL_AUTOCOMMIT connection option, can cause the data source to close the cursors and delete the access plans for all *hstmts* on an *hdbc*. For more information, see the SQL_CURSOR_COMMIT_BEHAVIOR and SQL_CURSOR_ROLLBACK_BEHAVIOR information types in **SQLGetInfo**.

ODBC Extensions for SQL Statements

ODBC extends the X/Open and SQL Access Group Call Level Interface to provide additional functions related to SQL statements. ODBC also extends the X/Open and SQL Access Group SQL CAE specification (1992) to provide common extensions to SQL. The remainder of this chapter describes these functions and SQL extensions.

To determine if a driver supports a specific function, an application calls **SQLGetFunctions**. To determine if a driver supports a specific ODBC extension to SQL, such as outer joins or procedure invocation, an application calls **SQLGetInfo**.

Retrieving Information About the Data Source's Catalog

The following functions, known as catalog functions, return information about a data source's catalog:

- **SQLTables** returns the names of tables stored in a data source.
- **SQLTablePrivileges** returns the privileges associated with one or more tables.
- **SQLColumns** returns the names of columns in one or more tables.
- **SQLColumnPrivileges** returns the privileges associated with each column in a single table.
- **SQLPrimaryKeys** returns the names of columns that comprise the primary key of a single table.
- **SQLForeignKeys** returns the names of columns in a single table that are foreign keys. It also returns the names of columns in other tables that refer to the primary key of the specified table.

- **SQLSpecialColumns** returns information about the optimal set of columns that uniquely identify a row in a single table or the columns in that table that are automatically updated when any value in the row is updated by a transaction.

- **SQLStatistics** returns statistics about a single table and the indexes associated with that table.

- **SQLProcedures** returns the names of procedures stored in a data source.

- **SQLProcedureColumns** returns a list of the input and output parameters, as well as the names of columns in the result set, for one or more procedures.

Each function returns the information as a result set. An application retrieves these results by calling **SQLBindCol** and **SQLFetch**.

Sending Parameter Data at Execution Time

To send parameter data at statement execution time, such as for parameters of the SQL_LONGVARCHAR or SQL_LONGVARBINARY types, an application uses the following three functions:

- **SQLBindParameter**
- **SQLParamData**
- **SQLPutData**

To indicate that it plans to send parameter data at statement execution time, an application calls **SQLBindParameter** and sets the *pcbValue* buffer for the parameter to the result of the SQL_LEN_DATA_AT_EXEC(*length*) macro. If the *fSqlType* argument is SQL_LONGVARBINARY or SQL_LONGVARCHAR and the driver returns "Y" for the SQL_NEED_LONG_DATA_LEN information type in **SQLGetInfo**, *length* is the total number of bytes of data to be sent for the parameter; otherwise, it is ignored.

The application sets the *rgbValue* argument to a value that, at run time, can be used to retrieve the data. For example, *rgbValue* might point to a storage location that will contain the data at statement execution time or to a file that contains the data. The driver returns the value to the application at statement execution time.

When the driver processes a call to **SQLExecute** or **SQLExecDirect** and the statement being executed includes a data-at-execution parameter, the driver returns SQL_NEED_DATA. To send the parameter data, the application:

1. Calls **SQLParamData**, which returns *rgbValue* (as set with **SQLBindParameter**) for the first data-at-execution parameter.

2. Calls **SQLPutData** one or more times to send data for the parameter. (More than one call will be needed if the data value is larger than the buffer; multiple

calls are allowed only if the C data type is character or binary and the SQL data type is character, binary, or data source–specific.)

3. Calls **SQLParamData** again to indicate that all data has been sent for the parameter. If there is another data-at-execution parameter, the driver returns *rgbValue* for that parameter and SQL_NEED_DATA for the function return code. Otherwise, it returns SQL_SUCCESS for the function return code.

4. Repeats steps 2 and 3 for the remaining data-at-execution parameters.

For additional information, see the description of **SQLBindParameter** in Chapter 22, "ODBC Function Reference."

Specifying Arrays of Parameter Values

To specify multiple sets of parameter values for a single SQL statement, an application calls **SQLParamOptions**. For example, if there are ten sets of column values to insert into a table—and the same SQL statement can be used for all ten operations—the application can set up an array of values, then submit a single **INSERT** statement.

If an application uses **SQLParamOptions**, it must allocate enough memory to handle the arrays of values.

Executing Functions Asynchronously

By default, a driver executes ODBC functions synchronously; the driver does not return control to an application until a function call completes. If a driver supports asynchronous execution, however, an application can request asynchronous execution for the functions listed below. (All of these functions either submit requests to a data source or retrieve data. These operations may require extensive processing.)

SQLColAttributes	**SQLForeignKeys**	**SQLProcedureColumns**
SQLColumnPrivileges	**SQLGetData**	**SQLProcedures**
SQLColumns	**SQLGetTypeInfo**	**SQLPutData**
SQLDescribeCol	**SQLMoreResults**	**SQLSetPos**
SQLDescribeParam	**SQLNumParams**	**SQLSpecialColumns**
SQLExecDirect	**SQLNumResultCols**	**SQLStatistics**
SQLExecute	**SQLParamData**	**SQLTablePrivileges**
SQLExtendedFetch	**SQLPrepare**	**SQLTables**
SQLFetch	**SQLPrimaryKeys**	

Asynchronous execution is performed on a statement-by-statement basis. To execute a statement asynchronously, an application:

1. Calls **SQLSetStmtOption** with the SQL_ASYNC_ENABLE option to enable asynchronous execution for an *hstmt*. (To enable asynchronous execution for all *hstmts* associated with an *hdbc*, an application calls **SQLSetConnectOption** with the SQL_ASYNC_ENABLE option.)

2. Calls one of the functions listed earlier in this section and passes it the *hstmt*. The driver begins asynchronous execution of the function and returns SQL_STILL_EXECUTING.

Note If the application calls a function that cannot be executed asynchronously, the driver executes the function synchronously.

---

3. Performs other operations while the function is executing asynchronously. The application can call any function with a different *hstmt* or an *hdbc* not associated with the original *hstmt*. With the original *hstmt* and the *hdbc* associated with that *hstmt*, the application can only call the original function, **SQLAllocStmt**, **SQLCancel**, or **SQLGetFunctions**.

4. Calls the asynchronously executing function to check if it has finished. While the arguments must be valid, the driver ignores all of them except the *hstmt* argument. For example, suppose an application called **SQLExecDirect** to execute a **SELECT** statement asynchronously. When the application calls **SQLExecDirect** again, the return value indicates the status of the **SELECT** statement, even if the *szSqlStr* argument contains an **INSERT** statement.

   If the function is still executing, the driver returns SQL_STILL_EXECUTING and the application must repeat steps 3 and 4. If the function has finished, the driver returns a different code, such as SQL_SUCCESS or SQL_ERROR. For information about canceling a function executing asynchronously, see "Terminating Statement Processing" in Chapter 9, "Terminating Transactions and Connections."

5. Repeats steps 2 through 4 as needed.

To disable asynchronous execution for an *hstmt*, an application calls **SQLSetStmtOption** with the SQL_ASYNC_ENABLE option. To disable asynchronous execution for all *hstmts* associated with an *hdbc*, an application calls **SQLSetConnectOption** with the SQL_ASYNC_ENABLE option.

Using ODBC Extensions to SQL

ODBC defines the following extensions to SQL, which are common to most DBMS's:

- Date, time, and timestamp data
- Scalar functions such as numeric, string, and data type conversion functions

- **LIKE** predicate escape characters
- Outer joins
- Procedures

The syntax defined by ODBC for these extensions uses the escape clause provided by the X/Open and SQL Access Group SQL CAE specification (1992) to cover vendor-specific extensions to SQL. Its format is:

--(*vendor(_vendor-name_**), product(**_product-name_**)** _extension_ ***)--**

For the ODBC extensions to SQL, _product-name_ is always "ODBC", since the product defining them is ODBC. _Vendor-name_ is always "Microsoft", since ODBC is a Microsoft product. ODBC also defines a shorthand syntax for these extensions:

{_extension_}

Most DBMS's provide the same extensions to SQL as does ODBC. Because of this, an application may be able to submit an SQL statement using one of these extensions in either of two ways:

- Use the syntax defined by ODBC. An application that uses the ODBC syntax will be interoperable among DBMS's.

- Use the syntax defined by the DBMS. An application that uses DBMS-specific syntax will not be interoperable among DBMS's.

Due to the difficulty in implementing some ODBC extensions to SQL, such as outer joins, a driver might only implement those ODBC extensions that are supported by its associated DBMS. To determine whether the driver and data source support all the ODBC extensions to SQL, an application calls **SQLGetInfo** with the SQL_ODBC_SQL_CONFORMANCE flag. For information about how an application determines whether a specific extension is supported, see the section that describes the extension.

Note Many DBMS's provide extensions to SQL other than those defined by ODBC. To use one of these extensions, an application uses the DBMS-specific syntax. The application will not be interoperable among DBMS's.

Date, Time, and Timestamp Data

The escape clauses ODBC uses for date, time, and timestamp data are:

--(*vendor(Microsoft),product(ODBC) d '_value_' ***)--**
--(*vendor(Microsoft),product(ODBC) t '_value_' ***)--**
--(*vendor(Microsoft),product(ODBC) ts '_value_' ***)--**

where **d** indicates *value* is a date in the "yyyy-mm-dd" format, **t** indicates *value* is a time in the "hh:mm:ss" format, and **ts** indicates *value* is a timestamp in the "yyyy-mm-dd hh:mm:ss[.f...]" format. The shorthand syntax for date, time, and timestamp data is:

{d *'value'*}
{t *'value'*}
{ts *'value'*}

For example, each of the following statements updates the birthday of John Smith in the EMPLOYEE table. The first statement uses the escape clause syntax. The second statement uses the shorthand syntax. The third statement uses the native syntax for a DATE column in DEC's Rdb and is not interoperable among DBMS's.

```
UPDATE EMPLOYEE
    SET BIRTHDAY=--(*vendor(Microsoft),product(ODBC) d '1967-01-15' *)--
    WHERE NAME='Smith, John'

UPDATE EMPLOYEE
    SET BIRTHDAY={d '1967-01-15'}
    WHERE NAME='Smith, John'

UPDATE EMPLOYEE
    SET BIRTHDAY='15-Jan-1967'
    WHERE NAME='Smith, John'
```

The ODBC escape clauses for date, time, and timestamp literals can be used in parameters with a C data type of SQL_C_CHAR. For example, the following statement uses a parameter to update the birthday of John Smith in the EMPLOYEE table:

```
UPDATE EMPLOYEE SET BIRTHDAY=? WHERE NAME='Smith, John'
```

A storage location of type SQL_C_CHAR bound to the parameter might contain any of the following values. The first value uses the escape clause syntax. The second value uses the shorthand syntax. The third value uses the native syntax for a DATE column in DEC's Rdb and is not interoperable among DBMS's.

```
"--(*vendor(Microsoft),product(ODBC) d '1967-01-15' *)--"

"{d '1967-01-15'}"

"'15-Jan-1967'"
```

An application can also send date, time, or timestamp values as parameters using the C structures defined by the C data types SQL_C_DATE, SQL_C_TIME, and SQL_C_TIMESTAMP.

To determine if a data source supports date, time, or timestamp data, an application calls **SQLGetTypeInfo**. If a driver supports date, time, or timestamp data, it must also support the escape clauses for date, time, or timestamp literals.

Scalar Functions

Scalar functions—such as string length, absolute value, or current date—can be used on columns of a result set and on columns that restrict rows of a result set. The escape clause ODBC uses for scalar functions is:

--(*vendor(Microsoft),product(ODBC) fn *scalar-function* ***)--**

where *scalar-function* is one of the functions listed in Appendix F, "Scalar Functions." The shorthand syntax for scalar functions is:

{fn *scalar-function***}**

For example, each of the following statements creates the same result set of uppercase employee names. The first statement uses the escape clause syntax. The second statement uses the shorthand syntax. The third statement uses the native syntax for Ingres™ for OS/2 and is not interoperable among DBMS's.

```
SELECT --(*vendor(Microsoft),product(ODBC) fn UCASE(NAME) *)--
    FROM EMPLOYEE

SELECT {fn UCASE(NAME)} FROM EMPLOYEE

SELECT uppercase(NAME) FROM EMPLOYEE
```

An application can mix scalar functions that use native syntax and scalar functions that use ODBC syntax. For example, the following statement creates a result set of last names of employees in the EMPLOYEE table. (Names in the EMPLOYEE table are stored as a last name, a comma, and a first name.) The statement uses the ODBC scalar function **SUBSTRING** and the SQL Server scalar function **CHARINDEX** and will only execute correctly on SQL Server.

```
SELECT {fn SUBSTRING(NAME, 1, CHARINDEX(',', NAME) - 1)} FROM EMPLOYEE
```

To determine which scalar functions are supported by a data source, an application calls **SQLGetInfo** with the SQL_NUMERIC_FUNCTIONS, SQL_STRING_FUNCTIONS, SQL_SYSTEM_FUNCTIONS, and SQL_TIMEDATE_FUNCTIONS flags.

Data Type Conversion Function

ODBC defines a special scalar function, **CONVERT**, that requests that the data source convert data from one SQL data type to another SQL data type. The escape clause ODBC uses for the **CONVERT** function is:

--(*vendor(Microsoft),product(ODBC)
  fn CONVERT(*value_exp*, *data_type*) *)--

where *value_exp* is a column name, the result of another scalar function, or a literal value, and *data_type* is a keyword that matches the **#define** name used by an ODBC SQL data type (as defined in Appendix D, "Data Types"). The shorthand syntax for the **CONVERT** function is:

{fn CONVERT(*value_exp*, *data_type*)**}**

For example, the following statement creates a result set of the names and ages of all employees in their twenties. It uses the **CONVERT** function to convert each employee's age from type SQL_SMALLINT to type SQL_CHAR. Each resulting character string is compared to the pattern "2%" to determine if the employee's age is in the twenties.

```
SELECT NAME, AGE FROM EMPLOYEE
    WHERE {fn CONVERT(AGE,SQL_CHAR)} LIKE '2%'
```

To determine if the **CONVERT** function is supported by a data source, an application calls **SQLGetInfo** with the SQL_CONVERT_FUNCTIONS flag. For more information about the **CONVERT** function, see Appendix F, "Scalar Functions."

LIKE Predicate Escape Characters

In a **LIKE** predicate, the percent character (%) matches zero or more of any character and the underscore character (_) matches any one character. The percent and underscore characters can be used as literals in a **LIKE** predicate by preceding them with an escape character. The escape clause ODBC uses to define the **LIKE** predicate escape character is:

--(*vendor(Microsoft),product(ODBC) escape '*escape-character*' *)--

where *escape-character* is any character supported by the data source. The shorthand syntax for the **LIKE** predicate escape character is:

{escape '*escape-character*'**}**

For example, each of the following statements creates the same result set of department names that start with the characters "%AAA". The first statement uses the escape clause syntax. The second statement uses the shorthand syntax. The third statement uses the native syntax for Ingres and is not interoperable among DBMS's. Note that the second percent character in each **LIKE** predicate is a wild-card character that matches zero or more of any character.

```
SELECT NAME FROM DEPT WHERE NAME
    LIKE '\%AAA%' --(*vendor(Microsoft),product(ODBC) escape '\'*)--

SELECT NAME FROM DEPT WHERE NAME LIKE '\%AAA%' {escape '\'}

SELECT NAME FROM DEPT WHERE NAME LIKE '\%AAA%' ESCAPE '\'
```

To determine whether **LIKE** predicate escape characters are supported by a data source, an application calls **SQLGetInfo** with the SQL_LIKE_ESCAPE_CLAUSE information type.

Outer Joins

ODBC supports the ANSI SQL-92 left outer join syntax. The escape clause ODBC uses for outer joins is:

--(*vendor(Microsoft),product(ODBC) oj *outer-join* ***)--**

where *outer-join* is:

table-reference **LEFT OUTER JOIN** {*table-reference* | *outer-join*}
    ON *search-condition*

table-reference specifies a table name, and *search-condition* specifies the join condition between the *table-references*. The shorthand syntax for outer joins is:

{**oj** *outer-join*}

An outer join request must appear after the **FROM** keyword and before the **WHERE** clause (if one exists). For complete syntax information, see Appendix C, "SQL Grammar."

For example, each of the following statements creates the same result set of the names and departments of employees working on project 544. The first statement uses the escape clause syntax. The second statement uses the shorthand syntax. The third statement uses the native syntax for Oracle and is not interoperable among DBMS's.

```
SELECT EMPLOYEE.NAME, DEPT.DEPTNAME
    FROM --(*vendor(Microsoft),product(ODBC) oj
        EMPLOYEE LEFT OUTER JOIN DEPT ON EMPLOYEE.DEPTID=DEPT.DEPTID*)--
    WHERE EMPLOYEE.PROJID=544

SELECT EMPLOYEE.NAME, DEPT.DEPTNAME
    FROM {oj EMPLOYEE LEFT OUTER JOIN DEPT
        ON EMPLOYEE.DEPTID=DEPT.DEPTID}
    WHERE EMPLOYEE.PROJID=544

SELECT EMPLOYEE.NAME, DEPT.DEPTNAME
    FROM EMPLOYEE, DEPT
    WHERE (EMPLOYEE.PROJID=544) AND (EMPLOYEE.DEPTID = DEPT.DEPTID (+))
```

To determine the level of outer joins a data source supports, an application calls **SQLGetInfo** with the SQL_OUTER_JOINS flag. Data sources can support two-table outer joins, partially support multi-table outer joins, fully support multi-table outer joins, or not support outer joins.

Procedures

An application can call a procedure in place of an SQL statement. The escape clause ODBC uses for calling a procedure is:

--(*vendor(Microsoft),product(ODBC)
   [?=] call *procedure-name*[([*parameter*][,[*parameter*]]...)] ***)--**

where *procedure-name* specifies the name of a procedure stored on the data source and *parameter* specifies a procedure parameter. A procedure can have zero or more parameters and can return a value. The shorthand syntax for procedure invocation is:

{[**?=**]**call** *procedure-name*[([*parameter*][,[*parameter*]]...)]}

For output parameters, *parameter* must be a parameter marker. For input and input/output parameters, *parameter* can be a literal, a parameter marker, or not specified. If *parameter* is a literal or is not specified for an input/output parameter, the driver discards the output value. If *parameter* is not specified for an input or input/output parameter, the procedure uses the default value of the parameter as the input value; the procedure also uses the default value if *parameter* is a parameter marker and the *pcbValue* argument in **SQLBindParameter** is SQL_DEFAULT_PARAM. If a procedure call includes parameter markers (including the "?=" parameter marker for the return value), the application must bind each marker by calling **SQLBindParameter** prior to calling the procedure.

Note   For some data sources, *parameter* cannot be a literal value. For all data sources, it can be a parameter marker. For maximum interoperability, applications should always use a parameter marker for *parameter*.

If an application specifies a return value parameter for a procedure that does not return a value, the driver sets the *pcbValue* buffer specified in **SQLBindParameter** for the parameter to SQL_NULL_DATA. If the application omits the return value parameter for a procedure returns a value, the driver ignores the value returned by the procedure.

If a procedure returns a result set, the application retrieves the data in the result set in the same manner as it retrieves data from any other result set.

For example, each of the following statements uses the procedure EMPS_IN_PROJ to create the same result set of names of employees working on a project. The first statement uses the escape clause syntax. The second statement uses the shorthand syntax. For an example of code that calls a procedure, see **SQLProcedures** in Chapter 22, "ODBC Function Reference."

```
--(*vendor(Microsoft),product(ODBC) call EMPS_IN_PROJ(?)*)--

{call EMPS_IN_PROJ(?)}
```

To determine if a data source supports procedures, an application calls **SQLGetInfo** with the SQL_PROCEDURES information type. To retrieve a list of the procedures stored in a data source, an application calls **SQLProcedures**. To retrieve a list of the input, input/output, and output parameters, as well as the return value and the columns that make up the result set (if any) returned by a procedure, an application calls **SQLProcedureColumns**.

Additional Extension Functions

ODBC also provides the following functions related to SQL statements. For more information about these functions, see Chapter 22, "ODBC Function Reference."

Function	Description
SQLDescribeParam	Retrieves information about prepared parameters.
SQLNativeSql	Retrieves the SQL statement as processed by the data source, with escape sequences translated to SQL code used by the data source.
SQLNumParams	Retrieves the number of parameters in an SQL statement.
SQLSetStmtOption **SQLSetConnectOption** **SQLGetStmtOption**	These functions set or retrieve statement options, such as asynchronous processing, orientation for binding rowsets, maximum amount of variable length data to return, maximum number of result set rows to return, and query timeout value. Note that **SQLSetConnectOption** sets options for all statements in a connection.

C H A P T E R   7

Retrieving Results

A **SELECT** statement is used to retrieve data that meets a given set of specifications. For example, **SELECT * FROM EMPLOYEE WHERE EMPNAME = "Jones"** is used to retrieve all columns of all rows in EMPLOYEE where the employee's name is Jones. ODBC extension functions also can retrieve data. For example, **SQLColumns** retrieves data about columns in the data source. These sets of data, called result sets, can contain zero or more rows.

Note that other SQL statements, such as **GRANT** or **REVOKE**, do not return result sets. For these statements, the return code from **SQLExecute** or **SQLExecDirect** is usually the only source of information as to whether the statement was successful. (For **INSERT**, **UPDATE**, and **DELETE** statements, an application can call **SQLRowCount** to return the number of affected rows.)

The steps an application takes to process a result set depends on what is known about it.

- **Known result set**   The application knows the exact form of the SQL statement, and therefore the result set, at compile time. For example, the query **SELECT EMPNO, EMPNAME FROM EMPLOYEE** returns two specific columns.

- **Unknown result set**   The application does not know the exact form of the SQL statement, and therefore the result set, at compile time. For example, the ad hoc query **SELECT * FROM EMPLOYEE** returns all currently defined columns in the EMPLOYEE table. The application may not be able to predict the format of these results prior to execution.

Assigning Storage for Results (Binding)

An application can assign storage for results before or after it executes an SQL statement. If an application prepares or executes the SQL statement first, it can inquire about the result set before it assigns storage for results. For example, if the result set is unknown, the application must retrieve the number of columns before it can assign storage for them.

To associate storage for a column of data, an application calls **SQLBindCol** and passes it the following information:

- The data type to which the data is to be converted. For more information, see "Converting Data from SQL to C Data Types" in Appendix D, "Data Types."

- The address of an output buffer for the data. The application must allocate this buffer and it must be large enough to hold the data in the form to which it is converted.

- The length of the output buffer. This value is ignored if the returned data has a fixed width in C, such as an integer, real number, or date structure.

- The address of a storage buffer in which to return the number of bytes of available data.

Determining the Characteristics of a Result Set

To determine the characteristics of a result set, an application can:

- Call **SQLNumResultCols** to determine how many columns a request returned.

- Call **SQLColAttributes** or **SQLDescribeCol** to describe a column in the result set.

If the result set is unknown, an application can use the information returned by these functions to bind the columns in the result set. An application can call these functions at any time after a statement is prepared or executed. Note that, although **SQLRowCount** can sometimes return the number of rows in a result set, it is not guaranteed to do so. Few data sources support this functionality and interoperable applications should not rely on it.

Note For optimal performance, an application should call **SQLColAttributes**, **SQLDescribeCol**, and **SQLNumResultCols** after a statement is executed. In data sources that emulate statement preparation, these functions sometimes execute more slowly before a statement is executed because the information returned by them is not readily available until after the statement is executed.

Fetching Result Data

To retrieve a row of data from the result set, an application:

1. Calls **SQLBindCol** to bind the columns of the result set to storage locations if it has not already done so.

2. Calls **SQLFetch** to move to the next row in the result set and retrieve data for all bound columns.

The following diagram shows the operations an application uses to retrieve data from the result set:

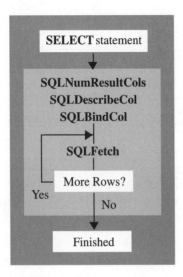

Using Cursors

To keep track of its position in the result set, a driver maintains a cursor. The cursor is so named because it indicates the current position in the result set, just as the cursor on a CRT screen indicates current position.

Each time an application calls **SQLFetch**, the driver moves the cursor to the next row and returns that row. The cursor supported by the core ODBC functions only scrolls forward, one row at a time. (To reretrieve a row of data that it has already retrieved from the result set, the application must close the cursor by calling **SQLFreeStmt** with the SQL_CLOSE option, reexecute the **SELECT** statement, and fetch rows with **SQLFetch** until the target row is retrieved.)

Important Committing or rolling back a transaction, either by calling **SQLTransact** or by using the SQL_AUTOCOMMIT connection option, can cause the data source to close the cursors for all *hstmts* on an *hdbc*. For more information, see the SQL_CURSOR_COMMIT_BEHAVIOR and SQL_CURSOR_ROLLBACK_BEHAVIOR information types in **SQLGetInfo**.

ODBC Extensions for Results

ODBC extends the X/Open and SQL Access Group Call Level Interface to provide additional functions related to retrieving results. The remainder of this chapter describes these functions. To determine if a driver supports a specific function, an application calls **SQLGetFunctions**.

Retrieving Data from Unbound Columns

To retrieve data from unbound columns—that is, columns for which storage has not been assigned with **SQLBindCol**—an application uses **SQLGetData**. The application first calls **SQLFetch** or **SQLExtendedFetch** to position the cursor on the next row. It then calls **SQLGetData** to retrieve data from specific unbound columns.

An application may retrieve data from both bound and unbound columns in the same row. It calls **SQLBindCol** to bind as many columns as desired. It calls **SQLFetch** or **SQLExtendedFetch** to position the cursor on the next row of the result set and retrieve all bound columns. It then calls **SQLGetData** to retrieve data from unbound columns.

If the data type of a column is character, binary, or data source–specific and the column contains more data than can be retrieved in a single call, an application may call **SQLGetData** more than once for that column, as long as the data is being transferred to a buffer of type SQL_C_CHAR or SQL_C_BINARY. For example, data of the SQL_LONGVARBINARY and SQL_LONGVARCHAR types may need to be retrieved in several parts.

For maximum interoperability, an application should only call **SQLGetData** for columns to the right of the rightmost bound column and then only in left-to-right order. To determine if a driver can return data with **SQLGetData** for any column (including unbound columns before the last bound column and any bound columns) or in any order, an application calls **SQLGetInfo** with the SQL_GETDATA_EXTENSIONS option.

Assigning Storage for Rowsets (Binding)

In addition to binding individual rows of data, an application can call **SQLBindCol** to assign storage for a *rowset* (one or more rows of data). By default, rowsets are bound in column-wise fashion. They can also be bound in row-wise fashion.

To specify how many rows of data are in a rowset, an application calls **SQLSetStmtOption** with the SQL_ROWSET_SIZE option.

Column-Wise Binding

To assign storage for column-wise bound results, an application performs the following steps for each column to be bound:

1. Allocates an array of data storage buffers. The array has as many elements as there are rows in the rowset.

2. Allocates an array of storage buffers to hold the number of bytes available to return for each data value. The array has as many elements as there are rows in the rowset.

3. Calls **SQLBindCol** and specifies the address of the data array, the size of one element of the data array, the address of the number-of-bytes array, and the type to which the data will be converted. When data is retrieved, the driver will use the array element size to determine where to store successive rows of data in the array.

Row-Wise Binding

To assign storage for row-wise bound results, an application performs the following steps:

1. Declares a structure that can hold a single row of retrieved data and the associated data lengths. (For each column to be bound, the structure contains one field to contain data and one field to contain the number of bytes of data available to return.)

2. Allocates an array of these structures. This array has as many elements as there are rows in the rowset.

3. Calls **SQLBindCol** for each column to be bound. In each call, the application specifies the address of the column's data field in the first array element, the size of the data field, the address of the column's number-of-bytes field in the first array element, and the type to which the data will be converted.

4. Calls **SQLSetStmtOption** with the SQL_BIND_TYPE option and specifies the size of the structure. When the data is retrieved, the driver will use the structure size to determine where to store successive rows of data in the array.

Retrieving Rowset Data

Before it retrieves rowset data, an application calls **SQLSetStmtOption** with the SQL_ROWSET_SIZE option to specify the number of rows in the rowset. It then binds columns in the rowset with **SQLBindCol**. The rowset may be bound in column-wise or row-wise fashion. For more information, see "Assigning Storage for Rowsets (Binding)" previous in this chapter.

To retrieve rowset data, an application calls **SQLExtendedFetch**.

For maximum interoperability, an application should not use **SQLGetData** to retrieve data from unbound columns in a block (more than one row) of data that has been retrieved with **SQLExtendedFetch**. To determine if a driver can return data with **SQLGetData** from a block of data, an application calls **SQLGetInfo** with the SQL_GETDATA_EXTENSIONS option.

Using Block and Scrollable Cursors

As originally designed, cursors in SQL only scroll forward through a result set, returning one row at a time. However, interactive applications often require forward and backward scrolling, absolute or relative positioning within the result set, and the ability to retrieve and update blocks of data, or *rowsets*.

To retrieve and update rowset data, ODBC provides a *block* cursor attribute. To allow an application to scroll forwards or backwards through the result set, or move to an absolute or relative position in the result set, ODBC provides a *scrollable* cursor attribute. Cursors may have one or both attributes.

Block Cursors

An application calls **SQLSetStmtOption** with the SQL_ROWSET_SIZE option to specify the rowset size. The application can call **SQLSetStmtOption** to change the rowset size at any time. Each time the application calls **SQLExtendedFetch**, the driver returns the next *rowset size* rows of data. After the data is returned, the cursor points to the first row in the rowset. By default, the rowset size is one.

Scrollable Cursors

Applications have different needs in their ability to sense changes in the tables underlying a result set. For example, when balancing financial data, an accountant needs data that appears static; it is impossible to balance books when the data is continually changing. When selling concert tickets, a clerk needs up-to-the minute, or dynamic, data on which tickets are still available. Various cursor models are designed to meet these needs, each of which requires different sensitivities to changes in the tables underlying the result set.

Static Cursors

At one extreme are *static* cursors, to which the data in the underlying tables appears to be static. The membership, order, and values in the result set used by a static cursor are generally fixed when the cursor is opened. Rows updated, deleted, or inserted by other users (including other cursors in the same application) are not detected by the cursor until it is closed and then reopened; the SQL_STATIC_SENSITIVITY information type returns whether the cursor can detect rows it has updated, deleted, or inserted.

Static cursors are commonly implemented by taking a snapshot of the data or locking the result set. Note that in the former case, the cursor diverges from the underlying tables as other users make changes; in the latter case, other users are prohibited from changing the data.

Dynamic Cursors

At the other extreme are *dynamic* cursors, to which the data appears to be dynamic. The membership, order, and values in the result set used by a dynamic cursor are ever-changing. Rows updated, deleted, or inserted by all users (the cursor, other cursors in the same application, and other applications) are detected by the cursor when data is next fetched. Although ideal for many situations, dynamic cursors are difficult to implement.

Keyset-Driven Cursors

Between static and dynamic cursors are *keyset-driven* cursors, which have some of the attributes of each. Like static cursors, the membership and ordering of the result set of a keyset-driven cursor is generally fixed when the cursor is opened. Like dynamic cursors, most changes to the values in the underlying result set are visible to the cursor when data is next fetched.

When a keyset-driven cursor is opened, the driver saves the keys for the entire result set, thus fixing the membership and order of the result set. As the cursor scrolls through the result set, the driver uses the keys in this *keyset* to retrieve the current data values for each row in the rowset. Because data values are retrieved only when the cursor scrolls to a given row, updates to that row by other users (including other cursors in the same application) after the cursor was opened are visible to the cursor.

If the cursor scrolls to a row of data that has been deleted by other users (including other cursors in the same application), the row appears as a *hole* in the result set, since the key is still in the keyset but the row is no longer in the result set. Updating the key values in a row is considered to be deleting the existing row and inserting a new row; therefore, rows of data for which the key values have been changed also appear as holes. When the driver encounters a hole in the result set, it returns a status code of SQL_ROW_DELETED for the row.

Rows of data inserted into the result set by other users (including other cursors in the same application) after the cursor was opened are not visible to the cursor, since the keys for those rows are not in the keyset.

The SQL_STATIC_SENSITIVITY information type returns whether the cursor can detect rows it has deleted or inserted. Because updating key values in a keyset-driven cursor is considered to be deleting the existing row and inserting a new row, keyset-driven cursors can always detect rows they have updated.

Mixed (Keyset/Dynamic) Cursors

If a result set is large, it may be impractical for the driver to save the keys for the entire result set. Instead, the application can use a *mixed* cursor. In a mixed cursor, the keyset is smaller than the result set, but larger than the rowset.

Within the boundaries of the keyset, a mixed cursor is keyset-driven, that is, the driver uses keys to retrieve the current data values for each row in the rowset. When a mixed cursor scrolls beyond the boundaries of the keyset, it becomes dynamic, that is, the driver simply retrieves the next *rowset size* rows of data. The driver then constructs a new keyset, which contains the new rowset.

For example, assume a result set has 1000 rows and uses a mixed cursor with a keyset size of 100 and a rowset size of 10. When the cursor is opened, the driver (depending on the implementation) saves keys for the first 100 rows and retrieves data for the first 10 rows. If another user deletes row 11 and the cursor then scrolls to row 11, the cursor will detect a hole in the result set; the key for row 11 is in the keyset but the data is no longer in the result set. This is the same behavior as a keyset-driven cursor. However, if another user deletes row 101 and the cursor then scrolls to row 101, the cursor will not detect a hole; the key for the row 101 is not in the keyset. Instead, the cursor will retrieve the data for the row that was originally row 102. This is the same behavior as a dynamic cursor.

Specifying the Cursor Type

To specify the cursor type, an application calls **SQLSetStmtOption** with the SQL_CURSOR_TYPE option. The application can specify a cursor that only scrolls forward, a static cursor, a dynamic cursor, a keyset-driven cursor, or a mixed cursor. If the application specifies a mixed cursor, it also specifies the size of the keyset used by the cursor.

Note To use the ODBC cursor library, an application calls **SQLSetConnectOption** with the SQL_ODBC_CURSORS option before it connects to the data source. The cursor library supports block scrollable cursors. It also supports positioned update and delete statements. For more information, see Appendix G, "ODBC Cursor Library."

Unless the cursor is a forward-only cursor, an application calls **SQLExtendedFetch** to scroll the cursor backwards, forwards, or to an absolute or relative position in the result set. The application calls **SQLSetPos** to refresh the row currently pointed to by the cursor.

Specifying Cursor Concurrency

Concurrency is the ability of more than one user to use the same data at the same time. A transaction is *serializable* if it is performed in a manner in which it appears as if no other transactions operate on the same data at the same time. For example, assume one transaction doubles data values and another adds 1 to data values. If the transactions are serializable and both attempt to operate on the values 0 and 10 at the same time, the final values will be 1 and 21 or 2 and 22, depending on which transaction is performed first. If the transactions are not serializable, the final values will be 1 and 21, 2 and 22, 1 and 22, or 2 and 21; the sets of values 1 and 22, and 2 and 21, are the result of the transactions acting on each value in a different order.

Serializability is considered necessary to maintain database integrity. For cursors, it is most easily implemented at the expense of concurrency by locking the result set. A compromise between serializability and concurrency is *optimistic concurrency control*. In a cursor using optimistic concurrency control, the driver does not lock rows when it retrieves them. When the application requests an update or delete operation, the driver or data source checks if the row has changed. If the row has not changed, the driver or data source prevents other transactions from changing the row until the operation is complete. If the row has changed, the transaction containing the update or delete operation fails.

To specify the concurrency used by a cursor, an application calls **SQLSetStmtOption** with the SQL_CONCURRENCY option. The application can specify that the cursor is read-only, locks the result set, uses optimistic concurrency control and compares row versions to determine if a row has changed, or uses optimistic concurrency control and compares data values to determine if a row has changed. The application calls **SQLSetPos** to lock the row currently pointed to by the cursor, regardless of the specified cursor concurrency.

Using Bookmarks

A bookmark is a 32-bit value that an application uses to return to a row. The application does not request that the driver places a bookmark on a row; instead, the application requests a bookmark that it can use to return to a row. For example, if a bookmark is a row number, an application requests the row number of a row and stores it. Later, the application passes this row number back to the driver and requests that the driver return to the row.

Before opening the cursor, an application must call **SQLSetStmtOption** with the SQL_USE_BOOKMARKS option to inform the driver it will use bookmarks. After opening the cursor, the application retrieves bookmarks either from column 0 of the result set or by calling **SQLGetStmtOption** with the SQL_GET_BOOKMARK option. To retrieve a bookmark from the result set, the application either binds column 0 and calls **SQLExtendedFetch** or calls **SQLGetData**; in either case, the *fCType* argument must be set to SQL_C_BOOKMARK. To return to the row specified by a bookmark, the application calls **SQLExtendedFetch** with a fetch type of SQL_FETCH_BOOKMARK.

If a bookmark requires more than 32 bits, such as when it is a key value, the driver maps the bookmarks requested by the application to 32-bit binary values. The 32-bit binary values are then returned to the application. Because this mapping may require considerable memory, applications should only bind column 0 of the result set if they will actually use bookmarks for most rows. Otherwise, they should call **SQLGetStmtOption** with the SQL_BOOKMARK statement option or call **SQLGetData** for column 0.

Before an application opens a cursor with which it will use bookmarks, it:

- Calls **SQLSetStmtOption** with the SQL_USE_BOOKMARKS option and a value of SQL_UB_ON.

To retrieve a bookmark for the current row, an application:

- Retrieves the value from column 0 of the rowset. The application can either call **SQLBindCol** to bind column 0 before it calls **SQLExtendedFetch** or call **SQLGetData** to retrieve the data after it calls **SQLExtendedFetch**. In either case, the *fCType* argument must be SQL_C_BOOKMARK.

Note To determine whether it can call **SQLGetData** for a block (more than one row) of data and whether it can call **SQLGetData** for a column before the last bound column, an application calls **SQLGetInfo** with the SQL_GETDATA_EXTENSIONS information type.

−Or−

Calls **SQLSetPos** with the SQL_POSITION option to position the cursor on the row and calls **SQLGetStmtOption** with the SQL_BOOKMARK option to retrieve the bookmark.

To return to the row specified by a bookmark (or a row a certain number of rows from the bookmark), an application:

- Calls **SQLExtendedFetch** with the *irow* argument set to the bookmark and the *fFetchType* argument set to SQL_FETCH_BOOKMARK. The driver returns the rowset starting with the row identified by the bookmark.

Modifying Result Set Data

ODBC provides two ways to modify data in the result set. Positioned update and delete statements are similar to such statements in embedded SQL. Calls to **SQLSetPos** allow an application to update, delete, or add new data without executing SQL statements.

Executing Positioned Update and Delete Statements

An application can update or delete the row in the result set currently pointed to by the cursor. This is known as a positioned update or delete statement. After executing a **SELECT** statement to create a result set, an application calls **SQLFetch** one or more times to position the cursor on the row to be updated or deleted. Alternatively, it fetches the rowset with **SQLExtendedFetch** and positions the cursor on the desired row by calling **SQLSetPos** with the SQL_POSITION option. To update or delete the row, the application then executes an SQL statement with the following syntax on a different *hstmt*:

UPDATE *table-name*
    SET *column-identifier* = {*expression* | **NULL**}
        [**,** *column-identifier* = {*expression* | **NULL**}]...
    WHERE CURRENT OF *cursor-name*

DELETE FROM *table-name* **WHERE CURRENT OF** *cursor-name*

Positioned update and delete statements require cursor names. An application can name a cursor with **SQLSetCursorName**. If the application has not named the cursor by the time the driver executes a **SELECT** statement, the driver generates a cursor name. To retrieve the cursor name for an *hstmt*, an application calls **SQLGetCursorName**.

To execute a positioned update or delete statement, an application must follow these guidelines:

- The **SELECT** statement that creates the result set must use a **FOR UPDATE** clause.

- The cursor name used in the **UPDATE** or **DELETE** statement must be the same as the cursor name associated with the **SELECT** statement.

- The application must use different *hstmts* for the **SELECT** statement and the **UPDATE** or **DELETE** statement.

- The *hstmts* for the **SELECT** statement and the **UPDATE** or **DELETE** statement must be on the same connection.

To determine if a data source supports positioned update and delete statements, an application calls **SQLGetInfo** with the SQL_POSITIONED_STATEMENTS option. For an example of code that performs a positioned update in a rowset, see **SQLSetPos** in Chapter 22, "ODBC Function Reference."

Note In ODBC 1.0, positioned update, positioned delete, and **SELECT FOR UPDATE** statements were part of the core SQL grammar; in ODBC 2.0, they are part of the extended grammar. Applications that use the SQL conformance level to determine whether these statements are supported also need to check the version number of the driver to correctly interpret the information. In particular, applications that use these features with ODBC 1.0 drivers need to explicitly check for these capabilities in ODBC 2.0 drivers.

Modifying Data with SQLSetPos

To add, update, and delete rows of data, an application calls **SQLSetPos** and specifies the operation, the row number, and how to lock the row. Where new rows of data are added to the result set, and whether they are visible to the cursor is data source–defined.

The row number determines both the number of the row in the rowset to update or delete and the index of the row in the rowset buffers from which to retrieve data to add or update. If the row number is 0, the operation affects all of the rows in the rowset.

SQLSetPos retrieves the data to update or add from the rowset buffers. It only updates those columns in a row that have been bound with **SQLBindCol** and do not have a length of SQL_IGNORE. However, it cannot add a new row of data unless all of the columns in the row are bound, are nullable, or have a default value.

Note The rowset buffers are used both to send and retrieve data. To avoid overwriting existing data when it adds a new row of data, an application can allocate an extra row at the end of the rowset buffers to use as an add buffer.

To add a new row of data to the result set, an application:

1. Places the data for each column the *rgbValue* buffers specified with **SQLBindCol**. To avoid overwriting an existing row of data, the application should allocate an extra row of the rowset buffers to use as an add buffer.

2. Places the length of each column in the *pcbValue* buffer specified with **SQLBindCol**; this only needs to be done for columns with an *fCType* of SQL_C_CHAR or SQL_C_BINARY. To use the default value for a column, the application specifies a length of SQL_IGNORE.

Note To add a new row of data to a result set, one of the following two conditions must be met:

- All columns in the underlying tables must be bound with **SQLBindCol**.

- All unbound columns and all bound columns for which the specified length is SQL_IGNORE must accept NULL values or have default values.

To determine if a row in a result set accepts NULL values, an application calls **SQLColAttributes**. To determine if a data source supports non-nullable columns, an application calls **SQLGetInfo** with the SQL_NON_NULLABLE flag.

3. Calls **SQLSetPos** with the *fOption* argument set to SQL_ADD. The *irow* argument determines the row in the rowset buffers from which the data is retrieved. For information about how an application sends data for data-at-execution columns, see **SQLSetPos** in Chapter 22, "ODBC Function Reference."

   After the row is added, the row the cursor points to is unchanged.

Note Columns for long data types, such as SQL_LONGVARCHAR and SQL_LONGVARBINARY, are generally not bound. However, if an application uses **SQLSetPos** to send data for these columns, it must bind them with **SQLBindCol**. Unless the driver returns the SQL_GD_BOUND bit for the SQL_GETDATA_EXTENSIONS information type, the application must unbind them before calling **SQLGetData** to retrieve data from them.

To update a row of data, an application:

1. Modifies the data of each column to be updated in the *rgbValue* buffer specified with **SQLBindCol**.

2. Places the length of each column to be updated in the *pcbValue* buffer specified with **SQLBindCol**. This only needs to be done for columns with an *fCType* of SQL_C_CHAR or SQL_C_BINARY.

3. Sets the value of the *pcbValue* buffer for each bound column that is not to be updated to SQL_IGNORE.

4. Calls **SQLSetPos** with the *fOption* argument set to SQL_UPDATE. The *irow* argument specifies the number of the row in the rowset to modify and the index of row in the rowset buffer from which to retrieve the data. The cursor points to this row after it is updated.

   For information about how an application sends data for data-at-execution columns, see **SQLSetPos** in Chapter 22, "ODBC Function Reference."

To delete a row of data, an application:

■ Calls **SQLSetPos** with the *fOption* argument set to SQL_DELETE. The *irow* argument specifies the number of the row in the rowset to delete. The cursor points to this row after it is deleted.

Note The application cannot perform any positioned operations, such as executing a positioned update or delete statement or calling **SQLGetData**, on a deleted row.

To determine what operations a data source supports for **SQLSetPos**, an application calls **SQLGetInfo** with the SQL_POS_OPERATIONS flag.

Processing Multiple Results

SELECT statements return result sets. **UPDATE, INSERT**, and **DELETE** statements return a count of affected rows. If any of these statements are batched, submitted with arrays of parameters, or in procedures, they can return multiple result sets or counts.

To process a batch of statements, statement with arrays of parameters, or procedure returning multiple result sets or row counts, an application:

1. Calls **SQLExecute** or **SQLExecDirect** to execute the statement or procedure.

2. Calls **SQLRowCount** to determine the number of rows affected by an **UPDATE, INSERT**, or **DELETE** statement. For statements or procedures that return result sets, the application calls functions to determine the characteristics of the result set and retrieve data from the result set.

3. Calls **SQLMoreResults** to determine if another result set or row count is available.

4. Repeats steps 2 and 3 until **SQLMoreResults** returns SQL_NO_DATA_FOUND.

CHAPTER 8

Retrieving Status and Error Information

This chapter defines the ODBC return codes and error handling protocol. The return codes indicate whether a function succeeded, succeeded but returned a warning, or failed. The error handling protocol defines how the components in an ODBC connection construct and return error messages through **SQLError**.

The protocol describes:

- Use of the error text to identify the source of an error.
- Rules to ensure consistent and useful error information.
- Responsibility for setting the ODBC SQLSTATE based on the native error.

Function Return Codes

When an application calls an ODBC function, the driver executes the function and returns a predefined code. These return codes indicate success, warning, or failure status. The following table defines the return codes.

Return Code	Description
SQL_SUCCESS	Function completed successfully; no additional information is available.
SQL_SUCCESS_WITH_INFO	Function completed successfully, possibly with a nonfatal error. The application can call **SQLError** to retrieve additional information.
SQL_NO_DATA_FOUND	All rows from the result set have been fetched.
SQL_ERROR	Function failed. The application can call **SQLError** to retrieve error information.
SQL_INVALID_HANDLE	Function failed due to an invalid environment handle, connection handle, or statement handle. This indicates a programming error. No additional information is available from **SQLError**.

Return Code	Description
SQL_STILL_EXECUTING	A function that was started asynchronously is still executing.
SQL_NEED_DATA	While processing a statement, the driver determined that the application needs to send parameter data values.

The application is responsible for taking the appropriate action based on the return code.

Retrieving Error Messages

If an ODBC function other than **SQLError** returns SQL_ERROR or SQL_SUCCESS_WITH_INFO, an application can call **SQLError** to obtain additional information. The application may need to call **SQLError** more than once to retrieve all the error messages from a function, since a function may return more than one error message. When the application calls a different function, the error messages from the previous function are deleted.

Additional error or status information can come from one of two sources:

- Error or status information from an ODBC function, indicating that a programming error was detected.
- Error or status information from the data source, indicating that an error occurred during SQL statement processing.

The information returned by **SQLError** is in the same format as that provided by SQLSTATE in the X/Open and SQL Access Group SQL CAE specification (1992). Note that **SQLError** never returns error information about itself.

ODBC Error Messages

ODBC defines a layered architecture to connect an application to a data source. At its simplest, an ODBC connection requires two components: the Driver Manager and a driver.

A more complex connection might include more components: the Driver Manager, a number of drivers, and a (possibly different) number of DBMS's. The connection might cross computing platforms and operating systems and use a variety of networking protocols.

As the complexity of an ODBC connection increases, so does the importance of providing consistent and complete error messages to the application, its users, and support personnel. Error messages must not only explain the error, but also provide the identity of the component in which it occurred. The identity of the component is particularly important to support personnel when an application uses ODBC components from more than one vendor. Because **SQLError** does not return the identity of the component in which the error occurred, this information must be embedded in the error text.

Error Text Format

Error messages returned by **SQLError** come from two sources: data sources and components in an ODBC connection. Typically, data sources do not directly support ODBC. Consequently, if a component in an ODBC connection receives an error message from a data source, it must identify the data source as the source of the error. It must also identify itself as the component that received the error.

If the source of an error is the component itself, the error message must explain this. Therefore, the error text returned by **SQLError** has two different formats: one for errors that occur in a data source and one for errors that occur in other components in an ODBC connection.

For errors that do not occur in a data source, the error text must use the format:

[*vendor-identifier*][*ODBC-component-identifier*]*component-supplied-text*

For errors that occur in a data source, the error text must use the format:

[*vendor-identifier*][*ODBC-component-identifier*][*data-source-identifier*]
    data-source-supplied-text

The following table shows the meaning of each element.

Element	Meaning
vendor-identifier	Identifies the vendor of the component in which the error occurred or that received the error directly from the data source.
ODBC-component-identifier	Identifies the component in which the error occurred or that received the error directly from the data source.
data-source-identifier	Identifies the data source. For single-tier drivers, this is typically a file format, such as Xbase[1]. For multiple-tier drivers, this is the DBMS product.
component-supplied-text	Generated by the ODBC component.
data-source-supplied-text	Generated by the data source.

1 In this case, the driver is acting as both the driver and the data source.

Note that the brackets ([ ]) are included in the error text; they do not indicate optional items.

Sample Error Messages

The following are examples of how various components in an ODBC connection might generate the text of error messages and how various drivers might return them to the application with **SQLError**. Note that these examples do not represent actual implementations of the error handling protocol. For more information on how an individual driver has implemented the protocol, see the documentation for that driver.

Single-Tier Driver

A single-tier driver acts both as an ODBC driver and as a data source. It can therefore generate errors both as a component in an ODBC connection and as a data source. Because it also is the component that interfaces with the Driver Manager, it formats and returns arguments for **SQLError**.

For example, if a Microsoft driver for dBASE® could not allocate sufficient memory, it might return the following arguments for **SQLError**:

```
szSQLState      =   "S1001"
pfNativeError   =   NULL
szErrorMsg      =   "[Microsoft][ODBC dBASE Driver]Unable to
                    ➡ allocate sufficient memory."
pcbErrorMsg     =   67
```

Because this error was not related to the data source, the driver only added prefixes to the error text for the vendor ([Microsoft]) and the driver ([ODBC dBASE Driver]).

If the driver could not find the file EMPLOYEE.DBF, it might return the following arguments for **SQLError**:

```
szSQLState      =   "S0002"
pfNativeError   =   NULL
szErrorMsg      =   "[Microsoft][ODBC dBASE Driver][dBASE]Invalid file
                    ➡ name;file EMPLOYEE.DBF not found."
pcbErrorMsg     =   83
```

Because this error was related to the data source, the driver added the file format of the data source ([dBASE]) as a prefix to the error text. Because the driver was also the component that interfaced with the data source, it added prefixes for the vendor ([Microsoft]) and the driver ([ODBC dBASE Driver]).

Multiple-Tier Driver

A multiple-tier driver sends requests to a DBMS and returns information to the application through the Driver Manager. Because it is the component that interfaces with the Driver Manager, it formats and returns arguments for **SQLError**.

For example, if a Microsoft driver for DEC's Rdb using SQL/Services encountered a duplicate cursor name, it might return the following arguments for **SQLError**:

```
szSQLState     =    "3C000"
pfNativeError  =    NULL
szErrorMsg     =    "[Microsoft][ODBC Rdb Driver]Duplicate cursor name:
                ➥ EMPLOYEE_CURSOR."
pcbErrorMsg    =    67
```

Because the error occurred in the driver, it added prefixes to the error text for the vendor ([Microsoft]) and the driver ([ODBC Rdb Driver]).

If the DBMS could not find the table EMPLOYEE, the driver might format and return the following arguments for **SQLError**:

```
szSQLState     =    "S0002"
pfNativeError  =    -1
szErrorMsg     =    "[Microsoft][ODBC Rdb Driver][Rdb]
                ➥ %SQL-F-RELNOTDEF, Table   EMPLOYEE is not defined
                ➥ in schema."
pcbErrorMsg    =    92
```

Because the error occurred in the data source, the driver added a prefix for the data source identifier ([Rdb]) to the error text. Because the driver was the component that interfaced with the data source, it added prefixes for its vendor ([Microsoft]) and identifier ([ODBC Rdb Driver]) to the error text.

Gateways

In a gateway architecture, a driver sends requests to a gateway that supports ODBC. The gateway sends the requests to a DBMS. Because it is the component that interfaces with the Driver Manager, the driver formats and returns arguments for **SQLError**.

For example, if DEC based a gateway to Rdb on Microsoft Open Data Services, and Rdb could not find the table EMPLOYEE, the gateway might generate the following error text:

```
"[S0002][-1][DEC][ODS Gateway][Rdb]%SQL-F-RELNOTDEF, Table EMPLOYEE
➥ is not defined in schema."
```

Because the error occurred in the data source, the gateway added a prefix for the data source identifier ([Rdb]) to the error text. Because the gateway was the component that interfaced with the data source, it added prefixes for its vendor ([DEC]) and identifier ([ODS Gateway]) to the error text. Note that it also added the SQLSTATE value and the Rdb error code to the beginning of the error text. This permitted it to preserve the semantics of its own message structure and still supply the ODBC error information to the driver.

Because the gateway driver is the component that interfaces with the Driver Manager, it would use the preceding error text to format and return the following arguments for **SQLError**:

```
szSQLState      =    "S0002"
pfNativeError   =    -1
szErrorMsg      =    "[DEC][ODS Gateway][Rdb]%SQL-F-RELNOTDEF, Table
                     ➥ EMPLOYEE is not defined in schema."
pcbErrorMsg     =    81
```

Driver Manager

The Driver Manager can also generate error messages. For example, if an application passed an invalid argument value to **SQLDataSources**, the Driver Manager might format and return the following arguments for **SQLError**:

```
szSQLState      =    "S1009"
pfNativeError   =    NULL
szErrorMsg      =    "[Microsoft][ODBC DLL]Invalid argument value:
                     ➥ SQLDataSources."
pcbErrorMsg     =    60
```

Because the error occurred in the Driver Manager, it added prefixes to the error text for its vendor ([Microsoft]) and its identifier ([ODBC DLL]).

Processing Error Messages

Applications should provide users with all the error information available through **SQLError**: the ODBC SQLSTATE, the native error code, the error text, and the source of the error. The application may parse the error text to separate the text from the information identifying the source of the error. It is the application's responsibility to take appropriate action based on the error or provide the user with a choice of actions.

CHAPTER 9

Terminating Transactions and Connections

The ODBC interface provides functions that terminate statements, transactions, and connections, and free statement (*hstmt*), connection (*hdbc*), and environment (*henv*) handles.

Terminating Statement Processing

To free resources associated with a statement handle, an application calls **SQLFreeStmt**. The **SQLFreeStmt** function has four options:

- **SQL_CLOSE**   Closes the cursor, if one exists, and discards pending results. The application can use the statement handle again later.
- **SQL_DROP**   Closes the cursor if one exists, discards pending results, and frees all resources associated with the statement handle.
- **SQL_UNBIND**   Frees all return buffers bound by **SQLBindCol** for the statement handle.
- **SQL_RESET_PARAMS**   Frees all parameter buffers requested by **SQLBindParameter** for the statement handle.

To cancel a statement that is executing asynchronously, an application:

- Calls **SQLCancel**. When and if the statement is actually canceled is driver- and data source–dependent.
- Calls the function that was executing the statement asynchronously. If the statement is still executing, the function returns SQL_STILL_EXECUTING; if it was successfully canceled, the function returns SQL_ERROR and SQLSTATE S1008 (Operation canceled); if it completed normal execution, the function returns any valid return code, such as SQL_SUCCESS or SQL_ERROR.
- Calls **SQLError** if the function returned SQL_ERROR. If the driver successfully canceled the function, the SQLSTATE will be S1008 (Operation canceled).

Terminating Transactions

An application calls **SQLTransact** to commit or roll back the current transaction.

Terminating Connections

To terminate a connection to a driver and data source, an application performs the following steps:

1. Calls **SQLDisconnect** to close the connection. The application can then use the handle to reconnect to the same data source or to a different data source.

2. Calls **SQLFreeConnect** to free the connection handle and free all resources associated with the handle.

3. Calls **SQLFreeEnv** to free the environment handle and free all resources associated with the handle.

C H A P T E R   1 0

Constructing an ODBC Application

This chapter provides two examples of C-language source code for ODBC-enabled applications. A summary of development, debugging, installation, and administration tools provided by the ODBC SDK 2.0 is included.

Sample Application Code

The following sections contain two ODBC examples that are written in the C programming language:

- An example that uses static SQL functions to create a table, add data to it, and select the inserted data.
- An example of interactive, ad-hoc query processing.

Static SQL Example

The following example constructs SQL statements within the application. The example comments include equivalent embedded SQL calls for illustrative purposes.

```
#include "SQL.H"
#include <string.h>

#ifndef NULL
#define NULL 0
#endif

#define MAX_NAME_LEN 50
#define MAX_STMT_LEN 100
int print_err(HDBC hdbc, HSTMT hstmt);

int example1(server, uid, pwd)
UCHAR * server;
UCHAR * uid;
UCHAR * pwd;
```

```
{
HENV    henv;
HDBC    hdbc;
HSTMT   hstmt;

SDWORD  id;
UCHAR   name[MAX_NAME_LEN + 1];
UCHAR   create[MAX_STMT_LEN]
UCHAR   insert[MAX_STMT_LEN]
UCHAR   select[MAX_STMT_LEN]
SDWORD  namelen;
RETCODE rc;

/* EXEC SQL CONNECT TO :server USER :uid USING :pwd; */
/* Allocate an environment handle.                   */
/* Allocate a connection handle.                     */
/* Connect to a data source.                         */
/* Allocate a statement handle.                      */

SQLAllocEnv(&henv);
SQLAllocConnect(henv, &hdbc);
rc = SQLConnect(hdbc, server, SQL_NTS, uid, SQL_NTS, pwd, SQL_NTS);
if (rc != SQL_SUCCESS && rc != SQL_SUCCESS_WITH_INFO)
    return(print_err(hdbc, SQL_NULL_HSTMT));
SQLAllocStmt(hdbc, &hstmt);

/* EXEC SQL CREATE TABLE NAMEID (ID integer, NAME varchar(50)); */
/* Execute the SQL statement.                                   */

lstrcpy(create, "CREATE TABLE NAMEID (ID INTEGER, NAME
        VARCHAR(50))");
rc = SQLExecDirect(hstmt, create, SQL_NTS);
if (rc != SQL_SUCCESS && rc != SQL_SUCCESS_WITH_INFO)
    return(print_err(hdbc, hstmt));
```

```
/* EXEC SQL COMMIT WORK;        */
/* Commit the table creation. */

/* Note that the default transaction mode for drivers that support    */
/* SQLSetConnectOption is auto-commit and SQLTransact has no effect. */

SQLTransact(hdbc, SQL_COMMIT);

/* EXEC SQL INSERT INTO NAMEID VALUES ( :id, :name ); */
/* Show the use of the SQLPrepare/SQLExecute method:  */
/* Prepare the insertion and bind parameters.         */
/* Assign parameter values.                           */
/* Execute the insertion.                             */

lstrcpy(insert, "INSERT INTO NAMEID VALUES (?, ?)");
if (SQLPrepare(hstmt, insert, SQL_NTS) != SQL_SUCCESS)
    return(print_err(hdbc, hstmt));
SQLBindParameter(hstmt, 1, SQL_PARAM_INPUT, SQL_C_SLONG, SQL_INTEGER,
                0, 0, &id, 0, NULL);
SQLBindParameter(hstmt, 2, SQL_PARAM_INPUT, SQL_C_CHAR, SQL_VARCHAR,
                MAX_NAME_LEN, 0, name, 0, NULL);
id=500;
lstrcpy(name, "Babbage");
if (SQLExecute(hstmt) != SQL_SUCCESS)
    return(print_err(hdbc, hstmt));

/* EXEC SQL COMMIT WORK; */
/* Commit the insertion. */

SQLTransact(hdbc, SQL_COMMIT);

/* EXEC SQL DECLARE c1 CURSOR FOR SELECT ID, NAME FROM NAMEID; */
/* EXEC SQL OPEN c1;                                          */
/* Show the use of the SQLExecDirect method.                 */
/* Execute the selection.                                    */
/* Note that the application does not declare a cursor.      */

lstrcpy(select, "SELECT ID, NAME FROM NAMEID");
if (SQLExecDirect(hstmt, select, SQL_NTS) != SQL_SUCCESS)
    return(print_err(hdbc, hstmt));

/* EXEC SQL FETCH c1 INTO :id, :name;                */
/* Bind the columns of the result set with SQLBindCol. */
/* Fetch the first row.                              */

SQLBindCol(hstmt, 1, SQL_C_SLONG, &id, 0, NULL);
SQLBindCol(hstmt, 2, SQL_C_CHAR, name, (SDWORD)sizeof(name), &namelen);
SQLFetch(hstmt);
```

```
/* EXEC SQL COMMIT WORK;   */
/* Commit the transaction. */

SQLTransact(hdbc, SQL_COMMIT);

/* EXEC SQL CLOSE c1;           */
/* Free the statement handle. */

SQLFreeStmt(hstmt, SQL_DROP);

/* EXEC SQL DISCONNECT;               */
/* Disconnect from the data source. */
/* Free the connection handle.       */
/* Free the environment handle.      */

SQLDisconnect(hdbc);
SQLFreeConnect(hdbc);
SQLFreeEnv(henv);

return(0);
}
```

Interactive Ad Hoc Query Example

The following example illustrates how an application can determine the nature of the result set prior to retrieving results.

```c
#include "SQL.H"
#include <string.h>
#include <stdlib.h>

#define MAXCOLS 100
#define max(a,b) (a>b?a:b)

int    print_err(HDBC hdbc, HSTMT hstmt);
UDWORD display_size(SWORD coltype, UDWORD collen, UCHAR *colname);

example2(server, uid, pwd, sqlstr)
UCHAR * server;
UCHAR * uid;
UCHAR * pwd;
UCHAR * sqlstr;
{
int    i;
HENV   henv;
HDBC   hdbc;
HSTMT  hstmt;
UCHAR  errmsg[256];
UCHAR  colname[32];
SWORD  coltype;
SWORD  colnamelen;
SWORD  nullable;
UDWORD collen[MAXCOLS];
SWORD  scale;
SDWORD outlen[MAXCOLS];
UCHAR * data[MAXCOLS];
SWORD  nresultcols;
SDWORD rowcount;
RETCODE rc;

/* Allocate environment and connection handles. */
/* Connect to the data source.                  */
/* Allocate a statement handle.                 */
SQLAllocEnv(&henv);
SQLAllocConnect(henv, &hdbc);
rc = SQLConnect(hdbc, server, SQL_NTS, uid, SQL_NTS, pwd, SQL_NTS);
if (rc != SQL_SUCCESS && rc != SQL_SUCCESS_WITH_INFO)
    return(print_err(hdbc, SQL_NULL_HSTMT));
SQLAllocStmt(hdbc, &hstmt);
```

```
/* Execute the SQL statement. */
if (SQLExecDirect(hstmt, sqlstr, SQL_NTS) != SQL_SUCCESS)
    return(print_err(hdbc, hstmt));

/* See what kind of statement it was.  If there are no result    */
/* columns, the statement is not a SELECT statement.  If the      */
/* number of affected rows is greater than 0, the statement was   */
/* probably an UPDATE, INSERT, or DELETE statement, so print the  */
/* number of affected rows.  If the number of affected rows is 0, */
/* the statement is probably a DDL statement, so print that the   */
/* operation was successful and commit it.                        */

SQLNumResultCols(hstmt, &nresultcols);
if (nresultcols == 0) {
    SQLRowCount(hstmt, &rowcount);
    if (rowcount > 0 ) {
        printf("%ld rows affected.\n", rowcount);
    } else {
        printf("Operation successful.\n");
    }
    SQLTransact(hdbc, SQL_COMMIT);

/* Otherwise, display the column names of the result set and use the */
/* display_size() function to compute the length needed by each data */
/* type.  Next, bind the columns and specify all data will be        */
/* converted to char.  Finally, fetch and print each row, printing   */
/* truncation messages as necessary.                                 */

} else {
    for (i = 0; i < nresultcols; i++) {
        SQLDescribeCol(hstmt, i + 1, colname, (SWORD)sizeof(colname),
                        &colnamelen, &coltype, &collen[i], &scale,
                        &nullable);
        collen[i] = display_size(coltype, collen[i], colname);
        printf("%*.*s", collen[i], collen[i], colname);
        data[i] = (UCHAR *) malloc(collen[i] + 1);
        SQLBindCol(hstmt, i + 1, SQL_C_CHAR, data[i], collen[i],
                    &outlen[i]);
    }
```

```
            while (TRUE) {
                rc = SQLFetch(hstmt);
                if (rc == SQL_SUCCESS || rc == SQL_SUCCESS_WITH_INFO) {
                    errmsg[0] = '\0';
                    for (i = 0; i < nresultcols; i++)
                        if (outlen[i] == SQL_NULL_DATA) {
                            lstrcpy(data[i], "NULL");
                        } else if (outlen[i] >= collen[i]) {
                            sprintf(&errmsg[strlen(errmsg)],
                                    "%d chars truncated, col %d\n",
                                    *outlen[i] - collen[i] + 1,
                                    colnum);
                        }
                        printf("%*.*s ", collen[i], collen[i], data[i]);
                    }
                    printf("\n%s", errmsg);
                } else {
                    break;
                }
            }
        }

        /* Free the data buffers. */
        for (i = 0; i < nresultcols; i++) {
            free(data[i]);
        }

        SQLFreeStmt(hstmt, SQL_DROP );  /* Free the statement handle.       */
        SQLDisconnect(hdbc);            /* Disconnect from the data source. */
        SQLFreeConnect(hdbc);           /* Free the connection handle.      */
        SQLFreeEnv(henv);               /* Free the environment handle.     */

        return(0);
        }
```

```
/**********************************************************/
/* The following function is included for completeness, but */
/* is not relevant for understanding the function of ODBC.  */
/**********************************************************/

#define MAX_NUM_PRECISION 15

/* Define max length of char string representation of number as:    */
/*   =  max(precision) + leading sign + E + exp sign + max exp length */
/*   =  15                + 1              + 1 + 1        + 2          */
/*   =  15 + 5                                                         */

#define MAX_NUM_STRING_SIZE (MAX_NUM_PRECISION + 5)

UDWORD  display_size(coltype, collen, colname)
SWORD   coltype;
UDWORD  collen;
UCHAR * colname;
{
switch (coltype) {

    case SQL_CHAR:
    case SQL_VARCHAR:
        return(max(collen, strlen(colname)));

    case SQL_SMALLINT:
        return(max(6, strlen(colname)));

    case SQL_INTEGER:
        return(max(11, strlen(colname)));

    case SQL_DECIMAL:
    case SQL_NUMERIC:
    case SQL_REAL:
    case SQL_FLOAT:
    case SQL_DOUBLE:
        return(max(MAX_NUM_STRING_SIZE, strlen(colname)));

    /* Note that this function only supports the core data types. */
    default:
        printf("Unknown datatype, %d\n", coltype);
        return(0);
    }
}
```

Testing and Debugging an Application

The ODBC SDK provides the following tools for application development:

- ODBC Test, an interactive utility that enables you to perform ad hoc and automated testing on drivers. A sample test DLL (the Quick Test) is included which covers basic areas of ODBC driver conformance.

- ODBC Spy, a debugging tool with which you can capture data source information, emulate drivers, and emulate applications.

- Sample applications, including source code and makefiles.

- A **#define**, ODBCVER, to specify which version of ODBC you want to compile your application with. By default, the SQL.H and SQLEXT.H files include all ODBC 2.0 constants and prototypes. To use only the ODBC 1.0 constants and prototypes, add the following line to your application code before including SQL.H and SQLEXT.H:

```
#define ODBCVER 0x0100
```

For additional infomation about the ODBC SDK tools, see the *Microsoft ODBC SDK Guide*.

Installing and Configuring ODBC Software

Users install ODBC software with a driver-specific setup program (built with the Driver Setup Toolkit that is shipped with the ODBC SDK) or an application-specific setup program. They configure the ODBC environment with the ODBC Administrator (also shipped with the ODBC SDK) or an application-specific administration program. Application developers must decide whether to redistribute these programs or write their own setup and administration programs. For more information about the Driver Setup Toolkit and the ODBC Administrator, see the *Microsoft ODBC SDK Guide*.

A setup program written by an application developer uses the installer DLL to retrieve information from the ODBC.INF file, which is created by a driver developer and describes the disks on which the ODBC software is shipped. The setup program also uses the installer DLL to retrieve the target directories for the Driver Manager and the drivers, record information about the installed drivers, and install ODBC software. For more information, see Chapter 19, "Installing ODBC Software."

Administration programs written by application developers use the installer DLL to retrieve information about the available drivers, to specify default drivers, and to configure data sources. For more information, see Chapter 20, "Configuring Data Sources."

Application developers who write their own setup and administration programs must ship the installer DLL and the ODBC.INF file.

PART 3

Developing Drivers

CHAPTER 11

Guidelines for Implementing ODBC Functions

Each driver supports a set of ODBC functions. These functions perform tasks such as allocating and deallocating memory, transmitting or processing SQL statements, and returning results and errors.

This chapter describes the role of the Driver Manager, the general characteristics of ODBC functions, supporting ODBC conformance levels, ODBC function arguments, and what ODBC functions return.

Role of the Driver Manager

ODBC function calls are passed through the Driver Manager to the driver. An application typically links with the Driver Manager import library (ODBC.LIB) to gain access to the Driver Manager. When an application calls an ODBC function, the Driver Manager performs one of the following actions:

- For **SQLDataSources** and **SQLDrivers**, the Driver Manager processes the call. It does not pass the call to the driver.

- For **SQLGetFunctions**, the Driver Manager passes the call to the driver associated with the connection. If the driver does not support **SQLGetFunctions**, the Driver Manager processes the call.

- For **SQLAllocEnv**, **SQLAllocConnect**, **SQLSetConnectOption**, **SQLFreeConnect**, and **SQLFreeEnv**, the Driver Manager processes the call. The Driver Manager calls **SQLAllocEnv**, **SQLAllocConnect**, and **SQLSetConnectOption** in the driver when the application calls a function to connect to the data source (**SQLConnect**, **SQLDriverConnect**, or **SQLBrowseConnect**). The Driver Manager calls **SQLFreeConnect** and **SQLFreeEnv** in the driver when the application calls **SQLFreeConnect**.

- For **SQLConnect**, **SQLDriverConnect**, **SQLBrowseConnect**, and **SQLError**, the Driver Manager performs initial processing, then sends the call to the driver associated with the connection.

- For any other ODBC function, the Driver Manager passes the call to the driver associated with the connection.

If requested, the Driver Manager records each called function in a trace file after checking the function call for errors. The name of each function that does not contain errors detectable by the Driver Manager is recorded, along with the values of the input arguments and the names of the output arguments (as listed in the function definitions).

The Driver Manager also checks function arguments and state transitions, and for other error conditions before passing the call to the driver associated with the connection. This reduces the amount of error handling that a driver needs to perform. However, the Driver Manager does not check all arguments, state transitions, or error conditions for a given function. For complete information about what the Driver Manager checks, see the following sections, the Diagnostics section of each function in Chapter 22, "ODBC Function Reference," and the state transition tables in Appendix B, "ODBC State Transition Tables."

Validating Arguments

The following general guidelines discuss the arguments or types of arguments checked by the Driver Manager. They are not intended to be exhaustive; the Diagnostics section of each function in Chapter 22, "ODBC Function Reference," lists those SQLSTATEs returned by the Driver Manager for that function. Unless otherwise noted, the Driver Manager returns the return code SQL_ERROR.

- Environment, connection, and statement handles are checked to make sure they are not null pointers and are the correct type of handle for the argument. For example, the Driver Manager checks that the application does not pass an *hdbc* where an *hstmt* is required. If the Driver Manager finds an invalid handle, it returns SQL_INVALID_HANDLE.

- Other required arguments, such as the *phenv* argument in **SQLAllocEnv** or the *szCursor* argument in **SQLSetCursorName**, are checked to make sure they are not null pointers.

- Option flags that cannot be extended by the driver are checked to make sure they specify only supported options. For example, the Driver Manager checks that the *fDriverCompletion* argument in **SQLDriverConnect** is a valid value.

- Option flags that can be extended by the driver, such as the *fInfoType* argument in **SQLGetInfo**, are checked only to make sure that values in the ranges reserved for ODBC options are valid; drivers must check that values in the ranges reserved for driver-specific options are valid. For more information, see "Driver-Specific Data Types, Descriptor Types, Information Types, and Options," later in this chapter.

- All option flags are checked to make sure that no ODBC 2.0 option values are sent to ODBC 1.0 drivers. For example, the Driver Manager returns an error if the *fInfoType* argument in **SQLGetInfo** is SQL_GROUP_BY and the driver is an ODBC 1.0 driver.

- Argument values that specify a column or parameter number are checked to make sure they are greater than 0 or greater than or equal to 0, depending on the function. The driver must check the upper limit of these argument values based on the current result set or SQL statement.

- Buffer length arguments are checked as possible to make sure that their values are appropriate for the corresponding buffer in the context of the given function. For example, *szTableName* in **SQLColumns** is an input argument. Therefore, the Driver Manager checks that if the corresponding length argument (*cbTableName*) is less than 0, it is SQL_NTS. The *szColName* argument in **SQLDescribeCol** is an output argument. Therefore, the Driver Manager checks that the corresponding length argument (*cbColNameMax*) is greater than or equal to 0.

  Note that the driver may also need to check the validity of buffer length arguments. For example, the driver must check that the *cbTableName* argument in **SQLColumns** is less than or equal to the maximum length of a table name in the data source.

Checking State Transitions

The Driver Manager validates the state of the *henv*, *hdbc* or *hstmt* in the context of the function's requirement. For example, an *hdbc* must be in an allocated state before the application can call **SQLConnect** and an *hstmt* must be in a prepared state before the application can call **SQLExecute**.

The state transition tables in Appendix B, "ODBC State Transition Tables," list those state transition errors detected by the Driver Manager for each function. The Driver Manager always returns the SQL_ERROR return code for state transition errors.

Checking for General Errors

The following general guidelines discuss general error checking done by the Driver Manager. They are not intended to be exhaustive; the Diagnostics section of each function in Chapter 22, "ODBC Function Reference," lists those SQLSTATEs returned by the Driver Manager for that function. The Driver Manager always returns the SQL_ERROR return code for general errors.

- Function calls are checked to make sure that the functions are supported by the associated driver.

- The Driver Manager completely implements **SQLDataSources** and **SQLDrivers**. Therefore, it checks for all errors in these functions.

- The Driver Manager checks if a driver implements **SQLGetFunctions**. If the driver does not implement **SQLGetFunctions**, the Driver Manager implements and checks for all errors in it.

- The Driver Manager partially implements **SQLAllocEnv**, **SQLAllocConnect**, **SQLConnect**, **SQLDriverConnect**, **SQLBrowseConnect**, **SQLFreeConnect**, **SQLFreeEnv**, and **SQLError**. Therefore, it checks for some errors in these functions. It may return the same errors as the driver for some of these functions, as both perform similar operations. For example, the Driver Manager or driver may return SQLSTATE IM008 (Dialog failed) if they are unable to display a login dialog box for **SQLDriverConnect**.

Elements of ODBC Functions

The following characteristics apply to all ODBC functions.

General Information

Each ODBC function name starts with the prefix "SQL". Each function includes one or more arguments. Arguments are defined for input (to the driver) or output (from the driver). Applications can include variable-length data where appropriate.

C programs that call ODBC functions include the SQL.H, SQLEXT.H, and WINDOWS.H header files. These files define Windows and ODBC constants and types and provide function prototypes for all ODBC functions.

Supporting ODBC Conformance Levels

ODBC defines conformance levels for drivers in two areas: the ODBC API and the ODBC SQL grammar (which includes the ODBC SQL data types). These levels establish standard sets of functionality. By returning the conformance levels it supports, a driver informs applications of the functionality it supports. For a complete discussion of ODBC conformance levels, see "ODBC Conformance Levels" in Chapter 1, "ODBC Theory of Operation."

To claim that it conforms to a given API or SQL conformance level, a driver must support all the functionality in that conformance level, regardless of whether that functionality is supported by the DBMS associated with the driver. A driver may support functionality beyond that in its stated conformance levels.

Note The following sections describe the functions through which a driver returns its conformance levels. Since these are Level 1 extension functions, a given driver may not support them. If a driver does not support these functions, the conformance levels it supports must be included in its documentation.

Supporting API Conformance Levels

ODBC functions are divided into core functions, which are defined in the X/Open and SQL Access Group Call Level Interface specification, and two levels of extension functions, with which ODBC extends this specification. A driver returns its function conformance level through **SQLGetInfo** with the SQL_ODBC_SAG_CLI_CONFORMANCE and SQL_ODBC_API_CONFORMANCE flags. Note that a driver can support one or more extension functions but not conform to ODBC extension Level 1 or 2. The Driver Manager or driver determines and returns whether the driver supports a particular function through **SQLGetFunctions**.

Important Many ODBC applications require that drivers support all of the functions in the Level 1 API conformance level. To ensure that their driver works with most ODBC applications, driver developers should implement all Level 1 functions.

Supporting SQL Conformance Levels

The ODBC SQL grammar, which includes SQL data types, is divided into a minimum grammar, a core grammar, which corresponds to the X/Open and SQL Access Group SQL CAE specification (1992), and an extended grammar, which provides common SQL extensions. A driver returns its SQL conformance level through **SQLGetInfo** with the SQL_ODBC_SQL_CONFORMANCE flag. It returns whether it supports a specific SQL extension through **SQLGetInfo** with a flag for that extension. It returns whether it supports specific SQL data types through **SQLGetTypeInfo**. For more information, see Appendix C, "SQL Grammar," and Appendix D, "Data Types."

Note If a driver supports SQL data types that map to the ODBC SQL date, time, or timestamp data types, the driver must also support the extended SQL grammar for specifying date, time, or timestamp literals.

Buffers

An application passes data to a driver in an input buffer. The driver returns data to an application in an output buffer. The application must allocate memory for both input and output buffers. (If the application will use the buffer to retrieve string data, the buffer must contain space for the null termination byte.)

Caution ODBC does not require drivers to correctly manage buffers that cross segment boundaries in Windows 3.1. The Driver Manager supports the use of such buffers, since it passes buffer addresses to drivers and does not operate on buffer contents. If a driver supports buffers that cross segment boundaries, the documentation for the driver should clearly state this.

If a driver does not support the use of buffers that cross segment boundaries, an application can still use such buffers. The application uses these buffers by passing them to ODBC functions in pieces, none of which crosses a segment boundary.

Input Buffers

An application passes the address and length of an input buffer to a driver. The length of the buffer must be one of the following values:

- A length greater than or equal to zero. This is the actual length of the data in the input buffer. For character data, a length of zero indicates that the data is an empty (zero length) string. Note that this is different from a null pointer. If the application specifies the length of character data, the character data does not need to be null-terminated.

- SQL_NTS. This specifies that a character data value is null-terminated.

- SQL_NULL_DATA. This tells the driver to ignore the value in the input buffer and use a NULL data value instead. It is only valid when the input buffer is used to provide the value of a parameter in an SQL statement.

The operation of ODBC functions on character data containing embedded null characters is undefined, and is not recommended for maximum interoperability. Unless it is specifically prohibited in the description of a given function, the address of an input buffer may be a null pointer. When the address of an input buffer is a null pointer, the value of the corresponding buffer length argument is ignored.

For more information about input buffers, see "Converting Data from C to SQL Data Types" in Appendix D, "Data Types."

Output Buffers

An application passes the following arguments to a driver, so that it can return data in an output buffer:

- The address of the buffer in which the driver returns the data (the output buffer). Unless it is specifically prohibited in a function description, the address of an output buffer can be a null pointer. In this case, the driver does not return anything in the buffer and, in the absence of other errors, returns SQL_SUCCESS.

If necessary, the driver converts data before returning it. The driver always null-terminates character data before returning it.

- The length of the buffer. This is ignored by the driver if the returned data has a fixed length in C, such as an integer, real number, or date structure.

- The address of a variable in which the driver returns the length of the data (the length buffer). The returned length of the data is SQL_NULL_DATA if the data is a NULL value in a result set. Otherwise, it is the number of bytes of data available to return. If the driver converts the data, it is the number of bytes after the conversion. For character data, it does not include the null-termination byte added by the driver.

If the output buffer is too small, the driver attempts to truncate the data. If the truncation does not cause a loss of significant data, the driver returns the truncated data in the output buffer, returns the length of the available data (as opposed to the length of the truncated data) in the length buffer, and returns SQL_SUCCESS_WITH_INFO. If the truncation causes a loss of significant data, the driver leaves the output and length buffers untouched and returns SQL_ERROR. The application calls **SQLError** to retrieve information about the truncation or the error.

For more information about output buffers, see "Converting Data from SQL to C Data Types" in Appendix D, "Data Types."

Environment, Connection, and Statement Handles

When so requested by an application, the Driver Manager and each driver allocate storage for information about the ODBC environment, each connection, and each SQL statement. The handles to these storage areas are returned to the application. The application then uses one or more of them in each call to an ODBC function.

The ODBC interface defines three types of handles:

- The **environment handle** identifies memory storage for global information, including the valid connection handles and current active connection handle. ODBC defines the environment handle as a variable of type HENV. An application uses a single environment handle; it must request this handle prior to connecting to a data source.

- **Connection handles** identify memory storage for information about a particular connection. ODBC defines connection handles as variables of type HDBC. An application must request a connection handle prior to connecting to a a data source. Each connection handle is associated with the environment handle. The environment handle can, however, have multiple connection handles associated with it.

- **Statement handles** identify memory storage for information about an SQL statement. ODBC defines statement handles as variables of type HSTMT. An application must request a statement handle prior to submitting SQL requests. Each statement handle is associated with exactly one connection handle. Each connection handle can, however, have multiple statement handles associated with it.

For more information about connection handles, see Chapter 13, "Establishing Connections." For more information about statement handles, see Chapter 14, "Processing an SQL Statement."

Data Type Support

ODBC defines SQL data types and C data types; a data source may define additional SQL data types. A driver supports these data types in the following ways:

- Accepts SQL and ODBC C data types as arguments in function calls.
- Translates ODBC SQL data types to SQL data types acceptable by the data source, if necessary.
- Converts C data from an application to the SQL data type required by the data source.
- Converts SQL data from a data source to the C data type requested by the application.
- Provides access to data type information through the **SQLDescribeCol** and **SQLColAttributes** functions. If a driver supports them, it also provides data type information through the **SQLGetTypeInfo** and **SQLDescribeParam** functions.

For more information on data types, see Appendix D, "Data Types." The C data types are defined in SQL.H and SQLEXT.H.

ODBC Function Return Codes

When an application calls an ODBC function, the driver executes the function and returns a predefined code. These return codes indicate success, warning, or failure status. The return codes are:

SQL_SUCCESS	SQL_INVALID_HANDLE
SQL_SUCCESS_WITH_INFO	SQL_STILL_EXECUTING
SQL_NO_DATA_FOUND	SQL_NEED_DATA
SQL_ERROR	

If the function returns SQL_SUCCESS_WITH_INFO or SQL_ERROR, the application can call **SQLError** to retrieve additional information. For a complete description of return codes and error handling, see Chapter 16, "Returning Status and Error Information."

Driver-Specific Data Types, Descriptor Types, Information Types, and Options

Drivers can allocate driver-specific values for the following items:

- SQL data types. These are used in the *fSqlType* argument in **SQLBindParameter** and **SQLGetTypeInfo** and returned by **SQLColAttributes**, **SQLColumns**, **SQLDescribeCol**, **SQLGetTypeInfo**, **SQLDescribeParam**, **SQLProcedureColumns**, and **SQLSpecialColumns**.

- Descriptor types. These are used in the *fDescType* argument in **SQLColAttributes**.

- Information types. These are used in the *fInfoType* argument in **SQLGetInfo**.

- Connection and statement options. These are used in the *fOption* argument in **SQLGetConnectOption**, **SQLGetStmtOption**, **SQLSetConnectOption**, and **SQLSetStmtOption**.

For each of these items, there are two ranges of values: a range reserved for use by ODBC, and a range reserved for use by drivers. If you want to implement driver-specific values, such as driver-specific SQL data types or driver-specific statement options, you must reserve a block of values in the driver-specific range. To do this, post a request to the section lead of the ODBC section of the WINEXT forum on CompuServe® or send a request by electronic mail to odbcwish@microsoft.com. Furthermore, you must describe all driver-specific data types, descriptor types, information types, statement options, and connection options in your driver's documentation.

When any of these values is passed to an ODBC function, the Driver Manager checks that values in the ODBC ranges are valid. Drivers must check that values in the driver-specific range are valid. In particular, drivers return SQLSTATE S1C00 (Driver not capable) for driver-specific values that apply to other drivers. The following table shows the ranges of the driver-specific values for each item:

Item	Driver-Specific Range
SQL data types	Less than or equal to SQL_TYPE_DRIVER_START
Descriptor types	Greater than or equal to SQL_COLUMN_DRIVER_START
Information types	Greater than or equal to SQL_INFO_DRIVER_START
Connection and statement options	Greater than or equal to SQL_CONNECT_OPT_DRVR_START

Yielding Control to Windows

Generally, drivers should not explicitly yield control back to Windows. In particular, drivers should not call **PeekMessage** in the Windows API with the PM_REMOVE value set, even when an ODBC function takes a long time, such as when it generates a large result set. Furthermore, driver developers should be careful not to use other, lower-level DLLs (such as network DLLs) that call **PeekMessage**.

If a driver attempted to yield with **PeekMessage**, it would not set the PM_NOYIELD flag. Furthermore, it would not set the PM_NOREMOVE flag, since the first message in the queue is usually for the current application and no other application could be scheduled until that message is removed. However, calling **PeekMessage** with the PM_REMOVE flag causes two problems: the application can be reentered and the **PeekMessage/DispatchMessage** loop in the driver will bypass any preprocessing of messages that may have otherwise been done by the application.

The application can be reentered when the driver dispatches the message; the driver is obligated to dispatch the message because it removed it from the message queue. Because many Windows applications do not guard against reentrancy, this is likely to cause unpredictable results in the application.

Many Windows applications extensively preprocess messages. Because the driver has no knowledge of this preprocessing, it simply calls **DispatchMessage** and is therefore likely to cause unpredictable results in the application. For example, suppose the accelerator key for the Save command is CTRL+S. The message-processing loop in the application calls **TranslateAccelerator** to translate the WM_KEYDOWN and WM_KEYUP messages for CTRL+S into a WM_COMMAND message and to dispatch this message to the menu window. By only calling **DispatchMessage**, the driver does not translate the messages and sends the wrong messages to the menu window.

CHAPTER 12

Application Use of the ODBC Interface

This chapter describes the basic flow of many applications that use ODBC. This information is included here for reference purposes.

To interact with a data source, an application:

1. Connects to the data source. It specifies the data source name and any additional information needed to complete the connection.

2. Processes one or more SQL statements:

   - The application places the SQL text string in a buffer. If the statement includes parameter markers, it sets the parameter values.

   - If the statement returns a result set, the application assigns a cursor name for the statement or allows the driver to do so.

   - The application submits the statement for prepared or immediate execution.

   - If the statement creates a result set, the application can inquire about the attributes of the result set, such as the number of columns and the name and type of a specific column. It assigns storage for each column in the result set and fetches the results.

   - If the statement causes an error, the application retrieves error information from the driver and takes appropriate action.

3. Ends each transaction by committing it or rolling it back.

4. Terminates the connection when it has finished interacting with the data source.

The following diagram lists the ODBC function calls that an application makes to connect to a data source, process SQL statements, and disconnect from the data source. Depending on its needs, an application may call other ODBC functions. For a listing of valid command flow sequences, see Appendix B, "ODBC State Transition Table."

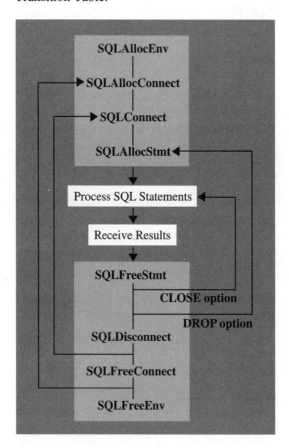

C H A P T E R   1 3

Establishing Connections

This chapter briefly describes data sources. It then describes how an application, Driver Manager, and driver work together to establish a connection to a data source.

About Data Sources

A data source consists of the data a user wants to access, its associated DBMS, the platform on which the DBMS resides, and the network (if any) used to access that platform. Each data source requires that a driver provide certain information in order to connect to it. At the core level, this is defined to be the name of the data source, a user ID, and a password. ODBC extensions allow drivers to specify additional information, such as a network address or additional passwords.

The connection information for each data source is stored in the ODBC.INI file or registry, which is created during installation and maintained with an administration program. A section in this file lists the available data sources. Additional sections describe each data source in detail, specifying the driver name, a description, and any additional information the driver needs to connect to the data source.

For example, suppose a user has three data sources: Personnel and Inventory, which use an Rdb DBMS, and Payroll, which uses an SQL Server DBMS. The section that lists the data sources might be:

```
[ODBC Data Sources]
Personnel=Rdb
Inventory=Rdb
Payroll=SQL Server
```

Suppose also that an Rdb driver needs the ID of the last user to log in, a server name, and a schema declaration statement. The section that describes the Personnel data source might be:

```
[Personnel]
Driver=c:\windows\system\rdb.dll
Description=Personnel database: CURLY
Lastuid=smithjo
Server=curly
Schema=declare schema personnel filename
➥ "sys$sysdevice:[corpdata]personnel.rdb"
```

For more information about data sources and how to configure them, see Chapter 20, "Configuring Data Sources."

Establishing a Connection to a Data Source

All drivers must support the following connection-related functions:

- **SQLAllocEnv** allows the driver to allocate storage for environment information.

- **SQLAllocConnect** allows the driver to allocate storage for connection information.

- **SQLConnect** allows an application to establish a connection with the data source. The application passes the following information in the call to **SQLConnect**:

  - **Data source name**   The name of the data source being requested by the application.

  - **User ID**   The login ID or account name for access to the data source, if appropriate (optional).

  - **Authentication string (password)**   A character string associated with the user ID that allows access to the remote data source (optional).

When an application calls **SQLConnect**, the Driver Manager uses the data source name to read the path of the driver DLL from the appropriate section of the ODBC.INI file or registry. It then loads the driver DLL and passes the **SQLConnect** arguments to it. If the driver needs additional information to connect to the data source, it reads this information from the same section of the ODBC.INI file or registry.

If the application specifies a data source name that is not in the ODBC.INI file or registry, or if the application does not specify a data source name, the Driver Manager searches for the default data source specification. If it finds the default data source, it loads the default driver DLL and passes the application-specified data source name to it. If there is no default data source, the Driver Manager returns an error.

The Driver Manager does not load a driver until the application calls a function (**SQLConnect**, **SQLDriverConnect**, or **SQLBrowseConnect**) to connect to the driver. Until that point, the Driver Manager works with its own handles and manages connection information. When the application calls a connection function, the Driver Manager checks if a driver is currently loaded for the specified *hdbc*:

- If a driver is not loaded, the Driver Manager loads the driver and calls **SQLAllocEnv**, **SQLAllocConnect**, **SQLSetConnectOption** (if the application specified any connection options), and the connection function in the driver. The Driver Manager returns SQLSTATE IM006 (Driver's SQLSetConnectOption failed) and SQL_SUCCESS_WITH_INFO for the connection function if the driver returned an error for **SQLSetConnectOption**.

- If the specified driver is already loaded on the *hdbc*, the Driver Manager only calls the connection function in the driver. In this case, the driver must ensure that all connection options for the *hdbc* maintain their current settings.

- If a different driver is loaded, the Driver Manager calls **SQLFreeConnect** and **SQLFreeEnv** in the loaded driver and then unloads that driver. It then performs the same operations as when a driver is not loaded.

The driver then allocates handles and initializes itself.

Note To resolve the addresses of the ODBC functions exported by the driver, the Driver Manager checks if the driver exports a dummy function with the ordinal 199. If it does not, the Driver Manager resolves the addresses by name. If it does, the Driver Manager resolves the addresses of the ODBC functions by ordinal, which is faster. The ordinal values of the ODBC functions must match the values of the *fFunction* argument in **SQLGetFunctions**; all other exported functions (such as **WEP**) must have ordinal values outside the range 1–199.

When the application calls **SQLDisconnect**, the Driver Manager calls **SQLDisconnect** in the driver. However, it does not unload the driver. This keeps the driver in memory for applications that repeatedly connect to and disconnect from a data source. When the application calls **SQLFreeConnect**, the Driver Manager calls **SQLFreeConnect** and **SQLFreeEnv** in the driver and then unloads the driver.

ODBC Extensions for Connections

ODBC extends the X/Open and SQL Access Group Call Level Interface to provide additional functions related to connections, drivers, and data sources. The remainder of this chapter describes these functions. A driver returns whether it supports a specific function with **SQLGetFunctions**.

Connecting to a Data Source With SQLDriverConnect

SQLDriverConnect supports:

- Data sources that require more connection information than the three arguments in **SQLConnect**.
- Dialog boxes to prompt the user for all connection information.
- Data sources that are not defined in the ODBC.INI file or registry.

SQLDriverConnect uses a connection string to specify the information needed to connect to a driver and data source.

A connection string contains the following information:

- Data source name or driver description
- Zero or more user IDs
- Zero or more passwords
- Zero or more data source–specific parameter values

The connection string is more flexible than the data source name, user ID, and password used by **SQLConnect**. For example, a driver needs to support **SQLDriveConnect** if its associated data source requires multiple levels of login authorizations or other data source–specific information.

An application calls **SQLDriverConnect** in one of three ways:

- Specify a connection string that contains a data source name. The Driver Manager retrieves the full path of the driver DLL associated with the data source from the ODBC.INI file or registry. To retrieve a list of data source names, an application calls **SQLDataSources**.
- Specify a connection string that contains a driver description. The Driver Manager retrieves the full path of the driver DLL. To retrieve a list of driver descriptions, an application calls **SQLDrivers**.
- Specify a connection string that does not contain a data source name or a driver name. The Driver Manager displays a dialog box from which the user selects a data source name. The Driver Manager then retrieves the full path of the driver DLL associated with the data source.

The Driver Manager then loads the driver DLL and passes the **SQLDriverConnect** arguments to it.

The application may pass all the connection information the driver needs. It may also request that the driver always prompt the user for connection information or only prompts the user for information it needs. Finally, if a data source is specified, the driver may read connection information from the appropriate section of the ODBC.INI file or registry. (For information on the structure of the ODBC.INI file or the keys used in the registry, see "Structure of the ODBC.INI File" in Chapter 20, "Configuring Data Sources.")

After the driver connects to the data source, it returns the connection information to the application. The application may store this information for future use.

If the application specifies a data source name that is not in the ODBC.INI file or registry, the Driver Manager searches for the default data source specification. If it finds the default data source, it loads the default driver DLL and passes the application-specified data source name to it. If there is no default data source, the Driver Manager returns an error.

The Driver Manager displays the following dialog box if the application calls **SQLDriverConnect** and requests that the user be prompted for information.

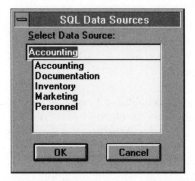

The following diagrams show sample login dialog boxes. A driver displays a login dialog box if the value of the **SQLDriverConnect** *fDriverCompletion* argument indicates that such a dialog box is necessary. The first is a basic login dialog box. The second would be displayed by a driver that requires additional information.

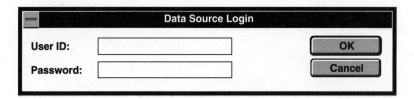

```
┌─────────────────────────────────────────────────────┐
│ ─         Data Source Login                          │
├─────────────────────────────────────────────────────┤
│                                                       │
│  Server:          [                ]    ┌──────────┐ │
│                                         │    OK    │ │
│  User ID:         [                ]    └──────────┘ │
│                                         ┌──────────┐ │
│  Password:        [                ]    │  Cancel  │ │
│                                         └──────────┘ │
│  Schema Statement: [               ]                 │
│                                                       │
└─────────────────────────────────────────────────────┘
```

Connection Browsing With SQLBrowseConnect

SQLBrowseConnect supports an iterative method of listing and specifying the attributes and attribute values required to connect to a data source. For each level of a connection, an application calls **SQLBrowseConnect** and specifies the connection attributes and attribute values for that level. First level connection attributes always include the data source name or driver description; the connection attributes for later levels are data source–dependent, but might include the host, user name, and database.

Each time **SQLBrowseConnect** is called, it validates the current attributes, returns the next level of attributes, and returns a user-friendly name for each attribute. It may also return a list of valid values for those attributes. (Note, however, that for some drivers and attributes, this list may not be complete.) After an application has specified each level of attributes and values, **SQLBrowseConnect** connects to the data source and returns a complete connection string. This string can be used in conjunction with **SQLDriverConnect** to connect to the data source at a later time.

Connection Browsing Example for SQL Server

The following example shows how **SQLBrowseConnect** might be used to browse the connections available with a driver for Microsoft's SQL Server. Although other drivers may require different connection attributes, this example illustrates the connection browsing model. (For the syntax of browse request and result strings, see **SQLBrowseConnect** in Chapter 22, "ODBC Function Reference.")

First, the application requests a connection handle:

```
SQLAllocConnect(henv, &hdbc);
```

Next, the application calls **SQLBrowseConnect** and specifies a data source name:

```
SQLBrowseConnect(hdbc, "DSN=MySQLServer", SQL_NTS,
                szBrowseResult, 100, &cb);
```

Because this is the first call to **SQLBrowseConnect**, the Driver Manager locates the data source name (MySQLServer) in the ODBC.INI file and loads the corresponding driver DLL (SQLSRVR.DLL). The Driver Manager then calls the driver's **SQLBrowseConnect** function with the same arguments it received from the application.

The driver determines that this is the first call to **SQLBrowseConnect** and returns the second level of connection attributes: server, user name, password, and application name. For the server attribute, it returns a list of valid server names. The return code from **SQLBrowseConnect** is SQL_NEED_DATA. The browse result string is:

```
"SERVER:Server={red,blue,green,yellow};UID:Login ID=?;PWD:Password=?;
➥ *APP:AppName=?;*WSID:WorkStation ID=?"
```

Note that each keyword in the browse result string is followed by a colon and one or more words before the equal sign. These words are the user-friendly name that an application can use as a prompt in a dialog box. The driver may change the value of this string for different languages and locales.

In its next call to **SQLBrowseConnect**, the application must supply a value for the **SERVER**, **UID**, and **PWD** keywords. Because they are prefixed by an asterisk, the **APP** and **WSID** keywords are optional and may be omitted. The value for the **SERVER** keyword may be one of the servers returned by **SQLBrowseConnect** or a user-supplied name.

The application calls **SQLBrowseConnect** again, specifying the green server and omitting the **APP** keyword and the user-friendly names after each keyword:

```
SQLBrowseConnect(hdbc, "SERVER=green;UID=Smith;PWD=Sesame", SQL_NTS,
                 szBrowseResult, 100, &cb);
```

The driver attempts to connect to the green server. If there are any nonfatal errors, such as a missing keyword-value pair, **SQLBrowseConnect** returns SQL_NEED_DATA and remains in the same state as prior to the error. The application can call **SQLError** to determine the error. If the connection is successful, the driver returns SQL_NEED_DATA and returns the browse result string:

```
"*DATABASE:Database={master,model,pubs,tempdb};
➥ *LANGUAGE:Language={us_english,Français}"
```

Since the attributes in this string are optional, the application can omit them. However, the application must call **SQLBrowseConnect** again. If the application chooses to omit the database name and language, it specifies an empty browse request string. In this example, the application chooses the pubs database and calls **SQLBrowseConnect** a final time, omitting the **LANGUAGE** keyword and the asterisk before the **DATABASE** keyword:

```
SQLBrowseConnect(hdbc, "DATABASE=pubs", SQL_NTS,
                    szBrowseResult, 100, &cb);
```

Since the **DATABASE** attribute is the final connection attribute of the data
source, the browsing process is complete, the application is connected to the data
source, and **SQLBrowseConnect** returns SQL_SUCCESS. **SQLBrowseConnect**
also returns the complete connection string as the browse result string:

```
"DSN=MySQLServer;SERVER=green;UID=Smith;PWD=Sesame;DATABASE=pubs"
```

The final connection string returned by the driver does not contain the user-
friendly names after each keyword, nor does it contain optional keywords not
specified by the application. The application can use this string with
SQLDriverConnect to reconnect to the data source on the current *hdbc* (after
disconnecting) or to connect to the data source on a different *hdbc*:

```
SQLDriverConnect(hdbc, szBrowseResult, SQL_NTS, szConnStrOut, 100, &cb,
                    SQL_DRIVER_NOPROMPT);
```

Connection Browsing Example for DAL

The following example shows how **SQLBrowseConnect** might be used in
conjunction with a driver that uses Apple's Data Access Language (DAL) to
access an Oracle host. To browse the available connections, an application
repeatedly calls **SQLBrowseConnect**:

```
retcode = SQLBrowseConnect(hdbc, szConnStrIn, SQL_NTS,
                             szConnStrOut, 200, &cb);
```

In the first call, the application specifies a data source name in *szConnStrIn*. In
each subsequent call, the application bases the value of *szConnStrIn* on the value
of *szConnStrOut* returned by the previous call. The application continues to call
SQLBrowseConnect as long as the function returns SQL_NEED_DATA. The
following list shows, for each call to **SQLBrowseConnect**, the value that the
application specifies for *szConnStrIn* and the values that the driver returns for
retcode and *szConnStrOut*. (For the syntax of the strings used in *szConnStrIn* and
szConnStrOut, see **SQLBrowseConnect** in Chapter 22, "ODBC Function
Reference.")

```
szConnStrIn  : "DSN=DAL"
szConnStrOut : "HOST:Host={MyVax,Direct,Unix};UID1:Host User Name=?;
             ➥ PWD1:Password=?"
retcode      : SQL_NEED_DATA

szConnStrIn  : "HOST=MyVax;UID1=Smith;PWD1=Sesame"
szConnStrOut : "DBMS:DBMS={Oracle,Informix,Sybase};UID2:DBMS User Name=?;
             ➥ PWD2:Password=?"
retcode      : SQL_NEED_DATA
```

```
szConnStrIn  : "DBMS=Oracle;UID2=John;PWD2=Lion"
szConnStrOut : "DATABASE:Database={DalDemo,Personnel,Production};
                ➥ *ALIAS:Alias=?;*UID3:User Name=?;*PWD3:Password=?"
retcode      : SQL_NEED_DATA

szConnStrIn  : "DATABASE=DalDemo;ALIAS=Demo"
szConnStrOut : "DSN=DAL;Host=MyVax;UID1=Smith;PWD1=Sesame;DBMS=Oracle;
                ➥ UID2=John;PWD2=Lion;DATABASE=DalDemo;ALIAS=Demo"
retcode      : SQL_SUCCESS
```

Note that the database alias, database user name, and database password are optional, as indicated by the asterisk before those attribute names. The application chooses not to specify the user name and password.

The driver can use several of DAL's capabilities to determine valid values for some of the connection attributes. It can retrieve the list of valid host names from the DAL Preferences file. To determine the list of available DBMS's, it can execute the DAL statement **DESCRIBE DBMS;FOR EACH {PRINT BRAND;}**. To determine the list of available databases, it can execute the DAL statement **DESCRIBE DATABASES; FOR EACH {PRINT NAME;}**.

Translating Data

An application and a data source can store data in different formats. For example, the application might use a different character set than the data source. ODBC provides a mechanism by which a driver can translate all data (data values, SQL statements, table names, row counts, and so on) that passes between the driver and the data source.

To translate data, the driver calls the functions **SQLDriverToDataSource** and **SQLDataSourceToDriver**. These functions reside in a translation DLL. A default translation DLL may be specified for a data source in the ODBC.INI file or registry. An application may specify a new translation DLL at any time by calling **SQLSetConnectOption**. (For more information about specifying a default translation DLL for a data source, see "Specifying a Default Translator" in Chapter 20, "Configuring Data Sources.")

If an application specifies a translation DLL with **SQLSetConnectOption** before the driver is connected to the data source, the driver stores the translation DLL name.

As part of the connection process, the driver loads the translation DLL (if one has been specified). The driver first checks for a translation DLL specified with **SQLSetConnectOption**. If none is found, it checks for a default translation DLL for the data source in the ODBC.INI file or registry.

If an application specifies a translation DLL with **SQLSetConnectOption** after the driver is connected to the data source, the driver frees the current translation DLL (if one exists) and loads the new translation DLL.

Translation functions may support several different types of translation. For example, a function that translates data from one character set to another might support a variety of character sets. To specify a particular type of translation, an application can specify an option flag by calling **SQLSetConnectOption**. The driver passes this flag in each call to **SQLDriverToDataSource** and **SQLDataSourceToDriver**.

Additional Extension Functions

ODBC also provides the following functions related to connections, drivers, and data sources. For more information about these functions, see Chapter 22, "ODBC Function Reference."

Function	Description
SQLDataSources	Returns a list of available data sources. The Driver Manager retrieves this information from the ODBC.INI file or registry.
SQLDrivers	Returns a list of installed drivers and their attributes. The Driver Manager retrieves this information from the ODBCINST.INI file or registry.
SQLGetFunctions	Returns functions supported by a driver. This function allows an application to determine at run time whether a particular function is supported by a driver.
SQLGetInfo	Returns general information about a driver and data source, including filenames, versions, conformance levels, and capabilities.
SQLGetTypeInfo	Returns the SQL data types supported by a driver and data source.
SQLSetConnectOption **SQLGetConnectOption**	These functions set or return connection options, such as the data source access mode, automatic transaction commitment, timeout values, function tracing, data translation options, and transaction isolation.

CHAPTER 14

Processing an SQL Statement

An application can submit any SQL statement supported by a data source. ODBC defines a standard syntax for SQL statements (listed in Appendix C, "SQL Grammar"). For maximum interoperability, an application should only submit SQL statements that use this syntax; the driver will translate these statements to the syntax used by the data source. If an application submits an SQL statement that does not use the ODBC syntax, the driver passes it directly to the data source.

The following diagram shows a simple sequence of ODBC function calls to execute SQL statements. Note that statements can be executed a single time with **SQLExecDirect** or prepared with **SQLPrepare** and executed multiple times with **SQLExecute**. Note also that an application calls **SQLTransact** to commit or roll back a transaction.

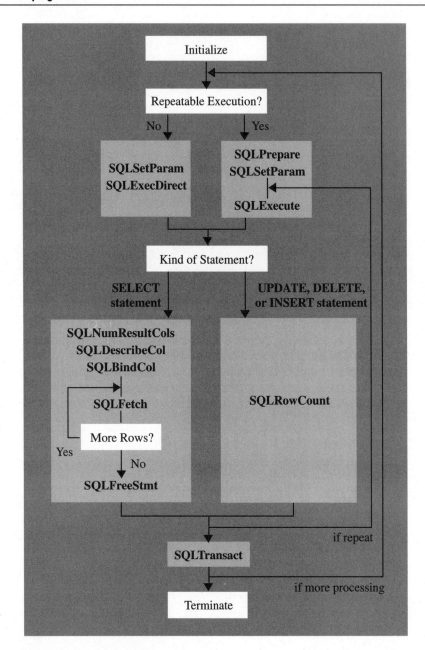

Allocating a Statement Handle

Before an application can submit an SQL statement, it must call **SQLAllocStmt** to request that the driver allocate storage for the statement. The application passes a connection handle and the address of a variable of type HSTMT to the driver.

The driver allocates storage for the statement, associates the statement with the connection referenced by the connection handle, and returns the statement handle in the variable.

A driver uses the statement handle to reference storage for names, parameter and binding information, error messages, and other information related to a statement processing stream.

Executing an SQL Statement

An application can submit an SQL statement for execution in two ways:

- **Prepared**   Call **SQLPrepare** and then call **SQLExecute**.
- **Direct**   Call **SQLExecDirect**.

These options are similar, though not identical to, the prepared and immediate options in embedded SQL. For a comparison of the ODBC functions and embedded SQL, see Appendix E, "Comparison Between Embedded SQL and ODBC."

Prepared Execution

Preparing a statement before it is executed provides the following advantages:

- It is the most efficient way to execute the statement more than once, especially if the statement is complex. The data source compiles the statement, produces an access plan, and returns an access plan identifier to the driver. The data source minimizes processing time by using the access plan each time it executes the statement.
- It allows the driver to send an access plan identifier instead of an entire statement each time the statement is to be executed. This minimizes network traffic.
- The driver can return information about a result set before executing the statement. For more information, see "Returning Information About a Result Set," in Chapter 15, "Returning Results."

Prepared execution is supported with **SQLPrepare** and **SQLExecute**. When an application calls **SQLPrepare**, the driver:

1. Modifies the statement to use the form of SQL supported by the data source, if necessary. In particular, the driver modifies the escape clauses used to define ODBC-specific SQL. These are discussed in "Supporting ODBC Extensions to SQL," later in this chapter.
2. Submits the statement to the data source for preparation.

3. Stores the returned access plan identifier for later execution (if the preparation succeeded) or returns errors to the application (if the preparation failed).

When an application calls **SQLExecute**, the driver:

1. Retrieves current parameter values, converts them as necessary, and sends them to the data source. For more information, see "Supporting Parameters" later in this chapter.
2. Sends the access plan identifier to the data source for execution.
3. Returns any errors.

Important   Some data sources delete the access plans for all *hstmts* on an *hdbc* when a transaction is committed or rolled back; transactions may be committed or rolled back with **SQLTransact** or automatically committed with the SQL_AUTOCOMMIT connection option. A driver reports this behavior with the SQL_CURSOR_COMMIT_BEHAVIOR and SQL_CURSOR_ROLLBACK_BEHAVIOR information types in **SQLGetInfo**.

If the data source does not support statement preparation, the driver must emulate it to the extent possible. For example, if the data source supports procedures, the driver might place the statement in a procedure and submit it for compilation when **SQLPrepare** is called. When **SQLExecute** is called, it would submit the compiled procedure for execution.

If the data source supports syntax checking without execution, the driver might submit the statement for checking when **SQLPrepare** is called and submit the statement for execution when **SQLExecute** is called.

If the driver cannot emulate statement preparation, it stores the statement when **SQLPrepare** is called and submits it for execution when **SQLExecute** is called. In this case, **SQLExecute** can return the errors normally returned by **SQLPrepare**.

Direct Execution

Executing a statement directly is the most efficient way to execute a statement a single time. Direct execution is supported through **SQLExecDirect**. When an application calls **SQLExecDirect**, the driver:

1. Modifies the statement to use the form of SQL supported by the data source, if necessary. In particular, the driver modifies the escape clauses used to define ODBC-specific SQL. These are discussed in "Supporting ODBC Extensions to SQL," later in this chapter.

2. Retrieves current parameter values, converts them as necessary, and sends them to the data source. For more information, see "Supporting Parameters" later in this chapter.

3. Submits the statement to the data source for execution.

4. Returns any errors.

Supporting Parameters

An SQL statement can contain parameter markers that indicate values that the driver retrieves from the application at execution time. For example, an application might use the following statement to insert a row of data into the EMPLOYEE table:

```
INSERT INTO EMPLOYEE (NAME, AGE, HIREDATE) VALUES (?, ?, ?)
```

At any time after an *hstmt* has been allocated, an application calls **SQLBindParameter** to specify information about a parameter. (If the application has previously called **SQLBindParameter** for a parameter, the driver replaces the old values with the new values.) The driver:

- Associates the address of the storage area with the parameter marker.

- Stores the data types of the storage location and the column associated with the parameter, as well as the precision and scale of the parameter.

Note When an application calls **SQLBindParameter**, it specifies the number of the parameter for which it is providing information. The driver stores the information without checking if a corresponding parameter marker exists in the statement. When the statement is executed, the driver only retrieves parameter values for those parameters with corresponding markers in the statement.

When the application calls **SQLExecute** or **SQLExecDirect** to execute the statement, the driver:

1. Checks that **SQLBindParameter** has been called for each parameter marker in the statement. If not, the driver returns an error.

2. Retrieves the current value of each parameter from its associated storage area.

3. Converts the value from the data type of the storage area to the data type of the associated column, if needed.

4. Passes the parameter values to the data source.

The driver releases information about parameters only when the application calls **SQLFreeStmt** with the SQL_RESET_PARAMS option or SQL_DROP option. Hence, parameter information persists after a statement has been executed.

Supporting Transactions

Drivers support two modes for transactions: *auto-commit* and *manual-commit*. In auto-commit mode, each SQL statement is a single, complete transaction; the driver commits one transaction for each statement. In manual-commit mode, a driver begins a transaction when an application submits an SQL statement and no transaction is open. It commits or rolls back the current transaction only when the application calls **SQLTransact**.

If a driver supports the SQL_AUTOCOMMIT connection option, the default transaction mode is auto-commit; otherwise, it is manual-commit. Applications call **SQLSetConnectOption** to switch between auto-commit and manual-commit mode. Note that if an application switches from manual-commit to auto-commit mode, the driver commits any open transactions on the connection.

Applications should call **SQLTransact**, rather than submitting a **COMMIT** or **ROLLBACK** statement, to commit or roll back a transaction. The result of a **COMMIT** or **ROLLBACK** statement depends on the driver and its associated data source.

Important   Some data sources delete the access plans and close the cursors for all *hstmts* on an *hdbc* when a transaction is committed or rolled back; transactions may be committed or rolled back with **SQLTransact** or automatically committed with the SQL_AUTOCOMMIT connection option. A driver reports this behavior with the SQL_CURSOR_COMMIT_BEHAVIOR and SQL_CURSOR_ROLLBACK_BEHAVIOR information types in **SQLGetInfo**.

ODBC Extensions for SQL Statements

ODBC extends the X/Open and SQL Access Group Call Level Interface to provide additional functions related to SQL statements. ODBC also extends the X/Open and SQL Access Group SQL CAE specification (1992) to provide common extensions to SQL. The remainder of this chapter describes these functions and SQL extensions.

A driver returns whether it supports a specific function with **SQLGetFunctions**. A driver returns whether it supports a specific extension to SQL with **SQLGetInfo**.

Returning Information About the Data Source's Catalog

To return information about a data source's catalog, a driver supports the following functions, known as the catalog functions:

- **SQLTables** returns the names of tables stored in a data source.

- **SQLTablePrivileges** returns the privileges associated with one or more tables.

- **SQLColumns** returns the names of columns in one or more tables.

- **SQLColumnPrivileges** returns the privileges associated with each column in a single table.

- **SQLPrimaryKeys** returns the names of columns that comprise the primary key of a single table.

- **SQLForeignKeys** returns the names of columns in a single table that are foreign keys. It also returns the names of columns in other tables that refer to the primary key of the specified table.

- **SQLSpecialColumns** returns information about the optimal set of columns that uniquely identify a row in a single table or the columns in that table that are automatically updated when any value in the row is updated by a transaction.

- **SQLStatistics** returns statistics about a single table and the indexes associated with that table.

- **SQLProcedures** returns the names of procedures stored in a data source.

- **SQLProcedureColumns** returns a list of the input and output parameters, as well as the names of columns in the result set, for one or more procedures.

Each function returns the information as a result set. The application retrieves these results by calling **SQLBindCol** and **SQLFetch**.

If the data source associated with a driver does not support catalog functions, the driver can implement these functions.

Accepting Parameter Data at Execution Time

To support the ability to send parameter data at statement execution time, such as for parameters of the SQL_LONGVARCHAR or SQL_LONGVARBINARY types, a driver has the following three functions:

- **SQLBindParameter**
- **SQLParamData**
- **SQLPutData**

To indicate that an application plans to send parameter data at statement execution time, it calls **SQLBindParameter** and sets the *pcbValue* buffer for the parameter to the result of the SQL_LEN_DATA_AT_EXEC(*length*) macro. If the *fSqlType* argument is SQL_LONGVARBINARY or SQL_LONGVARCHAR and the driver returns "Y" for the SQL_NEED_LONG_DATA_LEN information type in **SQLGetInfo**, *length* is the total number of bytes of data to be sent for the parameter; otherwise, it is ignored.

It sets *rgbValue* to a value that, at run time, can be used to retrieve the data. For example, *rgbValue* might point to a storage location that will contain the data at statement execution time or to a file that contains the data. The driver stores this value and returns it to the application at statement execution time.

When the driver processes a call to **SQLExecute** or **SQLExecDirect** and the statement being executed includes a data-at-execution parameter, the driver returns SQL_NEED_DATA. To send the parameter data, the application:

1. Calls **SQLParamData**. The driver returns *rgbValue* (which it stored when **SQLBindParameter** was called) for the first data-at-execution parameter.

2. Calls **SQLPutData** one or more times to send data for the parameter. (More than one call will be needed if the data value is larger than the buffer; multiple calls are allowed only if the C data type is character or binary and the SQL data type is character, binary, or data source–specific.)

3. Calls **SQLParamData** again to indicate that all data has been sent for the parameter. The driver finishes processing the parameter. If there is another data-at-execution parameter, the driver returns *rgbValue* for that parameter and SQL_NEED_DATA for the function return code. Otherwise, it returns SQL_SUCCESS for the function return code.

4. Repeats steps 2 and 3 for the remaining data-at-execution parameters.

For additional information, see the description of **SQLBindParameter** in Chapter 22, "ODBC Function Reference."

Accepting Arrays of Parameter Values

To support specification of multiple sets of parameter values for a single SQL statement, implement the **SQLParamOptions** function. For data sources that support multiple parameter values for a single SQL statement, **SQLParamOptions** can provide performance benefits. For example, an application can set up an array of values and submit a single **INSERT** statement.

Supporting Asynchronous Execution

By default, a driver executes ODBC functions synchronously; the driver does not return control to the application until a function call completes. If a driver supports asynchronous execution, however, the application can request asynchronous execution for the functions listed below. (All of these functions either submit requests to a data source or retrieve data. These operations may require extensive processing.)

SQLColAttributes	**SQLDescribeCol**	**SQLExecute**
SQLColumnPrivileges	**SQLDescribeParam**	**SQLExtendedFetch**
SQLColumns	**SQLExecDirect**	**SQLFetch**

SQLForeignKeys	**SQLParamData**	**SQLSetPos**
SQLGetData	**SQLPrepare**	**SQLSpecialColumns**
SQLGetTypeInfo	**SQLPrimaryKeys**	**SQLStatistics**
SQLMoreResults	**SQLProcedureColumns**	**SQLTablePrivileges**
SQLNumParams	**SQLProcedures**	**SQLTables**
SQLNumResultCols	**SQLPutData**	

Asynchronous execution is performed on a statement-by-statement basis. When an application calls **SQLSetStmtOption** with the SQL_ASYNC_ENABLE option, the driver enables or disables asynchronous execution for the *hstmt*. When an application calls **SQLSetConnectOption** with the SQL_ASYNC_ENABLE option, the driver enables or disables asynchronous execution for all *hstmts* associated with the *hdbc*.

For functions that can be executed asynchronously, the driver checks if asynchronous execution has been enabled for the *hstmt*. If this has been enabled, the driver begins executing the function asynchronously and returns SQL_STILL_EXECUTING. Otherwise, the driver executes the function synchronously.

While a function is executing asynchronously, an application can call any function with a different *hstmt* or an *hdbc* not associated with the original *hstmt*. With the original *hstmt* or the *hdbc* associated with that *hstmt*, the application can only call the original function, **SQLAllocStmt**, **SQLCancel**, or **SQLGetFunctions**. If it calls any other function with the original *hstmt* or the *hdbc* associated with that *hstmt*, the Driver Manager returns an error.

If the application calls the asynchronously executing function with the original *hstmt*, the driver ignores all arguments except the *hstmt* argument. It returns SQL_STILL_EXECUTING if the function is still executing. Otherwise, it returns a different code, such as SQL_SUCCESS or SQL_ERROR. For information about canceling an asynchronously execution, see "Terminating Statement Processing" in Chapter 17, "Terminating Transactions and Connections."

For functions that cannot be executed asynchronously, the driver ignores whether asynchronous execution is enabled for the *hstmt*.

Supporting ODBC Extensions to SQL

ODBC defines the following extensions to SQL, which are common to most DBMS's:

- Date, time, and timestamp data
- Scalar functions such as numeric, string, and data type conversion functions
- **LIKE** predicate escape characters

- Outer joins
- Procedures

The syntax defined by ODBC for these extensions uses the escape clause provided by the X/Open and SQL Access Group SQL CAE specification (1992) to cover vendor-specific extensions to SQL. Its format is:

--(*vendor(*vendor-name*)**, product**(*product-name*) *extension* ***)--**

For the ODBC extensions to SQL, *product-name* is always "ODBC", since the product defining them is ODBC. *Vendor-name* is always "Microsoft", since ODBC is a Microsoft product. ODBC also defines a shorthand syntax for these extensions:

{*extension*}

Most DBMS's provide the same extensions to SQL as does ODBC. Because of this, an application may be able to submit an SQL statement using one of these extensions in either of two ways:

- Use the syntax defined by ODBC. The driver translates the extension to its DBMS-specific syntax. An application that uses the ODBC syntax will be interoperable among DBMS's.

- Use the syntax defined by the DBMS. The driver does not translate the extension. An application that uses DBMS-specific syntax will not be interoperable among DBMS's.

In either case, the driver does not check the validity of the syntax except as needed to translate the ODBC syntax to the DBMS-specific syntax. For example, the driver does not perform type checking of the arguments of a scalar function.

Due to the difficulty in implementing some ODBC extensions to SQL, such as outer joins, a driver might only implement those ODBC extensions that are supported by its associated DBMS. A driver returns whether it and its associated data source support all the ODBC extensions to SQL through **SQLGetInfo** with the SQL_ODBC_SQL_CONFORMANCE flag. For information about how a driver returns whether a specific extension is supported, see the section that describes the extension.

Note Many DBMS's provide extensions to SQL other than those defined by ODBC. To use one of these extensions, an application uses the DBMS-specific syntax. The driver does not translate the extension. The application will not be interoperable among DBMS's.

Date, Time, and Timestamp Data

The escape clauses ODBC uses for date, time, and timestamp data are:

--(*vendor(Microsoft),product(ODBC) **d** '*value*' *)--
--(*vendor(Microsoft),product(ODBC) **t** '*value*' *)--
--(*vendor(Microsoft),product(ODBC) **ts** '*value*' *)--

where **d** indicates *value* is a date in the "yyyy-mm-dd" format, **t** indicates *value* is a time in the "hh:mm:ss" format, and **ts** indicates *value* is a timestamp in the "yyyy-mm-dd hh:mm:ss[.f...]" format. The shorthand syntax for date, time, and timestamp data is:

{**d** '*value*'}
{**t** '*value*'}
{**ts** '*value*'}

For example, each of the following statements updates the birthday of John Smith in the EMPLOYEE table. The first statement uses the escape clause syntax. The second statement uses the shorthand syntax. The third statement uses the native syntax for a DATE column in DEC's Rdb and is not interoperable among DBMS's.

```
UPDATE EMPLOYEE
    SET BIRTHDAY=--(*vendor(Microsoft),product(ODBC) d '1967-01-15' *)--
    WHERE NAME='Smith, John'

UPDATE EMPLOYEE
    SET BIRTHDAY={d '1967-01-15'}
    WHERE NAME='Smith, John'

UPDATE EMPLOYEE
    SET BIRTHDAY='15-Jan-1967'
    WHERE NAME='Smith, John'
```

The ODBC escape clauses for date, time, and timestamp literals can be used in parameters with a C data type of SQL_C_CHAR. For example, the following statement uses a parameter to update the birthday of John Smith in the EMPLOYEE table:

```
UPDATE EMPLOYEE SET BIRTHDAY=? WHERE NAME='Smith, John'
```

A storage location of type SQL_C_CHAR bound to the parameter might contain any of the following values. The first value uses the escape clause syntax. The second value uses the shorthand syntax. The third value uses the native syntax for a DATE column in DEC's Rdb and is not interoperable among DBMS's.

```
"--(*vendor(Microsoft),product(ODBC) d '1967-01-15' *)--"

"{d '1967-01-15'}"

"'15-Jan-1967'"
```

An application can also send date, time, or timestamp values as parameters using the C structures defined by the C data types SQL_C_DATE, SQL_C_TIME, and SQL_C_TIMESTAMP.

To determine if a data source supports date, time, or timestamp data, an application calls **SQLGetTypeInfo**. If a driver supports date, time, or timestamp data, it must also support the escape clauses for date, time, or timestamp literals.

Scalar Functions

Scalar functions—such as string length, absolute value, or current date—can be used on columns of a result set and on columns that restrict rows of a result set. The escape clause ODBC uses for scalar functions is:

--(*vendor(Microsoft),product(ODBC) fn *scalar-function* ***)--**

where *scalar-function* is one of the functions listed in Appendix F, "Scalar Functions." The shorthand syntax for scalar functions is:

{fn *scalar-function*}

For example, each of the following statements creates the same result set of uppercase employee names. The first statement uses the escape clause syntax. The second statement uses the shorthand syntax. The third statement uses the native syntax for Ingres for OS/2 and is not interoperable among DBMS's.

```
SELECT --(*vendor(Microsoft),product(ODBC) fn UCASE(NAME) *)--
    FROM EMPLOYEE

SELECT {fn UCASE(NAME)} FROM EMPLOYEE

SELECT uppercase(NAME) FROM EMPLOYEE
```

An application can mix scalar functions that use native syntax and scalar functions that use ODBC syntax. For example, the following statement creates a result set of last names of employees in the EMPLOYEE table. (Names in the EMPLOYEE table are stored as a last name, a comma, and a first name.) The statement uses the ODBC scalar function **SUBSTRING** and the SQL Server scalar function **CHARINDEX** and will only execute correctly on SQL Server.

```
SELECT {fn SUBSTRING(NAME, 1, CHARINDEX(',', NAME) - 1)} FROM EMPLOYEE
```

To determine which scalar functions are supported by a data source, an application calls **SQLGetInfo** with the SQL_NUMERIC_FUNCTIONS, SQL_STRING_FUNCTIONS, SQL_SYSTEM_FUNCTIONS, and SQL_TIMEDATE_FUNCTIONS flags.

Data Type Conversion Function

ODBC defines a special scalar function, **CONVERT**, that requests that the data source convert data from one SQL data type to another SQL data type. The escape clause ODBC uses for the **CONVERT** function is:

--(*vendor(Microsoft),product(ODBC)
    fn CONVERT(*value_exp***,** *data_type***) *)--**

where *value_exp* is a column name, the result of another scalar function, or a literal value, and *data_type* is a keyword that matches the **#define** name used by an ODBC SQL data type (as defined in Appendix D, "Data Types"). The shorthand syntax for the **CONVERT** function is:

{fn CONVERT(*value_exp***,** *data_type***)}**

For example, the following statement creates a result set of the names and ages of all employees in their twenties. It uses the **CONVERT** function to convert each employee's age from type SQL_SMALLINT to type SQL_CHAR. Each resulting character string is compared to the pattern "2%" to determine if the employee's age is in the twenties.

```
SELECT NAME, AGE FROM EMPLOYEE
    WHERE {fn CONVERT(AGE,SQL_CHAR)} LIKE '2%'
```

To determine if the **CONVERT** function is supported by a data source, an application calls **SQLGetInfo** with the SQL_CONVERT_FUNCTIONS flag. For more information about the **CONVERT** function, see Appendix F, "Scalar Functions."

LIKE Predicate Escape Characters

In a **LIKE** predicate, the percent character (%) matches zero or more of any character and the underscore character (_) matches any one character. The percent and underscore characters can be used as literals in a **LIKE** predicate by preceding them with an escape character. The escape clause ODBC uses to define the **LIKE** predicate escape character is:

--(*vendor(Microsoft),product(ODBC) escape '*escape-character***' *)--**

where *escape-character* is any character supported by the data source. The shorthand syntax for the **LIKE** predicate escape character is:

{escape '*escape-character***'}**

For example, each of the following statements creates the same result set of department names that start with the characters "%AAA". The first statement uses the escape clause syntax. The second statement uses the shorthand syntax. The third statement uses the native syntax for Ingres and is not interoperable among

DBMS's. Note that the second percent character in each **LIKE** predicate is a wild-card character that matches zero or more of any character.

```
SELECT NAME FROM DEPT WHERE NAME
    LIKE '\%AAA%' --(*vendor(Microsoft),product(ODBC) escape '\'*)--

SELECT NAME FROM DEPT WHERE NAME LIKE '\%AAA%' {escape '\'}

SELECT NAME FROM DEPT WHERE NAME LIKE '\%AAA%' ESCAPE '\'
```

To determine whether **LIKE** predicate escape characters are supported by a data source, an application calls **SQLGetInfo** with the SQL_LIKE_ESCAPE_CLAUSE information type.

Outer Joins

ODBC supports the ANSI SQL-92 left outer join syntax. The escape clause ODBC uses for outer joins is:

--(*vendor(Microsoft),product(ODBC) oj *outer-join* ***)--**

where *outer-join* is:

table-reference **LEFT OUTER JOIN** {*table-reference* | *outer-join*}
   ON *search-condition*

table-reference specifies a table name, and *search-condition* specifies the join condition between the *table-references*. The shorthand syntax for outer joins is:

{oj *outer-join*}

An outer join request must appear after the **FROM** keyword and before the **WHERE** clause (if one exists). For complete syntax information, see Appendix C, "SQL Grammar."

For example, each of the following statements creates the same result set of the names and departments of employees working on project 544. The first statement uses the escape clause syntax. The second statement uses the shorthand syntax. The third statement uses the native syntax for Oracle and is not interoperable among DBMS's.

```
SELECT EMPLOYEE.NAME, DEPT.DEPTNAME
    FROM --(*vendor(Microsoft),product(ODBC) oj
        EMPLOYEE LEFT OUTER JOIN DEPT ON EMPLOYEE.DEPTID=DEPT.DEPTID*)--
    WHERE EMPLOYEE.PROJID=544

SELECT EMPLOYEE.NAME, DEPT.DEPTNAME
    FROM {oj EMPLOYEE LEFT OUTER JOIN DEPT
        ON EMPLOYEE.DEPTID=DEPT.DEPTID}
    WHERE EMPLOYEE.PROJID=544

SELECT EMPLOYEE.NAME, DEPT.DEPTNAME
    FROM EMPLOYEE, DEPT
    WHERE (EMPLOYEE.PROJID=544) AND (EMPLOYEE.DEPTID = DEPT.DEPTID (+))
```

To determine the level of outer joins a data source supports, an application calls **SQLGetInfo** with the SQL_OUTER_JOINS flag. Data sources can support two-table outer joins, partially support multi-table outer joins, fully support multi-table outer joins, or not support outer joins.

Procedures

An application can call a procedure in place of an SQL statement. The escape clause ODBC uses for calling a procedure is:

--(*vendor(Microsoft),product(ODBC)
    [?=] call *procedure-name*[([*parameter*][,[*parameter*]]...)] ***)--**

where *procedure-name* specifies the name of a procedure stored on the data source and *parameter* specifies a procedure parameter. A procedure can have zero or more parameters and can return a value. The shorthand syntax for procedure invocation is:

{[[?=]**call** *procedure-name*[([*parameter*][,[*parameter*]]...)]}

For output parameters, *parameter* must be a parameter marker. For input and input/output parameters, *parameter* can be a literal, a parameter marker, or not specified. If *parameter* is a literal or is not specified for an input/output parameter, the driver discards the output value. If *parameter* is not specified for an input or input/output parameter, the procedure uses the default value of the parameter as the input value; the procedure also uses the default value if *parameter* is a parameter marker and the *pcbValue* argument in **SQLBindParameter** is SQL_DEFAULT_PARAM. If a procedure call includes parameter markers (including the "?=" parameter marker for the return value), the application must bind each marker by calling **SQLBindParameter** prior to calling the procedure.

Note For some data sources, *parameter* cannot be a literal value. For all data sources, it can be a parameter marker. For maximum interoperability, applications should always use a parameter marker for *parameter*.

If an application specifies a return value parameter for a procedure that does not return a value, the driver sets the *pcbValue* buffer specified in **SQLBindParameter** for the parameter to SQL_NULL_DATA. If the application omits the return value parameter for a procedure returns a value, the driver ignores the value returned by the procedure.

If a procedure returns a result set, the application retrieves the data in the result set in the same manner as it retrieves data from any other result set.

For example, each of the following statements uses the procedure EMPS_IN_PROJ to create the same result set of names of employees working on a project. The first statement uses the escape clause syntax. The second statement uses the shorthand syntax. For an example of code that calls a procedure, see **SQLProcedures** in Chapter 22, "ODBC Function Reference."

```
--(*vendor(Microsoft),product(ODBC) call EMPS_IN_PROJ(?)*)--
```

```
{call EMPS_IN_PROJ(?)}
```

To determine if a data source supports procedures, an application calls **SQLGetInfo** with the SQL_PROCEDURES information type. To retrieve a list of the procedures stored in a specific data source, an application calls **SQLProcedures**. To retrieve a list of the input, input/output, and output parameters, as well as the return value and the columns that make up the result set (if any) returned by a procedure, an application calls **SQLProcedureColumns**.

Additional Extension Functions

ODBC also provides the following functions related to SQL statements. For more information about these functions, see Chapter 22, "ODBC Function Reference."

Function	Description
SQLDescribeParam	Returns information about prepared parameters.
SQLNativeSql	Returns the SQL statement as processed by the data source, with escape sequences translated to SQL code used by the data source.
SQLNumParams	Returns the number of parameters in an SQL statement.
SQLSetStmtOption **SQLSetConnectOption** **SQLGetStmtOption**	These functions set or return statement options, such as asynchronous processing, orientation for binding rowsets, maximum amount of variable length data to return, maximum number of result set rows to return, and query timeout value. Note that **SQLSetConnectOption** sets options for all statements on a connection.

CHAPTER 15

Returning Results

A **SELECT** statement is used to retrieve data that meets a given set of specifications. For example, **SELECT * FROM EMPLOYEE WHERE EMPNAME = "Jones"** is used to retrieve all columns of all rows in EMPLOYEE where the employee's name is Jones. ODBC extension functions can also return data. For example, **SQLColumns** returns data about columns in the data source. These sets of data, called result sets, can contain zero or more rows.

Note that other SQL statements, such as **GRANT** or **REVOKE**, do not return result sets. For these statements, the code returned by the driver from **SQLExecute** or **SQLExecDirect** is usually the only source of information as to whether the statement was successful. (For **INSERT, UPDATE,** and **DELETE** statements, an application can call **SQLRowCount** to return the number of affected rows.)

An application may or may not know the form of an SQL statement prior to execution. Therefore, drivers support functions that allow an application to request information about the result set.

For functions and SQL statements that return a result set, an application calls ODBC functions to fetch the results.

Assigning Storage for Results (Binding)

An application can assign storage for result columns before or after submitting an SQL statement.

A driver binds storage to result columns using the information passed to it through **SQLBindCol**. The driver:

- Accepts pointer arguments that reference storage areas.
- Checks whether the pointers are null. If the *rgbValue* pointer is null, the driver unbinds the column. If the *pcbValue* pointer is null, the driver does not return length information to the application.

- Associates each column with the given storage area.
- Stores information about the data type to which to convert the result data.

The driver uses this information during subsequent fetch operations.

Returning Information About a Result Set

Each driver supports the following core functions:

- **SQLNumResultCols** returns the number of columns in the result set.
- **SQLColAttributes** and **SQLDescribeCol** provide information about a column in the result set.
- **SQLRowCount** returns the number of rows affected by an SQL statement.

An application can call **SQLColAttributes**, **SQLDescribeCol**, and **SQLNumResultCols** after it calls **SQLPrepare** and before it calls **SQLExecute**. If a data source cannot return this information before a statement has been executed, the driver must attempt to retrieve it in some other manner. For example, if the data source returns this information with a result set, then for a **SELECT** statement, the driver might generate an empty result set.

Returning Result Data

An application binds columns of the result set to storage locations with **SQLBindCol**. It retrieves a row of data with **SQLFetch**. Each time **SQLFetch** is called, a driver:

1. Moves the cursor to the next row.
2. Retrieves the data from the data source.
3. Converts the data for each bound column to the form specified by the *fCType* argument in **SQLBindCol**. The driver may truncate the data for some data type conversions.
4. Places the converted data for each bound column in the storage pointed to by the *rgbValue* argument in **SQLBindCol**. For some data types, the driver will truncate the data if the storage location is too small.

If the driver truncates data, it returns SQL_SUCCESS_WITH_INFO. For more information on converting and truncating data, see "Converting Data From SQL to C Data Types" in Appendix D, "Data Types."

Supporting Cursors

To keep track of its position in the result set, a driver maintains a cursor. The cursor is so named because it indicates the current position in the result set, just as the cursor on a CRT screen indicates current position. Each time an application calls **SQLFetch**, the driver moves the cursor to the next row and returns that row. The cursor supported by core ODBC functions only scrolls forward, one row at a time.

Important   Some data sources close the cursors for all *hstmts* on an *hdbc* when a transaction is committed or rolled back; transactions may be committed or rolled back with **SQLTransact** or automatically committed with the SQL_AUTOCOMMIT connection option. A driver reports this behavior with the SQL_CURSOR_COMMIT_BEHAVIOR and SQL_CURSOR_ROLLBACK_BEHAVIOR information types in **SQLGetInfo**.

ODBC Extensions for Results

ODBC extends the X/Open and SQL Access Group Call Level Interface to provide additional functions related to retrieving results. The remainder of this chapter describes these functions. A driver returns whether it supports a specific function with **SQLGetFunctions**.

Returning Data from Unbound Columns

SQLGetData returns data from a single column to a buffer. A driver may require that the column has not been bound by an earlier call to **SQLBindCol**, that the column be to the right of the rightmost bound column, and that, if data is returned from more than one column in a row with **SQLGetData**, these columns be accessed in left-to-right order. These restrictions are considered normal functionality and a driver returns whether it waives them through the SQL_GETDATA_EXTENSIONS option in **SQLGetInfo**.

SQLGetData cooperates with **SQLBindCol**, **SQLFetch**, and **SQLExtendedFetch**:

- **SQLGetData** can return data from each column in a row of a result set. The application must call **SQLFetch** or **SQLExtendedFetch** to move from row to row.

- The driver can return data from both bound and unbound columns in the same row. **SQLBindCol** is used to bind as many columns as desired. **SQLFetch** or **SQLExtendedFetch** positions the cursor on the next row of the result set and returns data for all bound columns. **SQLGetData** can then return data for unbound columns.

SQLGetData can be called more than once for the same column, as long as the type of the column is character, binary, or data source–specific and the data is being transferred to a buffer of type SQL_C_CHAR or SQL_C_BINARY. Each time it is called, it returns the next unreturned part of the data. For example, an application may need to retrieve data of the SQL_LONGVARCHAR and SQL_LONGVARBINARY types in several parts.

Assigning Storage for Rowsets (Binding)

In addition to binding individual rows of data, an application can call **SQLBindCol** to assign storage for a *rowset* (one or more rows of data). By default, the driver binds rowsets in column-wise fashion. It can also bind them in row-wise fashion.

To specify how many rows of data are in a rowset, an application calls **SQLSetStmtOption** with the SQL_ROWSET_SIZE option. The driver stores the number of rows for later reference.

Column-Wise Binding

To support column-wise binding of results, **SQLBindCol** performs the following tasks for each column:

- Accepts the address of an array of data storage buffers and the size of one element of the data array. When returning data, the driver will use the array element size to determine where to store successive rows of data in the array. If this address is null, the driver unbinds the column.

- Accepts the address of a second array. For each row, the driver will return the number of bytes of data available to return in an element in this array. If this address is null, the driver does not return the number of bytes of available data to the application.

- Associates the arrays with a column.

- Stores information about whether the data is to be converted to a different data type.

Row-Wise Binding

An application defines a structure in which to store row-wise bound results. For each column to be bound, this structure contains one field in which to return data and one field in which to return the number of bytes of data available to return.

To support row-wise binding of results:

- **SQLBindCol** performs the following tasks for each column:
  - Accepts the address of the data field for the column in the first element of an array of these structures. If this address is null, the driver unbinds the column.

- Accepts the size of the data field for the column.
- Accepts the address of the number-of-bytes field for the column in the first element of the array of structures. If this address is null, the driver does not return the number of bytes of available data to the application.
- Associates the addresses with the column.
- Stores information about whether the data in the column is to be converted to a different data type.

- **SQLSetStmtOption** accepts the size of the structure. When returning data, the driver uses the addresses and the size of the structure to determine where each successive row of data is stored.

Returning Rowset Data

To retrieve rowset data, an application calls **SQLExtendedFetch**. The driver retrieves the data from the data source. For each bound column in a row of data, the driver:

1. Converts the data to the type specified with **SQLBindCol**.

2. Calculates the location in the application where the data is to be stored.

   For column-wise bound data, it uses the current row number, the pointer to the data array, and the size of an element in the data array. The pointer to the data array and the size of an element in the data array are specified with **SQLBindCol**.

   For row-wise bound data, it uses the current row number, the pointer to the data field in the first element of the array of structures, and the size of the structure. The pointer to the data field is specified with **SQLBindCol**. The size of the structure is specified with **SQLSetStmtOption**.

3. Stores the converted data in the calculated location. If the size of the converted data is larger than the size of the data storage buffer (as specified in **SQLBindCol**), the driver truncates the data and returns SQL_SUCCESS_WITH_INFO or stops the processing and returns SQL_ERROR.

4. Calculates the location in the application where the number of available bytes to return is to be stored.

   For column-wise bound data, it uses the current row number, the pointer to the number-of-bytes array, and the size of an array element. The pointer to the number-of-bytes array is specified with **SQLBindCol**.

   For row-wise bound data, it uses the current row number, the pointer to the number-of-bytes field in the first element of the array of structures, and the size of the structure. The pointer to the number-of-bytes field is specified with **SQLBindCol**. The size of the structure is specified with **SQLSetStmtOption**.

5. Stores the number of bytes available to return in the calculated location.

The driver returns up to the number of rows of data specified with the SQL_ROWSET_SIZE statement option. For more information, see "Assigning Storage for Rowsets (Binding)" earlier in this chapter.

Note   Drivers are not required to support the use of **SQLGetData** with blocks (more than one row) of data. A driver returns whether it supports the use of **SQLGetData** with blocks of data through the SQL_GETDATA_EXTENSIONS option in **SQLGetInfo**.

Supporting Block and Scrollable Cursors

As originally designed, cursors in SQL only scroll forwards through a result set, returning one row at a time. However, interactive applications often require forward and backward scrolling, absolute or relative positioning within the result set, and the ability to retrieve and update blocks of data, or *rowsets*.

To retrieve and update rowset data, ODBC provides a *block* cursor attribute. To allow an application to scroll forwards or backwards through the result set, or move to an absolute or relative position in the result set, ODBC provides a *scrollable* cursor attribute. Cursors may have one or both attributes.

Block Cursors

An application calls **SQLSetStmtOption** with the SQL_ROWSET_SIZE option to specify the rowset size. The application can call **SQLSetStmtOption** to change the rowset size at any time. Each time the application calls **SQLExtendedFetch**, the driver returns the next *rowset size* rows of data. After the data is returned, the cursor points to the first row in the rowset. By default, the rowset size is one.

Scrollable Cursors

Applications have different needs in their ability to sense changes in the tables underlying a result set. For example, when balancing financial data, an accountant needs data that appears static; it is impossible to balance books when the data is continually changing. When selling concert tickets, a clerk needs up-to-the-minute, or dynamic, data on which tickets are still available. Various cursor models are designed to meet these needs, each of which requires different sensitivities to changes in the tables underlying the result set.

Static Cursors

At one extreme are *static* cursors, to which the data in the underlying tables appears to be static. The membership, order, and values in the result set used by a static cursor are generally fixed when the cursor is opened. Rows updated, deleted, or inserted by other users (including other cursors in the same application) are not detected by the cursor until it is closed and then reopened; the SQL_STATIC_SENSITIVITY information type returns whether the cursor can detect rows it has updated, deleted, or inserted.

Static cursors are commonly implemented by taking a snapshot of the data or locking the result set. Note that in the former case, the cursor diverges from the underlying tables as other users make changes; in the latter case, other users are prohibited from changing the data.

Dynamic Cursors

At the other extreme are *dynamic* cursors, to which the data appears to be dynamic. The membership, order, and values in the result set used by a dynamic cursor are ever-changing. Rows updated, deleted, or inserted by all users (the cursor, other cursors in the same application, and other applications) are detected by the cursor when data is next fetched. Although ideal for many situations, dynamic cursors are difficult to implement.

Keyset-Driven Cursors

Between static and dynamic cursors are *keyset-driven* cursors, which have some of the attributes of each. Like static cursors, the membership and ordering of the result set of a keyset-driven cursor is generally fixed when the cursor is opened. Like dynamic cursors, most changes to the values in the underlying result set are visible to the cursor when data is next fetched.

When a keyset-driven cursor is opened, the driver saves the keys for the entire result set, thus fixing the membership and order of the result set. As the cursor scrolls through the result set, the driver uses the keys in this *keyset* to retrieve the current data values for each row in the rowset. Because data values are retrieved only when the cursor scrolls to a given row, updates to that row by other users (including other cursors in the same application)after the cursor was opened are visible to the cursor.

If the cursor scrolls to a row of data that has been deleted by other users (including other cursors in the same application), the row appears as a *hole* in the result set, since the key is still in the keyset but the row is no longer in the result set. Updating the key values in a row is considered to be deleting the existing row and inserting a new row; therefore, rows of data for which the key values have been changed also appear as holes. When the driver encounters a hole in the result set, it returns a status code of SQL_ROW_DELETED for the row.

Rows of data inserted into the result set by other users (including other cursors in the same application) after the cursor was opened are not visible to the cursor, since the keys for those rows are not in the keyset.

The SQL_STATIC_SENSITIVITY information type returns whether the cursor can detect rows it has deleted or inserted. Because updating key values in a keyset-driven cursor is considered to be deleting the existing row and inserting a new row, keyset-driven cursors can always detect rows they have updated.

Mixed (Keyset/Dynamic) Cursors

If a result set is large, it may be impractical for the driver to save the keys for the entire result set. Instead, the application can use a *mixed* cursor. In a mixed cursor, the keyset is smaller than the result set, but larger than the rowset.

Within the boundaries of the keyset, a mixed cursor is keyset-driven, that is, the driver uses keys to retrieve the current data values for each row in the rowset. When a mixed cursor scrolls beyond the boundaries of the keyset, it becomes dynamic, that is, the driver simply retrieves the next *rowset size* rows of data. The driver then constructs a new keyset, which contains the new rowset.

For example, assume a result set has 1000 rows and uses a mixed cursor with a keyset size of 100 and a rowset size of 10. When the cursor is opened, the driver (depending on the implementation) saves keys for the first 100 rows and retrieves data for the first 10 rows. If another user deletes row 11 and the cursor then scrolls to row 11, the cursor will detect a hole in the result set; the key for row 11 is in the keyset but the data is no longer in the result set. This is the same behavior as a keyset-driven cursor. However, if another user deletes row 101 and the cursor then scrolls to row 101, the cursor will not detect a hole; the key for the row 101 is not in the keyset. Instead, the cursor will retrieve the data for the row that was originally row 102. This is the same behavior as a dynamic cursor.

Supporting the Cursor Types

To specify the cursor type, an application calls **SQLSetStmtOption** with the SQL_CURSOR_TYPE option. The application can specify a cursor that only scrolls forward, a static cursor, a dynamic cursor, a keyset-driven cursor, or a mixed cursor. If the application specifies a mixed cursor, it also specifies the size of the keyset used by the cursor.

Note To use the ODBC cursor library, an application calls **SQLSetConnectOption** with the SQL_ODBC_CURSORS option before it connects to the data source. The cursor library supports block scrollable cursors. It also supports positioned update and delete statements. For more information, see Appendix G, "ODBC Cursor Library."

Unless the cursor is a forward-only cursor, an application calls **SQLExtendedFetch** to scroll the cursor backwards, forwards, or to an absolute or relative position in the result set. The application calls **SQLSetPos** to refresh the row currently pointed to by the cursor.

If the data source does not support keyset-driven and mixed cursors, the driver can support **SQLExtendedFetch** and **SQLSetPos** by saving the keyset itself. The driver uses the keys in the keyset to position the cursor and return the requested results.

The driver can either build the entire keyset when the data source creates the result set, or build the keyset in pieces as the application fetches results from the result set. The keyset always contains keys for contiguous rows; that is, if the application positions the cursor more than *keyset-size* rows away from the current keyset, the current keyset is discarded and a new keyset is built.

The keyset is built from the optimal information that uniquely defines each row in the result set. This depends on the tables in the result set and may be a unique index, a unique key, or the entire row.

Supporting Cursor Concurrency

Concurrency is the ability of more than one user to use the same data at the same time. A transaction is *serializable* if it is performed in a manner in which it appears as if no other transactions operate on the same data at the same time. For example, assume one transaction doubles data values and another adds 1 to data values. If the transactions are serializable and both attempt to operate on the values 0 and 10 at the same time, the final values will be 1 and 21 or 2 and 22, depending on which transaction is performed first. If the transactions are not serializable, the final values will be 1 and 21, 2 and 22, 1 and 22, or 2 and 21; the sets of values 1 and 22, and 2 and 21, are the result of the transactions acting on each value in a different order.

Serializability is considered necessary to maintain database integrity. For cursors, it is most easily implemented at the expense of concurrency by locking the result set. A compromise between serializability and concurrency is *optimistic concurrency control*. In a cursor using optimistic concurrency control, the driver does not lock rows when it retrieves them. When the application requests an update or delete operation, the driver or data source checks if the row has changed. If the row has not changed, the driver or data source prevents other transactions from changing the row until the operation is complete. If the row has changed, the transaction containing the update or delete operation fails.

To specify the concurrency used by a cursor, an application calls **SQLSetStmtOption** with the SQL_CONCURRENCY option. The application can specify that the cursor is read-only, locks the result set, uses optimistic concurrency control and compares row versions to determine if a row has changed, or uses optimistic concurrency control and compares data values to determine if a row has changed. The application calls **SQLSetPos** to lock the row currently pointed to by the cursor, regardless of the specified cursor concurrency.

If the data source does not support optimistic concurrency control, the driver can support it by saving the timestamps or values for the entire rowset.

Using Bookmarks

A bookmark is a 32-bit value that an application uses to return to a row. The application does not request that the driver places a bookmark on a row; instead, the application requests a bookmark that it can use to return to a row. For example, if a bookmark is a row number, an application requests the row number of a row and stores it. Later, the application passes this row number back to the driver and requests that the driver return to the row.

Before opening the cursor, an application must call **SQLSetStmtOption** with the SQL_USE_BOOKMARKS option to inform the driver it will use bookmarks. After opening the cursor, the application retrieves bookmarks either from column 0 of the result set or by calling **SQLGetStmtOption** with the SQL_GET_BOOKMARK option. To retrieve a bookmark from the result set, the application either binds column 0 and calls **SQLExtendedFetch** or calls **SQLGetData**; in either case, the *fCType* argument must be set to SQL_C_BOOKMARK. To return to the row specified by a bookmark, the application calls **SQLExtendedFetch** with a fetch type of SQL_FETCH_BOOKMARK.

If a bookmark requires more than 32 bits, such as when it is a key value, the driver maps the bookmarks requested by the application to 32-bit binary values. The 32-bit values are then returned to the application. Because this mapping may require considerable memory, applications should only bind column 0 of the result set if they will actually use bookmarks for most rows. Otherwise, they should call **SQLGetStmtOption** with the SQL_GET_BOOKMARK statement option or call **SQLGetData** for column 0.

Modifying Result Set Data

ODBC provides two ways to modify data in the result set. Positioned update and delete statements are similar to such statements in embedded SQL. Calls to **SQLSetPos** allow an application to update, delete, or add new data without executing SQL statements.

Processing Positioned Update and Delete Statements

An application can update or delete the row in the rowset currently pointed to by the cursor. This is known as a positioned update or delete statement. After executing a **SELECT** statement to create a result set, an application calls **SQLFetch** one or more times to position the cursor on the row to be updated or deleted. Alternatively, it fetches the rowset with **SQLExtendedFetch** and positions the cursor on the desired row with **SQLSetPos**. To update or delete the row, the application then executes an SQL statement with the following syntax:

UPDATE *table-name*
   SET *column-identifier* = {*expression* | **NULL**}
    [**,** *column-identifier* = {*expression* | **NULL**}]...
   WHERE CURRENT OF *cursor-name*

DELETE FROM *table-name* **WHERE CURRENT OF** *cursor-name*

Positioned update and delete statements require cursor names. An application can name a cursor with **SQLSetCursorName**. The driver associates the cursor name with the SQL statement. If the application has not named the cursor by the time the driver executes a **SELECT** statement, the driver generates a cursor name. To retrieve the cursor name for an *hstmt*, an application calls **SQLGetCursorName**.

To support positioned update and delete statements, a driver or data source must check that:

- The **SELECT** statement that creates the result set has a **FOR UPDATE** clause.

- The cursor name used in the **UPDATE** or **DELETE** statement is the same as the cursor name associated with the **SELECT** statement.

- Different *hstmts* are used for the **SELECT** statement and the **UPDATE** or **DELETE** statement.

- The *hstmts* for the **SELECT** statement and the **UPDATE** or **DELETE** statement are on the same connection.

If the data source does not support positioned update and delete statements, the driver can support them by saving the keys for the entire rowset. (If the application requested a keyset-driven cursor, the driver may already have done this.) When the application executes a positioned update or delete statement, the action of the driver depends on the cursor concurrency:

- **Read Only**   The driver returns an error.

- **Locked**   The driver updates or deletes the row pointed to by the cursor.

- **Optimistic Concurrency Control Comparing Row Versions**   The driver retrieves and, at a minimum, locks the row pointed to by the cursor. It compares the new row version with the saved row version. If the row version is different, the driver returns an error.

- **Optimistic Concurrency Control Comparing Values**   The driver retrieves and, at a minimum, locks the row pointed to by the cursor. It compares the new values with the saved values. If any values are different, the driver returns an error.

A driver returns whether it supports positioned update and delete statements with the SQL_POSITIONED_STATEMENTS option in **SQLGetInfo**. For an example of code that performs a positioned update statement, see **SQLSetCursorName** in Chapter 22, "ODBC Function Reference."

Modifying Data with SQLSetPos

To add, update, and delete rows of data, an application calls **SQLSetPos** and specifies the operation, the row number, and how to lock the row. Where new rows of data are added to the result set, and whether they are visible to the cursor is data source–defined.

The row number determines both the number of the row in the rowset to update or delete and the index of the row in the rowset buffers from which to retrieve data to add or update. If the row number is 0, the operation affects all of the rows in the rowset.

SQLSetPos retrieves the data to update or add from the rowset buffers. It only updates those columns in a row that have been bound with **SQLBindCol** and do not have a length of SQL_IGNORE. However, it cannot add a new row of data unless all of the columns in the row are bound, are nullable, or have a default value.

To add a new row of data to the result set, a driver or data source:

1. Checks that one of the following two conditions is met:

    ▪ All columns in the underlying tables are bound.

    ▪ All unbound columns or bound columns for which the specified length is SQL_IGNORE accept NULL values or have default values.

    If neither condition is met, the driver returns an error.

2. Retrieves the data from array index *irow*–1 of each bound buffer for which the specified length is not SQL_IGNORE, converts the data as necessary, and adds the data to the new row in the data source. For information about how a driver retrieves data for data-at-execution columns, see **SQLSetPos** in Chapter 22, "ODBC Function Reference.".

3. Leaves the row locked in accordance with the *fLock* argument and the SQL_CONCURRENCY statement option.

4. Positions the cursor on the original row.

5. If *irow* is less than or equal to the rowset size, including when *irow* is 0, sets the corresponding value in the *rgfRowStatus* array to SQL_ROW_ADDED.

To update a row of data, a driver or data source:

1. Checks the value of the *irow* argument. If it is greater than the number of rows in the rowset, the driver returns an error.

2. Checks the value of the *rgfRowStatus* array. If it is SQL_ROW_DELETED, SQL_ROW_ERROR, or SQL_ROW_NOROW, the driver returns an error.

3. Retrieves the data from array index *irow*–1 of each bound buffer for which the specified length is not SQL_IGNORE, converts the data as necessary, and updates the corresponding row in the data source. For information about how a driver retrieves data for data-at-execution columns, see **SQLSetPos** in Chapter 22, "ODBC Function Reference."

4. Leaves the row locked in accordance with the *fLock* argument and the SQL_CONCURRENCY statement option.

5. Positions the cursor on the updated row.

6. Sets the value of the *irow*–1 element in the *rgfRowStatus* array to SQL_ROW_UPDATED.

To delete a row of data, a driver or data source:

1. Checks the value of the *irow* argument. If it is greater than the number of rows in the rowset, the driver returns an error.

2. Checks the value of the *rgfRowStatus* array. If it is SQL_ROW_DELETED, SQL_ROW_ERROR, or SQL_ROW_NOROW, the driver returns an error.

3. Deletes the row corresponding to row *irow* of the rowset.

4. Positions the cursor on the deleted row.

Note The application cannot perform any positioned operations, such as executing a positioned update or delete statement or calling **SQLGetData**, on a deleted row.

---

5. Sets the value of the *irow*–1 element in the *rgfRowStatus* array to SQL_ROW_DELETED.

Returning Multiple Results

SELECT statements return result sets. **UPDATE, INSERT**, and **DELETE** statements return a count of affected rows. If any of these statements are batched, submitted with arrays of parameters, or in procedures, they can return multiple result sets or counts.

For a batch of SQL statements or a statement with arrays of parameters, a driver:

- Returns SQL_SUCCESS for **SQLMoreResults** if another result set or row count is available. If another row count is available, performs the necessary processing so **SQLRowCount** will be able to return this count. If another result set is available, initializes the processing for that result set.

- Returns SQL_NO_DATA_FOUND for **SQLMoreResults** if no more result sets or row counts are available.

C H A P T E R   1 6

Returning Status and Error Information

This chapter defines the ODBC return codes and error handling protocol. The return codes indicate whether a function succeeded, succeeded but returned a warning, or failed. The error handling protocol defines how the components in an ODBC connection construct and return error messages through **SQLError**.

The protocol defines:

- Use of the error text to identify the source of an error.
- Rules to ensure consistent and useful error information.
- Responsibility for setting ODBC SQLSTATE based on the native error code.

Returning Return Codes

When an application calls an ODBC function, the driver executes the function and returns a predefined code. These return codes indicate success, warning, or failure status. The following table defines the return codes.

Return code	Description
SQL_SUCCESS	Function completed successfully; no additional information is available.
SQL_SUCCESS_WITH_INFO	Function completed successfully, possibly with a nonfatal error. The application can call **SQLError** to retrieve additional information.
SQL_NO_DATA_FOUND	All rows from the result set have been fetched.
SQL_ERROR	Function failed. The application can call **SQLError** to retrieve error information.
SQL_INVALID_HANDLE	Function failed due to an invalid environment handle, connection handle, or statement handle. This indicates a programming error. No additional information is available from **SQLError**.

Return code	Description
SQL_STILL_EXECUTING	A function that was started asynchronously is still executing.
SQL_NEED_DATA	While processing a statement, the driver determined that the application needs to send parameter data values.

Returning Error Messages

If an ODBC function other than **SQLError** returns SQL_SUCCESS_WITH_INFO or SQL_ERROR, an application can call **SQLError** to obtain additional information. Additional error or status information can come from one of two sources:

- Error or status information from an ODBC function, indicating that a programming error was detected.

- Error or status information from the data source, indicating that an error occurred during SQL statement processing.

The driver buffers errors or messages for the ODBC function it is currently executing. The function may store multiple errors in the driver's error buffer. After the driver has executed the function, an application can call **SQLError** to return error messages for the function. Each time the application calls **SQLError**, the driver returns the next error message in the buffer. When the application calls a different function, the driver discards the current contents of the error message buffer.

The information returned by **SQLError** is in the same format as that provided by SQLSTATE in the X/Open and SQL Access Group SQL CAE specification (1992). Note that **SQLError** never returns error information about itself.

For a list of error codes and the functions that return them, see Appendix A, "ODBC Error Codes."

Constructing ODBC Error Messages

ODBC defines a layered architecture to connect an application to a data source. At its simplest, an ODBC connection requires two components: the Driver Manager and a driver.

A more complex connection might include more components: the Driver Manager, a number of drivers, and a (possibly different) number of DBMS's. The connection might cross computing platforms and operating systems and use a variety of networking protocols.

As the complexity of an ODBC connection increases, so does the importance of providing consistent and complete error messages to the application, its users, and support personnel. Error messages must not only explain the error, but also provide the identity of the component in which it occurred. The identity of the component is particularly important to support personnel when an application uses ODBC components from more than one vendor. Because **SQLError** does not return the identity of the component in which the error occurred, this information must be embedded in the error text.

Error Text Format

Error messages returned by **SQLError** come from two sources: data sources and components in an ODBC connection. Typically, data sources do not directly support ODBC. Consequently, if a component in an ODBC connection receives an error message from a data source, it must identify the data source as the source of the error. It must also identify itself as the component that received the error.

If the source of an error is a component itself, the error message must explain this. Therefore, the error text returned by **SQLError** has two different formats: one for errors that occur in a data source and one for errors that occur in other components in an ODBC connection.

For errors that do not occur in a data source, the error text must use the format:

[*vendor-identifier*][*ODBC-component-identifier*]*component-supplied-text*

For errors that occur in a data source, the error text must use the format:

[*vendor-identifier*][*ODBC-component-identifier*][*data-source-identifier*]
    data-source-supplied-text

The following table shows the meaning of each element.

Element	Meaning
vendor-identifier	Identifies the vendor of the component in which the error occurred or that received the error directly from the data source.
ODBC-component-identifier	Identifies the component in which the error occurred or that received the error directly from the data source.
data-source-identifier	Identifies the data source. For single-tier drivers, this is typically a file format, such as Xbase [1]. For multiple-tier drivers, this is the DBMS product.
component-supplied-text	Generated by the ODBC component.
data-source-supplied-text	Generated by the data source.

1 In this case, the driver is acting as both the driver and the data source.

Note that the brackets ([ ]) must be included in the error text; they do not indicate optional items.

Error Handling Rules

Specific rules govern how each component in an ODBC connection handles errors.

All components in an ODBC connection:

- Must not replace, alter, or mask errors received from another component.
- May add an additional message to the error message queue when they receive an error message from another component. The added message must add real information value to the original message.

The component that directly interfaces a data source:

- Must prefix its vendor identifier, its component identifier, and the data source's identifier to the error text it receives from the data source.
- Must preserve the data source's error code.
- Must preserve the data source's error text.

Any component that generates an error independent of the data source:

- Must supply the correct ODBC SQLSTATE for the error.
- Must generate the text of the error message.
- Must prefix its vendor identifier and its component identifier to the error text.
- Must return a native error code, if one is available and meaningful.

The component that interfaces the Driver Manager:

- Must initialize the output arguments of **SQLError**.
- Must format and return the error information as output arguments of **SQLError** when that function is called.

One component other than the Driver Manager:

- Must set the ODBC SQLSTATE based on the native error. For one and two-tier drivers, the driver must set the ODBC SQLSTATE. For three-tier drivers, either the driver or a gateway that supports ODBC may set the ODBC SQLSTATE.

Documenting Error Mappings

The documentation for the component that formats and returns the arguments of **SQLError** should explain the correlation between those arguments and the native error information. This information is essential for creating and supporting ODBC applications.

For example, Digital Equipment Corporation's (DEC) SQL/Services uses a structure called an SQL Communications Area (SQLCA) to communicate between itself and a client. When an error occurs, it updates the fields in this structure. An ODBC driver for SQL/Services might use the **SQLCODE**, **SQLERRM.SQLERRMC**, **SQLERRM.SQLERRML**, and **SQLERRD[0]** fields from this structure to set the arguments of **SQLError**. Its documentation might include the following table:

SQLError Argument	SQLCA Fields
szSQLState	Derived from **SQLCODE** and **SQLERRD[0]**
pfNativeError	**SQLCODE** and **SQLERRD[0]**
szErrorMsg	**SQLERRM.SQLERRMC** (prefixed by ODBC vendor, ODBC component, and data source identifiers)
pcbErrorMsg	**SQLERRM.SQLERRML** plus the length of the identifiers

As another example, the **dbmsghandle** function in Microsoft's SQL Server installs a user function to handle SQL Server messages. An ODBC driver for SQL Server might call **dbmsghandle** to install a message handler, then use the *msgno* and *msgtext* arguments of the handler to set the arguments of **SQLError**. Its documentation might include the following table:

SQLError Argument	Message Handler Arguments
szSQLState	Derived from *msgno*
pfNativeError	*msgno*
szErrorMsg	*msgtext* (prefixed by ODBC vendor, ODBC component, and data source identifiers)
pcbErrorMsg	The length of *msgtext* plus the length of the identifiers

Sample Error Messages

The following are examples of how various components in an ODBC connection might generate the text of error messages and how various drivers might return them to the application with **SQLError**.

Single-Tier Driver

A single-tier driver acts both as an ODBC driver and as a data source. It can therefore generate errors both as a component in an ODBC connection and as a data source. Because it also is the component that interfaces with the Driver Manager, it formats and returns arguments for **SQLError**.

For example, if a Microsoft driver for dBASE could not allocate sufficient memory, it might return the following arguments for **SQLError**:

```
szSQLState      -    "S1001"
pfNativeError   -    NULL
szErrorMsg      -    "[Microsoft][ODBC dBASE Driver]Unable to
                     ➡ allocate sufficient memory."
pcbErrorMsg     -    67
```

Because this error was not related to the data source, the driver only added prefixes to the error text for the vendor ([Microsoft]) and the driver ([ODBC dBASE Driver]).

If the driver could not find the file EMPLOYEE.DBF, it might return the following arguments for **SQLError**:

```
szSQLState      -    "S0002"
pfNativeError   -    NULL
szErrorMsg      -    "[Microsoft][ODBC dBASE Driver][dBASE]Invalid file
                     ➡ name; file EMPLOYEE.DBF not found."
pcbErrorMsg     -    83
```

Because this error was related to the data source, the driver added the file format of the data source ([dBASE]) as a prefix to the error text. Because the driver was also the component that interfaced with the data source, it added prefixes for the vendor ([Microsoft]) and the driver ([ODBC dBASE Driver]).

Multiple-Tier Driver

A two-tier driver sends requests to a DBMS and returns information to the application through the Driver Manager. Because it is the component that interfaces with the Driver Manager, it formats and returns arguments for **SQLError**.

For example, if a Microsoft driver for DEC's Rdb using SQL/Services encountered a duplicate cursor name, it might return the following arguments for **SQLError**:

```
szSQLState      -    "3C000"
pfNativeError   -    NULL
szErrorMsg      -    "[Microsoft][ODBC Rdb Driver]Duplicate cursor name:
                     ➡ EMPLOYEE_CURSOR."
pcbErrorMsg     -    67
```

Because the error occurred in the driver, it added prefixes to the error text for the vendor ([Microsoft]) and the driver ([ODBC Rdb Driver]).

If the DBMS could not find the table EMPLOYEE, the driver might format and
return the following arguments for **SQLError**:

```
szSQLState      =   "S0002"
pfNativeError   =   -1
szErrorMsg      =   "[Microsoft][ODBC Rdb Driver][Rdb]
                    ➥ %SQL-F-RELNOTDEF, Table EMPLOYEE is not defined
                    ➥ in schema."
pcbErrorMsg     =   92
```

Because the error occurred in the data source, the driver added a prefix for the
data source identifier ([Rdb]) to the error text. Because the driver was the
component that interfaced with the data source, it added prefixes for its vendor
([Microsoft]) and identifier ([ODBC Rdb Driver]) to the error text.

Gateways

In a gateway architecture, a driver sends requests to a gateway that supports
ODBC. The gateway sends the requests to a DBMS. Because it is the component
that interfaces with the Driver Manager, the driver formats and returns arguments
for **SQLError**.

For example, if DEC based a gateway to Rdb on Microsoft Open Data Services,
and Rdb could not find the table EMPLOYEE, the gateway might generate the
error text:

```
"[S0002][-1][DEC][ODS Gateway][Rdb]%SQL-F-RELNOTDEF, Table EMPLOYEE is
➥ not defined in schema."
```

Because the error occurred in the data source, the gateway added a prefix for the
data source identifier ([Rdb]) to the error text. Because the gateway was the
component that interfaced with the data source, it added prefixes for its vendor
([DEC]) and identifier ([ODS Gateway]) to the error text. Note that it also added
the SQLSTATE value and the Rdb error code to the beginning of the error text.
This permitted it to preserve the semantics of its own message structure and still
supply the ODBC error information to the driver.

Because the gateway driver is the component that interfaces with the Driver
Manager, it would use the preceding error text to format and return the following
arguments for **SQLError**:

```
szSQLState      =   "S0002"
pfNativeError   =   -1
szErrorMsg      =   "[DEC][ODS Gateway][Rdb]%SQL-F-RELNOTDEF, Table
                    ➥ EMPLOYEE is not defined in schema."
pcbErrorMsg     =   81
```

Driver Manager

The Driver Manager can also generate error messages. For example, if an application passed an invalid argument value to **SQLDataSources**, the Driver Manager might format and return the following arguments for **SQLError**:

```
szSQLState     =   "S1009"
pfNativeError  =   NULL
szErrorMsg     =   "[Microsoft][ODBC DLL]Invalid argument value:
                   ↪ SQLDataSources."
pcbErrorMsg    =   60
```

Because the error occurred in the Driver Manager, it added prefixes to the error text for its vendor ([Microsoft]) and its identifier ([ODBC DLL]).

C H A P T E R   1 7

Terminating Transactions and Connections

The ODBC interface allows applications to terminate statements, transactions, and connections, and free statement (*hstmt*), connection (*hdbc*), and environment (*henv*) handles.

Terminating Statement Processing

The **SQLFreeStmt** function frees resources associated with a statement handle. The **SQLFreeStmt** function has four options:

- **SQL_CLOSE**   Closes the cursor if one exists, and discards pending results. The application can use the statement handle again later.
- **SQL_DROP**   Closes the cursor, if one exists, discards pending results, and frees all resources associated with the statement handle.
- **SQL_UNBIND**   Frees all return buffers bound by **SQLBindCol** for the statement handle.
- **SQL_RESET_PARAMS**   Frees all parameter buffers requested by **SQLBindParameter** for the statement handle.

SQLCancel requests that the currently executing statement be canceled. When and if the statement is actually canceled is driver- and data source–dependent. If the application calls the function that was executing the statement after the statement has been canceled, the driver returns SQL_STILL_EXECUTING if the statement is still executing, SQL_ERROR and SQLSTATE S1008 (Operation canceled) if the statement was successfully canceled, or any valid return code (such as SQL_SUCCESS or SQL_ERROR) if the statement completed execution.

Terminating Transactions

The **SQLTransact** function requests a commit or rollback operation for the current transaction. The driver must submit a commit or rollback request for all operations associated with the specified *hdbc*; this includes operations for all *hstmts* associated with the *hdbc*.

Terminating Connections

To allow an application to terminate the connection to a driver and the data source, the driver supports the following three functions:

1. **SQLDisconnect**   Closes a connection. The application can then use the handle to reconnect to the same data source or to a different data source.

2. **SQLFreeConnect**   Frees the connection handle and frees all resources associated with the handle.

3. **SQLFreeEnv**   Frees the environment handle and frees all resources associated with the handle.

C H A P T E R   1 8

Constructing an ODBC Driver

This chapter contains a summary of development, debugging, installation, and administration tools provided by the ODBC SDK 2.0.

Testing and Debugging a Driver

The ODBC SDK 2.0 provides the following tools for driver development:

- ODBC Test, an interactive utility that enables you to perform ad hoc and automated testing on drivers. A sample test DLL (the Quick Test) is included which covers basic areas of ODBC driver conformance.

- ODBC Spy, a debugging tool with which you can capture data source information, emulate drivers, and emulate applications.

- A sample driver template written in the C language that illustrates how to write an ODBC driver (16- and 32-bit versions).

- A **#define**, ODBCVER, to specify which version of ODBC you want to compile your driver with. By default, the SQL.H and SQLEXT.H files include all ODBC 2.0 constants and prototypes. To use only the ODBC 1.0 constants and prototypes, add the following line to your driver code before including SQL.H and SQLEXT.H:

```
#define ODBCVER 0x0100
```

For additional infomation about the ODBC SDK tools, see the *Microsoft ODBC SDK Guide*.

Installing and Configuring ODBC Software

Users install ODBC software with a setup program and configure the ODBC environment with an administration program. The setup program uses the installer DLL to retrieve information from the ODBC.INF file. This file is created by a driver developer and describes the disks on which the ODBC software is shipped. For more information, see "Constructing the ODBC.INF File" and "Structure of the ODBC.INF File" in Chapter 19, "Installing ODBC Software."

The administration program uses the installer DLL to configure data sources. The installer DLL calls a *setup DLL* to configure a data source. Driver developers must create a setup DLL for each driver; it may be the driver DLL or a separate DLL. For more information, see Chapter 20, "Configuring Data Sources," and Chapter 23, "Setup DLL Function Reference."

PART 4

Installing and Configuring ODBC Software

CHAPTER 19

Installing ODBC Software

This chapter describes the files that a developer must redistribute in order to enable users to install ODBC software. The ODBC SDK 2.0 provides you with two ways to install ODBC software components (the Driver Manager, drivers, translators, and so on) as follows:

- Use the Driver Setup Toolkit to create a driver setup program, which can be customized by the developer. For more information about using the Driver Setup Toolkit, see the *Microsoft ODBC SDK Guide*.

  Important The Driver Setup Toolkit is a subset of Windows Setup, designed specifically for driver installation. You cannot use it for customizing any other type of installation.

- Create your own setup program. Developers who want to install their own ODBC-enabled applications can use the Windows SDK setup utilities or setup software from other vendors. For more information about the Windows SDK setup utilities, see the Windows SDK documentation.

A setup program makes function calls to the installer DLL. The installer DLL reads information about the ODBC software to be installed from an installation file, ODBC.INF. The installer DLL records information about installed drivers and translators in the ODBCINST.INI file (or registry). The ODBCINST.INI file is used by the Driver Manager to determine which drivers and translators are currently installed. The structure of the ODBC.INF and ODBCINST.INI files is described in the sections that follow.

Redistributing ODBC Files

A number of files are shipped with the ODBC SDK that may be redistributed by application and driver developers. All developers who ship ODBC drivers must redistribute the following files for the specified environments:

ODBC Component	Windows 3.1, WOW (16-bit drivers)	Win32s	WOW (32-bit drivers)	Windows NT
Driver Manager	CTL3DV2.DLL ODBC.DLL	CTL3DV2.DLL ODBC.DLL ODBC16UT.DLL ODBC32.DLL[1]	CTL3D32.DLL ODBC.DLL ODBC16GT.DLL ODBC32GT.DLL	CTL3D32.DLL ODBC32.DLL[1]
Installer	CTL3DV2.DLL ODBC.INF[2] ODBCINST.DLL ODBCINST.HLP	CPN16UT.DLL CTL3DV2.DLL ODBC.INF[2] ODBCCP32.DLL[3] ODBCINST.DLL ODBCINST.HLP	CTL3D32.DLL DS16GT.DLL DS32GT.DLL ODBC.INF[2] ODBCINST.DLL ODBCINST.HLP	CTL3D32.DLL ODBC.INF[2] ODBCCP32.DLL[3] ODBCINST.HLP

[1] The ODBC32.DLL file shipped for use with Win32s® is different from the ODBC32.DLL file shipped for use with Windows NT. Under Win32s, it is a thunking layer that calls ODBC16UT.DLL, which in turn calls ODBC.DLL; under Windows NT, it is the Driver Manager. Applications created under Win32s or Windows NT that use the Win32s API will run under either environment.

[2] Developers must customize ODBC.INF for the files they ship. For more information, see "Constructing the ODBC.INF File," later in this chapter.

[3] The ODBCCP32.DLL file shipped for use with Win32s is different from the ODBCCP32.DLL file shipped for use with Windows NT. Under Win32s, it is a thunking layer that calls CPN16UT.DLL, which in turn calls ODBCINST.DLL; under Windows NT, it is the installer DLL. Applications created under Win32s or Windows NT that use the Win32s API will run under either environment.

Any developers who use the ODBC Driver Setup Toolkit, the program version of the ODBC Administrator, or the ODBC cursor library must redistribute the files required by these components, as listed in the following table. For information about the ODBC Administrator, see the *Microsoft ODBC SDK Guide*. For information about the ODBC cursor library, see Appendix G, "ODBC Cursor Library."

ODBC Component	Windows 3.1, WOW	Windows NT
Driver Setup Toolkit	_BOOTSTP.EXE _MSSETUP.EXE DRVSETUP.EXE [1, 2] SETUP.EXE SETUP.LST [2]	_BOOTSTP.EXE _MSSETUP.EXE DRVSETUP.EXE [1, 2] SETUP.EXE SETUP.LST [2]
Administrator [3]	ODBCADM.EXE	ODBCAD32.EXE
Cursor Library	ODBCCURS.DLL	ODBCCR32.DLL

[1] The DRVSETUP.EXE file shipped for setting up ODBC components on Windows 3.1 and WOW is a 16-bit program. The DRVSETUP.EXE file shipped for setting up ODBC components on Windows NT is a 32-bit program. All other files used by the driver setup program are the same.

[2] Developers must customize the DRVSETUP.EXE and SETUP.LST files for their product. For more information, see the *Microsoft ODBC SDK Guide*.

[3] The ODBC Administrator can be run as a control panel device or as a program on Windows 3.1 or later and on Windows NT. It can be run only as a program on Windows on Windows (WOW).

Creating Your Own Setup Program

If you decide to create your own setup program, it must use the installer DLL shipped with the ODBC SDK. The installer DLL provides functions that a program can call to set up drivers and other ODBC components. The installer can be used to install ODBC components interactively (with a dialog box interface) or silently. For more information about installer DLL functions, see Chapter 24, "Installer DLL Function Reference."

Installing the Software Interactively

To display a dialog box from which a user selects the ODBC components to install (Driver Manager, drivers, and translators), a program calls **SQLInstallODBC** in the installer DLL. It passes a window handle and the full path of the ODBC.INF file to the function. After the user has selected the components to install, **SQLInstallODBC** installs the selected components and records the installed drivers and translators in the ODBCINST.INI file (or registry).

Installing the Software Silently

To silently install the ODBC software, a program calls **SQLInstallODBC** in the installer DLL and passes it a null window handle, the full path of the ODBC.INF file, and, optionally, a list of drivers to install. **SQLInstallODBC** installs the drivers in the list (if any), the Driver Manager, and any translators that are listed in the ODBC.INF file and records the installed drivers and translators in the ODBCINST.INI file (or registry).

Installing Individual ODBC Components

A program can also install individual ODBC components. To install the Driver Manager, a program first calls **SQLInstallDriverManager** in the installer DLL to get the target directory for the Driver Manager. This is usually the directory in which Windows DLLs reside. The program then uses the information in the [ODBC Driver Manager] section of the ODBC.INF file to copy the Driver Manager and related files from the installation disk to this directory.

To install an individual driver, a program first calls **SQLInstallDriver** in the installer DLL to add the driver specification to the ODBCINST.INI file. **SQLInstallDriver** returns the driver's target directory—usually the directory in which Windows DLLs reside. The program then uses the information in the driver's section of the ODBC.INF file to copy the driver DLL and related files from the installation disk to this directory.

Constructing the ODBC.INF File

The ODBC.INF file must be constructed by anyone who ships drivers. The ODBC.INF file shipped with the ODBC SDK may be used as a template. Particular care should be taken to ensure that:

- All disks are described in the [Source Media Descriptions] section and each entry is placed in double quotation marks (") and separated by commas.

- The [ODBC Driver Manager] and [ODBC] sections are not modified and the [ODBC Administrator] section is not modified if the ODBC Administrator is being used.

- All drivers are listed in the [ODBC Drivers] section, each driver has a section describing all the files it needs, and each entry in the driver specification section has the correct number of commas.

- There is a data source specification section for each data source listed in a driver keyword section.

- All translators are listed in the [ODBC Translators] section, each translator has a section describing all the files it needs, and each entry in the translator specification section has the correct number of commas.

- The ODBC.INF file does not contain any tab characters.

Structure of the ODBC.INF File

The ODBC.INF file contains the following sections:

- The [Source Media Descriptions] section describes the disks used to install the ODBC software.

- The [ODBC Driver Manager] section describes the files shipped for the Driver Manager.

- The [ODBC] section describes the files shipped for the installer DLL.

- The [ODBC Administrator] section describes the files shipped for the ODBC Administrator.

- The [ODBC Drivers] and [ODBC Translators] sections describes the ODBC drivers and translators shipped on the disk.

- For each driver described in the [ODBC Drivers] section, there is a section that describes the files shipped for that driver and an optional section that lists driver attribute keywords. For each data source listed in a driver keyword section, there is a section that describes the data source. For each translator described in the [ODBC Translator] section, there is a section that describes the files shipped for that translator.

[Source Media Descriptions] Section

The entries in the [Source Media Descriptions] section describe each of the shipped disks. Each must be enclosed in double quotation marks (") and separated by a comma (,). The format of the section is:

[Source Media Descriptions]
"disk-ID-number1","disk-label1","tag-filename1","setup.exe-rel-path"
"disk-ID-number2","disk-label2","tag-filename2","setup.exe-rel-path"

$$\bullet$$
$$\bullet$$
$$\bullet$$

where each of the arguments has the following meaning:

Argument	Meaning
disk-ID-number	Disk identification number. A unique integer from 1 to 999.
disk-label	Disk label.
tag-filename	The name of a file residing on the disk. The setup program uses this to check that the correct disk has been placed in the drive.
setup.exe-rel-path	The relative path of SETUP.EXE. (This is used only if the installable files reside on a network disk drive.)

For example, if the ODBC software is shipped on a single disk, this section might be:

```
[Source Media Descriptions]
"1","ODBC Setup","SETUP.EXE","."
```

[ODBC Drivers] Section

The [ODBC Drivers] section lists the descriptions of the shipped drivers. A driver description is usually the name of the DBMS associated with that driver. Each entry in the section must start in column 1. The format of the section is:

[ODBC Drivers]
"driver-desc1"=
"driver-desc2"=

$$\bullet$$
$$\bullet$$
$$\bullet$$

For example, suppose drivers for formatted text files and SQL Server are shipped. The [ODBC Drivers] section might contain the following entries:

```
[ODBC Drivers]
"Text"=
"SQL Server"=
```

Driver Specification Sections

For each driver in the [ODBC Drivers] section, a separate section lists the disk
location, name, and installation properties of each file needed by the driver. The
section name is the driver description as listed in the [ODBC Drivers] section.
The driver DLL must be listed with the **Driver** keyword. If there is a separate
setup DLL, it must be listed with the **Setup** keyword. All other files, such as
network communication DLLs and driver data files, must be listed with their own
keywords. If any of these other files are to be placed in the \WINDOWS (as
opposed to the \WINDOWS\SYSTEM) directory, they must use the **Windows*nn***
keyword, where *nn* is a number from 00 to 99. The format of a driver
specification section is:

[*driver-desc*]
"Driver"=*driver-disk-ID,driver-DLL-filename,,,,Date,,,Replace,,,,,,*
➥ *Shared,Size,,,,Version,*
[**"Setup"**=*setup-disk-ID,setup-DLL-filename,,,,Date,,,Replace,,,,,,*
➥ *Shared,Size,,,,Version,*]
[*"keyword3"*=*disk-ID3,filename3,,,,Date,,,Replace,,,,,,Shared,Size,,,,Version,*]
[*"keyword4"*=*disk-ID4,filename4,,,,Date,,,Replace,,,,,,Shared,Size,,,,Version,*]

       •
       •
       •

where *Date*, *Replace*, *Shared*, *Size*, and *Version* are installation properties and
non-bold brackets ([]) indicate optional keywords. All commas (20 per line) must
be included, even if the properties are left blank. For more information, see
"Installation Properties" later in this section.

For example, suppose that a driver for formatted text files is created on May 11,
1992, has a separate setup DLL, and is shipped on the first installation disk.
Suppose also that a driver for SQL Server is created on May 15, 1992, does not
have a separate setup DLL, requires DBNMP3.DLL (a Microsoft SQL Server
Net-Library file) for network communications, and is shipped on the second
installation disk. The driver specification sections for these drivers might be:

```
[Text]
"Driver"=1,TEXT.DLL,,,,1992-05-11,,,,,,,,,,89302,,,,01.00.17.11,
"Setup"=1,TXTSETUP.DLL,,,,1992-05-11,,,,,,,,,,9601,,,,01.00.17.11,

[SQL Server]
"Driver"=2,SQLSRVR.DLL,,,,1992-05-15,,,,,,,,,,95264,,,,01.00.17.15,
"Sqlnet"=2,DBNMP3.DLL,,,,1992-05-15,,,,,,,,,SHARED,7473,,,,01.00.17.15,
```

Driver Keyword Sections

For each driver in the [ODBC Drivers] section, a separate section lists the driver attribute keywords. If a driver does not have any keywords that describe it, this section should not be included in the ODBC.INF file.

For each data source listed with the **CreateDSN** keyword, **SQLInstallODBC** creates a data source in the ODBC.INI file (or registry). For all other driver keywords, **SQLInstallODBC** copies the keywords and their values to the driver's specification section in the ODBCINST.INI file (or registry). To find out information about a driver before connecting to it, an application retrieves these keywords by calling **SQLDrivers**.

The format of a driver keyword section is:

[*driver-desc-***Keys**]
[**APILevel=0 | 1 | 2**]
[**CreateDSN=***data-source-name*[,*data-source-name*]...]
[**ConnectFunctions={Y|N}{Y|N}{Y|N}**]
[**DriverODBCVer=01.00 | 02.00**]
[**FileUsage=0 | 1 | 2**]
[**FileExtns=***.*file-extension1*[,*.*file-extension2*]...]
[**SQLLevel=0 | 1 | 2**]

where the use of each keyword is:

Keyword	Usage
APILevel	A number indicating the ODBC API conformance level supported by the driver:
	0 = None
	1 = Level 1 supported
	2 = Level 2 supported
	This must be the same as the value returned for the SQL_ODBC_API_CONFORMANCE information type in **SQLGetInfo**.
CreateDSN	The name of one or more data sources to be created when the driver is installed. The ODBC.INF file must include one data source specification section for each data source listed with the **CreateDSN** keyword. These sections should not include the **Driver** keyword, since this is specified in the driver specification section, but must include enough information for the **ConfigDSN** function in the driver-specific setup DLL to create a data source specification without displaying any dialog boxes. For the format of a data source specification section, see "Data Source Specification Sections" in Chapter 20, "Configuring Data Sources."

Keyword	Usage
ConnectFunctions	A three-character string indicating whether the driver supports **SQLConnect**, **SQLDriverConnect**, and **SQLBrowseConnect**. If the driver supports **SQLConnect**, the first character is "Y"; otherwise, it is "N". If the driver supports **SQLDriverConnect**, the second character is "Y"; otherwise, it is "N". If the driver supports **SQLBrowseConnect**, the third character is "Y"; otherwise, it is "N". For example, if a driver supports **SQLConnect** and **SQLDriverConnect**, but not **SQLBrowseConnect**, this is "YYN".
DriverODBCVer	A character string with the version of ODBC that the driver supports. The version is of the form ##.##, where the first two digits are the major version and the next two digits are the minor version. For the version of ODBC described in this manual, the driver must return "02.00". This must be the same as the value returned for the SQL_DRIVER_ODBC_VER information type in **SQLGetInfo.**
FileUsage	A number indicating how a single-tier driver directly treats files in a data source. 0 = The driver is not a single-tier driver. For example, an ORACLE driver is a two-tier driver. 1 = A single-tier driver treats files in a data source as tables. For example, an Xbase driver treats each Xbase file as a table. 2 = A single-tier driver treats files in a data source as a qualifier. For example, a Microsoft Access® driver treats each Microsoft Access file as a complete database. An application might use this to determine how users will select data. For example, Xbase and Paradox® users often think of data as stored in files, while ORACLE and Microsoft Access users generally think of data as stored in tables. When a user selects Open Data File from the File menu, an application could display the Windows File Open common dialog box. The list of file types would use the file extensions specified with the **FileExtns** keyword for drivers that specify a **FileUsage** value of 1 and "Y" as the second character of the value of the **ConnectFunctions** keyword. After the user selects a file, the application would call **SQLDriverConnect** with the **DRIVER** keyword, then execute a **SELECT * FROM** *table-name* statement. When the user selects Import Data from the File menu, an application could display a list of descriptions for drivers that specify a **FileUsage** value of 0 or 2 and "Y" as the second character of the value of the **ConnectFunctions** keyword. After the user selects a driver, the application would call **SQLDriverConnect** with the **DRIVER** keyword, then display a custom Select Table dialog box.

Keyword	Usage
FileExtns	For single-tier drivers, a comma-separated list of extensions of the files the driver can use. For example, a dBASE driver might specify *.dbf and a formatted text file driver might specify *.txt,*.csv. For an example of how an application might use this information, see the **FileUsage** keyword.
SQLLevel	A number indicating the ODBC SQL conformance level supported by the driver: 0 = Minimum grammar 1 = Core grammar 2 = Extended grammar This must be the same as the value returned for the SQL_ODBC_SQL_CONFORMANCE information type in **SQLGetInfo.**

For example, suppose a driver for formatted text files can use files with the .TXT and .CSV extensions and that a data source for this driver is to be created when it is installed. The driver keyword and data source specification sections might be:

```
[Text-Keys]
CreateDSN=Text Files
FileExtns=*.txt,*.csv
FileUsage=1

[Text Files]
Directory=#current directory#
TextFormat=Comma Delimited
```

[ODBC Translators] Section

The [ODBC Translators] section lists the descriptions of the shipped translators. Each entry in the section must start in column 1. The format of the section is:

[ODBC Translators]
"translator-desc1"=
"translator-desc2"=

.
.
.

For example, suppose only the Microsoft Code Page Translator is shipped. The [ODBC Translators] section might contain the following entry:

```
[ODBC Translators]
"MS Code Page Translator"=
```

Translator Specification Sections

For each translator in the [ODBC Translator] section, a separate section lists the disk location, name, and installation properties of each file needed by the translator. The section name is the translator description as listed in the [ODBC Translators] section. The translation DLL must be listed with the **Translator** keyword. If there is a separate translator setup DLL, it must be listed with the **Setup** keyword. All other files, such as translation tables for a code page translator, must be listed with their own keywords. If any of these other files are to be placed in the \WINDOWS directory, they must use the **Windows*nn*** keyword, where *nn* is a number from 00 to 99. The format of a translator specification section is:

[*translator-desc*]
"Translator"=*translator-disk-ID,translator-DLL-filename,,,,Date,,,Replace,,,,,,*
➥ *Shared,Size,,,,Version,*
["**Setup**"=*setup-disk-ID,setup-DLL-filename,,,,Date,,,Replace,,,,,,*
➥ *Shared,Size,,,,Version,*]
["*keyword3*"=*disk-ID3,filename3,,,,Date,,,Replace,,,,,,Shared,Size,,,,Version,*]
["*keyword4*"=*disk-ID4,filename4,,,,Date,,,Replace,,,,,,Shared,Size,,,,Version,*]

.
.
.

where *Date*, *Replace*, *Shared*, *Size*, and *Version* are installation properties and non-bold brackets ([]) indicate optional keywords. All commas (20 per line) must be included, even if the properties are left blank. For more information, see "Installation Properties" in the following section.

For example, suppose the Microsoft Code Page Translator is shipped with translation tables for the Multilingual (850) and Nordic (865) code pages. Suppose also that it does not have a separate setup DLL, that it requires the CTL3D.DLL file, and that the files are created on June 1, 1993. The translator specification section for this translator might be:

```
[MS Code Page Translator]
"Translator"=1,MSCPXLT.DLL,,,,1993-06-01,,,,,,,,,,10512,,,,01.01.27.25,
"Ctl3d"=1,CTL3D.DLL,,,,1993-06-01,,,,,,,,,SHARED,14480,,,,1.1.3.0,
"Code Page 850"=1,10070850.CPX,,,,1993-06-01,,,,,,,,,2216,,,,,
"Code Page 865"=1,10070865.CPX,,,,1993-06-01,,,,,,,,,2130,,,,,
```

Installation Properties

The following table describes the installation properties used in the driver specification and translator specification sections. A *blank* value means no value was specified for the property.

Property	Possible values	Meaning
Date	*blank*	The file has no date and is treated as if it was created before all other files.
	date in the format YYYY-MM-DD	Date the file was created. This should match the date in the version.
Replace	ALWAYS	Always overwrite an existing copy of the file.
	NEVER	Never overwrite an existing copy of the file.
	blank or OLDER	Overwrite an existing copy of the file if it is older.
	UNPROTECTED	Overwrite an existing copy of the file if it is unprotected.
Shared	*blank*	Do not treat the file as if it is a shared file.
	SHARED	Treat the file as if it is a shared file, that is, as if non-ODBC programs use it.
Size	*integer*	Approximate size of the uncompressed file in bytes.
	blank	0
Version	*blank*	00.00.00.00
	VV.vv.mm.dd	Version number of the file. The format is:
		VV: major version number
		vv: minor version number
		mm: month file was created (may be greater than 12)
		dd: date file was created

Structure of the ODBCINST.INI File

The ODBCINST.INI file is a Windows initialization file used in Windows 3.1 and WOW that contains the following sections:

- The [ODBC Drivers] section lists the description of each available driver.
- For each driver described in the [ODBC Drivers] section, there is a section that lists the driver DLL, the setup DLL, and any driver attribute keywords.
- An optional section that specifies the default driver.

- The [ODBC Translators] section lists the description of each available translator.

- For each translator described in the [ODBC Translators] section, there is a section that lists the translator DLL and the setup DLL.

On Windows NT, this information is stored in the registry. The key structure in which it is stored is:

HKEY_LOCAL_MACHINE
   Software
      ODBC
         ODBCINST.INI

A subkey of the ODBCINST.INI subkey is created for each section of the ODBCINST.INI file. A value is added to this subkey for each keyword-value pair in the section. The value's name is the same as the keyword, the value's data is the same as the value associated with the keyword, and the value's type is REG_SZ.

Note This section uses terminology for Windows initialization files. For the registry, you should substitute *ODBCINST.INI subkey* for *ODBCINST.INI file*, *subkey* for *section*, *value* for *keyword-value pair*, *value name* for *keyword*, and *value data* for *value*.

For information on the general structure of Windows initialization files, see the Windows SDK documentation. For information on the Windows NT registry, see the Windows NT SDK documentation.

[ODBC Drivers] Section

The [ODBC Drivers] section lists the descriptions of the installed drivers. A driver description is usually the name of the DBMS associated with that driver. Each entry in the section also states that the driver is installed (no other options are allowed). The format of the section is:

[ODBC Drivers]
driver-desc1=**Installed**
driver-desc2=**Installed**

      .
      .
      .

For example, suppose a user has installed drivers for formatted test files and SQL Server. The [ODBC Drivers] section might contain the following entries:

```
[ODBC Drivers]
Text=Installed
SQL Server=Installed
```

Driver Specification Sections

Each driver described in the [ODBC Drivers] section has a section of its own. The section name is the driver description from the [ODBC Drivers] section. It lists the full paths of the driver and setup DLLs, which are the same if the setup function is in the driver DLL. It also lists any driver attribute keywords. The format of a driver specification section is:

[*driver-desc*]
Driver=*driver-DLL-path*
Setup=*setup-DLL-path*
[**APILevel=0 | 1 | 2**]
[**ConnectFunctions={Y|N}{Y|N}{Y|N}**]
[**DriverODBCVer=01.00 | 02.00**]
[**FileUsage=0 | 1 | 2**]
[**FileExtns=****.file-extension1*[**,****.file-extension2*]...]
[**SQLLevel=0 | 1 | 2**]

For information about driver attribute keywords, see "Driver Keyword Sections" earlier in this chapter.

For example, suppose driver for formatted text files has a driver DLL named TEXT.DLL and a setup DLL named TXTSETUP.DLL, and that it can use files with the .TXT and .CSV extensions. Suppose also that a SQL Server driver has a driver DLL named SQLSRVR.DLL, which contains the setup function. The specification sections for these drivers might be:

```
[Text]
Driver=C:\WINDOWS\SYSTEM\TEXT.DLL
Setup=C:\WINDOWS\SYSTEM\TXTSETUP.DLL
FileExtns=*.txt,*.csv
FileUsage=1

[SQL Server]
Driver=C:\WINDOWS\SYSTEM\SQLSRVR.DLL
Setup=C:\WINDOWS\SYSTEM\SQLSRVR.DLL
```

Because the driver and setup DLLs are different for the formatted text file driver, two different files are listed; because they are the same for the SQL Server driver, the same file is listed twice.

Default Driver Specification Section

The ODBCINST.INI file may contain a default driver specification section. The section must be named [Default]. It contains a single entry, which gives the description of the default driver, which is the driver used by the default data source. (This driver must also be described in the [ODBC Drivers] section and in a driver specification section of its own.) The format of the default driver specification section is:

[Default]
Driver=*default-driver-desc*

For example, if the SQL Server driver is the default driver, the default driver specification section might be:

```
[Default]
Driver=SQL Server
```

[ODBC Translators] Section

The [ODBC Translators] section lists the descriptions of the installed translators. Each entry in the section also states that the translator is installed (no other options are allowed). The format of the section is:

[ODBC Translators]
translator-desc1=**Installed**
translator-desc2=**Installed**

> .
> .
> .

For example, suppose a user has installed the Microsoft Code Page Translator and a custom ASCII to EBCDIC translator. The [ODBC Translators] section might contain the following entries:

```
[ODBC Translators]
MS Code Page Translator=Installed
ASCII to EBCDIC=Installed
```

Translator Specification Sections

Each translator described in the [ODBC Translators] section has a section of its own. The section name is the translator description from the [ODBC Translator] section. It lists the full paths of the translation and setup DLLs, which are the same if the setup function is in the translator DLL. The format of a translator specification section is:

[*translator-desc*]
Driver=*translator-DLL-path*
Setup=*setup-DLL-path*

For example, suppose the Microsoft Code Page Translator has a translation DLL named MSCPXLT.DLL, which contains the setup function. Suppose also that a custom ASCII to EBCDIC translator has a translation DLL named ASCEBC.DLL and a setup DLL named ASCEBCST.DLL. The specification sections for these translators might be:

```
[MS Code Page Translator]
Translator=C:\WINDOWS\SYSTEM\MSCPXLT.DLL
Setup=C:\WINDOWS\SYSTEM\MSCPXLT.DLL

[ASCII to EBCDIC]
Translator=C:\WINDOWS\SYSTEM\ASCEBC.DLL
Setup=C:\WINDOWS\SYSTEM\ASCEBCST.DLL
```

Because the translator and setup DLLs are the same for the Microsoft Code Page Translator, the same file is listed twice; because they are different for the ASCII to EBCDIC translator, two different files are listed.

CHAPTER 20

Configuring Data Sources

This chapter describes the files that a developer must redistribute in order to enable users to configure ODBC data sources. The ODBC SDK 2.0 provides you with two ways to configure ODBC data sources, as follows:

- Use the ODBC Administrator (available as a program or as a Control Panel item). For more information about using the ODBC Administrator, see the *Microsoft ODBC SDK Guide.*

- Create your own program to configure data sources.

A program that configures data sources makes function calls to the installer DLL. The installer DLL calls a setup DLL to configure a data source. There is one setup DLL for each driver; it may be the driver DLL or a separate DLL. The setup DLL prompts the user for information that the driver needs to connect to the data source and the default translator, if supported. It then calls the installer DLL and the Windows API to record this information in the ODBC.INI file (or registry). The structure of the ODBC.INI file is described in the sections that follow.

Creating Your Own Data Source – Management Program

If you decide to create your own data source–management program, it must use the installer DLL shipped with the ODBC SDK. The installer DLL provides functions that a program can call to add, modify, and delete data sources, remove a default data source, and select a translator. These functions work with the driver's setup DLL, which returns the information a driver needs to connect to a data source, and the translator's setup DLL, which returns a default translation option for a data source. For more information about installer DLL functions, see Chapter 24, "Installer DLL Function Reference."

Adding, Modifying, and Deleting Data Sources

To display a dialog box with which a user can add, modify, and delete data sources, a program calls **SQLManageDataSources** in the installer DLL. This is the function that is invoked when the installer DLL is called from the Control Panel. To add, modify, or delete a data source, **SQLManageDataSources** calls **ConfigDSN** in the setup DLL for the driver associated with that data source.

To directly add, modify, or delete data sources, a program calls **SQLConfigDataSource** in the installer DLL. The program passes the name of the data source and an option that specifies the action to take. **SQLConfigDataSource** calls **ConfigDSN** in the setup DLL and passes it the arguments from **SQLConfigDataSource**.

For more information, see Chapter 23, "Setup DLL Function Reference," and Chapter 24, "Installer DLL Function Reference."

Specifying a Default Data Source

The default data source is the same as any other data source, except that it has the name Default. (Hence, the connection information includes the keyword-value pair DSN=Default.) To add or modify a default data source, a program performs the same steps that it does to add or modify any other data source. To remove the default data source, a program calls **SQLRemoveDefaultDataSource** in the installer DLL.

Specifying a Default Translator

If a driver supports translators, its setup DLL must provide a way for users to select the default translator and default translation option for a data source. To do this, a setup DLL can call **SQLGetTranslator**. This function displays a list of all installed translators. If the user selects a translator, **SQLGetTranslator** calls **ConfigTranslator** in the selected translator's setup DLL to get the default translation option. The user can also specify that there is no default translator. **SQLGetTranslator** returns the name, path, and option of the default translator (if any).

To add, modify, or delete the default translator and default translation option specified in the ODBC.INI file (or registry), the driver's setup DLL calls **SQLWritePrivateProfileString** in the installer DLL for the **TranslationName**, **TranslationDLL**, and **TranslationOption** keywords. These keywords have the following values:

Keyword	Value
TranslationName	Name of the translator as listed in the [ODBC Translators] section of the ODBCINST.INI file (or registry).
TranslationDLL	Full path of the translation DLL.
TranslationOption	ASCII representation of the 32-bit integer translation option.

Structure of the ODBC.INI File

The ODBC.INI file is a Windows initialization file used in Windows 3.1 and WOW. It is created by the installer DLL when data sources are first configured and contains the following sections:

- The [ODBC Data Sources] section lists the name of each available data source and the description of its associated driver.
- For each data source listed in the [ODBC Data Sources] section, there is a section that lists additional information about that data source.
- An optional section that specifies the default data source.
- An optional section that specifies ODBC options.

On Windows NT, this information is stored in the registry. The key structure in which it is stored is:

HKEY_CURRENT_USER
    Software
        ODBC
            ODBC.INI

A subkey of the ODBC.INI subkey is created for each section of the ODBC.INI file. A value is added to this subkey for each keyword-value pair in the section. The value's name is the same as the keyword, the value's data is the same as the value associated with the keyword, and the value's type is REG_SZ.

Note This section uses terminology for Windows initialization files. For the registry, you should substitute *ODBC.INI subkey* for *ODBC.INI file*, *subkey* for *section*, *value* for *keyword-value pair*, *value name* for *keyword*, and *value data* for *value*.

For information on the general structure of Windows initialization files, see the Windows SDK documentation. For information on the Windows NT registry, see the Windows NT SDK documentation.

[ODBC Data Sources] Section

The [ODBC Data Sources] section lists the data sources specified by the user. Each entry in the section lists a data source and the description of the driver it uses. The driver description is usually the name of the associated DBMS. The format of the section is:

[ODBC Data Sources]
data-source-name1=driver-desc1
data-source-name2=driver-desc2

     •

     •

     •

For example, suppose a user has three data sources: Personnel and Inventory, which use formatted text files, and Payroll, which uses an SQL Server DBMS. The [ODBC Data Sources] section might contain the following entries:

```
[ODBC Data Sources]
Personnel=Text
Inventory=Text
Payroll=SQL Server
```

Data Source Specification Sections

Each data source listed in the [ODBC Data Sources] section has a section of its own. The section name is the data source name from the [ODBC Data Sources] section. It must list the driver DLL and may list a description of the data source. If the driver supports translators, the section may list the name of a default translator, the default translation DLL, and the default translation option. The section may also list other information required by the driver to connect to the data source. For example, the driver might require a server name, database name, or schema name.

The format of a data source specification section is:

[*data-source-name*]
Driver=*driver-DLL-path*
[**Description**=*data-source-desc*]
[**TranslationDLL**=*translation-DLL-path*]
[**TranslationName**=*translator-name*]
[**TranslationOption**=*translation-option*]
[*keyword1=string1*]
[*keyword2=string2*]

     •

     •

     •

where brackets ([]) indicate optional keywords.

For example, suppose an Rdb driver requires the ID of the last user to log in, a server name, and a schema declaration statement. Suppose also that the Personnel data source uses the Microsoft Code Page Translator to translate between the Windows Latin 1 (1007) and Multilingual (850) code pages. The data source specification sections for the Personnel and Inventory data sources might be:

```
[Personnel]
Driver=C:\WINDOWS\SYSTEM\RDB.DLL
Description=Personnel database: CURLY
TranslationName=MS Code Page Translator
TranslationDLL=C:\WINDOWS\SYSTEM\MSCPXLT.DLL
TranslationOption=10070850
Lastuid=smithjo
Server=curly
Schema=declare schema personnel filename
➥ "sys$sysdevice:[corpdata]personnel.rdb"

[Inventory]
Driver=C:\WINDOWS\SYSTEM\RDB.DLL
Description=Western Region Inventory
Lastuid=smithjo
Server=larry
Schema=declare schema inventory filename
➥ "sys$sysdevice:[regionw]inventory.rdb"
```

Note that more than one data source can use the same driver.

Default Data Source Specification Section

The ODBC.INI file may contain a default data source specification section. The data source must be named Default and is not listed in the [ODBC Data Sources] section. The format of the default data source specification section is the same as the structure of any other data source specification section.

ODBC Options Section

The ODBC.INI file may contain a section that specifies ODBC options. These options are set in the Options dialog box displayed by the **SQLManageDataSources** function. The format of the ODBC options section is:

[ODBC]
Trace=0 | 1
TraceFile=*tracefile-path*
TraceAutoStop=0 | 1

where each keyword has the following meaning:

Keyword	Meaning
Trace	If the **Trace** keyword is set to 1 when an application calls **SQLAllocEnv**, then tracing is enabled. On Windows and WOW, it is enabled for all ODBC-enabled applications. On Windows NT, it is enabled only for the calling application.
	If the **Trace** keyword is set to 0 when an application calls **SQLAllocEnv**, then tracing is disabled. On Windows and WOW, it is disabled for all ODBC-enabled for all applications. On Windows NT, it is disabled only for the calling application. This is the default value.
	An application can enable or disable tracing with the SQL_OPT_TRACE connection option. However, doing so does not change the value of this keyword.
TraceFile	If tracing is enabled, the Driver Manager writes to the trace file specified by the **TraceFile** keyword.
	If no trace file is specified, the Driver Manager writes to the \SQL.LOG file in the current directory. This is the default value.
	On Windows NT, tracing should only be used for a single application or each application should specify a different trace file. Otherwise, two or more applications will attempt to open the same trace file at the same time, causing an error.
	An application can specify a new trace file with the SQL_OPT_TRACEFILE connection option. However, doing so does not change the value of this keyword.
TraceAutoStop	If the **TraceAutoStop** keyword is set to 1 when an application calls **SQLFreeEnv**, then tracing is disabled for all applications and the **Trace** keyword is set to 0. On Windows and WOW, it is disabled for all applications; on Windows NT, it is disabled for the calling application and any applications started after the application calls **SQLFreeEnv**. This is the default value.
	If the **TraceAutoStop** keyword is set to 0, then tracing must be disabled with the Options dialog box displayed by the **SQLManageDataSources** function.

PART 5

API Reference

CHAPTER 21

Function Summary

This chapter summarizes the functions used by ODBC-enabled applications and related software:

- ODBC functions
- Setup DLL functions
- Installer DLL functions
- Translation DLL functions

ODBC Function Summary

The following table lists ODBC functions, grouped by type of task, and includes the conformance designation and a brief description of the purpose of each function. For more information about conformance designations, see "ODBC Conformance Levels" in Chapter 1, "ODBC Theory of Operation." For more information about the syntax and semantics for each function, see Chapter 22, "ODBC Function Reference."

An application can call the **SQLGetInfo** function to obtain conformance information about a driver. To obtain information about support for a specific function in a driver, an application can call **SQLGetFunctions**.

Task	Function Name	Conformance	Purpose
Connecting to a Data Source	**SQLAllocEnv**	Core	Obtains an environment handle. One environment handle is used for one or more connections.
	SQLAllocConnect	Core	Obtains a connection handle.
	SQLConnect	Core	Connects to a specific driver by data source name, user ID, and password.
	SQLDriverConnect	Level 1	Connects to a specific driver by connection string or requests that the Driver Manager and driver display connection dialog boxes for the user.
	SQLBrowseConnect	Level 2	Returns successive levels of connection attributes and valid attribute values. When a value has been specified for each connection attribute, connects to the data source.
Obtaining Information about a Driver and Data Source	**SQLDataSources**	Level 2	Returns the list of available data sources.
	SQLDrivers	Level 2	Returns the list of installed drivers and their attributes.
	SQLGetInfo	Level 1	Returns information about a specific driver and data source.
	SQLGetFunctions	Level 1	Returns supported driver functions.
	SQLGetTypeInfo	Level 1	Returns information about supported data types.
Setting and Retrieving Driver Options	**SQLSetConnectOption**	Level 1	Sets a connection option.
	SQLGetConnectOption	Level 1	Returns the value of a connection option.
	SQLSetStmtOption	Level 1	Sets a statement option.
	SQLGetStmtOption	Level 1	Returns the value of a statement option.

Task	Function Name	Conformance	Purpose
Preparing SQL Requests	**SQLAllocStmt**	Core	Allocates a statement handle.
	SQLPrepare	Core	Prepares an SQL statement for later execution.
	SQLBindParameter	Level 1	Assigns storage for a parameter in an SQL statement.
	SQLParamOptions	Level 2	Specifies the use of multiple values for parameters.
	SQLGetCursorName	Core	Returns the cursor name associated with a statement handle.
	SQLSetCursorName	Core	Specifies a cursor name.
	SQLSetScrollOptions	Level 2	Sets options that control cursor behavior.
Submitting Requests	**SQLExecute**	Core	Executes a prepared statement.
	SQLExecDirect	Core	Executes a statement.
	SQLNativeSql	Level 2	Returns the text of an SQL statement as translated by the driver.
	SQLDescribeParam	Level 2	Returns the description for a specific parameter in a statement.
	SQLNumParams	Level 2	Returns the number of parameters in a statement.
	SQLParamData	Level 1	Used in conjunction with **SQLPutData** to supply parameter data at execution time. (Useful for long data values.)
	SQLPutData	Level 1	Send part or all of a data value for a parameter. (Useful for long data values.)

Task	Function Name	Conformance	Purpose
Retrieving Results and Information about Results	**SQLRowCount**	Core	Returns the number of rows affected by an insert, update, or delete request.
	SQLNumResultCols	Core	Returns the number of columns in the result set.
	SQLDescribeCol	Core	Describes a column in the result set.
	SQLColAttributes	Core	Describes attributes of a column in the result set.
	SQLBindCol	Core	Assigns storage for a result column and specifies the data type.
	SQLFetch	Core	Returns a result row.
	SQLExtendedFetch	Level 2	Returns multiple result rows.
	SQLGetData	Level 1	Returns part or all of one column of one row of a result set. (Useful for long data values.)
	SQLSetPos	Level 2	Positions a cursor within a fetched block of data.
	SQLMoreResults	Level 2	Determines whether there are more result sets available and, if so, initializes processing for the next result set.
	SQLError	Core	Returns additional error or status information.

Task	Function Name	Conformance	Purpose
Obtaining information about the data source's system tables (catalog functions)	**SQLColumnPrivileges**	Level 2	Returns a list of columns and associated privileges for one or more tables.
	SQLColumns	Level 1	Returns the list of column names in specified tables.
	SQLForeignKeys	Level 2	Returns a list of column names that comprise foreign keys, if they exist for a specified table.
	SQLPrimaryKeys	Level 2	Returns the list of column name(s) that comprise the primary key for a table.
	SQLProcedureColumns	Level 2	Returns the list of input and output parameters, as well as the columns that make up the result set for the specified procedures.
	SQLProcedures	Level 2	Returns the list of procedure names stored in a specific data source.
	SQLSpecialColumns	Level 1	Returns information about the optimal set of columns that uniquely identifies a row in a specified table, or the columns that are automatically updated when any value in the row is updated by a transaction.
	SQLStatistics	Level 1	Returns statistics about a single table and the list of indexes associated with the table.
	SQLTablePrivileges	Level 2	Returns a list of tables and the privileges associated with each table.
	SQLTables	Level 1	Returns the list of table names stored in a specific data source.
Terminating a Statement	**SQLFreeStmt**	Core	Ends statement processing and closes the associated cursor, discards pending results, and, optionally, frees all resources associated with the statement handle.
	SQLCancel	Core	Cancels an SQL statement.
	SQLTransact	Core	Commits or rolls back a transaction.
Terminating a Connection	**SQLDisconnect**	Core	Closes the connection.
	SQLFreeConnect	Core	Releases the connection handle.
	SQLFreeEnv	Core	Releases the environment handle.

Setup DLL Function Summary

The following table describes setup DLL functions. For more information about the syntax and semantics for each function, see Chapter 23, "Setup DLL Function Reference."

Task	Function Name	Purpose
Setting up data sources and translators	**ConfigDSN**	Adds, modifies, or deletes a data source.
	ConfigTranslator	Returns a default translation option.

Installer DLL Function Summary

The following table describes the functions in the Installer DLL. For more information about the syntax and semantics for each function, see Chapter 24, "Installer DLL Function Reference."

Task	Function Name	Purpose
Installing ODBC	**SQLGetAvailableDrivers**	Returns a list of drivers in the ODBC.INF file.
	SQLGetInstalledDrivers	Returns a list of installed drivers.
	SQLInstallDriver	Adds a driver to the ODBCINST.INI file (or registry).
	SQLInstallDriverManager	Returns the target directory for the Driver Manager.
	SQLInstallODBC	Installs the ODBC software interactively or silently.
Configuring data sources	**SQLConfigDataSource**	Calls the driver-specific setup DLL.
	SQLCreateDataSource	Displays a dialog box to add a data source.
	SQLGetPrivateProfileString	Writing a value to the ODBC.INI file or the registry
	SQLGetTranslator	Displays a dialog box to select a translator.
	SQLManageDataSources	Displays a dialog box to configure data sources and drivers
	SQLRemoveDefaultDataSource	Removes the default data source.
	SQLRemoveDSNFromIni	Removes a data source.
	SQLWriteDSNToIni	Adds a data source.
	SQLWritePrivateProfileString	Getting a value from the ODBC.INI file or the registry

Translation DLL Function Summary

The following table describes translation DLL functions. For more information about the syntax and semantics for each function, see Chapter 25, "Translation DLL Function Reference."

Task	Function Name	Purpose
Translating data	**SQLDriverToDataSource**	Translates all data flowing from the driver to the data source.
	SQLDataSourceToDriver	Translates all data flowing from the data source to the driver.

CHAPTER 22

ODBC Function Reference

The following pages describe each ODBC function in alphabetic order. Each function is defined as a C programming language function. Descriptions include the following:

- Purpose
- ODBC version
- Conformance level
- Syntax
- Arguments
- Return values
- Diagnostics
- Comments about usage and implementation
- Code example
- References to related functions

Error handling is described in the **SQLError** function description. The text associated with SQLSTATE values is included to provide a description of the condition, but is not intended to prescribe specific text.

Arguments

All function arguments use a naming convention of the following form:

[[*prefix*]...]*tag*[*qualifier*][*suffix*]

Optional elements are enclosed in square brackets ([]). The following prefixes are used:

Prefix	Description
c	Count of
h	Handle of
i	Index of
p	Pointer to
rg	Range (array) of

The following tags are used:

Tag	Description
b	Byte
col	Column (of a result set)
dbc	Database connection
env	Environment
f	Flag (enumerated type)
par	Parameter (of an SQL statement)
row	Row (of a result set)
stmt	Statement
sz	Character string (array of characters, terminated by zero)
v	Value of unspecified type

Prefixes and tags combine to correspond roughly to the ODBC C types listed below. Flags (f) and byte counts (cb) do not distinguish between SWORD, UWORD, SDWORD, and UDWORD.

Combined	Prefix	Tag	ODBC C Type(s)	Description
cb	c	b	SWORD, SDWORD, UDWORD	Count of bytes
crow	c	row	SDWORD, UDWORD, UWORD	Count of rows
f	–	f	SWORD, UWORD	Flag
hdbc	h	dbc	HDBC	Connection handle
henv	h	env	HENV	Environment handle
hstmt	h	stmt	HSTMT	Statement handle
hwnd	h	wnd	HWND	Window handle
ib	i	b	SWORD	Byte index

Combined	Prefix	Tag	ODBC C Type(s)	Description
icol	i	col	UWORD	Column index
ipar	i	par	UWORD	Parameter index
irow	i	row	SDWORD, UWORD	Row index
pcb	pc	b	SWORD FAR *, SDWORD FAR *, UDWORD FAR *	Pointer to byte count
pccol	pc	col	SWORD FAR *	Pointer to column count
pcpar	pc	par	SWORD FAR *	Pointer to parameter count
pcrow	pc	row	SDWORD FAR *, UDWORD FAR *	Pointer to row count
pf	p	f	SWORD, SDWORD, UWORD	Pointer to flag
phdbc	ph	dbc	HDBC FAR *	Pointer to connection handle
phenv	ph	env	HENV FAR *	Pointer to environment handle
phstmt	ph	stmt	HSTMT FAR *	Pointer to statement handle
pib	pi	b	SWORD FAR *	Pointer to byte index
pirow	pi	row	UDWORD FAR *	Pointer to row index
prgb	prg	b	PTR FAR *	Pointer to range (array) of bytes
pv	p	v	PTR	Pointer to value of unspecified type
rgb	rg	b	PTR	Range (array) of bytes
rgf	rg	f	UWORD FAR *	Range (array) of flags
sz	–	sz	UCHAR FAR *	String, zero terminated
v	–	v	UDWORD	Value of unspecified type

Qualifiers are used to distinguish specific variables of the same type. Qualifiers consist of the concatenation of one or more capitalized English words or abbreviations.

ODBC defines one value for the suffix *Max*, which denotes that the variable represents the largest value of its type for a given situation.

For example, the argument *cbErrorMsgMax* contains the largest possible byte count for an error message; in this case, the argument corresponds to the size in bytes of the argument *szErrorMsg*, a character string buffer. The argument *pcbErrorMsg* is a pointer to the count of bytes available to return in the argument *szErrorMsg*, not including the null termination character.

ODBC Include Files

The files SQL.H and SQLEXT.H contain function prototypes for all of the ODBC functions. They also contain all type definitions and **#define** names used by ODBC.

Diagnostics

The diagnostics provided with each function list the SQLSTATEs that may be returned for the function by the Driver Manager or a driver. Drivers can, however, return additional SQLSTATEs arising out of implementation-specific situations.

The character string value returned for an SQLSTATE consists of a two-character class value followed by a three-character subclass value. A class value of "01" indicates a warning and is accompanied by a return code of SQL_SUCCESS_WITH_INFO. Class values other than "01", except for the class "IM", indicate an error and are accompanied by a return code of SQL_ERROR. The class "IM" is specific to warnings and errors that derive from the implementation of ODBC itself. The subclass value "000" in any class is for implementation-defined conditions within the given class. The assignment of class and subclass values is defined by ANSI SQL-92.

Tables and Views

In ODBC functions, tables and views are interchangeable. The term *table* is used for both tables and views, except where view is used explicitly.

Catalog Functions

ODBC supports a set of functions that return information about the data source's system tables or catalog. These are sometimes referred to collectively as the *catalog functions*. For more information about catalog functions, see "Retrieving Information About the Data Source's Catalog" in Chapter 6, "Executing SQL

Statements," and "Returning Information About the Data Source's Catalog" in Chapter 14, "Processing an SQL Statement." The catalog functions are:

SQLColumnPrivileges	**SQLProcedures**
SQLColumns	**SQLSpecialColumns**
SQLForeignKeys	**SQLStatistics**
SQLPrimaryKeys	**SQLTablePrivileges**
SQLProcedureColumns	**SQLTables**

Search Pattern Arguments

Each catalog function returns information in the form of a result set. The information returned by a function may be constrained by a search pattern passed as an argument to that function. These search patterns can contain the metacharacters underscore (_) and percent (%) and a driver-defined escape character as follows:

- The underscore character represents any single character.

- The percent character represents any sequence of zero or more characters.

- The escape character permits the underscore and percent metacharacters to be used as literal characters in search patterns. To use a metacharacter as a literal character in the search pattern, precede it with the escape character. To use the escape character as a literal character in the search pattern, include it twice. To obtain the escape character for a driver, an application must call **SQLGetInfo** with the SQL_SEARCH_PATTERN_ESCAPE option.

- All other characters represent themselves.

For example, if the search pattern for a table name is "%A%", the function will return all tables with names that contain the character "A". If the search pattern for a table name is "B__" ("B" followed by two underscores), the function will return all tables with names that are three characters long and start with the character "B". If the search pattern for a table name is "%", the function will return all tables.

Suppose the search pattern escape character for a driver is a backslash (\). If the search pattern for a table name is "ABC\%", the function will return the table named "ABC%." If the search pattern for a table name is "\\%", the function will return all tables with names that start with a backslash. Failing to precede a metacharacter used as a literal with an escape character may return more results than expected. For example, if a table identifier, "MY_TABLE" was returned as the result of a call to **SQLTables** and an application wanted to retrieve a list of columns for "MY_TABLE" using **SQLColumns**, **SQLColumns** would return all of the tables that matched MY_TABLE, such as MY_TABLE, MY1TABLE, MY2TABLE, and so on, unless the escape character precedes the underscore.

Note A zero-length search pattern matches the empty string. A search pattern argument that is a null pointer means the search will not be constrained for that argument. (A null pointer and a search string of "%" should return the same values.)

SQLAllocConnect

Core

SQLAllocConnect allocates memory for a connection handle within the environment identified by *henv*.

Syntax

RETCODE **SQLAllocConnect**(*henv*, *phdbc*)

The **SQLAllocConnect** function accepts the following arguments.

Type	Argument	Use	Description
HENV	*henv*	Input	Environment handle.
HDBC FAR *	*phdbc*	Output	Pointer to storage for the connection handle.

Returns

SQL_SUCCESS, SQL_SUCCESS_WITH_INFO, SQL_ERROR, or SQL_INVALID_HANDLE.

If **SQLAllocConnect** returns SQL_ERROR, it will set the *hdbc* referenced by *phdbc* to SQL_NULL_HDBC. To obtain additional information, the application can call **SQLError** with the specified *henv* and with *hdbc* and *hstmt* set to SQL_NULL_HDBC and SQL_NULL_HSTMT, respectively.

Diagnostics

When **SQLAllocConnect** returns SQL_ERROR or SQL_SUCCESS_WITH_INFO, an associated SQLSTATE value may be obtained by calling **SQLError**. The following table lists the SQLSTATE values commonly returned by **SQLAllocConnect** and explains each one in the context of this function; the notation "(DM)" precedes the descriptions of SQLSTATEs returned by the Driver Manager. The return code associated with each SQLSTATE value is SQL_ERROR, unless noted otherwise.

SQLSTATE	Error	Description
01000	General warning	Driver-specific informational message. (Function returns SQL_SUCCESS_WITH_INFO.)
S1000	General error	An error occurred for which there was no specific SQLSTATE and for which no implementation-specific SQLSTATE was defined. The error message returned by **SQLError** in the argument *szErrorMsg* describes the error and its cause.
S1001	Memory allocation failure	(DM) The Driver Manager was unable to allocate memory for the connection handle.
		The driver was unable to allocate memory for the connection handle.
S1009	Invalid argument value	(DM) The argument *phdbc* was a null pointer.

Comments

A connection handle references information such as the valid statement handles on the connection and whether a transaction is currently open. To request a connection handle, an application passes the address of an *hdbc* to **SQLAllocConnect**. The driver allocates memory for the connection information and stores the value of the associated handle in the *hdbc*. On operating systems that support multiple threads, applications can use the same *hdbc* on different threads and drivers must therefore support safe, multithreaded access to this information. The application passes the *hdbc* value in all subsequent calls that require an *hdbc*.

The Driver Manager processes the **SQLAllocConnect** function and calls the driver's **SQLAllocConnect** function when the application calls **SQLConnect**, **SQLBrowseConnect**, or **SQLDriverConnect**. (For more information, see the description of the **SQLConnect** function.)

If the application calls **SQLAllocConnect** with a pointer to a valid *hdbc*, the driver overwrites the *hdbc* without regard to its previous contents.

Code Example

See **SQLBrowseConnect** and **SQLConnect**.

Related Functions

For information about	See
Connecting to a data source	**SQLConnect**
Freeing a connection handle	**SQLFreeConnect**

SQLAllocEnv

Core

SQLAllocEnv allocates memory for an environment handle and initializes the ODBC call level interface for use by an application. An application must call SQLAllocEnv prior to calling any other ODBC function.

Syntax

RETCODE SQLAllocEnv(*phenv*)

The **SQLAllocEnv** function accepts the following argument.

Type	Argument	Use	Description
HENV FAR *	*phenv*	Output	Pointer to storage for the environment handle.

Returns

SQL_SUCCESS or SQL_ERROR.

If **SQLAllocEnv** returns SQL_ERROR, it will set the *henv* referenced by *phenv* to SQL_NULL_HENV. In this case, the application can assume that the error was a memory allocation error.

Diagnostics

A driver cannot return SQLSTATE values directly after the call to **SQLAllocEnv**, since no valid handle will exist with which to call **SQLError**.

There are two levels of **SQLAllocEnv** functions, one within the Driver Manager and one within each driver. The Driver Manager does not call the driver-level function until the application calls **SQLConnect**, **SQLBrowseConnect**, or **SQLDriverConnect**. If an error occurs in the driver-level **SQLAllocEnv** function, then the Driver Manager–level **SQLConnect**, **SQLBrowseConnect**, or **SQLDriverConnect** function returns SQL_ERROR. A subsequent call to **SQLError** with *henv*, SQL_NULL_HDBC, and SQL_NULL_HSTMT returns SQLSTATE IM004 (Driver's **SQLAllocEnv** failed), followed by one of the following errors from the driver:

- SQLSTATE S1000 (General error).
- A driver-specific SQLSTATE value, ranging from S1000 to S19ZZ. For example, SQLSTATE S1001 (Memory allocation failure) indicates that the Driver Manager's call to the driver-level **SQLAllocEnv** returned SQL_ERROR, and the Driver Manager's *henv* was set to SQL_NULL_HENV.

For additional information about the flow of function calls between the Driver Manager and a driver, see the **SQLConnect** function description.

Comments

An environment handle references global information such as valid connection handles and active connection handles. To request an environment handle, an application passes the address of an *henv* to **SQLAllocEnv**. The driver allocates memory for the environment information and stores the value of the associated handle in the *henv*. On operating systems that support multiple threads, applications can use the same *henv* on different threads and drivers must therefore support safe, multithreaded access to this information. The application passes the *henv* value in all subsequent calls that require an *henv*.

There should never be more than one *henv* allocated at one time and the application should not call **SQLAllocEnv** when there is a current valid *henv*. If the application calls **SQLAllocEnv** with a pointer to a valid *henv*, the driver overwrites the *henv* without regard to its previous contents.

When the Driver Manager processes the **SQLAllocEnv** function, it checks the **Trace** keyword in the [ODBC] section of the ODBC.INI file or the ODBC subkey in the registry. If it is set to 1, the Driver Manager enables tracing for all applications on Windows 3.1 or for the current application on Windows NT.

Code Example	See **SQLBrowseConnect** and **SQLConnect**.

Related Functions

For information about	See
Allocating a connection handle	**SQLAllocConnect**
Connecting to a data source	**SQLConnect**
Freeing an environment handle	**SQLFreeEnv**

SQLAllocStmt

Core

SQLAllocStmt allocates memory for a statement handle and associates the statement handle with the connection specified by *hdbc*.

An application must call **SQLAllocStmt** prior to submitting SQL statements.

Syntax

RETCODE **SQLAllocStmt**(*hdbc*, *phstmt*)

The **SQLAllocStmt** function accepts the following arguments.

Type	Argument	Use	Description
HDBC	*hdbc*	Input	Connection handle.
HSTMT FAR *	*phstmt*	Output	Pointer to storage for the statement handle.

Returns

SQL_SUCCESS, SQL_SUCCESS_WITH_INFO, SQL_INVALID_HANDLE, or SQL_ERROR.

If **SQLAllocStmt** returns SQL_ERROR, it will set the *hstmt* referenced by *phstmt* to SQL_NULL_HSTMT. The application can then obtain additional information by calling **SQLError** with the *hdbc* and SQL_NULL_HSTMT.

Diagnostics

When **SQLAllocStmt** returns SQL_ERROR or SQL_SUCCESS_WITH_INFO, an associated SQLSTATE value may be obtained by calling **SQLError**. The following table lists the SQLSTATE values commonly returned by **SQLAllocStmt** and explains each one in the context of this function; the notation "(DM)" precedes the descriptions of SQLSTATEs returned by the Driver Manager. The return code associated with each SQLSTATE value is SQL_ERROR, unless noted otherwise.

SQLSTATE	Error	Description
01000	General warning	Driver-specific informational message. (Function returns SQL_SUCCESS_WITH_INFO.)
08003	Connection not open	(DM) The connection specified by the *hdbc* argument was not open. The connection process must be completed successfully (and the connection must be open) for the driver to allocate an *hstmt*.
IM001	Driver does not support this function	(DM) The driver associated with the *hdbc* does not support the function.

SQLSTATE	Error	Description
S1000	General error	An error occurred for which there was no specific SQLSTATE and for which no implementation-specific SQLSTATE was defined. The error message returned by **SQLError** in the argument *szErrorMsg* describes the error and its cause.
S1001	Memory allocation failure	(DM) The Driver Manager was unable to allocate memory for the statement handle.
		The driver was unable to allocate memory for the statement handle.
S1009	Invalid argument value	(DM) The argument *phstmt* was a null pointer.

Comments

A statement handle references statement information, such as network information, SQLSTATE values and error messages, cursor name, number of result set columns, and status information for SQL statement processing.

To request a statement handle, an application connects to a data source and then passes the address of an *hstmt* to **SQLAllocStmt**. The driver allocates memory for the statement information and stores the value of the associated handle in the *hstmt*. On operating systems that support multiple threads, applications can use the same *hstmt* on different threads and drivers must therefore support safe, multithreaded access to this information. The application passes the *hstmt* value in all subsequent calls that require an *hstmt.*

If the application calls **SQLAllocStmt** with a pointer to a valid *hstmt*, the driver overwrites the *hstmt* without regard to its previous contents.

Code Example

See **SQLBrowseConnect**, **SQLConnect**, and **SQLSetCursorName**.

Related Functions

For information about	See
Executing an SQL statement	**SQLExecDirect**
Executing a prepared SQL statement	**SQLExecute**
Freeing a statement handle	**SQLFreeStmt**
Preparing a statement for execution	**SQLPrepare**

SQLBindCol

Core

SQLBindCol assigns the storage and data type for a column in a result set, including:

- A storage buffer that will receive the contents of a column of data
- The length of the storage buffer
- A storage location that will receive the actual length of the column of data returned by the fetch operation
- Data type conversion

Syntax

RETCODE **SQLBindCol**(*hstmt, icol, fCType, rgbValue, cbValueMax, pcbValue*)

The **SQLBindCol** function accepts the following arguments.

Type	Argument	Use	Description
HSTMT	*hstmt*	Input	Statement handle.
UWORD	*icol*	Input	Column number of result data, ordered sequentially left to right, starting at 1. A column number of 0 is used to retrieve a bookmark for the row; bookmarks are not supported by ODBC 1.0 drivers or by **SQLFetch**.

Type	Argument	Use	Description
SWORD	*fCType*	Input	The C data type of the result data. This must be one of the following values:

SQL_C_BINARY
SQL_C_BIT
SQL_C_BOOKMARK
SQL_C_CHAR
SQL_C_DATE
SQL_C_DEFAULT
SQL_C_DOUBLE
SQL_C_FLOAT
SQL_C_SLONG
SQL_C_SSHORT
SQL_C_STINYINT
SQL_C_TIME
SQL_C_TIMESTAMP
SQL_C_ULONG
SQL_C_USHORT
SQL_C_UTINYINT

SQL_C_DEFAULT specifies that data be transferred to its default C data type.

Note Drivers must also support the following values of *fCType* from ODBC 1.0. Applications must use these values, rather than the ODBC 2.0 values, when calling an ODBC 1.0 driver:

SQL_C_LONG
SQL_C_SHORT
SQL_C_TINYINT

For more information, see "ODBC 1.0 C Data Types" in Appendix D, "Data Types."

For information about how data is converted, see "Converting Data from SQL to C Data Types" in Appendix D, "Data Types."

Type	Argument	Use	Description
PTR	*rgbValue*	Input	Pointer to storage for the data. If *rgbValue* is a null pointer, the driver unbinds the column. (To unbind all columns, an application calls **SQLFreeStmt** with the SQL_UNBIND option.)
			Note If a null pointer was passed for *rgbValue* in ODBC 1.0, the driver returned SQLSTATE S1009 (Invalid argument value); individual columns could not be unbound.
SDWORD	*cbValueMax*	Input	Maximum length of the *rgbValue* buffer. For character data, *rgbValue* must also include space for the null-termination byte. For more information about length, see "Precision, Scale, Length, and Display Size" in Appendix D, "Data Types."

Type	Argument	Use	Description
SDWORD FAR *	*pcbValue*	Input	SQL_NULL_DATA or the number of bytes (excluding the null termination byte for character data) available to return in *rgbValue* prior to calling **SQLExtendedFetch** or **SQLFetch**, or SQL_NO_TOTAL if the number of available bytes cannot be determined.
			For character data, if the number of bytes available to return is SQL_NO_TOTAL or is greater than or equal to *cbValueMax*, the data in *rgbValue* is truncated to *cbValueMax* – 1 bytes and is null-terminated by the driver.
			For binary data, if the number of bytes available to return is SQL_NO_TOTAL or is greater than *cbValueMax*, the data in *rgbValue* is truncated to *cbValueMax* bytes.
			For all other data types, the value of *cbValueMax* is ignored and the driver assumes the size of *rgbValue* is the size of the C data type specified with *fCType*.
			For more information about the value returned in *pcbValue* for each *fCType*, see "Converting Data from SQL to C Data Types" in Appendix D, "Data Types."

Returns   SQL_SUCCESS, SQL_SUCCESS_WITH_INFO, SQL_ERROR, or SQL_INVALID_HANDLE.

Diagnostics   When **SQLBindCol** returns SQL_ERROR or SQL_SUCCESS_WITH_INFO, an associated SQLSTATE value may be obtained by calling **SQLError**. The following table lists the SQLSTATE values commonly returned by **SQLBindCol** and explains each one in the context of this function; the notation "(DM)" precedes the descriptions of SQLSTATEs returned by the Driver Manager. The return code associated with each SQLSTATE value is SQL_ERROR, unless noted otherwise.

SQLSTATE	Error	Description
01000	General warning	Driver-specific informational message. (Function returns SQL_SUCCESS_WITH_INFO.)
IM001	Driver does not support this function	(DM) The driver associated with the *hstmt* does not support the function.
S1000	General error	An error occurred for which there was no specific SQLSTATE and for which no implementation-specific SQLSTATE was defined. The error message returned by **SQLError** in the argument *szErrorMsg* describes the error and its cause.
S1001	Memory allocation failure	The driver was unable to allocate memory required to support execution or completion of the function.
S1002	Invalid column number	The value specified for the argument *icol* was 0 and the driver was an ODBC 1.0 driver.
		The value specified for the argument *icol* exceeded the maximum number of columns supported by the data source.
S1003	Program type out of range	(DM) The argument *fCType* was not a valid data type or SQL_C_DEFAULT.
		The argument *icol* was 0 and the argument *fCType* was not SQL_C_BOOKMARK.
S1009	Invalid argument value	The driver supported ODBC 1.0 and the argument *rgbValue* was a null pointer.
S1010	Function sequence error	(DM) An asynchronously executing function was called for the *hstmt* and was still executing when this function was called.
		(DM) **SQLExecute, SQLExecDirect**, or **SQLSetPos** was called for the *hstmt* and returned SQL_NEED_DATA. This function was called before data was sent for all data-at-execution parameters or columns.
S1090	Invalid string or buffer length	(DM) The value specified for the argument *cbValueMax* was less than 0.

SQLSTATE	Error	Description
S1C00	Driver not capable	The driver does not support the data type specified in the argument *fCType*.
		The argument *icol* was 0 and the driver does not support bookmarks.
		The driver only supports ODBC 1.0 and the argument *fCType* was one of the following:

SQL_C_STINYINT
SQL_C_UTINYINT
SQL_C_SSHORT
SQL_C_USHORT
SQL_C_SLONG
SQL_C_ULONG

Comments   The ODBC interface provides two ways to retrieve a column of data:

- **SQLBindCol** assigns the storage location for a column of data before the data is retrieved. When **SQLFetch** or **SQLExtendedFetch** is called, the driver places the data for all bound columns in the assigned locations.

- **SQLGetData** (an extended function) assigns a storage location for a column of data after **SQLFetch** or **SQLExtendedFetch** has been called. It also places the data for the requested column in the assigned location. Because it can retrieve data from a column in parts, **SQLGetData** can be used to retrieve long data values.

An application may choose to bind every column with **SQLBindCol**, to do no binding and retrieve data only with **SQLGetData**, or to use a combination of the two. However, unless the driver provides extended functionality, **SQLGetData** can only be used to retrieve data from columns that occur after the last bound column.

An application calls **SQLBindCol** to pass the pointer to the storage buffer for a column of data to the driver and to specify how or if the data will be converted. It is the application's responsibility to allocate enough storage for the data. If the buffer will contain variable length data, the application must allocate as much storage as the maximum length of the bound column or the data may be truncated. For a list of valid data conversion types, see "Converting Data from SQL to C Data Types" in Appendix D, "Data Types."

At fetch time, the driver processes the data for each bound column according to the arguments specified in **SQLBindCol**. First, it converts the data according to the argument *fCType*. Next, it fills the buffer pointed to by *rgbValue*. Finally, it stores the available number of bytes in *pcbValue*; this is the number of bytes available prior to calling **SQLFetch** or **SQLExtendedFetch**.

- If SQL_MAX_LENGTH has been specified with **SQLSetStmtOption** and the available number of bytes is greater than SQL_MAX_LENGTH, the driver stores SQL_MAX_LENGTH in *pcbValue*.

- If the data is truncated because of SQL_MAX_LENGTH, but the user's buffer was large enough for SQL_MAX_LENGTH bytes of data, SQL_SUCCESS is returned.

Note The SQL_MAX_LENGTH statement option is intended to reduce network traffic and may not be supported by all drivers. To guarantee that data is truncated, an application should allocate a buffer of the desired size and specify this size in the *cbValueMax* argument.

- If the user's buffer causes the truncation, the driver returns SQL_SUCCESS_WITH_INFO and SQLSTATE 01004 (Data truncated) for the fetch function.

- If the data value for a column is NULL, the driver sets *pcbValue* to SQL_NULL_DATA.

- If the number of bytes available to return cannot be determined in advance, the driver sets *pcbValue* to SQL_NO_TOTAL.

When an application uses **SQLExtendedFetch** to retrieve more than one row of data, it only needs to call **SQLBindCol** once for each column of the result set (just as when it binds a column in order to retrieve a single row of data with **SQLFetch**). The **SQLExtendedFetch** function coordinates the placement of each row of data into subsequent locations in the rowset buffers. For additional information about binding rowset buffers, see the "Comments" topic for **SQLExtendedFetch**.

An application can call **SQLBindCol** to bind a column to a new storage location, regardless of whether data has already been fetched. The new binding replaces the old binding. Note that the new binding does not apply to data already fetched; the next time data is fetched, the data will be placed in the new storage location.

To unbind a single bound column, an application calls **SQLBindCol** and specifies a null pointer for *rgbValue*; if *rgbValue* is a null pointer and the column is not bound, **SQLBindCol** returns SQL_SUCCESS. To unbind all bound columns, an application calls **SQLFreeStmt** with the SQL_UNBIND option.

Code Example

In the following example, an application executes a **SELECT** statement to return a result set of the employee names, ages, and birthdays, which is sorted by birthday. It then calls **SQLBindCol** to bind the columns of data to local storage locations. Finally, the application fetches each row of data with **SQLFetch** and prints each employee's name, age, and birthday.

For more code examples, see **SQLColumns**, **SQLExtendedFetch**, and **SQLSetPos**.

```
#define NAME_LEN 30
#define BDAY_LEN 11

UCHAR   szName[NAME_LEN], szBirthday[BDAY_LEN];
SWORD   sAge;
SDWORD  cbName, cbAge, cbBirthday;

retcode = SQLExecDirect(hstmt,
            "SELECT NAME, AGE, BIRTHDAY FROM EMPLOYEE ORDER BY 3, 2, 1",
            SQL_NTS);

if (retcode == SQL_SUCCESS) {

    /* Bind columns 1, 2, and 3 */

    SQLBindCol(hstmt, 1, SQL_C_CHAR, szName, NAME_LEN, &cbName);
    SQLBindCol(hstmt, 2, SQL_C_SSHORT, &sAge, 0, &cbAge);
    SQLBindCol(hstmt, 3, SQL_C_CHAR, szBirthday, BDAY_LEN, &cbBirthday);

    /* Fetch and print each row of data.  On */
    /* an error, display a message and exit. */

    while (TRUE) {
        retcode = SQLFetch(hstmt);
        if (retcode == SQL_ERROR || retcode == SQL_SUCCESS_WITH_INFO) {
            show_error();
        }
        if (retcode == SQL_SUCCESS || retcode == SQL_SUCCESS_WITH_INFO){
            fprintf(out, "%-*s %-2d %*s", NAME_LEN-1, szName,
                    sAge, BDAY_LEN-1, szBirthday);
        } else {
            break;
        }
    }
}
```

Related Functions

For information about	See
Returning information about a column in a result set	**SQLDescribeCol**
Fetching a block of data or scrolling through a result set	**SQLExtendedFetch** (extension)
Fetching a row of data	**SQLFetch**
Freeing a statement handle	**SQLFreeStmt**
Fetching part or all of a column of data	**SQLGetData** (extension)
Returning the number of result set columns	**SQLNumResultCols**

SQLBindParameter

Level 1   **SQLBindParameter** binds a buffer to a parameter marker in an SQL statement.

Note This function replaces the ODBC 1.0 function **SQLSetParam**. For more information, see "Comments."

Syntax   RETCODE **SQLBindParameter**(*hstmt, ipar, fParamType, fCType, fSqlType, cbColDef, ibScale, rgbValue, cbValueMax, pcbValue*)

The **SQLBindParameter** function accepts the following arguments.

Type	Argument	Use	Description
HSTMT	*hstmt*	Input	Statement handle.
UWORD	*ipar*	Input	Parameter number, ordered sequentially left to right, starting at 1.
SWORD	*fParamType*	Input	The type of the parameter. For more information, see "fParamType Argument" in "Comments."
SWORD	*fCType*	Input	The C data type of the parameter. For more information, see "fCType Argument" in "Comments."
SWORD	*fSqlType*	Input	The SQL data type of the parameter. For more information, see "fSqlType Argument" in "Comments."
UDWORD	*cbColDef*	Input	The precision of the column or expression of the corresponding parameter marker. For more information, see "cbColDef Argument" in "Comments."
SWORD	*ibScale*	Input	The scale of the column or expression of the corresponding parameter marker. For further information concerning scale, see "Precision, Scale, Length, and Display Size," in Appendix D, "Data Types."
PTR	*rgbValue*	Input/ Output	A pointer to a buffer for the parameter's data. For more information, see "rgbValue Argument" in "Comments."

Type	Argument	Use	Description
SDWORD	*cbValueMax*	Input	Maximum length of the *rgbValue* buffer. For more information, see "cbValueMax Argument" in "Comments."
SDWORD FAR *	*pcbValue*	Input/ Output	A pointer to a buffer for the parameter's length. For more information, see "pcbValue Argument" in "Comments."

Returns

SQL_SUCCESS, SQL_SUCCESS_WITH_INFO, SQL_ERROR, or SQL_INVALID_HANDLE.

Diagnostics

When **SQLBindParameter** returns SQL_ERROR or SQL_SUCCESS_WITH_INFO, an associated SQLSTATE value may be obtained by calling **SQLError**. The following table lists the SQLSTATE values commonly returned by **SQLBindParameter** and explains each one in the context of this function; the notation "(DM)" precedes the descriptions of SQLSTATEs returned by the Driver Manager. The return code associated with each SQLSTATE value is SQL_ERROR, unless noted otherwise.

SQLSTATE	Error	Description
01000	General warning	Driver-specific informational message. (Function returns SQL_SUCCESS_WITH_INFO.)
07006	Restricted data type attribute violation	The data value identified by the *fCType* argument cannot be converted to the data type identified by the *fSqlType* argument.
IM001	Driver does not support this function	(DM) The driver associated with the *hstmt* does not support the function.
S1000	General error	An error occurred for which there was no specific SQLSTATE and for which no implementation-specific SQLSTATE was defined. The error message returned by **SQLError** in the argument *szErrorMsg* describes the error and its cause.
S1001	Memory allocation failure	The driver was unable to allocate memory required to support execution or completion of the function.
S1003	Program type out of range	(DM) The value specified by the argument *fCType* was not a valid data type or SQL_C_DEFAULT.

SQLSTATE	Error	Description
S1004	SQL data type out of range	(DM) The value specified for the argument *fSqlType* was in the block of numbers reserved for ODBC SQL data type indicators but was not a valid ODBC SQL data type indicator.
S1009	Invalid argument value	(DM) The argument *rgbValue* was a null pointer, the argument *pcbValue* was a null pointer, and the argument *fParamType* was not SQL_PARAM_OUTPUT.
S1010	Function sequence error	(DM) An asynchronously executing function was called for the *hstmt* and was still executing when this function was called.
		(DM) **SQLExecute**, **SQLExecDirect**, or **SQLSetPos** was called for the *hstmt* and returned SQL_NEED_DATA. This function was called before data was sent for all data-at-execution parameters or columns.
S1090	Invalid string or buffer length	(DM) The value specified for the argument *cbValueMax* was less than 0.
S1093	Invalid parameter number	(DM) The value specified for the argument *ipar* was less than 1.
		The value specified for the argument *ipar* was greater than the maximum number of parameters supported by the data source.
S1094	Invalid scale value	The value specified for the argument *ibScale* was outside the range of values supported by the data source for a column of the SQL data type specified by the *fSqlType* argument.
S1104	Invalid precision value	The value specified for the argument *cbColDef* was outside the range of values supported by the data source for a column of the SQL data type specified by the *fSqlType* argument.

SQLSTATE	Error	Description
S1105	Invalid parameter type	(DM) The value specified for the argument *fParamType* was invalid (see "Comments").
		The value specified for the argument *fParamType* was SQL_PARAM_OUTPUT and the parameter did not mark a return value from a procedure or a procedure parameter.
		The value specified for the argument *fParamType* was SQL_PARAM_INPUT and the parameter marked the return value from a procedure.
S1C00	Driver not capable	The driver or data source does not support the conversion specified by the combination of the value specified for the argument *fCType* and the driver-specific value specified for the argument *fSqlType*.
		The value specified for the argument *fSqlType* was a valid ODBC SQL data type indicator for the version of ODBC supported by the driver, but was not supported by the driver or data source.
		The value specified for the argument *fSqlType* was in the range of numbers reserved for driver-specific SQL data type indicators, but was not supported by the driver or data source.
		The driver only supports ODBC 1.0 and the argument *fCType* was one of the following:
		SQL_C_STINYINT SQL_C_UTINYINT SQL_C_SSHORT SQL_C_USHORT SQL_C_SLONG SQL_C_ULONG

Comments

An application calls **SQLBindParameter** to bind each parameter marker in an SQL statement. Bindings remain in effect until the application calls **SQLBindParameter** again or until the application calls **SQLFreeStmt** with the SQL_DROP or SQL_RESET_PARAMS option.

For more information concerning parameter data types and parameter markers, see "Parameter Data Types" and "Parameter Markers" in Appendix C, "SQL Grammar."

fParamType Argument

The *fParamType* argument specifies the type of the parameter. All parameters in SQL statements that do not call procedures, such as **INSERT** statements, are input parameters. Parameters in procedure calls can be input, input/output, or output parameters. (An application calls **SQLProcedureColumns** to determine the type of a parameter in a procedure call; parameters in procedure calls whose type cannot be determined are assumed to be input parameters.)

The *fParamType* argument is one of the following values:

- SQL_PARAM_INPUT. The parameter marks a parameter in an SQL statement that does not call a procedure, such as an **INSERT** statement, or it marks an input parameter in a procedure; these are collectively known as *input parameters*. For example, the parameters in **INSERT INTO Employee VALUES (?, ?, ?)** and {**call AddEmp(?, ?, ?)**} are input parameters.

  When the statement is executed, the driver sends data for the parameter to the data source; the *rgbValue* buffer must contain a valid input value or the *pcbValue* buffer must contain SQL_NULL_DATA, SQL_DATA_AT_EXEC, or the result of the SQL_LEN_DATA_AT_EXEC macro.

  If an application cannot determine the type of a parameter in a procedure call, it sets *fParamType* to SQL_PARAM_INPUT; if the data source returns a value for the parameter, the driver discards it.

- SQL_PARAM_INPUT_OUTPUT. The parameter marks an input/output parameter in a procedure. For example, the parameter in {**call GetEmpDept(?)**} is an input/output parameter that accepts an employee's name and returns the name of the employee's department.

  When the statement is executed, the driver sends data for the parameter to the data source; the *rgbValue* buffer must contain a valid input value or the *pcbValue* buffer must contain SQL_NULL_DATA, SQL_DATA_AT_EXEC, or the result of the SQL_LEN_DATA_AT_EXEC macro. After the statement is executed, the driver returns data for the parameter to the application; if the data source does not return a value for an input/output parameter, the driver sets the *pcbValue* buffer to SQL_NULL_DATA.

Note   When an ODBC 1.0 application calls **SQLSetParam** in an ODBC 2.0 driver, the Driver Manager converts this to a call to **SQLBindParameter** in which the *fParamType* argument is set to SQL_PARAM_INPUT_OUTPUT.

- SQL_PARAM_OUTPUT. The parameter marks the return value of a procedure or an output parameter in a procedure; these are collectively known as *output parameters*. For example, the parameter in {**?=call GetNextEmpID**} is an output parameter that returns the next employee ID.

  After the statement is executed, the driver returns data for the parameter to the application, unless the *rgbValue* and *pcbValue* arguments are both null pointers, in which case the driver discards the output value. If the data source does not return a value for an output parameter, the driver sets the *pcbValue* buffer to SQL_NULL_DATA.

fCType Argument

The C data type of the parameter. This must be one of the following values:

SQL_C_BINARY	SQL_C_SSHORT
SQL_C_BIT	SQL_C_STINYINT
SQL_C_CHAR	SQL_C_TIME
SQL_C_DATE	SQL_C_TIMESTAMP
SQL_C_DEFAULT	SQL_C_ULONG
SQL_C_DOUBLE	SQL_C_USHORT
SQL_C_FLOAT	SQL_C_UTINYINT
SQL_C_SLONG	

SQL_C_DEFAULT specifies that the parameter value be transferred from the default C data type for the SQL data type specified with *fSqlType*.

For more information, see "Default C Data Types" and "Converting Data from C to SQL Data Types" and "Converting Data from SQL to C Data Types" in Appendix D, "Data Types."

Note Drivers must also support the following values of *fCType* from ODBC 1.0. Applications must use these values, instead of the ODBC 2.0 values, when calling an ODBC 1.0 driver:

    SQL_C_LONG
    SQL_C_SHORT
    SQL_C_TINYINT

For more information, see "ODBC 1.0 C Data Types" in Appendix D, "Data Types."

---

fSqlType Argument

This must be one of the following values:

SQL_BIGINT	SQL_DECIMAL
SQL_BINARY	SQL_DOUBLE
SQL_BIT	SQL_FLOAT
SQL_CHAR	SQL_INTEGER
SQL_DATE	SQL_LONGVARBINARY

SQL_LONGVARCHAR   SQL_TIMESTAMP

SQL_NUMERIC   SQL_TINYINT

SQL_REAL   SQL_VARBINARY

SQL_SMALLINT   SQL_VARCHAR

SQL_TIME

or a driver-specific value. Values greater than SQL_TYPE_DRIVER_START are reserved by ODBC; values less than or equal to SQL_TYPE_DRIVER_START are driver-specific. For more information, see "Driver-Specific Data Types, Descriptor Types, Information Types, and Options" in Chapter 11, "Guidelines for Implementing ODBC Functions."

For information about how data is converted, see "Converting Data from C to SQL Data Types" and "Converting Data from SQL to C Data Types" in Appendix D, "Data Types."

cbColDef Argument

The *cbColDef* argument specifies the precision of the column or expression corresponding to the parameter marker, unless all of the following are true:

- An ODBC 2.0 application calls **SQLBindParameter** in an ODBC 1.0 driver or an ODBC 1.0 application calls **SQLSetParam** in an ODBC 2.0 driver. (Note that the Driver Manager converts these calls.)

- The *fSqlType* argument is SQL_LONGVARBINARY or SQL_LONGVARCHAR.

- The data for the parameter will be sent with **SQLPutData**.

In this case, the *cbColDef* argument contains the total number of bytes that will be sent for the parameter. For more information, see "Passing Parameter Values" and SQL_DATA_AT_EXEC in "pcbValue Argument."

rgbValue Argument

The *rgbValue* argument points to a buffer that, when **SQLExecute** or **SQLExecDirect** is called, contains the actual data for the parameter. The data must be in the form specified by the *fCType* argument.

If *rgbValue* points to a character string that contains a literal quote character ('), the driver ensures that each literal quote is translated into the form required by the data source. For example, if the data source required that embedded literal quotes be doubled, the driver would replace each quote character (') with two quote characters ('').

If *pcbValue* is the result of the SQL_LEN_DATA_AT_EXEC(*length*) macro or SQL_DATA_AT_EXEC, then *rgbValue* is an application-defined 32-bit value that is associated with the parameter. It is returned to the application through

SQLParamData. For example, *rgbValue* might be a token such as a parameter number, a pointer to data, or a pointer to a structure that the application used to bind input parameters. Note, however, that if the parameter is an input/output parameter, *rgbValue* must be a pointer to a buffer where the output value will be stored. If **SQLParamOptions** was called to specify multiple values for the parameter, the application can use the value of the *pirow* argument in **SQLParamOptions** in conjunction with the *rgbValue*. For example, *rgbValue* might point to an array of values and the application might use *pirow* to retrieve the correct value from the array. For more information, see "Passing Parameter Values."

If the *fParamType* argument is SQL_PARAM_INPUT_OUTPUT or SQL_PARAM_OUTPUT, *rgbValue* points to a buffer in which the driver returns the output value. If the procedure returns one or more result sets, the *rgbValue* buffer is not guaranteed to be set until all results have been fetched. (If *fParamType* is SQL_PARAM_OUTPUT and *rgbValue* and *pcbValue* are both null pointers, the driver discards the output value.)

If the application calls **SQLParamOptions** to specify multiple values for each parameter, *rgbValue* points to an array. A single SQL statement processes the entire array of input values for an input or input/output parameter and returns an array of output values for an input/output or output parameter.

cbValueMax Argument

For character and binary C data, the *cbValueMax* argument specifies the length of the *rgbValue* buffer (if it is a single element) or the length of an element in the *rgbValue* array (if the application calls **SQLParamOptions** to specify multiple values for each parameter). If the application specifies multiple values, *cbValueMax* is used to determine the location of values in the *rgbValue* array, both on input and on output. For input/output and output parameters, it is used to determine whether to truncate character and binary C data on output:

- For character C data, if the number of bytes available to return is greater than or equal to *cbValueMax*, the data in *rgbValue* is truncated to *cbValueMax* – 1 bytes and is null-terminated by the driver.

- For binary C data, if the number of bytes available to return is greater than *cbValueMax*, the data in *rgbValue* is truncated to *cbValueMax* bytes.

For all other types of C data, the *cbValueMax* argument is ignored. The length of the *rgbValue* buffer (if it is a single element) or the length of an element in the *rgbValue* array (if the application calls **SQLParamOptions** to specify multiple values for each parameter) is assumed to be the length of the C data type.

Note When an ODBC 1.0 application calls **SQLSetParam** in an ODBC 2.0 driver, the Driver Manager converts this to a call to **SQLBindParameter** in which the *cbValueMax* argument is always SQL_SETPARAM_VALUE_MAX. Because the Driver Manager returns an error if an ODBC 2.0 application sets *cbValueMax* to SQL_SETPARAM_VALUE_MAX, an ODBC 2.0 driver can use this to determine when it is called by an ODBC 1.0 application.

When an ODBC 2.0 application calls **SQLBindParameter** in an ODBC 1.0 driver, the Driver Manager converts this to a call to **SQLSetParam** and discards the *cbValueMax* argument.

In **SQLSetParam**, the way in which an application specifies the length of the *rgbValue* buffer so that the driver can return character or binary data and the way in which an application sends an array of character or binary parameter values to the driver are driver-defined. If an ODBC 2.0 application uses this functionality in an ODBC 1.0 driver, it must use the semantics defined by that driver. If an ODBC 2.0 driver supported this functionality as an ODBC 1.0 driver, it must continue to support this functionality for ODBC 1.0 applications.

pcbValue Argument

The *pcbValue* argument points to a buffer that, when **SQLExecute** or **SQLExecDirect** is called, contains one of the following:

- The length of the parameter value stored in *rgbValue*. This is ignored except for character or binary C data.

- SQL_NTS. The parameter value is a null-terminated string.

- SQL_NULL_DATA. The parameter value is NULL.

- SQL_DEFAULT_PARAM. A procedure is to use the default value of a parameter, rather than a value retrieved from the application. This value is valid only in a procedure call, and then only if the *fParamType* argument is SQL_PARAM_INPUT or SQL_PARAM_INPUT_OUTPUT. When *pcbValue* is SQL_DEFAULT_PARAM, the *fCType*, *fSqlType*, *cbColDef*, *ibScale*, *cbValueMax* and *rgbValue* arguments are ignored for input parameters and are used only to define the output parameter value for input/output parameters.

Note This value was introduced in ODBC 2.0.

- The result of the SQL_LEN_DATA_AT_EXEC(*length*) macro. The data for the parameter will be sent with **SQLPutData**. If the *fSqlType* argument is SQL_LONGVARBINARY, SQL_LONGVARCHAR, or a long, data source–specific data type and the driver returns "Y" for the SQL_NEED_LONG_DATA_LEN information type in **SQLGetInfo**, *length* is the number of bytes of data to be sent for the parameter; otherwise, *length* must be a nonnegative value and is ignored. For more information, see "Passing Parameter Values."

For example, to specify that 10,000 bytes of data will be sent with **SQLPutData** for an SQL_LONGVARCHAR parameter, an application sets *pcbValue* to SQL_LEN_DATA_AT_EXEC(10000).

Note This macro was introduced in ODBC 2.0.

- SQL_DATA_AT_EXEC. The data for the parameter will be sent with **SQLPutData**. This value is used by ODBC 2.0 applications when calling ODBC 1.0 drivers and by ODBC 1.0 applications when calling ODBC 2.0 drivers. For more information, see "Passing Parameter Values."

If *pcbValue* is a null pointer, the driver assumes that all input parameter values are non-NULL and that character and binary data are null-terminated. If *fParamType* is SQL_PARAM_OUTPUT and *rgbValue* and *pcbValue* are both null pointers, the driver discards the output value.

Note Application developers are strongly discouraged from specifying a null pointer for *pcbValue* when the data type of the parameter is SQL_C_BINARY. For SQL_C_BINARY data, a driver sends only the data preceding an occurrence of the null-termination character, 0x00. To ensure that a driver does not unexpectedly truncate SQL_C_BINARY data, *pcbValue* should contain a pointer to a valid length value.

If the *fParamType* argument is SQL_PARAM_INPUT_OUTPUT or SQL_PARAM_OUTPUT, *pcbValue* points to a buffer in which the driver returns SQL_NULL_DATA, the number of bytes available to return in *rgbValue* (excluding the null termination byte of character data), or SQL_NO_TOTAL if the number of bytes available to return cannot be determined. If the procedure returns one or more result sets, the *pcbValue* buffer is not guaranteed to be set until all results have been fetched.

If the application calls **SQLParamOptions** to specify multiple values for each parameter, *pcbValue* points to an array of SDWORD values. These can be any of the values listed earlier in this section and are processed with a single SQL statement.

Passing Parameter Values

An application can pass the value for a parameter either in the *rgbValue* buffer or with one or more calls to **SQLPutData**. Parameters whose data is passed with **SQLPutData** are known as *data-at-execution* parameters. These are commonly used to send data for SQL_LONGVARBINARY and SQL_LONGVARCHAR parameters and can be mixed with other parameters.

To pass parameter values, an application:

1. Calls **SQLBindParameter** for each parameter to bind buffers for the parameter's value (*rgbValue* argument) and length (*pcbValue* argument). For data-at-execution parameters, *rgbValue* is an application-defined 32-bit value such as a parameter number or a pointer to data. The value will be returned later and can be used to identify the parameter.

2. Places values for input and input/output parameters in the *rgbValue* and *pcbValue* buffers:

   ▪ For normal parameters, the application places the parameter value in the *rgbValue* buffer and the length of that value in the *pcbValue* buffer.

   ▪ For data-at-execution parameters, the application places the result of the SQL_LEN_DATA_AT_EXEC(*length*) macro (when calling an ODBC 2.0 driver) or SQL_DATA_AT_EXEC (when calling an ODBC 1.0 driver) in the *pcbValue* buffer.

3. Calls **SQLExecute** or **SQLExecDirect** to execute the SQL statement.

   ▪ If there are no data-at-execution parameters, the process is complete.

   ▪ If there are any data-at-execution parameters, the function returns SQL_NEED_DATA.

4. Calls **SQLParamData** to retrieve the application-defined value specified in the *rgbValue* argument for the first data-at-execution parameter to be processed.

Note Although data-at-execution parameters are similar to data-at-execution columns, the value returned by **SQLParamData** is different for each.

Data-at-execution parameters are parameters in an SQL statement for which data will be sent with **SQLPutData** when the statement is executed with **SQLExecDirect** or **SQLExecute**. They are bound with **SQLBindParameter**. The value returned by **SQLParamData** is a 32-bit value passed to **SQLBindParameter** in the *rgbValue* argument.

Data-at-execution columns are columns in a rowset for which data will be sent with **SQLPutData** when a row is updated or added with **SQLSetPos**. They are bound with **SQLBindCol**. The value returned by **SQLParamData** is the address of the row in the *rgbValue* buffer that is being processed.

---

5. Calls **SQLPutData** one or more times to send data for the parameter. More than one call is needed if the data value is larger than the *rgbValue* buffer specified in **SQLPutData**; note that multiple calls to **SQLPutData** for the same parameter are allowed only when sending character C data to a column with a character, binary, or data source–specific data type or when sending binary C data to a column with a character, binary, or data source–specific data type.

6. Calls **SQLParamData** again to signal that all data has been sent for the parameter.

- If there are more data-at-execution parameters, **SQLParamData** returns SQL_NEED_DATA and the application-defined value for the next data-at-execution parameter to be processed. The application repeats steps 5 and 6.

- If there are no more data-at-execution parameters, the process is complete. If the statement was successfully executed, **SQLParamData** returns SQL_SUCCESS or SQL_SUCCESS_WITH_INFO; if the execution failed, it returns SQL_ERROR. At this point, **SQLParamData** can return any SQLSTATE that can be returned by the function used to execute the statement (**SQLExecDirect** or **SQLExecute**).

Output values for any input/output or output parameters will be available in the *rgbValue* and *pcbValue* buffers after the application retrieves any result sets generated by the statement.

After **SQLExecute** or **SQLExecDirect** returns SQL_NEED_DATA, and before data is sent for all data-at-execution parameters, the statement is canceled, or an error occurs in **SQLParamData** or **SQLPutData**, the application can only call **SQLCancel**, **SQLGetFunctions**, **SQLParamData**, or **SQLPutData** with the *hstmt* or the *hdbc* associated with the *hstmt*. If it calls any other function with the *hstmt* or the *hdbc* associated with the *hstmt*, the function returns SQL_ERROR and SQLSTATE S1010 (Function sequence error).

If the application calls **SQLCancel** while the driver still needs data for data-at-execution parameters, the driver cancels statement execution; the application can then call **SQLExecute** or **SQLExecDirect** again. If the application calls **SQLParamData** or **SQLPutData** after canceling the statement, the function returns SQL_ERROR and SQLSTATE S1008 (Operation canceled).

Conversion of Calls to and from SQLSetParam

When an ODBC 1.0 application calls **SQLSetParam** in an ODBC 2.0 driver, the ODBC 2.0 Driver Manager maps the call as follows:

Call by ODBC 1.0 Application	**Call to ODBC 2.0 Driver**
```SQLSetParam(hstmt, ipar, fCType, fSqlType, cbColDef, ibScale, rgbValue, pcbValue);```	```SQLBindParameter(hstmt, ipar, SQL_PARAM_INPUT_OUTPUT, fCType, fSqlType, cbColDef, ibScale, rgbValue, SQL_SETPARAM_VALUE_MAX, pcbValue);```

When an ODBC 2.0 application calls **SQLBindParameter** in an ODBC 1.0 driver, the ODBC 2.0 Driver Manager maps the calls as follows:

Call by ODBC 2.0 Application	**Call to ODBC 1.0 Driver**
```SQLBindParameter(hstmt, ipar, fParamType, fCType, fSqlType, cbColDef, ibScale, rgbValue, cbValueMax, pcbValue);```	```SQLSetParam(hstmt, ipar, fCType, fSqlType, cbColDef, ibScale, rgbValue, pcbValue);```

Code Example

In the following example, an application prepares an SQL statement to insert data into the EMPLOYEE table. The SQL statement contains parameters for the NAME, AGE, and BIRTHDAY columns. For each parameter in the statement, the application calls **SQLBindParameter** to specify the ODBC C data type and the SQL data type of the parameter and to bind a buffer to each parameter. For each row of data, the application assigns data values to each parameter and calls **SQLExecute** to execute the statement.

For more code examples, see **SQLParamOptions**, **SQLProcedures**, **SQLPutData**, and **SQLSetPos**.

```
#define NAME_LEN 30

UCHAR       szName[NAME_LEN];
SWORD       sAge;
SDWORD      cbName = SQL_NTS, cbAge = 0, cbBirthday = 0;
DATE_STRUCT dsBirthday;

retcode = SQLPrepare(hstmt,
          "INSERT INTO EMPLOYEE (NAME, AGE, BIRTHDAY) VALUES (?, ?, ?)",
          SQL_NTS);

if (retcode == SQL_SUCCESS) {

    /* Specify data types and buffers.          */
    /* for Name, Age, Birthday parameter data.  */

    SQLBindParameter(hstmt, 1, SQL_PARAM_INPUT, SQL_C_CHAR,
                     SQL_CHAR, NAME_LEN, 0, szName, 0, &cbName);
    SQLBindParameter(hstmt, 2, SQL_PARAM_INPUT, SQL_C_SSHORT,
                     SQL_SMALLINT, 0, 0, &sAge, 0, &cbAge);
    SQLBindParameter(hstmt, 3, SQL_PARAM_INPUT, SQL_C_DATE,
                     SQL_DATE, 0, 0, &dsBirthday, 0, &cbBirthday);

    strcpy(szName, "Smith, John D.");   /* Specify first row of  */
    sAge = 40;                          /* parameter data        */
    dsBirthday.year = 1952;
    dsBirthday.month = 2;
    dsBirthday.day = 29;
    retcode = SQLExecute(hstmt);        /* Execute statement with */
                                        /* first row              */

    strcpy(szName, "Jones, Bob K.");    /* Specify second row of  */
    sAge = 52;                          /* parameter data         */
    dsBirthday.year = 1940;
    dsBirthday.month = 3;
    dsBirthday.day = 31;
    SQLExecute(hstmt);                  /* Execute statement with  */
                                        /* second row              */

}
```

Related Functions

For information about	See
Returning information about a parameter in a statement	**SQLDescribeParam** (extension)
Executing an SQL statement	**SQLExecDirect**
Executing a prepared SQL statement	**SQLExecute**
Returning the number of statement parameters	**SQLNumParams** (extension)
Returning the next parameter to send data for	**SQLParamData** (extension)
Specifying multiple parameter values	**SQLParamOptions** (extension)
Sending parameter data at execution time	**SQLPutData** (extension)

SQLBrowseConnect

Extension Level 2

SQLBrowseConnect supports an iterative method of discovering and enumerating the attributes and attribute values required to connect to a data source. Each call to **SQLBrowseConnect** returns successive levels of attributes and attribute values. When all levels have been enumerated, a connection to the data source is completed and a complete connection string is returned by **SQLBrowseConnect**. A return code of SQL_SUCCESS or SQL_SUCCESS_WITH_INFO indicates that all connection information has been specified and the application is now connected to the data source.

Syntax

RETCODE **SQLBrowseConnect**(*hdbc*, *szConnStrIn*, *cbConnStrIn*, *szConnStrOut*, *cbConnStrOutMax*, *pcbConnStrOut*)

The **SQLBrowseConnect** function accepts the following arguments:

Type	Argument	Use	Description
HDBC	*hdbc*	Input	Connection handle.
UCHAR FAR *	*szConnStrIn*	Input	Browse request connection string (see "szConnStrIn Argument" in "Comments").
SWORD	*cbConnStrIn*	Input	Length of *szConnStrIn*.
UCHAR FAR *	*szConnStrOut*	Output	Pointer to storage for the browse result connection string (see "szConnStrOut Argument" in "Comments").
SWORD	*cbConnStrOutMax*	Input	Maximum length of the *szConnStrOut* buffer.
SWORD FAR *	*pcbConnStrOut*	Output	The total number of bytes (excluding the null termination byte) available to return in *szConnStrOut*. If the number of bytes available to return is greater than or equal to *cbConnStrOutMax*, the connection string in *szConnStrOut* is truncated to *cbConnStrOutMax* – 1 bytes.

Returns

SQL_SUCCESS, SQL_SUCCESS_WITH_INFO, SQL_NEED_DATA, SQL_ERROR, or SQL_INVALID_HANDLE.

Diagnostics

When **SQLBrowseConnect** returns SQL_ERROR, SQL_SUCCESS_WITH_INFO, or SQL_NEED_DATA, an associated SQLSTATE value may be obtained by calling **SQLError**. The following table lists the SQLSTATE values commonly returned by **SQLBrowseConnect** and explains each one in the context of this function; the notation "(DM)" precedes the descriptions of SQLSTATEs returned by the Driver Manager. The return code associated with each SQLSTATE value is SQL_ERROR, unless noted otherwise.

SQLSTATE	Error	Description
01000	General warning	Driver-specific informational message. (Function returns SQL_SUCCESS_WITH_INFO.)
01004	Data truncated	The buffer *szConnStrOut* was not large enough to return entire browse result connection string, so the string was truncated. The argument *pcbConnStrOut* contains the length of the untruncated browse result connection string. (Function returns SQL_SUCCESS_WITH_INFO.)
01S00	Invalid connection string attribute	An invalid attribute keyword was specified in the browse request connection string (*szConnStrIn*). (Function returns SQL_NEED_DATA.)
		An attribute keyword was specified in the browse request connection string (*szConnStrIn*) that does not apply to the current connection level. (Function returns SQL_NEED_DATA.)
08001	Unable to connect to data source	The driver was unable to establish a connection with the data source.
08002	Connection in use	(DM) The specified *hdbc* had already been used to establish a connection with a data source and the connection was open.
08004	Data source rejected establishment of connection	The data source rejected the establishment of the connection for implementation defined reasons.
08S01	Communication link failure	The communication link between the driver and the data source to which the driver was attempting to connect failed before the function completed processing.
28000	Invalid authorization specification	Either the user identifier or the authorization string or both as specified in the browse request connection string (*szConnStrIn*) violated restrictions defined by the data source.
IM001	Driver does not support this function	(DM) The driver corresponding to the specified data source name does not support the function.

SQLSTATE	Error	Description
IM002	Data source not found and no default driver specified	(DM) The data source name specified in the browse request connection string (*szConnStrIn*) was not found in the ODBC.INI file or registry nor was there a default driver specification. (DM) The ODBC.INI file could not be found.
IM003	Specified driver could not be loaded	(DM) The driver listed in the data source specification in the ODBC.INI file or registry, or specified by the **DRIVER** keyword was not found or could not be loaded for some other reason.
IM004	Driver's SQLAllocEnv failed	(DM) During **SQLBrowseConnect**, the Driver Manager called the driver's **SQLAllocEnv** function and the driver returned an error.
IM005	Driver's SQLAllocConnect failed	(DM) During **SQLBrowseConnect**, the Driver Manager called the driver's **SQLAllocConnect** function and the driver returned an error.
IM006	Driver's SQLSetConnect-Option failed	(DM) During **SQLBrowseConnect**, the Driver Manager called the driver's **SQLSetConnectOption** function and the driver returned an error.
IM009	Unable to load translation DLL	The driver was unable to load the translation DLL that was specified for the data source or for the connection.
IM010	Data source name too long	(DM) The attribute value for the DSN keyword was longer than SQL_MAX_DSN_LENGTH characters.
IM011	Driver name too long	(DM) The attribute value for the DRIVER keyword was longer than 255 characters.
IM012	DRIVER keyword syntax error	(DM) The keyword-value pair for the DRIVER keyword contained a syntax error.
S1000	General error	An error occurred for which there was no specific SQLSTATE and for which no implementation-specific SQLSTATE was defined. The error message returned by **SQLError** in the argument *szErrorMsg* describes the error and its cause.

SQLSTATE	Error	Description
S1001	Memory allocation failure	(DM) The Driver Manager was unable to allocate memory required to support execution or completion of the function.
		The driver was unable to allocate memory required to support execution or completion of the function.
S1090	Invalid string or buffer length	(DM) The value specified for argument *cbConnStrIn* was less than 0 and was not equal to SQL_NTS.
		(DM) The value specified for argument *cbConnStrOutMax* was less than 0.
S1T00	Timeout expired	The timeout period expired before the connection to the data source completed. The timeout period is set through **SQLSetConnectOption**, SQL_LOGIN_TIMEOUT.

Comments

szConnStrIn Argument

A browse request connection string has the following syntax:

connection-string ::= attribute[;] | *attribute*; *connection-string*
attribute ::= attribute-keyword=attribute-value | DRIVER={*attribute-value*}
(The braces are literal; the application must specify them.)
attribute-keyword ::= DSN | UID | PWD
                    | *driver-defined-attribute-keyword*
attribute-value ::= character-string
driver-defined-attribute-keyword ::= identifier

where *character-string* has zero or more characters; *identifier* has one or more characters; *attribute-keyword* is case insensitive; *attribute-value* may be case sensitive; and the value of the **DSN** keyword does not consist solely of blanks. Because of connection string and initialization file grammar, keywords and attribute values that contain the characters []{}(),;?*=!@ should be avoided. Because of the registry grammar, keywords and data source names cannot contain the backslash (\) character.

Note The **DRIVER** keyword was introduced in ODBC 2.0 and is not supported by ODBC 1.0 drivers.

If any keywords are repeated in the browse request connection string, the driver uses the value associated with the first occurrence of the keyword. If the **DSN** and **DRIVER** keywords are included in the same browse request connection string, the Driver Manager and driver use whichever keyword appears first.

szConnStrOut Argument

The browse result connection string is a list of connection attributes. A connection attribute consists of an attribute keyword and a corresponding attribute value. The browse result connection string has the following syntax:

connection-string ::= *attribute*[;] | *attribute*; *connection-string*
attribute ::= [*]*attribute-keyword*=*attribute-value*
attribute-keyword ::= *ODBC-attribute-keyword*
                 | *driver-defined-attribute-keyword*
ODBC-attribute-keyword = {UID | PWD}[:*localized-identifier*]
driver-defined-attribute-keyword ::= *identifer*[:*localized-identifier*]
attribute-value ::= {*attribute-value-list*} | ?
(The braces are literal; they are returned by the driver.)
attribute-value-list ::= *character-string* | *character-string*, *attribute-value-list*

where *character-string* has zero or more characters; *identifier* and *localized-identifier* have one or more characters; *attribute-keyword* is case insensitive; and *attribute-value* may be case sensitive. Because of connection string and initialization file grammar, keywords, localized identifiers, and attribute values that contain the characters []{}(),;?*=!@ should be avoided. Because of the registry grammar, keywords and data source names cannot contain the backslash (\) character.

The browse result connection string syntax is used according to the following semantic rules:

- If an asterisk (*) precedes an *attribute-keyword*, the *attribute* is optional, and may be omitted in the next call to **SQLBrowseConnect**.

- The attribute keywords **UID** and **PWD** have the same meaning as defined in **SQLDriverConnect**.

- A *driver-defined-attribute-keyword* names the kind of attribute for which an attribute value may be supplied. For example, it might be **SERVER**, **DATABASE**, **HOST**, or **DBMS**.

- *ODBC-attribute-keywords* and *driver-defined-attribute-keywords* include a localized or user-friendly version of the keyword. This might be used by applications as a label in a dialog box. However, **UID**, **PWD**, or the *identifier* alone must be used when passing a browse request string to the driver.

- The {*attribute-value-list*} is an enumeration of actual values valid for the corresponding *attribute-keyword*. Note that the braces ({ }) do not indicate a list of choices; they are returned by the driver. For example, it might be a list of server names or a list of database names.

- If the *attribute-value* is a single question mark (?), a single value corresponds to the *attribute-keyword*. For example, UID=JohnS; PWD=Sesame.

- Each call to **SQLBrowseConnect** returns only the information required to satisfy the next level of the connection process. The driver associates state information with the connection handle so that the context can always be determined on each call.

Using SQLBrowseConnect

SQLBrowseConnect requires an allocated *hdbc*. The Driver Manager loads the driver that was specified in or that corresponds to the data source name specified in the initial browse request connection string; for information on when this occurs, see the "Comments" section in **SQLConnect**. It may establish a connection with the data source during the browsing process. If **SQLBrowseConnect** returns SQL_ERROR, outstanding connections are terminated and the *hdbc* is returned to an unconnected state.

When **SQLBrowseConnect** is called for the first time on an *hdbc*, the browse request connection string must contain the **DSN** keyword or the **DRIVER** keyword. If the browse request connection string contains the **DSN** keyword, the Driver Manager locates a corresponding data source specification in the ODBC.INI file or registry:

- If the Driver Manager finds the corresponding data source specification, it loads the associated driver DLL; the driver can retrieve information about the data source from the ODBC.INI file or registry.

- If the Driver Manager cannot find the corresponding data source specification, it locates the default data source specification and loads the associated driver DLL; the driver can retrieve information about the default data source from the ODBC.INI file or registry.

- If the Driver Manager cannot find the corresponding data source specification and there is no default data source specification, it returns SQL_ERROR with SQLSTATE IM002 (Data source not found and no default driver specified).

If the browse request connection string contains the **DRIVER** keyword, the Driver Manager loads the specified driver; it does not attempt to locate a data source in the ODBC.INI file or registry. Because the **DRIVER** keyword does not use information from the ODBC.INI file or registry, the driver must define enough keywords so that a driver can connect to a data source using only the information in the browse request connection strings.

On each call to **SQLBrowseConnect**, the application specifies the connection attribute values in the browse request connection string. The driver returns successive levels of attributes and attribute values in the browse result connection string; it returns SQL_NEED_DATA as long as there are connection attributes that have not yet been enumerated in the browse request connection string. The application uses the contents of the browse result connection string to build the browse request connection string for the next call to **SQLBrowseConnect**. Note that the application cannot use the contents of previous browse result connection strings when building the current browse request connection string; that is, it cannot specify different values for attributes set in previous levels.

When all levels of connection and their associated attributes have been enumerated, the driver returns SQL_SUCCESS, the connection to the data source is complete, and a complete connection string is returned to the application. The connection string is suitable to use in conjunction with **SQLDriverConnect** with the SQL_DRIVER_NOPROMPT option to establish another connection.

SQLBrowseConnect also returns SQL_NEED_DATA if there are recoverable, nonfatal errors during the browse process, for example, an invalid password supplied by the application or an invalid attribute keyword supplied by the application. When SQL_NEED_DATA is returned and the browse result connection string is unchanged, an error has occurred and the application must call **SQLError** to return the SQLSTATE for browse-time errors. This permits the application to correct the attribute and continue the browse.

An application may terminate the browse process at any time by calling **SQLDisconnect**. The driver will terminate any outstanding connections and return the *hdbc* to an unconnected state.

For more information, see "Connection Browsing With SQLBrowseConnect" in Chapter 5, "Establishing Connections."

If a driver supports **SQLBrowseConnect**, the driver keyword section of the ODBC.INF file for the driver must contain the **ConnectFunctions** keyword with the third character set to "Y". For more information, see "Driver Keyword Sections" in Chapter 19, "Installing ODBC Software."

Code Example

In the following example, an application calls **SQLBrowseConnect** repeatedly. Each time **SQLBrowseConnect** returns SQL_NEED_DATA, it passes back information about the data it needs in *szConnStrOut*. The application passes *szConnStrOut* to its routine **GetUserInput** (not shown). **GetUserInput** parses the information, builds and displays a dialog box, and returns the information entered by the user in *szConnStrIn*. The application passes the user's information to the driver in the next call to **SQLBrowseConnect**. After the application has provided all necessary information for the driver to connect to the data source, **SQLBrowseConnect** returns SQL_SUCCESS and the application proceeds.

For example, to connect to the data source My Source, the following actions might occur. First, the application passes the following string to **SQLBrowseConnect**:

```
"DSN=My Source"
```

The Driver Manager loads the driver associated with the data source My Source. It then calls the driver's **SQLBrowseConnect** function with the same arguments it received from the application. The driver returns the following string in *szConnStrOut*.

```
"HOST:Server={red,blue,green};UID:ID=?;PWD:Password=?"
```

The application passes this string to its **GetUserInput** routine, which builds a dialog box that asks the user to select the red, blue, or green server, and to enter a user ID and password. The routine passes the following user-specified information back in *szConnStrIn*, which the application passes to **SQLBrowseConnect**:

```
"HOST=red;UID=Smith;PWD=Sesame"
```

SQLBrowseConnect uses this information to connect to the red server as Smith with the password Sesame, then returns the following string in *szConnStrOut*:

```
"*DATABASE:Database={master,model,empdata}"
```

The application passes this string to its **GetUserInput** routine, which builds a dialog box that asks the user to select a database. The user selects empdata and the application calls **SQLBrowseConnect** a final time with the string:

```
"DATABASE=empdata"
```

This is the final piece of information the driver needs to connect to the data source; **SQLBrowseConnect** returns SQL_SUCCESS and *szConnStrOut* contains the completed connection string:

```
"DSN=My Source;HOST=red;UID=Smith;PWD=Sesame;DATABASE=empdata"
```

```
#define BRWS_LEN 100
HENV    henv;
HDBC    hdbc;
HSTMT   hstmt;
RETCODE retcode;
UCHAR   szConnStrIn[BRWS_LEN], szConnStrOut[BRWS_LEN];
SWORD   cbConnStrOut;

retcode = SQLAllocEnv(&henv);                    /* Environment handle */
if (retcode == SQL_SUCCESS) {
    retcode = SQLAllocConnect(henv, &hdbc);   /* Connection handle  */
    if (retcode == SQL_SUCCESS) {
```

```
/* Call SQLBrowseConnect until it returns a value other than */
/* SQL_NEED_DATA (pass the data source name the first time). */
/* If SQL_NEED_DATA is returned, call GetUserInput (not      */
/* shown) to build a dialog from the values in szConnStrOut. */
/* The user-supplied values are returned in szConnStrIn,     */
/* which is passed in the next call to SQLBrowseConnect.     */

lstrcpy(szConnStrIn, "DSN=MyServer");
do {
    retcode = SQLBrowseConnect(hstmt, szConnStrIn, SQL_NTS,
                        szConnStrOut, BRWS_LEN, &cbConnStrOut)
    if (retcode == SQL_NEED_DATA)
        GetUserInput(szConnStrOut, szConnStrIn);
} while (retcode == SQL_NEED_DATA);

if (retcode == SQL_SUCCESS || retcode == SQL_SUCCESS_WITH_INFO){

    /* Process data after successful connection */

    retcode = SQLAllocStmt(hdbc, &hstmt);
    if (retcode == SQL_SUCCESS) {
        ...;
        ...;
        ...;
        SQLFreeStmt(hstmt, SQL_DROP);
    }
    SQLDisconnect(hdbc);
  }
 }
SQLFreeConnect(hdbc);
}
SQLFreeEnv(henv);
```

Related Functions

For information about	See
Allocating a connection handle	**SQLAllocConnect**
Connecting to a data source	**SQLConnect**
Disconnecting from a data source	**SQLDisconnect**
Connecting to a data source using a connection string or dialog box	**SQLDriverConnect** (extension)
Returning driver descriptions and attributes	**SQLDrivers** (extension)
Freeing a connection handle	**SQLFreeConnect**

SQLCancel

ODBC 1.0

Core   **SQLCancel** cancels the processing on an *hstmt*.

Syntax   RETCODE **SQLCancel**(*hstmt*)

The **SQLCancel** function accepts the following argument.

Type	Argument	Use	Description
HSTMT	*hstmt*	Input	Statement handle.

Returns   SQL_SUCCESS, SQL_SUCCESS_WITH_INFO, SQL_ERROR, or
                SQL_INVALID_HANDLE.

Diagnostics When **SQLCancel** returns SQL_ERROR or SQL_SUCCESS_WITH_INFO, an
                associated SQLSTATE value may be obtained by calling **SQLError**. The
                following table lists the SQLSTATE values commonly returned by **SQLCancel**
                and explains each one in the context of this function; the notation "(DM)"
                precedes the descriptions of SQLSTATEs returned by the Driver Manager. The
                return code associated with each SQLSTATE value is SQL_ERROR, unless noted
                otherwise.

SQLSTATE	Error	Description
01000	General warning	Driver-specific informational message. (Function returns SQL_SUCCESS_WITH_INFO.)
70100	Operation aborted	The data source was unable to process the cancel request.
IM001	Driver does not support this function	(DM) The driver associated with the *hstmt* does not support the function.
S1000	General error	An error occurred for which there was no specific SQLSTATE and for which no implementation-specific SQLSTATE was defined. The error message returned by **SQLError** in the argument *szErrorMsg* describes the error and its cause.
S1001	Memory allocation failure	The driver was unable to allocate memory required to support execution or completion of the function.

Comments   **SQLCancel** can cancel the following types of processing on an *hstmt*:

- A function running asynchronously on the *hstmt*.
- A function on an *hstmt* that needs data.
- A function running on the *hstmt* on another thread.

If an application calls **SQLCancel** when no processing is being done on the *hstmt*, **SQLCancel** has the same effect as **SQLFreeStmt** with the SQL_CLOSE option; this behavior is defined only for completeness and applications should call **SQLFreeStmt** to close cursors.

Canceling Asynchronous Processing

After an application calls a function asynchronously, it calls the function repeatedly to determine whether it has finished processing. If the function is still processing, it returns SQL_STILL_EXECUTING. If the function has finished processing, it returns a different code.

After any call to the function that returns SQL_STILL_EXECUTING, an application can call **SQLCancel** to cancel the function. If the cancel request is successful, the driver returns SQL_SUCCESS. This message does not indicate that the function was actually canceled; it indicates that the cancel request was processed. When or if the function is actually canceled is driver- and data source– dependent. The application must continue to call the original function until the return code is not SQL_STILL_EXECUTING. If the function was successfully canceled, the return code is SQL_ERROR and SQLSTATE S1008 (Operation canceled). If the function completed its normal processing, the return code is SQL_SUCCESS or SQL_SUCCESS_WITH_INFO if the function succeeded or SQL_ERROR and a SQLSTATE other than S1008 (Operation canceled) if the function failed.

Canceling Functions that Need Data

After **SQLExecute** or **SQLExecDirect** returns SQL_NEED_DATA and before data has been sent for all data-at-execution parameters, an application can call **SQLCancel** to cancel the statement execution. After the statement has been canceled, the application can call **SQLExecute** or **SQLExecDirect** again. For more information, see **SQLBindParameter**.

After **SQLSetPos** returns SQL_NEED_DATA and before data has been sent for all data-at-execution columns, an application can call **SQLCancel** to cancel the operation. After the operation has been canceled, the application can call **SQLSetPos** again; canceling does not affect the cursor state or the current cursor position. For more information, see **SQLSetPos**.

Canceling Functions in Multithreaded Applications

In a multithreaded application, the application can cancel a function that is running synchronously on an *hstmt*. To cancel the function, the application calls **SQLCancel** with the same *hstmt* as that used by the target function, but on a different thread. As in canceling a function running asynchronously, the return code of the **SQLCancel** only indicates whether the driver processed the request successfully. The return code of the original function indicates whether it completed normally or was canceled.

Related Functions	For information about	See
	Assigning storage for a parameter	**SQLBindParameter**
	Executing an SQL statement	**SQLExecDirect**
	Executing a prepared SQL statement	**SQLExecute**
	Freeing a statement handle	**SQLFreeStmt**
	Positioning the cursor in a rowset	**SQLSetPos** (extension)
	Returning the next parameter to send data for	**SQLParamData** (extension)
	Sending parameter data at execution time	**SQLPutData** (extension)

SQLColAttributes

ODBC 1.0

Core

SQLColAttributes returns descriptor information for a column in a result set; it cannot be used to return information about the bookmark column (column 0). Descriptor information is returned as a character string, a 32-bit descriptor-dependent value, or an integer value.

Syntax

RETCODE **SQLColAttributes**(*hstmt, icol, fDescType, rgbDesc, cbDescMax, pcbDesc, pfDesc*)

The **SQLColAttributes** function accepts the following arguments.

Type	Argument	Use	Description
HSTMT	*hstmt*	Input	Statement handle.
UWORD	*icol*	Input	Column number of result data, ordered sequentially from left to right, starting at 1. Columns may be described in any order.
UWORD	*fDescType*	Input	A valid descriptor type (see "Comments").
PTR	*rgbDesc*	Output	Pointer to storage for the descriptor information. The format of the descriptor information returned depends on the *fDescType*.
SWORD	*cbDescMax*	Input	Maximum length of the *rgbDesc* buffer.
SWORD FAR *	*pcbDesc*	Output	Total number of bytes (excluding the null termination byte for character data) available to return in *rgbDesc*.
			For character data, if the number of bytes available to return is greater than or equal to *cbDescMax*, the descriptor information in *rgbDesc* is truncated to *cbDescMax* – 1 bytes and is null-terminated by the driver.
			For all other types of data, the value of *cbValueMax* is ignored and the driver assumes the size of *rgbValue* is 32 bits.
SDWORD FAR *	*pfDesc*	Output	Pointer to an integer value to contain descriptor information for numeric descriptor types, such as SQL_COLUMN_LENGTH.

Returns

SQL_SUCCESS, SQL_SUCCESS_WITH_INFO, SQL_STILL_EXECUTING, SQL_ERROR, or SQL_INVALID_HANDLE.

Diagnostics   When **SQLColAttributes** returns either SQL_ERROR or
SQL_SUCCESS_WITH_INFO, an associated SQLSTATE value may be obtained
by calling **SQLError**. The following table lists the SQLSTATE values commonly
returned by **SQLColAttributes** and explains each one in the context of this
function; the notation "(DM)" precedes the descriptions of SQLSTATEs returned
by the Driver Manager. The return code associated with each SQLSTATE value is
SQL_ERROR, unless noted otherwise.

SQLSTATE	Error	Description
01000	General warning	Driver-specific informational message. (Function returns SQL_SUCCESS_WITH_INFO.)
01004	Data truncated	The buffer *rgbDesc* was not large enough to return the entire string value, so the string value was truncated. The argument *pcbDesc* contains the length of the untruncated string value. (Function returns SQL_SUCCESS_WITH_INFO.)
24000	Invalid cursor state	The statement associated with the *hstmt* did not return a result set. There were no columns to describe.
IM001	Driver does not support this function	(DM) The driver associated with the *hstmt* does not support the function.
S1000	General error	An error occurred for which there was no specific SQLSTATE and for which no implementation-specific SQLSTATE was defined. The error message returned by **SQLError** in the argument *szErrorMsg* describes the error and its cause.
S1001	Memory allocation failure	The driver was unable to allocate memory required to support execution or completion of the function.
S1002	Invalid column number	(DM) The value specified for the argument *icol* was 0 and the argument *fDescType* was not SQL_COLUMN_COUNT.
		The value specified for the argument *icol* was greater than the number of columns in the result set and the argument *fDescType* was not SQL_COLUMN_COUNT.

SQLSTATE	Error	Description
S1008	Operation canceled	Asynchronous processing was enabled for the *hstmt*. The function was called and before it completed execution, **SQLCancel** was called on the *hstmt*. Then the function was called again on the *hstmt*.
		The function was called and, before it completed execution, **SQLCancel** was called on the *hstmt* from a different thread in a multithreaded application.
S1010	Function sequence error	(DM) The function was called prior to calling **SQLPrepare** or **SQLExecDirect** for the *hstmt*.
		(DM) An asynchronously executing function (not this one) was called for the *hstmt* and was still executing when this function was called.
		(DM) **SQLExecute**, **SQLExecDirect**, or **SQLSetPos** was called for the *hstmt* and returned SQL_NEED_DATA. This function was called before data was sent for all data-at-execution parameters or columns.
S1090	Invalid string or buffer length	(DM) The value specified for the argument *cbDescMax* was less than 0.
S1091	Descriptor type out of range	(DM) The value specified for the argument *fDescType* was in the block of numbers reserved for ODBC descriptor types but was not valid for the version of ODBC supported by the driver (see "Comments").
S1C00	Driver not capable	The value specified for the argument *fDescType* was in the range of numbers reserved for driver-specific descriptor types but was not supported by the driver.
S1T00	Timeout expired	The timeout period expired before the data source returned the requested information. The timeout period is set through **SQLSetStmtOption**, SQL_QUERY_TIMEOUT.

SQLColAttributes can return any SQLSTATE that can be returned by **SQLPrepare** or **SQLExecute** when called after **SQLPrepare** and before **SQLExecute** depending on when the data source evaluates the SQL statement associated with the *hstmt*.

Comments   **SQLColAttributes** returns information either in *pfDesc* or in *rgbDesc*. Integer information is returned in *pfDesc* as a 32-bit, signed value; all other formats of information are returned in *rgbDesc*. When information is returned in *pfDesc*, the driver ignores *rgbDesc*, *cbDescMax*, and *pcbDesc*. When information is returned in *rgbDesc*, the driver ignores *pfDesc*.

The currently defined descriptor types, the version of ODBC in which they were introduced, and the arguments in which information is returned for them are shown below; it is expected that more descriptor types will be defined to take advantage of different data sources. Descriptor types from 0 to 999 are reserved by ODBC; driver developers must reserve values greater than or equal to SQL_COLUMN_DRIVER_START for driver-specific use. For more information, see "Driver-Specific Data Types, Descriptor Types, Information Types, and Options" in Chapter 11, "Guidelines for Implementing ODBC Functions."

A driver must return a value for each of the descriptor types defined in the following table. If a descriptor type does not apply to a driver or data source, then, unless otherwise stated, the driver returns 0 in *pcbDesc* or an empty string in *rgbDesc*.

fDescType	Information returned in	Description
SQL_COLUMN_AUTO_INCREMENT (ODBC 1.0)	*pfDesc*	TRUE if the column is autoincrement.
		FALSE if the column is not autoincrement or is not numeric.
		Auto increment is valid for numeric data type columns only. An application can insert values into an autoincrement column, but cannot update values in the column.
SQL_COLUMN_CASE_SENSITIVE (ODBC 1.0)	*pfDesc*	TRUE if the column is treated as case sensitive for collations and comparisons.
		FALSE if the column is not treated as case sensitive for collations and comparisons or is noncharacter.
SQL_COLUMN_COUNT (ODBC 1.0)	*pfDesc*	Number of columns available in the result set. The *icol* argument is ignored.
SQL_COLUMN_DISPLAY_SIZE (ODBC 1.0)	*pfDesc*	Maximum number of characters required to display data from the column. For more information on display size, see "Precision, Scale, Length, and Display Size" in Appendix D, "Data Types."

fDescType	Information returned in	Description
SQL_COLUMN_LABEL (ODBC 2.0)	rgbDesc	The column label or title. For example, a column named EmpName might be labeled Employee Name.
		If a column does not have a label, the column name is returned. If the column is unlabeled and unnamed, an empty string is returned.
SQL_COLUMN_LENGTH (ODBC 1.0)	pfDesc	The length in bytes of data transferred on an **SQLGetData** or **SQLFetch** operation if SQL_C_DEFAULT is specified. For numeric data, this size may be different than the size of the data stored on the data source. For more length information, see "Precision, Scale, Length, and Display Size" in Appendix D, "Data Types."
SQL_COLUMN_MONEY (ODBC 1.0)	pfDesc	TRUE if the column is money data type.
		FALSE if the column is not money data type.
SQL_COLUMN_NAME (ODBC 1.0)	rgbDesc	The column name.
		If the column is unnamed, an empty string is returned.
SQL_COLUMN_NULLABLE (ODBC 1.0)	pfDesc	SQL_NO_NULLS if the column does not accept NULL values.
		SQL_NULLABLE if the column accepts NULL values.
		SQL_NULLABLE_UNKNOWN if it is not known if the column accepts NULL values.
SQL_COLUMN_OWNER_NAME (ODBC 2.0)	rgbDesc	The owner of the table that contains the column. The returned value is implementation-defined if the column is an expression or if the column is part of a view. If the data source does not support owners or the owner name cannot be determined, an empty string is returned.
SQL_COLUMN_PRECISION (ODBC 1.0)	pfDesc	The precision of the column on the data source. For more information on precision, see "Precision, Scale, Length, and Display Size" in Appendix D, "Data Types."
SQL_COLUMN_QUALIFIER_NAME (ODBC 2.0)	rgbDesc	The qualifier of the table that contains the column. The returned value is implementation-defined if the column is an expression or if the column is part of a view. If the data source does not support qualifiers or the qualifier name cannot be determined, an empty string is returned.

fDescType	Information returned in	Description
SQL_COLUMN_SCALE (ODBC 1.0)	*pfDesc*	The scale of the column on the data source. For more information on scale, see "Precision, Scale, Length, and Display Size" in Appendix D, "Data Types."
SQL_COLUMN_SEARCHABLE (ODBC 1.0)	*pfDesc*	SQL_UNSEARCHABLE if the column cannot be used in a **WHERE** clause.
		SQL_LIKE_ONLY if the column can be used in a **WHERE** clause only with the **LIKE** predicate.
		SQL_ALL_EXCEPT_LIKE if the column can be used in a **WHERE** clause with all comparison operators except **LIKE**.
		SQL_SEARCHABLE if the column can be used in a **WHERE** clause with any comparison operator.
		Columns of type SQL_LONGVARCHAR and SQL_LONGVARBINARY usually return SQL_LIKE_ONLY.
SQL_COLUMN_TABLE_NAME (ODBC 2.0)	*rgbDesc*	The name of the table that contains the column. The returned value is implementation-defined if the column is an expression or if the column is part of a view.
		If the table name cannot be determined, an empty string is returned.
SQL_COLUMN_TYPE (ODBC 1.0)	*pfDesc*	SQL data type. This can be an ODBC SQL data type or a driver-specific SQL data type. For a list of valid ODBC SQL data types, see "SQL Data Types" in Appendix D, "Data Types." For information about driver-specific SQL data types, see the driver's documentation.
SQL_COLUMN_TYPE_NAME (ODBC 1.0)	*rgbDesc*	Data source–dependent data type name; for example, "CHAR", "VARCHAR", "MONEY", "LONG VARBINARY", or "CHAR ( ) FOR BIT DATA".
		If the type is unknown, an empty string is returned.
SQL_COLUMN_UNSIGNED (ODBC 1.0)	*pfDesc*	TRUE if the column is unsigned (or not numeric).
		FALSE if the column is signed.

fDescType	Information returned in	Description
SQL_COLUMN_UPDATABLE (ODBC 1.0)	pfDesc	Column is described by the values for the defined constants:
		SQL_ATTR_READONLY SQL_ATTR_WRITE SQL_ATTR_READWRITE_UNKNOWN
		SQL_COLUMN_UPDATABLE describes the updatability of the column in the result set. Whether a column is updatable can be based on the data type, user privileges, and the definition of the result set itself. If it is unclear whether a column is updatable, SQL_ATTR_READWRITE_UNKNOWN should be returned.

This function is an extensible alternative to **SQLDescribeCol**. **SQLDescribeCol** returns a fixed set of descriptor information based on ANSI-89 SQL. **SQLColAttributes** allows access to the more extensive set of descriptor information available in ANSI SQL-92 and DBMS vendor extensions.

Related Functions	For information about	See
	Assigning storage for a column in a result set	**SQLBindCol**
	Canceling statement processing	**SQLCancel**
	Returning information about a column in a result set	**SQLDescribeCol**
	Fetching a block of data or scrolling through a result set	**SQLExtendedFetch** (extension)
	Fetching a row of data	**SQLFetch**

SQLColumnPrivileges

Extension Level 2　　**SQLColumnPrivileges** returns a list of columns and associated privileges for the specified table. The driver returns the information as a result set on the specified *hstmt*.

Syntax　　RETCODE **SQLColumnPrivileges**(*hstmt, szTableQualifier, cbTableQualifier, szTableOwner, cbTableOwner, szTableName, cbTableName, szColumnName, cbColumnName*)

The **SQLColumnPrivileges** function accepts the following arguments:

Type	Argument	Use	Description
HSTMT	*hstmt*	Input	Statement handle.
UCHAR FAR *	*szTableQualifier*	Input	Table qualifier. If a driver supports qualifiers for some tables but not for others, such as when the driver retrieves data from different DBMSs, an empty string ("") denotes those tables that do not have qualifiers.
SWORD	*cbTableQualifier*	Input	Length of *szTableQualifier*.
UCHAR FAR *	*szTableOwner*	Input	Owner name. If a driver supports owners for some tables but not for others, such as when the driver retrieves data from different DBMSs, an empty string ("") denotes those tables that do not have owners.
SWORD	*cbTableOwner*	Input	Length of *szTableOwner*.
UCHAR FAR *	*szTableName*	Input	Table name.
SWORD	*cbTableName*	Input	Length of *szTableName*.
UCHAR FAR *	*szColumnName*	Input	String search pattern for column names.
SWORD	*cbColumnName*	Input	Length of *szColumnName*.

Returns　　SQL_SUCCESS, SQL_SUCCESS_WITH_INFO, SQL_STILL_EXECUTING, SQL_ERROR, or SQL_INVALID_HANDLE.

Diagnostics   When **SQLColumnPrivileges** returns SQL_ERROR or
SQL_SUCCESS_WITH_INFO, an associated SQLSTATE value may be obtained
by calling **SQLError**. The following table lists the SQLSTATE values commonly
returned by **SQLColumnPrivileges** and explains each one in the context of this
function; the notation "(DM)" precedes the descriptions of SQLSTATEs returned
by the Driver Manager. The return code associated with each SQLSTATE value is
SQL_ERROR, unless noted otherwise.

SQLSTATE	Error	Description
01000	General warning	Driver-specific informational message. (Function returns SQL_SUCCESS_WITH_INFO.)
08S01	Communication link failure	The communication link between the driver and the data source to which the driver was connected failed before the function completed processing.
24000	Invalid cursor state	(DM) A cursor was open on the *hstmt* and **SQLFetch** or **SQLExtendedFetch** had been called.
		A cursor was open on the *hstmt* but **SQLFetch** or **SQLExtendedFetch** had not been called.
IM001	Driver does not support this function	(DM) The driver associated with the *hstmt* does not support the function.
S1000	General error	An error occurred for which there was no specific SQLSTATE and for which no implementation-specific SQLSTATE was defined. The error message returned by **SQLError** in the argument *szErrorMsg* describes the error and its cause.
S1001	Memory allocation failure	The driver was unable to allocate memory required to support execution or completion of the function.
S1008	Operation canceled	Asynchronous processing was enabled for the *hstmt*. The function was called and before it completed execution, **SQLCancel** was called on the *hstmt*. Then the function was called again on the *hstmt*.
		The function was called and, before it completed execution, **SQLCancel** was called on the *hstmt* from a different thread in a multithreaded application.

SQLSTATE	Error	Description
S1010	Function sequence error	(DM) An asynchronously executing function (not this one) was called for the *hstmt* and was still executing when this function was called.
		(DM) **SQLExecute**, **SQLExecDirect**, or **SQLSetPos** was called for the *hstmt* and returned SQL_NEED_DATA. This function was called before data was sent for all data-at-execution parameters or columns.
S1090	Invalid string or buffer length	(DM) The value of one of the name length arguments was less than 0, but not equal to SQL_NTS.
		The value of one of the name length arguments exceeded the maximum length value for the corresponding qualifier or name (see "Comments").
S1C00	Driver not capable	A table qualifier was specified and the driver or data source does not support qualifiers.
		A table owner was specified and the driver or data source does not support owners.
		A string search pattern was specified for the column name and the data source does not support search patterns for that argument.
		The combination of the current settings of the SQL_CONCURRENCY and SQL_CURSOR_TYPE statement options was not supported by the driver or data source.
S1T00	Timeout expired	The timeout period expired before the data source returned the result set. The timeout period is set through **SQLSetStmtOption**, SQL_QUERY_TIMEOUT.

Comments   **SQLColumnPrivileges** returns the results as a standard result set, ordered by TABLE_QUALIFIER, TABLE_OWNER, TABLE_NAME, COLUMN_NAME, and PRIVILEGE. The following table lists the columns in the result set.

Note **SQLColumnPrivileges** might not return privileges for all columns. For example, a driver might not return information about privileges for pseudo-columns, such as Oracle ROWID. Applications can use any valid column, regardless of whether it is returned by **SQLColumnPrivileges**.

The lengths of VARCHAR columns shown in the table are maximums; the actual lengths depend on the data source. To determine the actual lengths of the TABLE_QUALIFIER, TABLE_OWNER, TABLE_NAME, and COLUMN_NAME columns, an application can call **SQLGetInfo** with the SQL_MAX_QUALIFIER_NAME_LEN, SQL_MAX_OWNER_NAME_LEN, SQL_MAX_TABLE_NAME_LEN, and SQL_MAX_COLUMN_NAME_LEN options.

Column Name	Data Type	Comments
TABLE_QUALIFIER	Varchar(128)	Table qualifier identifier; NULL if not applicable to the data source. If a driver supports qualifiers for some tables but not for others, such as when the driver retrieves data from different DBMSs, it returns an empty string ("") for those tables that do not have qualifiers.
TABLE_OWNER	Varchar(128)	Table owner identifier; NULL if not applicable to the data source. If a driver supports owners for some tables but not for others, such as when the driver retrieves data from different DBMSs, it returns an empty string ("") for those tables that do not have owners.
TABLE_NAME	Varchar(128) not NULL	Table identifier.
COLUMN_NAME	Varchar(128) not NULL	Column identifier.
GRANTOR	Varchar(128)	Identifier of the user who granted the privilege; NULL if not applicable to the data source.
GRANTEE	Varchar(128) not NULL	Identifier of the user to whom the privilege was granted.

Column Name	Data Type	Comments
PRIVILEGE	Varchar(128) not NULL	Identifies the column privilege. May be one of the following or others supported by the data source when implementation-defined:
		SELECT: The grantee is permitted to retrieve data for the column.
		INSERT: The grantee is permitted to provide data for the column in new rows that are inserted into the associated table.
		UPDATE: The grantee is permitted to update data in the column.
		REFERENCES: The grantee is permitted to refer to the column within a constraint (for example, a unique, referential, or table check constraint).
IS_GRANTABLE	Varchar(3)	Indicates whether the grantee is permitted to grant the privilege to other users; "YES", "NO", or NULL if unknown or not applicable to the data source.

The *szColumnName* argument accepts a search pattern. For more information about valid search patterns, see "Search Pattern Arguments" earlier in this chapter.

Code Example   For a code example of a similar function, see **SQLColumns**.

Related Functions

For information about	See
Assigning storage for a column in a result set	**SQLBindCol**
Canceling statement processing	**SQLCancel**
Returning the columns in a table or tables	**SQLColumns** (extension)
Fetching a block of data or scrolling through a result set	**SQLExtendedFetch** (extension)
Fetching a row of data	**SQLFetch**
Returning privileges for a table or tables	**SQLTablePrivileges** (extension)
Returning a list of tables in a data source	**SQLTables** (extension)

SQLColumns

Extension Level 1   **SQLColumns** returns the list of column names in specified tables. The driver returns this information as a result set on the specified *hstmt*.

Syntax   RETCODE **SQLColumns**(*hstmt, szTableQualifier, cbTableQualifier, szTableOwner, cbTableOwner, szTableName, cbTableName, szColumnName, cbColumnName*)

The **SQLColumns** function accepts the following arguments:

Type	Argument	Use	Description
HSTMT	*hstmt*	Input	Statement handle.
UCHAR FAR *	*szTableQualifier*	Input	Qualifier name. If a driver supports qualifiers for some tables but not for others, such as when the driver retrieves data from different DBMSs, an empty string ("") denotes those tables that do not have qualifiers.
SWORD	*cbTableQualifier*	Input	Length of *szTableQualifier*.
UCHAR FAR *	*szTableOwner*	Input	String search pattern for owner names. If a driver supports owners for some tables but not for others, such as when the driver retrieves data from different DBMSs, an empty string ("") denotes those tables that do not have owners.
SWORD	*cbTableOwner*	Input	Length of *szTableOwner*.
UCHAR FAR *	*szTableName*	Input	String search pattern for table names.
SWORD	*cbTableName*	Input	Length of *szTableName*.
UCHAR FAR *	*szColumnName*	Input	String search pattern for column names.
SWORD	*cbColumnName*	Input	Length of *szColumnName*.

Returns   SQL_SUCCESS, SQL_SUCCESS_WITH_INFO, SQL_STILL_EXECUTING, SQL_ERROR, or SQL_INVALID_HANDLE.

Diagnostics   When **SQLColumns** returns SQL_ERROR or SQL_SUCCESS_WITH_INFO, an associated SQLSTATE value may be obtained by calling **SQLError**. The following table lists the SQLSTATE values commonly returned by **SQLColumns** and explains each one in the context of this function; the notation "(DM)" precedes the descriptions of SQLSTATEs returned by the Driver Manager. The return code associated with each SQLSTATE value is SQL_ERROR, unless noted otherwise.

SQLSTATE	Error	Description
01000	General warning	Driver-specific informational message. (Function returns SQL_SUCCESS_WITH_INFO.)
08S01	Communication link failure	The communication link between the driver and the data source to which the driver was connected failed before the function completed processing.
24000	Invalid cursor state	(DM) A cursor was open on the *hstmt* and **SQLFetch** or **SQLExtendedFetch** had been called.
		A cursor was open on the *hstmt* but **SQLFetch** or **SQLExtendedFetch** had not been called.
IM001	Driver does not support this function	(DM) The driver associated with the *hstmt* does not support the function.
S1000	General error	An error occurred for which there was no specific SQLSTATE and for which no implementation-specific SQLSTATE was defined. The error message returned by **SQLError** in the argument *szErrorMsg* describes the error and its cause.
S1001	Memory allocation failure	The driver was unable to allocate memory required to support execution or completion of the function.
S1008	Operation canceled	Asynchronous processing was enabled for the *hstmt*. The function was called and before it completed execution, **SQLCancel** was called on the *hstmt*. Then the function was called again on the *hstmt*.
		The function was called and, before it completed execution, **SQLCancel** was called on the *hstmt* from a different thread in a multithreaded application.

SQLSTATE	Error	Description
S1010	Function sequence error	(DM) An asynchronously executing function (not this one) was called for the *hstmt* and was still executing when this function was called.
		(DM) **SQLExecute, SQLExecDirect**, or **SQLSetPos** was called for the *hstmt* and returned SQL_NEED_DATA. This function was called before data was sent for all data-at-execution parameters or columns.
S1090	Invalid string or buffer length	(DM) The value of one of the name length arguments was less than 0, but not equal to SQL_NTS.
		The value of one of the name length arguments exceeded the maximum length value for the corresponding qualifier or name. The maximum length of each qualifier or name may be obtained by calling **SQLGetInfo** with the *fInfoType* values (see "Comments").
S1C00	Driver not capable	A table qualifier was specified and the driver or data source does not support qualifiers.
		A table owner was specified and the driver or data source does not support owners.
		A string search pattern was specified for the table owner, table name, or column name and the data source does not support search patterns for one or more of those arguments.
		The combination of the current settings of the SQL_CONCURRENCY and SQL_CURSOR_TYPE statement options was not supported by the driver or data source.
S1T00	Timeout expired	The timeout period expired before the data source returned the result set. The timeout period is set through **SQLSetStmtOption**, SQL_QUERY_TIMEOUT.

Comments   This function is typically used before statement execution to retrieve information about columns for a table or tables from the data source's catalog. Note by contrast, that the functions **SQLColAttributes** and **SQLDescribeCol** describe the columns in a result set and that the function **SQLNumResultCols** returns the number of columns in a result set.

Note **SQLColumns** might not return all columns. For example, a driver might not return information about pseudo-columns, such as Oracle ROWID. Applications can use any valid column, regardless of whether it is returned by **SQLColumns**.

SQLColumns returns the results as a standard result set, ordered by TABLE_QUALIFIER, TABLE_OWNER, and TABLE_NAME. The following table lists the columns in the result set. Additional columns beyond column 12 (REMARKS) can be defined by the driver.

The lengths of VARCHAR columns shown in the table are maximums; the actual lengths depend on the data source. To determine the actual lengths of the TABLE_QUALIFIER, TABLE_OWNER, TABLE_NAME, and COLUMN_NAME columns, an application can call **SQLGetInfo** with the SQL_MAX_QUALIFIER_NAME_LEN, SQL_MAX_OWNER_NAME_LEN, SQL_MAX_TABLE_NAME_LEN, and SQL_MAX_COLUMN_NAME_LEN options.

Column Name	Data Type	Comments
TABLE_QUALIFIER	Varchar(128)	Table qualifier identifier; NULL if not applicable to the data source. If a driver supports qualifiers for some tables but not for others, such as when the driver retrieves data from different DBMSs, it returns an empty string ("") for those tables that do not have qualifiers.
TABLE_OWNER	Varchar(128)	Table owner identifier; NULL if not applicable to the data source. If a driver supports owners for some tables but not for others, such as when the driver retrieves data from different DBMSs, it returns an empty string ("") for those tables that do not have owners.
TABLE_NAME	Varchar(128) not NULL	Table identifier.
COLUMN_NAME	Varchar(128) not NULL	Column identifier.
DATA_TYPE	Smallint not NULL	SQL data type. This can be an ODBC SQL data type or a driver-specific SQL data type. For a list of valid ODBC SQL data types, see "SQL Data Types" in Appendix D, "Data Types." For information about driver-specific SQL data types, see the driver's documentation.

Column Name	Data Type	Comments
TYPE_NAME	Varchar(128) not NULL	Data source–dependent data type name; for example, "CHAR", "VARCHAR", "MONEY", "LONG VARBINARY", or "CHAR ( ) FOR BIT DATA".
PRECISION	Integer	The precision of the column on the data source. For precision information, see "Precision, Scale, Length, and Display Size" in Appendix D, "Data Types."
LENGTH	Integer	The length in bytes of data transferred on an **SQLGetData** or **SQLFetch** operation if SQL_C_DEFAULT is specified. For numeric data, this size may be different than the size of the data stored on the data source. This value is the same as the PRECISION column for character or binary data. For more information about length, see "Precision, Scale, Length, and Display Size" in Appendix D, "Data Types."
SCALE	Smallint	The scale of the column on the data source. For more scale information, see "Precision, Scale, Length, and Display Size" in Appendix D, "Data Types." NULL is returned for data types where scale is not applicable.
RADIX	Smallint	For numeric data types, either 10 or 2. If it is 10, the values in PRECISION and SCALE give the number of decimal digits allowed for the column. For example, a DECIMAL(12,5) column would return a RADIX of 10, a PRECISION of 12, and a SCALE of 5; A FLOAT column could return a RADIX of 10, a PRECISION of 15 and a SCALE of NULL. If it is 2, the values in PRECISION and SCALE give the number of bits allowed in the column. For example, a FLOAT column could return a RADIX of 2, a PRECISION of 53, and a SCALE of NULL. NULL is returned for data types where radix is not applicable.

Column Name	Data Type	Comments
NULLABLE	Smallint not NULL	SQL_NO_NULLS if the column does not accept NULL values.
		SQL_NULLABLE if the column accepts NULL values.
		SQL_NULLABLE_UNKNOWN if it is not known if the column accepts NULL values.
REMARKS	Varchar(254)	A description of the column.

The *szTableOwner*, *szTableName*, and *szColumnName* arguments accept search patterns. For more information about valid search patterns, see "Search Pattern Arguments" earlier in this chapter.

Code Example

In the following example, an application declares storage locations for the result set returned by **SQLColumns**. It calls **SQLColumns** to return a result set that describes each column in the EMPLOYEE table. It then calls **SQLBindCol** to bind the columns in the result set to the storage locations. Finally, the application fetches each row of data with **SQLFetch** and processes it.

```
#define STR_LEN 128+1
#define REM_LEN 254+1

/* Declare storage locations for result set data */

UCHAR  szQualifier[STR_LEN], szOwner[STR_LEN];
UCHAR  szTableName[STR_LEN], szColName[STR_LEN];
UCHAR  szTypeName[STR_LEN], szRemarks[REM_LEN];
SDWORD Precision, Length;
SWORD  DataType, Scale, Radix, Nullable;

/* Declare storage locations for bytes available to return */

SDWORD cbQualifier, cbOwner, cbTableName, cbColName;
SDWORD cbTypeName, cbRemarks, cbDataType, cbPrecision;
SDWORD cbLength, cbScale, cbRadix, cbNullable;

retcode = SQLColumns(hstmt,
                NULL, 0,                /* All qualifiers */
                NULL, 0,                /* All owners     */
                "EMPLOYEE", SQL_NTS,    /* EMPLOYEE table */
                NULL, 0);               /* All columns    */
```

```
if (retcode == SQL_SUCCESS) {

    /* Bind columns in result set to storage locations */

    SQLBindCol(hstmt, 1, SQL_C_CHAR, szQualifier, STR_LEN,&cbQualifier);
    SQLBindCol(hstmt, 2, SQL_C_CHAR, szOwner, STR_LEN, &cbOwner);
    SQLBindCol(hstmt, 3, SQL_C_CHAR, szTableName, STR_LEN,&cbTableName);
    SQLBindCol(hstmt, 4, SQL_C_CHAR, szColName, STR_LEN, &cbColName);
    SQLBindCol(hstmt, 5, SQL_C_SSHORT, &DataType, 0, &cbDataType);
    SQLBindCol(hstmt, 6, SQL_C_CHAR, szTypeName, STR_LEN, &cbTypeName);
    SQLBindCol(hstmt, 7, SQL_C_SLONG, &Precision, 0, &cbPrecision);
    SQLBindCol(hstmt, 8, SQL_C_SLONG, &Length, 0, &cbLength);
    SQLBindCol(hstmt, 9, SQL_C_SSHORT, &Scale, 0, &cbScale);
    SQLBindCol(hstmt, 10, SQL_C_SSHORT, &Radix, 0, &cbRadix);
    SQLBindCol(hstmt, 11, SQL_C_SSHORT, &Nullable, 0, &cbNullable);
    SQLBindCol(hstmt, 12, SQL_C_CHAR, szRemarks, REM_LEN, &cbRemarks);

    while(TRUE) {
        retcode = SQLFetch(hstmt);
        if (retcode == SQL_ERROR || retcode == SQL_SUCCESS_WITH_INFO) {
            show_error( );
        }
        if (retcode == SQL_SUCCESS || retcode == SQL_SUCCESS_WITH_INFO){
            ...;  /* Process fetched data */
        } else {
            break;
        }
    }
}
```

Related Functions

For information about	See
Assigning storage for a column in a result set	**SQLBindCol**
Canceling statement processing	**SQLCancel**
Returning privileges for a column or columns	**SQLColumnPrivileges** (extension)
Fetching a block of data or scrolling through a result set	**SQLExtendedFetch** (extension)
Fetching a row of data	**SQLFetch**
Returning table statistics and indexes	**SQLStatistics** (extension)
Returning a list of tables in a data source	**SQLTables** (extension)
Returning privileges for a table or tables	**SQLTablePrivileges** (extension)

SQLConnect

Core

SQLConnect loads a driver and establishes a connection to a data source. The connection handle references storage of all information about the connection, including status, transaction state, and error information.

Syntax

RETCODE **SQLConnect**(*hdbc*, *szDSN*, *cbDSN*, *szUID*, *cbUID*, *szAuthStr*, *cbAuthStr*)

The **SQLConnect** function accepts the following arguments.

Type	Argument	Use	Description
HDBC	*hdbc*	Input	Connection handle.
UCHAR FAR *	*szDSN*	Input	Data source name.
SWORD	*cbDSN*	Input	Length of *szDSN*.
UCHAR FAR *	*szUID*	Input	User identifier.
SWORD	*cbUID*	Input	Length of *szUID*.
UCHAR FAR *	*szAuthStr*	Input	Authentication string (typically the password).
SWORD	*cbAuthStr*	Input	Length of *szAuthStr*.

Returns

SQL_SUCCESS, SQL_SUCCESS_WITH_INFO, SQL_ERROR, or SQL_INVALID_HANDLE.

Diagnostics

When **SQLConnect** returns SQL_ERROR or SQL_SUCCESS_WITH_INFO, an associated SQLSTATE value may be obtained by calling **SQLError**. The following table lists the SQLSTATE values commonly returned by **SQLConnect** and explains each one in the context of this function; the notation "(DM)" precedes the descriptions of SQLSTATEs returned by the Driver Manager. The return code associated with each SQLSTATE value is SQL_ERROR, unless noted otherwise.

SQLSTATE	Error	Description
01000	General warning	Driver-specific informational message. (Function returns SQL_SUCCESS_WITH_INFO.)
08001	Unable to connect to data source	The driver was unable to establish a connection with the data source.
08002	Connection in use	(DM) The specified *hdbc* had already been used to establish a connection with a data source and the connection was still open.
08004	Data source rejected establishment of connection	The data source rejected the establishment of the connection for implementation-defined reasons.

SQLSTATE	Error	Description
08S01	Communication link failure	The communication link between the driver and the data source to which the driver was attempting to connect failed before the function completed processing.
28000	Invalid authorization specification	The value specified for the argument *szUID* or the value specified for the argument *szAuthStr* violated restrictions defined by the data source.
IM001	Driver does not support this function	(DM) The driver specified by the data source name does not support the function.
IM002	Data source not found and no default driver specified	(DM) The data source name specified in the argument *szDSN* was not found in the ODBC.INI file or registry, nor was there a default driver specification.
		(DM) The ODBC.INI file could not be found.
IM003	Specified driver could not be loaded	(DM) The driver listed in the data source specification in the ODBC.INI file or registry was not found or could not be loaded for some other reason.
IM004	Driver's SQLAllocEnv failed	(DM) During **SQLConnect**, the Driver Manager called the driver's **SQLAllocEnv** function and the driver returned an error.
IM005	Driver's SQLAllocConnect failed	(DM) During **SQLConnect**, the Driver Manager called the driver's **SQLAllocConnect** function and the driver returned an error.
IM006	Driver's SQLSetConnect-Option failed	(DM) During **SQLConnect**, the Driver Manager called the driver's **SQLSetConnectOption** function and the driver returned an error. (Function returns SQL_SUCCESS_WITH_INFO).
IM009	Unable to load translation DLL	The driver was unable to load the translation DLL that was specified for the data source.
S1000	General error	An error occurred for which there was no specific SQLSTATE and for which no implementation-specific SQLSTATE was defined. The error message returned by **SQLError** in the argument *szErrorMsg* describes the error and its cause.

SQLSTATE	Error	Description
S1001	Memory allocation failure	(DM) The Driver Manager was unable to allocate memory required to support execution or completion of the function.
		The driver was unable to allocate memory required to support execution or completion of the function.
S1090	Invalid string or buffer length	(DM) The value specified for argument *cbDSN* was less than 0, but not equal to SQL_NTS.
		(DM) The value specified for argument *cbDSN* exceeded the maximum length for a data source name.
		(DM) The value specified for argument *cbUID* was less than 0, but not equal to SQL_NTS.
		(DM) The value specified for argument *cbAuthStr* was less than 0, but not equal to SQL_NTS.
S1T00	Timeout expired	The timeout period expired before the connection to the data source completed. The timeout period is set through **SQLSetConnectOption**, SQL_LOGIN_TIMEOUT.

Comments

The Driver Manager does not load a driver until the application calls a function (**SQLConnect**, **SQLDriverConnect**, or **SQLBrowseConnect**) to connect to the driver. Until that point, the Driver Manager works with its own handles and manages connection information. When the application calls a connection function, the Driver Manager checks if a driver is currently loaded for the specified *hdbc*:

- If a driver is not loaded, the Driver Manager loads the driver and calls **SQLAllocEnv**, **SQLAllocConnect**, **SQLSetConnectOption** (if the application specified any connection options), and the connection function in the driver. The Driver Manager returns SQLSTATE IM006 (Driver's SQLSetConnectOption failed) and SQL_SUCCESS_WITH_INFO for the connection function if the driver returned an error for **SQLSetConnectOption**.

- If the specified driver is already loaded on the *hdbc*, the Driver Manager only calls the connection function in the driver. In this case, the driver must ensure that all connection options for the *hdbc* maintain their current settings.

- If a different driver is loaded, the Driver Manager calls **SQLFreeConnect** and **SQLFreeEnv** in the loaded driver and then unloads that driver. It then performs the same operations as when a driver is not loaded.

The driver then allocates handles and initializes itself.

Note To resolve the addresses of the ODBC functions exported by the driver, the Driver Manager checks if the driver exports a dummy function with the ordinal 199. If it does not, the Driver Manager resolves the addresses by name. If it does, the Driver Manager resolves the addresses of the ODBC functions by ordinal, which is faster. The ordinal values of the ODBC functions must match the values of the *fFunction* argument in **SQLGetFunctions**; all other exported functions (such as **WEP**) must have ordinal values outside the range 1–199.

When the application calls **SQLDisconnect**, the Driver Manager calls **SQLDisconnect** in the driver. However, it does not unload the driver. This keeps the driver in memory for applications that repeatedly connect to and disconnect from a data source. When the application calls **SQLFreeConnect**, the Driver Manager calls **SQLFreeConnect** and **SQLFreeEnv** in the driver and then unloads the driver.

An ODBC application can establish more than one connection.

Driver Manager Guidelines

The contents of *szDSN* affect how the Driver Manager and a driver work together to establish a connection to a data source.

- If *szDSN* contains a valid data source name, the Driver Manager locates the corresponding data source specification in the ODBC.INI file or registry and loads the associated driver DLL. The Driver Manager passes each **SQLConnect** argument to the driver.

- If the data source name cannot be found or *szDSN* is a null pointer, the Driver Manager locates the default data source specification and loads the associated driver DLL. The Driver Manager passes each **SQLConnect** argument to the driver.

- If the data source name cannot be found or *szDSN* is a null pointer, and the default data source specification does not exist, the Driver Manager returns SQL_ERROR with SQLSTATE IM002 (Data source name not found and no default driver specified).

After being loaded by the Driver Manager, a driver can locate its corresponding data source specification in the ODBC.INI file or registry and use driver-specific information from the specification to complete its set of required connection information.

If a default translation DLL is specified in the ODBC.INI file or registry for the data source, the driver loads it. A different translation DLL can be loaded by calling **SQLSetConnectOption** with the SQL_TRANSLATE_DLL option. A translation option can be specified by calling **SQLSetConnectOption** with the SQL_TRANSLATE_OPTION option.

If a driver supports **SQLConnect**, the driver keyword section of the ODBC.INF file for the driver must contain the **ConnectFunctions** keyword with the first character set to "Y". For more information, see "Driver Keyword Sections" in Chapter 19, "Installing ODBC Software."

Code Example

In the following example, an application allocates environment and connection handles. It then connects to the EmpData data source with the user ID JohnS and the password Sesame and processes data. When it has finished processing data, it disconnects from the data source and frees the handles.

```
HENV     henv;
HDBC     hdbc;
HSTMT    hstmt;
RETCODE  retcode;

retcode = SQLAllocEnv(&henv);                 /* Environment handle */
if (retcode == SQL_SUCCESS) {
    retcode = SQLAllocConnect(henv, &hdbc); /* Connection handle */
    if (retcode == SQL_SUCCESS) {

        /* Set login timeout to 5 seconds. */

        SQLSetConnectOption(hdbc, SQL_LOGIN_TIMEOUT, 5);

        /* Connect to data source */

        retcode = SQLConnect(hdbc, "EmpData", SQL_NTS,
                                   "JohnS", SQL_NTS,
                                   "Sesame", SQL_NTS);

        if (retcode == SQL_SUCCESS || retcode == SQL_SUCCESS_WITH_INFO){

            /* Process data after successful connection */

            retcode = SQLAllocStmt(hdbc, &hstmt); /* Statement handle */
            if (retcode == SQL_SUCCESS) {
                ...;
                ...;
                ...;
                SQLFreeStmt(hstmt, SQL_DROP);
            }
            SQLDisconnect(hdbc);
        }
        SQLFreeConnect(hdbc);
    }
    SQLFreeEnv(henv);
}
```

Related Functions	**For information about**	**See**
	Allocating a connection handle	**SQLAllocConnect**
	Allocating a statement handle	**SQLAllocStmt**
	Discovering and enumerating values required to connect to a data source	**SQLBrowseConnect** (extension)
	Disconnecting from a data source	**SQLDisconnect**
	Connecting to a data source using a connection string or dialog box	**SQLDriverConnect** (extension)
	Returning the setting of a connection option	**SQLGetConnectOption** (extension)
	Setting a connection option	**SQLSetConnectOption** (extension)

SQLDataSources

ODBC 1.0

Extension Level 2   **SQLDataSources** lists data source names. This function is implemented solely by the Driver Manager.

Syntax   RETCODE **SQLDataSources**(*henv, fDirection, szDSN, cbDSNMax, pcbDSN, szDescription, cbDescriptionMax, pcbDescription*)

The **SQLDataSources** function accepts the following arguments:

Type	Argument	Use	Description
HENV	*henv*	Input	Environment handle.
UWORD	*fDirection*	Input	Determines whether the Driver Manager fetches the next data source name in the list (SQL_FETCH_NEXT) or whether the search starts from the beginning of the list (SQL_FETCH_FIRST).
UCHAR FAR *	*szDSN*	Output	Pointer to storage for the data source name.
SWORD	*cbDSNMax*	Input	Maximum length of the *szDSN* buffer; this does not need to be longer than SQL_MAX_DSN_LENGTH + 1.
SWORD FAR *	*pcbDSN*	Output	Total number of bytes (excluding the null termination byte) available to return in *szDSN*. If the number of bytes available to return is greater than or equal to *cbDSNMax*, the data source name in *szDSN* is truncated to *cbDSNMax* − 1 bytes.
UCHAR FAR *	*szDescription*	Output	Pointer to storage for the description of the driver associated with the data source. For example, dBASE or SQL Server.
SWORD	*cbDescriptionMax*	Input	Maximum length of the *szDescription* buffer; this should be at least 255 bytes.

Type	Argument	Use	Description
SWORD FAR *	*pcbDescription*	Output	Total number of bytes (excluding the null termination byte) available to return in *szDescription*. If the number of bytes available to return is greater than or equal to *cbDescriptionMax*, the driver description in *szDescription* is truncated to *cbDescriptionMax* – 1 bytes.

Returns

SQL_SUCCESS, SQL_SUCCESS_WITH_INFO, SQL_NO_DATA_FOUND, SQL_ERROR, or SQL_INVALID_HANDLE.

Diagnostics

When **SQLDataSources** returns either SQL_ERROR or SQL_SUCCESS_WITH_INFO, an associated SQLSTATE value may be obtained by calling **SQLError**. The following table lists the SQLSTATE values commonly returned by **SQLDataSources** and explains each one in the context of this function; the notation "(DM)" precedes the descriptions of SQLSTATEs returned by the Driver Manager. The return code associated with each SQLSTATE value is SQL_ERROR, unless noted otherwise.

SQLSTATE	Error	Description
01000	General warning	(DM) Driver Manager–specific informational message. (Function returns SQL_SUCCESS_WITH_INFO.)
01004	Data truncated	(DM) The buffer *szDSN* was not large enough to return the entire data source name, so the name was truncated. The argument *pcbDSN* contains the length of the entire data source name. (Function returns SQL_SUCCESS_WITH_INFO.)
		(DM) The buffer *szDescription* was not large enough to return the entire driver description, so the description was truncated. The argument *pcbDescription* contains the length of the untruncated data source description. (Function returns SQL_SUCCESS_WITH_INFO.)
S1000	General error	(DM) An error occurred for which there was no specific SQLSTATE and for which no implementation-specific SQLSTATE was defined. The error message returned by **SQLError** in the argument *szErrorMsg* describes the error and its cause.

SQLSTATE	Error	Description
S1001	Memory allocation failure	(DM) The Driver Manager was unable to allocate memory required to support execution or completion of the function.
S1090	Invalid string or buffer length	(DM) The value specified for argument *cbDSNMax* was less than 0.
		(DM) The value specified for argument *cbDescriptionMax* was less than 0.
S1103	Direction option out of range	(DM) The value specified for the argument *fDirection* was not equal to SQL_FETCH_FIRST or SQL_FETCH_NEXT.

Comments

Because **SQLDataSources** is implemented in the Driver Manager, it is supported for all drivers regardless of a particular driver's conformance level.

An application can call **SQLDataSources** multiple times to retrieve all data source names. The Driver Manager retrieves this information from the ODBC.INI file or the registry. When there are no more data source names, the Driver Manager returns SQL_NO_DATA_FOUND. If **SQLDataSources** is called with SQL_FETCH_NEXT immediately after it returns SQL_NO_DATA_FOUND, it will return the first data source name.

If SQL_FETCH_NEXT is passed to **SQLDataSources** the very first time it is called, it will return the first data source name.

The driver determines how data source names are mapped to actual data sources.

Related Functions

For information about	See
Discovering and listing values required to connect to a data source	**SQLBrowseConnect** (extension)
Connecting to a data source	**SQLConnect**
Connecting to a data source using a connection string or dialog box	**SQLDriverConnect** (extension)
Returning driver descriptions and attributes	**SQLDrivers** (extension)

SQLDescribeCol

Core

SQLDescribeCol returns the result descriptor—column name, type, precision, scale, and nullability—for one column in the result set; it cannot be used to return information about the bookmark column (column 0).

Syntax

RETCODE **SQLDescribeCol**(*hstmt*, *icol*, *szColName*, *cbColNameMax*, *pcbColName*, *pfSqlType*, *pcbColDef*, *pibScale*, *pfNullable*)

The **SQLDescribeCol** function accepts the following arguments.

Type	Argument	Use	Description
HSTMT	*hstmt*	Input	Statement handle.
UWORD	*icol*	Input	Column number of result data, ordered sequentially left to right, starting at 1.
UCHAR FAR *	*szColName*	Output	Pointer to storage for the column name. If the column is unnamed or the column name cannot be determined, the driver returns an empty string.
SWORD	*cbColNameMax*	Input	Maximum length of the *szColName* buffer.
SWORD FAR *	*pcbColName*	Output	Total number of bytes (excluding the null termination byte) available to return in *szColName*. If the number of bytes available to return is greater than or equal to *cbColNameMax*, the column name in *szColName* is truncated to *cbColNameMax* – 1 bytes.

Type	Argument	Use	Description
SWORD FAR *	*pfSqlType*	Output	The SQL data type of the column. This must be one of the following values:
			SQL_BIGINT SQL_BINARY SQL_BIT SQL_CHAR SQL_DATE SQL_DECIMAL SQL_DOUBLE SQL_FLOAT SQL_INTEGER SQL_LONGVARBINARY SQL_LONGVARCHAR SQL_NUMERIC SQL_REAL SQL_SMALLINT SQL_TIME SQL_TIMESTAMP SQL_TINYINT SQL_VARBINARY SQL_VARCHAR
			or a driver-specific SQL data type. If the data type cannot be determined, the driver returns 0.
			For more information, see "SQL Data Types" in Appendix D, "Data Types." For information about driver-specific SQL data types, see the driver's documentation.
UDWORD FAR *	*pcbColDef*	Output	The precision of the column on the data source. If the precision cannot be determined, the driver returns 0. For more information on precision, see "Precision, Scale, Length, and Display Size" in Appendix D, "Data Types."
SWORD FAR *	*pibScale*	Output	The scale of the column on the data source. If the scale cannot be determined or is not applicable, the driver returns 0. For more information on scale, see "Precision, Scale, Length, and Display Size" in Appendix D, "Data Types."

Type	Argument	Use	Description
SWORD FAR *	*pfNullable*	Output	Indicates whether the column allows NULL values. One of the following values:
			SQL_NO_NULLS: The column does not allow NULL values.
			SQL_NULLABLE: The column allows NULL values.
			SQL_NULLABLE_UNKNOWN: The driver cannot determine if the column allows NULL values.

Returns

SQL_SUCCESS, SQL_SUCCESS_WITH_INFO, SQL_STILL_EXECUTING, SQL_ERROR, or SQL_INVALID_HANDLE.

Diagnostics

When **SQLDescribeCol** returns either SQL_ERROR or SQL_SUCCESS_WITH_INFO, an associated SQLSTATE value may be obtained by calling **SQLError**. The following table lists the SQLSTATE values commonly returned by **SQLDescribeCol** and explains each one in the context of this function; the notation "(DM)" precedes the descriptions of SQLSTATEs returned by the Driver Manager. The return code associated with each SQLSTATE value is SQL_ERROR, unless noted otherwise.

SQLSTATE	Error	Description
01000	General warning	Driver-specific informational message. (Function returns SQL_SUCCESS_WITH_INFO.)
01004	Data truncated	The buffer *szColName* was not large enough to return the entire column name, so the column name was truncated. The argument *pcbColName* contains the length of the untruncated column name. (Function returns SQL_SUCCESS_WITH_INFO.)
24000	Invalid cursor state	The statement associated with the *hstmt* did not return a result set. There were no columns to describe.
IM001	Driver does not support this function	(DM) The driver associated with the *hstmt* does not support the function.
S1000	General error	An error occurred for which there was no specific SQLSTATE and for which no implementation-specific SQLSTATE was defined. The error message returned by **SQLError** in the argument *szErrorMsg* describes the error and its cause.

SQLSTATE	Error	Description
S1001	Memory allocation failure	The driver was unable to allocate memory required to support execution or completion of the function.
S1002	Invalid column number	(DM) The value specified for the argument *icol* was 0.
		The value specified for the argument *icol* was greater than the number of columns in the result set.
S1008	Operation canceled	Asynchronous processing was enabled for the *hstmt*. The function was called and before it completed execution, **SQLCancel** was called on the *hstmt*. Then the function was called again on the *hstmt*.
		The function was called and, before it completed execution, **SQLCancel** was called on the *hstmt* from a different thread in a multithreaded application.
S1010	Function sequence error	(DM) The function was called prior to calling **SQLPrepare** or **SQLExecDirect** for the *hstmt*.
		(DM) An asynchronously executing function (not this one) was called for the *hstmt* and was still executing when this function was called.
		(DM) **SQLExecute**, **SQLExecDirect**, or **SQLSetPos** was called for the *hstmt* and returned SQL_NEED_DATA. This function was called before data was sent for all data-at-execution parameters or columns.
S1090	Invalid string or buffer length	(DM) The value specified for argument *cbColNameMax* was less than 0.
S1T00	Timeout expired	The timeout period expired before the data source returned the result set. The timeout period is set through **SQLSetStmtOption**, SQL_QUERY_TIMEOUT.

SQLDescribeCol can return any SQLSTATE that can be returned by **SQLPrepare** or **SQLExecute** when called after **SQLPrepare** and before **SQLExecute** depending on when the data source evaluates the SQL statement associated with the *hstmt*.

Comments   An application typically calls **SQLDescribeCol** after a call to **SQLPrepare** and before or after the associated call to **SQLExecute**. An application can also call **SQLDescribeCol** after a call to **SQLExecDirect**.

SQLDescribeCol retrieves the column name, type, and length generated by a **SELECT** statement. If the column is an expression, *szColName* is either an empty string or a driver-defined name.

Note ODBC supports SQL_NULLABLE_UNKNOWN as an extension, even though the X/Open and SQL Access Group Call Level Interface specification does not specify the option for **SQLDescribeCol**.

Related Functions

For information about	See
Assigning storage for a column in a result set	**SQLBindCol**
Canceling statement processing	**SQLCancel**
Returning information about a column in a result set	**SQLColAttributes**
Fetching a row of data	**SQLFetch**
Returning the number of result set columns	**SQLNumResultCols**
Preparing a statement for execution	**SQLPrepare**

SQLDescribeParam

Extension Level 2   **SQLDescribeParam** returns the description of a parameter marker associated with a prepared SQL statement.

Syntax   RETCODE **SQLDescribeParam**(*hstmt, ipar, pfSqlType, pcbColDef, pibScale, pfNullable*)

The **SQLDescribeParam** function accepts the following arguments:

Type	Argument	Use	Description
HSTMT	*hstmt*	Input	Statement handle.
UWORD	*ipar*	Input	Parameter marker number ordered sequentially left to right, starting at 1.
SWORD FAR *	*pfSqlType*	Output	The SQL data type of the parameter. This must be one of the following values:

SQL_BIGINT
SQL_BINARY
SQL_BIT
SQL_CHAR
SQL_DATE
SQL_DECIMAL
SQL_DOUBLE
SQL_FLOAT
SQL_INTEGER
SQL_LONGVARBINARY
SQL_LONGVARCHAR
SQL_NUMERIC
SQL_REAL
SQL_SMALLINT
SQL_TIME
SQL_TIMESTAMP
SQL_TINYINT
SQL_VARBINARY
SQL_VARCHAR

or a driver-specific SQL data type.

For more information, see "SQL Data Types" in Appendix D, "Data Types." For information about driver-specific SQL data types, see the driver's documentation.

Type	Argument	Use	Description
UDWORD FAR *	*pcbColDef*	Output	The precision of the column or expression of the corresponding parameter marker as defined by the data source. For further information concerning precision, see "Precision, Scale, Length, and Display Size," in Appendix D, "Data Types."
SWORD FAR *	*pibScale*	Output	The scale of the column or expression of the corresponding parameter as defined by the data source. For more information on scale, see "Precision, Scale, Length, and Display Size," in Appendix D, "Data Types."
SWORD FAR *	*pfNullable*	Output	Indicates whether the parameter allows NULL values. One of the following:
			SQL_NO_NULLS: The parameter does not allow NULL values (this is the default value).
			SQL_NULLABLE: The parameter allows NULL values.
			SQL_NULLABLE_UNKNOWN: The driver cannot determine if the parameter allows NULL values.

Returns

SQL_SUCCESS, SQL_SUCCESS_WITH_INFO, SQL_STILL_EXECUTING, SQL_ERROR, or SQL_INVALID_HANDLE.

Diagnostics

When **SQLDescribeParam** returns SQL_ERROR or SQL_SUCCESS_WITH_INFO, an associated SQLSTATE value may be obtained by calling **SQLError**. The following table lists the SQLSTATE values commonly returned by **SQLDescribeParam** and explains each one in the context of this function; the notation "(DM)" precedes the descriptions of SQLSTATEs returned by the Driver Manager. The return code associated with each SQLSTATE value is SQL_ERROR, unless noted otherwise.

SQLSTATE	Error	Description
01000	General warning	Driver-specific informational message. (Function returns SQL_SUCCESS_WITH_INFO.)
IM001	Driver does not support this function	(DM) The driver associated with the *hstmt* does not support the function.

SQLSTATE	Error	Description
S1000	General error	An error occurred for which there was no specific SQLSTATE and for which no implementation-specific SQLSTATE was defined. The error message returned by **SQLError** in the argument *szErrorMsg* describes the error and its cause.
S1001	Memory allocation error	The driver was unable to allocate memory required to support execution or completion of the function.
S1008	Operation canceled	Asynchronous processing was enabled for the *hstmt*. The function was called and before it completed execution, **SQLCancel** was called on the *hstmt*. Then the function was called again on the *hstmt*.
		The function was called and, before it completed execution, **SQLCancel** was called on the *hstmt* from a different thread in a multithreaded application.
S1010	Function sequence error	(DM) The function was called prior to calling **SQLPrepare** or **SQLExecDirect** for the *hstmt*.
		(DM) An asynchronously executing function (not this one) was called for the *hstmt* and was still executing when this function was called.
		(DM) **SQLExecute**, **SQLExecDirect**, or **SQLSetPos** was called for the *hstmt* and returned SQL_NEED_DATA. This function was called before data was sent for all data-at-execution parameters or columns.
S1093	Invalid parameter number	(DM) The value specified for the argument *ipar* was 0.
		The value specified for the argument *ipar* was greater than the number of parameters in the associated SQL statement.
S1T00	Timeout expired	The timeout period expired before the data source returned the result set. The timeout period is set through **SQLSetStmtOption**, SQL_QUERY_TIMEOUT.

Comments   Parameter markers are numbered from left to right in the order they appear in the SQL statement.

SQLDescribeParam does not return the type (input, input/output, or output) of a parameter in an SQL statement. Except in calls to procedures, all parameters in SQL statements are input parameters. To determine the type of each parameter in a call to a procedure, an application calls **SQLProcedureColumns**.

Related Functions

For information about	See
Canceling statement processing	**SQLCancel**
Executing a prepared SQL statement	**SQLExecute**
Preparing a statement for execution	**SQLPrepare**
Assigning storage for a parameter	**SQLBindParameter**

SQLDisconnect

ODBC 1.0

Core

SQLDisconnect closes the connection associated with a specific connection handle.

Syntax

RETCODE **SQLDisconnect**(*hdbc*)

The **SQLDisconnect** function accepts the following argument.

Type	Argument	Use	Description
HDBC	*hdbc*	Input	Connection handle.

Returns

SQL_SUCCESS, SQL_SUCCESS_WITH_INFO, SQL_ERROR, or SQL_INVALID_HANDLE.

Diagnostics

When **SQLDisconnect** returns SQL_ERROR or SQL_SUCCESS_WITH_INFO, an associated SQLSTATE value may be obtained by calling **SQLError**. The following table lists the SQLSTATE values commonly returned by **SQLDisconnect** and explains each one in the context of this function; the notation "(DM)" precedes the descriptions of SQLSTATEs returned by the Driver Manager. The return code associated with each SQLSTATE value is SQL_ERROR, unless noted otherwise.

SQLSTATE	Error	Description
01000	General warning	Driver-specific informational message. (Function returns SQL_SUCCESS_WITH_INFO.)
01002	Disconnect error	An error occurred during the disconnect. However, the disconnect succeeded. (Function returns SQL_SUCCESS_WITH_INFO.)
08003	Connection not open	(DM) The connection specified in the argument *hdbc* was not open.
25000	Invalid transaction state	There was a transaction in process on the connection specified by the argument *hdbc*. The transaction remains active.
IM001	Driver does not support this function	(DM) The driver associated with the *hdbc* does not support the function.
S1000	General error	An error occurred for which there was no specific SQLSTATE and for which no implementation-specific SQLSTATE was defined. The error message returned by **SQLError** in the argument *szErrorMsg* describes the error and its cause.

SQLSTATE	Error	Description
S1001	Memory allocation failure	The driver was unable to allocate memory required to support execution or completion of the function.
S1010	Function sequence error	(DM) An asynchronously executing function was called for an *hstmt* associated with the *hdbc* and was still executing when **SQLDisconnect** was called.
		(DM) **SQLExecute**, **SQLExecDirect**, or **SQLSetPos** was called for an *hstmt* associated with the *hdbc* and returned SQL_NEED_DATA. This function was called before data was sent for all data-at-execution parameters or columns.

Comments

If an application calls **SQLDisconnect** after **SQLBrowseConnect** returns SQL_NEED_DATA and before it returns a different return code, the driver cancels the connection browsing process and returns the *hdbc* to an unconnected state.

If an application calls **SQLDisconnect** while there is an incomplete transaction associated with the connection handle, the driver returns SQLSTATE 25000 (Invalid transaction state), indicating that the transaction is unchanged and the connection is open. An incomplete transaction is one that has not been committed or rolled back with **SQLTransact**.

If an application calls **SQLDisconnect** before it has freed all *hstmts* associated with the connection, the driver frees those *hstmts* after it successfully disconnects from the data source. However, if one or more of the *hstmts* associated with the connection are still executing asynchronously, **SQLDisconnect** will return SQL_ERROR with a SQLSTATE value of S1010 (Function sequence error).

Code Example

See **SQLBrowseConnect** and **SQLConnect**.

Related Functions

For information about	See
Allocating a connection handle	**SQLAllocConnect**
Connecting to a data source	**SQLConnect**
Connecting to a data source using a connection string or dialog box	**SQLDriverConnect** (extension)
Freeing a connection handle	**SQLFreeConnect**
Executing a commit or rollback operation	**SQLTransact**

SQLDriverConnect

Extension Level 1   **SQLDriverConnect** is an alternative to **SQLConnect**. It supports data sources that require more connection information than the three arguments in **SQLConnect**; dialog boxes to prompt the user for all connection information; and data sources that are not defined in the ODBC.INI file or registry.

SQLDriverConnect provides the following connection options:

- Establish a connection using a connection string that contains the data source name, one or more user IDs, one or more passwords, and other information required by the data source.

- Establish a connection using a partial connection string or no additional information; in this case, the Driver Manager and the driver can each prompt the user for connection information.

- Establish a connection to a data source that is not defined in the ODBC.INI file or registry. If the application supplies a partial connection string, the driver can prompt the user for connection information.

Once a connection is established, **SQLDriverConnect** returns the completed connection string. The application can use this string for subsequent connection requests.

Syntax   RETCODE **SQLDriverConnect**(*hdbc, hwnd, szConnStrIn, cbConnStrIn, szConnStrOut, cbConnStrOutMax, pcbConnStrOut, fDriverCompletion*)

The **SQLDriverConnect** function accepts the following arguments:

Type	Argument	Use	Description
HDBC	*hdbc*	Input	Connection handle.
HWND	*hwnd*	Input	Window handle. The application can pass the handle of the parent window, if applicable, or a null pointer if either the window handle is not applicable or if **SQLDriverConnect** will not present any dialog boxes.
UCHAR FAR *	*szConnStrIn*	Input	A full connection string (see the syntax in "Comments"), a partial connection string, or an empty string.
SWORD	*cbConnStrIn*	Input	Length of *szConnStrIn*.

Type	Argument	Use	Description
UCHAR FAR *	*szConnStrOut*	Output	Pointer to storage for the completed connection string. Upon successful connection to the target data source, this buffer contains the completed connection string. Applications should allocate at least 255 bytes for this buffer.
SWORD	*cbConnStrOutMax*	Input	Maximum length of the *szConnStrOut* buffer.
SWORD FAR *	*pcbConnStrOut*	Output	Pointer to the total number of bytes (excluding the null termination byte) available to return in *szConnStrOut*. If the number of bytes available to return is greater than or equal to *cbConnStrOutMax*, the completed connection string in *szConnStrOut* is truncated to *cbConnStrOutMax* – 1 bytes.
UWORD	*fDriverCompletion*	Input	Flag which indicates whether Driver Manager or driver must prompt for more connection information: SQL_DRIVER_PROMPT, SQL_DRIVER_COMPLETE, SQL_DRIVER_COMPLETE_ REQUIRED, or SQL_DRIVER_NOPROMPT. (See "Comments," for additional information.)

Returns

SQL_SUCCESS, SQL_SUCCESS_WITH_INFO, SQL_NO_DATA_FOUND, SQL_ERROR, or SQL_INVALID_HANDLE.

Diagnostics

When **SQLDriverConnect** returns either SQL_ERROR or SQL_SUCCESS_WITH_INFO, an associated SQLSTATE value may be obtained by calling **SQLError**. The following table lists the SQLSTATE values commonly returned by **SQLDriverConnect** and explains each one in the context of this function; the notation "(DM)" precedes the descriptions of SQLSTATEs returned by the Driver Manager. The return code associated with each SQLSTATE value is SQL_ERROR, unless noted otherwise.

SQLSTATE	Error	Description
01000	General warning	Driver-specific informational message. (Function returns SQL_SUCCESS_WITH_INFO.)
01004	Data truncated	The buffer *szConnStrOut* was not large enough to return the entire connection string, so the connection string was truncated. The argument *pcbConnStrOut* contains the length of the untruncated connection string. (Function returns SQL_SUCCESS_WITH_INFO.)
01S00	Invalid connection string attribute	An invalid attribute keyword was specified in the connection string (*szConnStrIn*) but the driver was able to connect to the data source anyway. (Function returns SQL_SUCCESS_WITH_INFO.)
08001	Unable to connect to data source	The driver was unable to establish a connection with the data source.
08002	Connection in use	(DM) The specified *hdbc* had already been used to establish a connection with a data source and the connection was still open.
08004	Data source rejected establishment of connection	The data source rejected the establishment of the connection for implementation-defined reasons.
08S01	Communication link failure	The communication link between the driver and the data source to which the driver was attempting to connect failed before the function completed processing.
28000	Invalid authorization specification	Either the user identifier or the authorization string or both as specified in the connection string (*szConnStrIn*) violated restrictions defined by the data source.
IM001	Driver does not support this function	(DM) The driver corresponding to the specified data source name does not support the function.
IM002	Data source not found and no default driver specified	(DM) The data source name specified in the connection string (*szConnStrIn*) was not found in the ODBC.INI file or registry and there was no default driver specification. (DM) The ODBC.INI file could not be found.

SQLSTATE	Error	Description
IM003	Specified driver could not be loaded	(DM) The driver listed in the data source specification in the ODBC.INI file or registry, or specified by the **DRIVER** keyword, was not found or could not be loaded for some other reason.
IM004	Driver's SQLAllocEnv failed	(DM) During **SQLDriverConnect**, the Driver Manager called the driver's **SQLAllocEnv** function and the driver returned an error.
IM005	Driver's SQLAllocConnect failed	(DM) During **SQLDriverConnect**, the Driver Manager called the driver's **SQLAllocConnect** function and the driver returned an error.
IM006	Driver's SQLSetConnect-Option failed	(DM) During **SQLDriverConnect**, the Driver Manager called the driver's **SQLSetConnectOption** function and the driver returned an error.
IM007	No data source or driver specified; dialog prohibited	No data source name or driver was specified in the connection string and *fDriverCompletion* was SQL_DRIVER_NOPROMPT.
IM008	Dialog failed	(DM) The Driver Manager attempted to display the SQL Data Sources dialog box and failed.
		The driver attempted to display its login dialog box and failed.
IM009	Unable to load translation DLL	The driver was unable to load the translation DLL that was specified for the data source or for the connection.
IM010	Data source name too long	(DM) The attribute value for the DSN keyword was longer than SQL_MAX_DSN_LENGTH characters.
IM011	Driver name too long	(DM) The attribute value for the DRIVER keyword was longer than 255 characters.
IM012	DRIVER keyword syntax error	(DM) The keyword-value pair for the DRIVER keyword contained a syntax error.
S1000	General error	An error occurred for which there was no specific SQLSTATE and for which no implementation-specific SQLSTATE was defined. The error message returned by **SQLError** in the argument *szErrorMsg* describes the error and its cause.

SQLSTATE	Error	Description
S1001	Memory allocation failure	The Driver Manager was unable to allocate memory required to support execution or completion of the function.
		The driver was unable to allocate memory required to support execution or completion of the function.
S1090	Invalid string or buffer length	(DM) The value specified for argument *cbConnStrIn* was less than 0 and was not equal to SQL_NTS.
		(DM) The value specified for argument *cbConnStrOutMax* was less than 0.
S1110	Invalid driver completion	(DM) The value specified for the argument *fDriverCompletion* was not equal to SQL_DRIVER_PROMPT, SQL_DRIVER_COMPLETE, SQL_DRIVER_COMPLETE_REQUIRED or SQL_DRIVER_NOPROMPT.
S1T00	Timeout expired	The timeout period expired before the connection to the data source completed. The timeout period is set through **SQLSetConnectOption**, SQL_LOGIN_TIMEOUT.

Comments

Connection Strings

A connection string has the following syntax:

connection-string ::= *empty-string*[;] | *attribute*[;] | *attribute*; *connection-string*
empty-string ::=
attribute ::= *attribute-keyword*=*attribute-value* | DRIVER={*attribute-value*}
(The braces ({ }) are literal; the application must specify them.)
attribute-keyword ::= DSN | UID | PWD
                                | *driver-defined-attribute-keyword*
attribute-value ::= *character-string*
driver-defined-attribute-keyword ::= *identifier*

where *character-string* has zero or more characters; *identifier* has one or more characters; *attribute-keyword* is case insensitive; *attribute-value* may be case sensitive; and the value of the **DSN** keyword does not consist solely of blanks. Because of connection string and initialization file grammar, keywords and attribute values that contain the characters []{}(),;?*=!@ should be avoided. Because of the registry grammar, keywords and data source names cannot contain the backslash (\) character.

Note The **DRIVER** keyword was introduced in ODBC 2.0 and is not supported by ODBC 1.0 drivers.

The connection string may include any number of driver-defined keywords. Because the **DRIVER** keyword does not use information from the ODBC.INI file or registry, the driver must define enough keywords so that a driver can connect to a data source using only the information in the connection string. (For more information, see "Driver Guidelines," later in this section.) The driver defines which keywords are required in order to connect to the data source.

If any keywords are repeated in the connection string, the driver uses the value associated with the first occurrence of the keyword. If the **DSN** and **DRIVER** keywords are included in the same connection string, the Driver Manager and the driver use whichever keyword appears first. The following table describes the attribute values of the **DSN**, **DRIVER**, **UID**, and **PWD** keywords.

Keyword	Attribute value description
DSN	Name of a data source as returned by **SQLDataSources** or the data sources dialog box of **SQLDriverConnect**.
DRIVER	Description of the driver as returned by the **SQLDrivers** function. For example, Rdb or SQL Server.
UID	A user ID.
PWD	The password corresponding to the user ID, or an empty string if there is no password for the user ID (PWD=;).

Driver Manager Guidelines

The Driver Manager constructs a connection string to pass to the driver in the *szConnStrIn* argument of the driver's **SQLDriverConnect** function. Note that the Driver Manager does not modify the *szConnStrIn* argument passed to it by the application.

If the connection string specified by the application contains the **DSN** keyword or does not contain either the **DSN** or **DRIVER** keywords, the action of the Driver Manager is based on the value of the *fDriverCompletion* argument:

- SQL_DRIVER_PROMPT: The Driver Manager displays the Data Sources dialog box. It constructs a connection string from the data source name returned by the dialog box and any other keywords passed to it by the application. If the data source name returned by the dialog box is empty, the Driver Manager specifies the keyword-value pair DSN=Default.

- SQL_DRIVER_COMPLETE or SQL_DRIVER_COMPLETE_REQUIRED: If the connection string specified by the application includes the **DSN** keyword, the Driver Manager copies the connection string specified by the application. Otherwise, it takes the same actions as it does when *fDriverCompletion* is SQL_DRIVER_PROMPT.

- SQL_DRIVER_NOPROMPT: The Driver Manager copies the connection string specified by the application.

If the connection string specified by the application contains the **DRIVER** keyword, the Driver Manager copies the connection string specified by the application.

Using the connection string it has constructed, the Driver Manager determines which driver to use, loads that driver, and passes the connection string it has constructed to the driver; for more information about the interaction of the Driver Manager and the driver, see the "Comments" section in **SQLConnect**. If the connection string contains the **DSN** keyword or does not contain either the **DSN** or the **DRIVER** keyword, the Driver Manager determines which driver to use as follows:

1. If the connection string contains the **DSN** keyword, the Driver Manager retrieves the driver associated with the data source from the ODBC.INI file or registry.

2. If the connection string does not contain the **DSN** keyword or the data source is not found, the Driver Manager retrieves the driver associated with the Default data source from the ODBC.INI file or registry. However, the Driver Manager does not change the value of the **DSN** keyword in the connection string.

3. If the data source is not found and the Default data source is not found, the Driver Manager returns SQL_ERROR with SQLSTATE IM002 (Data source not found and no default driver specified).

Driver Guidelines

The driver checks if the connection string passed to it by the Driver Manager contains the **DSN** or **DRIVER** keyword. If the connection string contains the **DRIVER** keyword, the driver cannot retrieve information about the data source from the ODBC.INI file or registry. If the connection string contains the **DSN** keyword or does not contain either the **DSN** or the **DRIVER** keyword, the driver can retrieve information about the data source from the ODBC.INI file or registry as follows:

1. If the connection string contains the **DSN** keyword, the driver retrieves the information for the specified data source.

2. If the connection string does not contain the **DSN** keyword or the specified data source is not found, the driver retrieves the information for the Default data source.

The driver uses any information it retrieves from the ODBC.INI file or registry to augment the information passed to it in the connection string. If the information in the ODBC.INI file or registry duplicates information in the connection string, the driver uses the information in the connection string.

Based on the value of *fDriverCompletion*, the driver prompts the user for connection information, such as the user ID and password, and connects to the data source:

- SQL_DRIVER_PROMPT: The driver displays a dialog box, using the values from the connection string and ODBC.INI file or registry (if any) as initial values. When the user exits the dialog box, the driver connects to the data source. It also constructs a connection string from the value of the **DSN** or **DRIVER** keyword in *szConnStrIn* and the information returned from the dialog box. It places this connection string in the buffer referenced by *szConnStrOut*.

- SQL_DRIVER_COMPLETE or SQL_DRIVER_COMPLETE_REQUIRED: If the connection string contains enough information, and that information is correct, the driver connects to the data source and copies *szConnStrIn* to *szConnStrOut*. If any information is missing or incorrect, the driver takes the same actions as it does when *fDriverCompletion* is SQL_DRIVER_PROMPT, except that if *fDriverCompletion* is SQL_DRIVER_COMPLETE_REQUIRED, the driver disables the controls for any information not required to connect to the data source.

- SQL_DRIVER_NOPROMPT: If the connection string contains enough information, the driver connects to the data source and copies *szConnStrIn* to *szConnStrOut*. Otherwise, the driver returns SQL_ERROR for **SQLDriverConnect**.

On successful connection to the data source, the driver also sets *pcbConnStrOut* to the length of *szConnStrOut*.

If the user cancels a dialog box presented by the Driver Manager or the driver, **SQLDriverConnect** returns SQL_NO_DATA_FOUND.

For information about how the Driver Manager and the driver interact during the connection process, see **SQLConnect**.

If a driver supports **SQLDriverConnect**, the driver keyword section of the ODBC.INF file for the driver must contain the **ConnectFunctions** keyword with the second character set to "Y". For more information, see "Driver Keyword Sections" in Chapter 19, "Installing ODBC Software."

Connection Options

The SQL_LOGIN_TIMEOUT connection option, set using
SQLSetConnectOption, defines the number of seconds to wait for a login
request to complete before returning to the application. If the user is prompted to
complete the connection string, a waiting period for each login request begins
after the user has dismissed each dialog box.

The driver opens the connection in SQL_MODE_READ_WRITE access mode by
default. To set the access mode to SQL_MODE_READ_ONLY, the application
must call **SQLSetConnectOption** with the SQL_ACCESS_MODE option prior
to calling **SQLDriverConnect**.

If a default translation DLL is specified in the ODBC.INI file or registry for the
data source, the driver loads it. A different translation DLL can be loaded by
calling **SQLSetConnectOption** with the SQL_TRANSLATE_DLL option. A
translation option can be specified by calling **SQLSetConnectOption** with the
SQL_TRANSLATE_OPTION option.

Related Functions

For information about	See
Allocating a connection handle	**SQLAllocConnect**
Discovering and enumerating values required to connect to a data source	**SQLBrowseConnect** (extension)
Connecting to a data source	**SQLConnect**
Disconnecting from a data source	**SQLDisconnect**
Returning driver descriptions and attributes	**SQLDrivers** (extension)
Freeing a connection handle	**SQLFreeConnect**
Setting a connection option	**SQLSetConnectOption** (extension)

SQLDrivers

Extension Level 2 **SQLDrivers** lists driver descriptions and driver attribute keywords. This function is implemented solely by the Driver Manager.

Syntax RETCODE **SQLDrivers**(*henv, fDirection, szDriverDesc, cbDriverDescMax, pcbDriverDesc, szDriverAttributes, cbDrvrAttrMax, pcbDrvrAttr*)

The **SQLDrivers** function accepts the following arguments:

Type	Argument	Use	Description
HENV	*henv*	Input	Environment handle.
UWORD	*fDirection*	Input	Determines whether the Driver Manager fetches the next driver description in the list (SQL_FETCH_NEXT) or whether the search starts from the beginning of the list (SQL_FETCH_FIRST).
UCHAR FAR *	*szDriverDesc*	Output	Pointer to storage for the driver description.
SWORD	*cbDriverDescMax*	Input	Maximum length of the *szDriverDesc* buffer.
SWORD FAR *	*pcbDriverDesc*	Output	Total number of bytes (excluding the null termination byte) available to return in *szDriverDesc*. If the number of bytes available to return is greater than or equal to *cbDriverDescMax*, the driver description in *szDriverDesc* is truncated to *cbDriverDescMax* – 1 bytes.
UCHAR FAR *	*szDriverAttributes*	Output	Pointer to storage for the list of driver attribute value pairs (see "Comments").
SWORD	*cbDrvrAttrMax*	Input	Maximum length of the *szDriverAttributes* buffer.

Type	Argument	Use	Description
SWORD FAR *	*pcbDrvrAttr*	Output	Total number of bytes (excluding the null termination byte) available to return in *szDriverAttributes*. If the number of bytes available to return is greater than or equal to *cbDrvrAttrMax*, the list of attribute value pairs in *szDriverAttributes* is truncated to *cbDrvrAttrMax* – 1 bytes.

Returns

SQL_SUCCESS, SQL_SUCCESS_WITH_INFO, SQL_NO_DATA_FOUND, SQL_ERROR, or SQL_INVALID_HANDLE.

Diagnostics

When **SQLDrivers** returns either SQL_ERROR or SQL_SUCCESS_WITH_INFO, an associated SQLSTATE value may be obtained by calling **SQLError**. The following table lists the SQLSTATE values commonly returned by **SQLDrivers** and explains each one in the context of this function; the notation "(DM)" precedes the descriptions of SQLSTATEs returned by the Driver Manager. The return code associated with each SQLSTATE value is SQL_ERROR, unless noted otherwise.

SQLSTATE	Error	Description
01000	General warning	(DM) Driver Manager–specific informational message. (Function returns SQL_SUCCESS_WITH_INFO.)
01004	Data truncated	(DM) The buffer *szDriverDesc* was not large enough to return the entire driver description, so the description was truncated. The argument *pcbDriverDesc* contains the length of the entire driver description. (Function returns SQL_SUCCESS_WITH_INFO.)
		(DM) The buffer *szDriverAttributes* was not large enough to return the entire list of attribute value pairs, so the list was truncated. The argument *pcbDrvrAttr* contains the length of the untruncated list of attribute value pairs. (Function returns SQL_SUCCESS_WITH_INFO.)
S1000	General error	(DM) An error occurred for which there was no specific SQLSTATE and for which no implementation-specific SQLSTATE was defined. The error message returned by **SQLError** in the argument *szErrorMsg* describes the error and its cause.

SQLSTATE	Error	Description
S1001	Memory allocation failure	(DM) The Driver Manager was unable to allocate memory required to support execution or completion of the function.
S1090	Invalid string or buffer length	(DM) The value specified for argument *cbDriverDescMax* was less than 0.
		(DM) The value specified for argument *cbDrvrAttrMax* was less than 0 or equal to 1.
S1103	Direction option out of range	(DM) The value specified for the argument *fDirection* was not equal to SQL_FETCH_FIRST or SQL_FETCH_NEXT.

Comments   **SQLDrivers** returns the driver description in the *szDriverDesc* argument. It returns additional information about the driver in the *szDriverAttributes* argument as a list of keyword-value pairs. Each pair is terminated with a null byte, and the entire list is terminated with a null byte (that is, two null bytes mark the end of the list). For example, a dBASE driver might return the following list of attributes ("\0" represents a null byte):

```
FileUsage=1\0FileExtns=*.dbf\0\0
```

If *szDriverAttributes* is not large enough to hold the entire list, the list is truncated, **SQLDrivers** returns SQLSTATE 01004 (Data truncated), and the length of the list (excluding the final null termination byte) is returned in *pcbDrvrAttr*.

Driver attribute keywords are added from the ODBC.INF file when the driver is installed. For more information, see "Structure of the ODBC.INF File" and "Structure of the ODBCINST.INI File" in Chapter 19, "Installing ODBC Software."

An application can call **SQLDrivers** multiple times to retrieve all driver descriptions. The Driver Manager retrieves this information from the ODBCINST.INI file or the registry. When there are no more driver descriptions, **SQLDrivers** returns SQL_NO_DATA_FOUND. If **SQLDrivers** is called with SQL_FETCH_NEXT immediately after it returns SQL_NO_DATA_FOUND, it returns the first driver description.

If SQL_FETCH_NEXT is passed to **SQLDrivers** the very first time it is called, **SQLDrivers** returns the first data source name.

Because **SQLDrivers** is implemented in the Driver Manager, it is supported for all drivers regardless of a particular driver's conformance level.

Related Functions

For information about	See
Discovering and listing values required to connect to a data source	**SQLBrowseConnect** (extension)
Connecting to a data source	**SQLConnect**
Returning data source names	**SQLDataSources** (extension)
Connecting to a data source using a connection string or dialog box	**SQLDriverConnect** (extension)

SQLError

Core

SQLError returns error or status information.

Syntax

RETCODE **SQLError**(*henv, hdbc, hstmt, szSqlState, pfNativeError, szErrorMsg, cbErrorMsgMax, pcbErrorMsg*)

The **SQLError** function accepts the following arguments.

Type	Argument	Use	Description
HENV	*henv*	Input	Environment handle or SQL_NULL_HENV.
HDBC	*hdbc*	Input	Connection handle or SQL_NULL_HDBC.
HSTMT	*hstmt*	Input	Statement handle or SQL_NULL_HSTMT.
UCHAR FAR *	*szSqlState*	Output	SQLSTATE as null-terminated string. For a list of SQLSTATEs, see Appendix A, "ODBC Error Codes."
SDWORD FAR *	*pfNativeError*	Output	Native error code (specific to the data source).
UCHAR FAR *	*szErrorMsg*	Output	Pointer to storage for the error message text.
SWORD	*cbErrorMsgMax*	Input	Maximum length of the *szErrorMsg* buffer. This must be less than or equal to SQL_MAX_MESSAGE_LENGTH − 1.
SWORD FAR *	*pcbErrorMsg*	Output	Pointer to the total number of bytes (excluding the null termination byte) available to return in *szErrorMsg*. If the number of bytes available to return is greater than or equal to *cbErrorMsgMax*, the error message text in *szErrorMsg* is truncated to *cbErrorMsgMax* − 1 bytes.

Returns

SQL_SUCCESS, SQL_SUCCESS_WITH_INFO, SQL_NO_DATA_FOUND, SQL_ERROR, or SQL_INVALID_HANDLE.

Diagnostics

SQLError does not post error values for itself. **SQLError** returns SQL_NO_DATA_FOUND when it is unable to retrieve any error information, (in which case *szSqlState* equals 00000). If **SQLError** cannot access error values for any reason that would normally return SQL_ERROR, **SQLError** returns SQL_ERROR but does not post any error values. If the buffer for the error message is too short, **SQLError** returns SQL_SUCCESS_WITH_INFO but, again, does not return a SQLSTATE value for **SQLError**.

To determine that a truncation occurred in the error message, an application can compare *cbErrorMsgMax* to the actual length of the message text written to *pcbErrorMsg*.

Comments   An application typically calls **SQLError** when a previous call to an ODBC function returns SQL_ERROR or SQL_SUCCESS_WITH_INFO. However, any ODBC function can post zero or more errors each time it is called, so an application can call **SQLError** after any ODBC function call.

SQLError retrieves an error from the data structure associated with the rightmost non-null handle argument. An application requests error information as follows:

- To retrieve errors associated with an environment, the application passes the corresponding *henv* and includes SQL_NULL_HDBC and SQL_NULL_HSTMT in *hdbc* and *hstmt*, respectively. The driver returns the error status of the ODBC function most recently called with the same *henv*.

- To retrieve errors associated with a connection, the application passes the corresponding *hdbc* plus an *hstmt* equal to SQL_NULL_HSTMT. In such a case, the driver ignores the *henv* argument. The driver returns the error status of the ODBC function most recently called with the *hdbc*.

- To retrieve errors associated with a statement, an application passes the corresponding *hstmt*. If the call to **SQLError** contains a valid *hstmt*, the driver ignores the *hdbc* and *henv* arguments. The driver returns the error status of the ODBC function most recently called with the *hstmt*.

- To retrieve multiple errors for a function call, an application calls **SQLError** multiple times. For each error, the driver returns SQL_SUCCESS and removes that error from the list of available errors.

When there is no additional information for the rightmost non-null handle, **SQLError** returns SQL_NO_DATA_FOUND. In this case, *szSqlState* equals 00000 (Success), *pfNativeError* is undefined, *pcbErrorMsg* equals 0, and *szErrorMsg* contains a single null termination byte (unless *cbErrorMsgMax* equals 0).

The Driver Manager stores error information in its *henv*, *hdbc*, and *hstmt* structures. Similarly, the driver stores error information in its *henv*, *hdbc*, and *hstmt* structures. When the application calls **SQLError**, the Driver Manager checks if there are any errors in its structure for the specified handle. If there are errors for the specified handle, it returns the first error; if there are no errors, it calls **SQLError** in the driver.

The Driver Manager can store up to 64 errors with an *henv* and its associated *hdbcs* and *hstmts*. When this limit is reached, the Driver Manager discards any subsequent errors posted on the Driver Manager's *henv*, *hdbcs*, or *hstmts*. The number of errors that a driver can store is driver-dependent.

An error is removed from the structure associated with a handle when **SQLError** is called for that handle and returns that error. All errors stored for a given handle are removed when that handle is used in a subsequent function call. For example, errors on an *hstmt* that were returned by **SQLExecDirect** are removed when **SQLExecDirect** or **SQLTables** is called with that *hstmt*. The errors stored on a given handle are not removed as the result of a call to a function using an associated handle of a different type. For example, errors on an *hdbc* that were returned by **SQLNativeSql** are not removed when **SQLError** or **SQLExecDirect** is called with an *hstmt* associated with that *hdbc*.

For more information about error codes, see Appendix A, "ODBC Error Codes."

Related Functions   None.

SQLExecDirect

Core

SQLExecDirect executes a preparable statement, using the current values of the parameter marker variables if any parameters exist in the statement. **SQLExecDirect** is the fastest way to submit an SQL statement for one-time execution.

Syntax

RETCODE **SQLExecDirect**(*hstmt*, *szSqlStr*, *cbSqlStr*)

The **SQLExecDirect** function uses the following arguments.

Type	Argument	Use	Description
HSTMT	*hstmt*	Input	Statement handle.
UCHAR FAR *	*szSqlStr*	Input	SQL statement to be executed.
SDWORD	*cbSqlStr*	Input	Length of *szSqlStr*.

Returns

SQL_SUCCESS, SQL_SUCCESS_WITH_INFO, SQL_NEED_DATA, SQL_STILL_EXECUTING, SQL_ERROR, or SQL_INVALID_HANDLE.

Diagnostics

When **SQLExecDirect** returns either SQL_ERROR or SQL_SUCCESS_WITH_INFO, an associated SQLSTATE value may be obtained by calling **SQLError**. The following table lists the SQLSTATE values commonly returned by **SQLExecDirect** and explains each one in the context of this function; the notation "(DM)" precedes the descriptions of SQLSTATEs returned by the Driver Manager. The return code associated with each SQLSTATE value is SQL_ERROR, unless noted otherwise.

SQLSTATE	Error	Description
01000	General warning	Driver-specific informational message. (Function returns SQL_SUCCESS_WITH_INFO.)
01004	Data truncated	The argument *szSqlStr* contained an SQL statement that contained a character or binary parameter or literal and the value exceeded the maximum length of the associated table column.
		The argument *szSqlStr* contained an SQL statement that contained a numeric parameter or literal and the fractional part of the value was truncated.
		The argument *szSqlStr* contained an SQL statement that contained a date or time parameter or literal and a timestamp value was truncated.

SQLSTATE	Error	Description
01006	Privilege not revoked	The argument *szSqlStr* contained a **REVOKE** statement and the user did not have the specified privilege. (Function returns SQL_SUCCESS_WITH_INFO.)
01S03	No rows updated or deleted	The argument *szSqlStr* contained a positioned update or delete statement and no rows were updated or deleted. (Function returns SQL_SUCCESS_WITH_INFO.)
01S04	More than one row updated or deleted	The argument *szSqlStr* contained a positioned update or delete statement and more than one row was updated or deleted. (Function returns SQL_SUCCESS_WITH_INFO.)
07001	Wrong number of parameters	The number of parameters specified in **SQLBindParameter** was less than the number of parameters in the SQL statement contained in the argument *szSqlStr*.
08S01	Communication link failure	The communication link between the driver and the data source to which the driver was connected failed before the function completed processing.
21S01	Insert value list does not match column list	The argument *szSqlStr* contained an **INSERT** statement and the number of values to be inserted did not match the degree of the derived table.
21S02	Degree of derived table does not match column list	The argument *szSqlStr* contained a **CREATE VIEW** statement and the number of names specified is not the same degree as the derived table defined by the query specification.
22003	Numeric value out of range	The argument *szSqlStr* contained an SQL statement which contained a numeric parameter or literal and the value caused the whole (as opposed to fractional) part of the number to be truncated when assigned to the associated table column.
22005	Error in assignment	The argument *szSqlStr* contained an SQL statement that contained a parameter or literal and the value was incompatible with the data type of the associated table column.

SQLSTATE	Error	Description
22008	Datetime field overflow	The argument *szSqlStr* contained an SQL statement that contained a date, time, or timestamp parameter or literal and the value was, respectively, an invalid date, time, or timestamp.
22012	Division by zero	The argument *szSqlStr* contained an SQL statement which contained an arithmetic expression which caused division by zero.
23000	Integrity constraint violation	The argument *szSqlStr* contained an SQL statement which contained a parameter or literal. The parameter value was NULL for a column defined as NOT NULL in the associated table column, a duplicate value was supplied for a column constrained to contain only unique values, or some other integrity constraint was violated.
24000	Invalid cursor state	(DM) A cursor was open on the *hstmt* and **SQLFetch** or **SQLExtendedFetch** had been called. A cursor was open on the *hstmt* but **SQLFetch** or **SQLExtendedFetch** had not been called. The argument *szSqlStr* contained a positioned update or delete statement and the cursor was positioned before the start of the result set or after the end of the result set.
34000	Invalid cursor name	The argument *szSqlStr* contained a positioned update or delete statement and the cursor referenced by the statement being executed was not open.
37000	Syntax error or access violation	The argument *szSqlStr* contained an SQL statement that was not preparable or contained a syntax error.
40001	Serialization failure	The transaction to which the SQL statement contained in the argument *szSqlStr* belonged was terminated to prevent deadlock.
42000	Syntax error or access violation	The user did not have permission to execute the SQL statement contained in the argument *szSqlStr*.
IM001	Driver does not support this function	(DM) The driver associated with the *hstmt* does not support the function.

SQLSTATE	Error	Description
S0001	Base table or view already exists	The argument *szSqlStr* contained a **CREATE TABLE** or **CREATE VIEW** statement and the table name or view name specified already exists.
S0002	Table or view not found	The argument *szSqlStr* contained a **DROP TABLE** or a **DROP VIEW** statement and the specified table name or view name did not exist.
		The argument *szSqlStr* contained an **ALTER TABLE** statement and the specified table name did not exist.
		The argument *szSqlStr* contained a **CREATE VIEW** statement and a table name or view name defined by the query specification did not exist.
		The argument *szSqlStr* contained a **CREATE INDEX** statement and the specified table name did not exist.
		The argument *szSqlStr* contained a **GRANT** or **REVOKE** statement and the specified table name or view name did not exist.
		The argument *szSqlStr* contained a **SELECT** statement and a specified table name or view name did not exist.
		The argument *szSqlStr* contained a **DELETE, INSERT**, or **UPDATE** statement and the specified table name did not exist.
		The argument *szSqlStr* contained a **CREATE TABLE** statement and a table specified in a constraint (referencing a table other than the one being created) did not exist.
S0011	Index already exists	The argument *szSqlStr* contained a **CREATE INDEX** statement and the specified index name already existed.
S0012	Index not found	The argument *szSqlStr* contained a **DROP INDEX** statement and the specified index name did not exist.

SQLSTATE	Error	Description
S0021	Column already exists	The argument *szSqlStr* contained an **ALTER TABLE** statement and the column specified in the **ADD** clause is not unique or identifies an existing column in the base table.
S0022	Column not found	The argument *szSqlStr* contained a **CREATE INDEX** statement and one or more of the column names specified in the column list did not exist.
		The argument *szSqlStr* contained a **GRANT** or **REVOKE** statement and a specified column name did not exist.
		The argument *szSqlStr* contained a **SELECT, DELETE, INSERT,** or **UPDATE** statement and a specified column name did not exist.
		The argument *szSqlStr* contained a **CREATE TABLE** statement and a column specified in a constraint (referencing a table other than the one being created) did not exist.
S1000	General error	An error occurred for which there was no specific SQLSTATE and for which no implementation-specific SQLSTATE was defined. The error message returned by **SQLError** in the argument *szErrorMsg* describes the error and its cause.
S1001	Memory allocation failure	The driver was unable to allocate memory required to support execution or completion of the function.
S1008	Operation canceled	Asynchronous processing was enabled for the *hstmt*. The function was called and before it completed execution, **SQLCancel** was called on the *hstmt*. Then the function was called again on the *hstmt*.
		The function was called and, before it completed execution, **SQLCancel** was called on the *hstmt* from a different thread in a multithreaded application.
S1009	Invalid argument value	(DM) The argument *szSqlStr* was a null pointer.

SQLSTATE	Error	Description
S1010	Function sequence error	(DM) An asynchronously executing function (not this one) was called for the *hstmt* and was still executing when this function was called.
		(DM) **SQLExecute**, **SQLExecDirect**, or **SQLSetPos** was called for the *hstmt* and returned SQL_NEED_DATA. This function was called before data was sent for all data-at-execution parameters or columns.
S1090	Invalid string or buffer length	(DM) The argument *cbSqlStr* was less than or equal to 0, but not equal to SQL_NTS.
		A parameter value, set with **SQLBindParameter**, was a null pointer and the parameter length value was not 0, SQL_NULL_DATA, SQL_DATA_AT_EXEC, or less than or equal to SQL_LEN_DATA_AT_EXEC_OFFSET.
		A parameter value, set with **SQLBindParameter**, was not a null pointer and the parameter length value was less than 0, but was not SQL_NTS, SQL_NULL_DATA, SQL_DATA_AT_EXEC, or less than or equal to SQL_LEN_DATA_AT_EXEC_OFFSET.
S1109	Invalid cursor position	The argument *szSqlStr* contained a positioned update or delete statement and the cursor was positioned (by **SQLSetPos** or **SQLExtendedFetch**) on a row for which the value in the *rgfRowStatus* array in **SQLExtendedFetch** was SQL_ROW_DELETED or SQL_ROW_ERROR.
S1C00	Driver not capable	The combination of the current settings of the SQL_CONCURRENCY and SQL_CURSOR_TYPE statement options was not supported by the driver or data source.
S1T00	Timeout expired	The timeout period expired before the data source returned the result set. The timeout period is set through **SQLSetStmtOption**, SQL_QUERY_TIMEOUT.

Comments

The application calls **SQLExecDirect** to send an SQL statement to the data source. The driver modifies the statement to use the form of SQL used by the data source, then submits it to the data source. In particular, the driver modifies the escape clauses used to define ODBC-specific SQL. For a description of SQL statement grammar, see "Supporting ODBC Extensions to SQL" in Chapter 14 and Appendix C, "SQL Grammar."

The application can include one or more parameter markers in the SQL statement. To include a parameter marker, the application embeds a question mark (?) into the SQL statement at the appropriate position.

If the SQL statement is a **SELECT** statement, and if the application called **SQLSetCursorName** to associate a cursor with an *hstmt*, then the driver uses the specified cursor. Otherwise, the driver generates a cursor name.

If the data source is in manual-commit mode (requiring explicit transaction initiation), and a transaction has not already been initiated, the driver initiates a transaction before it sends the SQL statement.

If an application uses **SQLExecDirect** to submit a **COMMIT** or **ROLLBACK** statement, it will not be interoperable between DBMS products. To commit or roll back a transaction, call **SQLTransact**.

If **SQLExecDirect** encounters a data-at-execution parameter, it returns SQL_NEED_DATA. The application sends the data using **SQLParamData** and **SQLPutData**. See **SQLBindParameter**, **SQLParamOptions**, **SQLParamData**, and **SQLPutData** for more information.

Code Example

See **SQLBindCol**, **SQLExtendedFetch**, **SQLGetData**, and **SQLProcedures**.

Related Functions

For information about	See
Assigning storage for a column in a result set	**SQLBindCol**
Canceling statement processing	**SQLCancel**
Executing a prepared SQL statement	**SQLExecute**
Fetching a block of data or scrolling through a result set	**SQLExtendedFetch** (extension)
Fetching a row of data	**SQLFetch**
Returning a cursor name	**SQLGetCursorName**
Fetching part or all of a column of data	**SQLGetData** (extension)
Returning the next parameter to send data for	**SQLParamData** (extension)

For information about	See
Preparing a statement for execution	**SQLPrepare**
Sending parameter data at execution time	**SQLPutData** (extension)
Setting a cursor name	**SQLSetCursorName**
Setting a statement option	**SQLSetStmtOption** (extension)
Executing a commit or rollback operation	**SQLTransact**

SQLExecute

Core

SQLExecute executes a prepared statement, using the current values of the parameter marker variables if any parameter markers exist in the statement.

Syntax

RETCODE **SQLExecute**(*hstmt*)

The **SQLExecute** statement accepts the following argument.

Type	Argument	Use	Description
HSTMT	*hstmt*	Input	Statement handle.

Returns

SQL_SUCCESS, SQL_SUCCESS_WITH_INFO, SQL_NEED_DATA, SQL_STILL_EXECUTING, SQL_ERROR, or SQL_INVALID_HANDLE.

Diagnostics

When **SQLExecute** returns either SQL_ERROR or SQL_SUCCESS_WITH_INFO, an associated SQLSTATE value may be obtained by calling **SQLError**. The following table lists the SQLSTATE values commonly returned by **SQLExecute** and explains each one in the context of this function; the notation "(DM)" precedes the descriptions of SQLSTATEs returned by the Driver Manager. The return code associated with each SQLSTATE value is SQL_ERROR, unless noted otherwise.

SQLSTATE	Error	Description
01000	General warning	Driver-specific informational message. (Function returns SQL_SUCCESS_WITH_INFO.)
01004	Data truncated	The prepared statement associated with the *hstmt* contained a character or binary parameter or literal and the value exceeded the maximum length of the associated table column.
		The prepared statement associated with the *hstmt* contained a numeric parameter or literal and the fractional part of the value was truncated.
		The prepared statement associated with the *hstmt* contained a date or time parameter or literal and a timestamp value was truncated.
01006	Privilege not revoked	The prepared statement associated with the *hstmt* was **REVOKE** and the user did not have the specified privilege. (Function returns SQL_SUCCESS_WITH_INFO.)

SQLSTATE	Error	Description
01S03	No rows updated or deleted	The prepared statement associated with the *hstmt* was a positioned update or delete statement and no rows were updated or deleted. (Function returns SQL_SUCCESS_WITH_INFO.)
01S04	More than one row updated or deleted	The prepared statement associated with the *hstmt* was a positioned update or delete statement and more than one row was updated or deleted. (Function returns SQL_SUCCESS_WITH_INFO.)
07001	Wrong number of parameters	The number of parameters specified in **SQLBindParameter** was less than the number of parameters in the prepared statement associated with the *hstmt*.
08S01	Communication link failure	The communication link between the driver and the data source to which the driver was connected failed before the function completed processing.
22003	Numeric value out of range	The prepared statement associated with the *hstmt* contained a numeric parameter and the parameter value caused the whole (as opposed to fractional) part of the number to be truncated when assigned to the associated table column.
22005	Error in assignment	The prepared statement associated with the *hstmt* contained a parameter and the value was incompatible with the data type of the associated table column.
22008	Datetime field overflow	The prepared statement associated with the *hstmt* contained a date, time, or timestamp parameter or literal and the value was, respectively, an invalid date, time, or timestamp.
22012	Division by zero	The prepared statement associated with the *hstmt* contained an arithmetic expression which caused division by zero.
23000	Integrity constraint violation	The prepared statement associated with the *hstmt* contained a parameter. The parameter value was NULL for a column defined as NOT NULL in the associated table column, a duplicate value was supplied for a column constrained to contain only unique values, or some other integrity constraint was violated.

SQLSTATE	Error	Description
24000	Invalid cursor state	(DM) A cursor was open on the *hstmt* and **SQLFetch** or **SQLExtendedFetch** had been called.
		A cursor was open on the *hstmt* but **SQLFetch** or **SQLExtendedFetch** had not been called.
		The prepared statement associated with the *hstmt* contained a positioned update or delete statement and the cursor was positioned before the start of the result set or after the end of the result set.
40001	Serialization failure	The transaction to which the prepared statement associated with the *hstmt* belonged was terminated to prevent deadlock.
42000	Syntax error or access violation	The user did not have permission to execute the prepared statement associated with the *hstmt*.
IM001	Driver does not support this function	(DM) The driver associated with the *hstmt* does not support the function.
S1000	General error	An error occurred for which there was no specific SQLSTATE and for which no implementation-specific SQLSTATE was defined. The error message returned by **SQLError** in the argument *szErrorMsg* describes the error and its cause.
S1001	Memory allocation failure	The driver was unable to allocate memory required to support execution or completion of the function.
S1008	Operation canceled	Asynchronous processing was enabled for the *hstmt*. The function was called and before it completed execution, **SQLCancel** was called on the *hstmt*. Then the function was called again on the *hstmt*.
		The function was called and, before it completed execution, **SQLCancel** was called on the *hstmt* from a different thread in a multithreaded application.

SQLSTATE	Error	Description
S1010	Function sequence error	(DM) An asynchronously executing function (not this one) was called for the *hstmt* and was still executing when this function was called.
		(DM) **SQLExecute, SQLExecDirect,** or **SQLSetPos** was called for the *hstmt* and returned SQL_NEED_DATA. This function was called before data was sent for all data-at-execution parameters or columns.
		(DM) The *hstmt* was not prepared. Either the *hstmt* was not in an executed state, or a cursor was open on the *hstmt* and **SQLFetch** or **SQLExtendedFetch** had been called.
		The *hstmt* was not prepared. It was in an executed state and either no result set was associated with the *hstmt* or **SQLFetch** or **SQLExtendedFetch** had not been called.
S1090	Invalid string or buffer length	A parameter value, set with **SQLBindParameter**, was a null pointer and the parameter length value was not 0, SQL_NULL_DATA, SQL_DATA_AT_EXEC, or less than or equal to SQL_LEN_DATA_AT_EXEC_OFFSET.
		A parameter value, set with **SQLBindParameter**, was not a null pointer and the parameter length value was less than 0, but was not SQL_NTS, SQL_NULL_DATA, or SQL_DATA_AT_EXEC, or less than or equal to SQL_LEN_DATA_AT_EXEC_OFFSET.
S1109	Invalid cursor position	The prepared statement was a positioned update or delete statement and the cursor was positioned (by **SQLSetPos** or **SQLExtendedFetch**) on a row for which the value in the *rgfRowStatus* array in **SQLExtendedFetch** was SQL_ROW_DELETED or SQL_ROW_ERROR.

SQLSTATE	Error	Description
S1C00	Driver not capable	The combination of the current settings of the SQL_CONCURRENCY and SQL_CURSOR_TYPE statement options was not supported by the driver or data source.
S1T00	Timeout expired	The timeout period expired before the data source returned the result set. The timeout period is set through **SQLSetStmtOption**, SQL_QUERY_TIMEOUT.

SQLExecute can return any SQLSTATE that can be returned by **SQLPrepare** based on when the data source evaluates the SQL statement associated with the *hstmt*.

Comments   **SQLExecute** executes a statement prepared by **SQLPrepare**. Once the application processes or discards the results from a call to **SQLExecute**, the application can call **SQLExecute** again with new parameter values.

To execute a **SELECT** statement more than once, the application must call **SQLFreeStmt** with the SQL_CLOSE parameter before reissuing the **SELECT** statement.

If the data source is in manual-commit mode (requiring explicit transaction initiation), and a transaction has not already been initiated, the driver initiates a transaction before it sends the SQL statement.

If an application uses **SQLPrepare** to prepare and **SQLExecute** to submit a **COMMIT** or **ROLLBACK** statement, it will not be interoperable between DBMS products. To commit or roll back a transaction, call **SQLTransact**.

If **SQLExecute** encounters a data-at-execution parameter, it returns SQL_NEED_DATA. The application sends the data using **SQLParamData** and **SQLPutData**. See **SQLBindParameter**, **SQLParamOptions**, **SQLParamData**, and **SQLPutData** for more information.

Code Example   See **SQLBindParameter**, **SQLParamOptions**, **SQLPutData**, and **SQLSetPos**.

Related Functions

For information about	See
Assigning storage for a column in a result set	**SQLBindCol**
Canceling statement processing	**SQLCancel**
Executing an SQL statement	**SQLExecDirect**
Fetching a block of data or scrolling through a result set	**SQLExtendedFetch** (extension)
Fetching a row of data	**SQLFetch**

For information about	See
Freeing a statement handle	**SQLFreeStmt**
Returning a cursor name	**SQLGetCursorName**
Fetching part or all of a column of data	**SQLGetData** (extension)
Returning the next parameter to send data for	**SQLParamData** (extension)
Preparing a statement for execution	**SQLPrepare**
Sending parameter data at execution time	**SQLPutData** (extension)
Setting a cursor name	**SQLSetCursorName**
Setting a statement option	**SQLSetStmtOption** (extension)
Executing a commit or rollback operation	**SQLTransact**

SQLExtendedFetch

ODBC 1.0

Extension Level 2

SQLExtendedFetch extends the functionality of **SQLFetch** in the following ways:

- It returns rowset data (one or more rows), in the form of an array, for each bound column.
- It scrolls through the result set according to the setting of a scroll-type argument.

SQLExtendedFetch works in conjunction with **SQLSetStmtOption**.

To fetch one row of data at a time in a forward direction, an application should call **SQLFetch**.

For more information about scrolling through result sets, see "Using Block and Scrollable Cursors" in Chapter 7, "Retrieving Results."

Syntax

RETCODE **SQLExtendedFetch**(*hstmt, fFetchType, irow, pcrow, rgfRowStatus*)

The **SQLExtendedFetch** function accepts the following arguments:

Type	Argument	Use	Description
HSTMT	*hstmt*	Input	Statement handle.
UWORD	*fFetchType*	Input	Type of fetch. For more information, see the "Comments" section.
SDWORD	*irow*	Input	Number of the row to fetch. For more information, see the "Comments" section.
UDWORD FAR *	*pcrow*	Output	Number of rows actually fetched.
UWORD FAR *	*rgfRowStatus*	Output	An array of status values. For more information, see the "Comments" section.

Returns

SQL_SUCCESS, SQL_SUCCESS_WITH_INFO, SQL_NO_DATA_FOUND, SQL_STILL_EXECUTING, SQL_ERROR, or SQL_INVALID_HANDLE.

Diagnostics

When **SQLExtendedFetch** returns either SQL_ERROR or SQL_SUCCESS_WITH_INFO, an associated SQLSTATE value may be obtained by calling **SQLError**. The following table lists the SQLSTATE values commonly returned by **SQLExtendedFetch** and explains each one in the context of this function; the notation "(DM)" precedes the descriptions of SQLSTATEs returned by the Driver Manager. The return code associated with each SQLSTATE value is SQL_ERROR, unless noted otherwise.

SQLSTATE	Error	Description
01000	General warning	Driver-specific informational message. (Function returns SQL_SUCCESS_WITH_INFO.)
01004	Data truncated	The data returned for one or more columns was truncated. String values are right truncated. For numeric values, the fractional part of number was truncated. (Function returns SQL_SUCCESS_WITH_INFO.)
01S01	Error in row	An error occurred while fetching one or more rows. (Function returns SQL_SUCCESS_WITH_INFO.)
07006	Restricted data type attribute violation	A data value could not be converted to the C data type specified by *fCType* in **SQLBindCol**.
08S01	Communication link failure	The communication link between the driver and the data source to which the driver was connected failed before the function completed processing.
22003	Numeric value out of range	Returning the numeric value (as numeric or string) for one or more columns would have caused the whole (as opposed to fractional) part of the number to be truncated.
		Returning the binary value for one or more columns would have caused a loss of binary significance.
		For more information, see Appendix D, "Data Types."
22012	Division by zero	A value from an arithmetic expression was returned which resulted in division by zero.
24000	Invalid cursor state	The *hstmt* was in an executed state but no result set was associated with the *hstmt*.
40001	Serialization failure	The transaction in which the fetch was executed was terminated to prevent deadlock.
IM001	Driver does not support this function	(DM) The driver associated with the *hdbc* does not support the function.
S1000	General error	An error occurred for which there was no specific SQLSTATE and for which no implementation-specific SQLSTATE was defined. The error message returned by **SQLError** in the argument *szErrorMsg* describes the error and its cause.

SQLSTATE	Error	Description
S1001	Memory allocation failure	The driver was unable to allocate memory required to support execution or completion of the function.
S1002	Invalid column number	A column number specified in the binding for one or more columns was greater than the number of columns in the result set.
		Column 0 was bound with **SQLBindCol** and the SQL_USE_BOOKMARKS statement option was set to SQL_UB_OFF.
S1008	Operation canceled	Asynchronous processing was enabled for the *hstmt*. The function was called and before it completed execution, **SQLCancel** was called on the *hstmt*. Then the function was called again on the *hstmt*.
		The function was called and, before it completed execution, **SQLCancel** was called on the *hstmt* from a different thread in a multithreaded application.
S1010	Function sequence error	(DM) The specified *hstmt* was not in an executed state. The function was called without first calling **SQLExecDirect**, **SQLExecute**, or a catalog function..
		(DM) An asynchronously executing function (not this one) was called for the *hstmt* and was still executing when this function was called.
		(DM) **SQLExecute**, **SQLExecDirect**, or **SQLSetPos** was called for the *hstmt* and returned SQL_NEED_DATA. This function was called before data was sent for all data-at-execution parameters or columns.
		(DM) **SQLExtendedFetch** was called for an *hstmt* after **SQLFetch** was called and before **SQLFreeStmt** was called with the SQL_CLOSE option.
S1106	Fetch type out of range	(DM) The value specified for the argument *fFetchType* was invalid (see "Comments").
		The value of the SQL_CURSOR_TYPE statement option was SQL_CURSOR_FORWARD_ONLY and the value of argument *fFetchType* was not SQL_FETCH_NEXT.

SQLSTATE	Error	Description
S1107	Row value out of range	The value specified with the SQL_CURSOR_TYPE statement option was SQL_CURSOR_KEYSET_DRIVEN, but the value specified with the SQL_KEYSET_SIZE statement option was greater than 0 and less than the value specified with the SQL_ROWSET_SIZE statement option.
S1111	Invalid bookmark value	The argument *fFetchType* was SQL_FETCH_BOOKMARK and the bookmark specified in the *irow* argument was not valid.
S1C00	Driver not capable	Driver or data source does not support the specified fetch type.
		The driver or data source does not support the conversion specified by the combination of the *fCType* in **SQLBindCol** and the SQL data type of the corresponding column. This error only applies when the SQL data type of the column was mapped to a driver-specific SQL data type.
		The argument *fFetchType* was SQL_FETCH_RESUME and the driver supports ODBC 2.0.
S1T00	Timeout expired	The timeout period expired before the data source returned the result set. The timeout period is set through **SQLSetStmtOption**, SQL_QUERY_TIMEOUT.

Comments

SQLExtendedFetch returns one rowset of data to the application. An application cannot mix calls to **SQLExtendedFetch** and **SQLFetch** for the same cursor.

An application specifies the number of rows in the rowset by calling **SQLSetStmtOption** with the SQL_ROWSET_SIZE statement option.

Binding

If any columns in the result set have been bound with **SQLBindCol**, the driver converts the data for the bound columns as necessary and stores it in the locations bound to those columns. The result set can be bound in a column-wise (the default) or row-wise fashion.

Column-Wise Binding

To bind a result set in column-wise fashion, an application specifies SQL_BIND_BY_COLUMN for the SQL_BIND_TYPE statement option. (This is the default value.) For each column to be bound, the application:

1. Allocates an array of data storage buffers. The array has as many elements as there are rows in the rowset, plus an additional element if the application will search for key values or append new rows of data. Each buffer's size is the maximum size of the C data that can be returned for the column. For example, when the C data type is SQL_C_DEFAULT, each buffer's size is the column length. When the C data type is SQL_C_CHAR, each buffer's size is the display size of the data. For more information, see "Converting Data from SQL to C Data Types" and "Precision, Scale, Length, and Display Size" in Appendix D, "Data Types."

2. Allocates an array of SDWORDs to hold the number of bytes available to return for each row in the column. The array has as many elements as there are rows in the rowset.

3. Calls **SQLBindCol**:

   - The *rgbValue* argument specifies the address of the data storage array.

   - The *cbValueMax* argument specifies the size of each buffer in the data storage array.

   - The *pcbValue* argument specifies the address of the number-of-bytes array.

When the application calls **SQLExtendedFetch**, the driver retrieves the data and the number of bytes available to return and stores them in the buffers allocated by the application:

- For each bound column, the driver stores the data in the *rgbValue* buffer bound to the column. It stores the first row of data at the start of the buffer and each subsequent row of data at an offset of *cbValueMax* bytes from the data for the previous row.

- For each bound column, the driver stores the number of bytes available to return in the *pcbValue* buffer bound to the column. This is the number of bytes available prior to calling **SQLExtendedFetch**. (If the number of bytes available to return cannot be determined in advance, the driver sets *pcbValue* to SQL_NO_TOTAL. If the data for the column is NULL, the driver sets *pcbValue* to SQL_NULL_DATA.) It stores the number of bytes available to return for the first row at the start of the buffer and the number of bytes available to return for each subsequent row at an offset of **sizeof(SDWORD)** from the value for the previous row.

Row-Wise Binding

To bind a result set in row-wise fashion, an application:

1. Declares a structure that can hold a single row of retrieved data and the associated data lengths. For each bound column, the structure contains one field for the data and one SDWORD field for the number of bytes available to return. The data field's size is the maximum size of the C data that can be returned for the column.

2. Calls **SQLSetStmtOption** with *fOption* set to SQL_BIND_TYPE and *vParam* set to the size of the structure.

3. Allocates an array of these structures. The array has as many elements as there are rows in the rowset, plus an additional element if the application will search for key values or append new rows of data.

4. Calls **SQLBindCol** for each column to be bound:

   - The *rgbValue* argument specifies the address of the column's data field in the first array element.

   - The *cbValueMax* argument specifies the size of the column's data field.

   - The *pcbValue* argument specifies the address of the column's number-of-bytes field in the first array element.

When the application calls **SQLExtendedFetch**, the driver retrieves the data and the number of bytes available to return and stores them in the buffers allocated by the application:

- For each bound column, the driver stores the first row of data at the address specified by *rgbValue* for the column and each subsequent row of data at an offset of *vParam* bytes from the data for the previous row.

- For each bound column, the driver stores the number of bytes available to return for the first row at the address specified by *pcbValue* and the number of bytes available to return for each subsequent row at an offset of *vParam* bytes from the value for the previous row. This is the number of bytes available prior to calling **SQLExtendedFetch**. (If the number of bytes available to return cannot be determined in advance, the driver sets *pcbValue* to SQL_NO_TOTAL. If the data for the column is NULL, the driver sets *pcbValue* to SQL_NULL_DATA.)

Positioning the Cursor

The following operations require a cursor position:

- Positioned update and delete statements.

- Calls to **SQLGetData**.

- Calls to **SQLSetPos** with the SQL_DELETE, SQL_REFRESH, and SQL_UPDATE options.

An application can specify a cursor position when it calls **SQLSetPos**. Before it executes a positioned update or delete statement or calls **SQLGetData**, the application must position the cursor by calling **SQLExtendedFetch** to retrieve a rowset; the cursor points to the first row in the rowset. To position the cursor to a different row in the rowset, the application calls **SQLSetPos**.

The following table shows the rowset and return code returned when the application requests different rowsets.

Requested Rowset	Return Code	Cursor Position	Returned Rowset
Before start of result set	SQL_NO_DATA_FOUND	Before start of result set	None. The contents of the rowset buffers are undefined.
Overlaps start of result set	SQL_SUCCESS	Row 1 of rowset	First rowset in result set.
Within result set	SQL_SUCCESS	Row 1 of rowset	Requested rowset.
Overlaps end of result set	SQL_SUCCESS	Row 1 of rowset	For rows in the rowset that overlap the result set, data is returned. For rows in the rowset outside the result set, the contents of the *rgbValue* and *pcbValue* buffers are undefined and the *rgfRowStatus* array contains SQL_ROW_NOROW.
After end of result set	SQL_NO_DATA_FOUND	After end of result set	None. The contents of the rowset buffers are undefined.

For example, suppose a result set has 100 rows and the rowset size is 5. The following table shows the rowset and return code returned by **SQLExtendedFetch** for different values of *irow* when the fetch type is SQL_FETCH_RELATIVE:

Current Rowset	*irow*	Return Code	New Rowset
1 to 5	–5	SQL_NO_DATA_FOUND	None.
1 to 5	–3	SQL_SUCCESS	1 to 5
96 to 100	5	SQL_NO_DATA_FOUND	None.
96 to 100	3	SQL_SUCCESS	99 and 100. For rows 3, 4, and 5 in the rowset, the *rgfRowStatusArray* is set to SQL_ROW_NOROW.

Before **SQLExtendedFetch** is called the first time, the cursor is positioned before the start of the result set.

For the purpose of moving the cursor, deleted rows (that is, rows with an entry in the *rgfRowStatus* array of SQL_ROW_DELETED) are treated no differently than other rows. For example, calling **SQLExtendedFetch** with *fFetchType* set to

SQL_FETCH_ABSOLUTE and *irow* set to 15 returns the rowset starting at row 15, even if the *rgfRowStatus* array for row 15 is SQL_ROW_DELETED.

Processing Errors

If an error occurs that pertains to the entire rowset, such as SQLSTATE S1T00 (Timeout expired), the driver returns SQL_ERROR and the appropriate SQLSTATE. The contents of the rowset buffers are undefined and the cursor position is unchanged.

If an error occurs that pertains to a single row, the driver:

- Sets the element in the *rgfRowStatus* array for the row to SQL_ROW_ERROR.
- Posts SQLSTATE 01S01 (Error in row) in the error queue.
- Posts zero or more additional SQLSTATEs for the error after SQLSTATE 01S01 (Error in row) in the error queue.

After it has processed the error or warning, the driver continues the operation for the remaining rows in the rowset and returns SQL_SUCCESS_WITH_INFO. Thus, for each error that pertains to a single row, the error queue contains SQLSTATE 01S01 (Error in row) followed by zero or more additional SQLSTATEs.

After it has processed the error, the driver fetches the remaining rows in the rowset and returns SQL_SUCCESS_WITH_INFO. Thus, for each row that returned an error, the error queue contains SQLSTATE 01S01 (Error in row) followed by zero or more additional SQLSTATEs.

If the rowset contains rows that have already been fetched, the driver is not required to return SQLSTATEs for errors that occurred when the rows were first fetched. It is, however, required to return SQLSTATE 01S01 (Error in row) for each row in which an error originally occurred and to return SQL_SUCCESS_WITH_INFO. For example, a static cursor that maintains a cache might cache row status information (so it can determine which rows contain errors) but might not cache the SQLSTATE associated with those errors.

Error rows do not affect relative cursor movements. For example, suppose the result set size is 100 and the rowset size is 10. If the current rowset is rows 11 through 20 and the element in the *rgfRowStatus* array for row 11 is SQL_ROW_ERROR, calling **SQLExtendedFetch** with the SQL_FETCH_NEXT fetch type still returns rows 21 through 30.

If the driver returns any warnings, such as SQLSTATE 01004 (Data truncated), it returns warnings that apply to the entire rowset or to unknown rows in the rowset before it returns error information applying to specific rows. It returns warnings for specific rows along with any other error information about those rows.

fFetchType Argument

The *fFetchType* argument specifies how to move through the result set. It is one of the following values:

SQL_FETCH_NEXT	SQL_FETCH_ABSOLUTE
SQL_FETCH_FIRST	SQL_FETCH_RELATIVE
SQL_FETCH_LAST	SQL_FETCH_BOOKMARK
SQL_FETCH_PRIOR	

If the value of the SQL_CURSOR_TYPE statement option is SQL_CURSOR_FORWARD_ONLY, the *fFetchType* argument must be SQL_FETCH_NEXT.

Note In ODBC 1.0, **SQLExtendedFetch** supported the SQL_FETCH_RESUME fetch type. In ODBC 2.0, SQL_FETCH_RESUME is obsolete and the Driver Manager returns SQLSTATE S1C00 (Driver not capable) if an application specifies it for an ODBC 2.0 driver.

The SQL_FETCH_BOOKMARK fetch type was introduced in ODBC 2.0; the Driver Manager returns SQLSTATE S1106 (Fetch type out of range) if it is specified for an ODBC 1.0 driver.

Moving by Row Position

SQLExtendedFetch supports the following values of the *fFetchType* argument to move relative to the current rowset:

fFetchType Argument	Action
SQL_FETCH_NEXT	The driver returns the next rowset. If the cursor is positioned before the start of the result set, this is equivalent to SQL_FETCH_FIRST.
SQL_FETCH_PRIOR	The driver returns the prior rowset. If the cursor is positioned after the end of the result set, this is equivalent to SQL_FETCH_LAST.
SQL_FETCH_RELATIVE	The driver returns the rowset *irow* rows from the start of the current rowset. If *irow* equals 0, the driver refreshes the current rowset. If the cursor is positioned before the start of the result set and *irow* is greater than 0 or if the cursor is positioned after the end of the result set and *irow* is less than 0, this is equivalent to SQL_FETCH_ABSOLUTE.

It supports the following values of the *fFetchType* argument to move to an absolute position in the result set:

fFetchType Argument	Action
SQL_FETCH_FIRST	The driver returns the first rowset in the result set.
SQL_FETCH_LAST	The driver returns the last complete rowset in the result set.
SQL_FETCH_ABSOLUTE	If *irow* is greater than 0, the driver returns the rowset starting at row *irow*.
	If *irow* equals 0, the driver returns SQL_NO_DATA_FOUND and the cursor is positioned before the start of the result set.
	If *irow* is less than 0, the driver returns the rowset starting at row $n+irow+1$, where *n* is the number of rows in the result set. For example, if *irow* is –1, the driver returns the rowset starting at the last row in the result set. If the result set size is 10 and *irow* is –10, the driver returns the rowset starting at the first row in the result set.

Positioning to a Bookmark

When an application calls **SQLExtendedFetch** with the
SQL_FETCH_BOOKMARK fetch type, the driver retrieves the rowset starting
with the row specified by the bookmark in the *irow* argument.

To inform the driver that it will use bookmarks, the application calls
SQLSetStmtOption with the SQL_USE_BOOKMARKS option before opening
the cursor. To retrieve the bookmark for a row, the application either positions the
cursor on the row and calls **SQLGetStmtOption** with the
SQL_GET_BOOKMARK option, or retrieves the bookmark from column 0 of the
result set. If the application retrieves a bookmark from column 0 of the result set,
it must set *fCType* in **SQLBindCol** or **SQLGetData** to SQL_C_BOOKMARK.
The application stores the bookmarks for those rows in each rowset to which it
will return later.

Bookmarks are 32-bit binary values; if a bookmark requires more than 32 bits,
such as when it is a key value, the driver maps the bookmarks requested by the
application to 32-bit binary values. The 32-bit binary values are then returned to
the application. Because this mapping may require considerable memory,
applications should only bind column 0 of the result set if they will actually use
bookmarks for most rows. Otherwise, applications should call
SQLGetStmtOption with the SQL_GET_BOOKMARK statement option or call
SQLGetData for column 0.

irow Argument

For the SQL_FETCH_ABSOLUTE fetch type, **SQLExtendedFetch** returns the
rowset starting at the row number specified by the *irow* argument.

For the SQL_FETCH_RELATIVE fetch type, **SQLExtendedFetch** returns the
rowset starting *irow* rows from the first row in the current rowset.

For the SQL_FETCH_BOOKMARK fetch type, the *irow* argument specifies the bookmark that marks the first row in the requested rowset.

The *irow* argument is ignored for the SQL_FETCH_NEXT, SQL_FETCH_PRIOR, SQL_FETCH_FIRST, and SQL_FETCH_LAST, fetch types.

rgfRowStatus Argument

In the *rgfRowStatus* array, **SQLExtendedFetch** returns any changes in status to each row since it was last retrieved from the data source. Rows may be unchanged (SQL_ROW_SUCCESS), updated (SQL_ROW_UPDATED), deleted (SQL_ROW_DELETED), added (SQL_ROW_ADDED), or were unretrievable due to an error (SQL_ROW_ERROR). For static cursors, this information is available for all rows. For keyset, mixed, and dynamic cursors, this information is only available for rows in the keyset; the driver does not save data outside the keyset and therefore cannot compare the newly retrieved data to anything.

Note Some drivers cannot detect changes to data. To determine whether a driver can detect changes to refetched rows, an application calls **SQLGetInfo** with the SQL_ROW_UPDATES option.

The number of elements must equal the number of rows in the rowset (as defined by the SQL_ROWSET_SIZE statement option). If the number of rows fetched is less than the number of elements in the status array, the driver sets remaining status elements to SQL_ROW_NOROW.

When an application calls **SQLSetPos** with *fOption* set to SQL_DELETE or SQL_UPDATE, **SQLSetPos** changes the *rgfRowStatus* array for the changed row to SQL_ROW_DELETED or SQL_ROW_UPDATED.

Note For keyset, mixed, and dynamic cursors, if a key value is updated, the row of data is considered to have been deleted and a new row added.

Code Example   The following two examples show how an application could use column-wise or row-wise binding to bind storage locations to the same result set.

For more code examples, see **SQLSetPos**.

Column-Wise Binding

In the following example, an application declares storage locations for column-wise bound data and the returned numbers of bytes. Because column-wise binding is the default, there is no need, as in the row-wise binding example, to request column-wise binding with **SQLSetStmtOption**. However, the application does call **SQLSetStmtOption** to specify the number of rows in the rowset.

The application then executes a **SELECT** statement to return a result set of the employee names and birthdays, which is sorted by birthday. It calls **SQLBindCol** to bind the columns of data, passing the addresses of storage locations for both the data and the returned numbers of bytes. Finally, the application fetches the rowset data with **SQLExtendedFetch** and prints each employee's name and birthday.

```
#define ROWS 100
#define NAME_LEN 30
#define BDAY_LEN 11

UCHAR     szName[ROWS][NAME_LEN], szBirthday[ROWS][BDAY_LEN];
SWORD     sAge[ROWS];
SDWORD    cbName[ROWS], cbAge[ROWS], cbBirthday[ROWS];

UDWORD    crow, irow;
UWORD     rgfRowStatus[ROWS];

SQLSetStmtOption(hstmt, SQL_CONCURRENCY, SQL_CONCUR_READ_ONLY);
SQLSetStmtOption(hstmt, SQL_CURSOR_TYPE, SQL_CURSOR_KEYSET_DRIVEN);
SQLSetStmtOption(hstmt, SQL_ROWSET_SIZE, ROWS);
retcode = SQLExecDirect(hstmt,
            "SELECT NAME, AGE, BIRTHDAY FROM EMPLOYEE ORDER BY 3, 2, 1",
            SQL_NTS);

if (retcode == SQL_SUCCESS) {
    SQLBindCol(hstmt, 1, SQL_C_CHAR, szName, NAME_LEN, cbName);
    SQLBindCol(hstmt, 2, SQL_C_SSHORT, sAge, 0, cbAge);
    SQLBindCol(hstmt, 3, SQL_C_CHAR, szBirthday, BDAY_LEN,
            cbBirthday);

    /* Fetch the rowset data and print each row. */
    /* On an error, display a message and exit.  */

    while (TRUE) {
        retcode = SQLExtendedFetch(hstmt, SQL_FETCH_NEXT, 1, &crow,
                            rgfRowStatus);
        if (retcode == SQL_ERROR || retcode == SQL_SUCCESS_WITH_INFO) {
            show_error();
        }
        if (retcode == SQL_SUCCESS || retcode == SQL_SUCCESS_WITH_INFO){
            for (irow = 0; irow < crow; irow++) {
                if (rgfRowStatus[irow] != SQL_ROW_DELETED &&
                    rgfRowStatus[irow] != SQL_ROW_ERROR)
                    fprintf(out, "%-*s  %-2d  %*s",
                            NAME_LEN-1, szName[irow], sAge[irow],
                            BDAY_LEN-1, szBirthday[irow]);
            }
        } else {
            break;
        }
    }
}
```

Row-Wise Binding

In the following example, an application declares an array of structures to hold row-wise bound data and the returned numbers of bytes. Using **SQLSetStmtOption**, it requests row-wise binding and passes the size of the structure to the driver. The driver will use this size to find successive storage locations in the array of structures. Using **SQLSetStmtOption**, it specifies the size of the rowset.

The application then executes a **SELECT** statement to return a result set of the employee names and birthdays, which is sorted by birthday. It calls **SQLBindCol** to bind the columns of data, passing the addresses of storage locations for both the data and the returned numbers of bytes. Finally, the application fetches the rowset data with **SQLExtendedFetch** and prints each employee's name and birthday.

```
#define ROWS 100
#define NAME_LEN 30
#define BDAY_LEN 11

typedef struct {
    UCHAR      szName[NAME_LEN];
    SDWORD     cbName;
    SWORD      sAge;
    SDWORD     cbAge;
    UCHAR      szBirthday[BDAY_LEN];
    SDWORD     cbBirthday;
    }  EmpTable;

EmpTable rget[ROWS];
UDWORD   crow, irow;
UWORD    rgfRowStatus[ROWS];

SQLSetStmtOption(hstmt, SQL_BIND_TYPE, sizeof(EmpTable));
SQLSetStmtOption(hstmt, SQL_CONCURRENCY, SQL_CONCUR_READ_ONLY);
SQLSetStmtOption(hstmt, SQL_CURSOR_TYPE, SQL_CURSOR_KEYSET_DRIVEN);
SQLSetStmtOption(hstmt, SQL_ROWSET_SIZE, ROWS);
retcode = SQLExecDirect(hstmt,
            "SELECT NAME, AGE, BIRTHDAY FROM EMPLOYEE ORDER BY 3, 2, 1",
            SQL_NTS);

if (retcode == SQL_SUCCESS) {
    SQLBindCol(hstmt, 1, SQL_C_CHAR, rget[0].szName, NAME_LEN,
            &rget[0].cbName);
    SQLBindCol(hstmt, 2, SQL_C_SSHORT, &rget[0].sAge, 0,
            &rget[0].cbAge);
    SQLBindCol(hstmt, 3, SQL_C_CHAR, rget[0].szBirthday, BDAY_LEN,
            &rget[0].cbBirthday);
```

```
                    /* Fetch the rowset data and print each row. */
                    /* On an error, display a message and exit.  */

                    while (TRUE) {
                        retcode = SQLExtendedFetch(hstmt, SQL_FETCH_NEXT, 1, &crow,
                                              rgfRowStatus);
                        if (retcode == SQL_ERROR || retcode == SQL_SUCCESS_WITH_INFO) {
                            show_error();
                        }
                        if (retcode == SQL_SUCCESS || retcode == SQL_SUCCESS_WITH_INFO){
                            for (irow = 0; irow < crow; irow++) {
                                if (rgfRowStatus[irow] != SQL_ROW_DELETED &&
                                    rgfRowStatus[irow] != SQL_ROW_ERROR)
                                    fprintf(out, "%-*s  %-2d  %*s",
                                        NAME_LEN-1, rget[irow].szName, rget[irow].sAge,
                                        BDAY_LEN-1, rget[irow].szBirthday);
                            }
                        } else {
                            break;
                        }
                    }
                }
```

Related Functions	For information about	See
	Assigning storage for a column in a result set	**SQLBindCol**
	Canceling statement processing	**SQLCancel**
	Returning information about a column in a result set	**SQLDescribeCol**
	Executing an SQL statement	**SQLExecDirect**
	Executing a prepared SQL statement	**SQLExecute**
	Returning the number of result set columns	**SQLNumResultCols**
	Positioning the cursor in a rowset	**SQLSetPos** (extension)
	Setting a statement option	**SQLSetStmtOption** (extension)

SQLFetch

Core

SQLFetch fetches a row of data from a result set. The driver returns data for all columns that were bound to storage locations with **SQLBindCol**.

Syntax

RETCODE **SQLFetch**(*hstmt*)

The **SQLFetch** function accepts the following argument.

Type	Argument	Use	Description
HSTMT	*hstmt*	Input	Statement handle.

Returns

SQL_SUCCESS, SQL_SUCCESS_WITH_INFO, SQL_NO_DATA_FOUND, SQL_STILL_EXECUTING, SQL_ERROR, or SQL_INVALID_HANDLE.

Diagnostics

When **SQLFetch** returns either SQL_ERROR or SQL_SUCCESS_WITH_INFO, an associated SQLSTATE value may be obtained by calling **SQLError**. The following table lists the SQLSTATE values commonly returned by **SQLFetch** and explains each one in the context of this function; the notation "(DM)" precedes the descriptions of SQLSTATEs returned by the Driver Manager. The return code associated with each SQLSTATE value is SQL_ERROR, unless noted otherwise.

SQLSTATE	Error	Description
01000	General warning	Driver-specific informational message. (Function returns SQL_SUCCESS_WITH_INFO.)
01004	Data truncated	The data returned for one or more columns was truncated. String values are right truncated. For numeric values, the fractional part of number was truncated. (Function returns SQL_SUCCESS_WITH_INFO.)
07006	Restricted data type attribute violation	The data value could not be converted to the data type specified by *fCType* in **SQLBindCol**.
08S01	Communication link failure	The communication link between the driver and the data source to which the driver was connected failed before the function completed processing.

SQLSTATE	Error	Description
22003	Numeric value out of range	Returning the numeric value (as numeric or string) for one or more columns would have caused the whole (as opposed to fractional) part of the number to be truncated.
		Returning the binary value for one or more columns would have caused a loss of binary significance.
		For more information, see "Converting Data from SQL to C Data Types" in Appendix D, "Data Types."
22012	Division by zero	A value from an arithmetic expression was returned which resulted in division by zero.
24000	Invalid cursor state	The *hstmt* was in an executed state but no result set was associated with the *hstmt*.
40001	Serialization failure	The transaction in which the fetch was executed was terminated to prevent deadlock.
IM001	Driver does not support this function	(DM) The driver associated with the *hstmt* does not support the function.
S1000	General error	An error occurred for which there was no specific SQLSTATE and for which no implementation-specific SQLSTATE was defined. The error message returned by **SQLError** in the argument *szErrorMsg* describes the error and its cause.
S1001	Memory allocation failure	The driver was unable to allocate memory required to support execution or completion of the function.
S1002	Invalid column number	A column number specified in the binding for one or more columns was greater than the number of columns in the result set.
		A column number specified in the binding for a column was 0; **SQLFetch** cannot be used to retrieve bookmarks.
S1008	Operation canceled	Asynchronous processing was enabled for the *hstmt*. The function was called and before it completed execution, **SQLCancel** was called on the *hstmt*. Then the function was called again on the *hstmt*.
		The function was called and, before it completed execution, **SQLCancel** was called on the *hstmt* from a different thread in a multithreaded application.

SQLSTATE	Error	Description
S1010	Function sequence error	(DM) The specified *hstmt* was not in an executed state. The function was called without first calling **SQLExecDirect**, **SQLExecute**, or a catalog function..
		(DM) An asynchronously executing function (not this one) was called for the *hstmt* and was still executing when this function was called.
		(DM) **SQLExecute**, **SQLExecDirect**, or **SQLSetPos** was called for the *hstmt* and returned SQL_NEED_DATA. This function was called before data was sent for all data-at-execution parameters or columns.
		(DM) **SQLExtendedFetch** was called for an *hstmt* after **SQLFetch** was called and before **SQLFreeStmt** was called with the SQL_CLOSE option.
S1C00	Driver not capable	The driver or data source does not support the conversion specified by the combination of the *fCType* in **SQLBindCol** and the SQL data type of the corresponding column. This error only applies when the SQL data type of the column was mapped to a driver-specific SQL data type.
S1T00	Timeout expired	The timeout period expired before the data source returned the result set. The timeout period is set through **SQLSetStmtOption**, SQL_QUERY_TIMEOUT.

Comments

SQLFetch positions the cursor on the next row of the result set. Before **SQLFetch** is called the first time, the cursor is positioned before the start of the result set. When the cursor is positioned on the last row of the result set, **SQLFetch** returns SQL_NO_DATA_FOUND and the cursor is positioned after the end of the result set. An application cannot mix calls to **SQLExtendedFetch** and **SQLFetch** for the same cursor.

If the application called **SQLBindCol** to bind columns, **SQLFetch** stores data into the locations specified by the calls to **SQLBindCol**. If the application does not call **SQLBindCol** to bind any columns, **SQLFetch** doesn't return any data; it just moves the cursor to the next row. An application can call **SQLGetData** to retrieve data that is not bound to a storage location.

The driver manages cursors during the fetch operation and places each value of a bound column into the associated storage. The driver follows these guidelines when performing a fetch operation:

- **SQLFetch** accesses column data in left-to-right order.
- After each fetch, *pcbValue* (specified in **SQLBindCol**) contains the number of bytes available to return for the column. This is the number of bytes available prior to calling **SQLFetch**. If the number of bytes available to return cannot be determined in advance, the driver sets *pcbValue* to SQL_NO_TOTAL. (If SQL_MAX_LENGTH has been specified with **SQLSetStmtOption** and the number of bytes available to return is greater than SQL_MAX_LENGTH, *pcbValue* contains SQL_MAX_LENGTH.)

Note The SQL_MAX_LENGTH statement option is intended to reduce network traffic and may not be supported by all drivers. To guarantee that data is truncated, an application should allocate a buffer of the desired size and specify this size in the *cbValueMax* argument.

- If *rgbValue* is not large enough to hold the entire result, the driver stores part of the value and returns SQL_SUCCESS_WITH_INFO. A subsequent call to **SQLError** indicates that a truncation occurred. The application can compare *pcbValue* to *cbValueMax* (specified in **SQLBindCol**) to determine which column or columns were truncated. If *pcbValue* is greater than or equal to *cbValueMax*, then truncation occurred.
- If the data value for the column is NULL, the driver stores SQL_NULL_DATA in *pcbValue*.

SQLFetch is valid only after a call that returns a result set.

For information about conversions allowed by **SQLBindCol** and **SQLGetData**, see "Converting Data from SQL to C Data Types" in Appendix D, "Data Types."

Code Example   See **SQLBindCol**, **SQLColumns**, **SQLGetData**, and **SQLProcedures**.

Related Functions

For information about	See
Assigning storage for a column in a result set	**SQLBindCol**
Canceling statement processing	**SQLCancel**
Returning information about a column in a result set	**SQLDescribeCol**
Executing an SQL statement	**SQLExecDirect**
Executing a prepared SQL statement	**SQLExecute**
Fetching a block of data or scrolling through a result set	**SQLExtendedFetch** (extension)
Freeing a statement handle	**SQLFreeStmt**
Fetching part or all of a column of data	**SQLGetData** (extension)
Returning the number of result set columns	**SQLNumResultCols**
Preparing a statement for execution	**SQLPrepare**

SQLForeignKeys

Extension Level 2

SQLForeignKeys can return:

- A list of foreign keys in the specified table (columns in the specified table that refer to primary keys in other tables).
- A list of foreign keys in other tables that refer to the primary key in the specified table.

The driver returns each list as a result set on the specified *hstmt*.

Syntax

RETCODE **SQLForeignKeys**(*hstmt, szPkTableQualifier, cbPkTableQualifier, szPkTableOwner, cbPkTableOwner, szPkTableName, cbPkTableName, szFkTableQualifier, cbFkTableQualifier, szFkTableOwner, cbFkTableOwner, szFkTableName, cbFkTableName*)

The **SQLForeignKeys** function accepts the following arguments.

Type	Argument	Use	Description
HSTMT	*hstmt*	Input	Statement handle.
UCHAR FAR *	*szPkTableQualifier*	Input	Primary key table qualifier. If a driver supports qualifiers for some tables but not for others, such as when the driver retrieves data from different DBMSs, an empty string ("") denotes those tables that do not have qualifiers.
SWORD	*cbPkTableQualifier*	Input	Length of *szPkTableQualifier*.
UCHAR FAR *	*szPkTableOwner*	Input	Primary key owner name. If a driver supports owners for some tables but not for others, such as when the driver retrieves data from different DBMSs, an empty string ("") denotes those tables that do not have owners.
SWORD	*cbPkTableOwner*	Input	Length of *szPkTableOwner*.
UCHAR FAR *	*szPkTableName*	Input	Primary key table name.
SWORD	*cbPkTableName*	Input	Length of *szPkTableName*.

Type	Argument	Use	Description
UCHAR FAR *	*szFkTableQualifier*	Input	Foreign key table qualifier. If a driver supports qualifiers for some tables but not for others, such as when the driver retrieves data from different DBMSs, an empty string ("") denotes those tables that do not have qualifiers.
SWORD	*cbFkTableQualifier*	Input	Length of *szFkTableQualifier*.
UCHAR FAR *	*szFkTableOwner*	Input	Foreign key owner name. If a driver supports owners for some tables but not for others, such as when the driver retrieves data from different DBMSs, an empty string ("") denotes those tables that do not have owners.
SWORD	*cbFkTableOwner*	Input	Length of *szFkTableOwner*.
UCHAR FAR *	*szFkTableName*	Input	Foreign key table name.
SWORD	*cbFkTableName*	Input	Length of *szFkTableName*.

Returns

SQL_SUCCESS, SQL_SUCCESS_WITH_INFO, SQL_STILL_EXECUTING, SQL_ERROR, or SQL_INVALID_HANDLE.

Diagnostics

When **SQLForeignKeys** returns SQL_ERROR or SQL_SUCCESS_WITH_INFO, an associated SQLSTATE value may be obtained by calling **SQLError**. The following table lists the SQLSTATE values commonly returned by **SQLForeignKeys** and explains each one in the context of this function; the notation "(DM)" precedes the descriptions of SQLSTATEs returned by the Driver Manager. The return code associated with each SQLSTATE value is SQL_ERROR, unless noted otherwise.

SQLSTATE	Error	Description
01000	General warning	Driver-specific informational message. (Function returns SQL_SUCCESS_WITH_INFO.)
08S01	Communication link failure	The communication link between the driver and the data source to which the driver was connected failed before the function completed processing.

SQLSTATE	Error	Description
24000	Invalid cursor state	(DM) A cursor was open on the *hstmt* and **SQLFetch** or **SQLExtendedFetch** had been called.
		A cursor was open on the *hstmt* but **SQLFetch** or **SQLExtendedFetch** had not been called.
IM001	Driver does not support this function	(DM) The driver associated with the *hstmt* does not support the function.
S1000	General error	An error occurred for which there was no specific SQLSTATE and for which no implementation-specific SQLSTATE was defined. The error message returned by **SQLError** in the argument *szErrorMsg* describes the error and its cause.
S1001	Memory allocation failure	The driver was unable to allocate memory required to support execution or completion of the function.
S1008	Operation canceled	Asynchronous processing was enabled for the *hstmt*. The function was called and before it completed execution, **SQLCancel** was called on the *hstmt*. Then the function was called again on the *hstmt*.
		The function was called and, before it completed execution, **SQLCancel** was called on the *hstmt* from a different thread in a multithreaded application.
S1009	Invalid argument value	(DM) The arguments *szPkTableName* and *szFkTableName* were both null pointers.
S1010	Function sequence error	(DM) An asynchronously executing function (not this one) was called for the *hstmt* and was still executing when this function was called.
		(DM) **SQLExecute**, **SQLExecDirect**, or **SQLSetPos** was called for the *hstmt* and returned SQL_NEED_DATA. This function was called before data was sent for all data-at-execution parameters or columns.

SQLSTATE	Error	Description
S1090	Invalid string or buffer length	(DM) The value of one of the name length arguments was less than 0, but not equal to SQL_NTS.
		The value of one of the name length arguments exceeded the maximum length value for the corresponding qualifier or name (see "Comments").
S1C00	Driver not capable	A table qualifier was specified and the driver or data source does not support qualifiers.
		A table owner was specified and the driver or data source does not support owners.
		The combination of the current settings of the SQL_CONCURRENCY and SQL_CURSOR_TYPE statement options was not supported by the driver or data source.
S1T00	Timeout expired	The timeout period expired before the data source returned the result set. The timeout period is set through **SQLSetStmtOption**, SQL_QUERY_TIMEOUT.

Comments

If *szPkTableName* contains a table name, **SQLForeignKeys** returns a result set containing the primary key of the specified table and all of the foreign keys that refer to it.

If *szFkTableName* contains a table name, **SQLForeignKeys** returns a result set containing all of the foreign keys in the specified table and the primary keys (in other tables) to which they refer.

If both *szPkTableName* and *szFkTableName* contain table names, **SQLForeignKeys** returns the foreign keys in the table specified in *szFkTableName* that refer to the primary key of the table specified in *szPkTableName*. This should be one key at most.

SQLForeignKeys returns results as a standard result set. If the foreign keys associated with a primary key are requested, the result set is ordered by FKTABLE_QUALIFIER, FKTABLE_OWNER, FKTABLE_NAME, and KEY_SEQ. If the primary keys associated with a foreign key are requested, the result set is ordered by PKTABLE_QUALIFIER, PKTABLE_OWNER, PKTABLE_NAME, and KEY_SEQ. The following table lists the columns in the result set.

The lengths of VARCHAR columns shown in the table are maximums; the actual lengths depend on the data source. To determine the actual lengths of the TABLE_QUALIFIER, TABLE_OWNER, TABLE_NAME, and

COLUMN_NAME columns, an application can call **SQLGetInfo** with the SQL_MAX_QUALIFIER_NAME_LEN, SQL_MAX_OWNER_NAME_LEN, SQL_MAX_TABLE_NAME_LEN, and SQL_MAX_COLUMN_NAME_LEN options.

Column Name	Data Type	Comments
PKTABLE_QUALIFIER	Varchar(128)	Primary key table qualifier identifier; NULL if not applicable to the data source. If a driver supports qualifiers for some tables but not for others, such as when the driver retrieves data from different DBMSs, it returns an empty string ("") for those tables that do not have qualifiers.
PKTABLE_OWNER	Varchar(128)	Primary key table owner identifier; NULL if not applicable to the data source. If a driver supports owners for some tables but not for others, such as when the driver retrieves data from different DBMSs, it returns an empty string ("") for those tables that do not have owners.
PKTABLE_NAME	Varchar(128) not NULL	Primary key table identifier.
PKCOLUMN_NAME	Varchar(128) not NULL	Primary key column identifier.
FKTABLE_QUALIFIER	Varchar(128)	Foreign key table qualifier identifier; NULL if not applicable to the data source. If a driver supports qualifiers for some tables but not for others, such as when the driver retrieves data from different DBMSs, it returns an empty string ("") for those tables that do not have qualifiers.
FKTABLE_OWNER	Varchar(128)	Foreign key table owner identifier; NULL if not applicable to the data source. If a driver supports owners for some tables but not for others, such as when the driver retrieves data from different DBMSs, it returns an empty string ("") for those tables that do not have owners.
FKTABLE_NAME	Varchar(128) not NULL	Foreign key table identifier.
FKCOLUMN_NAME	Varchar(128) not NULL	Foreign key column identifier.

Column Name	Data Type	Comments
KEY_SEQ	Smallint not NULL	Column sequence number in key (starting with 1).
UPDATE_RULE	Smallint	Action to be applied to the foreign key when the SQL operation is **UPDATE**:
		SQL_CASCADE SQL_RESTRICT SQL_SET_NULL
		NULL if not applicable to the data source.
DELETE_RULE	Smallint	Action to be applied to the foreign key when the SQL operation is **DELETE**:
		SQL_CASCADE SQL_RESTRICT SQL_SET_NULL
		NULL if not applicable to the data source.
FK_NAME	Varchar(128)	Foreign key identifier. NULL if not applicable to the data source.
PK_NAME	Varchar(128)	Primary key identifier. NULL if not applicable to the data source.

Note The FK_NAME and PK_NAME columns were added in ODBC 2.0. ODBC 1.0 drivers may return different, driver-specific columns with the same column numbers.

Code Example

This example uses four tables:

SALES_ORDER	SALES_LINE	CUSTOMER	EMPLOYEE
SALES_ID	SALES_ID	CUSTOMER_ID	EMPLOYEE_ID
CUSTOMER_ID	LINE_NUMBER	CUST_NAME	NAME
EMPLOYEE_ID	PART_ID	ADDRESS	AGE
TOTAL_PRICE	QUANTITY	PHONE	BIRTHDAY
	PRICE		

In the SALES_ORDER table, CUSTOMER_ID identifies the customer to whom the sale has been made. It is a foreign key that refers to CUSTOMER_ID in the CUSTOMER table. EMPLOYEE_ID identifies the employee who made the sale. It is a foreign key that refers to EMPLOYEE_ID in the EMPLOYEE table.

In the SALES_LINE table, SALES_ID identifies the sales order with which the line item is associated. It is a foreign key that refers to SALES_ID in the SALES_ORDER table.

This example calls **SQLPrimaryKeys** to get the primary key of the SALES_ORDER table. The result set will have one row and the significant columns are:

TABLE_NAME	COLUMN_NAME	KEY_SEQ
SALES_ORDER	SALES_ID	1

Next, the example calls **SQLForeignKeys** to get the foreign keys in other tables that reference the primary key of the SALES_ORDER table. The result set will have one row and the significant columns are:

PKTABLE_NAME	PKCOLUMN_NAME	FKTABLE_NAME	FKCOLUMN_NAME	KEY_SEQ
SALES_ORDER	SALES_ID	SALES_LINE	SALES_ID	1

Finally, the example calls **SQLForeignKeys** to get the foreign keys in the SALES_ORDER table the refer to the primary keys of other tables. The result set will have two rows and the significant columns are:

PKTABLE_NAME	PKCOLUMN_NAME	FKTABLE_NAME	FKCOLUMN_NAME	KEY_SEQ
CUSTOMER	CUSTOMER_ID	SALES_ORDER	CUSTOMER_ID	1
EMPLOYEE	EMPLOYEE_ID	SALES_ORDER	EMPLOYEE_ID	1

```
#define TAB_LEN SQL_MAX_TABLE_NAME_LEN + 1
#define COL_LEN SQL_MAX_COLUMN_NAME_LEN + 1

LPSTR     szTable;              /* Table to display      */

UCHAR     szPkTable[TAB_LEN];  /* Primary key table name */
UCHAR     szFkTable[TAB_LEN];  /* Foreign key table name */
UCHAR     szPkCol[COL_LEN];    /* Primary key column     */
UCHAR     szFkCol[COL_LEN];    /* Foreign key column     */

HSTMT        hstmt;
SDWORD       cbPkTable, cbPkCol, cbFkTable, cbFkCol, cbKeySeq;
SWORD        iKeySeq;
RETCODE      retcode;

/* Bind the columns that describe the primary and foreign keys.  */
/* Ignore the table owner, name, and qualifier for this example. */

SQLBindCol(hstmt, 3, SQL_C_CHAR, szPkTable, TAB_LEN, &cbPkTable);
SQLBindCol(hstmt, 4, SQL_C_CHAR, szPkCol, COL_LEN, &cbPkCol);
SQLBindCol(hstmt, 5, SQL_C_SSHORT, &iKeySeq, TAB_LEN, &cbKeySeq);
SQLBindCol(hstmt, 7, SQL_C_CHAR, szFkTable, TAB_LEN, &cbFkTable);
SQLBindCol(hstmt, 8, SQL_C_CHAR, szFkCol, COL_LEN, &cbFkCol);
```

```
strcpy(szTable, "SALES_ORDER");

/* Get the names of the columns in the primary key.              */

retcode = SQLPrimaryKeys(hstmt,
                        NULL, 0,            /* Table qualifier  */
                        NULL, 0,            /* Table owner      */
                        szTable, SQL_NTS); /* Table name       */

while ((retcode == SQL_SUCCESS) || (retcode == SQL SUCCESS_WITH_INFO)) {

    /* Fetch and display the result set. This will be a list of the */
    /* columns in the primary key of the SALES_ORDER table.        */

    retcode = SQLFetch(hstmt);
    if (retcode == SQL_SUCCESS || retcode != SQL_SUCCESS_WITH_INFO)
        fprintf(out, "Column: %s    Key Seq: %hd \n", szPkCol, iKeySeq);
}

/* Close the cursor (the hstmt is still allocated).              */

SQLFreeStmt(hstmt, SQL_CLOSE);

/* Get all the foreign keys that refer to SALES_ORDER primary key. */

retcode = SQLForeignKeys(hstmt,
                        NULL, 0,            /* Primary qualifier  */
                        NULL, 0,            /* Primary owner      */
                        szTable, SQL_NTS,  /* Primary table      */
                        NULL, 0,            /* Foreign qualifier  */
                        NULL, 0,            /* Foreign owner      */
                        NULL, 0);           /* Foreign table      */

while ((retcode == SQL_SUCCESS) || (retcode == SQL_SUCCESS_WITH_INFO)) {

    /* Fetch and display the result set. This will be all of the  */
    /* foreign keys in other tables that refer to the SALES_ORDER */
    /* primary key.                                               */

    retcode = SQLFetch(hstmt);
    if (retcode == SQL_SUCCESS || retcode == SQL_SUCCESS_WITH_INFO)
        fprintf(out, "%-s ( %-s ) <-- %-s ( %-s )\n", szPkTable,
                szPkCol, szFkTable, szFkCol);
}
```

```
                    /* Close the cursor (the hstmt is still allocated).         */

                    SQLFreeStmt(hstmt, SQL_CLOSE);

                    /* Get all the foreign keys in the SALES_ORDER table.        */

                    retcode = SQLForeignKeys(hstmt,
                                    NULL, 0,         /* Primary qualifier   */
                                    NULL, 0,         /* Primary owner       */
                                    NULL, 0,         /* Primary table       */
                                    NULL, 0,         /* Foreign qualifier   */
                                    NULL, 0,         /* Foreign owner       */
                                    szTable, SQL_NTS); /* Foreign table     */

                    while ((retcode == SQL_SUCCESS) || (retcode == SQL_SUCCESS_WITH_INFO)) {

                        /* Fetch and display the result set. This will be all of the  */
                        /* primary keys in other tables that are referred to by foreign */
                        /* keys in the SALES_ORDER table.                             */

                        retcode = SQLFetch(hstmt);
                        if (retcode == SQL_SUCCESS || retcode == SQL_SUCCESS_WITH_INFO)
                            fprintf(out, "%-s ( %-s )--> %-s ( %-s )\n", szFkTable, szFkCol,
                                    szPkTable, szPkCol);
                    }

                    /* Free the hstmt. */

                    SQLFreeStmt(hstmt, SQL_DROP);
```

Related Functions

For information about	See
Assigning storage for a column in a result set	**SQLBindCol**
Canceling statement processing	**SQLCancel**
Fetching a block of data or scrolling through a result set	**SQLExtendedFetch** (extension)
Fetching a row of data	**SQLFetch**
Returning the columns of a primary key	**SQLPrimaryKeys** (extension)
Returning table statistics and indexes	**SQLStatistics** (extension)

SQLFreeConnect

Core

SQLFreeConnect releases a connection handle and frees all memory associated with the handle.

Syntax

RETCODE **SQLFreeConnect**(*hdbc*)

The **SQLFreeConnect** function accepts the following argument.

Type	Argument	Use	Description
HDBC	*hdbc*	Input	Connection handle.

Returns

SQL_SUCCESS, SQL_SUCCESS_WITH_INFO, SQL_ERROR, or SQL_INVALID_HANDLE.

Diagnostics

When **SQLFreeConnect** returns SQL_ERROR or SQL_SUCCESS_WITH_INFO, an associated SQLSTATE value may be obtained by calling **SQLError**. The following table lists the SQLSTATE values commonly returned by **SQLFreeConnect** and explains each one in the context of this function; the notation "(DM)" precedes the descriptions of SQLSTATEs returned by the Driver Manager. The return code associated with each SQLSTATE value is SQL_ERROR, unless noted otherwise.

SQLSTATE	Error	Description
01000	General warning	Driver-specific informational message. (Function returns SQL_SUCCESS_WITH_INFO.)
08S01	Communication link failure	The communication link between the driver and the data source to which the driver was connected failed before the function completed processing.
S1000	General error	An error occurred for which there was no specific SQLSTATE and for which no implementation-specific SQLSTATE was defined. The error message returned by **SQLError** in the argument *szErrorMsg* describes the error and its cause.
S1010	Function sequence error	(DM) The function was called prior to calling **SQLDisconnect** for the *hdbc*.

Comments

Prior to calling **SQLFreeConnect,** an application must call **SQLDisconnect** for the *hdbc*. Otherwise, **SQLFreeConnect** returns SQL_ERROR and the *hdbc* remains valid. Note that **SQLDisconnect** automatically drops any *hstmts* open on the *hdbc*.

Code Example

See **SQLBrowseConnect** and **SQLConnect**.

Related Functions

For information about	See
Allocating a statement handle	**SQLAllocConnect**
Connecting to a data source	**SQLConnect**
Disconnecting from a data source	**SQLDisconnect**
Connecting to a data source using a connection string or dialog box	**SQLDriverConnect** (extension)
Freeing an environment handle	**SQLFreeEnv**
Freeing a statement handle	**SQLFreeStmt**

SQLFreeEnv

Core

SQLFreeEnv frees the environment handle and releases all memory associated with the environment handle.

Syntax

RETCODE **SQLFreeEnv**(*henv*)

The **SQLFreeEnv** function accepts the following argument.

Type	Argument	Use	Description
HENV	*henv*	Input	Environment handle.

Returns

SQL_SUCCESS, SQL_SUCCESS_WITH_INFO, SQL_ERROR, or SQL_INVALID_HANDLE.

Diagnostics

When **SQLFreeEnv** returns SQL_ERROR or SQL_SUCCESS_WITH_INFO, an associated SQLSTATE value may be obtained by calling **SQLError**. The following table lists the SQLSTATE values commonly returned by **SQLFreeEnv** and explains each one in the context of this function; the notation "(DM)" precedes the descriptions of SQLSTATEs returned by the Driver Manager. The return code associated with each SQLSTATE value is SQL_ERROR, unless noted otherwise.

SQLSTATE	Error	Description
01000	General warning	Driver-specific informational message. (Function returns SQL_SUCCESS_WITH_INFO.)
S1000	General error	An error occurred for which there was no specific SQLSTATE and for which no implementation-specific SQLSTATE was defined. The error message returned by **SQLError** in the argument *szErrorMsg* describes the error and its cause.
S1010	Function sequence error	(DM) There was at least one *hdbc* in an allocated or connected state. Call **SQLDisconnect** and **SQLFreeConnect** for each *hdbc* before calling **SQLFreeEnv**.

Comments

Prior to calling **SQLFreeEnv**, an application must call **SQLFreeConnect** for any *hdbc* allocated under the *henv*. Otherwise, **SQLFreeEnv** returns SQL_ERROR and the *henv* and any active *hdbc* remains valid.

When the Driver Manager processes the **SQLFreeEnv** function, it checks the **TraceAutoStop** keyword in the [ODBC] section of the ODBC.INI file or the ODBC subkey of the registry. If it is set to 1, the Driver Manager disables tracing for all applications and sets the **Trace** keyword in the [ODBC] section of the ODBC.INI file or the ODBC subkey of the registry to 0.

Code Example   See **SQLBrowseConnect** and **SQLConnect**.

Related Functions

For information about	See
Allocating an environment handle	**SQLAllocEnv**
Freeing a connection handle	**SQLFreeConnect**

SQLFreeStmt

Core

SQLFreeStmt stops processing associated with a specific *hstmt*, closes any open cursors associated with the *hstmt*, discards pending results, and, optionally, frees all resources associated with the statement handle.

Syntax

RETCODE **SQLFreeStmt**(*hstmt*, *fOption*)

The **SQLFreeStmt** function accepts the following arguments.

Type	Argument	Use	Description
HSTMT	*hstmt*	Input	Statement handle
UWORD	*fOption*	Input	One of the following options:
			SQL_ CLOSE: Close the cursor associated with *hstmt* (if one was defined) and discard all pending results. The application can reopen this cursor later by executing a **SELECT** statement again with the same or different parameter values. If no cursor is open, this option has no effect for the application.
			SQL_DROP: Release the *hstmt*, free all resources associated with it, close the cursor (if one is open), and discard all pending rows. This option terminates all access to the *hstmt*. The *hstmt* must be reallocated to be reused.
			SQL_UNBIND: Release all column buffers bound by **SQLBindCol** for the given *hstmt*.
			SQL_RESET_PARAMS: Release all parameter buffers set by **SQLBindParameter** for the given *hstmt*.

Returns

SQL_SUCCESS, SQL_SUCCESS_WITH_INFO, SQL_ERROR, or SQL_INVALID_HANDLE.

Diagnostics

When **SQLFreeStmt** returns SQL_ERROR or SQL_SUCCESS_WITH_INFO, an associated SQLSTATE value may be obtained by calling **SQLError**. The following table lists the SQLSTATE values commonly returned by

SQLFreeStmt and explains each one in the context of this function; the notation "(DM)" precedes the descriptions of SQLSTATEs returned by the Driver Manager. The return code associated with each SQLSTATE value is SQL_ERROR, unless noted otherwise.

SQLSTATE	Error	Description
01000	General warning	Driver-specific informational message. (Function returns SQL_SUCCESS_WITH_INFO.)
IM001	Driver does not support this function	(DM) The driver associated with the *hstmt* does not support the function.
S1000	General error	An error occurred for which there was no specific SQLSTATE and for which no implementation-specific SQLSTATE was defined. The error message returned by **SQLError** in the argument *szErrorMsg* describes the error and its cause.
S1001	Memory allocation failure	The driver was unable to allocate memory required to support execution or completion of the function.
S1010	Function sequence error	(DM) An asynchronously executing function was called for the *hstmt* and was still executing when this function was called.
		(DM) **SQLExecute**, **SQLExecDirect**, or **SQLSetPos** was called for the *hstmt* and returned SQL_NEED_DATA. This function was called before data was sent for all data-at-execution parameters or columns.
S1092	Option type out of range	(DM) The value specified for the argument *fOption* was not: SQL_CLOSE SQL_DROP SQL_UNBIND SQL_RESET_PARAMS

Comments   An application can call **SQLFreeStmt** to terminate processing of a **SELECT** statement with or without canceling the statement handle.

The SQL_DROP option frees all resources that were allocated by the **SQLAllocStmt** function.

Code Example   See **SQLBrowseConnect** and **SQLConnect**.

Related Functions

For information about	See
Allocating a statement handle	**SQLAllocStmt**
Canceling statement processing	**SQLCancel**
Setting a cursor name	**SQLSetCursorName**

SQLGetConnectOption

Extension Level 1   **SQLGetConnectOption** returns the current setting of a connection option.

Syntax   RETCODE **SQLGetConnectOption**(*hdbc*, *fOption*, *pvParam*)

The **SQLGetConnectOption** function accepts the following arguments:

Type	Argument	Use	Description
HDBC	*hdbc*	Input	Connection handle.
UWORD	*fOption*	Input	Option to retrieve.
PTR	*pvParam*	Output	Value associated with *fOption*. Depending on the value of *fOption*, a 32-bit integer value or a pointer to a null-terminated character string will be returned in *pvParam*.

Returns   SQL_SUCCESS, SQL_SUCCESS_WITH_INFO, SQL_NO_DATA_FOUND, SQL_ERROR, or SQL_INVALID_HANDLE.

Diagnostics   When **SQLGetConnectOption** returns SQL_ERROR or SQL_SUCCESS_WITH_INFO, an associated SQLSTATE value may be obtained by calling **SQLError**. The following table lists the SQLSTATE values commonly returned by **SQLGetConnectOption** and explains each one in the context of this function; the notation "(DM)" precedes the descriptions of SQLSTATEs returned by the Driver Manager. The return code associated with each SQLSTATE value is SQL_ERROR, unless noted otherwise.

SQLSTATE	Error	Description
01000	General warning	Driver-specific informational message. (Function returns SQL_SUCCESS_WITH_INFO.)
08003	Connection not open	(DM) An *fOption* value was specified that required an open connection.
IM001	Driver does not support this function	(DM) The driver corresponding to the *hdbc* does not support the function.
S1000	General error	An error occurred for which there was no specific SQLSTATE and for which no implementation-specific SQLSTATE was defined. The error message returned by **SQLError** in the argument *szErrorMsg* describes the error and its cause.
S1001	Memory allocation failure	The driver was unable to allocate memory required to support execution or completion of the function.

SQLSTATE	Error	Description
S1010	Function sequence error	(DM) **SQLBrowseConnect** was called for the *hdbc* and returned SQL_NEED_DATA. This function was called before **SQLBrowseConnect** returned SQL_SUCCESS_WITH_INFO or SQL_SUCCESS.
S1092	Option type out of range	(DM) The value specified for the argument *fOption* was in the block of numbers reserved for ODBC connection and statement options, but was not valid for the version of ODBC supported by the driver.
S1C00	Driver not capable	The value specified for the argument *fOption* was a valid ODBC connection option for the version of ODBC supported by the driver, but was not supported by the driver.
		The value specified for the argument *fOption* was in the block of numbers reserved for driver-specific connection and statement options, but was not supported by the driver.

Comments

For a list of options, see **SQLSetConnectOption**. Note that if *fOption* specifies an option that returns a string, *pvParam* must be a pointer to storage for the string. The maximum length of the string will be SQL_MAX_OPTION_STRING_LENGTH bytes (excluding the null termination byte).

Depending on the option, an application does not need to establish a connection prior to calling **SQLGetConnectOption**. However, if **SQLGetConnectOption** is called and the specified option does not have a default and has not been set by a prior call to **SQLSetConnectOption**, **SQLGetConnnectOption** will return SQL_NO_DATA_FOUND.

While an application can set statement options using **SQLSetConnectOption**, an application cannot use **SQLGetConnectOption** to retrieve statement option values; it must call **SQLGetStmtOption** to retrieve the setting of statement options.

Related Functions

For information about	See
Returning the setting of a statement option	**SQLGetStmtOption** (extension)
Setting a connection option	**SQLSetConnectOption** (extension)
Setting a statement option	**SQLSetStmtOption** (extension)

SQLGetCursorName

Core

SQLGetCursorName returns the cursor name associated with a specified *hstmt*.

Syntax

RETCODE **SQLGetCursorName**(*hstmt*, *szCursor*, *cbCursorMax*, *pcbCursor*)

The **SQLGetCursorName** function accepts the following arguments.

Type	Argument	Use	Description
HSTMT	*hstmt*	Input	Statement handle.
UCHAR FAR *	*szCursor*	Output	Pointer to storage for the cursor name.
SWORD	*cbCursorMax*	Input	Length of *szCursor*.
SWORD FAR *	*pcbCursor*	Output	Total number of bytes (excluding the null termination byte) available to return in *szCursor*. If the number of bytes available to return is greater than or equal to *cbCursorMax*, the cursor name in *szCursor* is truncated to *cbCursorMax* − 1 bytes.

Returns

SQL_SUCCESS, SQL_SUCCESS_WITH_INFO, SQL_ERROR, or SQL_INVALID_HANDLE.

Diagnostics

When **SQLGetCursorName** returns either SQL_ERROR or SQL_SUCCESS_WITH_INFO, an associated SQLSTATE value may be obtained by calling **SQLError**. The following table lists the SQLSTATE values commonly returned by **SQLGetCursorName** and explains each one in the context of this function; the notation "(DM)" precedes the descriptions of SQLSTATEs returned by the Driver Manager. The return code associated with each SQLSTATE value is SQL_ERROR, unless noted otherwise.

SQLSTATE	Error	Description
01000	General warning	Driver-specific informational message. (Function returns SQL_SUCCESS_WITH_INFO.)
01004	Data truncated	The buffer *szCursor* was not large enough to return the entire cursor name, so the cursor name was truncated. The argument *pcbCursor* contains the length of the untruncated cursor name. (Function returns SQL_SUCCESS_WITH_INFO.)
IM001	Driver does not support this function	(DM) The driver associated with the *hstmt* does not support the function.

SQLSTATE	Error	Description
S1000	General error	An error occurred for which there was no specific SQLSTATE and for which no implementation-specific SQLSTATE was defined. The error message returned by **SQLError** in the argument *szErrorMsg* describes the error and its cause.
S1001	Memory allocation failure	The driver was unable to allocate memory required to support execution or completion of the function.
S1010	Function sequence error	(DM) An asynchronously executing function was called for the *hstmt* and was still executing when this function was called.
		(DM) **SQLExecute**, **SQLExecDirect**, or **SQLSetPos** was called for the *hstmt* and returned SQL_NEED_DATA. This function was called before data was sent for all data-at-execution parameters or columns.
S1015	No cursor name available	(DM) There was no open cursor on the *hstmt* and no cursor name had been set with **SQLSetCursorName**.
S1090	Invalid string or buffer length	(DM) The value specified in the argument *cbCursorMax* was less than 0.

Comments

The only ODBC SQL statements that use a cursor name are positioned update and delete (for example, **UPDATE** *table-name* ...**WHERE CURRENT OF** *cursor-name*). If the application does not call **SQLSetCursorName** to define a cursor name, on execution of a **SELECT** statement the driver generates a name that begins with the letters SQL_CUR and does not exceed 18 characters in length.

SQLGetCursorName returns the name of a cursor regardless of whether the name was created explicitly or implicitly.

A cursor name that is set either explicitly or implicitly remains set until the *hstmt* with which it is associated is dropped, using **SQLFreeStmt** with the SQL_DROP option.

Related Functions

For information about	See
Executing an SQL statement	**SQLExecDirect**
Executing a prepared SQL statement	**SQLExecute**
Preparing a statement for execution	**SQLPrepare**
Setting a cursor name	**SQLSetCursorName**
Setting cursor scrolling options	**SQLSetScrollOptions** (extension)

SQLGetData

Extension Level 1   **SQLGetData** returns result data for a single unbound column in the current row. The application must call **SQLFetch**, or **SQLExtendedFetch** and (optionally) **SQLSetPos** to position the cursor on a row of data before it calls **SQLGetData**. It is possible to use **SQLBindCol** for some columns and use **SQLGetData** for others within the same row. This function can be used to retrieve character or binary data values in parts from a column with a character, binary, or data source–specific data type (for example, data from SQL_LONGVARBINARY or SQL_LONGVARCHAR columns).

Syntax   RETCODE **SQLGetData**(*hstmt, icol, fCType, rgbValue, cbValueMax, pcbValue*)

The **SQLGetData** function accepts the following arguments:

Type	Argument	Use	Description
HSTMT	*hstmt*	Input	Statement handle.
UWORD	*icol*	Input	Column number of result data, ordered sequentially left to right, starting at 1. A column number of 0 is used to retrieve a bookmark for the row; bookmarks are not supported by ODBC 1.0 drivers or **SQLFetch**.

Type	Argument	Use	Description
SWORD	*fCType*	Input	The C data type of the result data. This must be one of the following values:
			SQL_C_BINARY SQL_C_BIT SQL_C_BOOKMARK SQL_C_CHAR SQL_C_DATE SQL_C_DEFAULT SQL_C_DOUBLE SQL_C_FLOAT SQL_C_SLONG SQL_C_SSHORT SQL_C_STINYINT SQL_C_TIME SQL_C_TIMESTAMP SQL_C_ULONG SQL_C_USHORT SQL_C_UTINYINT
			SQL_C_DEFAULT specifies that data be converted to its default C data type.
			Note Drivers must also support the following values of *fCType* from ODBC 1.0. Applications must use these values, rather than the ODBC 2.0 values, when calling an ODBC 1.0 driver:
			SQL_C_LONG SQL_C_SHORT SQL_C_TINYINT
			For information about how data is converted, see "Converting Data from SQL to C Data Types" in Appendix D, "Data Types."
PTR	*rgbValue*	Output	Pointer to storage for the data.

Type	Argument	Use	Description
SDWORD	*cbValueMax*	Input	Maximum length of the *rgbValue* buffer. For character data, *rgbValue* must also include space for the null-termination byte.
			For character and binary C data, *cbValueMax* determines the amount of data that can be received in a single call to **SQLGetData**. For all other types of C data, *cbValueMax* is ignored; the driver assumes that the size of *rgbValue* is the size of the C data type specified with *fCType* and returns the entire data value. For more information about length, see "Precision, Scale, Length, and Display Size" in Appendix D, "Data Types."
SDWORD FAR *	*pcbValue*	Output	SQL_NULL_DATA, the total number of bytes (excluding the null termination byte for character data) available to return in *rgbValue* prior to the current call to **SQLGetData**, or SQL_NO_TOTAL if the number of available bytes cannot be determined.
			For character data, if *pcbValue* is SQL_NO_TOTAL or is greater than or equal to *cbValueMax*, the data in *rgbValue* is truncated to *cbValueMax* – 1 bytes and is null-terminated by the driver.
			For binary data, if *pcbValue* is SQL_NO_TOTAL or is greater than *cbValueMax*, the data in *rgbValue* is truncated to *cbValueMax* bytes.
			For all other data types, the value of *cbValueMax* is ignored and the driver assumes the size of *rgbValue* is the size of the C data type specified with *fCType*.

Returns SQL_SUCCESS, SQL_SUCCESS_WITH_INFO, SQL_NO_DATA_FOUND, SQL_STILL_EXECUTING, SQL_ERROR, or SQL_INVALID_HANDLE.

Diagnostics When **SQLGetData** returns either SQL_ERROR or SQL_SUCCESS_WITH_INFO, an associated SQLSTATE value may be obtained by calling **SQLError**. The following table lists the SQLSTATE values commonly returned by **SQLGetData** and explains each one in the context of this function; the notation "(DM)" precedes the descriptions of SQLSTATEs returned by the Driver Manager. The return code associated with each SQLSTATE value is SQL_ERROR, unless noted otherwise.

SQLSTATE	Error	Description
01000	General warning	Driver-specific informational message. (Function returns SQL_SUCCESS_WITH_INFO.)
01004	Data truncated	All of the data for the specified column, *icol*, could not be retrieved in a single call to the function. The argument *pcbValue* contains the length of the data remaining in the specified column prior to the current call to **SQLGetData**. (Function returns SQL_SUCCESS_WITH_INFO.) For more information on using multiple calls to **SQLGetData** for a single column, see "Comments."
07006	Restricted data type attribute violation	The data value cannot be converted to the C data type specified by the argument *fCType*.
08S01	Communication link failure	The communication link between the driver and the data source to which the driver was connected failed before the function completed processing.
22003	Numeric value out of range	Returning the numeric value (as numeric or string) for the column would have caused the whole (as opposed to fractional) part of the number to be truncated.
		Returning the binary value for the column would have caused a loss of binary significance.
		For more information, see Appendix D, "Data Types."
22005	Error in assignment	The data for the column was incompatible with the data type into which it was to be converted. For more information, see Appendix D, "Data Types."

SQLSTATE	Error	Description
22008	Datetime field overflow	The data for the column was not a valid date, time, or timestamp value. For more information, see Appendix D, "Data Types."
24000	Invalid cursor state	(DM) The *hstmt* was in an executed state but no result set was associated with the *hstmt*.
		(DM) A cursor was open on the *hstmt* but **SQLFetch** or **SQLExtendedFetch** had not been called.
		A cursor was open on the *hstmt* and **SQLFetch** or **SQLExtendedFetch** had been called, but the cursor was positioned before the start of the result set or after the end of the result set.
IM001	Driver does not support this function	(DM) The driver corresponding to the *hstmt* does not support the function.
S1000	General error	An error occurred for which there was no specific SQLSTATE and for which no implementation-specific SQLSTATE was defined. The error message returned by **SQLError** in the argument *szErrorMsg* describes the error and its cause.
S1001	Memory allocation failure	The driver was unable to allocate memory required to support execution or completion of the function.

SQLSTATE	Error	Description
S1002	Invalid column number	The value specified for the argument *icol* was 0 and the driver was an ODBC 1.0 driver.
		The value specified for the argument *icol* was 0 and **SQLFetch** was used to fetch the data.
		The value specified for the argument *icol* was 0 and the SQL_USE_BOOKMARKS statement option was set to SQL_UB_OFF.
		The specified column was greater than the number of result columns.
		The specified column was bound through a call to **SQLBindCol**. This description does not apply to drivers that return the SQL_GD_BOUND bitmask for the SQL_GETDATA_EXTENSIONS option in **SQLGetInfo**.
		The specified column was at or before the last bound column specified through **SQLBindCol**. This description does not apply to drivers that return the SQL_GD_ANY_COLUMN bitmask for the SQL_GETDATA_EXTENSIONS option in **SQLGetInfo**.
		The application has already called **SQLGetData** for the current row. The column specified in the current call was before the column specified in the preceding call. This description does not apply to drivers that return the SQL_GD_ANY_ORDER bitmask for the SQL_GETDATA_EXTENSIONS option in **SQLGetInfo**.
S1003	Program type out of range	(DM) The argument *fCType* was not a valid data type or SQL_C_DEFAULT.
		The argument *icol* was 0 and the argument *fCType* was not SQL_C_BOOKMARK.

SQLSTATE	Error	Description
S1008	Operation canceled	Asynchronous processing was enabled for the *hstmt*. The function was called and before it completed execution, **SQLCancel** was called on the *hstmt*. Then the function was called again on the *hstmt*.
		The function was called and, before it completed execution, **SQLCancel** was called on the *hstmt* from a different thread in a multithreaded application.
S1009	Invalid argument value	(DM) The argument *rgbValue* was a null pointer.
S1010	Function sequence error	(DM) The specified *hstmt* was not in an executed state. The function was called without first calling **SQLExecDirect**, **SQLExecute**, or a catalog function.
		(DM) An asynchronously executing function (not this one) was called for the *hstmt* and was still executing when this function was called.
		(DM) **SQLExecute**, **SQLExecDirect**, or **SQLSetPos** was called for the *hstmt* and returned SQL_NEED_DATA. This function was called before data was sent for all data-at-execution parameters or columns.
S1090	Invalid string or buffer length	(DM) The value specified for argument *cbValueMax* was less than 0.
S1109	Invalid cursor position	The cursor was positioned (by **SQLSetPos** or **SQLExtendedFetch**) on a row for which the value in the *rgfRowStatus* array in **SQLExtendedFetch** was SQL_ROW_DELETED or SQL_ROW_ERROR.

SQLSTATE	Error	Description
S1C00	Driver not capable	The driver or data source does not support use of **SQLGetData** with multiple rows in **SQLExtendedFetch**. This description does not apply to drivers that return the SQL_GD_BLOCK bitmask for the SQL_GETDATA_EXTENSIONS option in **SQLGetInfo**.
		The driver or data source does not support the conversion specified by the combination of the *fCType* argument and the SQL data type of the corresponding column. This error only applies when the SQL data type of the column was mapped to a driver-specific SQL data type.
		The argument *icol* was 0 and the driver does not support bookmarks.
		The driver only supports ODBC 1.0 and the argument *fCType* was one of the following:
		SQL_C_STINYINT SQL_C_UTINYINT SQL_C_SSHORT SQL_C_USHORT SQL_C_SLONG SQL_C_ULONG
S1T00	Timeout expired	The timeout period expired before the data source returned the result set. The timeout period is set through **SQLSetStmtOption**, SQL_QUERY_TIMEOUT.

Comments

With each call, the driver sets *pcbValue* to the number of bytes that were available in the result column prior to the current call to **SQLGetData**. (If SQL_MAX_LENGTH has been set with **SQLSetStmtOption**, and the total number of bytes available on the first call is greater than SQL_MAX_LENGTH, the available number of bytes is set to SQL_MAX_LENGTH. Note that the SQL_MAX_LENGTH statement option is intended to reduce network traffic and may not be supported by all drivers. To guarantee that data is truncated, an application should allocate a buffer of the desired size and specify this size in the *cbValueMax* argument.) If the total number of bytes in the result column cannot be determined in advance, the driver sets *pcbValue* to SQL_NO_TOTAL. If the data value for the column is NULL, the driver stores SQL_NULL_DATA in *pcbValue*.

SQLGetData can convert data to a different data type. The result and success of the conversion is determined by the rules for assignment specified in "Converting Data from SQL to C Data Types" in Appendix D, "Data Types."

If more than one call to **SQLGetData** is required to retrieve data from a single column with a character, binary, or data source–specific data type, the driver returns SQL_SUCCESS_WITH_INFO. A subsequent call to **SQLError** returns SQLSTATE 01004 (Data truncated). The application can then use the same column number to retrieve subsequent parts of the data until **SQLGetData** returns SQL_SUCCESS, indicating that all data for the column has been retrieved. **SQLGetData** will return SQL_NO_DATA_FOUND when it is called for a column after all of the data has been retrieved and before data is retrieved for a subsequent column. The application can ignore excess data by proceeding to the next result column.

Note An application can use **SQLGetData** to retrieve data from a column in parts only when retrieving character C data from a column with a character,binary, or data source–specific data type or when retrieving binary C data from a column with a character, binary, or data source–specific data type. If **SQLGetData** is called more than one time in a row for a column under any other conditions, it returns SQL_NO_DATA_FOUND for all calls after the first.

For maximum interoperability, applications should call **SQLGetData** only for unbound columns with numbers greater than the number of the last bound column. Within a single row of data, the column number in each call to **SQLGetData** should be greater than or equal to the column number in the previous call (that is, data should be retrieved in increasing order of column number). As extended functionality, drivers can return data through **SQLGetData** from bound columns, from columns before the last bound column, or from columns in any order. To determine whether a driver supports these extensions, an application calls **SQLGetInfo** with the SQL_GETDATA_EXTENSIONS option.

Furthermore, applications that use **SQLExtendedFetch** to retrieve data should call **SQLGetData** only when the rowset size is 1. As extended functionality, drivers can return data through **SQLGetData** when the rowset size is greater than 1. The application calls **SQLSetPos** to position the cursor on a row and calls **SQLGetData** to retrieve data from an unbound column. To determine whether a driver supports this extension, an application calls **SQLGetInfo** with the SQL_GETDATA_EXTENSIONS option.

Code Example   In the following example, an application executes a **SELECT** statement to return a result set of the employee names, ages, and birthdays sorted by birthday, age, and name. For each row of data, it calls **SQLFetch** to position the cursor to the next row. It calls **SQLGetData** to retrieve the fetched data; the storage locations for the data and the returned number of bytes are specified in the call to **SQLGetData**. Finally, it prints each employee's name, age, and birthday.

```
#define NAME_LEN 30
#define BDAY_LEN 11

UCHAR     szName[NAME_LEN], szBirthday[BDAY_LEN];
SWORD     sAge;
SDWORD    cbName, cbAge, cbBirthday;

retcode = SQLExecDirect(hstmt,
             "SELECT NAME, AGE, BIRTHDAY FROM EMPLOYEE ORDER BY 3, 2, 1",
             SQL_NTS);

if (retcode == SQL_SUCCESS) {
    while (TRUE) {
        retcode = SQLFetch(hstmt);
        if (retcode == SQL_ERROR || retcode == SQL_SUCCESS_WITH_INFO) {
            show_error();
        }
        if (retcode == SQL_SUCCESS || retcode == SQL_SUCCESS_WITH_INFO){

            /* Get data for columns 1, 2, and 3 */
            /* Print the row of data            */

            SQLGetData(hstmt, 1, SQL_C_CHAR, szName, NAME_LEN, &cbName);
            SQLGetData(hstmt, 2, SQL_C_SSHORT, &sAge, 0, &cbAge);
            SQLGetData(hstmt, 3, SQL_C_CHAR, szBirthday, BDAY_LEN,
                          &cbBirthday);

            fprintf(out, "%-*s %-2d %*s", NAME_LEN-1, szName, sAge,
                        BDAY_LEN-1, szBirthday);
        } else {
            break;
        }
    }
}
```

Related Functions

For information about	See
Assigning storage for a column in a result set	**SQLBindCol**
Canceling statement processing	**SQLCancel**
Executing an SQL statement	**SQLExecDirect**
Executing a prepared SQL statement	**SQLExecute**
Fetching a block of data or scrolling through a result set	**SQLExtendedFetch** (extension)
Fetching a row of data	**SQLFetch**
Sending parameter data at execution time	**SQLPutData** (extension)

SQLGetFunctions

Extension Level 1   **SQLGetFunctions** returns information about whether a driver supports a specific ODBC function. This function is implemented in the Driver Manager; it can also be implemented in drivers. If a driver implements **SQLGetFunctions**, the Driver Manager calls the function in the driver. Otherwise, it executes the function itself.

Syntax   RETCODE **SQLGetFunctions**(*hdbc*, *fFunction*, *pfExists*)

The **SQLGetFunctions** function accepts the following arguments:

Type	Argument	Use	Description
HDBC	*hdbc*	Input	Connection handle.
UWORD	*fFunction*	Input	SQL_API_ALL_FUNCTIONS or a **#define** value that identifies the ODBC function of interest. For a list of **#define** values that identify ODBC functions, see the tables in "Comments."
UWORD FAR *	*pfExists*	Output	If *fFunction* is SQL_API_ALL_FUNCTIONS, *pfExists* points to a UWORD array with 100 elements. The array is indexed by **#define** values used by *fFunction* to identify each ODBC function; some elements of the array are unused and reserved for future use. An element is TRUE if it identifies an ODBC function supported by the driver. It is FALSE if it identifies an ODBC function not supported by the driver or does not identify an ODBC function.

Note The *fFunction* value SQL_API_ALL_FUNCTIONS was added in ODBC 2.0.

If *fFunction* identifies a single ODBC function, *pfExists* points to single UWORD. *pfExists* is TRUE if the specified function is supported by the driver; otherwise, it is FALSE.

Returns	SQL_SUCCESS, SQL_SUCCESS_WITH_INFO, SQL_ERROR, or SQL_INVALID_HANDLE.
Diagnostics	When **SQLGetFunctions** returns SQL_ERROR or SQL_SUCCESS_WITH_INFO, an associated SQLSTATE value may be obtained by calling **SQLError**. The following table lists the SQLSTATE values commonly returned by **SQLGetFunctions** and explains each one in the context of this function; the notation "(DM)" precedes the descriptions of SQLSTATEs returned by the Driver Manager. The return code associated with each SQLSTATE value is SQL_ERROR, unless noted otherwise.

SQLSTATE	Error	Description
01000	General warning	Driver-specific informational message. (Function returns SQL_SUCCESS_WITH_INFO.)
S1000	General error	An error occurred for which there was no specific SQLSTATE and for which no implementation-specific SQLSTATE was defined. The error message returned by **SQLError** in the argument *szErrorMsg* describes the error and its cause.
S1001	Memory allocation failure	The driver was unable to allocate memory required to support execution or completion of the function.
S1010	Function sequence error	(DM) **SQLGetFunctions** was called before **SQLConnect**, **SQLBrowseConnect**, or **SQLDriverConnect**.
		(DM) **SQLBrowseConnect** was called for the *hdbc* and returned SQL_NEED_DATA. This function was called before **SQLBrowseConnect** returned SQL_SUCCESS_WITH_INFO or SQL_SUCCESS.
S1095	Function type out of range	(DM) An invalid *fFunction* value was specified.

Comments	**SQLGetFunctions** always returns that **SQLGetFunctions**, **SQLDataSources**, and **SQLDrivers** are supported. It does this because these functions are implemented in the Driver Manager.

The following table lists valid values for *fFunction* for ODBC core functions.

SQL_API_SQLALLOCCONNECT	SQL_API_SQLFETCH
SQL_API_SQLALLOCENV	SQL_API_SQLFREECONNECT
SQL_API_SQLALLOCSTMT	SQL_API_SQLFREEENV
SQL_API_SQLBINDCOL	SQL_API_SQLFREESTMT
SQL_API_SQLCANCEL	SQL_API_SQLGETCURSORNAME
SQL_API_SQLCOLATTRIBUTES	SQL_API_SQLNUMRESULTCOLS
SQL_API_SQLCONNECT	SQL_API_SQLPREPARE
SQL_API_SQLDESCRIBECOL	SQL_API_SQLROWCOUNT
SQL_API_SQLDISCONNECT	SQL_API_SQLSETCURSORNAME
SQL_API_SQLERROR	SQL_API_SQLSETPARAM
SQL_API_SQLEXECDIRECT	SQL_API_SQLTRANSACT
SQL_API_SQLEXECUTE	

Note For ODBC 1.0 drivers, **SQLGetFunctions** returns TRUE in *pfExists* if *fFunction* is SQL_API_SQLBINDPARAMETER or SQL_API_SQLSETPARAM and the driver supports **SQLSetParam**. For ODBC 2.0 drivers, **SQLGetFunctions** returns TRUE in *pfExists* if *fFunction* is SQL_API_SQLSETPARAM or SQL_API_SQLBINDPARAMETER and the driver supports **SQLBindParameter**.

The following table lists valid values for *fFunction* for ODBC extension level 1 functions.

SQL_API_SQLBINDPARAMETER	SQL_API_SQLGETTYPEINFO
SQL_API_SQLCOLUMNS	SQL_API_SQLPARAMDATA
SQL_API_SQLDRIVERCONNECT	SQL_API_SQLPUTDATA
SQL_API_SQLGETCONNECTOPTION	SQL_API_SQLSETCONNECTOPTION
SQL_API_SQLGETDATA	SQL_API_SQLSETSTMTOPTION
SQL_API_SQLGETFUNCTIONS	SQL_API_SQLSPECIALCOLUMNS
SQL_API_SQLGETINFO	SQL_API_SQLSTATISTICS
SQL_API_SQLGETSTMTOPTION	SQL_API_SQLTABLES

The following table lists valid values for *fFunction* for ODBC extension level 2 functions.

SQL_API_SQLBROWSECONNECT	SQL_API_SQLNUMPARAMS
SQL_API_SQLCOLUMNPRIVILEGES	SQL_API_SQLPARAMOPTIONS
SQL_API_SQLDATASOURCES	SQL_API_SQLPRIMARYKEYS
SQL_API_SQLDESCRIBEPARAM	SQL_API_SQLPROCEDURECOLUMNS
SQL_API_SQLDRIVERS	SQL_API_SQLPROCEDURES
SQL_API_SQLEXTENDEDFETCH	SQL_API_SQLSETPOS
SQL_API_SQLFOREIGNKEYS	SQL_API_SQLSETSCROLLOPTIONS
SQL_API_SQLMORERESULTS	SQL_API_SQLTABLEPRIVILEGES
SQL_API_SQLNATIVESQL	

Code Example

The following two examples show how an application uses **SQLGetFunctions** to determine if a driver supports **SQLTables**, **SQLColumns**, and **SQLStatistics**. If the driver does not support these functions, the application disconnects from the driver. The first example calls **SQLGetFunctions** once for each function.

```
UWORD TablesExists, ColumnsExists, StatisticsExists;

SQLGetFunctions(hdbc, SQL_API_SQLTABLES, &TablesExists);
SQLGetFunctions(hdbc, SQL_API_SQLCOLUMNS, &ColumnsExists);
SQLGetFunctions(hdbc, SQL_API_SQLSTATISTICS, &StatisticsExists);

if (TablesExists && ColumnsExists && StatisticsExists) {

    /* Continue with application */

}

SQLDisconnect(hdbc);
```

The second example calls **SQLGetFunctions** a single time and passes it an array in which **SQLGetFunctions** returns information about all ODBC functions.

```
UWORD fExists[100];

SQLGetFunctions(hdbc, SQL_API_ALL_FUNCTIONS, fExists);

if (fExists[SQL_API_SQLTABLES] &&
    fExists[SQL_API_SQLCOLUMNS] &&
    fExists[SQL_API_SQLSTATISTICS]) {

    /* Continue with application */

}

SQLDisconnect(hdbc);
```

Related Functions

For information about	See
Returning the setting of a connection option	**SQLGetConnectOption** (extension)
Returning information about a driver or data source	**SQLGetInfo** (extension)
Returning the setting of a statement option	**SQLGetStmtOption** (extension)

SQLGetInfo

Extension Level 1   **SQLGetInfo** returns general information about the driver and data source associated with an *hdbc*.

Syntax   RETCODE **SQLGetInfo**(*hdbc*, *fInfoType*, *rgbInfoValue*, *cbInfoValueMax*, *pcbInfoValue*)

The **SQLGetInfo** function accepts the following arguments.

Type	Argument	Use	Description
HDBC	*hdbc*	Input	Connection handle.
UWORD	*fInfoType*	Input	Type of information. *fInfoType* must be a value representing the type of interest (see "Comments").
PTR	*rgbInfoValue*	Output	Pointer to storage for the information. Depending on the *fInfoType* requested, the information returned will be one of the following: a null-terminated character string, a 16-bit integer value, a 32-bit flag, or a 32-bit binary value.
SWORD	*cbInfoValueMax*	Input	Maximum length of the *rgbInfoValue* buffer.
SWORD FAR *	*pcbInfoValue*	Output	The total number of bytes (excluding the null termination byte for character data) available to return in *rgbInfoValue*.
			For character data, if the number of bytes available to return is greater than or equal to *cbInfoValueMax*, the information in *rgbInfoValue* is truncated to *cbInfoValueMax* – 1 bytes and is null-terminated by the driver.
			For all other types of data, the value of *cbValueMax* is ignored and the driver assumes the size of *rgbValue* is 32 bits.

Returns   SQL_SUCCESS, SQL_SUCCESS_WITH_INFO, SQL_ERROR, or SQL_INVALID_HANDLE.

Diagnostics   When **SQLGetInfo** returns either SQL_ERROR or
SQL_SUCCESS_WITH_INFO, an associated SQLSTATE value may be obtained
by calling **SQLError**. The following table lists the SQLSTATE values commonly
returned by **SQLGetInfo** and explains each one in the context of this function;
the notation "(DM)" precedes the descriptions of SQLSTATEs returned by the
Driver Manager. The return code associated with each SQLSTATE value is
SQL_ERROR, unless noted otherwise.

SQLSTATE	Error	Description
01000	General warning	Driver-specific informational message. (Function returns SQL_SUCCESS_WITH_INFO.)
01004	Data truncated	The buffer *rgbInfoValue* was not large enough to return all of the requested information, so the information was truncated. The argument *pcbInfoValue* contains the length of the requested information in its untruncated form. (Function returns SQL_SUCCESS_WITH_INFO.)
08003	Connection not open	(DM) The type of information requested in *fInfoType* requires an open connection. Of the information types reserved by ODBC, only SQL_ODBC_VER can be returned without an open connection.
22003	Numeric value out of range	Returning the requested information would have caused a loss of numeric or binary significance.
IM001	Driver does not support this function	(DM) The driver corresponding to the *hdbc* does not support the function.
S1000	General error	An error occurred for which there was no specific SQLSTATE and for which no implementation-specific SQLSTATE was defined. The error message returned by **SQLError** in the argument *szErrorMsg* describes the error and its cause.
S1001	Memory allocation failure	The driver was unable to allocate memory required to support execution or completion of the function.
S1009	Invalid argument value	(DM) The *fInfoType* was SQL_DRIVER_HSTMT, and the value pointed to by *rgbInfoValue* was not a valid statement handle.
S1090	Invalid string or buffer length	(DM) The value specified for argument *cbInfoValueMax* was less than 0.

SQLSTATE	Error	Description
S1096	Information type out of range	(DM) The value specified for the argument *fOption* was in the block of numbers reserved for ODBC information types, but was not valid for the version of ODBC supported by the driver.
S1C00	Driver not capable	The value specified for the argument *fOption* was in the range of numbers reserved for driver-specific information types, but was not supported by the driver.
S1T00	Timeout expired	The timeout period expired before the data source returned the requested information. The timeout period is set through **SQLSetStmtOption**, SQL_QUERY_TIMEOUT.

Comments

The currently defined information types are shown below; it is expected that more will be defined to take advantage of different data sources. Information types from 0 to 999 are reserved by ODBC; driver developers must reserve values greater than or equal to SQL_INFO_DRIVER_START for driver-specific use. For more information, see "Driver-Specific Data Types, Descriptor Types, Information Types, and Options" in Chapter 11, "Guidelines for Implementing ODBC Functions."

The format of the information returned in *rgbInfoValue* depends on the *fInfoType* requested. **SQLGetInfo** will return information in one of five different formats:

- A null-terminated character string,
- A 16-bit integer value,
- A 32-bit bitmask,
- A 32-bit integer value,
- Or a 32-bit binary value.

The format of each of the following information types is noted in the type's description. The application must cast the value returned in *rgbInfoValue* accordingly. For an example of how an application could retrieve data from a 32-bit bitmask, see "Code Example."

A driver must return a value for each of the information types defined in the following tables. If an information type does not apply to the driver or data source, then the driver returns one of the following values:

Format of *rgbInfoValue*	Returned value
Character string ("Y" or "N")	"N"
Character string (not "Y" or "N")	Empty string
16-bit integer	0
32-bit bitmask or 32-bit binary value	0L

For example, if a data source does not support procedures, **SQLGetInfo** returns the following values for the values of *fInfoType* that are related to procedures:

fInfoType	Returned value
SQL_PROCEDURES	"N"
SQL_ACCESSIBLE_PROCEDURES	"N"
SQL_MAX_PROCEDURE_NAME_LEN	0
SQL_PROCEDURE_TERM	Empty string

SQLGetInfo returns SQLSTATE S1096 (Invalid argument value) for values of *fInfoType* that are in the range of information types reserved for use by ODBC but are not defined by the version of ODBC supported by the driver. To determine what version of ODBC a driver conforms to, an application calls **SQLGetInfo** with the SQL_DRIVER_ODBC_VER information type. **SQLGetInfo** returns SQLSTATE S1C00 (Driver not capable) for values of *fInfoType* that are in the range of information types reserved for driver-specific use but are not supported by the driver.

Note Application developers should be aware that ODBC 1.0 drivers might return SQL_ERROR and SQLSTATE S1C00 (Driver not capable) for values of *fInfoType* that were defined in ODBC 1.0 but do not apply to the driver or the data source.

Information Types

This section lists the information types supported by **SQLGetInfo**. Information types are grouped categorically and listed alphabetically.

Driver Information

The following values of *fInfoType* return information about the ODBC driver, such as the number of active statements, the data source name, and the API conformance levels.

SQL_ACTIVE_CONNECTIONS	SQL_DRIVER_HENV
SQL_ACTIVE_STATEMENTS	SQL_DRIVER_HLIB
SQL_DATA_SOURCE_NAME	SQL_DRIVER_HSTMT
SQL_DRIVER_HDBC	SQL_DRIVER_NAME

SQL_DRIVER_ODBC_VER

SQL_DRIVER_VER

SQL_FETCH_DIRECTION

SQL_FILE_USAGE

SQL_GETDATA_EXTENSIONS

SQL_LOCK_TYPES

SQL_ODBC_API_CONFORMANCE

SQL_ODBC_SAG_CLI_CONFORMANCE

SQL_ODBC_VER

SQL_POS_OPERATIONS

SQL_ROW_UPDATES

SQL_SEARCH_PATTERN_ESCAPE

SQL_SERVER_NAME

DBMS Product Information

The following values of *fInfoType* return information about the DBMS product, such as the DBMS name and version.

SQL_DATABASE_NAME

SQL_DBMS_NAME

SQL_DBMS_VER

Data Source Information

The following values of *fInfoType* return information about the data source, such as cursor characteristics and transaction capabilities.

SQL_ACCESSIBLE_PROCEDURES

SQL_ACCESSIBLE_TABLES

SQL_BOOKMARK_PERSISTENCE

SQL_CONCAT_NULL_BEHAVIOR

SQL_CURSOR_COMMIT_BEHAVIOR

SQL_CURSOR_ROLLBACK_BEHAVIOR

SQL_DATA_SOURCE_READ_ONLY

SQL_DEFAULT_TXN_ISOLATION

SQL_MULT_RESULT_SETS

SQL_MULTIPLE_ACTIVE_TXN

SQL_NEED_LONG_DATA_LEN

SQL_NULL_COLLATION

SQL_OWNER_TERM

SQL_PROCEDURE_TERM

SQL_QUALIFIER_TERM

SQL_SCROLL_CONCURRENCY

SQL_SCROLL_OPTIONS

SQL_STATIC_SENSITIVITY

SQL_TABLE_TERM

SQL_TXN_CAPABLE

SQL_TXN_ISOLATION_OPTION

SQL_USER_NAME

Supported SQL

The following values of *fInfoType* return information about the SQL statements supported by the data source. These information types do not exhaustively describe the entire ODBC SQL grammar. Instead, they describe those parts of the grammar for which data sources commonly offer different levels of support.

Applications should determine the general level of supported grammar from the SQL_ODBC_SQL_CONFORMANCE information type and use the other information types to determine variations from the stated conformance level.

SQL_ALTER_TABLE

SQL_COLUMN_ALIAS

SQL_CORRELATION_NAME

SQL_EXPRESSIONS_IN_ORDERBY

SQL_GROUP_BY

SQL_IDENTIFIER_CASE

SQL_IDENTIFIER_QUOTE_CHAR

SQL_KEYWORDS

SQL_LIKE_ESCAPE_CLAUSE

SQL_NON_NULLABLE_COLUMNS

SQL_ODBC_SQL_CONFORMANCE

SQL_ODBC_SQL_OPT_IEF

SQL_ORDER_BY_COLUMNS_IN_ SELECT

SQL_OUTER_JOINS

SQL_OWNER_USAGE

SQL_POSITIONED_STATEMENTS

SQL_PROCEDURES

SQL_QUALIFIER_LOCATION

SQL_QUALIFIER_NAME_ SEPARATOR

SQL_QUALIFIER_USAGE

SQL_QUOTED_IDENTIFIER_CASE

SQL_SPECIAL_CHARACTERS

SQL_SUBQUERIES

SQL_UNION

SQL Limits

The following values of *fInfoType* return information about the limits applied to identifiers and clauses in SQL statements, such as the maximum lengths of identifiers and the maximum number of columns in a select list. Limitations may be imposed by either the driver or the data source.

SQL_MAX_BINARY_LITERAL_LEN

SQL_MAX_CHAR_LITERAL_LEN

SQL_MAX_COLUMN_NAME_LEN

SQL_MAX_COLUMNS_IN_ GROUP_BY

SQL_MAX_COLUMNS_IN_ ORDER_BY

SQL_MAX_COLUMNS_IN_INDEX

SQL_MAX_COLUMNS_IN_SELECT

SQL_MAX_COLUMNS_IN_TABLE

SQL_MAX_CURSOR_NAME_LEN

SQL_MAX_INDEX_SIZE

SQL_MAX_OWNER_NAME_LEN

SQL_MAX_PROCEDURE_NAME_ LEN

SQL_MAX_QUALIFIER_NAME_LEN

SQL_MAX_ROW_SIZE

SQL_MAX_ROW_SIZE_INCLUDES_ LONG

SQL_MAX_STATEMENT_LEN

SQL_MAX_TABLE_NAME_LEN

SQL_MAX_TABLES_IN_SELECT

SQL_MAX_USER_NAME_LEN

Scalar Function Information

The following values of *fInfoType* return information about the scalar functions supported by the data source and the driver. For more information about scalar functions, see Appendix F, "Scalar Functions."

SQL_CONVERT_FUNCTIONS	SQL_TIMEDATE_ADD_INTERVALS
SQL_NUMERIC_FUNCTIONS	SQL_TIMEDATE_DIFF_INTERVALS
SQL_STRING_FUNCTIONS	SQL_TIMEDATE_FUNCTIONS
SQL_SYSTEM_FUNCTIONS	

Conversion Information

The following values of *fInfoType* return a list of the SQL data types to which the data source can convert the specified SQL data type with the **CONVERT** scalar function.

SQL_CONVERT_BIGINT	SQL_CONVERT_LONGVARCHAR
SQL_CONVERT_BINARY	SQL_CONVERT_NUMERIC
SQL_CONVERT_BIT	SQL_CONVERT_REAL
SQL_CONVERT_CHAR	SQL_CONVERT_SMALLINT
SQL_CONVERT_DATE	SQL_CONVERT_TIME
SQL_CONVERT_DECIMAL	SQL_CONVERT_TIMESTAMP
SQL_CONVERT_DOUBLE	SQL_CONVERT_TINYINT
SQL_CONVERT_FLOAT	SQL_CONVERT_VARBINARY
SQL_CONVERT_INTEGER	SQL_CONVERT_VARCHAR
SQL_CONVERT_LONGVARBINARY	

Information Type Descriptions

The following table alphabetically lists each information type, the version of ODBC in which it was introduced, and its description.

InfoType	Returns
SQL_ACCESSIBLE_PROCEDURES (ODBC 1.0)	A character string: "Y" if the user can execute all procedures returned by **SQLProcedures**, "N" if there may be procedures returned that the user cannot execute.
SQL_ACCESSIBLE_TABLES (ODBC 1.0)	A character string: "Y" if the user is guaranteed **SELECT** privileges to all tables returned by **SQLTables**, "N" if there may be tables returned that the user cannot access.
SQL_ACTIVE_CONNECTIONS (ODBC 1.0)	A 16-bit integer value specifying the maximum number of active *hdbcs* that the driver can support. This value can reflect a limitation imposed by either the driver or the data source. If there is no specified limit or the limit is unknown, this value is set to zero.

InfoType	Returns
SQL_ACTIVE_STATEMENTS (ODBC 1.0)	A 16-bit integer value specifying the maximum number of active *hstmts* that the driver can support for an *hdbc*. This value can reflect a limitation imposed by either the driver or the data source. If there is no specified limit or the limit is unknown, this value is set to zero.
SQL_ALTER_TABLE (ODBC 2.0)	A 32-bit bitmask enumerating the clauses in the **ALTER TABLE** statement supported by the data source.
	The following bitmask is used to determine which clauses are supported:
	SQL_AT_ADD_COLUMN SQL_AT_DROP_COLUMN
SQL_BOOKMARK_PERSISTENCE (ODBC 2.0)	A 32-bit bitmask enumerating the operations through which bookmarks persist.
	The following bitmasks are used in conjunction with the flag to determine through which options bookmarks persist:
	SQL_BP_CLOSE = Bookmarks are valid after an application calls **SQLFreeStmt** with the SQL_CLOSE option to close the cursor associated with an *hstmt*.
	SQL_BP_DELETE = The bookmark for a row is valid after that row has been deleted.
	SQL_BP_DROP = Bookmarks are valid after an *hstmt* an application calls **SQLFreeStmt** with the SQL_DROP option to drop an *hstmt*.
	SQL_BP_SCROLL = Bookmarks are valid after any scrolling operation (call to **SQLExtendedFetch**). Because all bookmarks must remain valid after **SQLExtendedFetch** is called, this value can be used by applications to determine whether bookmarks are supported.
	SQL_BP_TRANSACTION = Bookmarks are valid after an application commits or rolls back a transaction.
	SQL_BP_UPDATE = The bookmark for a row is valid after any column in that row has been updated, including key columns.
	SQL_BP_OTHER_HSTMT = A bookmark associated with one *hstmt* can be used with another *hstmt*.
SQL_COLUMN_ALIAS (ODBC 2.0)	A character string: "Y" if the data source supports column aliases; otherwise, "N".
SQL_CONCAT_NULL_BEHAVIOR (ODBC 1.0)	A 16-bit integer value indicating how the data source handles the concatenation of NULL valued character data type columns with non-NULL valued character data type columns:
	SQL_CB_NULL = Result is NULL valued.
	SQL_CB_NON_NULL = Result is concatenation of non-NULL valued column or columns.

InfoType	Returns
SQL_CONVERT_BIGINT SQL_CONVERT_BINARY SQL_CONVERT_BIT SQL_CONVERT_CHAR SQL_CONVERT_DATE SQL_CONVERT_DECIMAL SQL_CONVERT_DOUBLE SQL_CONVERT_FLOAT SQL_CONVERT_INTEGER SQL_CONVERT_LONGVARBINARY SQL_CONVERT_LONGVARCHAR SQL_CONVERT_NUMERIC SQL_CONVERT_REAL SQL_CONVERT_SMALLINT SQL_CONVERT_TIME SQL_CONVERT_TIMESTAMP SQL_CONVERT_TINYINT SQL_CONVERT_VARBINARY SQL_CONVERT_VARCHAR (ODBC 1.0)	A 32-bit bitmask. The bitmask indicates the conversions supported by the data source with the CONVERT scalar function for data of the type named in the *fInfoType*. If the bitmask equals zero, the data source does not support any conversions for data of the named type, including conversion to the same data type. For example, to find out if a data source supports the conversion of SQL_INTEGER data to the SQL_BIGINT data type, an application calls **SQLGetInfo** with the *fInfoType* of SQL_CONVERT_INTEGER. The application ANDs the returned bitmask with SQL_CVT_BIGINT. If the resulting value is nonzero, the conversion is supported. The following bitmasks are used to determine which conversions are supported: SQL_CVT_BIGINT SQL_CVT_BINARY SQL_CVT_BIT SQL_CVT_CHAR SQL_CVT_DATE SQL_CVT_DECIMAL SQL_CVT_DOUBLE SQL_CVT_FLOAT SQL_CVT_INTEGER SQL_CVT_LONGVARBINARY SQL_CVT_LONGVARCHAR SQL_CVT_NUMERIC SQL_CVT_REAL SQL_CVT_SMALLINT SQL_CVT_TIME SQL_CVT_TIMESTAMP SQL_CVT_TINYINT SQL_CVT_VARBINARY SQL_CVT_VARCHAR
SQL_CONVERT_FUNCTIONS (ODBC 1.0)	A 32-bit bitmask enumerating the scalar conversion functions supported by the driver and associated data source. The following bitmask is used to determine which conversion functions are supported: SQL_FN_CVT_CONVERT
SQL_CORRELATION_NAME (ODBC 1.0)	A 16-bit integer indicating if table correlation names are supported: SQL_CN_NONE = Correlation names are not supported. SQL_CN_DIFFERENT = Correlation names are supported, but must differ from the names of the tables they represent. SQL_CN_ANY = Correlation names are supported and can be any valid user-defined name.

InfoType	Returns
SQL_CURSOR_COMMIT_BEHAVIOR (ODBC 1.0)	A 16-bit integer value indicating how a **COMMIT** operation affects cursors and prepared statements in the data source:
	SQL_CB_DELETE = Close cursors and delete prepared statements. To use the cursor again, the application must reprepare and reexecute the *hstmt*.
	SQL_CB_CLOSE = Close cursors. For prepared statements, the application can call **SQLExecute** on the *hstmt* without calling **SQLPrepare** again.
	SQL_CB_PRESERVE = Preserve cursors in the same position as before the **COMMIT** operation. The application can continue to fetch data or it can close the cursor and reexecute the *hstmt* without repreparing it.
SQL_CURSOR_ROLLBACK_ BEHAVIOR (ODBC 1.0)	A 16-bit integer value indicating how a **ROLLBACK** operation affects cursors and prepared statements in the data source:
	SQL_CB_DELETE = Close cursors and delete prepared statements. To use the cursor again, the application must reprepare and reexecute the *hstmt*.
	SQL_CB_CLOSE = Close cursors. For prepared statements, the application can call **SQLExecute** on the *hstmt* without calling **SQLPrepare** again.
	SQL_CB_PRESERVE = Preserve cursors in the same position as before the **ROLLBACK** operation. The application can continue to fetch data or it can close the cursor and reexecute the *hstmt* without repreparing it.
SQL_DATA_SOURCE_NAME (ODBC 1.0)	A character string with the data source name used during connection. If the application called **SQLConnect**, this is the value of the *szDSN* argument. If the application called **SQLDriverConnect** or **SQLBrowseConnect**, this is the value of the DSN keyword in the connection string passed to the driver. If the connection string did not contain the DSN keyword (such as when it contains the DRIVER keyword), this is an empty string.
SQL_DATA_SOURCE_READ_ONLY (ODBC 1.0)	A character string. "Y" if the data source is set to READ ONLY mode, "N" if it is otherwise.
	This characteristic pertains only to the data source itself, it is not a characteristic of the driver that enables access to the data source.
SQL_DATABASE_NAME (ODBC 1.0)	A character string with the name of the current database in use, if the data source defines a named object called "database."
	Note In ODBC 2.0, this value of *fInfoType* has been replaced by the SQL_CURRENT_QUALIFIER connection option. ODBC 2.0 drivers should continue to support the SQL_DATABASE_NAME information type, and ODBC 2.0 applications should only use it with ODBC 1.0 drivers.

InfoType	Returns
SQL_DBMS_NAME (ODBC 1.0)	A character string with the name of the DBMS product accessed by the driver.
SQL_DBMS_VER (ODBC 1.0)	A character string indicating the version of the DBMS product accessed by the driver. The version is of the form ##.##.####, where the first two digits are the major version, the next two digits are the minor version, and the last four digits are the release version. The driver must render the DBMS product version in this form, but can also append the DBMS product-specific version as well. For example, "04.01.0000 Rdb 4.1".
SQL_DEFAULT_TXN_ISOLATION (ODBC 1.0)	A 32-bit integer that indicates the default transaction isolation level supported by the driver or data source, or zero if the data source does not support transactions. The following terms are used to define transaction isolation levels:

Dirty Read   Transaction 1 changes a row. Transaction 2 reads the changed row before transaction 1 commits the change. If transaction 1 rolls back the change, transaction 2 will have read a row that is considered to have never existed.

Nonrepeatable Read   Transaction 1 reads a row. Transaction 2 updates or deletes that row and commits this change. If transaction 1 attempts to reread the row, it will receive different row values or discover that the row has been deleted.

Phantom   Transaction 1 reads a set of rows that satisfy some search criteria. Transaction 2 inserts a row that matches the search criteria. If transaction 1 reexecutes the statement that read the rows, it receives a different set of rows.

If the data source supports transactions, the driver returns one of the following bitmasks:

SQL_TXN_READ_UNCOMMITTED = Dirty reads, nonrepeatable reads, and phantoms are possible.

SQL_TXN_READ_COMMITTED = Dirty reads are not possible. Nonrepeatable reads and phantoms are possible.

SQL_TXN_REPEATABLE_READ = Dirty reads and nonrepeatable reads are not possible. Phantoms are possible.

SQL_TXN_SERIALIZABLE = Transactions are serializable. Dirty reads, nonrepeatable reads, and phantoms are not possible.

SQL_TXN_VERSIONING = Transactions are serializable, but higher concurrency is possible than with SQL_TXN_SERIALIZABLE. Dirty reads are not possible. Typically, SQL_TXN_SERIALIZABLE is implemented by using locking protocols that reduce concurrency and SQL_TXN_VERSIONING is implemented by using a non-locking protocol such as record versioning. Oracle's Read Consistency isolation level is an example of SQL_TXN_VERSIONING.

InfoType	Returns
SQL_DRIVER_HDBC SQL_DRIVER_HENV (ODBC 1.0)	A 32-bit value, the driver's environment handle or connection handle, determined by the argument *hdbc*. These information types are implemented by the Driver Manager alone.
SQL_DRIVER_HLIB (ODBC 2.0)	A 32-bit value, the library handle returned to the Driver Manager when it loaded the driver DLL. The handle is only valid for the *hdbc* specified in the call to **SQLGetInfo**. This information type is implemented by the Driver Manager alone.
SQL_DRIVER_HSTMT (ODBC 1.0)	A 32-bit value, the driver's statement handle determined by the Driver Manager statement handle, which must be passed on input in *rgbInfoValue* from the application. Note that in this case, *rgbInfoValue* is both an input and an output argument. The input *hstmt* passed in *rgbInfoValue* must have been an *hstmt* allocated on the argument *hdbc*. This information type is implemented by the Driver Manager alone.
SQL_DRIVER_NAME (ODBC 1.0)	A character string with the filename of the driver used to access the data source.
SQL_DRIVER_ODBC_VER (ODBC 2.0)	A character string with the version of ODBC that the driver supports. The version is of the form ##.##, where the first two digits are the major version and the next two digits are the minor version. SQL_SPEC_MAJOR and SQL_SPEC_MINOR define the major and minor version numbers. For the version of ODBC described in this manual, these are 2 and 0, and the driver should return "02.00". If a driver supports **SQLGetInfo** but does not support this value of the *fInfoType* argument, the Driver Manager returns "01.00".
SQL_DRIVER_VER (ODBC 1.0)	A character string with the version of the driver and, optionally a description of the driver. At a minimum, the version is of the form ##.##.####, where the first two digits are the major version, the next two digits are the minor version, and the last four digits are the release version.
SQL_EXPRESSIONS_IN_ORDERBY (ODBC 1.0)	A character string: "Y" if the data source supports expressions in the **ORDER BY** list; "N" if it does not.

InfoType	Returns
SQL_FETCH_DIRECTION (ODBC 1.0) The information type was introduced in ODBC 1.0; each bitmask is labeled with the version in which it was introduced.	A 32-bit bitmask enumerating the supported fetch direction options. The following bitmasks are used in conjunction with the flag to determine which options are supported: SQL_FD_FETCH_NEXT (ODBC 1.0) SQL_FD_FETCH_FIRST (ODBC 1.0) SQL_FD_FETCH_LAST (ODBC 1.0) SQL_FD_FETCH_PRIOR (ODBC 1.0) SQL_FD_FETCH_ABSOLUTE (ODBC 1.0) SQL_FD_FETCH_RELATIVE (ODBC 1.0) SQL_FD_FETCH_RESUME (ODBC 1.0) SQL_FD_FETCH_BOOKMARK (ODBC 2.0)
SQL_FILE_USAGE (ODBC 2.0)	A 16-bit integer value indicating how a single-tier driver directly treats files in a data source: SQL_FILE_NOT_SUPPORTED = The driver is not a single-tier driver. For example, an ORACLE driver is a two-tier driver. SQL_FILE_TABLE = A single-tier driver treats files in a data source as tables. For example, an Xbase driver treats each Xbase file as a table. SQL_FILE_QUALIFIER = A single-tier driver treats files in a data source as a qualifier. For example, a Microsoft Access driver treats each Microsoft Access file as a complete database. An application might use this to determine how users will select data. For example, Xbase users often think of data as stored in files, while ORACLE and Microsoft Access users generally think of data as stored in tables. When a user selects an Xbase data source, the application could display the Windows File Open common dialog box; when the user selects a Microsoft Access or ORACLE data source, the application could display a custom Select Table dialog box.

InfoType	Returns
SQL_GETDATA_EXTENSIONS (ODBC 2.0)	A 32-bit bitmask enumerating extensions to **SQLGetData**.
	The following bitmasks are used in conjunction with the flag to determine what common extensions the driver supports for **SQLGetData**:
	SQL_GD_ANY_COLUMN = **SQLGetData** can be called for any unbound column, including those before the last bound column. Note that the columns must be called in order of ascending column number unless SQL_GD_ANY_ORDER is also returned.
	SQL_GD_ANY_ORDER = **SQLGetData** can be called for unbound columns in any order. Note that **SQLGetData** can only be called for columns after the last bound column unless SQL_GD_ANY_COLUMN is also returned.
	SQL_GD_BLOCK = **SQLGetData** can be called for an unbound column in any row in a block (more than one row) of data after positioning to that row with **SQLSetPos**.
	SQL_GD_BOUND = **SQLGetData** can be called for bound columns as well as unbound columns. A driver cannot return this value unless it also returns SQL_GD_ANY_COLUMN.
	SQLGetData is only required to return data from unbound columns that occur after the last bound column, are called in order of increasing column number, and are not in a row in a block of rows.
SQL_GROUP_BY (ODBC 2.0)	A 16-bit integer value specifying the relationship between the columns in the **GROUP BY** clause and the non-aggregated columns in the select list:
	SQL_GB_NOT_SUPPORTED = **GROUP BY** clauses are not supported.
	SQL_GB_GROUP_BY_EQUALS_SELECT = The **GROUP BY** clause must contain all non-aggregated columns in the select list. It cannot contain any other columns. For example, **SELECT DEPT, MAX(SALARY) FROM EMPLOYEE GROUP BY DEPT**.
	SQL_GB_GROUP_BY_CONTAINS_SELECT = The **GROUP BY** clause must contain all non-aggregated columns in the select list. It can contain columns that are not in the select list. For example, **SELECT DEPT, MAX(SALARY) FROM EMPLOYEE GROUP BY DEPT, AGE**.
	SQL_GB_NO_RELATION = The columns in the **GROUP BY** clause and the select list are not related. The meaning of non-grouped, non-aggregated columns in the select list is data source–dependent. For example, **SELECT DEPT, SALARY FROM EMPLOYEE GROUP BY DEPT, AGE**.

InfoType	Returns
SQL_IDENTIFIER_CASE (ODBC 1.0)	A 16-bit integer value as follows: SQL_IC_UPPER = Identifiers in SQL are case insensitive and are stored in upper case in system catalog. SQL_IC_LOWER = Identifiers in SQL are case insensitive and are stored in lower case in system catalog. SQL_IC_SENSITIVE = Identifiers in SQL are case sensitive and are stored in mixed case in system catalog. SQL_IC_MIXED = Identifiers in SQL are case insensitive and are stored in mixed case in system catalog.
SQL_IDENTIFIER_QUOTE_CHAR (ODBC 1.0)	The character string used as the starting and ending delimiter of a quoted (delimited) identifiers in SQL statements. (Identifiers passed as arguments to ODBC functions do not need to be quoted.) If the data source does not support quoted identifiers, a blank is returned.
SQL_KEYWORDS (ODBC 2.0)	A character string containing a comma-separated list of all data source–specific keywords. This list does not contain keywords specific to ODBC or keywords used by both the data source and ODBC. For a list of ODBC keywords, see "List of Reserved Keywords" in Appendix C, "SQL Grammar." The **#define** value SQL_ODBC_KEYWORDS contains a comma-separated list of ODBC keywords.
SQL_LIKE_ESCAPE_CLAUSE (ODBC 2.0)	A character string: "Y" if the data source supports an escape character for the percent character (%) and underscore character (_) in a **LIKE** predicate and the driver supports the ODBC syntax for defining a **LIKE** predicate escape character; "N" otherwise.
SQL_LOCK_TYPES (ODBC 2.0)	A 32-bit bitmask enumerating the supported lock types for the *fLock* argument in **SQLSetPos**. The following bitmasks are used in conjunction with the flag to determine which lock types are supported: SQL_LCK_NO_CHANGE SQL_LCK_EXCLUSIVE SQL_LCK_UNLOCK
SQL_MAX_BINARY_LITERAL_LEN (ODBC 2.0)	A 32-bit integer value specifying the maximum length (number of hexadecimal characters, excluding the literal prefix and suffix returned by **SQLGetTypeInfo**) of a binary literal in an SQL statement. For example, the binary literal 0xFFAA has a length of 4. If there is no maximum length or the length is unknown, this value is set to zero.

InfoType	Returns
SQL_MAX_CHAR_LITERAL_LEN (ODBC 2.0)	A 32-bit integer value specifying the maximum length (number of characters, excluding the literal prefix and suffix returned by **SQLGetTypeInfo**) of a character literal in an SQL statement. If there is no maximum length or the length is unknown, this value is set to zero.
SQL_MAX_COLUMN_NAME_LEN (ODBC 1.0)	A 16-bit integer value specifying the maximum length of a column name in the data source. If there is no maximum length or the length is unknown, this value is set to zero.
SQL_MAX_COLUMNS_IN_GROUP_BY (ODBC 2.0)	A 16-bit integer value specifying the maximum number of columns allowed in a **GROUP BY** clause. If there is no specified limit or the limit is unknown, this value is set to zero.
SQL_MAX_COLUMNS_IN_INDEX (ODBC 2.0)	A 16-bit integer value specifying the maximum number of columns allowed in an index. If there is no specified limit or the limit is unknown, this value is set to zero.
SQL_MAX_COLUMNS_IN_ORDER_BY (ODBC 2.0)	A 16-bit integer value specifying the maximum number of columns allowed in an **ORDER BY** clause. If there is no specified limit or the limit is unknown, this value is set to zero.
SQL_MAX_COLUMNS_IN_SELECT (ODBC 2.0)	A 16-bit integer value specifying the maximum number of columns allowed in a select list. If there is no specified limit or the limit is unknown, this value is set to zero.
SQL_MAX_COLUMNS_IN_TABLE (ODBC 2.0)	A 16-bit integer value specifying the maximum number of columns allowed in a table. If there is no specified limit or the limit is unknown, this value is set to zero.
SQL_MAX_CURSOR_NAME_LEN (ODBC 1.0)	A 16-bit integer value specifying the maximum length of a cursor name in the data source. If there is no maximum length or the length is unknown, this value is set to zero.
SQL_MAX_INDEX_SIZE (ODBC 2.0)	A 32-bit integer value specifying the maximum number of bytes allowed in the combined fields of an index. If there is no specified limit or the limit is unknown, this value is set to zero.
SQL_MAX_OWNER_NAME_LEN (ODBC 1.0)	A 16-bit integer value specifying the maximum length of an owner name in the data source. If there is no maximum length or the length is unknown, this value is set to zero.
SQL_MAX_PROCEDURE_NAME_LEN (ODBC 1.0)	A 16-bit integer value specifying the maximum length of a procedure name in the data source. If there is no maximum length or the length is unknown, this value is set to zero.
SQL_MAX_QUALIFIER_NAME_LEN (ODBC 1.0)	A 16-bit integer value specifying the maximum length of a qualifier name in the data source. If there is no maximum length or the length is unknown, this value is set to zero.
SQL_MAX_ROW_SIZE (ODBC 2.0)	A 32-bit integer value specifying the maximum length of a single row in a table. If there is no specified limit or the limit is unknown, this value is set to zero.

InfoType	Returns
SQL_MAX_ROW_SIZE_INCLUDES_ LONG (ODBC 2.0)	A character string: "Y" if the maximum row size returned for the SQL_MAX_ROW_SIZE information type includes the length of all SQL_LONGVARCHAR and SQL_LONGVARBINARY columns in the row; "N" otherwise.
SQL_MAX_STATEMENT_LEN (ODBC 2.0)	A 32-bit integer value specifying the maximum length (number of characters, including white space) of an SQL statement. If there is no maximum length or the length is unknown, this value is set to zero.
SQL_MAX_TABLE_NAME_LEN (ODBC 1.0)	A 16-bit integer value specifying the maximum length of a table name in the data source. If there is no maximum length or the length is unknown, this value is set to zero.
SQL_MAX_TABLES_IN_SELECT (ODBC 2.0)	A 16-bit integer value specifying the maximum number of tables allowed in the **FROM** clause of a **SELECT** statement. If there is no specified limit or the limit is unknown, this value is set to zero.
SQL_MAX_USER_NAME_LEN (ODBC 2.0)	A 16-bit integer value specifying the maximum length of a user name in the data source. If there is no maximum length or the length is unknown, this value is set to zero.
SQL_MULT_RESULT_SETS (ODBC 1.0)	A character string: "Y" if the data source supports multiple result sets, "N" if it does not.
SQL_MULTIPLE_ACTIVE_TXN (ODBC 1.0)	A character string: "Y" if active transactions on multiple connections are allowed, "N" if only one connection at a time can have an active transaction.
SQL_NEED_LONG_DATA_LEN (ODBC 2.0)	A character string: "Y" if the data source needs the length of a long data value (the data type is SQL_LONGVARCHAR, SQL_LONGVARBINARY, or a long, data source–specific data type) before that value is sent to the data source, "N" if it does not. For more information, see **SQLBindParameter** and **SQLSetPos**.
SQL_NON_NULLABLE_COLUMNS (ODBC 1.0)	A 16-bit integer specifying whether the data source supports non-nullable columns: SQL_NNC_NULL = All columns must be nullable. SQL_NNC_NON_NULL = Columns may be non-nullable (the data source supports the **NOT NULL** column constraint in **CREATE TABLE** statements).
SQL_NULL_COLLATION (ODBC 2.0)	A 16-bit integer value specifying where NULLs are sorted in a list: SQL_NC_END = NULLs are sorted at the end of the list, regardless of the sort order. SQL_NC_HIGH = NULLs are sorted at the high end of the list. SQL_NC_LOW = NULLs are sorted at the low end of the list. SQL_NC_START = NULLs are sorted at the start of the list, regardless of the sort order.

InfoType	Returns
SQL_NUMERIC_FUNCTIONS (ODBC 1.0)	A 32-bit bitmask enumerating the scalar numeric functions supported by the driver and associated data source.
The information type was introduced in ODBC 1.0; each bitmask is labeled with the version in which it was introduced.	The following bitmasks are used to determine which numeric functions are supported:

SQL_FN_NUM_ABS	(ODBC 1.0)
SQL_FN_NUM_ACOS	(ODBC 1.0)
SQL_FN_NUM_ASIN	(ODBC 1.0)
SQL_FN_NUM_ATAN	(ODBC 1.0)
SQL_FN_NUM_ATAN2	(ODBC 1.0)
SQL_FN_NUM_CEILING	(ODBC 1.0)
SQL_FN_NUM_COS	(ODBC 1.0)
SQL_FN_NUM_COT	(ODBC 1.0)
SQL_FN_NUM_DEGREES	(ODBC 2.0)
SQL_FN_NUM_EXP	(ODBC 1.0)
SQL_FN_NUM_FLOOR	(ODBC 1.0)
SQL_FN_NUM_LOG	(ODBC 1.0)
SQL_FN_NUM_LOG10	(ODBC 2.0)
SQL_FN_NUM_MOD	(ODBC 1.0)
SQL_FN_NUM_PI	(ODBC 1.0)
SQL_FN_NUM_POWER	(ODBC 2.0)
SQL_FN_NUM_RADIANS	(ODBC 2.0)
SQL_FN_NUM_RAND	(ODBC 1.0)
SQL_FN_NUM_ROUND	(ODBC 2.0)
SQL_FN_NUM_SIGN	(ODBC 1.0)
SQL_FN_NUM_SIN	(ODBC 1.0)
SQL_FN_NUM_SQRT	(ODBC 1.0)
SQL_FN_NUM_TAN	(ODBC 1.0)
SQL_FN_NUM_TRUNCATE	(ODBC 2.0)

InfoType	Returns
SQL_ODBC_API_CONFORMANCE (ODBC 1.0)	A 16-bit integer value indicating the level of ODBC conformance: SQL_OAC_NONE = None SQL_OAC_LEVEL1 = Level 1 supported SQL_OAC_LEVEL2 = Level 2 supported (For a list of functions and conformance levels, see Chapter 21, "Function Summary.")
SQL_ODBC_SAG_CLI_ CONFORMANCE (ODBC 1.0)	A 16-bit integer value indicating compliance to the functions of the SAG specification: SQL_OSCC_NOT_COMPLIANT = Not SAG-compliant; one or more core functions are not supported SQL_OSCC_COMPLIANT = SAG-compliant

InfoType	Returns
SQL_ODBC_SQL_CONFORMANCE (ODBC 1.0)	A 16-bit integer value indicating SQL grammar supported by the driver:
	SQL_OSC_MINIMUM = Minimum grammar supported
	SQL_OSC_CORE = Core grammar supported
	SQL_OSC_EXTENDED = Extended grammar supported
SQL_ODBC_SQL_OPT_IEF (ODBC 1.0)	A character string: "Y" if the data source supports the optional Integrity Enhancement Facility; "N" if it does not.
SQL_ODBC_VER (ODBC 1.0)	A character string with the version of ODBC to which the Driver Manager conforms. The version is of the form ##.##, where the first two digits are the major version and the next two digits are the minor version. This is implemented solely in the Driver Manager.
SQL_ORDER_BY_COLUMNS_IN_ SELECT (ODBC 2.0)	A character string: "Y" if the columns in the **ORDER BY** clause must be in the select list; otherwise, "N".
SQL_OUTER_JOINS (ODBC 1.0) The information type was introduced in ODBC 1.0; each return value is labeled with the version in which it was introduced.	A character string:
	"N" = No. The data source does not support outer joins. (ODBC 1.0)
	"Y" = Yes. The data source supports two-table outer joins, and the driver supports the ODBC outer join syntax except for nested outer joins. However, columns on the left side of the comparison operator in the ON clause must come from the left-hand table in the outer join, and columns on the right side of the comparison operator must come from the right-hand table. (ODBC 1.0)
	"P" = Partial. The data source partially supports nested outer joins, and the driver supports the ODBC outer join syntax. However, columns on the left side of the comparison operator in the ON clause must come from the left-hand table in the outer join and columns on the right side of the comparison operator must come from the right-hand table. Also, the right-hand table of an outer join cannot be included in an inner join. (ODBC 2.0)
	"F" = Full. The data source fully supports nested outer joins, and the driver supports the ODBC outer join syntax. (ODBC 2.0)
SQL_OWNER_TERM (ODBC 1.0)	A character string with the data source vendor's name for an owner; for example, "owner", "Authorization ID", or "Schema".

InfoType	Returns
SQL_OWNER_USAGE (ODBC 2.0)	A 32-bit bitmask enumerating the statements in which owners can be used: SQL_OU_DML_STATEMENTS = Owners are supported in all Data Manipulation Language statements: **SELECT, INSERT, UPDATE, DELETE,** and, if supported, **SELECT FOR UPDATE** and positioned update and delete statements. SQL_OU_PROCEDURE_INVOCATION = Owners are supported in the ODBC procedure invocation statement. SQL_OU_TABLE_DEFINITION = Owners are supported in all table definition statements: **CREATE TABLE, CREATE VIEW, ALTER TABLE, DROP TABLE,** and **DROP VIEW.** SQL_OU_INDEX_DEFINITION = Owners are supported in all index definition statements: **CREATE INDEX** and **DROP INDEX.** SQL_OU_PRIVILEGE_DEFINITION = Owners are supported in all privilege definition statements: **GRANT** and **REVOKE.**
SQL_POS_OPERATIONS (ODBC 2.0)	A 32-bit bitmask enumerating the supported operations in **SQLSetPos.** The following bitmasks are used to in conjunction with the flag to determine which options are supported: SQL_POS_POSITION SQL_POS_REFRESH SQL_POS_UPDATE SQL_POS_DELETE SQL_POS_ADD
SQL_POSITIONED_STATEMENTS (ODBC 2.0)	A 32-bit bitmask enumerating the supported positioned SQL statements. The following bitmasks are used to determine which statements are supported: SQL_PS_POSITIONED_DELETE SQL_PS_POSITIONED_UPDATE SQL_PS_SELECT_FOR_UPDATE
SQL_PROCEDURE_TERM (ODBC 1.0)	A character string with the data source vendor's name for a procedure; for example, "database procedure", "stored procedure", or "procedure".
SQL_PROCEDURES (ODBC 1.0)	A character string: "Y" if the data source supports procedures and the driver supports the ODBC procedure invocation syntax; "N" otherwise.

InfoType	Returns
SQL_QUALIFIER_LOCATION (ODBC 2.0)	A 16-bit integer value indicating the position of the qualifier in a qualified table name: SQL_QL_START SQL_QL_END For example, an Xbase driver returns SQL_QL_START because the directory (qualifier) name is at the start of the table name, as in \EMPDATA\EMP.DBF. An ORACLE Server driver returns SQL_QL_END, because the qualifier is at the end of the table name, as in ADMIN.EMP@EMPDATA.
SQL_QUALIFIER_NAME_SEPARATOR (ODBC 1.0)	A character string: the character or characters that the data source defines as the separator between a qualifier name and the qualified name element that follows it.
SQL_QUALIFIER_TERM (ODBC 1.0)	A character string with the data source vendor's name for a qualifier; for example, "database" or "directory".
SQL_QUALIFIER_USAGE (ODBC 2.0)	A 32-bit bitmask enumerating the statements in which qualifiers can be used. The following bitmasks are used to determine where qualifiers can be used: SQL_QU_DML_STATEMENTS = Qualifiers are supported in all Data Manipulation Language statements: **SELECT, INSERT, UPDATE, DELETE**, and, if supported, **SELECT FOR UPDATE** and positioned update and delete statements. SQL_QU_PROCEDURE_INVOCATION = Qualifiers are supported in the ODBC procedure invocation statement. SQL_QU_TABLE_DEFINITION = Qualifiers are supported in all table definition statements: **CREATE TABLE, CREATE VIEW, ALTER TABLE, DROP TABLE**, and **DROP VIEW**. SQL_QU_INDEX_DEFINITION = Qualifiers are supported in all index definition statements: **CREATE INDEX** and **DROP INDEX**. SQL_QU_PRIVILEGE_DEFINITION = Qualifiers are supported in all privilege definition statements: **GRANT** and **REVOKE**.
SQL_QUOTED_IDENTIFIER_CASE (ODBC 2.0)	A 16-bit integer value as follows: SQL_IC_UPPER = Quoted identifiers in SQL are case insensitive and are stored in upper case in system catalog. SQL_IC_LOWER = Quoted identifiers in SQL are case insensitive and are stored in lower case in system catalog. SQL_IC_SENSITIVE = Quoted identifiers in SQL are case sensitive and are stored in mixed case in system catalog. SQL_IC_MIXED = Quoted identifiers in SQL are case insensitive and are stored in mixed case in system catalog.

InfoType	Returns
SQL_ROW_UPDATES (ODBC 1.0)	A character string: "Y" if a keyset-driven or mixed cursor maintains row versions or values for all fetched rows and therefore can detect any changes made to a row by any user since the row was last fetched; otherwise, "N".
SQL_SCROLL_CONCURRENCY (ODBC 1.0)	A 32-bit bitmask enumerating the concurrency control options supported for scrollable cursors.
	The following bitmasks are used to determine which options are supported:
	SQL_SCCO_READ_ONLY = Cursor is read only. No updates are allowed.
	SQL_SCCO_LOCK = Cursor uses the lowest level of locking sufficient to ensure that the row can be updated.
	SQL_SCCO_OPT_ROWVER = Cursor uses optimistic concurrency control, comparing row versions, such as SQLBase® ROWID or Sybase TIMESTAMP.
	SQL_SCCO_OPT_VALUES = Cursor uses optimistic concurrency control, comparing values.
	For information about cursor concurrency, see "Specifying Cursor Concurrency" in Chapter 7, "Retrieving Results."
SQL_SCROLL_OPTIONS (ODBC 1.0) The information type was introduced in ODBC 1.0; each bitmask is labeled with the version in which it was introduced.	A 32-bit bitmask enumerating the scroll options supported for scrollable cursors.
	The following bitmasks are used to determine which options are supported:
	SQL_SO_FORWARD_ONLY = The cursor only scrolls forward. (ODBC 1.0)
	SQL_SO_STATIC = The data in the result set is static. (ODBC 2.0)
	SQL_SO_KEYSET_DRIVEN = The driver saves and uses the keys for every row in the result set. (ODBC 1.0)
	SQL_SO_DYNAMIC = The driver keeps the keys for every row in the rowset (the keyset size is the same as the rowset size). (ODBC 1.0)
	SQL_SO_MIXED = The driver keeps the keys for every row in the keyset, and the keyset size is greater than the rowset size. The cursor is keyset-driven inside the keyset and dynamic outside the keyset. (ODBC 1.0)
	For information about scrollable cursors, see "Scrollable Cursors" in Chapter 7, "Retrieving Results."

InfoType	Returns
SQL_SEARCH_PATTERN_ESCAPE (ODBC 1.0)	A character string specifying what the driver supports as an escape character that permits the use of the pattern match metacharacters underscore (_) and percent (%) as valid characters in search patterns. This escape character applies only for those catalog function arguments that support search strings. If this string is empty, the driver does not support a search-pattern escape character. This *fInfoType* is limited to catalog functions. For a description of the use of the escape character in search pattern strings, see "Search Pattern Arguments" earlier in this chapter.
SQL_SERVER_NAME (ODBC 1.0)	A character string with the actual data source–specific server name; useful when a data source name is used during **SQLConnect, SQLDriverConnect,** and **SQLBrowseConnect**.
SQL_SPECIAL_CHARACTERS (ODBC 2.0)	A character string containing all special characters (that is, all characters except a through z, A through Z, 0 through 9, and underscore) that can be used in an object name, such as a table, column, or index name, on the data source. For example, "#$^".
SQL_STATIC_SENSITIVITY (ODBC 2.0)	A 32-bit bitmask enumerating whether changes made by an application to a static or keyset-driven cursor through **SQLSetPos** or positioned update or delete statements can be detected by that application: SQL_SS_ADDITIONS = Added rows are visible to the cursor; the cursor can scroll to these rows. Where these rows are added to the cursor is driver-dependent. SQL_SS_DELETIONS = Deleted rows are no longer available to the cursor and do not leave a "hole" in the result set; after the cursor scrolls from a deleted row, it cannot return to that row. SQL_SS_UPDATES = Updates to rows are visible to the cursor; if the cursor scrolls from and returns to an updated row, the data returned by the cursor is the updated data, not the original data. Because updating key values in a keyset-driven cursor is considered to be deleting the existing row and adding a new row, this value is always returned for keyset-driven cursors. Whether an application can detect changes made to the result set by other users, including other cursors in the same application, depends on the cursor type. For more information, see "Scrollable Cursors" in Chapter 7, "Retrieving Results."

InfoType	Returns
SQL_STRING_FUNCTIONS (ODBC 1.0)	A 32-bit bitmask enumerating the scalar string functions supported by the driver and associated data source.
The information type was introduced in ODBC 1.0; each bitmask is labeled with the version in which it was introduced.	The following bitmasks are used to determine which string functions are supported:

SQL_FN_STR_ASCII   (ODBC 1.0)
SQL_FN_STR_CHAR   (ODBC 1.0)
SQL_FN_STR_CONCAT   (ODBC 1.0)
SQL_FN_STR_DIFFERENCE (ODBC 2.0)
SQL_FN_STR_INSERT   (ODBC 1.0)
SQL_FN_STR_LCASE   (ODBC 1.0)
SQL_FN_STR_LEFT   (ODBC 1.0)
SQL_FN_STR_LENGTH   (ODBC 1.0)
SQL_FN_STR_LOCATE   (ODBC 1.0)
SQL_FN_STR_LOCATE_2   (ODBC 2.0)
SQL_FN_STR_LTRIM   (ODBC 1.0)
SQL_FN_STR_REPEAT   (ODBC 1.0)
SQL_FN_STR_REPLACE   (ODBC 1.0)
SQL_FN_STR_RIGHT   (ODBC 1.0)
SQL_FN_STR_RTRIM   (ODBC 1.0)
SQL_FN_STR_SOUNDEX   (ODBC 2.0)
SQL_FN_STR_SPACE   (ODBC 2.0)
SQL_FN_STR_SUBSTRING   (ODBC 1.0)
SQL_FN_STR_UCASE   (ODBC 1.0)

If an application can call the LOCATE scalar function with the *string_exp1*, *string_exp2*, and *start* arguments, the driver returns the SQL_FN_STR_LOCATE bitmask. If an application can call the LOCATE scalar function with only the *string_exp1* and *string_exp2* arguments, the driver returns the SQL_FN_STR_LOCATE_2 bitmask. Drivers that fully support the LOCATE scalar function return both bitmasks.

InfoType	Returns
SQL_SUBQUERIES (ODBC 2.0)	A 32-bit bitmask enumerating the predicates that support subqueries:

SQL_SQ_CORRELATED_SUBQUERIES
SQL_SQ_COMPARISON
SQL_SQ_EXISTS
SQL_SQ_IN
SQL_SQ_QUANTIFIED

The SQL_SQ_CORRELATED_SUBQUERIES bitmask indicates that all predicates that support subqueries support correlated subqueries.

InfoType	Returns
SQL_SYSTEM_FUNCTIONS (ODBC 1.0)	A 32-bit bitmask enumerating the scalar system functions supported by the driver and associated data source.
	The following bitmasks are used to determine which system functions are supported:
	SQL_FN_SYS_DBNAME SQL_FN_SYS_IFNULL SQL_FN_SYS_USERNAME
SQL_TABLE_TERM (ODBC 1.0)	A character string with the data source vendor's name for a table; for example, "table" or "file".
SQL_TIMEDATE_ADD_INTERVALS (ODBC 2.0)	A 32-bit bitmask enumerating the timestamp intervals supported by the driver and associated data source for the TIMESTAMPADD scalar function.
	The following bitmasks are used to determine which intervals are supported:
	SQL_FN_TSI_FRAC_SECOND SQL_FN_TSI_SECOND SQL_FN_TSI_MINUTE SQL_FN_TSI_HOUR SQL_FN_TSI_DAY SQL_FN_TSI_WEEK SQL_FN_TSI_MONTH SQL_FN_TSI_QUARTER SQL_FN_TSI_YEAR
SQL_TIMEDATE_DIFF_INTERVALS (ODBC 2.0)	A 32-bit bitmask enumerating the timestamp intervals supported by the driver and associated data source for the TIMESTAMPDIFF scalar function.
	The following bitmasks are used to determine which intervals are supported:
	SQL_FN_TSI_FRAC_SECOND SQL_FN_TSI_SECOND SQL_FN_TSI_MINUTE SQL_FN_TSI_HOUR SQL_FN_TSI_DAY SQL_FN_TSI_WEEK SQL_FN_TSI_MONTH SQL_FN_TSI_QUARTER SQL_FN_TSI_YEAR

InfoType	Returns
SQL_TIMEDATE_FUNCTIONS (ODBC 1.0)	A 32-bit bitmask enumerating the scalar date and time functions supported by the driver and associated data source.
The information type was introduced in ODBC 1.0; each bitmask is labeled with the version in which it was introduced.	The following bitmasks are used to determine which date and time functions are supported:

SQL_FN_TD_CURDATE   (ODBC 1.0)
SQL_FN_TD_CURTIME   (ODBC 1.0)
SQL_FN_TD_DAYNAME   (ODBC 2.0)
SQL_FN_TD_DAYOFMONTH   (ODBC 1.0)
SQL_FN_TD_DAYOFWEEK   (ODBC 1.0)
SQL_FN_TD_DAYOFYEAR   (ODBC 1.0)
SQL_FN_TD_HOUR   (ODBC 1.0)
SQL_FN_TD_MINUTE   (ODBC 1.0)
SQL_FN_TD_MONTH   (ODBC 1.0)
SQL_FN_TD_MONTHNAME   (ODBC 2.0)
SQL_FN_TD_NOW   (ODBC 1.0)
SQL_FN_TD_QUARTER   (ODBC 1.0)
SQL_FN_TD_SECOND   (ODBC 1.0)
SQL_FN_TD_TIMESTAMPADD   (ODBC 2.0)
SQL_FN_TD_TIMESTAMPDIFF   (ODBC 2.0)
SQL_FN_TD_WEEK   (ODBC 1.0)
SQL_FN_TD_YEAR   (ODBC 1.0)

InfoType	Returns
SQL_TXN_CAPABLE (ODBC 1.0)	A 16-bit integer value describing the transaction support in the driver or data source:
The information type was introduced in ODBC 1.0; each return value is labeled with the version in which it was introduced	SQL_TC_NONE = Transactions not supported. (ODBC 1.0)

SQL_TC_DML = Transactions can only contain Data Manipulation Language (DML) statements (**SELECT, INSERT, UPDATE, DELETE**). Data Definition Language (DDL) statements encountered in a transaction cause an error. (ODBC 1.0)

SQL_TC_DDL_COMMIT = Transactions can only contain DML statements. DDL statements (**CREATE TABLE, DROP INDEX,** an so on) encountered in a transaction cause the transaction to be committed. (ODBC 2.0)

SQL_TC_DDL_IGNORE = Transactions can only contain DML statements. DDL statements encountered in a transaction are ignored. (ODBC 2.0)

SQL_TC_ALL = Transactions can contain DDL statements and DML statements in any order. (ODBC 1.0)

InfoType	Returns
SQL_TXN_ISOLATION_OPTION (ODBC 1.0)	A 32-bit bitmask enumerating the transaction isolation levels available from the driver or data source. The following bitmasks are used in conjunction with the flag to determine which options are supported:
	SQL_TXN_READ_UNCOMMITTED SQL_TXN_READ_COMMITTED SQL_TXN_REPEATABLE_READ SQL_TXN_SERIALIZABLE SQL_TXN_VERSIONING
	For descriptions of these isolation levels, see the description of SQL_DEFAULT_TXN_ISOLATION.
SQL_UNION (ODBC 2.0)	A 32-bit bitmask enumerating the support for the **UNION** clause:
	SQL_U_UNION = The data source supports the **UNION** clause.
	SQL_U_UNION_ALL = The data source supports the **ALL** keyword in the **UNION** clause. (**SQLGetInfo** returns both SQL_U_UNION and SQL_U_UNION_ALL in this case.)
SQL_USER_NAME (ODBC 1.0)	A character string with the name used in a particular database, which can be different than login name.

Code Example

SQLGetInfo returns lists of supported options as a 32-bit bitmask in *rgbInfoValue*. The bitmask for each option is used in conjunction with the flag to determine whether the option is supported.

For example, an application could use the following code to determine whether the SUBSTRING scalar function is supported by the driver associated with the *hdbc*:

```
UDWORD    fFuncs;

SQLGetInfo(hdbc,
            SQL_STRING_FUNCTIONS,
            (PTR)&fFuncs,
            sizeof(fFuncs),
            NULL);

if (fFuncs & SQL_FN_STR_SUBSTRING) /* SUBSTRING supported */
    ...;
else                                /* SUBSTRING not supported */
    ...;
```

Related Functions

For information about	See
Returning the setting of a connection option	**SQLGetConnectOption** (extension)
Determining if a driver supports a function	**SQLGetFunctions** (extension)
Returning the setting of a statement option	**SQLGetStmtOption** (extension)
Returning information about a data source's data types	**SQLGetTypeInfo** (extension)

SQLGetStmtOption

Extension Level 1   SQLGetStmtOption returns the current setting of a statement option.

Syntax   RETCODE **SQLGetStmtOption**(*hstmt*, *fOption*, *pvParam*)

The **SQLGetStmtOption** function accepts the following arguments:

Type	Argument	Use	Description
HSTMT	*hstmt*	Input	Statement handle.
UWORD	*fOption*	Input	Option to retrieve.
PTR	*pvParam*	Output	Value associated with *fOption*. Depending on the value of *fOption*, a 32-bit integer value or a pointer to a null-terminated character string will be returned in *pvParam*.

Returns   SQL_SUCCESS, SQL_SUCCESS_WITH_INFO, SQL_ERROR, or SQL_INVALID_HANDLE.

Diagnostics   When **SQLGetStmtOption** returns SQL_ERROR or SQL_SUCCESS_WITH_INFO, an associated SQLSTATE value may be obtained by calling **SQLError**. The following table lists the SQLSTATE values commonly returned by **SQLGetStmtOption** and explains each one in the context of this function; the notation "(DM)" precedes the descriptions of SQLSTATEs returned by the Driver Manager. The return code associated with each SQLSTATE value is SQL_ERROR, unless noted otherwise.

SQLSTATE	Error	Description
01000	General warning	Driver-specific informational message. (Function returns SQL_SUCCESS_WITH_INFO.)
24000	Invalid cursor state	The argument *fOption* was SQL_ROW_NUMBER or SQL_GET_BOOKMARK and the cursor was not open, or the cursor was positioned before the start of the result set or after the end of the result set.
IM001	Driver does not support this function	(DM) The driver corresponding to the *hstmt* does not support the function.

SQLSTATE	Error	Description
S1000	General error	An error occurred for which there was no specific SQLSTATE and for which no implementation-specific SQLSTATE was defined. The error message returned by **SQLError** in the argument *szErrorMsg* describes the error and its cause.
S1001	Memory allocation failure	The driver was unable to allocate memory required to support execution or completion of the function.
S1010	Function sequence error	(DM) An asynchronously executing function was called for the *hstmt* and was still executing when this function was called.
		(DM) **SQLExecute**, **SQLExecDirect**, or **SQLSetPos** was called for the *hstmt* and returned SQL_NEED_DATA. This function was called before data was sent for all data-at-execution parameters or columns.
S1011	Operation invalid at this time	The *fOption* argument was SQL_GET_BOOKMARK and the value of the SQL_USE_BOOKMARKS statement option was SQL_UB_OFF.
S1092	Option type out of range	(DM) The value specified for the argument *fOption* was in the block of numbers reserved for ODBC connection and statement options, but was not valid for the version of ODBC supported by the driver.
S1109	Invalid cursor position	The *fOption* argument was SQL_GET_BOOKMARK or SQL_ROW_NUMBER and the value in the *rgfRowStatus* array in **SQLExtendedFetch** for the current row was SQL_ROW_DELETED or SQL_ROW_ERROR.
S1C00	Driver not capable	The value specified for the argument *fOption* was a valid ODBC statement option for the version of ODBC supported by the driver, but was not supported by the driver.
		The value specified for the argument *fOption* was in the block of numbers reserved for driver-specific connection and statement options, but was not supported by the driver.

Comments   The following table lists statement options for which corresponding values can be returned, but not set. The table also lists the version of ODBC in which they were introduced. For a list of options that can be set and retrieved, see **SQLSetStmtOption**. If *fOption* specifies an option that returns a string, *pvParam* must be a pointer to storage for the string. The maximum length of the string will be SQL_MAX_OPTION_STRING_LENGTH bytes (excluding the null termination byte).

fOption	*pvParam* contents
SQL_GET_BOOKMARK (ODBC 2.0)	A 32-bit integer value that is the bookmark for the current row. Before using this option, an application must set the SQL_USE_BOOKMARKS statement option to SQL_UB_ON, create a result set, and call **SQLExtendedFetch**.
	To return to the rowset starting with the row marked by this bookmark, an application calls **SQLExtendedFetch** with the SQL_FETCH_BOOKMARK fetch type and *irow* set to this value.
	Bookmarks are also returned as column 0 of the result set.
SQL_ROW_NUMBER (ODBC 2.0)	A 32-bit integer value that specifies the number of the current row in the entire result set. If the number of the current row cannot be determined or there is no current row, the driver returns 0.

Related Functions

For information about	See
Returning the setting of a connection option	**SQLGetConnectOption** (extension)
Setting a connection option	**SQLSetConnectOption** (extension)
Setting a statement option	**SQLSetStmtOption** (extension)

SQLGetTypeInfo

Extension Level 1   **SQLGetTypeInfo** returns information about data types supported by the data source. The driver returns the information in the form of an SQL result set.

Important Applications must use the type names returned in the TYPE_NAME column in **ALTER TABLE** and **CREATE TABLE** statements; they must not use the sample type names listed in Appendix C, "SQL Grammar." **SQLGetTypeInfo** may return more than one row with the same value in the DATA_TYPE column.

Syntax   RETCODE **SQLGetTypeInfo**(*hstmt, fSqlType*)

The **SQLGetTypeInfo** function accepts the following arguments:

Type	Argument	Use	Description
HSTMT	*hstmt*	Input	Statement handle for the result set.
SWORD	*fSqlType*	Input	The SQL data type. This must be one of the following values:

SQL_BIGINT
SQL_BINARY
SQL_BIT
SQL_CHAR
SQL_DATE
SQL_DECIMAL
SQL_DOUBLE
SQL_FLOAT
SQL_INTEGER
SQL_LONGVARBINARY
SQL_LONGVARCHAR
SQL_NUMERIC
SQL_REAL
SQL_SMALLINT
SQL_TIME
SQL_TIMESTAMP
SQL_TINYINT
SQL_VARBINARY
SQL_VARCHAR

or a driver-specific SQL data type. SQL_ALL_TYPES specifies that information about all data types should be returned.

For information about ODBC SQL data types, see "SQL Data Types" in Appendix D, "Data Types." For information about driver-specific SQL data types, see the driver's documentation.

Returns

SQL_SUCCESS, SQL_SUCCESS_WITH_INFO, SQL_STILL_EXECUTING, SQL_ERROR, or SQL_INVALID_HANDLE.

Diagnostics

When **SQLGetTypeInfo** returns SQL_ERROR or SQL_SUCCESS_WITH_INFO, an associated SQLSTATE value may be obtained by calling **SQLError**. The following table lists the SQLSTATE values commonly returned by **SQLGetTypeInfo** and explains each one in the context of this function; the notation "(DM)" precedes the descriptions of SQLSTATEs returned by the Driver Manager. The return code associated with each SQLSTATE value is SQL_ERROR, unless noted otherwise.

SQLSTATE	Error	Description
01000	General warning	Driver specific informational message. (Function returns SQL_SUCCESS_WITH_INFO.)
08S01	Communication link failure	The communication link between the driver and the data source to which the driver was connected failed before the function completed processing.
24000	Invalid cursor state	(DM) A cursor was open on the *hstmt* and **SQLFetch** or **SQLExtendedFetch** had not been called.
		A result set was open on the *hstmt* but **SQLFetch** or **SQLExtendedFetch** had not been called.
IM001	Driver does not support this function	(DM) The driver corresponding to the *hstmt* does not support the function.
S1000	General error	An error occurred for which there was no specific SQLSTATE and for which no implementation-specific SQLSTATE was defined. The error message returned by **SQLError** in the argument *szErrorMsg* describes the error and its cause.
S1001	Memory allocation failure	The driver was unable to allocate memory required to support execution or completion of the function.
S1004	SQL data type out of range	(DM) The value specified for the argument *fSqlType* was in the block of numbers reserved for ODBC SQL data type indicators but was not a valid ODBC SQL data type indicator.
S1008	Operation canceled	Asynchronous processing was enabled for the *hstmt*, then the function was called and before it completed execution, **SQLCancel** was called on the *hstmt*. Then the function was called again on the *hstmt*.
		The function was called and, before it completed execution, **SQLCancel** was called on the *hstmt* from a different thread in a multithreaded application.

SQLSTATE	Error	Description
S1010	Function sequence error	(DM) An asynchronously executing function (not this one) was called for the *hstmt* and was still executing when this function was called.
		(DM) **SQLExecute**, **SQLExecDirect**, or **SQLSetPos** was called for the *hstmt* and returned SQL_NEED_DATA. This function was called before data was sent for all data-at-execution parameters or columns.
S1C00	Driver not capable	The value specified for the argument *fSqlType* was in the range of numbers reserved for driver-specific SQL data type indicators, but was not supported by the driver or data source.
		The combination of the current settings of the SQL_CONCURRENCY and SQL_CURSOR_TYPE statement options was not supported by the driver or data source.
S1T00	Timeout expired	The timeout period expired before the data source returned the result set. The timeout period is set through **SQLSetStmtOption**, SQL_QUERY_TIMEOUT.

Comments

SQLGetTypeInfo returns the results as a standard result set, ordered by DATA_TYPE and TYPE_NAME. The following table lists the columns in the result set.

Note **SQLGetTypeInfo** might not return all data types. For example, a driver might not return user-defined data types. Applications can use any valid data type, regardless of whether it is returned by **SQLGetTypeInfo**.

The lengths of VARCHAR columns shown in the table are maximums; the actual lengths depend on the data source.

Column Name	Data Type	Comments
TYPE_NAME	Varchar(128) not NULL	Data source–dependent data type name; for example, "CHAR", "VARCHAR", "MONEY", "LONG VARBINARY", or "CHAR ( ) FOR BIT DATA". Applications must use this name in **CREATE TABLE** and **ALTER TABLE** statements.
DATA_TYPE	Smallint not NULL	SQL data type. This can be an ODBC SQL data type or a driver-specific SQL data type. For a list of valid ODBC SQL data types, see "SQL Data Types" in Appendix D, "Data Types." For information about driver-specific SQL data types, see the driver's documentation.
PRECISION	Integer	The maximum precision of the data type on the data source. NULL is returned for data types where precision is not applicable. For more information on precision, see "Precision, Scale, Length, and Display Size" in Appendix D, "Data Types."
LITERAL_PREFIX	Varchar(128)	Character or characters used to prefix a literal; for example, a single quote (') for character data types or 0x for binary data types; NULL is returned for data types where a literal prefix is not applicable.
LITERAL_SUFFIX	Varchar(128)	Character or characters used to terminate a literal; for example, a single quote (') for character data types; NULL is returned for data types where a literal suffix is not applicable.
CREATE_PARAMS	Varchar(128)	Parameters for a data type definition. For example, CREATE_PARAMS for DECIMAL would be "precision,scale"; CREATE_PARAMS for VARCHAR would equal "max length"; NULL is returned if there are no parameters for the data type definition, for example INTEGER. The driver supplies the CREATE_PARAMS text in the language of the country where it is used.

Column Name	Data Type	Comments
NULLABLE	Smallint not NULL	Whether the data type accepts a NULL value:
		SQL_NO_NULLS if the data type does not accept NULL values.
		SQL_NULLABLE if the data type accepts NULL values.
		SQL_NULLABLE_UNKNOWN if it is not known if the column accepts NULL values.
CASE_SENSITIVE	Smallint not NULL	Whether a character data type is case sensitive in collations and comparisons:
		TRUE if the data type is a character data type and is case sensitive.
		FALSE if the data type is not a character data type or is not case sensitive.
SEARCHABLE	Smallint not NULL	How the data type is used in a **WHERE** clause:
		SQL_UNSEARCHABLE if the data type cannot be used in a **WHERE** clause.
		SQL_LIKE_ONLY if the data type can be used in a **WHERE** clause only with the **LIKE** predicate.
		SQL_ALL_EXCEPT_LIKE if the data type can be used in a **WHERE** clause with all comparison operators except **LIKE**.
		SQL_SEARCHABLE if the data type can be used in a **WHERE** clause with any comparison operator.
UNSIGNED_ATTRIBUTE	Smallint	Whether the data type is unsigned:
		TRUE if the data type is unsigned.
		FALSE if the data type is signed.
		NULL is returned if the attribute is not applicable to the data type or the data type is not numeric.
MONEY	Smallint not NULL	Whether the data type is a money data type:
		TRUE if it is a money data type.
		FALSE if it is not.

Column Name	Data Type	Comments
AUTO_INCREMENT	Smallint	Whether the data type is autoincrementing:
		TRUE if the data type is autoincrementing.
		FALSE if the data type is not autoincrementing.
		NULL is returned if the attribute is not applicable to the data type or the data type is not numeric.
		An application can insert values into a column having this attribute, but cannot update the values in the column.
LOCAL_TYPE_NAME	Varchar(128)	Localized version of the data source–dependent name of the data type. NULL is returned if a localized name is not supported by the data source. This name is intended for display only, such as in dialog boxes.
MINIMUM_SCALE	Smallint	The minimum scale of the data type on the data source. If a data type has a fixed scale, the MINIMUM_SCALE and MAXIMUM_SCALE columns both contain this value. For example, an SQL_TIMESTAMP column might have a fixed scale for fractional seconds. NULL is returned where scale is not applicable. For more information, see "Precision, Scale, Length, and Display Size" in Appendix D, "Data Types."
MAXIMUM_SCALE	Smallint	The maximum scale of the data type on the data source. NULL is returned where scale is not applicable. If the maximum scale is not defined separately on the data source, but is instead defined to be the same as the maximum precision, this column contains the same value as the PRECISION column. For more information, see "Precision, Scale, Length, and Display Size" in Appendix D, "Data Types."

Note The MINIMUM_SCALE and MAXIMUM_SCALE columns were added in ODBC 2.0. ODBC 1.0 drivers may return different, driver-specific columns with the same column numbers.

Attribute information can apply to data types or to specific columns in a result set. **SQLGetTypeInfo** returns information about attributes associated with data types; **SQLColAttributes** returns information about attributes associated with columns in a result set.

Related Functions	**For information about**	**See**
	Assigning storage for a column in a result set	**SQLBindCol**
	Canceling statement processing	**SQLCancel**
	Returning information about a column in a result set	**SQLColAttributes**
	Fetching a block of data or scrolling through a result set	**SQLExtendedFetch** (extension)
	Fetching a row of data	**SQLFetch**
	Returning information about a driver or data source	**SQLGetInfo** (extension)

SQLMoreResults

Extension Level 2   **SQLMoreResults** determines whether there are more results available on an *hstmt* containing **SELECT**, **UPDATE**, **INSERT**, or **DELETE** statements and, if so, initializes processing for those results.

Syntax   RETCODE **SQLMoreResults**(*hstmt*)

The **SQLMoreResults** function accepts the following argument:

Type	Argument	Use	Description
HSTMT	*hstmt*	Input	Statement handle.

Returns   SQL_SUCCESS, SQL_SUCCESS_WITH_INFO, SQL_STILL_EXECUTING, SQL_NO_DATA_FOUND, SQL_ERROR, or SQL_INVALID_HANDLE.

Diagnostics   When **SQLMoreResults** returns SQL_ERROR or SQL_SUCCESS_WITH_INFO, an associated SQLSTATE value may be obtained by calling **SQLError**. The following table lists the SQLSTATE values commonly returned by **SQLMoreResults** and explains each one in the context of this function; the notation "(DM)" precedes the descriptions of SQLSTATEs returned by the Driver Manager. The return code associated with each SQLSTATE value is SQL_ERROR, unless noted otherwise.

SQLSTATE	Error	Description
01000	General warning	Driver-specific informational message. (Function returns SQL_SUCCESS_WITH_INFO.)
IM001	Driver does not support this function	(DM) The driver associated with the *hstmt* does not support the function.
S1000	General error	An error occurred for which there was no specific SQLSTATE and for which no implementation-specific SQLSTATE was defined. The error message returned by **SQLError** in the argument *szErrorMsg* describes the error and its cause.
S1001	Memory allocation failure	The driver was unable to allocate memory required to support execution or completion of the function.

SQLSTATE	Error	Description
S1008	Operation canceled	Asynchronous processing was enabled for the *hstmt*. The function was called and before it completed execution, **SQLCancel** was called on the *hstmt*. Then the function was called again on the *hstmt*.
		The function was called and, before it completed execution, **SQLCancel** was called on the *hstmt* from a different thread in a multithreaded application.
S1010	Function sequence error	(DM) An asynchronously executing function (not this one) was called for the *hstmt* and was still executing when this function was called.
		(DM) **SQLExecute, SQLExecDirect**, or **SQLSetPos** was called for the *hstmt* and returned SQL_NEED_DATA. This function was called before data was sent for all data-at-execution parameters or columns.
S1T00	Timeout expired	The timeout period expired before the data source returned the result set. The timeout period is set through **SQLSetStmtOption**, SQL_QUERY_TIMEOUT.

Comments

SELECT statements return result sets. **UPDATE, INSERT**, and **DELETE** statements return a count of affected rows. If any of these statements are batched, submitted with arrays of parameters, or in procedures, they can return multiple result sets or counts.

If another result set or count is available, **SQLMoreResults** returns SQL_SUCCESS and initializes the result set or count for additional processing. After calling **SQLMoreResults** for **SELECT** statements, an application can call functions to determine the characteristics of the result set and to retrieve data from the result set. After calling **SQLMoreResults** for **UPDATE, INSERT**, or **DELETE** statements, an application can call **SQLRowCount**.

If all results have been processed, **SQLMoreResults** returns SQL_NO_DATA_FOUND.

Note that if there is a current result set with unfetched rows, **SQLMoreResults** discards that result set and makes the next result set or count available.

If a batch of statements or a procedure mixes other SQL statements with **SELECT, UPDATE, INSERT**, and **DELETE** statements, these other statements do not affect **SQLMoreResults**.

For additional information about the valid sequencing of result-processing functions, see Appendix B, "ODBC State Transition Tables."

Related Functions

For information about	See
Canceling statement processing	**SQLCancel**
Fetching a block of data or scrolling through a result set	**SQLExtendedFetch** (extension)
Fetching a row of data	**SQLFetch**
Fetching part or all of a column of data	**SQLGetData** (extension)

SQLNativeSql

Extension Level 2   **SQLNativeSql** returns the SQL string as translated by the driver.

Syntax   RETCODE **SQLNativeSql**(*hdbc*, *szSqlStrIn*, *cbSqlStrIn*, *szSqlStr*, *cbSqlStrMax*, *pcbSqlStr*)

The **SQLNativeSql** function accepts the following arguments:

Type	Argument	Use	Description
HDBC	*hdbc*	Input	Connection handle.
UCHAR FAR *	*szSqlStrIn*	Input	SQL text string to be translated.
SDWORD	*cbSqlStrIn*	Input	Length of *szSqlStrIn* text string.
UCHAR FAR *	*szSqlStr*	Output	Pointer to storage for the translated SQL string.
SDWORD	*cbSqlStrMax*	Input	Maximum length of the *szSqlStr* buffer.
SDWORD FAR *	*pcbSqlStr*	Output	The total number of bytes (excluding the null termination byte) available to return in *szSqlStr*. If the number of bytes available to return is greater than or equal to *cbSqlStrMax*, the translated SQL string in *szSqlStr* is truncated to *cbSqlStrMax* – 1 bytes.

Returns   SQL_SUCCESS, SQL_SUCCESS_WITH_INFO, SQL_ERROR, or SQL_INVALID_HANDLE.

Diagnostics   When **SQLNativeSql** returns either SQL_ERROR or SQL_SUCCESS_WITH_INFO, an associated SQLSTATE value may be obtained by calling **SQLError**. The following table lists the SQLSTATE values commonly returned by **SQLNativeSql** and explains each one in the context of this function; the notation "(DM)" precedes the descriptions of SQLSTATEs returned by the Driver Manager. The return code associated with each SQLSTATE value is SQL_ERROR, unless noted otherwise.

SQLSTATE	Error	Description
01000	General warning	Driver-specific informational message. (Function returns SQL_SUCCESS_WITH_INFO.)
01004	Data truncated	The buffer *szSqlStr* was not large enough to return the entire SQL string, so the SQL string was truncated. The argument *pcbSqlStr* contains the length of the untruncated SQL string. (Function returns SQL_SUCCESS_WITH_INFO.)
08003	Connection not open	The *hdbc* was not in a connected state.
37000	Syntax error or access violation	The argument *szSqlStrIn* contained an SQL statement that was not preparable or contained a syntax error.
IM001	Driver does not support this function	(DM) The driver associated with the *hdbc* does not support the function.
S1000	General error	An error occurred for which there was no specific SQLSTATE and for which no implementation-specific SQLSTATE was defined. The error message returned by **SQLError** in the argument *szErrorMsg* describes the error and its cause.
S1001	Memory allocation failure	The driver was unable to allocate memory required to support execution or completion of the function.
S1009	Invalid argument value	(DM) The argument *szSqlStrIn* was a null pointer.
S1090	Invalid string or buffer length	(DM) The argument *cbSqlStrIn* was less than 0, but not equal to SQL_NTS.
		(DM) The argument *cbSqlStrMax* was less than 0 and the argument *szSqlStr* was not a null pointer..

Comments   The following are examples of what **SQLNativeSql** might return for the following input SQL string containing the scalar function CONVERT. Assume that the column empid is of type INTEGER in the data source:

```
SELECT { fn CONVERT (empid, SQL_SMALLINT) } FROM employee
```

A driver for SQL Server might return the following translated SQL string:

```
SELECT convert (smallint, empid) FROM employee
```

A driver for ORACLE Server might return the following translated SQL string:

```
SELECT to_number (empid) FROM employee
```

A driver for Ingres might return the following translated SQL string:

```
SELECT int2 (empid) FROM employee
```

Related Functions   None.

SQLNumParams

Extension Level 2 **SQLNumParams** returns the number of parameters in an SQL statement.

Syntax RETCODE **SQLNumParams**(*hstmt, pcpar*)

The **SQLNumParams** function accepts the following arguments.

Type	Argument	Use	Description
HSTMT	*hstmt*	Input	Statement handle.
SWORD FAR *	*pcpar*	Output	Number of parameters in the statement.

Returns SQL_SUCCESS, SQL_SUCCESS_WITH_INFO, SQL_STILL_EXECUTING, SQL_ERROR, or SQL_INVALID_HANDLE.

Diagnostics When **SQLNumParams** returns SQL_ERROR or SQL_SUCCESS_WITH_INFO, an associated SQLSTATE value may be obtained by calling **SQLError**. The following table lists the SQLSTATE values commonly returned by **SQLNumParams** and explains each one in the context of this function; the notation "(DM)" precedes the descriptions of SQLSTATEs returned by the Driver Manager. The return code associated with each SQLSTATE value is SQL_ERROR, unless noted otherwise.

SQLSTATE	Error	Description
01000	General warning	Driver-specific informational message. (Function returns SQL_SUCCESS_WITH_INFO.)
IM001	Driver does not support this function	(DM) The driver associated with the *hstmt* does not support the function.
S1000	General error	An error occurred for which there was no specific SQLSTATE and for which no implementation-specific SQLSTATE was defined. The error message returned by **SQLError** in the argument *szErrorMsg* describes the error and its cause.
S1001	Memory allocation failure	The driver was unable to allocate memory required to support execution or completion of the function.

SQLSTATE	Error	Description
S1008	Operation canceled	Asynchronous processing was enabled for the *hstmt*. The function was called and before it completed execution, **SQLCancel** was called on the *hstmt*. Then the function was called again on the *hstmt*.
		The function was called and, before it completed execution, **SQLCancel** was called on the *hstmt* from a different thread in a multithreaded application.
S1010	Function sequence error	(DM) The function was called prior to calling **SQLPrepare** or **SQLExecDirect** for the *hstmt*.
		(DM) An asynchronously executing function (not this one) was called for the *hstmt* and was still executing when this function was called.
		(DM) **SQLExecute**, **SQLExecDirect**, or **SQLSetPos** was called for the *hstmt* and returned SQL_NEED_DATA. This function was called before data was sent for all data-at-execution parameters or columns.
S1T00	Timeout expired	The timeout period expired before the data source returned the result set. The timeout period is set through **SQLSetStmtOption**, SQL_QUERY_TIMEOUT.

Comments

SQLNumParams can only be called after **SQLPrepare** has been called.

If the statement associated with *hstmt* does not contain parameters, **SQLNumParams** sets *pcpar* to 0.

Related Functions

For information about	See
Returning information about a parameter in a statement	**SQLDescribeParam** (extension)
Assigning storage for a parameter	**SQLBindParameter**

SQLNumResultCols

Core

SQLNumResultCols returns the number of columns in a result set.

Syntax

RETCODE **SQLNumResultCols**(*hstmt*, *pccol*)

The **SQLNumResultCols** function accepts the following arguments.

Type	Argument	Use	Description
HSTMT	*hstmt*	Input	Statement handle.
SWORD FAR *	*pccol*	Output	Number of columns in the result set.

Returns

SQL_SUCCESS, SQL_SUCCESS_WITH_INFO, SQL_STILL_EXECUTING, SQL_ERROR, or SQL_INVALID_HANDLE.

Diagnostics

When **SQLNumResultCols** returns SQL_ERROR or SQL_SUCCESS_WITH_INFO, an associated SQLSTATE value may be obtained by calling **SQLError**. The following table lists the SQLSTATE values commonly returned by **SQLNumResultCols** and explains each one in the context of this function; the notation "(DM)" precedes the descriptions of SQLSTATEs returned by the Driver Manager. The return code associated with each SQLSTATE value is SQL_ERROR, unless noted otherwise.

SQLSTATE	Error	Description
01000	General warning	Driver-specific informational message. (Function returns SQL_SUCCESS_WITH_INFO.)
IM001	Driver does not support this function	(DM) The driver associated with the *hstmt* does not support the function.
S1000	General error	An error occurred for which there was no specific SQLSTATE and for which no implementation-specific SQLSTATE was defined. The error message returned by **SQLError** in the argument *szErrorMsg* describes the error and its cause.
S1001	Memory allocation failure	The driver was unable to allocate memory required to support execution or completion of the function.

SQLSTATE	Error	Description
S1008	Operation canceled	Asynchronous processing was enabled for the *hstmt*. The function was called and before it completed execution, **SQLCancel** was called on the *hstmt*. Then the function was called again on the *hstmt*.
		The function was called and, before it completed execution, **SQLCancel** was called on the *hstmt* from a different thread in a multithreaded application.
S1010	Function sequence error	(DM) The function was called prior to calling **SQLPrepare** or **SQLExecDirect** for the *hstmt*.
		(DM) An asynchronously executing function (not this one) was called for the *hstmt* and was still executing when this function was called.
		(DM) **SQLExecute**, **SQLExecDirect**, or **SQLSetPos** was called for the *hstmt* and returned SQL_NEED_DATA. This function was called before data was sent for all data-at-execution parameters or columns.
S1T00	Timeout expired	The timeout period expired before the data source returned the result set. The timeout period is set through **SQLSetStmtOption**, SQL_QUERY_TIMEOUT.

SQLNumResultCols can return any SQLSTATE that can be returned by **SQLPrepare** or **SQLExecute** when called after **SQLPrepare** and before **SQLExecute** depending on when the data source evaluates the SQL statement associated with the *hstmt*.

Comments

SQLNumResultCols can be called successfully only when the *hstmt* is in the prepared, executed, or positioned state.

If the statement associated with *hstmt* does not return columns, **SQLNumResultCols** sets *pccol* to 0.

Related Functions

For information about	See
Assigning storage for a column in a result set	**SQLBindCol**
Canceling statement processing	**SQLCancel**
Returning information about a column in a result set	**SQLColAttributes**
Returning information about a column in a result set	**SQLDescribeCol**
Fetching a block of data or scrolling through a result set	**SQLExtendedFetch** (extension)
Fetching a row of data	**SQLFetch**
Fetching part or all of a column of data	**SQLGetData** (extension)
Setting cursor scrolling options	**SQLSetScrollOptions** (extension)

SQLParamData

Extension Level 1   **SQLParamData** is used in conjunction with **SQLPutData** to supply parameter data at statement execution time.

Syntax   RETCODE **SQLParamData**(*hstmt*, *prgbValue*)

The **SQLParamData** function accepts the following arguments.

Type	Argument	Use	Description
HSTMT	*hstmt*	Input	Statement handle.
PTR FAR *	*prgbValue*	Output	Pointer to storage for the value specified for the *rgbValue* argument in **SQLBindParameter** (for parameter data) or the address of the *rgbValue* buffer specified in **SQLBindCol** (for column data).

Returns   SQL_SUCCESS, SQL_SUCCESS_WITH_INFO, SQL_NEED_DATA, SQL_STILL_EXECUTING, SQL_ERROR, or SQL_INVALID_HANDLE.

Diagnostics   When **SQLParamData** returns SQL_ERROR or SQL_SUCCESS_WITH_INFO, an associated SQLSTATE value may be obtained by calling **SQLError**. The following table lists the SQLSTATE values commonly returned by **SQLParamData** and explains each one in the context of this function; the notation "(DM)" precedes the descriptions of SQLSTATEs returned by the Driver Manager. The return code associated with each SQLSTATE value is SQL_ERROR, unless noted otherwise.

SQLSTATE	Error	Description
01000	General warning	Driver-specific informational message. (Function returns SQL_SUCCESS_WITH_INFO.)
08S01	Communication link failure	The communication link between the driver and the data source to which the driver was connected failed before the function completed processing.

SQLSTATE	Error	Description
22026	String data, length mismatch	The SQL_NEED_LONG_DATA_LEN information type in **SQLGetInfo** was "Y" and less data was sent for a long parameter (the data type was SQL_LONGVARCHAR, SQL_LONGVARBINARY, or a long, data source–specific data type) than was specified with the *pcbValue* argument in **SQLBindParameter**.
		The SQL_NEED_LONG_DATA_LEN information type in **SQLGetInfo** was "Y" and less data was sent for a long column (the data type was SQL_LONGVARCHAR, SQL_LONGVARBINARY, or a long, data source–specific data type) than was specified in the length buffer corresponding to a column in a row of data that was added or updated with **SQLSetPos**.
IM001	Driver does not support this function	(DM) The driver that corresponds the *hstmt* does not support the function.
S1000	General error	An error occurred for which there was no specific SQLSTATE and for which no implementation-specific SQLSTATE was defined. The error message returned by **SQLError** in the argument *szErrorMsg* describes the error and its cause.
S1001	Memory allocation failure	The driver was unable to allocate memory required to support execution or completion of the function.
S1008	Operation canceled	Asynchronous processing was enabled for the *hstmt*. The function was called and before it completed execution, **SQLCancel** was called on the *hstmt*. Then the function was called again on the *hstmt*.
		The function was called and, before it completed execution, **SQLCancel** was called on the *hstmt* from a different thread in a multithreaded application.
		SQLExecute, **SQLExecDirect**, or **SQLSetPos** was called for the *hstmt* and returned SQL_NEED_DATA. **SQLCancel** was called before data was sent for all data-at-execution parameters or columns.

SQLSTATE	Error	Description
S1010	Function sequence error	(DM) The previous function call was not a call to **SQLExecDirect**, **SQLExecute**, or **SQLSetPos** where the return code was SQL_NEED_DATA or a call to **SQLPutData**.
		The previous function call was a call to **SQLParamData**.
		(DM) An asynchronously executing function (not this one) was called for the *hstmt* and was still executing when this function was called.
S1T00	Timeout expired	The timeout period expired before the data source completed processing the parameter value. The timeout period is set through **SQLSetStmtOption**, SQL_QUERY_TIMEOUT.

If **SQLParamData** is called while sending data for a parameter in an SQL statement, it can return any SQLSTATE that can be returned by the function called to execute the statement (**SQLExecute** or **SQLExecDirect**). If it is called while sending data for a column being updated or added with **SQLSetPos**, it can return any SQLSTATE that can be returned by **SQLSetPos**.

Comments

For an explanation of how data-at-execution parameter data is passed at statement execution time, see "Passing Parameter Values" in **SQLBindParameter**. For an explanation of how data-at-execution column data is updated or added, see "Using SQLSetPos" in **SQLSetPos**.

Code Example

See **SQLPutData**.

Related Functions

For information about	See
Canceling statement processing	**SQLCancel**
Returning information about a parameter in a statement	**SQLDescribeParam** (extension)
Executing an SQL statement	**SQLExecDirect**
Executing a prepared SQL statement	**SQLExecute**
Sending parameter data at execution time	**SQLPutData** (extension)
Assigning storage for a parameter	**SQLBindParameter**

SQLParamOptions

Extension Level 2   **SQLParamOptions** allows an application to specify multiple values for the set of parameters assigned by **SQLBindParameter**. The ability to specify multiple values for a set of parameters is useful for bulk inserts and other work that requires the data source to process the same SQL statement multiple times with various parameter values. An application can, for example, specify three sets of values for the set of parameters associated with an **INSERT** statement, and then execute the **INSERT** statement once to perform the three insert operations.

Syntax   RETCODE **SQLParamOptions**(*hstmt, crow, pirow*)

The **SQLParamOptions** function accepts the following arguments:

Type	Argument	Use	Description
HSTMT	*hstmt*	Input	Statement handle.
UDWORD	*crow*	Input	Number of values for each parameter. If *crow* is greater than 1, the *rgbValue* argument in **SQLBindParameter** points to an array of parameter values and *pcbValue* points to an array of lengths.
UDWORD FAR *	*pirow*	Input	Pointer to storage for the current row number. As each row of parameter values is processed, *pirow* is set to the number of that row. No row number will be returned if *pirow* is set to a null pointer.

Returns   SQL_SUCCESS, SQL_SUCCESS_WITH_INFO, SQL_ERROR, or SQL_INVALID_HANDLE.

Diagnostics   When **SQLParamOptions** returns SQL_ERROR or SQL_SUCCESS_WITH_INFO, an associated SQLSTATE value may be obtained by calling **SQLError**. The following table lists the SQLSTATE values commonly returned by **SQLParamOptions** and explains each one in the context of this function; the notation "(DM)" precedes the descriptions of SQLSTATEs returned by the Driver Manager. The return code associated with each SQLSTATE value is SQL_ERROR, unless noted otherwise.

SQLSTATE	Error	Description
01000	General warning	Driver-specific informational message. (Function returns SQL_SUCCESS_WITH_INFO.)
IM001	Driver does not support this function	(DM) The driver associated with the *hstmt* does not support the function.
S1000	General error	An error occurred for which there was no specific SQLSTATE and for which no implementation-specific SQLSTATE was defined. The error message returned by **SQLError** in the argument *szErrorMsg* describes the error and its cause.
S1001	Memory allocation failure	The driver was unable to allocate memory required to support execution or completion of the function.
S1010	Function sequence error	(DM) An asynchronously executing function was called for the *hstmt* and was still executing when this function was called.
		(DM) **SQLExecute**, **SQLExecDirect**, or **SQLSetPos** was called for the *hstmt* and returned SQL_NEED_DATA. This function was called before data was sent for all data-at-execution parameters or columns.
S1107	Row value out of range	(DM) The value specified for the argument *crow* was equal to 0.

Comments

As a statement executes, the driver sets *pirow* to the number of the current row of parameter values; the first row is row number 1. The contents of *pirow* can be used as follows:

- When **SQLParamData** returns SQL_NEED_DATA for data-at-execution parameters, the application can access the value in *pirow* to determine which row of parameters is being executed.

- When **SQLExecute** or **SQLExecDirect** returns an error, the application can access the value in *pirow* to find out which row of parameters failed.

- When **SQLExecute**, **SQLExecDirect**, **SQLParamData**, or **SQLPutData** succeed, the value in *pirow* is set to *crow*—the total number of rows of parameters processed.

Code Example

In the following example, an application specifies an array of parameter values with **SQLBindParameter** and **SQLParamOptions**. It then inserts those values into a table with a single **INSERT** statement and checks for any errors. If the first row fails, the application rolls back all changes. If any other row fails, the application commits the transaction, skips the failed row, rebinds the remaining parameters, and continues processing. (Note that **irow** is 1-based and **szData[ ]** is 0-based, so the **irow** entry of **szData[ ]** is skipped by rebinding at **szData[irow]**.)

```
#define CITY_LEN 256
SDWORD cbValue[ ] = {SQL_NTS, SQL_NTS, SQL_NTS, SQL_NTS, SQL_NTS};
UCHAR  szData[ ][CITY_LEN] = {"Boston","New York","Keokuk","Seattle",
                             "Eugene"};
UDWORD irow;
SQLSetConnectOption(hdbc, SQL_AUTOCOMMIT, 0);
SQLBindParameter(hstmt, 1, SQL_PARAM_INPUT, SQL_C_DEFAULT, SQL_CHAR,
                 CITY_LEN, 0, szData, 0, cbValue);
SQLPrepare(hstmt, "INSERT INTO CITIES VALUES (?)", SQL_NTS);
SQLParamOptions(hstmt, 5, &irow);

while (TRUE) {

    retcode = SQLExecute(hstmt);

    /* Done if execution was successful */

    if (retcode != SQL_ERROR) {
        break;
    }

    /* On an error, print the error.  If the error is in row 1, roll */
    /* back the transaction and quit.  If the error is in another    */
    /* row, commit the transaction and, unless the error is in the   */
    /* last row, rebind to the next row and continue processing.     */

    show_error();
    if (irow == 1) {
        SQLTransact(henv, hstmt, SQL_ROLLBACK);
        break;
    } else {
        SQLTransact(henv, hstmt, SQL_COMMIT);
        if (irow == 5) {
            break;
        } else {
            SQLBindParameter(hstmt, 1, SQL_PARAM_INPUT,
                             SQL_C_DEFAULT, SQL_CHAR, CITY_LEN, 0,
                             szData[irow], 0, cbValue[irow]);
            SQLParamOptions(hstmt, 5-irow, &irow);
        }
    }
}
```

Related Functions

For information about	See
Returning information about a parameter in a statement	**SQLDescribeParam** (extension)
Assigning storage for a parameter	**SQLBindParameter**

SQLPrepare

ODBC 1.0

Core

SQLPrepare prepares an SQL string for execution.

Syntax

RETCODE **SQLPrepare**(*hstmt*, *szSqlStr*, *cbSqlStr*)

The **SQLPrepare** function accepts the following arguments.

Type	Argument	Use	Description
HSTMT	*hstmt*	Input	Statement handle.
UCHAR FAR *	*szSqlStr*	Input	SQL text string.
SDWORD	*cbSqlStr*	Input	Length of *szSqlStr*.

Returns

SQL_SUCCESS, SQL_SUCCESS_WITH_INFO, SQL_STILL_EXECUTING, SQL_ERROR, or SQL_INVALID_HANDLE.

Diagnostics

When **SQLPrepare** returns SQL_ERROR or SQL_SUCCESS_WITH_INFO, an associated SQLSTATE value may be obtained by calling **SQLError**. The following table lists the SQLSTATE values commonly returned by **SQLPrepare** and explains each one in the context of this function; the notation "(DM)" precedes the descriptions of SQLSTATEs returned by the Driver Manager. The return code associated with each SQLSTATE value is SQL_ERROR, unless noted otherwise.

SQLSTATE	Error	Description
01000	General warning	Driver-specific informational message. (Function returns SQL_SUCCESS_WITH_INFO.)
08S01	Communication link failure	The communication link between the driver and the data source to which the driver was connected failed before the function completed processing.
21S01	Insert value list does not match column list	The argument *szSqlStr* contained an **INSERT** statement and the number of values to be inserted did not match the degree of the derived table.
21S02	Degree of derived table does not match column list	The argument *szSqlStr* contained a **CREATE VIEW** statement and the number of names specified is not the same degree as the derived table defined by the query specification.
22005	Error in assignment	The argument *szSqlStr* contained an SQL statement that contained a literal or parameter and the value was incompatible with the data type of the associated table column.

SQLSTATE	Error	Description
24000	Invalid cursor state	(DM) A cursor was open on the *hstmt* and **SQLFetch** or **SQLExtendedFetch** had been called.
		A cursor was open on the *hstmt* but **SQLFetch** or **SQLExtendedFetch** had not been called.
34000	Invalid cursor name	The argument *szSqlStr* contained a positioned **DELETE** or a positioned **UPDATE** and the cursor referenced by the statement being prepared was not open.
37000	Syntax error or access violation	The argument *szSqlStr* contained an SQL statement that was not preparable or contained a syntax error.
42000	Syntax error or access violation	The argument *szSqlStr* contained a statement for which the user did not have the required privileges.
IM001	Driver does not support this function	(DM) The driver associated with the *hstmt* does not support the function.
S0001	Base table or view already exists	The argument *szSqlStr* contained a **CREATE TABLE** or **CREATE VIEW** statement and the table name or view name specified already exists.

SQLSTATE	Error	Description
S0002	Base table not found	The argument *szSqlStr* contained a **DROP TABLE** or a **DROP VIEW** statement and the specified table name or view name did not exist.
		The argument *szSqlStr* contained an **ALTER TABLE** statement and the specified table name did not exist.
		The argument *szSqlStr* contained a **CREATE VIEW** statement and a table name or view name defined by the query specification did not exist.
		The argument *szSqlStr* contained a **CREATE INDEX** statement and the specified table name did not exist.
		The argument *szSqlStr* contained a **GRANT** or **REVOKE** statement and the specified table name or view name did not exist.
		The argument *szSqlStr* contained a **SELECT** statement and a specified table name or view name did not exist.
		The argument *szSqlStr* contained a **DELETE, INSERT,** or **UPDATE** statement and the specified table name did not exist.
		The argument *szSqlStr* contained a **CREATE TABLE** statement and a table specified in a constraint (referencing a table other than the one being created) did not exist.
S0011	Index already exists	The argument *szSqlStr* contained a **CREATE INDEX** statement and the specified index name already existed.
S0012	Index not found	The argument *szSqlStr* contained a **DROP INDEX** statement and the specified index name did not exist.
S0021	Column already exists	The argument *szSqlStr* contained an **ALTER TABLE** statement and the column specified in the **ADD** clause is not unique or identifies an existing column in the base table.

SQLSTATE	Error	Description
S0022	Column not found	The argument *szSqlStr* contained a **CREATE INDEX** statement and one or more of the column names specified in the column list did not exist.
		The argument *szSqlStr* contained a **GRANT** or **REVOKE** statement and a specified column name did not exist.
		The argument *szSqlStr* contained a **SELECT, DELETE, INSERT,** or **UPDATE** statement and a specified column name did not exist.
		The argument *szSqlStr* contained a **CREATE TABLE** statement and a column specified in a constraint (referencing a table other than the one being created) did not exist.
S1000	General error	An error occurred for which there was no specific SQLSTATE and for which no implementation-specific SQLSTATE was defined. The error message returned by **SQLError** in the argument *szErrorMsg* describes the error and its cause.
S1001	Memory allocation failure	The driver was unable to allocate memory required to support execution or completion of the function.
S1008	Operation canceled	Asynchronous processing was enabled for the *hstmt*. The function was called and before it completed execution, **SQLCancel** was called on the *hstmt*. Then the function was called again on the *hstmt*.
		The function was called and, before it completed execution, **SQLCancel** was called on the *hstmt* from a different thread in a multithreaded application.
S1009	Invalid argument value	(DM) The argument *szSqlStr* was a null pointer.

SQLSTATE	Error	Description
S1010	Function sequence error	(DM) An asynchronously executing function (not this one) was called for the *hstmt* and was still executing when this function was called.
		(DM) **SQLExecute**, **SQLExecDirect**, or **SQLSetPos** was called for the *hstmt* and returned SQL_NEED_DATA. This function was called before data was sent for all data-at-execution parameters or columns.
S1090	Invalid string or buffer length	(DM) The argument *cbSqlStr* was less than or equal to 0, but not equal to SQL_NTS.
S1T00	Timeout expired	The timeout period expired before the data source returned the result set. The timeout period is set through **SQLSetStmtOption**, SQL_QUERY_TIMEOUT.

Comments

The application calls **SQLPrepare** to send an SQL statement to the data source for preparation. The application can include one or more parameter markers in the SQL statement. To include a parameter marker, the application embeds a question mark (?) into the SQL string at the appropriate position.

Note If an application uses **SQLPrepare** to prepare and **SQLExecute** to submit a **COMMIT** or **ROLLBACK** statement, it will not be interoperable between DBMS products. To commit or roll back a transaction, call **SQLTransact**.

The driver modifies the statement to use the form of SQL used by the data source, then submits it to the data source for preparation. In particular, the driver modifies the escape clauses used to define ODBC-specific SQL. (For a description of SQL statement grammar, see "Supporting ODBC Extensions to SQL" in Chapter 14, "Processing an SQL Statement," and Appendix C, "SQL Grammar.") For the driver, an *hstmt* is similar to a statement identifier in embedded SQL code. If the data source supports statement identifiers, the driver can send a statement identifier and parameter values to the data source.

Once a statement is prepared, the application uses *hstmt* to refer to the statement in later function calls. The prepared statement associated with the *hstmt* may be reexecuted by calling **SQLExecute** until the application frees the *hstmt* with a call to **SQLFreeStmt** with the SQL_DROP option or until the *hstmt* is used in a call to **SQLPrepare**, **SQLExecDirect**, or one of the catalog functions (**SQLColumns**, **SQLTables**, and so on). Once the application prepares a statement, it can request information about the format of the result set.

Some drivers cannot return syntax errors or access violations when the application calls **SQLPrepare**. A driver may handle syntax errors and access violations, only syntax errors, or neither syntax errors nor access violations. Therefore, an application must be able to handle these conditions when calling subsequent related functions such as **SQLNumResultCols**, **SQLDescribeCol**, **SQLColAttributes**, and **SQLExecute**.

Depending on the capabilities of the driver and data source and on whether the application has called **SQLBindParameter**, parameter information (such as data types) might be checked when the statement is prepared or when it is executed. For maximum interoperability, an application should unbind all parameters that applied to an old SQL statement before preparing a new SQL statement on the same *hstmt*. This prevents errors that are due to old parameter information being applied to the new statement.

Important Committing or rolling back a transaction, either by calling **SQLTransact** or by using the SQL_AUTOCOMMIT connection option, can cause the data source to delete the access plans for all *hstmts* on an *hdbc*. For more information, see the SQL_CURSOR_COMMIT_BEHAVIOR and SQL_CURSOR_ROLLBACK_BEHAVIOR information types in **SQLGetInfo**.

Code Example   See **SQLBindParameter**, **SQLParamOptions**, **SQLPutData**, and **SQLSetPos**.

Related Functions

For information about	See
Allocating a statement handle	**SQLAllocStmt**
Assigning storage for a column in a result set	**SQLBindCol**
Canceling statement processing	**SQLCancel**
Executing an SQL statement	**SQLExecDirect**
Executing a prepared SQL statement	**SQLExecute**
Returning the number of rows affected by a statement	**SQLRowCount**
Setting a cursor name	**SQLSetCursorName**
Assigning storage for a parameter	**SQLBindParameter**
Executing a commit or rollback operation	**SQLTransact**

SQLPrimaryKeys

Extension Level 2   **SQLPrimaryKeys** returns the column names that comprise the primary key for a table. The driver returns the information as a result set. This function does not support returning primary keys from multiple tables in a single call.

Syntax   RETCODE **SQLPrimaryKeys**(*hstmt, szTableQualifier, cbTableQualifier, szTableOwner, cbTableOwner, szTableName, cbTableName*)

The **SQLPrimaryKeys** function accepts the following arguments:

Type	Argument	Use	Description
HSTMT	*hstmt*	Input	Statement handle.
UCHAR FAR *	*szTableQualifier*	Input	Qualifier name. If a driver supports qualifiers for some tables but not for others, such as when the driver retrieves data from different DBMSs, an empty string ("") denotes those tables that do not have qualifiers.
SWORD	*cbTableQualifier*	Input	Length of *szTableQualifier*.
UCHAR FAR *	*szTableOwner*	Input	Table owner. If a driver supports owners for some tables but not for others, such as when the driver retrieves data from different DBMSs, an empty string ("") denotes those tables that do not have owners.
SWORD	*cbTableOwner*	Input	Length of *szTableOwner*.
UCHAR FAR *	*szTableName*	Input	Table name.
SWORD	*cbTableName*	Input	Length of *szTableName*.

Returns   SQL_SUCCESS, SQL_SUCCESS_WITH_INFO, SQL_STILL_EXECUTING, SQL_ERROR, or SQL_INVALID_HANDLE.

Diagnostics   When **SQLPrimaryKeys** returns SQL_ERROR or SQL_SUCCESS_WITH_INFO, an associated SQLSTATE value may be obtained by calling **SQLError**. The following table lists the SQLSTATE values commonly returned by **SQLPrimaryKeys** and explains each one in the context of this function; the notation "(DM)" precedes the descriptions of SQLSTATEs returned by the Driver Manager. The return code associated with each SQLSTATE value is SQL_ERROR, unless noted otherwise.

SQLSTATE	Error	Description
01000	General warning	Driver-specific informational message. (Function returns SQL_SUCCESS_WITH_INFO.)
08S01	Communication link failure	The communication link between the driver and the data source to which the driver was connected failed before the function completed processing.
24000	Invalid cursor state	(DM) A cursor was open on the *hstmt* and **SQLFetch** or **SQLExtendedFetch** had been called.
		A cursor was open on the *hstmt* but **SQLFetch** or **SQLExtendedFetch** had not been called.
IM001	Driver does not support this function	(DM) The driver associated with the *hstmt* does not support the function.
S1000	General error	An error occurred for which there was no specific SQLSTATE and for which no implementation-specific SQLSTATE was defined. The error message returned by **SQLError** in the argument *szErrorMsg* describes the error and its cause.
S1001	Memory allocation failure	The driver was unable to allocate memory required to support execution or completion of the function.
S1008	Operation canceled	Asynchronous processing was enabled for the *hstmt*. The function was called and before it completed execution, **SQLCancel** was called on the *hstmt*. Then the function was called again on the *hstmt*.
		The function was called and, before it completed execution, **SQLCancel** was called on the *hstmt* from a different thread in a multithreaded application.
S1010	Function sequence error	(DM) An asynchronously executing function (not this one) was called for the *hstmt* and was still executing when this function was called.
		(DM) **SQLExecute**, **SQLExecDirect**, or **SQLSetPos** was called for the *hstmt* and returned SQL_NEED_DATA. This function was called before data was sent for all data-at-execution parameters or columns.

SQLSTATE	Error	Description
S1090	Invalid string or buffer length	(DM) The value of one of the name length arguments was less than 0, but not equal to SQL_NTS.
		The value of one of the name length arguments exceeded the maximum length value for the corresponding qualifier or name.
S1C00	Driver not capable	A table qualifier was specified and the driver or data source does not support qualifiers.
		A table owner was specified and the driver or data source does not support owners.
		The combination of the current settings of the SQL_CONCURRENCY and SQL_CURSOR_TYPE statement options was not supported by the driver or data source.
S1T00	Timeout expired	The timeout period expired before the data source returned the requested result set. The timeout period is set through **SQLSetStmtOption**, SQL_QUERY_TIMEOUT.

Comments

SQLPrimaryKeys returns the results as a standard result set, ordered by TABLE_QUALIFIER, TABLE_OWNER, TABLE_NAME, and KEY_SEQ. The following table lists the columns in the result set.

Note **SQLPrimaryKeys** might not return all primary keys. For example, a Paradox driver might only return primary keys for files (tables) in the current directory.

The lengths of VARCHAR columns shown in the table are maximums; the actual lengths depend on the data source. To determine the actual lengths of the TABLE_QUALIFIER, TABLE_OWNER, TABLE_NAME, and COLUMN_NAME columns, call **SQLGetInfo** with the SQL_MAX_QUALIFIER_NAME_LEN, SQL_MAX_OWNER_NAME_LEN, SQL_MAX_TABLE_NAME_LEN, and SQL_MAX_COLUMN_NAME_LEN options.

Column Name	Data Type	Comments
TABLE_QUALIFIER	Varchar(128)	Primary key table qualifier identifier; NULL if not applicable to the data source. If a driver supports qualifiers for some tables but not for others, such as when the driver retrieves data from different DBMSs, it returns an empty string ("") for those tables that do not have qualifiers.
TABLE_OWNER	Varchar(128)	Primary key table owner identifier; NULL if not applicable to the data source. If a driver supports owners for some tables but not for others, such as when the driver retrieves data from different DBMSs, it returns an empty string ("") for those tables that do not have owners.
TABLE_NAME	Varchar(128) not NULL	Primary key table identifier.
COLUMN_NAME	Varchar(128) not NULL	Primary key column identifier.
KEY_SEQ	Smallint not NULL	Column sequence number in key (starting with 1).
PK_NAME	Varchar(128)	Primary key identifier. NULL if not applicable to the data source.

Note The PK_NAME column was added in ODBC 2.0. ODBC 1.0 drivers may return a different, driver-specific column with the same column number.

Code Example See **SQLForeignKeys**.

Related Functions

For information about	See
Assigning storage for a column in a result set	**SQLBindCol**
Canceling statement processing	**SQLCancel**
Fetching a block of data or scrolling through a result set	**SQLExtendedFetch** (extension)
Fetching a row of data	**SQLFetch**
Returning the columns of foreign keys	**SQLForeignKeys** (extension)
Returning table statistics and indexes	**SQLStatistics** (extension)

SQLProcedureColumns

Extension Level 2   **SQLProcedureColumns** returns the list of input and output parameters, as well as the columns that make up the result set for the specified procedures. The driver returns the information as a result set on the specified *hstmt*.

Syntax   RETCODE **SQLProcedureColumns**(*hstmt*, *szProcQualifier*, *cbProcQualifier*, *szProcOwner*, *cbProcOwner*, *szProcName*, *cbProcName*, *szColumnName*, *cbColumnName*)

The **SQLProcedureColumns** function accepts the following arguments:

Type	Argument	Use	Description
HSTMT	*hstmt*	Input	Statement handle.
UCHAR FAR *	*szProcQualifier*	Input	Procedure qualifier name. If a driver supports qualifiers for some procedures but not for others, such as when the driver retrieves data from different DBMSs, an empty string ("") denotes those procedures that do not have qualifiers.
SWORD	*cbProcQualifier*	Input	Length of *szProcQualifier*.
UCHAR FAR *	*szProcOwner*	Input	String search pattern for procedure owner names. If a driver supports owners for some procedures but not for others, such as when the driver retrieves data from different DBMSs, an empty string ("") denotes those procedures that do not have owners.
SWORD	*cbProcOwner*	Input	Length of *szProcOwner*.
UCHAR FAR *	*szProcName*	Input	String search pattern for procedure names.
SWORD	*cbProcName*	Input	Length of *szProcName*.
UCHAR FAR *	*szColumnName*	Input	String search pattern for column names.
SWORD	*cbColumnName*	Input	Length of *szColumnName*.

Returns   SQL_SUCCESS, SQL_SUCCESS_WITH_INFO, SQL_STILL_EXECUTING, SQL_ERROR, or SQL_INVALID_HANDLE.

Diagnostics

When **SQLProcedureColumns** returns SQL_ERROR or SQL_SUCCESS_WITH_INFO, an associated SQLSTATE value may be obtained by calling **SQLError**. The following table lists the SQLSTATE values commonly returned by **SQLProcedureColumns** and explains each one in the context of this function; the notation "(DM)" precedes the descriptions of SQLSTATEs returned by the Driver Manager. The return code associated with each SQLSTATE value is SQL_ERROR, unless noted otherwise.

SQLSTATE	Error	Description
01000	General warning	Driver-specific informational message. (Function returns SQL_SUCCESS_WITH_INFO.)
08S01	Communication link failure	The communication link between the driver and the data source to which the driver was connected failed before the function completed processing.
24000	Invalid cursor state	(DM) A cursor was open on the *hstmt* and **SQLFetch** or **SQLExtendedFetch** had been called.
		A cursor was open on the *hstmt* but **SQLFetch** or **SQLExtendedFetch** had not been called.
IM001	Driver does not support this function	(DM) The driver associated with the *hstmt* does not support the function.
S1000	General error	An error occurred for which there was no specific SQLSTATE and for which no implementation-specific SQLSTATE was defined. The error message returned by **SQLError** in the argument *szErrorMsg* describes the error and its cause.
S1001	Memory allocation failure	The driver was unable to allocate memory required to support execution or completion of the function.
S1008	Operation canceled	Asynchronous processing was enabled for the *hstmt*. The function was called and before it completed execution, **SQLCancel** was called on the *hstmt*. Then the function was called again on the *hstmt*.
		The function was called and, before it completed execution, **SQLCancel** was called on the *hstmt* from a different thread in a multithreaded application.

SQLSTATE	Error	Description
S1010	Function sequence error	(DM) An asynchronously executing function (not this one) was called for the *hstmt* and was still executing when this function was called.
		(DM) **SQLExecute**, **SQLExecDirect**, or **SQLSetPos** was called for the *hstmt* and returned SQL_NEED_DATA. This function was called before data was sent for all data-at-execution parameters or columns.
S1090	Invalid string or buffer length	(DM) The value of one of the name length arguments was less than 0, but not equal to SQL_NTS.
		The value of one of the name length arguments exceeded the maximum length value for the corresponding qualifier or name.
S1C00	Driver not capable	A procedure qualifier was specified and the driver or data source does not support qualifiers.
		A procedure owner was specified and the driver or data source does not support owners.
		A string search pattern was specified for the procedure owner, procedure name, or column name and the data source does not support search patterns for one or more of those arguments.
		The combination of the current settings of the SQL_CONCURRENCY and SQL_CURSOR_TYPE statement options was not supported by the driver or data source.
S1T00	Timeout expired	The timeout period expired before the data source returned the result set. The timeout period is set through **SQLSetStmtOption**, SQL_QUERY_TIMEOUT.

Comments   This function is typically used before statement execution to retrieve information about procedure parameters and columns from the data source's catalog. For more information about stored procedures, see "Using ODBC Extensions to SQL" in Chapter 6, "Executing SQL Statements."

Note **SQLProcedureColumns** might not return all columns used by a procedure. For example, a driver might only return information about the parameters used by a procedure and not the columns in a result set it generates.

The *szProcOwner*, *szProcName*, and *szColumnName* arguments accept search patterns. For more information about valid search patterns, see "Search Pattern Arguments" earlier in this chapter.

SQLProcedureColumns returns the results as a standard result set, ordered by PROCEDURE_QUALIFIER, PROCEDURE_OWNER, PROCEDURE_NAME, and COLUMN_TYPE. The following table lists the columns in the result set. Additional columns beyond column 13 (REMARKS) can be defined by the driver.

The lengths of VARCHAR columns shown in the table are maximums; the actual lengths depend on the data source. To determine the actual lengths of the PROCEDURE_QUALIFIER, PROCEDURE_OWNER, PROCEDURE_NAME, and COLUMN_NAME columns, an application can call **SQLGetInfo** with the SQL_MAX_QUALIFIER_NAME_LEN, SQL_MAX_OWNER_NAME_LEN, SQL_MAX_PROCEDURE_NAME_LEN, and SQL_MAX_COLUMN_NAME_LEN options.

Column Name	Data Type	Comments
PROCEDURE_QUALIFIER	Varchar(128)	Procedure qualifer identifier; NULL if not applicable to the data source. If a driver supports qualifiers for some procedures but not for others, such as when the driver retrieves data from different DBMSs, it returns an empty string ("") for those procedures that do not have qualifiers.
PROCEDURE_OWNER	Varchar(128)	Procedure owner identifier; NULL if not applicable to the data source. If a driver supports owners for some procedures but not for others, such as when the driver retrieves data from different DBMSs, it returns an empty string ("") for those procedures that do not have owners.
PROCEDURE_NAME	Varchar(128) not NULL	Procedure identifier.
COLUMN_NAME	Varchar(128) not NULL	Procedure column identifier.

Column Name	Data Type	Comments
COLUMN_TYPE	Smallint not NULL	Defines the procedure column as parameter or a result set column:
		SQL_PARAM_TYPE_UNKNOWN: The procedure column is a parameter whose type is unknown. (ODBC 1.0)
		SQL_PARAM_INPUT: The procedure column is an input parameter. (ODBC 1.0)
		SQL_PARAM_INPUT_OUTPUT: the procedure column is an input/output parameter. (ODBC 1.0)
		SQL_PARAM_OUTPUT: The procedure column is an output parameter. (ODBC 1.0)
		SQL_RETURN_VALUE: The procedure column is the return value of the procedure. (ODBC 2.0)
		SQL_RESULT_COL: The procedure column is a result set column. (ODBC 1.0)
DATA_TYPE	Smallint not NULL	SQL data type. This can be an ODBC SQL data type or a driver-specific SQL data type. For a list of valid ODBC SQL data types, see "SQL Data Types" in Appendix D, "Data Types." For information about driver-specific SQL data types, see the driver's documentation.
TYPE_NAME	Varchar(128) not NULL	Data source–dependent data type name; for example, "CHAR", "VARCHAR", "MONEY", "LONG VARBINARY", or "CHAR ( ) FOR BIT DATA".
PRECISION	Integer	The precision of the procedure column on the data source. NULL is returned for data types where precision is not applicable. For more information concerning precision, see "Precision, Scale, Length, and Display Size," in Appendix D, "Data Types."

Column Name	Data Type	Comments
LENGTH	Integer	The length in bytes of data transferred on an **SQLGetData** or **SQLFetch** operation if SQL_C_DEFAULT is specified. For numeric data, this size may be different than the size of the data stored on the data source. For more information, see "Precision, Scale, Length, and Display Size," in Appendix D, "Data Types."
SCALE	Smallint	The scale of the procedure column on the data source. NULL is returned for data types where scale is not applicable. For more information concerning scale, see "Precision, Scale, Length, and Display Size," in Appendix D, "Data Types."
RADIX	Smallint	For numeric data types, either 10 or 2. If it is 10, the values in PRECISION and SCALE give the number of decimal digits allowed for the column. For example, a DECIMAL(12,5) column would return a RADIX of 10, a PRECISION of 12, and a SCALE of 5; a FLOAT column could return a RADIX of 10, a PRECISION of 15 and a SCALE of NULL.
		If it is 2, the values in PRECISION and SCALE give the number of bits allowed in the column. For example, a FLOAT column could return a RADIX of 2, a PRECISION of 53, and a SCALE of NULL.
		NULL is returned for data types where radix is not applicable.
NULLABLE	Smallint not NULL	Whether the procedure column accepts a NULL value:
		SQL_NO_NULLS: The procedure column does not accept NULL values.
		SQL_NULLABLE: The procedure column accepts NULL values.
		SQL_NULLABLE_UNKNOWN: It is not known if the procedure column accepts NULL values.
REMARKS	Varchar(254)	A description of the procedure column.

Code Example   See **SQLProcedures**.

Related Functions

For information about	See
Assigning storage for a column in a result set	**SQLBindCol**
Canceling statement processing	**SQLCancel**
Fetching a block of data or scrolling through a result set	**SQLExtendedFetch** (extension)
Fetching a row of data	**SQLFetch**
Returning a list of procedures in a data source	**SQLProcedures** (extension)

SQLProcedures

Extension Level 2   **SQLProcedures** returns the list of procedure names stored in a specific data source. *Procedure* is a generic term used to describe an *executable object*, or a named entity that can be invoked using input and output parameters, and which can return result sets similar to the results returned by SQL **SELECT** expressions.

Syntax   RETCODE **SQLProcedures**(*hstmt, szProcQualifier, cbProcQualifier, szProcOwner, cbProcOwner, szProcName, cbProcName*)

The **SQLProcedures** function accepts the following arguments:

Type	Argument	Use	Description
HSTMT	*hstmt*	Input	Statement handle.
UCHAR FAR *	*szProcQualifier*	Input	Procedure qualifier. If a driver supports qualifiers for some tables but not for others, such as when the driver retrieves data from different DBMSs, an empty string ("") denotes those tables that do not have qualifiers.
SWORD	*cbProcQualifier*	Input	Length of *szProcQualifier*.
UCHAR FAR *	*szProcOwner*	Input	String search pattern for procedure owner names. If a driver supports owners for some procedures but not for others, such as when the driver retrieves data from different DBMSs, an empty string ("") denotes those procedures that do not have owners.
SWORD	*cbProcOwner*	Input	Length of *szProcOwner*.
UCHAR FAR *	*szProcName*	Input	String search pattern for procedure names.
SWORD	*cbProcName*	Input	Length of *szProcName*.

Returns   SQL_SUCCESS, SQL_SUCCESS_WITH_INFO, SQL_STILL_EXECUTING, SQL_ERROR, or SQL_INVALID_HANDLE.

Diagnostics   When **SQLProcedures** returns SQL_ERROR or SQL_SUCCESS_WITH_INFO, an associated SQLSTATE value may be obtained by calling **SQLError**. The following table lists the SQLSTATE values commonly returned by **SQLProcedures** and explains each one in the context of this function; the notation "(DM)" precedes the descriptions of SQLSTATEs returned by the Driver Manager. The return code associated with each SQLSTATE value is SQL_ERROR, unless noted otherwise.

SQLSTATE	Error	Description
01000	General warning	Driver-specific informational message. (Function returns SQL_SUCCESS_WITH_INFO.)
08S01	Communication link failure	The communication link between the driver and the data source to which the driver was connected failed before the function completed processing.
24000	Invalid cursor state	(DM) A cursor was open on the *hstmt* and **SQLFetch** or **SQLExtendedFetch** had been called.
		A cursor was open on the *hstmt* but **SQLFetch** or **SQLExtendedFetch** had not been called.
IM001	Driver does not support this function	(DM) The driver associated with the *hstmt* does not support this function.
S1000	General error	An error occurred for which there was no specific SQLSTATE and for which no implementation-specific SQLSTATE was defined. The error message returned by **SQLError** in the argument *szErrorMsg* describes the error and its cause.
S1001	Memory allocation failure	The driver was unable to allocate memory required to support execution or completion of the function.
S1008	Operation canceled	Asynchronous processing was enabled for the *hstmt*. The function was called and before it completed execution, **SQLCancel** was called on the *hstmt*. Then the function was called again on the *hstmt*.
		The function was called and, before it completed execution, **SQLCancel** was called on the *hstmt* from a different thread in a multithreaded application.

SQLSTATE	Error	Description
S1010	Function sequence error	(DM) An asynchronously executing function (not this one) was called for the *hstmt* and was still executing when this function was called.
		(DM) **SQLExecute**, **SQLExecDirect**, or **SQLSetPos** was called for the *hstmt* and returned SQL_NEED_DATA. This function was called before data was sent for all data-at-execution parameters or columns.
S1090	Invalid string or buffer length	(DM) The value of one of the name length arguments was less than 0, but not equal to SQL_NTS.
		The value of one of the name length arguments exceeded the maximum length value for the corresponding qualifier or name.
S1C00	Driver not capable	A procedure qualifier was specified and the driver or data source does not support qualifiers.
		A procedure owner was specified and the driver or data source does not support owners.
		A string search pattern was specified for the procedure owner or procedure name and the data source does not support search patterns for one or more of those arguments.
		The combination of the current settings of the SQL_CONCURRENCY and SQL_CURSOR_TYPE statement options was not supported by the driver or data source.
S1T00	Timeout expired	The timeout period expired before the data source returned the requested result set. The timeout period is set through **SQLSetStmtOption**, SQL_QUERY_TIMEOUT.

Comments   **SQLProcedures** lists all procedures in the requested range. A user may or may not have permission to execute any of these procedures. To check accessibility, an application can call **SQLGetInfo** and check the SQL_ACCESSIBLE_PROCEDURES information value. Otherwise, the application must be able to handle a situation where the user selects a procedure which it cannot execute.

Note **SQLProcedures** might not return all procedures. Applications can use any valid procedure, regardless of whether it is returned by **SQLProcedures**.

SQLProcedures returns the results as a standard result set, ordered by PROCEDURE_QUALIFIER, PROCEDURE_OWNER, and PROCEDURE_NAME. The following table lists the columns in the result set.

The lengths of VARCHAR columns shown in the table are maximums; the actual lengths depend on the data source. To determine the actual lengths of the PROCEDURE_QUALIFIER, PROCEDURE_OWNER, and PROCEDURE_NAME columns, an application can call **SQLGetInfo** with the SQL_MAX_QUALIFIER_NAME_LEN, SQL_MAX_OWNER_NAME_LEN, and SQL_MAX_PROCEDURE_NAME_LEN options.

Column Name	Data Type	Comments
PROCEDURE_QUALIFIER	Varchar(128)	Procedure qualifier identifier; NULL if not applicable to the data source. If a driver supports qualifiers for some procedures but not for others, such as when the driver retrieves data from different DBMSs, it returns an empty string ("") for those procedures that do not have qualifiers.
PROCEDURE_OWNER	Varchar(128)	Procedure owner identifier; NULL if not applicable to the data source. If a driver supports owners for some procedures but not for others, such as when the driver retrieves data from different DBMSs, it returns an empty string ("") for those procedures that do not have owners.
PROCEDURE_NAME	Varchar(128) not NULL	Procedure identifier.
NUM_INPUT_PARAMS	N/A	Reserved for future use. Applications should not rely on the data returned in these result columns.
NUM_OUTPUT_PARAMS	N/A	Reserved for future use. Applications should not rely on the data returned in these result columns.
NUM_RESULT_SETS	N/A	Reserved for future use. Applications should not rely on the data returned in these result columns.
REMARKS	Varchar(254)	A description of the procedure.

Column Name	Data Type	Comments
PROCEDURE_TYPE	Smallint	Defines the procedure type:
		SQL_PT_UNKNOWN: It cannot be determined whether the procedure returns a value.
		SQL_PT_PROCEDURE: The returned object is a procedure; that is, it does not have a return value.
		SQL_PT_FUNCTION: The returned object is a function; that is, it has a return value.

Note The PROCEDURE_TYPE column was added in ODBC 2.0. ODBC 1.0 drivers might return a different, driver-specific column with the same column number.

The *szProcOwner* and *szProcName* arguments accept search patterns. For more information about valid search patterns, see "Search Pattern Arguments" earlier in this chapter.

Code Example

In this example, an application uses the procedure **AddEmployee** to insert data into the EMPLOYEE table. The procedure contains input parameters for NAME, AGE, and BIRTHDAY columns. It also contains one output parameter that returns a remark about the new employee. The example also shows the use of a return value from a stored procedure. For the return value and each parameter in the procedure, the application calls **SQLBindParameter** to specify the ODBC C data type and the SQL data type of the parameter and to specify the storage location and length of the parameter. The application assigns data values to the storage locations for each parameter and calls **SQLExecDirect** to execute the procedure. If **SQLExecDirect** returns SQL_SUCCESS or SQL_SUCCESS_WITH_INFO, the return value and the value of each output or input/output parameter is automatically put into the storage location defined for the parameter in **SQLBindParameter**.

```
#define NAME_LEN 30
#define REM_LEN 128

UCHAR       szName[NAME_LEN], szRemark[REM_LEN];
SWORD       sAge, sEmpId;
SDWORD      cbEmpId, cbName, cbAge = 0, cbBirthday = 0, cbRemark;
DATE_STRUCT dsBirthday;
```

```
/* Define parameter for return value (Employee ID) from procedure. */

SQLBindParameter(hstmt, 1, SQL_PARAM_OUTPUT, SQL_C_SLONG, SQL_INTEGER,
                 0, 0, &sEmpId, 0, &cbEmpId);

/* Define data types and storage locations for Name, Age, Birthday */
/* input parameter data.                                           */

SQLBindParameter(hstmt, 2, SQL_PARAM_INPUT, SQL_C_CHAR, SQL_CHAR,
                 NAME_LEN, 0, szName, 0, &cbName);
SQLBindParameter(hstmt, 3, SQL_PARAM_INPUT, SQL_C_SSHORT, SQL_SMALLINT,
                 0, 0, &sAge, 0, &cbAge);
SQLBindParameter(hstmt, 4, SQL_PARAM_INPUT, SQL_C_DATE, SQL_DATE,
                 0, 0, &dsBirthday, 0, &cbBirthday);

/* Define data types and storage location for Remark output parameter */

SQLBindParameter(hstmt, 5, SQL_PARAM_OUTPUT, SQL_C_CHAR, SQL_CHAR,
                 REM_LEN, 0, szRemark, REM_LEN, &cbRemark);

strcpy(szName, "Smith, John D.");    /* Specify first row of */
sAge = 40;                            /* parameter data.      */
dsBirthday.year = 1952;
dsBirthday.month = 2;
dsBirthday.day = 29;
cbName = SQL_NTS;

/* Execute procedure with first row of data. After the procedure */
/* is executed, sEmpId and szRemark will have the values         */
/* returned by AddEmployee.                                      */

retcode = SQLExecDirect(hstmt, "{?=call AddEmployee(?,?,?,?)}",SQL_NTS);

strcpy(szName, "Jones, Bob K.");     /* Specify second row of */
sAge = 52;                            /* parameter data        */
dsBirthday.year = 1940;
dsBirthday.month = 3;
dsBirthday.day = 31;

/* Execute procedure with second row of data. After the procedure */
/* is executed, sEmpId and szRemark will have the new values      */
/* returned by AddEmployee.                                       */

retcode = SQLExecDirect(hstmt,
                        "{?=call AddEmployee(?,?,?,?)}", SQL_NTS);
```

Related Functions	**For information about**	**See**
	Assigning storage for a column in a result set	**SQLBindCol**
	Canceling statement processing	**SQLCancel**
	Fetching a block of data or scrolling through a result set	**SQLExtendedFetch** (extension)
	Fetching a row of data	**SQLFetch**
	Returning information about a driver or data source	**SQLGetInfo** (extension)
	Returning the parameters and result set columns of a procedure	**SQLProcedureColumns** (extension)
	Syntax for invoking stored procedures	**Chapter 6**, "Executing SQL Statements"

SQLPutData

Extension Level 1   **SQLPutData** allows an application to send data for a parameter or column to the driver at statement execution time. This function can be used to send character or binary data values in parts to a column with a character, binary, or data source–specific data type (for example, parameters of the SQL_LONGVARBINARY or SQL_LONGVARCHAR types).

Syntax   RETCODE **SQLPutData**(*hstmt*, *rgbValue*, *cbValue*)

The **SQLPutData** function accepts the following arguments.

Type	Argument	Use	Description
HSTMT	*hstmt*	Input	Statement handle.
PTR	*rgbValue*	Input	Pointer to storage for the actual data for the parameter or column. The data must use the C data type specified in the *fCType* argument of **SQLBindParameter** (for parameter data) or **SQLBindCol** (for column data).

Type	Argument	Use	Description
SDWORD	*cbValue*	Input	Length of *rgbValue*. Specifies the amount of data sent in a call to **SQLPutData**. The amount of data can vary with each call for a given parameter or column. *cbValue* is ignored unless it is SQL_NTS, SQL_NULL_DATA, or SQL_DEFAULT_PARAM; the C data type specified in **SQLBindParameter** or **SQLBindCol** is SQL_C_CHAR or SQL_C_BINARY; or the C data type is SQL_C_DEFAULT and the default C data type for the specified SQL data type is SQL_C_CHAR or SQL_C_BINARY. For all other types of C data, if *cbValue* is not SQL_NULL_DATA or SQL_DEFAULT_PARAM, the driver assumes that the size of *rgbValue* is the size of the C data type specified with *fCType* and sends the entire data value. For more information, see "Converting Data from C to SQL Data Types" in Appendix D, "Data Types."

Returns

SQL_SUCCESS, SQL_SUCCESS_WITH_INFO, SQL_STILL_EXECUTING, SQL_ERROR, or SQL_INVALID_HANDLE.

Diagnostics

When **SQLPutData** returns SQL_ERROR or SQL_SUCCESS_WITH_INFO, an associated SQLSTATE value may be obtained by calling **SQLError**. The following table lists the SQLSTATE values commonly returned by **SQLPutData** and explains each one in the context of this function; the notation "(DM)" precedes the descriptions of SQLSTATEs returned by the Driver Manager. The return code associated with each SQLSTATE value is SQL_ERROR, unless noted otherwise.

SQLSTATE	Error	Description
01000	General warning	Driver-specific informational message. (Function returns SQL_SUCCESS_WITH_INFO.)

SQLSTATE	Error	Description
01004	Data truncated	The data sent for a character or binary parameter or column in one or more calls to **SQLPutData** exceeded the maximum length of the associated character or binary column.
		The fractional part of the data sent for a numeric or bit parameter or column was truncated.
		Timestamp data sent for a date or time parameter or column was truncated.
08S01	Communication link failure	The communication link between the driver and the data source to which the driver was connected failed before the function completed processing.
22001	String data right truncation	The SQL_NEED_LONG_DATA_LEN information type in **SQLGetInfo** was "Y" and more data was sent for a long parameter (the data type was SQL_LONGVARCHAR, SQL_LONGVARBINARY, or a long, data source–specific data type) than was specified with the *pcbValue* argument in **SQLBindParameter**.
		The SQL_NEED_LONG_DATA_LEN information type in **SQLGetInfo** was "Y" and more data was sent for a long column (the data type was SQL_LONGVARCHAR, SQL_LONGVARBINARY, or a long, data source–specific data type) than was specified in the length buffer corresponding to a column in a row of data that was added or updated with **SQLSetPos**.
22003	Numeric value out of range	**SQLPutData** was called more than once for a parameter or column and it was not being used to send character C data to a column with a character, binary, or data source–specific data type or to send binary C data to a column with a character, binary, or data source–specific data type.
		The data sent for a numeric parameter or column caused the whole (as opposed to fractional) part of the number to be truncated when assigned to the associated table column.

SQLSTATE	Error	Description
22005	Error in assignment	The data sent for a parameter ór column was incompatible with the data type of the associated table column.
22008	Datetime field overflow	The data sent for a date, time, or timestamp parameter or column was, respectively, an invalid date, time, or timestamp.
IM001	Driver does not support this function	(DM) The driver associated with the *hstmt* does not support the function.
S1000	General error	An error occurred for which there was no specific SQLSTATE and for which no implementation-specific SQLSTATE was defined. The error message returned by **SQLError** in the argument *szErrorMsg* describes the error and its cause.
S1001	Memory allocation failure	The driver was unable to allocate memory required to support execution or completion of the function.
S1008	Operation canceled	Asynchronous processing was enabled for the *hstmt*. The function was called and before it completed execution, **SQLCancel** was called on the *hstmt*. Then the function was called again on the *hstmt*.
		The function was called and, before it completed execution, **SQLCancel** was called on the *hstmt* from a different thread in a multithreaded application.
		SQLExecute, **SQLExecDirect**, or **SQLSetPos** was called for the *hstmt* and returned SQL_NEED_DATA. **SQLCancel** was called before data was sent for all data-at-execution parameters or columns.
S1009	Invalid argument value	(DM) The argument *rgbValue* was a null pointer and the argument *cbValue* was not 0, SQL_DEFAULT_PARAM, or SQL_NULL_DATA.

SQLSTATE	Error	Description
S1010	Function sequence error	(DM) The previous function call was not a call to **SQLPutData** or **SQLParamData**.
		The previous function call was a call to **SQLExecDirect**, **SQLExecute**, or **SQLSetPos** where the return code was SQL_NEED_DATA.
		(DM) An asynchronously executing function (not this one) was called for the *hstmt* and was still executing when this function was called.
S1090	Invalid string or buffer length	The argument *rgbValue* was not a null pointer and the argument *cbValue* was less than 0, but not equal to SQL_NTS or SQL_NULL_DATA.
S1T00	Timeout expired	The timeout period expired before the data source completed processing the parameter value. The timeout period is set through **SQLSetStmtOption**, SQL_QUERY_TIMEOUT.

Comments

For an explanation of how data-at-execution parameter data is passed at statement execution time, see "Passing Parameter Values" in **SQLBindParameter**. For an explanation of how data-at-execution column data is updated or added, see "Using SQLSetPos" in **SQLSetPos**.

Note An application can use **SQLPutData** to send data in parts only when sending character C data to a column with a character, binary, or data source–specific data type or when sending binary C data to a column with a character, binary, or data source–specific data type. If **SQLPutData** is called more than once under any other conditions, it returns SQL_ERROR and SQLSTATE 22003 (Numeric value out of range).

Code Example

In the following example, an application prepares an SQL statement to insert data into the EMPLOYEE table. The statement contains parameters for the NAME, ID, and PHOTO columns. For each parameter, the application calls **SQLBindParameter** to specify the C and SQL data types of the parameter. It also specifies that the data for the first and third parameters will be passed at execution time, and passes the values 1 and 3 for later retrieval by **SQLParamData**. These values will identify which parameter is being processed.

The application calls **GetNextID** to get the next available employee ID number. It then calls **SQLExecute** to execute the statement. **SQLExecute** returns SQL_NEED_DATA when it needs data for the first and third parameters. The application calls **SQLParamData** to retrieve the value it stored with **SQLBindParameter**; it uses this value to determine which parameter to send data for. For each parameter, the application calls **InitUserData** to initialize the data routine. It repeatedly calls **GetUserData** and **SQLPutData** to get and send the parameter data. Finally, it calls **SQLParamData** to indicate it has sent all the data for the parameter and to retrieve the value for the next parameter. After data has been sent for both parameters, **SQLParamData** returns SQL_SUCCESS.

For the first parameter, **InitUserData** does not do anything and **GetUserData** calls a routine to prompt the user for the employee name. For the third parameter, **InitUserData** calls a routine to prompt the user for the name of a file containing a bitmap photo of the employee and opens the file. **GetUserData** retrieves the next MAX_DATA_LEN bytes of photo data from the file. After it has retrieved all the photo data, it closes the photo file.

Note that some application routines are omitted for clarity.

```
#define NAME_LEN 30
#define MAX_DATA_LEN 1024
SDWORD   cbNameParam, cbID = 0; cbPhotoParam, cbData;
SWORD    sID;
PTR      pToken, InitValue;
UCHAR    Data[MAX_DATA_LEN];

retcode = SQLPrepare(hstmt,
          "INSERT INTO EMPLOYEE (NAME, ID, PHOTO) VALUES (?, ?, ?)",
          SQL_NTS);
if (retcode == SQL_SUCCESS) {

    /* Bind the parameters. For parameters 1 and 3, pass the     */
    /* parameter number in rgbValue instead of a buffer address. */

    SQLBindParameter(hstmt, 1, SQL_PARAM_INPUT, SQL_C_CHAR, SQL_CHAR,
                NAME_LEN, 0, 1, 0, &cbNameParam);
    SQLBindParameter(hstmt, 2, SQL_PARAM_INPUT, SQL_C_SSHORT,
                    SQL_SMALLINT, 0, 0, &sID, 0, &cbID);
    SQLBindParameter(hstmt, 3, SQL_PARAM_INPUT,
                    SQL_C_BINARY, SQL_LONGVARBINARY,
                    0, 0, 3, 0, &cbPhotoParam);
```

```
                    /* Set values so data for parameters 1 and 3 will be passed  */
                    /* at execution. Note that the length parameter in the macro */
                    /* SQL_LEN_DATA_AT_EXEC is 0. This assumes that the driver   */
                    /* returns "N" for the SQL_NEED_LONG_DATA_LEN information     */
                    /* type in SQLGetInfo.                                        */

                    cbNameParam = cbPhotoParam = SQL_LEN_DATA_AT_EXEC(0);

                    sID = GetNextID();  /* Get next available employee ID number. */

                    retcode = SQLExecute(hstmt);

                    /* For data-at-execution parameters, call SQLParamData to get the */
                    /* parameter number set by SQLBindParameter. Call InitUserData.   */
                    /* Call GetUserData and SQLPutData repeatedly to get and put all   */
                    /* data for the parameter. Call SQLParamData to finish processing */
                    /* this parameter and start processing the next parameter.        */

                    while (retcode == SQL_NEED_DATA) {
                        retcode = SQLParamData(hstmt, &pToken);
                        if (retcode == SQL_NEED_DATA) {
                            InitUserData((SWORD)pToken, InitValue);
                            while (GetUserData(InitValue, (SWORD)pToken, Data, &cbData))
                                SQLPutData(hstmt, Data, cbData);
                        }
                    }
                }

        VOID InitUserData(sParam, InitValue)
        SWORD sParam;
        PTR   InitValue;
        {
        UCHAR  szPhotoFile[MAX_FILE_NAME_LEN];
        switch sParam {
            case 3:

                /* Prompt user for bitmap file containing employee photo.   */
                /* OpenPhotoFile opens the file and returns the file handle. */

                PromptPhotoFileName(szPhotoFile);
                OpenPhotoFile(szPhotoFile, (FILE *)InitValue);
                break;
        }
        }
```

```
BOOL GetUserData(InitValue, sParam, Data, cbData)
PTR     InitValue;
SWORD   sParam;
UCHAR   *Data;
SDWORD  *cbData;

{

switch sParam {
    case 1:
        /* Prompt user for employee name. */

        PromptEmployeeName(Data);
        *cbData = SQL_NTS;
        return (TRUE);

    case 3:
        /* GetNextPhotoData returns the next piece of photo data and   */
        /* the number of bytes of data returned (up to MAX_DATA_LEN). */

        Done = GetNextPhotoData((FILE *)InitValue, Data,
                                MAX_DATA_LEN, &cbData);
        if (Done) {
            ClosePhotoFile((FILE *)InitValue);
            return (TRUE);
        }
        return (FALSE);
}
return (FALSE);
}
```

For information about	**See**
Canceling statement processing	**SQLCancel**
Executing an SQL statement	**SQLExecDirect**
Executing a prepared SQL statement	**SQLExecute**
Returning the next parameter to send data for	**SQLParamData** (extension)
Assigning storage for a parameter	**SQLBindParameter**

Related Functions

SQLRowCount

Core

SQLRowCount returns the number of rows affected by an **UPDATE**, **INSERT**, or **DELETE** statement or by a SQL_UPDATE, SQL_ADD, or SQL_DELETE operation in **SQLSetPos**.

Syntax

RETCODE **SQLRowCount**(*hstmt*, *pcrow*)

The **SQLRowCount** function accepts the following arguments.

Type	Argument	Use	Description
HSTMT	*hstmt*	Input	Statement handle.
SDWORD FAR *	*pcrow*	Output	For **UPDATE**, **INSERT**, and **DELETE** statements and for the SQL_UPDATE, SQL_ADD, and SQL_DELETE operations in **SQLSetPos**, *pcrow* is the number of rows affected by the request or –1 if the number of affected rows is not available.
			For other statements and functions, the driver may define the value of *pcrow*. For example, some data sources may be able to return the number of rows returned by a **SELECT** statement or a catalog function before fetching the rows.
			Note Many data sources cannot return the number of rows in a result set before fetching them; for maximum interoperability, applications should not rely on this behavior.

Returns

SQL_SUCCESS, SQL_SUCCESS_WITH_INFO, SQL_ERROR, or SQL_INVALID_HANDLE.

Diagnostics

When **SQLRowCount** returns SQL_ERROR or SQL_SUCCESS_WITH_INFO, an associated SQLSTATE value may be obtained by calling **SQLError**. The following table lists the SQLSTATE values commonly returned by **SQLRowCount** and explains each one in the context of this function; the notation "(DM)" precedes the descriptions of SQLSTATEs returned by the Driver

Manager. The return code associated with each SQLSTATE value is SQL_ERROR, unless noted otherwise.

SQLSTATE	Error	Description
01000	General warning	Driver-specific informational message. (Function returns SQL_SUCCESS_WITH_INFO.)
IM001	Driver does not support this function	(DM) The driver associated with the *hstmt* does not support the function.
S1000	General error	An error occurred for which there was no specific SQLSTATE and for which no implementation-specific SQLSTATE was defined. The error message returned by **SQLError** in the argument *szErrorMsg* describes the error and its cause.
S1001	Memory allocation failure	The driver was unable to allocate memory required to support execution or completion of the function.
S1010	Function sequence error	(DM) The function was called prior to calling **SQLExecute**, **SQLExecDirect**, **SQLSetPos** for the *hstmt*.
		(DM) An asynchronously executing function was called for the *hstmt* and was still executing when this function was called.
		(DM) **SQLExecute**, **SQLExecDirect**, or **SQLSetPos** was called for the *hstmt* and returned SQL_NEED_DATA. This function was called before data was sent for all data-at-execution parameters or columns.

Comments

If the last executed statement associated with *hstmt* was not an **UPDATE**, **INSERT**, or **DELETE** statement, or if the *fOption* argument in the previous call to **SQLSetPos** was not SQL_UPDATE, SQL_ADD, or SQL_DELETE, the value of *pcrow* is driver-defined.

Related Functions

For information about	See
Executing an SQL statement	**SQLExecDirect**
Executing a prepared SQL statement	**SQLExecute**

SQLSetConnectOption

ODBC 1.0

Extension Level 1   **SQLSetConnectOption** sets options that govern aspects of connections.

Syntax   RETCODE **SQLSetConnectOption**(*hdbc, fOption, vParam*)

The **SQLSetConnectOption** function accepts the following arguments:

Type	Argument	Use	Description
HDBC	*hdbc*	Input	Connection handle.
UWORD	*fOption*	Input	Option to set, listed in "Comments."
UDWORD	*vParam*	Input	Value associated with *fOption*. Depending on the value of *fOption*, *vParam* will be a 32-bit integer value or point to a null-terminated character string.

Returns   SQL_SUCCESS, SQL_SUCCESS_WITH_INFO, SQL_ERROR, or SQL_INVALID_HANDLE.

Diagnostics   When **SQLSetConnectOption** returns SQL_ERROR or SQL_SUCCESS_WITH_INFO, an associated SQLSTATE value may be obtained by calling **SQLError**. The following table lists the SQLSTATE values commonly returned by **SQLSetConnectOption** and explains each one in the context of this function; the notation "(DM)" precedes the descriptions of SQLSTATEs returned by the Driver Manager. The return code associated with each SQLSTATE value is SQL_ERROR, unless noted otherwise.

The driver can return SQL_SUCCESS_WITH_INFO to provide information about the result of setting an option. For example, setting SQL_ACCESS_MODE to read-only during a transaction might cause the transaction to be committed. The driver could use SQL_SUCCESS_WITH_INFO—and information returned with **SQLError**—to inform the application of the commit action.

SQLSTATE	Error	Description
01000	General warning	Driver-specific informational message. (Function returns SQL_SUCCESS_WITH_INFO.)
01S02	Option value changed	The driver did not support the specified value of the *vParam* argument and substituted a similar value. (Function returns SQL_SUCCESS_WITH_INFO.)
08002	Connection in use	The argument *fOption* was SQL_ODBC_CURSORS and the driver was already connected to the data source.

SQLSTATE	Error	Description
08003	Connection not open	An *fOption* value was specified that required an open connection, but the *hdbc* was not in a connected state.
08S01	Communication link failure	The communication link between the driver and the data source to which the driver was connected failed before the function completed processing.
IM001	Driver does not support this function	(DM) The driver associated with the *hdbc* does not support the function.
IM009	Unable to load translation DLL	The driver was unable to load the translation DLL that was specified for the connection. This error can only be returned when *fOption* is SQL_TRANSLATE_DLL.
S1000	General error	An error occurred for which there was no specific SQLSTATE and for which no implementation-specific SQLSTATE was defined. The error message returned by **SQLError** in the argument *szErrorMsg* describes the error and its cause.
S1001	Memory allocation failure	The driver was unable to allocate memory required to support execution or completion of the function.
S1009	Invalid argument value	Given the specified *fOption* value, an invalid value was specified for the argument *vParam*. (The Driver Manager returns this SQLSTATE only for connection and statement options that accept a discrete set of values, such as SQL_ACCESS_MODE or SQL_ASYNC_ENABLE. For all other connection and statement options, the driver must verify the value of the argument *vParam*.)

SQLSTATE	Error	Description
S1010	Function sequence error	(DM) An asynchronously executing function was called for an *hstmt* associated with the *hdbc* and was still executing when **SQLSetConnectOption** was called.
		(DM) **SQLExecute**, **SQLExecDirect**, or **SQLSetPos** was called for an *hstmt* associated with the *hdbc* and returned SQL_NEED_DATA. This function was called before data was sent for all data-at-execution parameters or columns.
		(DM) **SQLBrowseConnect** was called for the *hdbc* and returned SQL_NEED_DATA. This function was called before **SQLBrowseConnect** returned SQL_SUCCESS_WITH_INFO or SQL_SUCCESS.
S1011	Operation invalid at this time	The argument *fOption* was SQL_TXN_ISOLATION and a transaction was open.
S1092	Option type out of range	(DM) The value specified for the argument *fOption* was in the block of numbers reserved for ODBC connection and statement options, but was not valid for the version of ODBC supported by the driver.
S1C00	Driver not capable	The value specified for the argument *fOption* was a valid ODBC connection or statement option for the version of ODBC supported by the driver, but was not supported by the driver.
		The value specified for the argument *fOption* was in the block of numbers reserved for driver-specific connection and statement options, but was not supported by the driver.

When *fOption* is a statement option, **SQLSetConnectOption** can return any SQLSTATEs returned by **SQLSetStmtOption**.

Comments   The currently defined options and the version of ODBC in which they were introduced are shown below; it is expected that more will be defined to take advantage of different data sources. Options from 0 to 999 are reserved by ODBC; driver developers must reserve values greater than or equal to SQL_CONNECT_OPT_DRVR_START for driver-specific use. For more information, see "Driver-Specific Data Types, Descriptor Types, Information Types, and Options" in Chapter 11, "Guidelines for Implementing ODBC Functions."

An application can call **SQLSetConnectOption** and include a statement option. The driver sets the statement option for any *hstmts* associated with the specified *hdbc* and establishes the statement option as a default for any *hstmts* later allocated for that *hdbc*. For a list of statement options, see **SQLSetStmtOption**.

All connection and statement options successfully set by the application for the *hdbc* persist until **SQLFreeConnect** is called on the *hdbc*. For example, if an application calls **SQLSetConnectOption** before connecting to a data source, the option persists even if **SQLSetConnectOption** fails in the driver when the application connects to the data source; if an application sets a driver-specific option, the option persists even if the application connects to a different driver on the *hdbc*.

Some connection and statement options support substitution of a similar value if the data source does not support the specified value of *vParam*. In such cases, the driver returns SQL_SUCCESS_WITH_INFO and SQLSTATE 01S02 (Option value changed). For example, if *fOption* is SQL_PACKET_SIZE and *vParam* exceeds the maximum packet size, the driver substitutes the maximum size. To determine the substituted value, an application calls **SQLGetConnectOption** (for connection options) or **SQLGetStmtOption** (for statement options).

The format of information set through *vParam* depends on the specified *fOption*. **SQLSetConnectOption** will accept option information in one of two different formats: a null-terminated character string or a 32-bit integer value. The format of each is noted in the option's description. Character strings pointed to by the *vParam* argument of **SQLSetConnectOption** have a maximum length of SQL_MAX_OPTION_STRING_LENGTH bytes (excluding the null termination byte).

fOption	*vParam* Contents
SQL_ACCESS_MODE (ODBC 1.0)	A 32-bit integer value. SQL_MODE_READ_ONLY is used by the driver or data source as an indicator that the connection is not required to support SQL statements that cause updates to occur. This mode can be used to optimize locking strategies, transaction management, or other areas as appropriate to the driver or data source. The driver is not required to prevent such statements from being submitted to the data source. The behavior of the driver and data source when asked to process SQL statements that are not read-only during a read-only connection is implementation defined. SQL_MODE_READ_WRITE is the default.
SQL_AUTOCOMMIT (ODBC 1.0)	A 32-bit integer value that specifies whether to use auto-commit or manual-commit mode: SQL_AUTOCOMMIT_OFF = The driver uses manual-commit mode, and the application must explicitly commit or roll back transactions with **SQLTransact**. SQL_AUTOCOMMIT_ON = The driver uses auto-commit mode. Each statement is committed immediately after it is executed. This is the default. Note that changing from manual-commit mode to auto-commit mode commits any open transactions on the connection.
	Important Some data sources delete the access plans and close the cursors for all *hstmts* on an *hdbc* each time a statement is committed; autocommit mode can cause this to happen after each statement is executed. For more information, see the SQL_CURSOR_COMMIT_BEHAVIOR and SQL_CURSOR_ROLLBACK_BEHAVIOR information types in **SQLGetInfo**.
SQL_CURRENT_QUALIFIER (ODBC 2.0)	A null-terminated character string containing the name of the qualifier to be used by the data source. For example, in SQL Server, the qualifier is a database, so the driver sends a **USE** *database* statement to the data source, where *database* is the database specified in *vParam*. For a single-tier driver, the qualifier might be a directory, so the driver changes its current directory to the directory specified in *vParam*.
SQL_LOGIN_TIMEOUT (ODBC 1.0)	A 32-bit integer value corresponding to the number of seconds to wait for a login request to complete before returning to the application. The default is driver-dependent and must be nonzero. If *vParam* is 0, the timeout is disabled and a connection attempt will wait indefinitely. If the specified timeout exceeds the maximum login timeout in the data source, the driver substitutes that value and returns SQLSTATE 01S02 (Option value changed).

fOption	*vParam* **Contents**
SQL_ODBC_CURSORS (ODBC 2.0)	A 32-bit option specifying how the Driver Manager uses the ODBC cursor library: SQL_CUR_USE_IF_NEEDED = The Driver Manager uses the ODBC cursor library only if it is needed. If the driver supports the SQL_FETCH_PRIOR option in **SQLExtendedFetch**, the Driver Manager uses the scrolling capabilities of the driver. Otherwise, it uses the ODBC cursor library. SQL_CUR_USE_ODBC = The Driver Manager uses the ODBC cursor library. SQL_CUR_USE_DRIVER = The Driver Manager uses the scrolling capabilities of the driver. This is the default setting. For more information about the ODBC cursor library, see Appendix G, "ODBC Cursor Library."
SQL_OPT_TRACE (ODBC 1.0)	A 32-bit integer value telling the Driver Manager whether to perform tracing: SQL_OPT_TRACE_OFF = Tracing off (the default) SQL_OPT_TRACE_ON = Tracing on When tracing is on, the Driver Manager writes each ODBC function call to the trace file. On Windows and WOW, the Driver Manager writes to the trace file each time any application calls a function. On Windows NT, the Driver Manager writes to the trace file only for the application that turned tracing on.

> **Note** When tracing is on, the Driver Manager can return SQLSTATE IM013 (Trace file error) from any function.

An application specifies a trace file with the SQL_OPT_TRACEFILE option. If the file already exists, the Driver Manager appends to the file. Otherwise, it creates the file. If tracing is on and no trace file has been specified, the Driver Manager writes to the file \SQL.LOG. On Windows NT, tracing should only be used for a single application or each application should specify a different trace file. Otherwise, two or more applications will attempt to open the same trace file at the same time, causing an error.

If the **Trace** keyword in the [ODBC] section of the ODBC.INI file (or registry) is set to 1 when an application calls **SQLAllocEnv**, tracing is enabled. On Windows and WOW, it is enabled for all applications; on Windows NT it is enabled only for the application that called **SQLAllocEnv**. For more information, see "ODBC Options Section" in Chapter 20, "Configuring Data Sources."

fOption	*vParam* **Contents**
SQL_OPT_TRACEFILE (ODBC 1.0)	A null-terminated character string containing the name of the trace file. The default value of the SQL_OPT_TRACEFILE option is specified with the TraceFile keyname in the [ODBC] section of the ODBC.INI file (or registry). For more information, see "ODBC Options Section" in Chapter 20, "Configuring Data Sources."
SQL_PACKET_SIZE (ODBC 2.0)	A 32-bit integer value specifying the network packet size in bytes. **Note** Many data sources either do not support this option or can only return the network packet size. If the specified size exceeds the maximum packet size or is smaller than the minimum packet size, the driver substitutes that value and returns SQLSTATE 01S02 (Option value changed).
SQL_QUIET_MODE (ODBC 2.0)	A 32-bit window handle (*hwnd*). If the window handle is a null pointer, the driver does not display any dialog boxes. If the window handle is not a null pointer, it should be the parent window handle of the application. The driver uses this handle to display dialog boxes. This is the default. If the application has not specified a parent window handle for this option, the driver uses a null parent window handle to display dialog boxes or return in **SQLGetConnectOption**. **Note** The SQL_QUIET_MODE connection option does not apply to dialog boxes displayed by **SQLDriverConnect**.
SQL_TRANSLATE_DLL (ODBC 1.0)	A null-terminated character string containing the name of a DLL containing the functions **SQLDriverToDataSource** and **SQLDataSourceToDriver** that the driver loads and uses to perform tasks such as character set translation. This option may only be specified if the driver has connected to the data source. For more information about translating data, see Chapter 25, "Translation DLL Function Reference."
SQL_TRANSLATE_OPTION (ODBC 1.0)	A 32-bit flag value that is passed to the translatation DLL. This option may only be specified if the driver has connected to the data source.

fOption	vParam Contents
SQL_TXN_ISOLATION (ODBC 1.0)	A 32-bit bitmask that sets the transaction isolation level for the current *hdbc*. An application must call **SQLTransact** to commit or roll back all open transactions on an *hdbc*, before calling **SQLSetConnectOption** with this option.

The valid values for *vParam* can be determined by calling **SQLGetInfo** with *fInfoType* equal to SQL_TXN_ISOLATION_OPTIONS. The following terms are used to define transaction isolation levels:

Dirty Read   Transaction 1 changes a row. Transaction 2 reads the changed row before transaction 1 commits the change. If transaction 1 rolls back the change, transaction 2 will have read a row that is considered to have never existed.

Nonrepeatable Read   Transaction 1 reads a row. Transaction 2 updates or deletes that row and commits this change. If transaction 1 attempts to reread the row, it will receive different row values or discover that the row has been deleted.

Phantom   Transaction 1 reads a set of rows that satisfy some search criteria. Transaction 2 inserts a row that matches the search criteria. If transaction 1 reexecutes the statement that read the rows, it receives a different set of rows.

vParam must be one of the following values:

SQL_TXN_READ_UNCOMMITTED = Dirty reads, nonrepeatable reads, and phantoms are possible.

SQL_TXN_READ_COMMITTED = Dirty reads are not possible. Nonrepeatable reads and phantoms are possible.

SQL_TXN_REPEATABLE_READ = Dirty reads and nonrepeatable reads are not possible. Phantoms are possible.

SQL_TXN_SERIALIZABLE = Transactions are serializable. Dirty reads, nonrepeatable reads, and phantoms are not possible.

SQL_TXN_VERSIONING = Transactions are serializable, but higher concurrency is possible than with SQL_TXN_SERIALIZABLE. Dirty reads are not possible. Typically, SQL_TXN_SERIALIZABLE is implemented by using locking protocols that reduce concurrency and SQL_TXN_VERSIONING is implemented by using a non-locking protocol such as record versioning. Oracle's Read Consistency isolation level is an example of SQL_TXN_VERSIONING.

Data Translation

Data translation will be performed for all data flowing between the driver and the data source.

The translation option (set with the SQL_TRANSLATE_OPTION option) can be any 32-bit value. Its meaning depends on the translation DLL being used. A new option can be set at any time. The new option will be applied to the next exchange of data following the call to **SQLSetConnectOption**. A default translation DLL may be specified for the data source in its data source specification in the ODBC.INI file or registry. The default translation DLL is loaded by the driver at connection time. A translation option (SQL_TRANSLATE_OPTION) may be specified in the data source specification as well.

To change the translation DLL for a connection, an application calls **SQLSetConnectOption** with the SQL_TRANSLATE_DLL option after it has connected to the data source. The driver will attempt to load the specified DLL and, if the attempt fails, return SQL_ERROR with the SQLSTATE IM009 (Unable to load translation DLL).

If no translation DLL has been specified in the ODBC initialization file or by calling **SQLSetConnectOption**, the driver will not attempt to translate data. Any value set for the translation option will be ignored.

For more information about translating data, see "Translating Data" in Chapter 13, "Establishing Connections"; "Specifying a Default Translator" in Chapter 20, "Configuring Data Sources"; and Chapter 25, "Translation Function DLL Reference."

Code Example   See **SQLConnect** and **SQLParamOptions**.

Related Functions

For information about	See
Returning the setting of a connection option	**SQLGetConnectOption** (extension)
Returning the setting of a statement option	**SQLGetStmtOption** (extension)
Setting a statement option	**SQLSetStmtOption** (extension)

SQLSetCursorName

Core

SQLSetCursorName associates a cursor name with an active *hstmt*. If an application does not call **SQLSetCursorName**, the driver generates cursor names as needed for SQL statement processing.

Syntax

RETCODE **SQLSetCursorName**(*hstmt*, *szCursor*, *cbCursor*)

The **SQLSetCursorName** function accepts the following arguments.

Type	Argument	Use	Description
HSTMT	*hstmt*	Input	Statement handle.
UCHAR FAR *	*szCursor*	Input	Cursor name.
SWORD	*cbCursor*	Input	Length of *szCursor*.

Returns

SQL_SUCCESS, SQL_SUCCESS_WITH_INFO, SQL_ERROR, or SQL_INVALID_HANDLE.

Diagnostics

When **SQLSetCursorName** returns SQL_ERROR or SQL_SUCCESS_WITH_INFO, an associated SQLSTATE value may be obtained by calling **SQLError**. The following table lists the SQLSTATE values commonly returned by **SQLSetCursorName** and explains each one in the context of this function; the notation "(DM)" precedes the descriptions of SQLSTATEs returned by the Driver Manager. The return code associated with each SQLSTATE value is SQL_ERROR, unless noted otherwise.

SQLSTATE	Error	Description
01000	General warning	Driver-specific informational message. (Function returns SQL_SUCCESS_WITH_INFO.)
24000	Invalid cursor state	The statement corresponding to *hstmt* was already in an executed or cursor-positioned state.
34000	Invalid cursor name	The cursor name specified by the argument *szCursor* was invalid. For example, the cursor name exceeded the maximum length as defined by the driver.
3C000	Duplicate cursor name	The cursor name specified by the argument *szCursor* already exists.
IM001	Driver does not support this function	(DM) The driver associated with the *hstmt* does not support the function.

SQLSTATE	Error	Description
S1000	General error	An error occurred for which there was no specific SQLSTATE and for which no implementation-specific SQLSTATE was defined. The error message returned by **SQLError** in the argument *szErrorMsg* describes the error and its cause.
S1001	Memory allocation failure	The driver was unable to allocate memory required to support execution or completion of the function.
S1009	Invalid argument value	(DM) The argument *szCursor* was a null pointer.
S1010	Function sequence error	(DM) An asynchronously executing function was called for the *hstmt* and was still executing when this function was called.
		(DM) **SQLExecute**, **SQLExecDirect**, or **SQLSetPos** was called for the *hstmt* and returned SQL_NEED_DATA. This function was called before data was sent for all data-at-execution parameters or columns.
S1090	Invalid string or buffer length	(DM) The argument *cbCursor* was less than 0, but not equal to SQL_NTS.

Comments

The only ODBC SQL statements that use a cursor name are a positioned update and delete (for example, **UPDATE** *table-name* ...**WHERE CURRENT OF** *cursor-name*). If the application does not call **SQLSetCursorName** to define a cursor name, on execution of a **SELECT** statement the driver generates a name that begins with the letters SQL_CUR and does not exceed 18 characters in length.

All cursor names within the *hdbc* must be unique. The maximum length of a cursor name is defined by the driver. For maximum interoperability, it is recommended that applications limit cursor names to no more than 18 characters.

A cursor name that is set either explicitly or implicitly remains set until the *hstmt* with which it is associated is dropped, using **SQLFreeStmt** with the SQL_DROP option.

Code Example

In the following example, an application uses **SQLSetCursorName** to set a cursor name for an *hstmt*. It then uses that *hstmt* to retrieve results from the EMPLOYEE table. Finally, it performs a positioned update to change the name of 25-year-old John Smith to John D. Smith. Note that the application uses different *hstmts* for the **SELECT** and **UPDATE** statements.

For more code examples, see **SQLSetPos**.

```
#define NAME_LEN 30

HSTMT     hstmtSelect,
HSTMT     hstmtUpdate;
UCHAR     szName[NAME_LEN];
SWORD     sAge;
SDWORD    cbName;
SDWORD    cbAge;

/* Allocate the statements and set the cursor name */

SQLAllocStmt(hdbc, &hstmtSelect);
SQLAllocStmt(hdbc, &hstmtUpdate);
SQLSetCursorName(hstmtSelect, "C1", SQL_NTS);

/* SELECT the result set and bind its columns to local storage */

SQLExecDirect(hstmtSelect,
              "SELECT NAME, AGE FROM EMPLOYEE FOR UPDATE",
              SQL_NTS);
SQLBindCol(hstmtSelect, 1, SQL_C_CHAR, szName, NAME_LEN, &cbName);
SQLBindCol(hstmtSelect, 2, SQL_C_SSHORT, &sAge, 0, &cbAge);

/* Read through the result set until the cursor is       */
/* positioned on the row for the 25-year-old John Smith */

do
    retcode = SQLFetch(hstmtSelect);
while ((retcode == SQL_SUCCESS || retcode == SQL_SUCCESS_WITH_INFO) &&
       (strcmp(szName, "Smith, John") != 0 || sAge != 25));

/* Perform a positioned update of John Smith's name */

if (retcode == SQL_SUCCESS || retcode == SQL_SUCCESS_WITH_INFO) {
    SQLExecDirect(hstmtUpdate,
       "UPDATE EMPLOYEE SET NAME=\"Smith, John D.\" WHERE CURRENT OF C1",
       SQL_NTS);
}
```

Related Functions

For information about	See
Executing an SQL statement	**SQLExecDirect**
Executing a prepared SQL statement	**SQLExecute**
Returning a cursor name	**SQLGetCursorName**
Setting cursor scrolling options	**SQLSetScrollOptions** (extension)

SQLSetParam

Deprecated   In ODBC 2.0, the ODBC 1.0 function **SQLSetParam** has been replaced by
SQLBindParameter. For more information, see **SQLBindParameter**.

SQLSetPos

Extension Level 2

SQLSetPos sets the cursor position in a rowset and allows an application to refresh, update, delete, or add data to the rowset.

Syntax

RETCODE **SQLSetPos**(*hstmt*, *irow*, *fOption*, *fLock*)

The **SQLSetPos** function accepts the following arguments:

Type	Argument	Use	Description
HSTMT	*hstmt*	Input	Statement handle.
UWORD	*irow*	Input	Position of the row in the rowset on which to perform the operation specified with the *fOption* argument. If *irow* is 0, the operation applies to every row in the rowset.
			For additional information, see "Comments."
UWORD	*fOption*	Input	Operation to perform:
			SQL_POSITION SQL_REFRESH SQL_UPDATE SQL_DELETE SQL_ADD
			For more information, see "Comments."
UWORD	*fLock*	Input	Specifies how to lock the row after performing the operation specified in the *fOption* argument.
			SQL_LOCK_NO_CHANGE SQL_LOCK_EXCLUSIVE SQL_LOCK_UNLOCK
			For more information, see "Comments."

Returns

SQL_SUCCESS, SQL_SUCCESS_WITH_INFO, SQL_NEED_DATA, SQL_STILL_EXECUTING, SQL_ERROR, or SQL_INVALID_HANDLE.

Diagnostics

When **SQLSetPos** returns SQL_ERROR or SQL_SUCCESS_WITH_INFO, an associated SQLSTATE value may be obtained by calling **SQLError**. The following table lists the SQLSTATE values commonly returned by **SQLSetPos** and explains each one in the context of this function; the notation "(DM)" precedes the descriptions of SQLSTATEs returned by the Driver Manager. The return code associated with each SQLSTATE value is SQL_ERROR, unless noted otherwise.

SQLSTATE	Error	Description
01000	General warning	Driver-specific informational message. (Function returns SQL_SUCCESS_WITH_INFO.)
01004	Data truncated	The argument *fOption* was SQL_ADD or SQL_UPDATE and the value specified for a character or binary column exceeded the maximum length of the associated table column. (Function returns SQL_SUCCESS_WITH_INFO.)
		The argument *fOption* was SQL_ADD or SQL_UPDATE and the fractional part of the value specified for a numeric column was truncated. (Function returns SQL_SUCCESS_WITH_INFO.)
		The argument *fOption* was SQL_ADD or SQL_UPDATE and a timestamp value specified for a date or time column was truncated. (Function returns SQL_SUCCESS_WITH_INFO.)
01S01	Error in row	The *irow* argument was 0 and an error occurred in one or more rows while performing the operation specified with the *fOption* argument. (Function returns SQL_SUCCESS_WITH_INFO.)
01S03	No rows updated or deleted	The argument *fOption* was SQL_UPDATE or SQL_DELETE and no rows were updated or deleted. (Function returns SQL_SUCCESS_WITH_INFO.)
01S04	More than one row updated or deleted	The argument *fOption* was SQL_UPDATE or SQL_DELETE and more than one row was updated or deleted. (Function returns SQL_SUCCESS_WITH_INFO.)
21S02	Degree of derived table does not match column list	The argument *fOption* was SQL_ADD or SQL_UPDATE and no columns were bound with **SQLBindCol**.
22003	Numeric value out of range	The argument *fOption* was SQL_ADD or SQL_UPDATE and the whole part of a numeric value was truncated.
22005	Error in assignment	The argument *fOption* was SQL_ADD or SQL_UPDATE and a value was incompatible with the data type of the associated column.

SQLSTATE	Error	Description
22008	Datetime field overflow	The argument *fOption* was SQL_ADD or SQL_UPDATE and a date, time, or timestamp value was, respectively, an invalid date, time, or timestamp.
23000	Integrity constraint violation	The argument *fOption* was SQL_ADD or SQL_UPDATE and a value was NULL for a column defined as NOT NULL in the associated column or some other integrity constraint was violated.
		The argument *fOption* was SQL_ADD and a column that was not bound with **SQLBindCol** is defined as NOT NULL or has no default.
24000	Invalid cursor state	(DM) The *hstmt* was in an executed state but no result set was associated with the *hstmt*.
		(DM) A cursor was open on the *hstmt* but **SQLFetch** or **SQLExtendedFetch** had not been called.
		A cursor was open on the *hstmt* and **SQLExtendedFetch** had been called, but the cursor was positioned before the start of the result set or after the end of the result set.
		The argument *fOption* was SQL_DELETE, SQL_REFRESH, or SQL_UPDATE and the cursor was positioned before the start of the result set or after the end of the result set.
42000	Syntax error or access violation	The driver was unable to lock the row as needed to perform the operation requested in the argument *fOption*.
		The driver was unable to lock the row as requested in the argument *fLock*.
IM001	Driver does not support this function	(DM) The driver associated with the *hstmt* does not support the function.

SQLSTATE	Error	Description
S0023	No default for column	The *fOption* argument was SQL_ADD and a column that was not bound did not have a default value and could not be set to NULL.
		The *fOption* argument was SQL_ADD, the length specified in the *pcbValue* buffer bound by **SQLBindCol** was SQL_IGNORE, and the column did not have a default value.
S1000	General error	An error occurred for which there was no specific SQLSTATE and for which no implementation-specific SQLSTATE was defined. The error message returned by **SQLError** in the argument *szErrorMsg* describes the error and its cause.
S1001	Memory allocation failure	The driver was unable to allocate memory required to support execution or completion of the function.
S1008	Operation canceled	Asynchronous processing was enabled for the *hstmt*. The function was called and before it completed execution, **SQLCancel** was called on the *hstmt*. Then the function was called again on the *hstmt*.
		The function was called and, before it completed execution, **SQLCancel** was called on the *hstmt* from a different thread in a multithreaded application.
S1009	Invalid argument value	(DM) The value specified for the argument *fOption* was invalid.
		(DM) The value specified for the argument *fLock* was invalid.
		The argument *irow* was greater than the number of rows in the rowset and the *fOption* argument was not SQL_ADD.
		The value specified for the argument *fOption* was SQL_ADD, SQL_UPDATE, or SQL_DELETE, the value specified for the argument *fLock* was SQL_LOCK_NO_CHANGE, and the SQL_CONCURRENCY statement option was SQL_CONCUR_READ_ONLY.

SQLSTATE	Error	Description
S1010	Function sequence error	(DM) The specified *hstmt* was not in an executed state. The function was called without first calling **SQLExecDirect**, **SQLExecute**, or a catalog function.
		(DM) An asynchronously executing function (not this one) was called for the *hstmt* and was still executing when this function was called.
		(DM) **SQLExecute**, **SQLExecDirect**, or **SQLSetPos** was called for the *hstmt* and returned SQL_NEED_DATA. This function was called before data was sent for all data-at-execution parameters or columns.
S1090	Invalid string or buffer length	The *fOption* argument was SQL_ADD or SQL_UPDATE, a data value was a null pointer, and the column length value was not 0, SQL_DATA_AT_EXEC, SQL_IGNORE, SQL_NULL_DATA, or less than or equal to SQL_LEN_DATA_AT_EXEC_OFFSET.
		The *fOption* argument was SQL_ADD or SQL_UPDATE, a data value was not a null pointer, and the column length value was less than 0, but not equal to SQL_DATA_AT_EXEC, SQL_IGNORE, SQL_NTS, or SQL_NULL_DATA, or less than or equal to SQL_LEN_DATA_AT_EXEC_OFFSET.
S1107	Row value out of range	The value specified for the argument *irow* was greater than the number of rows in the rowset and the *fOption* argument was not SQL_ADD.
S1109	Invalid cursor position	The cursor associated with the *hstmt* was defined as forward only, so the cursor could not be positioned within the rowset. See the description for the SQL_CURSOR_TYPE option in **SQLSetStmtOption**.
		The *fOption* argument was SQL_REFRESH, SQL_UPDATE, or SQL_DELETE and the value in the *rgfRowStatus* array for the row specified by the *irow* argument was SQL_ROW_DELETED or SQL_ROW_ERROR.

SQLSTATE	Error	Description
S1C00	Driver not capable	The driver or data source does not support the operation requested in the *fOption* argument or the *fLock* argument.
S1T00	Timeout expired	The timeout period expired before the data source returned the result set. The timeout period is set through **SQLSetStmtOption**, SQL_QUERY_TIMEOUT.

Comments

irow Argument

The *irow* argument specifies the number of the row in the rowset on which to perform the operation specified by the *fOption* argument. If *irow* is 0, the operation applies to every row in the rowset. Except for the SQL_ADD operation, *irow* must be a value from 0 to the number of rows in the rowset. For the SQL_ADD operation, *irow* can be any value; generally it is either 0 (to add as many rows as there are in the rowset) or the number of rows in the rowset plus 1 (to add the data from an extra row of buffers allocated for this purpose).

Note In the C language, arrays are 0-based, while the *irow* argument is 1-based. For example, to update the fifth row of the rowset, an application modifies the rowset buffers at array index 4, but specifies an *irow* of 5.

All operations except for SQL_ADD position the cursor on the row specified by *irow*; the SQL_ADD operation does not change the cursor position. The following operations require a cursor position:

- Positioned update and delete statements.
- Calls to **SQLGetData**.
- Calls to **SQLSetPos** with the SQL_DELETE, SQL_REFRESH, and SQL_UPDATE options.

For example, if the cursor is positioned on the second row of the rowset, a positioned delete statement deletes that row; if it is positioned on the entire rowset (*irow* is 0), a positioned delete statement deletes every row in the rowset.

An application can specify a cursor position when it calls **SQLSetPos**. Generally, it calls **SQLSetPos** with the SQL_POSITION or SQL_REFRESH operation to position the cursor before executing a positioned update or delete statement or calling **SQLGetData**.

fOption Argument

The *fOption* argument supports the following operations. To determine which options are supported by a data source, an application calls **SQLGetInfo** with the SQL_POS_OPERATIONS information type.

fOption Argument	Operation
SQL_POSITION	The driver positions the cursor on the row specified by *irow*.
	This is the same as the FALSE value of this argument in ODBC 1.0.
SQL_REFRESH	The driver positions the cursor on the row specified by *irow* and refreshes data in the rowset buffers for that row. For more information about how the driver returns data in the rowset buffers, see the descriptions of row-wise and column-wise binding in **SQLExtendedFetch**.
	This is the same as the TRUE value of this argument in ODBC 1.0.
SQL_UPDATE	The driver positions the cursor on the row specified by *irow* and updates the underlying row of data with the values in the rowset buffers (the *rgbValue* argument in **SQLBindCol**). It retrieves the lengths of the data from the number-of-bytes buffers (the *pcbValue* argument in **SQLBindCol**). If the length of any column is SQL_IGNORE, the column is not updated. After updating the row, the driver changes the *rgfRowStatus* array specified in **SQLExtendedFetch** to SQL_ROW_UPDATED.
SQL_DELETE	The driver positions the cursor on the row specified by *irow* and deletes the underlying row of data. It changes the *rgfRowStatus* array specified in **SQLExtendedFetch** to SQL_ROW_DELETED. After the row has been deleted, positioned update and delete statements, calls to **SQLGetData** and calls to **SQLSetPos** with *fOption* set to anything except SQL_POSITION are not valid for the row.
	Whether the row remains visible depends on the cursor type. For example, deleted rows are visible to static and keyset-driven cursors but invisible to dynamic cursors.

fOption Argument	Operation
SQL_ADD	The driver adds a new row of data to the data source. Where the row is added to the data source and whether it is visible in the result set is driver-defined.
	The driver retrieves the data from the rowset buffers (the *rgbValue* argument in **SQLBindCol**) according to the value of the *irow* argument. It retrieves the lengths of the data from the number-of-bytes buffers (the *pcbValue* argument in **SQLBindCol**). Generally, the application allocates an extra row of buffers for this purpose.
	For columns not bound to the rowset buffers, the driver uses default values (if they are available) or NULL values (if default values are not available). For columns with a length of SQL_IGNORE, the driver uses default values.
	If *irow* is less than or equal to the rowset size, the driver changes the *rgfRowStatus* array specified in **SQLExtendedFetch** to SQL_ROW_ADDED after adding the row. At this point, the rowset buffers do not match the cursors for the row. To restore the rowset buffers to match the data in the cursor, an application calls **SQLSetPos** with the SQL_REFRESH option.
	This operation does not affect the cursor position.

fLock Argument

The *fLock* argument provides a way for applications to control concurrency and simulate transactions on data sources that do not support them. Generally, data sources that support concurrency levels and transactions will only support the SQL_LOCK_NO_CHANGE value of the *fLock* argument.

The *fLock* argument specifies the lock state of the row after **SQLSetPos** has been executed. To simulate a transaction, an application uses the SQL_LOCK_RECORD macro to lock each of the rows in the transaction. It then uses the SQL_UPDATE_RECORD or SQL_DELETE_RECORD macro to update or delete each row; the driver may temporarily change the lock state of the row while performing the operation specified by the *fOption* argument. Finally, it uses the SQL_LOCK_RECORD macro to unlock each row. For an example of how an application might do this, see the second code example. Note that if the driver is unable to lock the row either to perform the requested operation or to satisfy the *fLock* argument, it returns SQL_ERROR and SQLSTATE 42000 (Syntax error or access violation).

Although the *fLock* argument is specified for an *hstmt*, the lock accords the same privileges to all *hstmts* on the connection. In particular, a lock that is acquired by one *hstmt* on a connection can be unlocked by a different *hstmt* on the same connection.

A row locked through **SQLSetPos** remains locked until the application calls **SQLSetPos** for the row with *fLock* set to SQL_LOCK_UNLOCK or the application calls **SQLFreeStmt** with the SQL_CLOSE or SQL_DROP option.

The *fLock* argument supports the following types of locks. To determine which locks are supported by a data source, an application calls **SQLGetInfo** with the SQL_LOCK_TYPES information type.

fLock Argument	Lock Type
SQL_LOCK_NO_CHANGE	The driver or data source ensures that the row is in the same locked or unlocked state as it was before **SQLSetPos** was called. This value of *fLock* allows data sources that do not support explicit row-level locking to use whatever locking is required by the current concurrency and transaction isolation levels.
	This is the same as the FALSE value of the *fLock* argument in ODBC 1.0.
SQL_LOCK_EXCLUSIVE	The driver or data source locks the row exclusively. An *hstmt* on a different *hdbc* or in a different application cannot be used to acquire any locks on the row.
	This is the same as the TRUE value of the *fLock* argument in ODBC 1.0.
SQL_LOCK_UNLOCK	The driver or data source unlocks the row.

For the add, update, and delete operations in **SQLSetPos**, the application uses the *fLock* argument as follows:

- To guarantee that a row does not change after it is retrieved, an application calls **SQLSetPos** with *fOption* set to SQL_REFRESH and *fLock* set to SQL_LOCK_EXCLUSIVE.

- If the application sets *fLock* to SQL_LOCK_NO_CHANGE, the driver guarantees an update, or delete operation will succeed only if the application specified SQL_CONCUR_LOCK for the SQL_CONCURRENCY statement option.

- If the application specifies SQL_CONCUR_ROWVER or SQL_CONCUR_VALUES for the SQL_CONCURRENCY statement option, the driver compares row versions or values and rejects the operation if the row has changed since the application fetched the row.

- If the application specifies SQL_CONCUR_READ_ONLY for the SQL_CONCURRENCY statement option, the driver rejects any update or delete operation.

For more information about the SQL_CONCURRENCY statement option, see **SQLSetStmtOption**.

Using SQLSetPos

Before an application calls **SQLSetPos**, it must:

1. If the application will call **SQLSetPos** with *fOption* set to SQL_ADD or
   SQL_UPDATE, call **SQLBindCol** for each column to specify its data type
   and associate storage for the column's data and length.
2. Call **SQLExecDirect**, **SQLExecute**, or a catalog function to create a result
   set.
3. Call **SQLExtendedFetch** to retrieve the data.

To delete data with **SQLSetPos**, an application:

- Calls **SQLSetPos** with *irow* set to the number of the row to delete.

An application can pass the value for a column either in the *rgbValue* buffer or
with one or more calls to **SQLPutData**. Columns whose data is passed with
SQLPutData are known as *data-at-execution* columns. These are commonly used
to send data for SQL_LONGVARBINARY and SQL_LONGVARCHAR
columns and can be mixed with other columns.

To update or add data with **SQLSetPos**, an application:

1. Places values in the *rgbValue* and *pcbValue* buffers bound with **SQLBindCol**:
   - For normal columns, the application places the new column value in the
     rgbValue buffer and the length of that value in the *pcbValue* buffer. If the
     row is being updated and the column is not to be changed, the application
     places SQL_IGNORE in the *pcbValue* buffer.
   - For data-at-execution columns, the application places an application-
     defined value, such as the column number, in the *rgbValue* buffer. The
     value can be used later to identify the column.

     It places the result of the SQL_LEN_DATA_AT_EXEC(*length*) macro in
     the *pcbValue* buffer. If the SQL data type of the column is
     SQL_LONGVARBINARY, SQL_LONGVARCHAR, or a long, data
     source–specific data type and the driver returns "Y" for the
     SQL_NEED_LONG_DATA_LEN information type in **SQLGetInfo**,
     length is the number of bytes of data to be sent for the parameter;
     otherwise, it must be a nonnegative value and is ignored.

2. Calls **SQLSetPos** or uses an **SQLSetPos** macro to update or add the row of
   data.
   - If there are no data-at-execution columns, the process is complete.
   - If there are any data-at-execution columns, the function returns
     SQL_NEED_DATA.

3. Calls **SQLParamData** to retrieve the address of the *rgbValue* buffer for the first data-at-execution column to be processed. The application retrieves the application-defined value from the *rgbValue* buffer.

Note Although data-at-execution parameters are similar to data-at-execution columns, the value returned by **SQLParamData** is different for each.

Data-at-execution parameters are parameters in an SQL statement for which data will be sent with **SQLPutData** when the statement is executed with **SQLExecDirect** or **SQLExecute**. They are bound with **SQLBindParameter**. The value returned by **SQLParamData** is a 32-bit value passed to **SQLBindParameter** in the *rgbValue* argument.

Data-at-execution columns are columns in a rowset for which data will be sent with **SQLPutData** when a row is updated or added with **SQLSetPos**. They are bound with **SQLBindCol**. The value returned by **SQLParamData** is the address of the row in the *rgbValue* buffer that is being processed.

---

4. Calls **SQLPutData** one or more times to send data for the column. More than one call is needed if the data value is larger than the *rgbValue* buffer specified in **SQLPutData**; note that multiple calls to **SQLPutData** for the same column are allowed only when sending character C data to a column with a character, binary, or data source–specific data type or when sending binary C data to a column with a character, binary, or data source–specific data type.

5. Calls **SQLParamData** again to signal that all data has been sent for the column.

   - If there are more data-at-execution columns, **SQLParamData** returns SQL_NEED_DATA and the address of the *rgbValue* buffer for the next data-at-execution column to be processed. The application repeats steps 4 and 5.

   - If there are no more data-at-execution columns, the process is complete. If the statement was executed successfully, **SQLParamData** returns SQL_SUCCESS or SQL_SUCCESS_WITH_INFO; if the execution failed, it returns SQL_ERROR. At this point, **SQLParamData** can return any SQLSTATE that can be returned by **SQLSetPos**.

After **SQLSetPos** returns SQL_NEED_DATA, and before data is sent for all data-at-execution columns, the operation is canceled, or an error occurs in **SQLParamData** or **SQLPutData**, the application can only call **SQLCancel**, **SQLGetFunctions**, **SQLParamData**, or **SQLPutData** with the *hstmt* or the *hdbc* associated with the *hstmt*. If it calls any other function with the *hstmt* or the *hdbc* associated with the *hstmt*, the function returns SQL_ERROR and SQLSTATE S1010 (Function sequence error).

If the application calls **SQLCancel** while the driver still needs data for data-at-execution columns, the driver cancels the operation; the application can then call **SQLSetPos** again; canceling does not affect the cursor state or the current cursor position. If the application calls **SQLParamData** or **SQLPutData** after canceling the operation, the function returns SQL_ERROR and SQLSTATE S1008 (Operation canceled).

Performing Bulk Operations

If the *irow* argument is 0, the driver performs the operation specified in the *fOption* argument for every row in the rowset. If an error occurs that pertains to the entire rowset, such as SQLSTATE S1T00 (Timeout expired), the driver returns SQL_ERROR and the appropriate SQLSTATE. The contents of the rowset buffers are undefined and the cursor position is unchanged.

If an error occurs that pertains to a single row, the driver:

- Sets the element in the *rgfRowStatus* array for the row to SQL_ROW_ERROR.
- Posts SQLSTATE 01S01 (Error in row) in the error queue.
- Posts one or more additional SQLSTATEs for the error after SQLSTATE 01S01 (Error in row) in the error queue.

After it has processed the error or warning, the driver continues the operation for the remaining rows in the rowset and returns SQL_SUCCESS_WITH_INFO. Thus, for each row that returned an error, the error queue contains SQLSTATE 01S01 (Error in row) followed by zero or more additional SQLSTATEs.

If the driver returns any warnings, such as SQLSTATE 01004 (Data truncated), it returns warnings that apply to the entire rowset or to unknown rows in the rowset before it returns the error information that applies to specific rows. It returns warnings for specific rows along with any other error information about those rows.

SQLSetPos Macros

As an aid to programming, the following macros for calling **SQLSetPos** are defined in the SQLEXT.H file.

Macro name	Function call
SQL_POSITION_TO(*hstmt*, *irow*)	**SQLSetPos**(*hstmt*, *irow*, SQL_POSITION, SQL_LOCK_NO_CHANGE)
SQL_LOCK_RECORD(*hstmt*, *irow*, *fLock*)	**SQLSetPos**(*hstmt*, *irow*, SQL_POSITION, *fLock*)
SQL_REFRESH_RECORD(*hstmt*, *irow*, *fLock*)	**SQLSetPos**(*hstmt*, *irow*, SQL_REFRESH, *fLock*)
SQL_UPDATE_RECORD(*hstmt*, *irow*)	**SQLSetPos**(*hstmt*, *irow*, SQL_UPDATE, SQL_LOCK_NO_CHANGE)
SQL_DELETE_RECORD(*hstmt*, *irow*)	**SQLSetPos**(*hstmt*, *irow*, SQL_DELETE, SQL_LOCK_NO_CHANGE)
SQL_ADD_RECORD(*hstmt*, *irow*)	**SQLSetPos**(*hstmt*, *irow*, SQL_ADD, SQL_LOCK_NO_CHANGE)

Code Example   In the following example, an application allows a user to browse the EMPLOYEE table and update employee birthdays. The cursor is keyset-driven with a rowset size of 20 and uses optimistic concurrency control comparing row versions. After each rowset is fetched, the application prints them and allows the user to select and update an employee's birthday. The application uses **SQLSetPos** to position the cursor on the selected row and performs a positioned update of the row. (Error handling is omitted for clarity.)

```
#define ROWS 20
#define NAME_LEN 30
#define BDAY_LEN 11

UCHAR   szName[ROWS][NAME_LEN], szBirthday[ROWS][BDAY_LEN], szReply[3];
SDWORD  cbName[ROWS], cbBirthday[ROWS];
UWORD   rgfRowStatus[ROWS];
UDWORD  crow, irow;
HSTMT   hstmtS, hstmtU;

SQLSetStmtOption(hstmtS, SQL_CONCURRENCY, SQL_CONCUR_ROWVER);
SQLSetStmtOption(hstmtS, SQL_CURSOR_TYPE, SQL_CURSOR_KEYSET_DRIVEN);
SQLSetStmtOption(hstmtS, SQL_ROWSET_SIZE, ROWS);
SQLSetCursorName(hstmtS, "C1", SQL_NTS);
SQLExecDirect(hstmtS,
            "SELECT NAME, BIRTHDAY FROM EMPLOYEE FOR UPDATE OF BIRTHDAY",
            SQL_NTS);

SQLBindCol(hstmtS, 1, SQL_C_CHAR, szName, NAME_LEN, cbName);
SQLBindCol(hstmtS, 1, SQL_C_CHAR, szBirthday, BDAY_LEN,
            cbBirthday);
```

```
while (SQLExtendedFetch(hstmtS, FETCH_NEXT, 0, &crow, rgfRowStatus) !=
        SQL_ERROR) {
    for (irow = 0; irow < crow; irow++) {
        if (rgfRowStatus[irow] != SQL_ROW_DELETED)
            printf("%d %-*s %*s\n", irow, NAME_LEN-1, szName[irow],
                    BDAY_LEN-1, szBirthday[irow]);
    }
    while (TRUE) {
        printf("\nRow number to update?");
        gets(szReply);
        irow = atoi(szReply);
        if (irow > 0 && irow <= crow) {
            printf("\nNew birthday?");
            gets(szBirthday[irow-1]);
            SQLSetPos(hstmtS, irow, SQL_POSITION, SQL_LOCK_NO_CHANGE);
            SQLPrepare(hstmtU,
                "UPDATE EMPLOYEE SET BIRTHDAY=? WHERE CURRENT OF C1",
                SQL_NTS);
            SQLBindParameter(hstmtU, 1, SQL_PARAM_INPUT,
                            SQL_C_CHAR, SQL_DATE,
                            BDAY_LEN, 0, szBirthday, 0, NULL);
            SQLExecute(hstmtU);
        } else if (irow == 0) {
            break;
        }
    }
}
```

In the following code fragment, an application simulates a transaction for rows 1 and 2. It locks the rows, updates them, then unlocks them. The code uses the **SQLSetPos** macros.

```
/* Lock rows 1 and 2                                          */

SQL_LOCK_RECORD(hstmt, 1, SQL_LOCK_EXCLUSIVE);
SQL_LOCK_RECORD(hstmt, 2, SQL_LOCK_EXCLUSIVE);


/* Modify the rowset buffers for rows 1 and 2 (not shown).*/
/* Update rows 1 and 2.                                       */

SQL_UPDATE_RECORD(hstmt, 1);
SQL_UPDATE_RECORD(hstmt, 2);


/* Unlock rows 1 and 2                                        */

SQL_LOCK_RECORD(hstmt, 1, SQL_LOCK_UNLOCK);
SQL_LOCK_RECORD(hstmt, 2, SQL_LOCK_UNLOCK);
```

Related Functions

For information about	See
Assigning storage for a column in a result set	**SQLBindCol**
Canceling statement processing	**SQLCancel**
Fetching a block of data or scrolling through a result set	**SQLExtendedFetch** (extension)
Setting a statement option	**SQLSetStmtOption** (extension)

SQLSetScrollOptions

Extension Level 2

SQLSetScrollOptions sets options that control the behavior of cursors associated with an *hstmt*. **SQLSetScrollOptions** allows the application to specify the type of cursor behavior desired in three areas: concurrency control, sensitivity to changes made by other transactions, and rowset size.

Note In ODBC 2.0, **SQLSetScrollOptions** has been superceded by the SQL_CURSOR_TYPE, SQL_CONCURRENCY, SQL_KEYSET_SIZE, and SQL_ROWSET_SIZE statement options. ODBC 2.0 drivers must support this function for backwards compatibility; ODBC 2.0 applications should only call this function in ODBC 1.0 drivers.

If an application calls **SQLSetScrollOptions**, a driver must be able to return the values of the aforementioned statement options with **SQLGetStmtOption**. For more information, see **SQLSetStmtOption**.

Syntax

RETCODE **SQLSetScrollOptions**(*hstmt*, *fConcurrency*, *crowKeyset*, *crowRowset*)

The **SQLSetScrollOptions** function accepts the following arguments:

Type	Argument	Use	Description
HSTMT	*hstmt*	Input	Statement handle.
UWORD	*fConcurrency*	Input	Specifies concurrency control for the cursor and must be one of the following values:
			SQL_CONCUR_READ_ONLY: Cursor is read-only. No updates are allowed.
			SQL_CONCUR_LOCK: Cursor uses the lowest level of locking sufficient to ensure that the row can be updated.
			SQL_CONCUR_ROWVER: Cursor uses optimistic concurrency control, comparing row versions, such as SQLBase ROWID or Sybase TIMESTAMP.
			SQL_CONCUR_VALUES: Cursor uses optimistic concurrency control, comparing values.

Type	Argument	Use	Description
SDWORD	*crowKeyset*	Input	Number of rows for which to buffer keys. This value must be greater than or equal to *crowRowset* or one of the following values:
			SQL_SCROLL_FORWARD_ONLY: The cursor only scrolls forward.
			SQL_SCROLL_STATIC: The data in the result set is static.
			SQL_SCROLL_KEYSET_DRIVEN: The driver saves and uses the keys for every row in the result set.
			SQL_SCROLL_DYNAMIC: The driver sets *crowKeyset* to the value of *crowRowset*.
			If *crowKeyset* is a value greater than *crowRowset*, the value defines the number of rows in the keyset that are to be buffered by the driver. This reflects a mixed scrollable cursor; the cursor is keyset driven within the keyset and dynamic outside of the keyset.
UWORD	*crowRowset*	Input	Number of rows in a rowset. *crowRowset* defines the number of rows fetched by each call to **SQLExtendedFetch**; the number of rows that the application buffers.

Returns

SQL_SUCCESS, SQL_SUCCESS_WITH_INFO, SQL_ERROR, or SQL_INVALID_HANDLE.

Diagnostics

When **SQLSetScrollOptions** returns SQL_ERROR or SQL_SUCCESS_WITH_INFO, an associated SQLSTATE value may be obtained by calling **SQLError**. The following table lists the SQLSTATE values commonly returned by **SQLSetScrollOptions** and explains each one in the context of this function; the notation "(DM)" precedes the descriptions of SQLSTATEs returned by the Driver Manager. The return code associated with each SQLSTATE value is SQL_ERROR, unless noted otherwise.

SQLSTATE	Error	Description
01000	General warning	Driver-specific informational message. (Function returns SQL_SUCCESS_WITH_INFO.)
IM001	Driver does not support this function	(DM) The driver associated with the *hstmt* does not support the function.
S1000	General error	An error occurred for which there was no specific SQLSTATE and for which no implementation-specific SQLSTATE was defined. The error message returned by **SQLError** in the argument *szErrorMsg* describes the error and its cause.
S1001	Memory allocation failure	The driver was unable to allocate memory required to support execution or completion of the function.
S1010	Function sequence error	(DM) The specified *hstmt* was in a prepared or executed state. The function must be called before calling **SQLPrepare** or **SQLExecDirect**.
		(DM) An asynchronously executing function was called for the *hstmt* and was still executing when this function was called.
		(DM) **SQLExecute**, **SQLExecDirect**, or **SQLSetPos** was called for the *hstmt* and returned SQL_NEED_DATA. This function was called before data was sent for all data-at-execution parameters or columns.
S1107	Row value out of range	(DM) The value specified for the argument *crowKeyset* was less than 1, but was not equal to SQL_SCROLL_FORWARD_ONLY, SQL_SCROLL_STATIC, SQL_SCROLL_KEYSET_DRIVEN, or SQL_SCROLL_DYNAMIC.
		(DM) The value specified for the argument *crowKeyset* is greater than 0, but less than *crowRowset*.
		(DM) The value specified for the argument *crowRowset* was 0.

SQLSTATE	Error	Description
S1108	Concurrency option out of range	(DM) The value specified for the argument *fConcurrency* was not equal to SQL_CONCUR_READ_ONLY, SQL_CONCUR_LOCK, SQL_CONCUR_ROWVER, or SQL_CONCUR_VALUES.
S1C00	Driver not capable	The driver or data source does not support the concurrency control option specified in the argument *fConcurrency*.
		The driver does not support the cursor model specified in the argument *crowKeyset*.

Comments

If an application calls **SQLSetScrollOptions** for an *hstmt*, it must do so before it calls **SQLPrepare** or **SQLExecDirect** or creating a result set with a catalog function.

The application must specify a buffer in a call to **SQLBindCol** that is large enough to hold the number of rows specified in *crowRowset*.

If the application does not call **SQLSetScrollOptions**, *crowRowset* has a default value of 1, *crowKeyset* has a default value of SQL_SCROLL_FORWARD_ONLY, and *fConcurrency* equals SQL_CONCUR_READ_ONLY.

For more information concerning scrollable cursors, see "Using Block and Scrollable Cursors" in Chapter 7, "Retrieving Results."

Related Functions

For information about	See
Assigning storage for a column in a result set	**SQLBindCol**
Fetching a block of data or scrolling through a result set	**SQLExtendedFetch** (extension)
Positioning the cursor in a rowset	**SQLSetPos** (extension)
Setting a statement option	**SQLSetStmtOption**

SQLSetStmtOption

ODBC 1.0

Extension Level 1 **SQLSetStmtOption** sets options related to an *hstmt*. To set an option for all statements associated with a specific *hdbc*, an application can call **SQLSetConnectOption**.

Syntax RETCODE **SQLSetStmtOption**(*hstmt, fOption, vParam*)

The **SQLSetStmtOption** function accepts the following arguments:

Type	Argument	Use	Description
HSTMT	*hstmt*	Input	Statement handle.
UWORD	*fOption*	Input	Option to set, listed in "Comments."
UDWORD	*vParam*	Input	Value associated with *fOption*. Depending on the value of *fOption*, *vParam* will be a 32-bit integer value or point to a null-terminated character string.

Returns SQL_SUCCESS, SQL_SUCCESS_WITH_INFO, SQL_ERROR, or SQL_INVALID_HANDLE.

Diagnostics When **SQLSetStmtOption** returns SQL_ERROR or SQL_SUCCESS_WITH_INFO, an associated SQLSTATE value may be obtained by calling **SQLError**. The following table lists the SQLSTATE values commonly returned by **SQLSetStmtOption** and explains each one in the context of this function; the notation "(DM)" precedes the descriptions of SQLSTATEs returned by the Driver Manager. The return code associated with each SQLSTATE value is SQL_ERROR, unless noted otherwise.

SQLSTATE	Error	Description
01000	General warning	Driver-specific informational message. (Function returns SQL_SUCCESS_WITH_INFO.)
01S02	Option value changed	The driver did not support the specified value of the *vParam* argument and substituted a similar value. (Function returns SQL_SUCCESS_WITH_INFO.)
08S01	Communication link failure	The communication link between the driver and the data source to which the driver was connected failed before the function completed processing.

SQLSTATE	Error	Description
24000	Invalid cursor state	The *fOption* was SQL_CONCURRENCY, SQL_CURSOR_TYPE, SQL_SIMULATE_CURSOR, or SQL_USE_BOOKMARKS and the cursor was open.
IM001	Driver does not support this function	(DM) The driver associated with the *hstmt* does not support the function.
S1000	General error	An error occurred for which there was no specific SQLSTATE and for which no implementation-specific SQLSTATE was defined. The error message returned by **SQLError** in the argument *szErrorMsg* describes the error and its cause.
S1001	Memory allocation failure	The driver was unable to allocate memory required to support execution or completion of the function.
S1009	Invalid argument value	Given the specified *fOption* value, an invalid value was specified for the argument *vParam*. (The Driver Manager returns this SQLSTATE only for statement options that accept a discrete set of values, such as SQL_ASYNC_ENABLE. For all other statement options, the driver must verify the value of the argument *vParam*.)
S1010	Function sequence error	(DM) An asynchronously executing function was called for the *hstmt* and was still executing when this function was called.
		(DM) **SQLExecute**, **SQLExecDirect**, or **SQLSetPos** was called for the *hstmt* and returned SQL_NEED_DATA. This function was called before data was sent for all data-at-execution parameters or columns.
S1011	Operation invalid at this time	The *fOption* was SQL_CONCURRENCY, SQL_CURSOR_TYPE, SQL_SIMULATE_CURSOR, or SQL_USE_BOOKMARKS and the statement was prepared.
S1092	Option type out of range	(DM) The value specified for the argument *fOption* was in the block of numbers reserved for ODBC connection and statement options, but was not valid for the version of ODBC supported by the driver.

SQLSTATE	Error	Description
S1C00	Driver not capable	The value specified for the argument *fOption* was a valid ODBC statement option for the version of ODBC supported by the driver, but was not supported by the driver.
		The value specified for the argument *fOption* was in the block of numbers reserved for driver-specific connection and statement options, but was not supported by the driver.

Comments   Statement options for an *hstmt* remain in effect until they are changed by another call to **SQLSetStmtOption** or the *hstmt* is dropped by calling **SQLFreeStmt** with the SQL_DROP option. Calling **SQLFreeStmt** with the SQL_CLOSE, SQL_UNBIND, or SQL_RESET_PARAMS options does not reset statement options.

Some statement options support substitution of a similar value if the data source does not support the specified value of *vParam*. In such cases, the driver returns SQL_SUCCESS_WITH_INFO and SQLSTATE 01S02 (Option value changed). For example, if *fOption* is SQL_CONCURRENCY, *vParam* is SQL_CONCUR_ROWVER, and the data source does not support this, the driver substitutes SQL_CONCUR_VALUES. To determine the substituted value, an application calls **SQLGetStmtOption**.

The currently defined options and the version of ODBC in which they were introduced are shown below; it is expected that more will be defined to take advantage of different data sources. Options from 0 to 999 are reserved by ODBC; driver developers must reserve values greater than or equal to SQL_CONNECT_OPT_DRVR_START for driver-specific use. For more information, see "Driver-Specific Data Types, Descriptor Types, Information Types, and Options" in Chapter 11, "Guidelines for Implementing ODBC Functions."

The format of information set with *vParam* depends on the specified *fOption*. **SQLSetStmtOption** accepts option information in one of two different formats: a null-terminated character string or a 32-bit integer value. The format of each is noted in the option's description. This format applies to the information returned for each option in **SQLGetStmtOption**. Character strings pointed to by the *vParam* argument of **SQLSetStmtOption** have a maximum length of SQL_MAX_OPTION_STRING_LENGTH bytes (excluding the null termination byte).

fOption	*vParam* Contents
SQL_ASYNC_ENABLE (ODBC 1.0)	A 32-bit integer value that specifies whether a function called with the specified *hstmt* is executed asynchronously:

SQL_ASYNC_ENABLE_OFF = Off (the default)
SQL_ASYNC_ENABLE_ON = On

Once a function has been called asynchronously, no other functions can be called on the *hstmt* or the *hdbc* associated with the *hstmt* except for the original function, **SQLAllocStmt**, **SQLCancel**, or **SQLGetFunctions**, until the original function returns a code other than SQL_STILL_EXECUTING. Any other function called on the *hstmt* returns SQL_ERROR with an SQLSTATE of S1010 (Function sequence error). Functions can be called on other *hstmts*. For more information, see "Executing Functions Asynchronously" in Chapter 6 and "Supporting Asynchronous Execution" in Chapter 14.

The following functions can be executed asynchronously:

SQLColAttributes	**SQLNumParams**
SQLColumnPrivileges	**SQLNumResultCols**
SQLColumns	**SQLParamData**
SQLDescribeCol	**SQLPrepare**
SQLDescribeParam	**SQLPrimaryKeys**
SQLExecDirect	**SQLProcedureColumns**
SQLExecute	**SQLProcedures**
SQLExtendedFetch	**SQLPutData**
SQLFetch	**SQLSetPos**
SQLForeignKeys	**SQLSpecialColumns**
SQLGetData	**SQLStatistics**
SQLGetTypeInfo	**SQLTablePrivileges**
SQLMoreResults	**SQLTables**

fOption	*vParam* Contents
SQL_BIND_TYPE (ODBC 1.0)	A 32-bit integer value that sets the binding orientation to be used when **SQLExtendedFetch** is called on the associated *hstmt*. Column-wise binding is selected by supplying the defined constant SQL_BIND_BY_COLUMN for the argument *vParam*. Row-wise binding is selected by supplying a value for *vParam* specifying the length of a structure or an instance of a buffer into which result columns will be bound.

The length specified in *vParam* must include space for all of the bound columns and any padding of the structure or buffer to ensure that when the address of a bound column is incremented with the specified length, the result will point to the beginning of the same column in the next row. When using the **sizeof** operator with structures or unions in ANSI C, this behavior is guaranteed.

Column-wise binding is the default binding orientation for **SQLExtendedFetch**.

fOption	*vParam* **Contents**
SQL_CONCURRENCY (ODBC 2.0)	A 32-bit integer value that specifies the cursor concurrency: SQL_CONCUR_READ_ONLY = Cursor is read-only. No updates are allowed. SQL_CONCUR_LOCK = Cursor uses the lowest level of locking sufficient to ensure that the row can be updated. SQL_CONCUR_ROWVER = Cursor uses optimistic concurrency control, comparing row versions, such as SQLBase ROWID or Sybase TIMESTAMP. SQL_CONCUR_VALUES = Cursor uses optimistic concurrency control, comparing values. The default value is SQL_CONCUR_READ_ONLY. This option cannot be specified for an open cursor and can also be set through the *fConcurrency* argument in **SQLSetScrollOptions**. If the specified concurrency is not supported by the data source, the driver substitutes a different concurrency and returns SQLSTATE 01S02 (Option value changed). For SQL_CONCUR_VALUES, the driver substitutes SQL_CONCUR_ROWVER, and vice versa. For SQL_CONCUR_LOCK, the driver substitutes, in order, SQL_CONCUR_ROWVER or SQL_CONCUR_VALUES.
SQL_CURSOR_TYPE (ODBC 2.0)	A 32-bit integer value that specifies the cursor type: SQL_CURSOR_FORWARD_ONLY = The cursor only scrolls forward. SQL_CURSOR_STATIC = The data in the result set is static. SQL_CURSOR_KEYSET_DRIVEN = The driver saves and uses the keys for the number of rows specified in the SQL_KEYSET_SIZE statement option. SQL_CURSOR_DYNAMIC = The driver only saves and uses the keys for the rows in the rowset. The default value is SQL_CURSOR_FORWARD_ONLY. This option cannot be specified for an open cursor and can also be set through the *crowKeyset* argument in **SQLSetScrollOptions**. If the specified cursor type is not supported by the data source, the driver substitutes a different cursor type and returns SQLSTATE 01S02 (Option value changed). For a mixed or dynamic cursor, the driver substitutes, in order, a keyset-driven or static cursor. For a keyset-driven cursor, the driver substitutes a static cursor.

fOption	vParam Contents
SQL_KEYSET_SIZE (ODBC 2.0)	A 32-bit integer value that specifies the number of rows in the keyset for a keyset-driven cursor. If the keyset size is 0 (the default), the cursor is fully keyset-driven. If the keyset size is greater than 0, the cursor is mixed (keyset-driven within the keyset and dynamic outside of the keyset). The default keyset size is 0. If the specified size exceeds the maximum keyset size, the driver substitutes that size and returns SQLSTATE 01S02 (Option value changed). **SQLExtendedFetch** returns an error if the keyset size is greater than 0 and less than the rowset size.
SQL_MAX_LENGTH (ODBC 1.0)	A 32-bit integer value that specifies the maximum amount of data that the driver returns from a character or binary column. If *vParam* is less than the length of the available data, **SQLFetch** or **SQLGetData** truncates the data and returns SQL_SUCCESS. If *vParam* is 0 (the default), the driver attempts to return all available data. If the specified length is less than the minimum amount of data that the data source can return (the minimum is 254 bytes on many data sources), or greater than the maximum amount of data that the data source can return, the driver substitutes that value and returns SQLSTATE 01S02 (Option value changed). This option is intended to reduce network traffic and should only be supported when the data source (as opposed to the driver) in a multiple-tier driver can implement it. To truncate data, an application should specify the maximum buffer length in the *cbValueMax* argument in **SQLBindCol** or **SQLGetData**. **Note** In ODBC 1.0, this statement option only applied to SQL_LONGVARCHAR and SQL_LONGVARBINARY columns.
SQL_MAX_ROWS (ODBC 1.0)	A 32-bit integer value corresponding to the maximum number of rows to return to the application for a **SELECT** statement. If *vParam* equals 0 (the default), then the driver returns all rows. This option is intended to reduce network traffic. Conceptually, it is applied when the result set is created and limits the result set to the first *vParam* rows. If the specified number of rows exceeds the number of rows that can be returned by the data source, the driver substitutes that value and returns SQLSTATE 01S02 (Option value changed).

fOption	*vParam* **Contents**
SQL_NOSCAN (ODBC 1.0)	A 32-bit integer value that specifies whether the driver does not scan SQL strings for escape clauses: SQL_NOSCAN_OFF = The driver scans SQL strings for escape clauses (the default). SQL_NOSCAN_ON = The driver does not scan SQL strings for escape clauses. Instead, the driver sends the statement directly to the data source.
SQL_QUERY_TIMEOUT (ODBC 1.0)	A 32-bit integer value corresponding to the number of seconds to wait for an SQL statement to execute before returning to the application. If *vParam* equals 0 (the default), then there is no time out. If the specified timeout exceeds the maximum timeout in the data source or is smaller than the minimum timeout, the driver substitutes that value and returns SQLSTATE 01S02 (Option value changed). Note that the application need not call **SQLFreeStmt** with the SQL_CLOSE option to reuse the *hstmt* if a **SELECT** statement timed out.
SQL_RETRIEVE_DATA (ODBC 2.0)	A 32-bit integer value: SQL_RD_ON = **SQLExtendedFetch** retrieves data after it positions the cursor to the specified location. This is the default. SQL_RD_OFF = **SQLExtendedFetch** does not retrieve data after it positions the cursor. By setting SQL_RETRIEVE_DATA to SQL_RD_OFF, an application can verify if a row exists or retrieve a bookmark for the row without incurring the overhead of retrieving rows.
SQL_ROWSET_SIZE (ODBC 2.0)	A 32-bit integer value that specifies the number of rows in the rowset. This is the number of rows returned by each call to **SQLExtendedFetch**. The default value is 1. If the specified rowset size exceeds the maximum rowset size supported by the data source, the driver substitutes that value and returns SQLSTATE 01S02 (Option value changed). This option can be specified for an open cursor and can also be set through the *crowRowset* argument in **SQLSetScrollOptions**.

fOption	*vParam* Contents
SQL_SIMULATE_CURSOR (ODBC 2.0)	A 32-bit integer value that specifies whether drivers that simulate positioned update and delete statements guarantee that such statements affect only one single row.
	To simulate positioned update and delete statements, most drivers construct a searched **UPDATE** or **DELETE** statement containing a **WHERE** clause that specifies the value of each column in the current row. Unless these columns comprise a unique key, such a statement may affect more than one row.
	To guarantee that such statements affect only one row, the driver determines the columns in a unique key and adds these columns to the result set. If an application guarantees that the columns in the result set comprise a unique key, the driver is not required to do so. This may reduce execution time.
	SQL_SC_NON_UNIQUE = The driver does not guarantee that simulated positioned update or delete statements will affect only one row; it is the application's responsibility to do so. If a statement affects more than one row, **SQLExecute** or **SQLExecDirect** returns SQLSTATE 01000 (General warning).
	SQL_SC_TRY_UNIQUE = The driver attempts to guarantee that simulated positioned update or delete statements affect only one row. The driver always executes such statements, even if they might affect more than one row, such as when there is no unique key. If a statement affects more than one row, **SQLExecute** or **SQLExecDirect** returns SQLSTATE 01000 (General warning).
	SQL_SC_UNIQUE = The driver guarantees that simulated positioned update or delete statements affect only one row. If the driver cannot guarantee this for a given statement, **SQLExecDirect** or **SQLPrepare** returns an error.
	If the specified cursor simulation type is not supported by the data source, the driver substitutes a different simulation type and returns SQLSTATE 01S02 (Option value changed). For SQL_SC_UNIQUE, the driver substitutes, in order, SQL_SC_TRY_UNIQUE or SQL_SC_NON_UNIQUE. For SQL_SC_TRY_UNIQUE, the driver substitutes SQL_SC_NON_UNIQUE.
	If a driver does not simulate positioned update and delete statements, it returns SQLSTATE S1C00 (Driver not capable).
SQL_USE_BOOKMARKS (ODBC 2.0)	A 32-bit integer value that specifies whether an application will use bookmarks with a cursor:
	SQL_UB_OFF = Off (the default) SQL_UB_ON = On
	To use bookmarks with a cursor, the application must specify this option with the SQL_UB_ON value before opening the cursor.

Code Example   See **SQLExtendedFetch**.

Related Functions

For information about	See
Canceling statement processing	**SQLCancel**
Returning the setting of a connection option	**SQLGetConnectOption** (extension)
Returning the setting of a statement option	**SQLGetStmtOption** (extension)
Setting a connection option	**SQLSetConnectOption** (extension)

SQLSpecialColumns

Extension Level 1   **SQLSpecialColumns** retrieves the following information about columns within a specified table:

- The optimal set of columns that uniquely identifies a row in the table.
- Columns that are automatically updated when any value in the row is updated by a transaction.

Syntax   RETCODE **SQLSpecialColumns**(*hstmt, fColType, szTableQualifier, cbTableQualifier, szTableOwner, cbTableOwner, szTableName, cbTableName, fScope, fNullable*)

The **SQLSpecialColumns** function accepts the following arguments:

Type	Argument	Use	Description
HSTMT	*hstmt*	Input	Statement handle.
UWORD	*fColType*	Input	Type of column to return. Must be one of the following values:
			SQL_BEST_ROWID: Returns the optimal column or set of columns that, by retrieving values from the column or columns, allows any row in the specified table to be uniquely identified. A column can be either a pseudocolumn specifically designed for this purpose (as in Oracle ROWID or Ingres TID) or the column or columns of any unique index for the table.
			SQL_ROWVER: Returns the column or columns in the specified table, if any, that are automatically updated by the data source when any value in the row is updated by any transaction (as in SQLBase ROWID or Sybase TIMESTAMP).
UCHAR FAR *	*szTableQualifier*	Input	Qualifier name for the table. If a driver supports qualifiers for some tables but not for others, such as when the driver retrieves data from different DBMSs, an empty string ("") denotes those tables that do not have qualifiers.

Type	Argument	Use	Description
SWORD	*cbTableQualifier*	Input	Length of *szTableQualifier*.
UCHAR FAR *	*szTableOwner*	Input	Owner name for the table. If a driver supports owners for some tables but not for others, such as when the driver retrieves data from different DBMSs, an empty string ("") denotes those tables that do not have owners.
SWORD	*cbTableOwner*	Input	Length of *szTableOwner*.
UCHAR FAR *	*szTableName*	Input	Table name.
SWORD	*cbTableName*	Input	Length of *szTableName*.
UWORD	*fScope*	Input	Minimum required scope of the rowid. The returned rowid may be of greater scope. Must be one of the following:
			SQL_SCOPE_CURROW: The rowid is guaranteed to be valid only while positioned on that row. A later reselect using rowid may not return a row if the row was updated or deleted by another transaction.
			SQL_SCOPE_TRANSACTION: The rowid is guaranteed to be valid for the duration of the current transaction.
			SQL_SCOPE_SESSION: The rowid is guaranteed to be valid for the duration of the session (across transaction boundaries).
UWORD	*fNullable*	Input	Determines whether to return special columns that can have a NULL value. Must be one of the following:
			SQL_NO_NULLS: Exclude special columns that can have NULL values.
			SQL_NULLABLE: Return special columns even if they can have NULL values.

Returns   SQL_SUCCESS, SQL_SUCCESS_WITH_INFO, SQL_STILL_EXECUTING, SQL_ERROR, or SQL_INVALID_HANDLE.

Diagnostics

When **SQLSpecialColumns** returns SQL_ERROR or SQL_SUCCESS_WITH_INFO, an associated SQLSTATE value may be obtained by calling **SQLError**. The following table lists the SQLSTATE values commonly returned by **SQLSpecialColumns** and explains each one in the context of this function; the notation "(DM)" precedes the descriptions of SQLSTATEs returned by the Driver Manager. The return code associated with each SQLSTATE value is SQL_ERROR, unless noted otherwise.

SQLSTATE	Error	Description
01000	General warning	Driver-specific informational message. (Function returns SQL_SUCCESS_WITH_INFO.)
08S01	Communication link failure	The communication link between the driver and the data source to which the driver was connected failed before the function completed processing.
24000	Invalid cursor state	(DM) A cursor was open on the *hstmt* and **SQLFetch** or **SQLExtendedFetch** had been called.
		A cursor was open on the *hstmt* but **SQLFetch** or **SQLExtendedFetch** had not been called.
IM001	Driver does not support this function	(DM) The driver associated with the *hstmt* does not support the function.
S1000	General error	An error occurred for which there was no specific SQLSTATE and for which no implementation-specific SQLSTATE was defined. The error message returned by **SQLError** in the argument *szErrorMsg* describes the error and its cause.
S1001	Memory allocation failure	The driver was unable to allocate memory required to support execution or completion of the function.
S1008	Operation canceled	Asynchronous processing was enabled for the *hstmt*. The function was called and before it completed execution, **SQLCancel** was called on the *hstmt*. Then the function was called again on the *hstmt*.
		The function was called and, before it completed execution, **SQLCancel** was called on the *hstmt* from a different thread in a multithreaded application.

SQLSTATE	Error	Description
S1010	Function sequence error	(DM) An asynchronously executing function (not this one) was called for the *hstmt* and was still executing when this function was called.
		(DM) **SQLExecute**, **SQLExecDirect**, or **SQLSetPos** was called for the *hstmt* and returned SQL_NEED_DATA. This function was called before data was sent for all data-at-execution parameters or columns.
S1090	Invalid string or buffer length	(DM) The value of one of the length arguments was less than 0, but not equal to SQL_NTS.
		The value of one of the length arguments exceeded the maximum length value for the corresponding qualifier or name. The maximum length of each qualifier or name may be obtained by calling **SQLGetInfo** with the *fInfoType* values: SQL_MAX_QUALIFIER_NAME_LEN, SQL_MAX_OWNER_NAME_LEN, or SQL_MAX_TABLE_NAME_LEN.
S1097	Column type out of range	(DM) An invalid *fColType* value was specified.
S1098	Scope type out of range	(DM) An invalid *fScope* value was specified.
S1099	Nullable type out of range	(DM) An invalid *fNullable* value was specified.
S1C00	Driver not capable	A table qualifier was specified and the driver or data source does not support qualifiers.
		A table owner was specified and the driver or data source does not support owners.
		The combination of the current settings of the SQL_CONCURRENCY and SQL_CURSOR_TYPE statement options was not supported by the driver or data source.
S1T00	Timeout expired	The timeout period expired before the data source returned the requested result set. The timeout period is set through **SQLSetStmtOption**, SQL_QUERY_TIMEOUT.

Comments

SQLSpecialColumns is provided so that applications can provide their own custom scrollable-cursor functionality, similar to that provided by **SQLExtendedFetch** and **SQLSetStmtOption**.

When the *fColType* argument is SQL_BEST_ROWID, **SQLSpecialColumns** returns the column or columns that uniquely identify each row in the table. These columns can always be used in a *select-list* or **WHERE** clause. However, **SQLColumns** does not necessarily return these columns. For example, **SQLColumns** might not return the Oracle ROWID pseudo-column ROWID. If there are no columns that uniquely identify each row in the table, **SQLSpecialColumns** returns a rowset with no rows; a subsequent call to **SQLFetch** or **SQLExtendedFetch** on the *hstmt* returns SQL_NO_DATA_FOUND.

If the *fColType*, *fScope*, or *fNullable* arguments specify characteristics that are not supported by the data source, **SQLSpecialColumns** returns a result set with no rows (as opposed to the function returning SQL_ERROR with SQLSTATE S1C00 (Driver not capable)). A subsequent call to **SQLFetch** or **SQLExtendedFetch** on the *hstmt* will return SQL_NO_DATA_FOUND.

SQLSpecialColumns returns the results as a standard result set, ordered by SCOPE. The following table lists the columns in the result set.

The lengths of VARCHAR columns shown in the table are maximums; the actual lengths depend on the data source. To determine the actual length of the COLUMN_NAME column, an application can call **SQLGetInfo** with the SQL_MAX_COLUMN_NAME_LEN option.

Column Name	Data Type	Comments
SCOPE	Smallint	Actual scope of the rowid. Contains one of the following values:
		SQL_SCOPE_CURROW SQL_SCOPE_TRANSACTION SQL_SCOPE_SESSION
		NULL is returned when *fColType* is SQL_ROWVER. For a description of each value, see the description of *fScope* in the "Syntax" section above.
COLUMN_NAME	Varchar(128) not NULL	Column identifier.

Column Name	Data Type	Comments
DATA_TYPE	Smallint not NULL	SQL data type. This can be an ODBC SQL data type or a driver-specific SQL data type. For a list of valid ODBC SQL data types, see "SQL Data Types" in Appendix D, "Data Types." For information about driver-specific SQL data types, see the driver's documentation.
TYPE_NAME	Varchar(128) not NULL	Data source–dependent data type name; for example, "CHAR", "VARCHAR", "MONEY", "LONG VARBINARY", or "CHAR ( ) FOR BIT DATA".
PRECISION	Integer	The precision of the column on the data source. NULL is returned for data types where precision is not applicable. For more information concerning precision, see "Precision, Scale, Length, and Display Size," in Appendix D, "Data Types."
LENGTH	Integer	The length in bytes of data transferred on an **SQLGetData** or **SQLFetch** operation if SQL_C_DEFAULT is specified. For numeric data, this size may be different than the size of the data stored on the data source. This value is the same as the PRECISION column for character or binary data. For more information, see "Precision, Scale, Length, and Display Size," in Appendix D, "Data Types."
SCALE	Smallint	The scale of the column on the data source. NULL is returned for data types where scale is not applicable. For more information concerning scale, see "Precision, Scale, Length, and Display Size," in Appendix D, "Data Types."
PSEUDO_COLUMN	Smallint	Indicates whether the column is a pseudo-column, such as Oracle ROWID: SQL_PC_UNKNOWN SQL_PC_PSEUDO SQL_PC_NOT_PSEUDO

Note For maximum interoperability, pseudo-columns should not be quoted with the identifier quote character returned by **SQLGetInfo**.

Note The PSEUDO_COLUMN column was added in ODBC 2.0. ODBC 1.0 drivers might return a different, driver-specific column with the same column number.

Once the application retrieves values for SQL_BEST_ROWID, the application can use these values to reselect that row within the defined scope. The **SELECT** statement is guaranteed to return either no rows or one row.

If an application reselects a row based on the rowid column or columns and the row is not found, then the application can assume that the row was deleted or the rowid columns were modified. The opposite is not true: even if the rowid has not changed, the other columns in the row may have changed.

Columns returned for column type SQL_BEST_ROWID are useful for applications that need to scroll forwards and backwards within a result set to retrieve the most recent data from a set of rows. The column or columns of the rowid are guaranteed not to change while positioned on that row.

The column or columns of the rowid may remain valid even when the cursor is not positioned on the row; the application can determine this by checking the SCOPE column in the result set.

Columns returned for column type SQL_ROWVER are useful for applications that need the ability to check if any columns in a given row have been updated while the row was reselected using the rowid. For example, after reselecting a row using rowid, the application can compare the previous values in the SQL_ROWVER columns to the ones just fetched. If the value in a SQL_ROWVER column differs from the previous value, the application can alert the user that data on the display has changed.

Code Example   For a code example of a similar function, see **SQLColumns**.

Related Functions

For information about	See
Assigning storage for a column in a result set	**SQLBindCol**
Canceling statement processing	**SQLCancel**
Returning the columns in a table or tables	**SQLColumns** (extension)
Fetching a block of data or scrolling through a result set	**SQLExtendedFetch** (extension)
Fetching a row of data	**SQLFetch**
Returning the columns of a primary key	**SQLPrimaryKeys** (extension)

SQLStatistics

ODBC 1.0

Extension Level 1   **SQLStatistics** retrieves a list of statistics about a single table and the indexes associated with the table. The driver returns the information as a result set.

Syntax   RETCODE **SQLStatistics**(*hstmt, szTableQualifier, cbTableQualifier, szTableOwner, cbTableOwner, szTableName, cbTableName, fUnique, fAccuracy*)

The **SQLStatistics** function accepts the following arguments:

Type	Argument	Use	Description
HSTMT	*hstmt*	Input	Statement handle.
UCHAR FAR *	*szTableQualifier*	Input	Qualifier name. If a driver supports qualifiers for some tables but not for others, such as when the driver retrieves data from different DBMSs, an empty string ("") denotes those tables that do not have qualifiers.
SWORD	*cbTableQualifier*	Input	Length of *szTableQualifier*.
UCHAR FAR *	*szTableOwner*	Input	Owner name. If a driver supports owners for some tables but not for others, such as when the driver retrieves data from different DBMSs, an empty string ("") denotes those tables that do not have owners.
SWORD	*cbTableOwner*	Input	Length of *szTableOwner*.
UCHAR FAR *	*szTableName*	Input	Table name.
SWORD	*cbTableName*	Input	Length of *szTableName*.
UWORD	*fUnique*	Input	Type of index: SQL_INDEX_UNIQUE or SQL_INDEX_ALL.

Type	Argument	Use	Description
UWORD	*fAccuracy*	Input	The importance of the CARDINALITY and PAGES columns in the result set:
			SQL_ENSURE requests that the driver unconditionally retrieve the statistics.
			SQL_QUICK requests that the driver retrieve results only if they are readily available from the server. In this case, the driver does not ensure that the values are current.

Returns

SQL_SUCCESS, SQL_SUCCESS_WITH_INFO, SQL_STILL_EXECUTING, SQL_ERROR, or SQL_INVALID_HANDLE.

Diagnostics

When **SQLStatistics** returns SQL_ERROR or SQL_SUCCESS_WITH_INFO, an associated SQLSTATE value may be obtained by calling **SQLError**. The following table lists the SQLSTATE values commonly returned by **SQLStatistics** and explains each one in the context of this function; the notation "(DM)" precedes the descriptions of SQLSTATEs returned by the Driver Manager. The return code associated with each SQLSTATE value is SQL_ERROR, unless noted otherwise.

SQLSTATE	Error	Description
01000	General warning	Driver-specific informational message. (Function returns SQL_SUCCESS_WITH_INFO.)
08S01	Communication link failure	The communication link between the driver and the data source to which the driver was connected failed before the function completed processing.
24000	Invalid cursor state	(DM) A cursor was open on the *hstmt* and **SQLFetch** or **SQLExtendedFetch** had been called.
		A cursor was open on the *hstmt* but **SQLFetch** or **SQLExtendedFetch** had not been called.
IM001	Driver does not support this function	(DM) The driver associated with the *hstmt* does not support the function.

SQLSTATE	Error	Description
S1000	General error	An error occurred for which there was no specific SQLSTATE and for which no implementation-specific SQLSTATE was defined. The error message returned by **SQLError** in the argument *szErrorMsg* describes the error and its cause.
S1001	Memory allocation failure	The driver was unable to allocate memory required to support execution or completion of the function.
S1008	Operation canceled	Asynchronous processing was enabled for the *hstmt*. The function was called and before it completed execution, **SQLCancel** was called on the *hstmt*. Then the function was called again on the *hstmt*.
		The function was called and, before it completed execution, **SQLCancel** was called on the *hstmt* from a different thread in a multithreaded application.
S1010	Function sequence error	(DM) An asynchronously executing function (not this one) was called for the *hstmt* and was still executing when this function was called.
		(DM) **SQLExecute**, **SQLExecDirect**, or **SQLSetPos** was called for the *hstmt* and returned SQL_NEED_DATA. This function was called before data was sent for all data-at-execution parameters or columns.
S1090	Invalid string or buffer length	(DM) The value of one of the name length arguments was less than 0, but not equal to SQL_NTS.
		The value of one of the name length arguments exceeded the maximum length value for the corresponding qualifier or name.
S1100	Uniqueness option type out of range	(DM) An invalid *fUnique* value was specified.
S1101	Accuracy option type out of range	(DM) An invalid *fAccuracy* value was specified.

SQLSTATE	Error	Description
S1C00	Driver not capable	A table qualifier was specified and the driver or data source does not support qualifiers.
		A table owner was specified and the driver or data source does not support owners.
		The combination of the current settings of the SQL_CONCURRENCY and SQL_CURSOR_TYPE statement options was not supported by the driver or data source.
S1T00	Timeout expired	The timeout period expired before the data source returned the requested result set. The timeout period is set through **SQLSetStmtOption**, SQL_QUERY_TIMEOUT.

Comments

SQLStatistics returns information about a single table as a standard result set, ordered by NON_UNIQUE, TYPE, INDEX_QUALIFIER, INDEX_NAME, and SEQ_IN_INDEX. The result set combines statistics information for the table with information about each index. The following table lists the columns in the result set.

Note **SQLStatistics** might not return all indexes. For example, an Xbase driver might only return indexes in files in the current directory. Applications can use any valid index, regardless of whether it is returned by **SQLStatistics**.

The lengths of VARCHAR columns shown in the table are maximums; the actual lengths depend on the data source. To determine the actual lengths of the TABLE_QUALIFIER, TABLE_OWNER, TABLE_NAME, and COLUMN_NAME columns, an application can call **SQLGetInfo** with the SQL_MAX_QUALIFIER_NAME_LEN, SQL_MAX_OWNER_NAME_LEN, SQL_MAX_TABLE_NAME_LEN, and SQL_MAX_COLUMN_NAME_LEN options.

Column Name	Data Type	Comments
TABLE_QUALIFIER	Varchar(128)	Table qualifier identifier of the table to which the statistic or index applies; NULL if not applicable to the data source. If a driver supports qualifiers for some tables but not for others, such as when the driver retrieves data from different DBMSs, it returns an empty string ("") for those tables that do not have qualifiers.

Column Name	Data Type	Comments
TABLE_OWNER	Varchar(128)	Table owner identifier of the table to which the statistic or index applies; NULL if not applicable to the data source. If a driver supports owners for some tables but not for others, such as when the driver retrieves data from different DBMSs, it returns an empty string ("") for those tables that do not have owners.
TABLE_NAME	Varchar(128) not NULL	Table identifier of the table to which the statistic or index applies.
NON_UNIQUE	Smallint	Indicates whether the index prohibits duplicate values: TRUE if the index values can be nonunique. FALSE if the index values must be unique. NULL is returned if TYPE is SQL_TABLE_STAT.
INDEX_QUALIFIER	Varchar(128)	The identifier that is used to qualify the index name doing a **DROP INDEX**; NULL is returned if an index qualifier is not supported by the data source or if TYPE is SQL_TABLE_STAT. If a non-null value is returned in this column, it must be used to qualify the index name on a **DROP INDEX** statement; otherwise the TABLE_OWNER name should be used to qualify the index name.
INDEX_NAME	Varchar(128)	Index identifier; NULL is returned if TYPE is SQL_TABLE_STAT.
TYPE	Smallint not NULL	Type of information being returned: SQL_TABLE_STAT indicates a statistic for the table. SQL_INDEX_CLUSTERED indicates a clustered index. SQL_INDEX_HASHED indicates a hashed index. SQL_INDEX_OTHER indicates another type of index.

Column Name	Data Type	Comments
SEQ_IN_INDEX	Smallint	Column sequence number in index (starting with 1); NULL is returned if TYPE is SQL_TABLE_STAT.
COLUMN_NAME	Varchar(128)	Column identifier. If the column is based on an expression, such as SALARY + BENEFITS, the expression is returned; if the expression cannot be determined, an empty string is returned. If the index is a filtered index, each column in the filter condition is returned; this may require more than one row. NULL is returned if TYPE is SQL_TABLE_STAT.
COLLATION	Char(1)	Sort sequence for the column; "A" for ascending; "D" for descending; NULL is returned if column sort sequence is not supported by the data source or if TYPE is SQL_TABLE_STAT.
CARDINALITY	Integer	Cardinality of table or index; number of rows in table if TYPE is SQL_TABLE_STAT; number of unique values in the index if TYPE is not SQL_TABLE_STAT; NULL is returned if the value is not available from the data source.
PAGES	Integer	Number of pages used to store the index or table; number of pages for the table if TYPE is SQL_TABLE_STAT; number of pages for the index if TYPE is not SQL_TABLE_STAT; NULL is returned if the value is not available from the data source, or if not applicable to the data source.
FILTER_CONDITION	Varchar(128)	If the index is a filtered index, this is the filter condition, such as SALARY > 30000; if the filter condition cannot be determined, this is an empty string.
		NULL if the index is not a filtered index, it cannot be determined whether the index is a filtered index, or TYPE is SQL_TABLE_STAT.

Note The FILTER_CONDITION column was added in ODBC 2.0. ODBC 1.0 drivers might return a different, driver-specific column with the same column number.

If the row in the result set corresponds to a table, the driver sets TYPE to SQL_TABLE_STAT and sets NON_UNIQUE, INDEX_QUALIFIER, INDEX_NAME, SEQ_IN_INDEX, COLUMN_NAME, and COLLATION to NULL. If CARDINALITY or PAGES are not available from the data source, the driver sets them to NULL.

Code Example   For a code example of a similar function, see **SQLColumns**.

Related Functions

For information about	See
Assigning storage for a column in a result set	**SQLBindCol**
Canceling statement processing	**SQLCancel**
Fetching a block of data or scrolling through a result set	**SQLExtendedFetch** (extension)
Fetching a row of data	**SQLFetch**
Returning the columns of foreign keys	**SQLForeignKeys** (extension)
Returning the columns of a primary key	**SQLPrimaryKeys** (extension)

SQLTablePrivileges

Extension Level 2

SQLTablePrivileges returns a list of tables and the privileges associated with each table. The driver returns the information as a result set on the specified *hstmt*.

Syntax

RETCODE **SQLTablePrivileges**(*hstmt, szTableQualifier, cbTableQualifier, szTableOwner, cbTableOwner, szTableName, cbTableName*)

The **SQLTablePrivileges** function accepts the following arguments.

Type	Argument	Use	Description
HSTMT	*hstmt*	Input	Statement handle.
UCHAR FAR *	*szTableQualifier*	Input	Table qualifier. If a driver supports qualifiers for some tables but not for others, such as when the driver retrieves data from different DBMSs, an empty string ("") denotes those tables that do not have qualifiers.
SWORD	*cbTableQualifier*	Input	Length of *szTableQualifier*.
UCHAR FAR *	*szTableOwner*	Input	String search pattern for owner names. If a driver supports owners for some tables but not for others, such as when the driver retrieves data from different DBMSs, an empty string ("") denotes those tables that do not have owners.
SWORD	*cbTableOwner*	Input	Length of *szTableOwner*.
UCHAR FAR *	*szTableName*	Input	String search pattern for table names.
SWORD	*cbTableName*	Input	Length of *szTableName*.

Returns

SQL_SUCCESS, SQL_SUCCESS_WITH_INFO, SQL_STILL_EXECUTING, SQL_ERROR, or SQL_INVALID_HANDLE.

Diagnostics

When **SQLTablePrivileges** returns SQL_ERROR or SQL_SUCCESS_WITH_INFO, an associated SQLSTATE value may be obtained by calling **SQLError**. The following table lists the SQLSTATE values commonly returned by **SQLTablePrivileges** and explains each one in the context of this function; the notation "(DM)" precedes the descriptions of SQLSTATEs returned by the Driver Manager. The return code associated with each SQLSTATE value is SQL_ERROR, unless noted otherwise.

SQLSTATE	Error	Description
01000	General warning	Driver-specific informational message. (Function returns SQL_SUCCESS_WITH_INFO.)
08S01	Communication link failure	The communication link between the driver and the data source to which the driver was connected failed before the function completed processing.
24000	Invalid cursor state	(DM) A cursor was open on the *hstmt* and **SQLFetch** or **SQLExtendedFetch** had been called.
		A cursor was open on the *hstmt* but **SQLFetch** or **SQLExtendedFetch** had not been called.
IM001	Driver does not support this function	(DM) The driver associated with the *hstmt* does not support the function.
S1000	General error	An error occurred for which there was no specific SQLSTATE and for which no implementation-specific SQLSTATE was defined. The error message returned by **SQLError** in the argument *szErrorMsg* describes the error and its cause.
S1001	Memory allocation failure	The driver was unable to allocate memory required to support execution or completion of the function.
S1008	Operation canceled	Asynchronous processing was enabled for the *hstmt*. The function was called and before it completed execution, **SQLCancel** was called on the *hstmt*. Then the function was called again on the *hstmt*.
		The function was called and, before it completed execution, **SQLCancel** was called on the *hstmt* from a different thread in a multithreaded application.
S1010	Function sequence error	(DM) An asynchronously executing function (not this one) was called for the *hstmt* and was still executing when this function was called.
		(DM) **SQLExecute**, **SQLExecDirect**, or **SQLSetPos** was called for the *hstmt* and returned SQL_NEED_DATA. This function was called before data was sent for all data-at-execution parameters or columns.

SQLSTATE	Error	Description
S1090	Invalid string or buffer length	(DM) The value of one of the name length arguments was less than 0, but not equal to SQL_NTS.
		The value of one of the name length arguments exceeded the maximum length value for the corresponding qualifier or name.
S1C00	Driver not capable	A table qualifier was specified and the driver or data source does not support qualifiers.
		A table owner was specified and the driver or data source does not support owners.
		A string search pattern was specified for the table owner, table name, or column name and the data source does not support search patterns for one or more of those arguments.
		The combination of the current settings of the SQL_CONCURRENCY and SQL_CURSOR_TYPE statement options was not supported by the driver or data source.
S1T00	Timeout expired	The timeout period expired before the data source returned the result set. The timeout period is set through **SQLSetStmtOption**, SQL_QUERY_TIMEOUT.

Comments

The *szTableOwner* and *szTableName* arguments accept search patterns. For more information about valid search patterns, see "Search Pattern Arguments" earlier in this chapter.

SQLTablePrivileges returns the results as a standard result set, ordered by TABLE_QUALIFIER, TABLE_OWNER, TABLE_NAME, and PRIVILEGE. The following table lists the columns in the result set.

Note **SQLTablePrivileges** might not return privileges for all tables. For example, an Xbase driver might only return privileges for files (tables) in the current directory. Applications can use any valid table, regardless of whether it is returned by **SQLTablePrivileges**.

The lengths of VARCHAR columns shown in the table are maximums; the actual lengths depend on the data source. To determine the actual lengths of the TABLE_QUALIFIER, TABLE_OWNER, and TABLE_NAME columns, an application can call **SQLGetInfo** with the SQL_MAX_QUALIFIER_NAME_LEN, SQL_MAX_OWNER_NAME_LEN, and SQL_MAX_TABLE_NAME_LEN options.

Column Name	Data Type	Comments
TABLE_QUALIFIER	Varchar(128)	Table qualifier identifier; NULL if not applicable to the data source. If a driver supports qualifiers for some tables but not for others, such as when the driver retrieves data from different DBMSs, it returns an empty string ("") for those tables that do not have qualifiers.
TABLE_OWNER	Varchar(128)	Table owner identifier; NULL if not applicable to the data source. If a driver supports owners for some tables but not for others, such as when the driver retrieves data from different DBMSs, it returns an empty string ("") for those tables that do not have owners.
TABLE_NAME	Varchar(128) not NULL	Table identifier.
GRANTOR	Varchar(128)	Identifier of the user who granted the privilege; NULL if not applicable to the data source.
GRANTEE	Varchar(128) not NULL	Identifier of the user to whom the privilege was granted.

Column Name	Data Type	Comments
PRIVILEGE	Varchar(128) not NULL	Identifies the table privilege. May be one of the following or a data source–specific privilege.
		SELECT: The grantee is permitted to retrieve data for one or more columns of the table.
		INSERT: The grantee is permitted to insert new rows containing data for one or more columns into to the table.
		UPDATE: The grantee is permitted to update the data in one or more columns of the table.
		DELETE: The grantee is permitted to delete rows of data from the table.
		REFERENCES: The grantee is permitted to refer to one or more columns of the table within a constraint (for example, a unique, referential, or table check constraint).
		The scope of action permitted the grantee by a given table privilege is data source–dependent. For example, the UPDATE privilege might permit the grantee to update all columns in a table on one data source and only those columns for which the grantor has the UPDATE privilege on another data source.
IS_GRANTABLE	Varchar(3)	Indicates whether the grantee is permitted to grant the privilege to other users; "YES", "NO", or NULL if unknown or not applicable to the data source.

Code Example For a code example of a similar function, see **SQLColumns**.

Related Functions

For information about	See
Assigning storage for a column in a result set	**SQLBindCol**
Canceling statement processing	**SQLCancel**
Returning privileges for a column or columns	**SQLColumnPrivileges** (extension)
Returning the columns in a table or tables	**SQLColumns** (extension)
Fetching a block of data or scrolling through a result set	**SQLExtendedFetch** (extension)
Fetching a row of data	**SQLFetch**
Returning table statistics and indexes	**SQLStatistics** (extension)
Returning a list of tables in a data source	**SQLTables** (extension)

SQLTables

Extension Level 1   **SQLTables** returns the list of table names stored in a specific data source. The driver returns the information as a result set.

Syntax   RETCODE **SQLTables**(*hstmt, szTableQualifier, cbTableQualifier, szTableOwner, cbTableOwner, szTableName, cbTableName, szTableType, cbTableType*)

The **SQLTables** function accepts the following arguments:

Type	Argument	Use	Description
HSTMT	*hstmt*	Input	Statement handle for retrieved results.
UCHAR FAR *	*szTableQualifier*	Input	Qualifier name. If a driver supports qualifiers for some tables but not for others, such as when a driver retrieves data from different DBMSs, an empty string ("") denotes those tables that do not have qualifiers.
SWORD	*cbTableQualifier*	Input	Length of *szTableQualifier*.
UCHAR FAR *	*szTableOwner*	Input	String search pattern for owner names.
SWORD	*cbTableOwner*	Input	Length of *szTableOwner*.
UCHAR FAR *	*szTableName*	Input	String search pattern for table names. If a driver supports owners for some tables but not for others, such as when the driver retrieves data from different DBMSs, an empty string ("") denotes those tables that do not have owners.
SWORD	*cbTableName*	Input	Length of *szTableName*.
UCHAR FAR *	*szTableType*	Input	List of table types to match.
SWORD	*cbTableType*	Input	Length of *szTableType*.

Returns   SQL_SUCCESS, SQL_SUCCESS_WITH_INFO, SQL_STILL_EXECUTING, SQL_ERROR or SQL_INVALID_HANDLE.

Diagnostics   When **SQLTables** returns SQL_ERROR or SQL_SUCCESS_WITH_INFO, an associated SQLSTATE value may be obtained by calling **SQLError**. The following table lists the SQLSTATE values commonly returned by **SQLTables** and explains each one in the context of this function; the notation "(DM)" precedes the descriptions of SQLSTATEs returned by the Driver Manager. The return code associated with each SQLSTATE value is SQL_ERROR, unless noted otherwise.

SQLSTATE	Error	Description
01000	General warning	Driver-specific informational message. (Function returns SQL_SUCCESS_WITH_INFO.)
08S01	Communication link failure	The communication link between the driver and the data source to which the driver was connected failed before the function completed processing.
24000	Invalid cursor state	(DM) A cursor was open on the *hstmt* and **SQLFetch** or **SQLExtendedFetch** had been called.
		A cursor was open on the *hstmt* but **SQLFetch** or **SQLExtendedFetch** had not been called.
IM001	Driver does not support this function	(DM) The driver associated with the *hstmt* does not support the function.
S1000	General error	An error occurred for which there was no specific SQLSTATE and for which no implementation-specific SQLSTATE was defined. The error message returned by **SQLError** in the argument *szErrorMsg* describes the error and its cause.
S1001	Memory allocation failure	The driver was unable to allocate memory required to support execution or completion of the function.
S1008	Operation canceled	Asynchronous processing was enabled for the *hstmt*. The function was called and before it completed execution, **SQLCancel** was called on the *hstmt*. Then the function was called again on the *hstmt*.
		The function was called and, before it completed execution, **SQLCancel** was called on the *hstmt* from a different thread in a multithreaded application.

SQLSTATE	Error	Description
S1010	Function sequence error	(DM) An asynchronously executing function (not this one) was called for the *hstmt* and was still executing when this function was called.
		(DM) **SQLExecute**, **SQLExecDirect**, or **SQLSetPos** was called for the *hstmt* and returned SQL_NEED_DATA. This function was called before data was sent for all data-at-execution parameters or columns.
S1090	Invalid string or buffer length	(DM) The value of one of the name length arguments was less than 0, but not equal to SQL_NTS.
		The value of one of the name length arguments exceeded the maximum length value for the corresponding qualifier or name.
S1C00	Driver not capable	A table qualifier was specified and the driver or data source does not support qualifiers.
		A table owner was specified and the driver or data source does not support owners.
		A string search pattern was specified for the table owner or table name and the data source does not support search patterns for one or more of those arguments.
		The combination of the current settings of the SQL_CONCURRENCY and SQL_CURSOR_TYPE statement options was not supported by the driver or data source.
S1T00	Timeout expired	The timeout period expired before the data source returned the requested result set. The timeout period is set through **SQLSetStmtOption**, SQL_QUERY_TIMEOUT.

Comments   **SQLTables** lists all tables in the requested range. A user may or may not have SELECT privileges to any of these tables. To check accessibility, an application can:

- Call **SQLGetInfo** and check the SQL_ACCESSIBLE_TABLES info value.
- Call **SQLTablePrivileges** to check the privileges for each table.

Otherwise, the application must be able to handle a situation where the user selects a table for which SELECT privileges are not granted.

The *szTableOwner* and *szTableName* arguments accept search patterns. For more information about valid search patterns, see "Search Pattern Arguments" earlier in this chapter.

To support enumeration of qualifiers, owners, and table types, **SQLTables** defines the following special semantics for the *szTableQualifier*, *szTableOwner*, *szTableName*, and *szTableType* arguments:

- If *szTableQualifier* is a single percent character (%) and *szTableOwner* and *szTableName* are empty strings, then the result set contains a list of valid qualifiers for the data source. (All columns except the TABLE_QUALIFIER column contain NULLs.)
- If *szTableOwner* is a single percent character (%) and *szTableQualifier* and *szTableName* are empty strings, then the result set contains a list of valid owners for the data source. (All columns except the TABLE_OWNER column contain NULLs.)
- If *szTableType* is a single percent character (%) and *szTableQualifier*, *szTableOwner*, and *szTableName* are empty strings, then the result set contains a list of valid table types for the data source. (All columns except the TABLE_TYPE column contain NULLs.)

If *szTableType* is not an empty string, it must contain a list of comma-separated, values for the types of interest; each value may be enclosed in single quotes (') or unquoted. For example, "'TABLE','VIEW'" or "TABLE, VIEW". If the data source does not support a specified table type, **SQLTables** does not return any results for that type.

SQLTables returns the results as a standard result set, ordered by TABLE_TYPE, TABLE_QUALIFIER, TABLE_OWNER, and TABLE_NAME. The following table lists the columns in the result set.

Note **SQLTables** might not return all qualifiers, owners, or tables. For example, an Xbase driver, for which a qualifier is a directory, might only return the current directory instead of all directories on the system. It might also only return files (tables) in the current directory. Applications can use any valid qualifier, owner, or table, regardless of whether it is returned by **SQLTables**.

The lengths of VARCHAR columns shown in the table are maximums; the actual lengths depend on the data source. To determine the actual lengths of the TABLE_QUALIFIER, TABLE_OWNER, and TABLE_NAME columns, an application can call **SQLGetInfo** with the SQL_MAX_QUALIFIER_NAME_LEN, SQL_MAX_OWNER_NAME_LEN, and SQL_MAX_TABLE_NAME_LEN options.

Column Name	Data Type	Comments
TABLE_QUALIFIER	Varchar(128)	Table qualifier identifier; NULL if not applicable to the data source. If a driver supports qualifiers for some tables but not for others, such as when the driver retrieves data from different DBMSs, it returns an empty string ("") for those tables that do not have qualifiers.
TABLE_OWNER	Varchar(128)	Table owner identifier; NULL if not applicable to the data source. If a driver supports owners for some tables but not for others, such as when the driver retrieves data from different DBMSs, it returns an empty string ("") for those tables that do not have owners.
TABLE_NAME	Varchar(128)	Table identifier.
TABLE_TYPE	Varchar(128)	Table type identifier; one of the following: "TABLE", "VIEW", "SYSTEM TABLE", "GLOBAL TEMPORARY", "LOCAL TEMPORARY", "ALIAS", "SYNONYM" or a data source–specific type identifier.
REMARKS	Varchar(254)	A description of the table.

Code Example   For a code example of a similar function, see **SQLColumns**.

Related Functions

For information about	See
Assigning storage for a column in a result set	**SQLBindCol**
Canceling statement processing	**SQLCancel**
Returning privileges for a column or columns	**SQLColumnPrivileges** (extension)
Returning the columns in a table or tables	**SQLColumns** (extension)
Fetching a block of data or scrolling through a result set	**SQLExtendedFetch** (extension)
Fetching a row of data	**SQLFetch**
Returning table statistics and indexes	**SQLStatistics** (extension)
Returning privileges for a table or tables	**SQLTablePrivileges** (extension)

SQLTransact

ODBC 1.0

Core

SQLTransact requests a commit or rollback operation for all active operations on all *hstmts* associated with a connection. **SQLTransact** can also request that a commit or rollback operation be performed for all connections associated with the *henv*.

Syntax

RETCODE **SQLTransact**(*henv*, *hdbc*, *fType*)

The **SQLTransact** function accepts the following arguments.

Type	Argument	Use	Description
HENV	*henv*	Input	Environment handle.
HDBC	*hdbc*	Input	Connection handle.
UWORD	*fType*	Input	One of the following two values: SQL_COMMIT SQL_ROLLBACK

Returns

SQL_SUCCESS, SQL_SUCCESS_WITH_INFO, SQL_ERROR, or SQL_INVALID_HANDLE.

Diagnostics

When **SQLTransact** returns SQL_ERROR or SQL_SUCCESS_WITH_INFO, an associated SQLSTATE value may be obtained by calling **SQLError**. The following table lists the SQLSTATE values commonly returned by **SQLTransact** and explains each one in the context of this function; the notation "(DM)" precedes the descriptions of SQLSTATEs returned by the Driver Manager. The return code associated with each SQLSTATE value is SQL_ERROR, unless noted otherwise.

SQLSTATE	Error	Description
01000	General warning	Driver-specific informational message. (Function returns SQL_SUCCESS_WITH_INFO.)
08003	Connection not open	(DM) The *hdbc* was not in a connected state.
08007	Connection failure during transaction	The connection associated with the *hdbc* failed during the execution of the function and it cannot be determined whether the requested **COMMIT** or **ROLLBACK** occurred before the failure.
IM001	Driver does not support this function	(DM) The driver associated with the *hdbc* does not support the function.

SQLSTATE	Error	Description
S1000	General error	An error occurred for which there was no specific SQLSTATE and for which no implementation-specific SQLSTATE was defined. The error message returned by **SQLError** in the argument *szErrorMsg* describes the error and its cause.
S1001	Memory allocation failure	The driver was unable to allocate memory required to support execution or completion of the function.
S1010	Function sequence error	(DM) An asynchronously executing function was called for an *hstmt* associated with the *hdbc* and was still executing when **SQLTransact** was called.
		(DM) **SQLExecute**, **SQLExecDirect**, or **SQLSetPos** was called for an *hstmt* associated with the *hdbc* and returned SQL_NEED_DATA. This function was called before data was sent for all data-at-execution parameters or columns.
S1012	Invalid transaction operation code	(DM) The value specified for the argument *fType* was neither SQL_COMMIT nor SQL_ROLLBACK.
S1C00	Driver not capable	The driver or data source does not support the **ROLLBACK** operation.

Comments

If *hdbc* is SQL_NULL_HDBC and *henv* is a valid environment handle, then the Driver Manager will attempt to commit or roll back transactions on all *hdbcs* that are in a connected state. The Driver Manager calls **SQLTransact** in the driver associated with each *hdbc*. The Driver Manager will return SQL_SUCCESS only if it receives SQL_SUCCESS for each *hdbc*. If the Driver Manager receives SQL_ERROR on one or more *hdbcs*, it will return SQL_ERROR to the application. To determine which connection(s) failed during the commit or rollback operation, the application can call **SQLError** for each *hdbc*.

Note The Driver Manager does not simulate a global transaction across all *hdbcs* and therefore does not use two-phase commit protocols.

If *hdbc* is a valid connection handle, *henv* is ignored and the Driver Manager calls **SQLTransact** in the driver for the *hdbc*.

If *hdbc* is SQL_NULL_HDBC and *henv* is SQL_NULL_HENV, **SQLTransact** returns SQL_INVALID_HANDLE.

If *fType* is SQL_COMMIT, **SQLTransact** issues a commit request for all active operations on any *hstmt* associated with an affected *hdbc*. If *fType* is

SQL_ROLLBACK, **SQLTransact** issues a rollback request for all active operations on any *hstmt* associated with an affected *hdbc*. If no transactions are active, **SQLTransact** returns SQL_SUCCESS with no effect on any data sources.

If the driver is in manual-commit mode (by calling **SQLSetConnectOption** with the SQL_AUTOCOMMIT option set to zero), a new transaction is implicitly started when an SQL statement that can be contained within a transaction is executed against the current data source.

To determine how transaction operations affect cursors, an application calls **SQLGetInfo** with the SQL_CURSOR_ROLLBACK_BEHAVIOR and SQL_CURSOR_COMMIT_BEHAVIOR options.

If the SQL_CURSOR_ROLLBACK_BEHAVIOR or SQL_CURSOR_COMMIT_BEHAVIOR value equals SQL_CB_DELETE, **SQLTransact** closes and deletes all open cursors on all *hstmts* associated with the *hdbc* and discards all pending results. **SQLTransact** leaves any *hstmt* present in an allocated (unprepared) state; the application can reuse them for subsequent SQL requests or can call **SQLFreeStmt** to deallocate them.

If the SQL_CURSOR_ROLLBACK_BEHAVIOR or SQL_CURSOR_COMMIT_BEHAVIOR value equals SQL_CB_CLOSE, **SQLTransact** closes all open cursors on all *hstmts* associated with the *hdbc*. **SQLTransact** leaves any *hstmt* present in a prepared state; the application can call **SQLExecute** for an *hstmt* associated with the *hdbc* without first calling **SQLPrepare**.

If the SQL_CURSOR_ROLLBACK_BEHAVIOR or SQL_CURSOR_COMMIT_BEHAVIOR value equals SQL_CB_PRESERVE, **SQLTransact** does not affect open cursors associated with the *hdbc*. Cursors remain at the row they pointed to prior to the call to **SQLTransact**.

For drivers and data sources that support transactions, calling **SQLTransact** with either SQL_COMMIT or SQL_ROLLBACK when no transaction is active will return SQL_SUCCESS (indicating that there is no work to be committed or rolled back) and have no effect on the data source.

Drivers or data sources that do not support transactions (**SQLGetInfo** *fOption* SQL_TXN_CAPABLE is 0) are effectively always in autocommit mode. Therefore, calling **SQLTransact** with SQL_COMMIT will return SQL_SUCCESS. However, calling **SQLTransact** with SQL_ROLLBACK will result in SQLSTATE S1C00 (Driver not capable), indicating that a rollback can never be performed.

Code Example   See **SQLParamOptions**.

Related Functions

For information about	See
Returning information about a driver or data source	**SQLGetInfo** (extension)
Freeing a statement handle	**SQLFreeStmt**

CHAPTER 23

Setup DLL Function Reference

This chapter describes the syntax of the driver setup DLL API, which consists of a single function (**ConfigDSN**). **ConfigDSN** may be either in the driver DLL or in a separate setup DLL.

It also describes the syntax of the translator setup DLL API, which consists of a single function (**ConfigTranslator**). **ConfigTranslator** may be either in the translator DLL or in a separate setup DLL.

Each function is labeled with the version of ODBC in which it was introduced.

For information on argument naming conventions, see Chapter 22, "ODBC Function Reference".

ConfigDSN

Purpose   **ConfigDSN** adds, modifies, or deletes data sources from the ODBC.INI file (or registry). It may prompt the user for connection information. It can be in the driver DLL or a separate setup DLL.

Syntax   BOOL **ConfigDSN**(*hwndParent, fRequest, lpszDriver, lpszAttributes*)

The **ConfigDSN** function accepts the following arguments.

Type	Argument	Use	Description
HWND	*hwndParent*	Input	Parent window handle. The function will not display any dialog boxes if the handle is null.
UINT	*fRequest*	Input	Type of request. *fRequest* must contain one of the following values:
			ODBC_ADD_DSN: add a new data source.
			ODBC_CONFIG_DSN: configure (modify) an existing data source.
			ODBC_REMOVE_DSN: remove an existing data source.
LPCSTR	*lpszDriver*	Input	Driver description (usually the name of the associated DBMS) presented to users instead of the physical driver name.
LPCSTR	*lpszAttributes*	Input	List of attributes in the form of keyword-value pairs. For information about the list structure, see "Comments."

Returns   The function returns TRUE if it is successful. It returns FALSE if it fails.

Comments   **ConfigDSN** receives connection information from the installer DLL as a list of attributes in the form of keyword-value pairs. Each pair is terminated with a null byte and the entire list is terminated with a null byte (that is, two null bytes mark the end of the list). The keywords used by **ConfigDSN** are the same as those used by **SQLBrowseConnect** and **SQLDriverConnect**, except that **ConfigDSN** does not accept the **DRIVER** keyword. As in **SQLBrowseConnect** and **SQLDriverConnect**, the keywords and their values should not contain the []{}(),;?*=!@ characters, and the value of the **DSN** keyword cannot consist only of blanks. Because of the registry grammar, keywords and data source names cannot contain the backslash (\) character.

For example, to configure a data source that requires a user ID, password, and database name, a setup application might pass the following keyword-value pairs:

```
DSN=Personnel Data\0UID=Smith\0PWD=Sesame\0DATABASE=Personnel\0\0
```

For more information about these keywords, see **SQLDriverConnect** and each driver's documentation.

In order to display a dialog box, *hwndParent* must not be null.

Adding a Data Source

If a data source name is passed to **ConfigDSN** in *lpszAttributes*, **ConfigDSN** checks that the name is valid. If the data source name matches an existing data source name and *hwndParent* is null, **ConfigDSN** overwrites the existing name. If it matches an existing name and *hwndParent* is not null, **ConfigDSN** prompts the user to overwrite the existing name.

If *lpszAttributes* contains enough information to connect to a data source, **ConfigDSN** can add the data source or display a dialog box with which the user can change the connection information. If *lpszAttributes* does not contain enough information to connect to a data source, **ConfigDSN** must determine the necessary information; if *hwndParent* is not null, it displays a dialog box to retrieve the information from the user.

If **ConfigDSN** displays a dialog box, it must display any connection information passed to it in *lpszAttributes*. In particular, if a data source name was passed to it, **ConfigDSN** displays that name but does not allow the user to change it. **ConfigDSN** can supply default values for connection information not passed to it in *lpszAttributes*.

If **ConfigDSN** cannot get complete connection information for a data source, it returns FALSE.

If **ConfigDSN** can get complete connection information for a data source, it calls **SQLWriteDSNToIni** in the installer DLL to add the new data source specification to the ODBC.INI file (or registry). **SQLWriteDSNToIni** adds the data source name to the [ODBC Data Sources] section, creates the data source specification section, and adds the **Driver** keyword with the driver description as its value. **ConfigDSN** calls **SQLWritePrivateProfileString** in the installer DLL to add any additional keywords and values used by the driver.

Modifying a Data Source

To modify a data source, a data source name must be passed to **ConfigDSN** in *lpszAttributes*. **ConfigDSN** checks that the data source name is in the ODBC.INI file (or registry).

If *hwndParent* is null, **ConfigDSN** uses the information in *lpszAttributes* to modify the information in the ODBC.INI file (or registry). If *hwndParent* is not null, **ConfigDSN** displays a dialog box using the information in *lpszAttributes*; for information not in *lpszAttributes*, it uses information from the ODBC.INI file (or registry). The user can modify the information before **ConfigDSN** stores it in the ODBC.INI file (or registry).

If the data source name was changed, **ConfigDSN** first calls **SQLRemoveDSNFromIni** in the installer DLL to remove the existing data source specification from the ODBC.INI file (or registry). It then follows the steps in the previous section to add the new data source specification. If the data source name was not changed, **ConfigDSN** calls **SQLWritePrivateProfileString** in the installer DLL to make any other changes. **ConfigDSN** may not delete or change the value of the **Driver** keyword.

Deleting a Data Source

To delete a data source, a data source name must be passed to **ConfigDSN** in *lpszAttributes*. **ConfigDSN** checks that the data source name is in the ODBC.INI file (or registry). It then calls **SQLRemoveDSNFromIni** in the installer DLL to remove the data source.

Related Functions

For information about	See
Adding, modifying, or removing a data source	**SQLConfigDataSource**
Getting a value from the ODBC.INI file or the registry	**SQLGetPrivateProfileString**
Removing the default data source	**SQLRemoveDefaultDataSource**
Removing a data source name from ODBC.INI (or registry)	**SQLRemoveDSNFromIni**
Adding a data source name to ODBC.INI (or registry)	**SQLWriteDSNToIni**
Writing a value to the ODBC.INI file or the registry	**SQLWritePrivateProfileString**

ConfigTranslator

Purpose

ConfigTranslator returns a default translation option for a translator. It can be in the translator DLL or a separate setup DLL.

Syntax

BOOL **ConfigTranslator**(*hwndParent*, *pvOption*)

The **ConfigTranslator** function accepts the following arguments.

Type	Argument	Use	Description
HWND	*hwndParent*	Input	Parent window handle. The function will not display any dialog boxes if the handle is null.
DWORD FAR *	*pvOption*	Output	A 32-bit translation option.

Returns

The function returns TRUE if it is successful. It returns FALSE if it fails.

Comments

If the translator supports only a single translation option, **ConfigTranslator** returns TRUE and sets *pvOption* to the 32-bit option. Otherwise, it determines the default translation option to use. **ConfigTranslator** can display a dialog box with which a user selects a default translation option.

Related Functions

For information about	See
Getting a translation option	**SQLGetConnectOption**
Selecting a translator	**SQLGetTranslator**
Setting a translation option	**SQLSetConnectOption**

C H A P T E R   2 4

Installer DLL Function Reference

This chapter describes the syntax of the functions in the installer DLL API. The installer DLL API consists of twelve functions. Three of these functions, **SQLGetTranslator**, **SQLRemoveDSNFromIni**, and **SQLWriteDSNToIni**, are called only by setup DLLs. The other functions are called by the setup and administration programs.

Each function is labeled with the version of ODBC in which it was introduced.

For information on argument naming conventions, see Chapter 22, "ODBC Function Reference."

SQLConfigDataSource

Purpose   **SQLConfigDataSource** adds, modifies, or deletes data sources.

Syntax   BOOL **SQLConfigDataSource**(*hwndParent*, *fRequest*, *lpszDriver*, *lpszAttributes*)

The **SQLConfigDataSource** function accepts the following arguments.

Type	Argument	Use	Description
HWND	*hwndParent*	Input	Parent window handle. The function will not display any dialog boxes if the handle is null.
UINT	*fRequest*	Input	Type of request. *fRequest* must contain one of the following values: ODBC_ADD_DSN: add a new data source. ODBC_CONFIG_DSN: configure (modify) an existing data source. ODBC_REMOVE_DSN: remove an existing data source.
LPCSTR	*lpszDriver*	Input	Driver description (usually the name of the associated DBMS) presented to users instead of the physical driver name.
LPCSTR	*lpszAttributes*	Input	List of attributes in the form of keyword-value pairs. For more information, see **ConfigDSN** in Chapter 23, "Setup DLL Function Reference."

Returns   The function returns TRUE if it is successful. It returns FALSE if it fails.

Comments   **SQLConfigDataSource** uses the value of *lpszDriver* to read the full path of the setup DLL for the driver from the ODBCINST.INI file (or registry). It loads the DLL and calls **ConfigDSN** with the same arguments that were passed to it.

SQLConfigDataSource returns FALSE if it is unable to find or load the setup DLL. Otherwise, it returns the status it received from **ConfigDSN**.

Related Functions

For information about	See
Adding, modifying, or removing a data source	**ConfigDSN**
Removing the default data source	**SQLRemoveDefaultDataSource**
Removing a data source name from ODBC.INI (or registry)	**SQLRemoveDSNFromIni**
Adding a data source name to ODBC.INI (or registry)	**SQLWriteDSNToIni**

SQLCreateDataSource

Purpose   **SQLCreateDataSource** displays a dialog box with which the user can add a data source.

Syntax   BOOL **SQLCreateDataSource**(*hwnd*, *lpszDS*)

The **SQLCreateDataSource** function accepts the following arguments.

Type	Argument	Use	Description
HWND	*hwnd*	Input	Parent window handle.
LPSTR	*lpszDS*	Input	Data source name. *lpszDS* can be a null pointer or an empty string.

Returns   **SQLCreateDataSource** returns TRUE if the data source is created. Otherwise, it returns FALSE.

Comments   If *hwnd* is null, **SQLCreateDataSource** returns FALSE. Otherwise, it displays the Add Data Source dialog box:

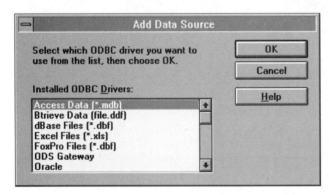

The dialog box displays a list of installed drivers. If the user chooses a driver, **SQLCreateDataSource** calls **ConfigDSN** in the setup DLL and passes it the ODBC_ADD_DSN option.

Related Functions

For information about	See
Installing ODBC software	**SQLInstallODBC**
Managing data sources	**SQLManageDataSources**

SQLGetAvailableDrivers

`ODBC 1.0`

Purpose

SQLGetAvailableDrivers reads the [ODBC Drivers] section of the ODBC.INF file and returns the descriptions of the drivers that the user may install.

Syntax

BOOL **SQLGetAvailableDrivers**(*lpszInfFile*, *lpszBuf*, *cbBufMax*, *pcbBufOut*)

The **SQLGetAvailableDrivers** function accepts the following arguments.

Type	Argument	Use	Description
LPCSTR	*lpszInfFile*	Input	Full path of the ODBC.INF file.
LPSTR	*lpszBuf*	Output	List of descriptions of the available drivers. For information about the list structure, see "Comments."
UINT	*cbBufMax*	Input	Length of *lpszBuf*.
UINT FAR *	*pcbBufOut*	Output	Total number of bytes (excluding the null termination byte) returned in *lpszBuf*. If the number of bytes available to return is greater than or equal to *cbBufMax*, the list of driver descriptions in *lpszBuf* is truncated to *cbBufMax* − 1 bytes.

Returns

The function returns TRUE if it is successful. It returns FALSE if it fails.

Comments

Each driver description is terminated with a null byte and the entire list is terminated with a null byte (that is, two null bytes mark the end of the list). If the allocated buffer is not large enough to hold the entire list, the list is truncated without error.

Related Functions

For information about	See
Returning driver descriptions and attributes	**SQLDrivers** (extension)
Getting a list of installed drivers	**SQLGetInstalledDrivers**

SQLGetInstalledDrivers

Purpose

SQLGetInstalledDrivers reads the [ODBC Drivers] section of the ODBCINST.INI file and returns a list of descriptions of the installed drivers.

Syntax

BOOL **SQLGetInstalledDrivers**(*lpszBuf, cBufMax, pcbBufOut*)

The **SQLGetInstalledDrivers** function accepts the following arguments.

Type	Argument	Use	Description
LPSTR	*lpszBuf*	Output	List of descriptions of the installed drivers. For information about the list structure, see "Comments."
UINT	*cBufMax*	Input	Length of *lpszBuf*.
UINT FAR *	*pcbBufOut*	Output	Total number of bytes (excluding the null termination byte) returned in *lpszBuf*. If the number of bytes available to return is greater than or equal to *cBufMax*, the list of driver descriptions in *lpszBuf* is truncated to *cBufMax* – 1 bytes.

Returns

The function returns TRUE if it is successful. It returns FALSE if it fails.

Comments

Each driver description is terminated with a null byte and the entire list is terminated with a null byte (that is, two null bytes mark the end of the list). If the allocated buffer is not large enough to hold the entire list, the list is truncated without error.

Related Functions

For information about	See
Returning driver descriptions and attributes	**SQLDrivers** (extension)
Getting a list of shipped drivers	**SQLGetAvailableDrivers**

SQLGetPrivateProfileString

Purpose

On Windows, **SQLGetPrivateProfileString** is a macro that calls **GetPrivateProfileString** in the Windows API. On Windows NT, **SQLGetPrivateProfileString** gets a list of names of values or data corresponding to a value of the ODBC.INI subkey of the registry.

Syntax

The syntax and return values of **SQLGetPrivateProfileString** are the same as those of **GetPrivateProfileString** in the Windows and Win32 APIs, except that *lpszFilename* can only be "ODBC.INI". For more information, see the *Microsoft Win32 SDK Programmer's Reference*.

Comments

SQLGetPrivateProfileString is provided as a simple way to port drivers and driver setup DLLs from Windows to Windows NT. Calls to **GetPrivateProfileString** that retrieve a profile string from the ODBC.INI file should be replaced with calls to **SQLGetPrivateProfileString**. **SQLGetPrivateProfileString** calls functions in the Win32 API to retrieve the requested names of values or data corresponding to a value of the ODBC.INI subkey of the registry.

Related Functions

For information about	See
Writing a value to the ODBC.INI file or the registry	**SQLWritePrivateProfileString**

SQLGetTranslator

Purpose   **SQLGetTranslator** displays a dialog box from which a user can select a translator.

Syntax   BOOL **SQLGetTranslator**(*hwndParent, lpszName, cbNameMax, pcbNameOut, lpszPath, cbPathMax, pcbPathOut, pvOption*)

The **SQLGetTranslator** function accepts the following arguments.

Type	Argument	Use	Description
HWND	*hwndParent*	Input	Parent window handle.
LPSTR	*lpszName*	Input/ Output	Name of the translator from the ODBCINST.INI file (or registry).
UINT	*cbNameMax*	Input	Maximum length of the *lpszName* buffer.
UINT FAR *	*pcbNameOut*	Input/ Output	Total number of bytes (excluding the null termination byte) passed or returned in *lpszName*. If the number of bytes available to return is greater than or equal to *cbNameMax*, the translator name in *lpszName* is truncated to *cbNameMax* – 1 bytes.
LPSTR	*lpszPath*	Output	Full path of the translation DLL.
UINT	*cbPathMax*	Input	Maximum length of the *lpszPath* buffer.
UINT FAR *	*pcbPathOut*	Output	Total number of bytes (excluding the null termination byte) returned in *lpszPath*. If the number of bytes available to return is greater than or equal to *cbPathMax*, the translation DLL path in *lpszPath* is truncated to *cbPathMax* – 1 bytes.
DWORD FAR *	*pvOption*	Output	32-bit translation option.

Returns   The function returns TRUE if it is successful. It returns FALSE if it fails or the user cancels the dialog box.

Comments   If *hwnd* is null, **SQLGetTranslator** returns FALSE. Otherwise, it displays the list of installed translators in the following dialog box:

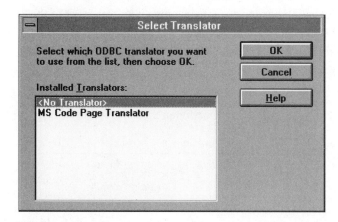

If *lpszName* contains a valid translator name, it is highlighted. Otherwise, <No Translator> is highlighted.

If the user chooses <No Translator>, the contents of *lpszName*, *lpszPath*, and *pvOption* are not touched. **SQLGetTranslator** sets *pcbNameOut* and *pcbPathOut* to 0 and returns TRUE.

If the user chooses a translator, **SQLGetTranslator** calls **ConfigTranslator** in the translator's setup DLL. If **ConfigTranslator** returns FALSE, **SQLGetTranslator** returns to its dialog box. If **ConfigTranslator** returns TRUE, **SQLGetTranslator** returns TRUE, along with the selected translator name, path, and translation option.

Related Functions

For information about	See
Configuring a translator	**ConfigTranslator**
Getting a translation option	**SQLGetConnectOption**
Setting a translation option	**SQLSetConnectOption**

SQLInstallDriver

Purpose

SQLInstallDriver adds information about the driver to the ODBCINST.INI file and returns the path of the target directory for the installation. The calling program must actually copy the driver's files to the target directory.

Syntax

BOOL **SQLInstallDriver**(*lpszInfFile*, *lpszDriver*, *lpszPath*, *cbPathMax*, *pcbPathOut*)

The **SQLInstallDriver** function accepts the following arguments.

Type	Argument	Use	Description
LPCSTR	*lpszInfFile*	Input	Full path of the ODBC.INF file or a null pointer. If *lpszInfFile* is a null pointer, *lpszDriver* must contain a list of keyword-value pairs describing the driver.
LPCSTR	*lpszDriver*	Input	If *lpszInfFile* is the path of the ODBC.INF file, *lpszDriver* must be the driver description (usually the name of the associated DBMS) presented to users instead of the physical driver name.
			If *lpszInfFile* is a null pointer, *lpszDriver* must contain a list of keyword-value pairs describing the driver.
			For more information, see "Comments."
LPSTR	*lpszPath*	Output	Path of the target directory of the installation.
UINT	*cbPathMax*	Input	Length of *lpszPath*. This must be at least _MAX_PATH bytes.
UINT FAR *	*pcbPathOut*	Output	Total number of bytes (excluding the null termination byte) returned in *lpszPath*. If the number of bytes available to return is greater than or equal to *cbPathMax*, the path in *lpszPath* is truncated to *cbPathMax* – 1 bytes.

Returns

The function returns TRUE if it is successful. It returns FALSE if it fails.

Comments

If *lpszInfFile* is a null pointer, *lpszDriver* is a list of attributes in the form of keyword-value pairs; note that this functionality is not supported by the 1.0 version of the installer DLL. Each pair is terminated with a null byte and the entire list is terminated with a null byte (that is, two null bytes mark the end of the list). The format of this list is:

*driver-desc***\0Driver=***driver-DLL-filename***\0**[**Setup=***setup-DLL-filename***\0**]
➥[*driver-attr-keyword1=value1***\0**][*driver-attr-keyword2=value2***\0**]...**\0**

where \0 is a null byte and *driver-attr-keywordn* is any driver attribute keyword described in "Driver Keyword Sections" in Chapter 19, "Installing ODBC Software." The keywords must appear in the specified order. For example, suppose a driver for formatted text files has separate driver and setup DLLs and can use files with the .TXT and .CSV extensions. The *lpszDriver* argument for this driver might be:

```
Text\0Driver=TEXT.DLL\0Setup=TXTSETUP.DLL\0FileUsage=1\0
➥FileExtns=*.txt,*.csv\0\0
```

Suppose that a driver for SQL Server does not have a separate setup DLL and does not have any driver attribute keywords. The *lpszDriver* argument for this driver might be:

```
SQL Server\0Driver=SQLSRVR.DLL\0\0
```

After **SQLInstallDriver** retrieves information about the driver from the *lpszDriver* argument or the ODBC.INF file, it adds the driver description to the [ODBC Drivers] section of the ODBCINST.INI file. It then creates a section titled with the driver's description and adds the full paths of the driver DLL and the setup DLL. Finally, it returns the path of the target directory of the installation but does not copy the driver files to it. The calling program must actually copy the driver files to the target directory.

Related Functions

For information about	See
Installing the Driver Manager	**SQLInstallDriverManager**

SQLInstallDriverManager

Purpose   **SQLInstallDriverManager** returns the path of the target directory for the installation. The calling program must actually copy the Driver Manager's files to the target directory.

Syntax   BOOL **SQLInstallDriverManager**(*lpszPath*, *cbPathMax*, *pcbPathOut*)

The **SQLInstallDriverManager** function accepts the following arguments.

Type	Argument	Use	Description
LPSTR	*lpszPath*	Output	Path of the target directory of the installation.
UINT	*cbPathMax*	Input	Length of *lpszPath*. This must be at least _MAX_PATH bytes.
UINT FAR *	*pcbPathOut*	Output	Total number of bytes (excluding the null termination byte) returned in *lpszPath*. If the number of bytes available to return is greater than or equal to *cbPathMax*, the path in *lpszPath* is truncated to *cbPathMax* – 1 bytes.

Returns   The function returns TRUE if it is successful. It returns FALSE if it fails.

Related Functions

For information about	See
Installing a driver	**SQLInstallDriver**

SQLInstallODBC

Purpose

SQLInstallODBC installs the ODBC software from a disk or hard drive. The hard drive can be a network drive. **SQLInstallODBC** adds information about the installed drivers and translators to the ODBCINST.INI file (or registry).

Syntax

BOOL **SQLInstallODBC**(*hwnd*, *lpszINF*, *lpszSrc*, *lpszDrivers*)

The **SQLInstallODBC** function accepts the following arguments.

Type	Argument	Use	Description
HWND	*hwnd*	Input	Parent window handle. The function does not display any dialog boxes if the handle is null.
LPSTR	*lpszINF*	Input	Full path of the .INF file describing the ODBC software to be installed. For example, A:\ODBC\ODBC.INF.
LPSTR	*lpszSrc*	Input	Absolute directory name specifying the location of the files to be installed. This can be different from the directory containing the .INF file. If *lpszSrc* is a null pointer or an empty string, the files to be installed are assumed to be in the directory containing the .INF file.
LPSTR	*lpszDrivers*	Input	List of drivers to install. For more information, see "Comments."

Returns

SQLInstallODBC returns TRUE if the ODBC software is successfully installed. Otherwise, it returns FALSE. Reasons for failure include, but are not limited to:

- The .INF file specified in *lpszINF* is not found or does not use the correct format.
- The user cancels the installation.
- The installation fails for any reason, such as insufficient disk space.

Comments

lpszDrivers Argument

If *lpszDrivers* is not a null pointer and is not an empty string, it must contain a list of driver names. The name of each driver in the list must be null-terminated and the entire list must be null-terminated (that is, two null bytes mark the end of the list). **SQLInstallODBC** installs the drivers in the list and the rest of the ODBC software.

If *lpszDrivers* is a null pointer or an empty string and *hwndParent* is not null, **SQLInstallODBC** displays a dialog box that allows the user to select the drivers to install. After the user has selected the drivers, **SQLInstallODBC** installs the drivers and the rest of the ODBC software.

If *lpszDrivers* is a null pointer or an empty string and *hwndParent* is a null pointer, **SQLInstallODBC** installs all ODBC software except drivers.

Installing the ODBC Software

SQLInstallODBC can check the version of shipped ODBC components (Driver Manager, drivers, translators, and so on) against the version of previously installed ODBC components. If *hwndParent* is not null, the user controls version checking with the Advanced Installation Options dialog box (described later in this section). If the version of an ODBC component (a driver, the Driver Manager, the installer DLL, or a translator) is less than the version of an installed component and *hwndParent* is not null, **SQLInstallODBC** asks if the user wants to overwrite the installed component; if the version of a new component is less than the version of an installed component and *hwndParent* is null, **SQLInstallODBC** does not install the component.

Note If the user disables version checking, **SQLInstallODBC** still checks the versions of files labeled SHARED in the .INF file.

To determine the version number of a driver, **SQLInstallODBC** checks the version number of the file specified with the **Driver** keyword in the .INF file. To determine the version number of a translator, **SQLInstallODBC** checks the version number of the file specified with the **Translator** keyword in the .INF file.

SQLInstallODBC installs all files in the directory containing the Windows system DLLs (usually the C:\WINDOWS\SYSTEM directory).

On Windows 3.1, **SQLInstallODBC** adds ODBCINST.DLL to the list of control panel devices in the [MMCPL] section of the CONTROL.INI file. On Windows NT, **SQLInstallODBC** adds the value named ODBC with data consisting of the path of ODBCCP32.DLL to the HKEY_CURRENT_USER \ CONTROL PANEL \ MMCPL keys in the registry.

Creating Data Sources

If the .INF file contains the **CreateDSN** keyword, **SQLInstallODBC** calls **ConfigDSN** in the driver setup DLL with a null parent window handle to silently add each listed data source. In the *lpszAttributes* argument, it passes the **DSN** keyword and the listed data source name; the **Driver** keyword and the driver description; and any keyword-value pairs listed in the section of the .INF file that describes the data source.

Adding Driver Attribute Keywords

If the .INF file contains any driver attribute keywords, **SQLInstallODBC** adds them to the section of the ODBCINST.INI file (or the registry) that describes the driver.

Displaying Dialog Boxes

If *hwndParent* is not null, **SQLInstallODBC** can display three dialog boxes. The Install Drivers dialog box displays a list of drivers to install:

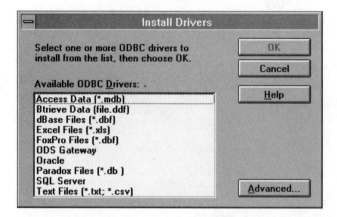

SQLInstallODBC retrieves the list of drivers from the [ODBC Drivers] section of the .INF file. The user selects the drivers, if any, to install. If the user chooses the Advanced button, **SQLInstallODBC** displays the Advanced Installation Options dialog box:

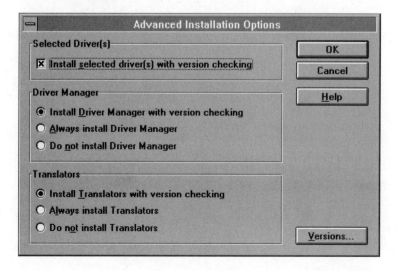

The user selects whether to use version checking when the drivers are installed, how and if the Driver Manager is installed, and how and if the translators (listed in the [ODBC Translators] section of the .INF file) are installed.

Note The Driver Manager section of the Advanced Installation Options dialog box controls the installation of the redistributable ODBC components, including the Driver Manager, the installer DLL, and the cursor library.

If the user chooses the Versions button, **SQLInstallODBC** displays the Versions dialog box:

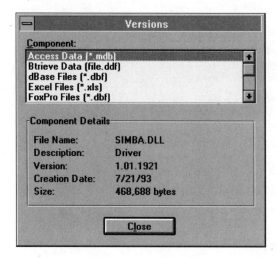

The user selects the driver for which information is to be displayed.

Related Functions

For information about	See
Creating data sources	**SQLCreateDataSource**
Managing data sources	**SQLManageDataSources**

SQLManageDataSources

Purpose

SQLManageDataSources displays a dialog box with which users can set up, add, and delete data sources. Users can also add and delete drivers.

Syntax

BOOL **SQLManageDataSources**(*hwnd*)

The **SQLManageDataSources** function accepts the following arguments.

Type	Argument	Use	Description
HWND	*hwnd*	Input	Parent window handle.

Returns

SQLManageDataSources returns FALSE if *hwnd* is not a valid window handle. Otherwise, it returns TRUE.

Comments

Managing Data Sources

SQLManageDataSources initially displays the Data Sources dialog box:

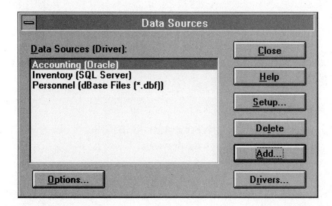

The dialog box displays the data sources listed in the ODBC.INI file (or registry). If the user double-clicks a data source or selects a data source and chooses the Setup button, **SQLManageDataSources** calls **ConfigDSN** in the setup DLL with the ODBC_CONFIG_DSN option.

If the user chooses the Add button, **SQLManageDataSources** displays the Add Data Source dialog box:

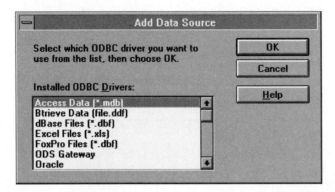

The dialog box displays a list of installed drivers. If the user double-clicks a driver or selects a driver and chooses the OK button, **SQLManageDataSources** calls **ConfigDSN** in the setup DLL and passes it the ODBC_ADD_DSN option.

If the user selects a data source and chooses the Delete button, **SQLManageDataSources** asks if the user wants to delete the data source. If the user chooses the Yes button, **SQLManageDataSources** calls **ConfigDSN** in the setup DLL with the ODBC_REMOVE_DSN option.

Managing Drivers

If the user chooses the Drivers button in the Data Sources dialog box, **SQLManageDataSources** displays the Drivers dialog box:

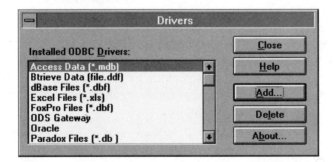

If the user chooses the Add button, **SQLManageDataSources** displays a dialog box in which the user can enter or browse for the name of a directory containing the ODBC.INF file. **SQLManageDataSources** then displays a dialog box from which the user can select drivers to install. **SQLManageDataSources** installs the selected drivers and other ODBC components.

If the user selects a driver and chooses the Delete button, **SQLManageDataSources** asks if the user wants to delete the driver and all associated data sources. If the user chooses the Yes button, **SQLManageDataSources** calls **ConfigDSN** in the setup DLL with the ODBC_REMOVE_DSN option for each data source that uses the driver. It then deletes the driver DLL and any associated files, and removes references to the driver from the ODBCINST.INI file (or registry).

If the user selects a driver and chooses the About button, **SQLManageDataSources** displays information about the selected driver.

Setting Options

If the user chooses the Options button in the Data Sources dialog box, **SQLManageDataSources** displays the Options dialog box:

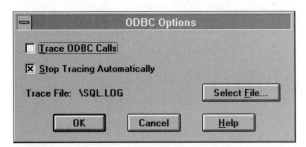

If the user selects or clears the Trace ODBC Calls check box and chooses the OK button, **SQLManageDataSources** sets the **Trace** keyword in the [ODBC] section of the ODBC.INI file (or registry) to 1 or 0 accordingly.

If the user selects or clears the Stop Tracing Automatically check box and chooses the OK button, **SQLManageDataSources** sets the **TraceAutoStop** keyword in the [ODBC] section of the ODBC.INI file (or registry) to 1 or 0 accordingly.

If the user specifies the name of a trace file with the Select File button, **SQLManageDataSources** displays the name of the trace file. When the user chooses the OK button, **SQLManageDataSources** sets the **TraceFile** keyword in the [ODBC] section of the ODBC.INI file (or registry) to the specified name.

For more information about the **Trace**, **TraceAutoStop**, and **TraceFile** keywords, see "ODBC Options Section" in Chapter 20, "Configuring Data Sources."

Related Functions	**For information about**	**See**
	Creating data sources	**SQLCreateDataSource**
	Installing ODBC software	**SQLInstallODBC**

SQLRemoveDefaultDataSource

Purpose   **SQLRemoveDefaultDataSource** removes the default data source specification section from the ODBC.INI file (or registry). It also removes the default driver specification section from the ODBCINST.INI file (or registry).

Syntax   BOOL **SQLRemoveDefaultDataSource**(*void*)

The **SQLRemoveDefaultDataSource** function does not accept any arguments.

Returns   The function returns TRUE if it is successful. It returns FALSE if it fails.

Related Functions

For information about	See
Adding, modifying, or removing a data source	**ConfigDSN**
Adding, modifying, or removing a data source	**SQLConfigDataSource**

SQLRemoveDSNFromIni

Purpose

SQLRemoveDSNFromIni removes a data source from the ODBC.INI file (or registry).

Syntax

BOOL **SQLRemoveDSNFromIni**(*lpszDSN*)

The **SQLRemoveDSNFromIni** function accepts the following arguments.

Type	Argument	Use	Description
LPCSTR	*lpszDSN*	Input	Name of the data source to remove.

Returns

The function returns TRUE if it removes the data source or the data source was not in the ODBC.INI file. It returns FALSE if it fails to remove the data source.

Comments

SQLRemoveDSNFromIni removes the data source name from the [ODBC Data Sources] section of the ODBC.INI file (or registry). It also removes the data source specification section from the file (or registry).

This function should only be called from a setup DLL.

Related Functions

For information about	See
Adding, modifying, or removing a data source	**ConfigDSN**
Adding, modifying, or removing a data source	**SQLConfigDataSource**
Removing the default data source	**SQLRemoveDefaultDataSource**
Adding a data source name to ODBC.INI (or registry)	**SQLWriteDSNToIni**

SQLWriteDSNTolni

ODBC 1.0

Purpose   **SQLWriteDSNToIni** adds a data source to the ODBC.INI file (or registry).

Syntax   BOOL **SQLWriteDSNToIni**(*lpszDSN*, *lpszDriver*)

The **SQLWriteDSNToIni** function accepts the following arguments.

Type	Argument	Use	Description
LPCSTR	*lpszDSN*	Input	Name of the data source to add.
LPCSTR	*lpszDriver*	Input	Driver description (usually the name of the associated DBMS) presented to users instead of the physical driver name.

Returns   The function returns TRUE if it is successful. It returns FALSE if it fails.

Comments   **SQLWriteDSNToIni** adds the data source to the [ODBC Data Sources] section of the ODBC.INI file (or registry). It then creates a specification section for the data source and adds a single keyword (Driver) with the name of the driver DLL as its value. If the data source specification section already exists, **SQLWriteDSNToIni** removes the old section before creating the new one.

The caller of this function must add any driver-specific keywords and values to the data source specification section of the ODBC.INI file (or registry).

If the name of the data source is Default, **SQLWriteDSNToIni** also creates the default driver specification section in the ODBCINST.INI file (or registry).

This function should only be called from a setup DLL.

Related Functions

For information about	See
Adding, modifying, or removing a data source	**ConfigDSN**
Adding, modifying, or removing a data source	**SQLConfigDataSource**
Removing a data source name from ODBC.INI (or registry)	**SQLRemoveDSNFromIni**

SQLWritePrivateProfileString

Purpose
On Windows, **SQLWritePrivateProfileString** is a macro that calls **WritePrivateProfileString** in the Windows API. On Windows NT, **SQLWritePrivateProfileString** writes a value name and data to the ODBC.INI subkey of the registry.

Syntax
The syntax and return values of **SQLWritePrivateProfileString** are the same as those of **WritePrivateProfileString** in the Windows and Win32 APIs, except that *lpszFilename* can only be "ODBC.INI". For more information, see the *Microsoft Win32 SDK Programmer's Reference*.

Comments
SQLWritePrivateProfileString is provided as a simple way to port drivers and driver setup DLLs from Windows to Windows NT. Calls to **WritePrivateProfileString** that write a profile string to the ODBC.INI file should be replaced with calls to **SQLWritePrivateProfileString**. **SQLWritePrivateProfileString** calls functions in the Win32 API to add the specified value name and data to the ODBC.INI subkey of the registry.

Related Functions

For information about	See
Getting a value from the ODBC.INI file or the registry	**SQLGetPrivateProfileString**

CHAPTER 25

Translation DLL Function Reference

The following section describes the syntax of the translation DLL API, which consists of two functions: **SQLDriverToDataSource** and **SQLDataSourceToDriver**. These functions must be included in the DLL which performs translation for the driver.

For information on argument naming conventions, see Chapter 22, "ODBC Function Reference."

SQLDataSourceToDriver

Extension Level 2   **SQLDataSourceToDriver** supports translations for ODBC drivers. This function is not called by ODBC-enabled applications; applications request translation through **SQLSetConnectOption**. The driver associated with the *hdbc* specified in **SQLSetConnectOption** calls the specified DLL to perform translations of all data flowing from the data source to the driver. A default translation DLL can be specified in the ODBC initialization file.

Syntax   BOOL **SQLDataSourceToDriver**(*fOption, fSqlType, rgbValueIn, cbValueIn, rgbValueOut, cbValueOutMax, pcbValueOut, szErrorMsg, cbErrorMsgMax, pcbErrorMsg*)

The **SQLDataSourceToDriver** function accepts the following arguments:

Type	Argument	Use	Description
UDWORD	*fOption*	Input	Option value.
SWORD	*fSqlType*	Input	The SQL data type. This argument tells the driver how to convert *rgbValueIn* into a form acceptable by the application. This must be one of the following values:
			SQL_BIGINT
			SQL_BINARY
			SQL_BIT
			SQL_CHAR
			SQL_DATE
			SQL_DECIMAL
			SQL_DOUBLE
			SQL_FLOAT
			SQL_INTEGER
			SQL_LONGVARBINARY
			SQL_LONGVARCHAR
			SQL_NUMERIC
			SQL_REAL
			SQL_SMALLINT
			SQL_TIME
			SQL_TIMESTAMP
			SQL_TINYINT
			SQL_VARBINARY
			SQL_VARCHAR
			For information about SQL data types, see "SQL Data Types" in Appendix D, "Data Types."

Type	Argument	Use	Description
PTR	*rgbValueIn*	Input	Value to translate.
SDWORD	*cbValueIn*	Input	Length of *rgbValueIn*.
PTR	*rgbValueOut*	Output	Result of the translation.
			Note The translation DLL does not null-terminate this value.
SDWORD	*cbValueOutMax*	Input	Length of *rgbValueOut*.
SDWORD FAR *	*pcbValueOut*	Output	The total number of bytes (excluding the null termination byte) available to return in *rgbValueOut*. For character or binary data, if this is greater than or equal to *cbValueOutMax*, the data in *rgbValueOut* is truncated to *cbValueOutMax* bytes. For all other data types, the value of *cbValueOutMax* is ignored and the translation DLL assumes the size of *rgbValueOut* is the size of the default C data type of the SQL data type specified with *fSqlType*.
UCHAR FAR *	*szErrorMsg*	Output	Pointer to storage for an error message. This is an empty string unless the translation failed.
SWORD	*cbErrorMsgMax*	Input	Length of *szErrorMsg*.
SWORD FAR *	*pcbErrorMsg*	Output	Pointer to the total number of bytes (excluding the null termination byte) available to return in *szErrorMsg*. If this is greater than or equal to *cbErrorMsg*, the data in *szErrorMsg* is truncated to *cbErrorMsgMax* – 1 bytes.

Returns   TRUE if the translation was successful.

FALSE if the translation failed.

Comments

The driver calls **SQLDataSourceToDriver** to translate *all* data (result set data, table names, row counts, error messages, and so on) passing from the data source to the driver. The translation DLL may not translate some data, depending on the data's type and the purpose of the translation DLL; for example, a DLL that translates character data from one code page to another ignores all numeric and binary data.

The value of *fOption* is set to the value of *vParam* specified by calling **SQLSetConnectOption** with the SQL_TRANSLATE_OPTION option. It is a 32-bit value which has a specific meaning for a given translation DLL. For example, it could specify a certain character set translation.

If the same buffer is specified for *rgbValueIn* and *rgbValueOut*, the translation of data in the buffer will be performed in place.

Note that, although *cbValueIn*, *cbValueOutMax*, and *pcbValueOut* are of the type SDWORD, **SQLDataSourceToDriver** does not necessarily support huge pointers.

If **SQLDataSourceToDriver** returns FALSE, data truncation may have occurred during translation. If *pcbValueOut*, the number of bytes available to return in the output buffer, is greater than *cbValueOutMax*, the length of the output buffer, then truncation occurred. The driver must determine whether the truncation was acceptable. If truncation did not occur, the **SQLDataSourceToDriver** returned FALSE due to another error. In either case, a specific error message is returned in *szErrorMsg*.

For more information about translating data, see "Translating Data" in Chapter 13, "Establishing Connections."

Related Functions

For information about	See
Translating data being sent to the data source	**SQLDriverToDataSource**
Returning the setting of a connection option	**SQLGetConnectOption** (extension)
Setting a connection option	**SQLSetConnectOption** (extension)

SQLDriverToDataSource

Extension Level 2   **SQLDriverToDataSource** supports translations for ODBC drivers. This function is not called by ODBC-enabled applications; applications request translation through **SQLSetConnectOption**. The driver associated with the *hdbc* specified in **SQLSetConnectOption** calls the specified DLL to perform translations of all data flowing from the driver to the data source. A default translation DLL can be specified in the ODBC initialization file.

Syntax   BOOL **SQLDriverToDataSource**(*fOption*, *fSqlType*, *rgbValueIn*, *cbValueIn*, *rgbValueOut*, *cbValueOutMax*, *pcbValueOut*, *szErrorMsg*, *cbErrorMsg*, *pcbErrorMsg*)

The **SQLDriverToDataSource** function accepts the following arguments:

Type	Argument	Use	Description
UDWORD	*fOption*	Input	Option value.
SWORD	*fSqlType*	Input	The ODBC SQL data type. This argument tells the driver how to convert *rgbValueIn* into a form acceptable by the data source. This must be one of the following values:
			SQL_BIGINT
			SQL_BINARY
			SQL_BIT
			SQL_CHAR
			SQL_DATE
			SQL_DECIMAL
			SQL_DOUBLE
			SQL_FLOAT
			SQL_INTEGER
			SQL_LONGVARBINARY
			SQL_LONGVARCHAR
			SQL_NUMERIC
			SQL_REAL
			SQL_SMALLINT
			SQL_TIME
			SQL_TIMESTAMP
			SQL_TINYINT
			SQL_VARBINARY
			SQL_VARCHAR
			For information about SQL data types, see "SQL Data Types" in Appendix D, "Data Types."
PTR	*rgbValueIn*	Input	Value to translate.

Type	Argument	Use	Description
SDWORD	cbValueIn	Input	Length of rgbValueIn.
PTR	rgbValueOut	Output	Result of the translation.
			Note The translation DLL does not null-terminate this value.
SDWORD	cbValueOutMax	Input	Length of rgbValueOut.
SDWORD FAR *	pcbValueOut	Output	The total number of bytes (excluding the null termination byte) available to return in rgbValueOut.
			For character or binary data, if this is greater than or equal to cbValueOutMax, the data in rgbValueOut is truncated to cbValueOutMax bytes.
			For all other data types, the value of cbValueOutMax is ignored and the translation DLL assumes the size of rgbValueOut is the size of the default C data type of the SQL data type specified with fSqlType.
UCHAR FAR *	szErrorMsg	Output	Pointer to storage for an error message. This is an empty string unless the translation failed.
SWORD	cbErrorMsgMax	Input	Length of szErrorMsg.
SWORD FAR *	pcbErrorMsg	Output	Pointer to the total number of bytes (excluding the null termination byte) available to return in szErrorMsg. If this is greater than or equal to cbErrorMsg, the data in szErrorMsg is truncated to cbErrorMsgMax − 1 bytes.

Returns TRUE if the translation was successful.

FALSE if the translation failed.

Comments   The driver calls **SQLDriverToDataSource** to translate *all* data (SQL statements, parameters, and so on) passing from the driver to the data source. The translation DLL may not translate some data, depending on the data's type and the purpose of the translation DLL. For example, a DLL that translates character data from one code page to another ignores all numeric and binary data.

The value of *fOption* is set to the value of *vParam* specified by calling **SQLSetConnectOption** with the SQL_TRANSLATE_OPTION option. It is a 32-bit value which has a specific meaning for a given translation DLL. For example, it could specify a certain character set translation.

If the same buffer is specified for *rgbValueIn* and *rgbValueOut*, the translation of data in the buffer will be performed in-place.

Note that, although *cbValueIn*, *cbValueOutMax*, and *pcbValueOut* are of the type SDWORD, **SQLDriverToDataSource** does not necessarily support huge pointers.

If **SQLDriverToDataSource** returns FALSE, data truncation may have occurred during translation. If *pcbValueOut*, the number of bytes available to return in the output buffer, is greater than *cbValueOutMax*, the length of the output buffer, then truncation occurred. The driver must determine whether or not the truncation was acceptable. If truncation did not occur, the **SQLDriverToDataSource** returned FALSE due to another error. In either case, a specific error message is returned in *szErrorMsg*.

For more information about translating data, see "Translating Data" in Chapter 13, "Establishing Connections."

Related Functions

For information about	See
Translating data returned from the data source	**SQLDataSourceToDriver**
Returning the setting of a connection option	**SQLGetConnectOption** (extension)
Setting a connection option	**SQLSetConnectOption** (extension)

Appendixes

APPENDIX A

ODBC Error Codes

SQLError returns SQLSTATE values as defined by the X/Open and SQL Access Group SQL CAE specification (1992). SQLSTATE values are strings that contain five characters. The following table lists SQLSTATE values that a driver can return for **SQLError**.

The character string value returned for an SQLSTATE consists of a two character class value followed by a three character subclass value. A class value of "01" indicates a warning and is accompanied by a return code of SQL_SUCCESS_WITH_INFO. Class values other than "01", except for the class "IM", indicate an error and are accompanied by a return code of SQL_ERROR. The class "IM" is specific to warnings and errors that derive from the implementation of ODBC itself. The subclass value "000" in any class is for implementation defined conditions within the given class. The assignment of class and subclass values is defined by ANSI SQL-92.

Note Although successful execution of a function is normally indicated by a return value of SQL_SUCCESS, the SQLSTATE 00000 also indicates success.

SQLSTATE	Error	Can be returned from
01000	General warning	All ODBC functions except:
		SQLAllocEnv
		SQLError
01002	Disconnect error	**SQLDisconnect**

SQLSTATE	Error	Can be returned from
01004	Data truncated	**SQLBrowseConnect** **SQLColAttributes** **SQLDataSources** **SQLDescribeCol** **SQLDriverConnect** **SQLDrivers** **SQLExecDirect** **SQLExecute** **SQLExtendedFetch** **SQLFetch** **SQLGetCursorName** **SQLGetData** **SQLGetInfo** **SQLNativeSql** **SQLPutData** **SQLSetPos**
01006	Privilege not revoked	**SQLExecDirect** **SQLExecute**
01S00	Invalid connection string attribute	**SQLBrowseConnect** **SQLDriverConnect**
01S01	Error in row	**SQLExtendedFetch** **SQLSetPos**
01S02	Option value changed	**SQLSetConnectOption** **SQLSetStmtOption**
01S03	No rows updated or deleted	**SQLExecDirect** **SQLExecute** **SQLSetPos**
01S04	More than one row updated or deleted	**SQLExecDirect** **SQLExecute** **SQLSetPos**
07001	Wrong number of parameters	**SQLExecDirect** **SQLExecute**
07006	Restricted data type attribute violation	**SQLBindParameter** **SQLExtendedFetch** **SQLFetch** **SQLGetData**
08001	Unable to connect to data source	**SQLBrowseConnect** **SQLConnect** **SQLDriverConnect**
08002	Connection in use	**SQLBrowseConnect** **SQLConnect** **SQLDriverConnect** **SQLSetConnectOption**

SQLSTATE	Error	Can be returned from
08003	Connection not open	**SQLAllocStmt** **SQLDisconnect** **SQLGetConnectOption** **SQLGetInfo** **SQLNativeSql** **SQLSetConnectOption** **SQLTransact**
08004	Data source rejected establishment of connection	**SQLBrowseConnect** **SQLConnect** **SQLDriverConnect**
08007	Connection failure during transaction	**SQLTransact**
08S01	Communication link failure	**SQLBrowseConnect** **SQLColumnPrivileges** **SQLColumns** **SQLConnect** **SQLDriverConnect** **SQLExecDirect** **SQLExecute** **SQLExtendedFetch** **SQLFetch** **SQLForeignKeys** **SQLFreeConnect** **SQLGetData** **SQLGetTypeInfo** **SQLParamData** **SQLPrepare** **SQLPrimaryKeys** **SQLProcedureColumns** **SQLProcedures** **SQLPutData** **SQLSetConnectOption** **SQLSetStmtOption** **SQLSpecialColumns** **SQLStatistics** **SQLTablePrivileges** **SQLTables**
21S01	Insert value list does not match column list	**SQLExecDirect** **SQLPrepare**
21S02	Degree of derived table does not match column list	**SQLExecDirect** **SQLPrepare** **SQLSetPos**
22001	String data right truncation	**SQLPutData**

SQLSTATE	Error	Can be returned from
22003	Numeric value out of range	**SQLExecDirect** **SQLExecute** **SQLExtendedFetch** **SQLFetch** **SQLGetData** **SQLGetInfo** **SQLPutData** **SQLSetPos**
22005	Error in assignment	**SQLExecDirect** **SQLExecute** **SQLGetData** **SQLPrepare** **SQLPutData** **SQLSetPos**
22008	Datetime field overflow	**SQLExecDirect** **SQLExecute** **SQLGetData** **SQLPutData** **SQLSetPos**
22012	Division by zero	**SQLExecDirect** **SQLExecute** **SQLExtendedFetch** **SQLFetch**
22026	String data, length mismatch	**SQLParamData**
23000	Integrity constraint violation	**SQLExecDirect** **SQLExecute** **SQLSetPos**

SQLSTATE	Error	Can be returned from
24000	Invalid cursor state	**SQLColAttributes** **SQLColumnPrivileges** **SQLColumns** **SQLDescribeCol** **SQLExecDirect** **SQLExecute** **SQLExtendedFetch** **SQLFetch** **SQLForeignKeys** **SQLGetData** **SQLGetStmtOption** **SQLGetTypeInfo** **SQLPrepare** **SQLPrimaryKeys** **SQLProcedureColumns** **SQLProcedures** **SQLSetCursorName** **SQLSetPos** **SQLSetStmtOption** **SQLSpecialColumns** **SQLStatistics** **SQLTablePrivileges** **SQLTables**
25000	Invalid transaction state	**SQLDisconnect**
28000	Invalid authorization specification	**SQLBrowseConnect** **SQLConnect** **SQLDriverConnect**
34000	Invalid cursor name	**SQLExecDirect** **SQLPrepare** **SQLSetCursorName**
37000	Syntax error or access violation	**SQLExecDirect** **SQLNativeSql** **SQLPrepare**
3C000	Duplicate cursor name	**SQLSetCursorName**
40001	Serialization failure	**SQLExecDirect** **SQLExecute** **SQLExtendedFetch** **SQLFetch**
42000	Syntax error or access violation	**SQLExecDirect** **SQLExecute** **SQLPrepare** **SQLSetPos**
70100	Operation aborted	**SQLCancel**

SQLSTATE	Error	Can be returned from
IM001	Driver does not support this function	All ODBC functions except: **SQLAllocConnect** **SQLAllocEnv** **SQLDataSources** **SQLDrivers** **SQLError** **SQLFreeConnect** **SQLFreeEnv** **SQLGetFunctions**
IM002	Data source name not found and no default driver specified	**SQLBrowseConnect** **SQLConnect** **SQLDriverConnect**
IM003	Specified driver could not be loaded	**SQLBrowseConnect** **SQLConnect** **SQLDriverConnect**
IM004	Driver's **SQLAllocEnv** failed	**SQLBrowseConnect** **SQLConnect** **SQLDriverConnect**
IM005	Driver's **SQLAllocConnect** failed	**SQLBrowseConnect** **SQLConnect** **SQLDriverConnect**
IM006	Driver's **SQLSetConnect-Option** failed	**SQLBrowseConnect** **SQLConnect** **SQLDriverConnect**
IM007	No data source or driver specified; dialog prohibited	**SQLDriverConnect**
IM008	Dialog failed	**SQLDriverConnect**
IM009	Unable to load translation DLL	**SQLBrowseConnect** **SQLConnect** **SQLDriverConnect** **SQLSetConnectOption**
IM010	Data source name too long	**SQLBrowseConnect** **SQLDriverConnect**
IM011	Driver name too long	**SQLBrowseConnect** **SQLDriverConnect**
IM012	DRIVER keyword syntax error	**SQLBrowseConnect** **SQLDriverConnect**
IM013	Trace file error	All ODBC functions.
S0001	Base table or view already exists	**SQLExecDirect** **SQLPrepare**

SQLSTATE	Error	Can be returned from
S0002	Base table not found	**SQLExecDirect** **SQLPrepare**
S0011	Index already exists	**SQLExecDirect** **SQLPrepare**
S0012	Index not found	**SQLExecDirect** **SQLPrepare**
S0021	Column already exists	**SQLExecDirect** **SQLPrepare**
S0022	Column not found	**SQLExecDirect** **SQLPrepare**
S0023	No default for column	**SQLSetPos**
S1000	General error	All ODBC functions except: **SQLAllocEnv** **SQLError**
S1001	Memory allocation failure	All ODBC functions except: **SQLAllocEnv** **SQLError** **SQLFreeConnect** **SQLFreeEnv**
S1002	Invalid column number	**SQLBindCol** **SQLColAttributes** **SQLDescribeCol** **SQLExtendedFetch** **SQLFetch** **SQLGetData**
S1003	Program type out of range	**SQLBindCol** **SQLBindParameter** **SQLGetData**
S1004	SQL data type out of range	**SQLBindParameter** **SQLGetTypeInfo**

SQLSTATE	Error	Can be returned from
S1008	Operation canceled	All ODBC functions that can be processed asynchronously: **SQLColAttributes** **SQLColumnPrivileges** **SQLColumns** **SQLDescribeCol** **SQLDescribeParam** **SQLExecDirect** **SQLExecute** **SQLExtendedFetch** **SQLFetch** **SQLForeignKeys** **SQLGetData** **SQLGetTypeInfo** **SQLMoreResults** **SQLNumParams** **SQLNumResultCols** **SQLParamData** **SQLPrepare** **SQLPrimaryKeys** **SQLProcedureColumns** **SQLProcedures** **SQLPutData** **SQLSetPos** **SQLSpecialColumns** **SQLStatistics** **SQLTablePrivileges** **SQLTables**
S1009	Invalid argument value	**SQLAllocConnect** **SQLAllocStmt** **SQLBindCol** **SQLBindParameter** **SQLExecDirect** **SQLForeignKeys** **SQLGetData** **SQLGetInfo** **SQLNativeSql** **SQLPrepare** **SQLPutData** **SQLSetConnectOption** **SQLSetCursorName** **SQLSetPos** **SQLSetStmtOption**

SQLSTATE	Error	Can be returned from
S1010	Function sequence error	**SQLBindCol**
		SQLBindParameter
		SQLColAttributes
		SQLColumnPrivileges
		SQLColumns
		SQLDescribeCol
		SQLDescribeParam
		SQLDisconnect
		SQLExecDirect
		SQLExecute
		SQLExtendedFetch
		SQLFetch
		SQLForeignKeys
		SQLFreeConnect
		SQLFreeEnv
		SQLFreeStmt
		SQLGetConnectOption
		SQLGetCursorName
		SQLGetData
		SQLGetFunctions
		SQLGetStmtOption
		SQLGetTypeInfo
		SQLMoreResults
		SQLNumParams
		SQLNumResultCols
		SQLParamData
		SQLParamOptions
		SQLPrepare
		SQLPrimaryKeys
		SQLProcedureColumns
		SQLProcedures
		SQLPutData
		SQLRowCount
		SQLSetConnectOption
		SQLSetCursorName
		SQLSetPos
		SQLSetScrollOptions
		SQLSetStmtOption
		SQLSpecialColumns
		SQLStatistics
		SQLTablePrivileges
		SQLTables
		SQLTransact
S1011	Operation invalid at this time	**SQLGetStmtOption**
		SQLSetConnectOption
		SQLSetStmtOption

SQLSTATE	Error	Can be returned from
S1012	Invalid transaction operation code specified	**SQLTransact**
S1015	No cursor name available	**SQLGetCursorName**
S1090	Invalid string or buffer length	**SQLBindCol** **SQLBindParameter** **SQLBrowseConnect** **SQLColAttributes** **SQLColumnPrivileges** **SQLColumns** **SQLConnect** **SQLDataSources** **SQLDescribeCol** **SQLDriverConnect** **SQLDrivers** **SQLExecDirect** **SQLExecute** **SQLForeignKeys** **SQLGetCursorName** **SQLGetData** **SQLGetInfo** **SQLNativeSql** **SQLPrepare** **SQLPrimaryKeys** **SQLProcedureColumns** **SQLProcedures** **SQLPutData** **SQLSetCursorName** **SQLSetPos** **SQLSpecialColumns** **SQLStatistics** **SQLTablePrivileges** **SQLTables**
S1091	Descriptor type out of range	**SQLColAttributes**
S1092	Option type out of range	**SQLFreeStmt** **SQLGetConnectOption** **SQLGetStmtOption** **SQLSetConnectOption** **SQLSetStmtOption**
S1093	Invalid parameter number	**SQLBindParameter** **SQLDescribeParam**
S1094	Invalid scale value	**SQLBindParameter**

SQLSTATE	Error	Can be returned from
S1095	Function type out of range	**SQLGetFunctions**
S1096	Information type out of range	**SQLGetInfo**
S1097	Column type out of range	**SQLSpecialColumns**
S1098	Scope type out of range	**SQLSpecialColumns**
S1099	Nullable type out of range	**SQLSpecialColumns**
S1100	Uniqueness option type out of range	**SQLStatistics**
S1101	Accuracy option type out of range	**SQLStatistics**
S1103	Direction option out of range	**SQLDataSources** **SQLDrivers**
S1104	Invalid precision value	**SQLBindParameter**
S1105	Invalid parameter type	**SQLBindParameter**
S1106	Fetch type out of range	**SQLExtendedFetch**
S1107	Row value out of range	**SQLExtendedFetch** **SQLParamOptions** **SQLSetPos** **SQLSetScrollOptions**
S1108	Concurrency option out of range	**SQLSetScrollOptions**
S1109	Invalid cursor position	**SQLExecute** **SQLExecDirect** **SQLGetData** **SQLGetStmtOption** **SQLSetPos**
S1110	Invalid driver completion	**SQLDriverConnect**
S1111	Invalid bookmark value	**SQLExtendedFetch**

SQLSTATE	Error	Can be returned from
S1C00	Driver not capable	**SQLBindCol**
		SQLBindParameter
		SQLColAttributes
		SQLColumnPrivileges
		SQLColumns
		SQLExecDirect
		SQLExecute
		SQLExtendedFetch
		SQLFetch
		SQLForeignKeys
		SQLGetConnectOption
		SQLGetData
		SQLGetInfo
		SQLGetStmtOption
		SQLGetTypeInfo
		SQLPrimaryKeys
		SQLProcedureColumns
		SQLProcedures
		SQLSetConnectOption
		SQLSetPos
		SQLSetScrollOptions
		SQLSetStmtOption
		SQLSpecialColumns
		SQLStatistics
		SQLTablePrivileges
		SQLTables
		SQLTransact

SQLSTATE	Error	Can be returned from
S1T00	Timeout expired	**SQLBrowseConnect**
		SQLColAttributes
		SQLColumnPrivileges
		SQLColumns
		SQLConnect
		SQLDescribeCol
		SQLDescribeParam
		SQLDriverConnect
		SQLExecDirect
		SQLExecute
		SQLExtendedFetch
		SQLFetch
		SQLForeignKeys
		SQLGetData
		SQLGetInfo
		SQLGetTypeInfo
		SQLMoreResults
		SQLNumParams
		SQLNumResultCols
		SQLParamData
		SQLPrepare
		SQLPrimaryKeys
		SQLProcedureColumns
		SQLProcedures
		SQLPutData
		SQLSetPos
		SQLSpecialColumns
		SQLStatistics
		SQLTablePrivileges
		SQLTables

A P P E N D I X   B

ODBC State Transition Tables

The tables in this appendix show how ODBC functions cause transitions of the environment, connection, and statement states. Generally speaking, the state of the environment, connection, or statement dictates when functions that use the corresponding type of handle (*henv*, *hdbc*, or *hstmt*) can be called. The environment, connection, and statement states overlap as follows, although the exact overlap of connection states C5 and C6 and statement states S1 through S12 is data source–dependent, since transactions begin at different times on different data sources. For a description of each state, see "Environment Transitions," "Connection Transitions," and "Statement Transitions," later in this appendix.

```
Environment: E0 E1                                    E2
Connection:  C0 C1 C2 C3 C4    C5                      C6
Statement:                  S0 S1 S2 S3 S4 S5 S6 S7 S8 S9 S10 S11 S12
```

Each entry in a transition table can be one of the following values:

- **--**. The state is unchanged after executing the function.

- **E**n, **C**n, or **S**n. The environment, connection, or statement state moves to the specified state.

- **(IH)**. The function returned SQL_INVALID_HANDLE. Although this error is possible in any state, it is shown only when it is the only possible outcome of calling the function in the specified state. This error does not change the state and is always detected by the Driver Manager, as indicated by the parentheses.

- **NS**. Next State. The statement transition is the same as if the statement had not gone through the asynchronous states. For example, suppose a statement that creates a result set enters state S11 from state S1 because **SQLExecDirect** returned SQL_STILL_EXECUTING. The NS notation in state S11 means that the transitions for the statement are the same as those for a statement in state S1 that creates a result set: if **SQLExecDirect** returns an error; the statement remains in state S1; if it succeeds, the statement moves to state S5; if it needs data, the statement moves to state S8; and if it is still executing, it remains in state S11.

- *XXXXX* or (*XXXXX*). An SQLSTATE that is related to the transition table; SQLSTATEs detected by the Driver Manager are enclosed in parentheses. The function returned SQL_ERROR and the specified SQLSTATE, but the state does not change. For example, if **SQLExecute** is called before **SQLPrepare**, it returns SQLSTATE S1010 (Function sequence error).

Note The tables do not show errors unrelated to the transition tables that do not change the state. For example, when **SQLAllocConnect** is called in environment state E1 and returns SQLSTATE S1001 (Memory allocation failure), the environment remains in state E1; this is not shown in the environment transition table for **SQLAllocConnect**.

If the environment, connection, or statement can move to more than one state, each possible state is shown and one or more footnotes explains the conditions under which each transition takes place. The following footnotes may appear in any table:

Footnote	Meaning
b	Before or after. The cursor was positioned before the start of the result set or after the end of the result set.
c	Current function. The current function was executing asynchronously.
d	Need data. The function returned SQL_NEED_DATA.
e	Error. The function returned SQL_ERROR.
i	Invalid row. The cursor was positioned on a row in the result set and the value in the *rgfRowStatus* array in **SQLExtendedFetch** for the row was SQL_DELETED or SQL_ERROR.
nf	Not found. The function returned SQL_NO_DATA_FOUND.
np	Not prepared. The statement was not prepared.
nr	No results. The statement will not or did not create a result set.
o	Other function. Another function was executing asynchronously.
p	Prepared. The statement was prepared.
r	Results. The statement will or did create a (possibly empty) result set.
s	Success. The function returned SQL_SUCCESS_WITH_INFO or SQL_SUCCESS.
v	Valid row. The cursor was positioned on a row in the result set and the value in the *rgfRowStatus* array in **SQLExtendedFetch** for the row was SQL_ADDED, SQL_SUCCESS, or SQL_UPDATED.
x	Executing. The function returned SQL_STILL_EXECUTING.

For example, the environment state transition table for **SQLFreeEnv** is:

SQLFreeEnv

E0 Unallocated	E1 Allocated	E2 *hdbc*
(IH)	E0	(S1010)

If **SQLFreeEnv** is called in environment state E0, the Driver Manager returns SQL_INVALID_HANDLE. If it is called in state E1, the environment moves to state E0 if the function succeeds and remains in state E1 if the function fails. If it is called in state E2, the Driver Manager always returns SQL_ERROR and SQLSTATE S1010 (Function sequence error) and the environment remains in state E2.

Environment Transitions

The ODBC environment has the following three states:

State	Description
E0	Unallocated *henv*
E1	Allocated *henv*, unallocated *hdbc*
E2	Allocated *henv*, allocated *hdbc*

The following tables show how each ODBC function affects the environment state.

SQLAllocConnect

E0 Unallocated	E1 Allocated	E2 *hdbc*
(IH)	E2	-- [1]

[1] Calling **SQLAllocConnect** with a pointer to a valid *hdbc* overwrites that *hdbc*. This may be an application programming error.

SQLAllocEnv

E0 Unallocated	E1 Allocated	E2 *hdbc*
E1	-- [1]	E1 [1]

[1] Calling **SQLAllocEnv** with a pointer to a valid *henv* overwrites that *henv*. This may be an application programming error.

SQLDataSources and SQLDrivers

E0 Unallocated	E1 Allocated	E2 *hdbc*
(IH)	--	--

SQLError

E0 Unallocated	E1 Allocated	E2 *hdbc*
(IH) [1]	--	--

1 This row shows transitions when *henv* was non-null, *hdbc* was SQL_NULL_HDBC, and *hstmt* was SQL_NULL_HSTMT.

SQLFreeConnect

E0 Unallocated	E1 Allocated	E2 *hdbc*
(IH)	(IH)	-- [1] E1 [2]

1 There were other allocated *hdbcs*.

2 The *hdbc* was the only allocated *hdbc*.

SQLFreeEnv

E0 Unallocated	E1 Allocated	E2 *hdbc*
(IH)	E0	(S1010)

SQLTransact

E0 Unallocated	E1 Allocated	E2 *hdbc*
(IH)	-- [1]	-- [1]

1 The *hdbc* argument was SQL_NULL_HDBC.

All Other ODBC Functions

E0 Unallocated	E1 Allocated	E2 *hdbc*
(IH)	(IH)	--

Connection Transitions

ODBC connections have the following states:

State	Description
C0	Unallocated *henv*, unallocated *hdbc*
C1	Allocated *henv*, unallocated *hdbc*
C2	Allocated *henv*, allocated *hdbc*
C3	Connection function needs data
C4	Connected *hdbc*
C5	Connected *hdbc*, allocated *hstmt*
C6	Connected *hdbc*, transaction in progress

The following tables show how each ODBC function affects the connection state.

SQLAllocConnect

C0 No *henv*	C1 Unallocated	C2 Allocated	C3 Need Data	C4 Connected	C5 *hstmt*	C6 Transaction
(IH)	C2	-- [1]	C2 [1]	C2 [1]	C2 [1]	C2 [1]

1 Calling **SQLAllocConnect** with a pointer to a valid *hdbc* overwrites that *hdbc*. This may be an application programming error.

SQLAllocEnv

C0 No *henv*	C1 Unallocated	C2 Allocated	C3 Need Data	C4 Connected	C5 *hstmt*	C6 Transaction
C1	-- [1]	C1 [1]	C1 [1]	C1 [1]	C1 [1]	C1 [1]

1 Calling **SQLAllocEnv** with a pointer to a valid *henv* overwrites that *henv*. This may be an application programming error.

SQLAllocStmt

C0 No *henv*	C1 Unallocated	C2 Allocated	C3 Need Data	C4 Connected	C5 *hstmt*	C6 Transaction
(IH)	(IH)	(08003)	(08003)	C5	-- [1]	C5 [1]

1 Calling **SQLAllocStmt** with a pointer to a valid *hstmt* overwrites that *hstmt*. This may be an application programming error.

SQLBrowseConnect

C0 No *henv*	C1 Unallocated	C2 Allocated	C3 Need Data	C4 Connected	C5 *hstmt*	C6 Transaction
(IH)	(IH)	C3 [d] C4 [s]	-- [d] C2 [e] C4 [s]	(08002)	(08002)	(08002)

SQLColumnPrivileges, SQLColumns, SQLForeignKeys, SQLGetTypeInfo, SQLPrimaryKeys, SQLProcedureColumns, SQLProcedures, SQLSpecialColumns, SQLStatistics, SQLTablePrivileges, and **SQLTables**

C0 No *henv*	C1 Unallocated	C2 Allocated	C3 Need Data	C4 Connected	C5 *hstmt*	C6 Transaction
(IH)	(IH)	(IH)	(IH)	(IH)	-- [1] C6 [2]	--

1 The data source was in auto-commit mode or did not begin a transaction.

2 The data source was in manual-commit mode and began a transaction.

SQLColumns: see SQLColumnPrivileges

SQLConnect and **SQLDriverConnect**

C0 No *henv*	C1 Unallocated	C2 Allocated	C3 Need Data	C4 Connected	C5 *hstmt*	C6 Transaction
(IH)	(IH)	C4	(08002)	(08002)	(08002)	(08002)

SQLDataSources and **SQLDrivers**

C0 No *henv*	C1 Unallocated	C2 Allocated	C3 Need Data	C4 Connected	C5 *hstmt*	C6 Transaction
(IH)	--	--	--	--	--	--

SQLDisconnect

C0 No *henv*	C1 Unallocated	C2 Allocated	C3 Need Data	C4 Connected	C5 *hstmt*	C6 Transaction
(IH)	(IH)	(08003)	C2	C2	C2	25000

SQLDriverConnect: see SQLConnect

SQLDrivers: see SQLDataSources

SQLError

C0 No *henv*	C1 Unallocated	C2 Allocated	C3 Need Data	C4 Connected	C5 *hstmt*	C6 Transaction
(IH) [1]	(IH)	--	--	--	--	--

1 This row shows transitions when *hdbc* was non-null and *hstmt* was SQL_NULL_HSTMT.

SQLExecDirect and **SQLExecute**

C0 No *henv*	C1 Unallocated	C2 Allocated	C3 Need Data	C4 Connected	C5 *hstmt*	C6 Transaction
(IH)	(IH)	(IH)	(IH)	(IH)	-- [1] C6 [2]	--

1 The data source was in auto-commit mode or did not begin a transaction.

2 The data source was in manual-commit mode and began a transaction.

SQLExecute: see SQLExecDirect

SQLForeignKeys: see SQLColumnPrivileges

SQLFreeConnect

C0 No *henv*	C1 Unallocated	C2 Allocated	C3 Need Data	C4 Connected	C5 *hstmt*	C6 Transaction
(IH)	(IH)	C1	(S1010)	(S1010)	(S1010)	(S1010)

SQLFreeEnv

C0 No *henv*	C1 Unallocated	C2 Allocated	C3 Need Data	C4 Connected	C5 *hstmt*	C6 Transaction
(IH)	C0 [1] (S1010) [2]	(S1010)	(S1010)	(S1010)	(S1010)	(S1010)

1 The *hdbc* was the only allocated *hdbc*.

2 There were other allocated *hdbcs*.

SQLFreeStmt

C0 No *henv*	C1 Unallocated	C2 Allocated	C3 Need Data	C4 Connected	C5 *hstmt*	C6 Transaction
(IH)	(IH)	(IH)	(IH)	(IH)	-- [1] C4 [2]	-- [1] C4 [2]

1 The *fOption* argument was SQL_CLOSE, SQL_UNBIND, or SQL_RESET_PARAMS.

2 The *fOption* argument was SQL_DROP.

SQLGetConnectOption

C0 No *henv*	C1 Unallocated	C2 Allocated	C3 Need Data	C4 Connected	C5 *hstmt*	C6 Transaction
(IH)	(IH)	-- [1] (08003) [2]	(S1010)	--	--	--

[1] The *fOption* argument was SQL_ACCESS_MODE or SQL_AUTOCOMMIT, or a value had been set for the connection option.

[2] The *fOption* argument was not SQL_ACCESS_MODE or SQL_AUTOCOMMIT, and a value had not been set for the connection option.

SQLGetFunctions

C0 No *henv*	C1 Unallocated	C2 Allocated	C3 Need Data	C4 Connected	C5 *hstmt*	C6 Transaction
(IH)	(IH)	(S1010)	(S1010)	--	--	--

SQLGetInfo

C0 No *henv*	C1 Unallocated	C2 Allocated	C3 Need Data	C4 Connected	C5 *hstmt*	C6 Transaction
(IH)	(IH)	-- [1] (08003) [2]	(08003)	--	--	--

[1] The *fInfoType* argument was SQL_ODBC_VER.

[2] The *fInfoType* argument was not SQL_ODBC_VER.

SQLGetTypeInfo: see SQLColumnPrivileges

SQLNativeSql

C0 No *henv*	C1 Unallocated	C2 Allocated	C3 Need Data	C4 Connected	C5 *hstmt*	C6 Transaction
(IH)	(IH)	(08003)	(08003)	--	--	--

SQLPrepare

C0 No *henv*	C1 Unallocated	C2 Allocated	C3 Need Data	C4 Connected	C5 *hstmt*	C6 Transaction
(IH)	(IH)	(IH)	(IH)	(IH)	-- [1] C6 [2]	--

[1] The data source was in auto-commit mode or did not begin a transaction.

[2] The data source was in manual commit mode and began a transaction.

SQLPrimaryKeys: see **SQLColumnPrivileges**

SQLProcedureColumns: see **SQLColumnPrivileges**

SQLProcedures: see **SQLColumnPrivileges**

SQLSetConnectOption

C0 No *henv*	C1 Unallocated	C2 Allocated	C3 Need Data	C4 Connected	C5 *hstmt*	C6 Transaction
(IH)	(IH)	-- [1] (08003) [2]	(S1010)	-- [3] (08002) [4]	-- [3] (08002) [4]	-- [3 and 5] C5 [6] (08002) [4] S1011 [7]

1 The *fOption* argument was not SQL_TRANSLATE_DLL or SQL_TRANSLATE_OPTION.

2 The *fOption* argument was SQL_TRANSLATE_DLL or SQL_TRANSLATE_OPTION.

3 The *fOption* argument was not SQL_ODBC_CURSORS.

4 The *fOption* argument was SQL_ODBC_CURSORS.

5 If the *fOption* argument was SQL_AUTOCOMMIT, then the data source was in manual-commit mode or the *vParam* argument was SQL_AUTOCOMMIT_OFF.

6 The data source was in manual-commit mode, the *fOption* argument was SQL_AUTOCOMMIT, and the *vParam* argument was SQL_AUTOCOMMIT_ON.

7 The data source was in manual-commit mode and the *fOption* argument was SQL_TXN_ISOLATION.

SQLSpecialColumns: see **SQLColumnPrivileges**

SQLStatistics: see **SQLColumnPrivileges**

SQLTablePrivileges: see **SQLColumnPrivileges**

SQLTables: see **SQLColumnPrivileges**

SQLTransact

C0 No *henv*	C1 Unallocated	C2 Allocated	C3 Need Data	C4 Connected	C5 *hstmt*	C6 Transaction
(IH) [1]	(IH)	(IH)	(IH)	(IH)	(IH)	(IH)
(IH) [2]	--	(08003)	(08003)	--	--	-- e and 4 C5 [s or 5]
(IH) [3]	(IH)	(08003)	(08003)	--	--	-- e C5 [s]

1 This row shows transitions when *henv* was SQL_NULL_HENV and *hdbc* was SQL_NULL_HDBC.

2 This row shows transitions when *henv* was a valid environment handle and *hdbc* was SQL_NULL_HDBC.

3 This row shows transitions when *hdbc* was a valid connection handle.

4 The commit or rollback failed on the connection.

5 The function returned SQL_ERROR but the commit or rollback succeeded on the connection.

All Other ODBC Functions

C0 No *henv*	C1 Unallocated	C2 Allocated	C3 Need Data	C4 Connected	C5 *hstmt*	C6 Transaction
(IH)	(IH)	(IH)	(IH)	(IH)	--	--

Statement Transitions

ODBC statements have the following states:

State	Description
S0	Unallocated *hstmt*. (The connection state must be C4. For more information, see "Connection Transitions.")
S1	Allocated *hstmt*.
S2	Prepared statement. No result set will be created.
S3	Prepared statement. A (possibly empty) result set will be created.
S4	Statement executed and no result set was created.
S5	Statement executed and a (possibly empty) result set was created. The cursor is open and positioned before the first row of the result set.
S6	Cursor positioned with **SQLFetch**.
S7	Cursor positioned with **SQLExtendedFetch**.
S8	Function needs data. **SQLParamData** has not been called.
S9	Function needs data. **SQLPutData** has not been called.
S10	Function needs data. **SQLPutData** has been called.
S11	Still executing.
S12	Asynchronous execution canceled. In S12, an application must call the canceled function until it returns a value other than SQL_STILL_EXECUTING. The function was canceled successfully only if the function returns SQL_ERROR and SQLSTATE S1008 (Operation canceled). If it returns any other value, such as SQL_SUCCESS, the cancel operation failed and the function executed normally.

States S2 and S3 are known as the prepared states, states S5 through S7 as the cursor states, states S8 through S10 as the need data states, and states S11 and S12 as the asynchronous states. In each of these groups, the transitions are shown separately only when they are different for each state in the group; generally, the transitions for each state in each a group are the same.

The following tables show how each ODBC function affects the statement state.

SQLAllocConnect

S0 Unallocated	S1 Allocated	S2 – S3 Prepared	S4 Executed	S5 – S7 Cursor	S8 – S10 Need Data	S11 – S12 Async
-- [1]	S0 [1]	S0 [1]	S0 [1]	S0 [1]	S0 [1]	S0 [1]

1 Calling **SQLAllocConnect** with a pointer to a valid *hdbc* overwrites that *hdbc*. This may be an application programming error. Furthermore, this returns the connection state to C2; the connection state must be C4 before the statement state is S0.

SQLAllocEnv

S0 Unallocated	S1 Allocated	S2 – S3 Prepared	S4 Executed	S5 – S7 Cursor	S8 – S10 Need Data	S11 – S12 Async
-- [1]	S0 [1]	S0 [1]	S0 [1]	S0 [1]	S0 [1]	S0 [1]

1 Calling **SQLAllocEnv** with a pointer to a valid *henv* overwrites that *henv*. This may be an application programming error. Furthermore, this returns the connection state to C1; the connection state must be C4 before the statement state is S0.

SQLAllocStmt

S0 Unallocated	S1 Allocated	S2 – S3 Prepared	S4 Executed	S5 – S7 Cursor	S8 – S10 Need Data	S11 – S12 Async
S1	-- [1]	S1 [1]	S1 [1]	S1 [1]	S1 [1]	S1 [1]

1 Calling **SQLAllocStmt** with a pointer to a valid *hstmt* overwrites that *hstmt*. This may be an application programming error.

SQLBindCol

S0 Unallocated	S1 Allocated	S2 – S3 Prepared	S4 Executed	S5 – S7 Cursor	S8 – S10 Need Data	S11 – S12 Async
(IH)	--	--	--	--	(S1010)	(S1010)

SQLBindParameter

S0 Unallocated	S1 Allocated	S2 – S3 Prepared	S4 Executed	S5 – S7 Cursor	S8 – S10 Need Data	S11 – S12 Async
(IH)	--	--	--	--	(S1010)	(S1010)

SQLBrowseConnect, SQLConnect, and **SQLDriverConnect**

S0 Unallocated	S1 Allocated	S2 – S3 Prepared	S4 Executed	S5 – S7 Cursor	S8 – S10 Need Data	S11 – S12 Async
(08002)	(08002)	(08002)	(08002)	(08002)	(08002)	(08002)

SQLCancel [1]

S0 Unallocated	S1 Allocated	S2 – S3 Prepared	S4 Executed	S5 – S7 Cursor	S8 – S10 Need Data	S11 – S12 Async
(IH)	--	--	S1 [np] S2 [p]	S1 [np] S3 [p]	S1 [2] S2 [nr and 3] S3 [r and 3] S7 [4]	S12

1 This table does not cover cancellation of a function running synchronously on one thread when an application calls **SQLCancel** on a different thread with the same *hstmt*. In this case, the driver must note that **SQLCancel** was called and return the correct return code and SQLSTATE (if any) from the synchronous function. The statement transition when that function finishes is NS (Next State). That is, the statement transition is the same as if the function completed processing normally; the only difference is that it is possible for the function to return SQL_ERROR and SQLSTATE S1008 (Operation canceled).

2 **SQLExecDirect** returned SQL_NEED_DATA.

3 **SQLExecute** returned SQL_NEED_DATA.

4 **SQLSetPos** returned SQL_NEED_DATA.

SQLColAttributes

S0 Unallocated	S1 Allocated	S2 – S3 Prepared	S4 Executed	S5 – S7 Cursor	S8 – S10 Need Data	S11 – S12 Async
(IH)	(S1010)	see below	24000	-- [s] S11 [x]	(S1010)	NS [c] (S1010) [o]

SQLColAttributes (Prepared states)

S2 No Results	S3 Results
24000	-- [s] S11 [x]

SQLColumnPrivileges, SQLColumns, SQLForeignKeys, SQLGetTypeInfo, SQLPrimaryKeys, SQLProcedureColumns, SQLProcedures, SQLSpecialColumns, SQLStatistics, SQLTablePrivileges, and SQLTables

S0 Unallocated	S1 Allocated	S2 – S3 Prepared	S4 Executed	S5 – S7 Cursor	S8 – S10 Need Data	S11 – S12 Async
(IH)	S5 [s] S11 [x]	S1 [e] S5 [s] S11 [x]	S1 [e] S5 [s] S11 [x]	see below	(S1010)	NS [c] (S1010) [o]

SQLColumnPrivileges, SQLColumns, SQLForeignKeys, SQLGetTypeInfo, SQLPrimaryKeys, SQLProcedureColumns, SQLProcedures, SQLSpecialColumns, SQLStatistics, SQLTablePrivileges, and **SQLTables** (Cursor states)

S5 Opened	S6 SQLFetch	S7 SQLExtendedFetch
24000	(24000)	(24000)

SQLColumns: see **SQLColumnPrivileges**

SQLConnect: see **SQLBrowseConnect**

SQLDataSources and **SQLDrivers**

S0 Unallocated	S1 Allocated	S2 – S3 Prepared	S4 Executed	S5 – S7 Cursor	S8 – S10 Need Data	S11 – S12 Async
--	--	--	--	--	--	--

SQLDescribeCol

S0 Unallocated	S1 Allocated	S2 – S3 Prepared	S4 Executed	S5 – S7 Cursor	S8 – S10 Need Data	S11 – S12 Async
(IH)	(S1010)	see below	24000	-- [s] S11 [x]	(S1010)	NS [c] (S1010) [o]

SQLDescribeCol (Prepared states)

S2 No Results	S3 Results
24000	-- [s] S11 [x]

SQLDescribeParam

S0 Unallocated	S1 Allocated	S2 – S3 Prepared	S4 Executed	S5 – S7 Cursor	S8 – S10 Need Data	S11 – S12 Async
(IH)	(S1010)	-- [s] S11 [x]	-- [s] S11 [x]	-- [s] S11 [x]	(S1010)	NS [c] (S1010) [o]

SQLDisconnect

S0 Unallocated	S1 Allocated	S2 – S3 Prepared	S4 Executed	S5 – S7 Cursor	S8 – S10 Need Data	S11 – S12 Async
-- [1]	S0 [1]	S0 [1]	S0 [1]	S0 [1]	(S1010)	(S1010)

1 Calling **SQLDisconnect** frees all *hstmts* associated with the *hdbc*. Furthermore, this returns the connection state to C2; the connection state must be C4 before the statement state is S0.

SQLDriverConnect: see SQLBrowseConnect

SQLDrivers: see SQLDataSources

SQLError

S0 Unallocated	S1 Allocated	S2 – S3 Prepared	S4 Executed	S5 – S7 Cursor	S8 – S10 Need Data	S11 – S12 Async
(IH) [1]	--	--	--	--	--	--

1 This row shows transitions when *hstmt* was non-null.

SQLExecDirect

S0 Unallocated	S1 Allocated	S2 – S3 Prepared	S4 Executed	S5 – S7 Cursor	S8 – S10 Need Data	S11 – S12 Async
(IH)	S4 [s and nr] S5 [s and r] S8 [d] S11 [x]	S1 [e] S4 [s and nr] S5 [s and r] S8 [d] S11 [x]	S1 [e] S4 [s and nr] S5 [s and r] S8 [d] S11 [x]	see below	(S1010)	NS [c] (S1010) [o]

SQLExecDirect (Cursor states)

S5 Opened	S6 SQLFetch	S7 SQLExtendedFetch
24000	(24000)	(24000)

SQLExecute

S0 Unallocated	S1 Allocated	S2 – S3 Prepared	S4 Executed	S5 – S7 Cursor	S8 – S10 Need Data	S11 – S12 Async
(IH)	(S1010)	see below	S2 [e and p] S4 [s, p, and nr] S8 [d and p] S11 [x and p] (S1010) [np]	see below	(S1010)	NS [c] (S1010) [o]

SQLExecute (Prepared states)

S2 No Results	S3 Results
S4 [s]	S5 [s]
S8 [d]	S8 [d]
S11 [x]	S11 [x]

SQLExecute (Cursor states)

S5 Opened	S6 SQLFetch	S7 SQLExtendedFetch
24000 [p]	(24000) [p]	(24000) [p]
(S1010) [np]	(S1010) [np]	(S1010) [np]

SQLExtendedFetch

S0 Unallocated	S1 Allocated	S2 – S3 Prepared	S4 Executed	S5 – S7 Cursor	S8 – S10 Need Data	S11 – S12 Async
(IH)	(S1010)	(S1010)	24000	see below	(S1010)	NS [c] (S1010) [o]

SQLExtendedFetch (Cursor states)

S5 Opened	S6 SQLFetch	S7 SQLExtendedFetch
S7 [s or nf]	(S1010)	-- [s or nf]
S11 [x]		S11 [x]

SQLFetch

S0 Unallocated	S1 Allocated	S2 – S3 Prepared	S4 Executed	S5 – S7 Cursor	S8 – S10 Need Data	S11 – S12 Async
(IH)	(S1010)	(S1010)	24000	see below	(S1010)	NS [c] (S1010) [o]

SQLFetch (Cursor states)

S5 Opened	S6 SQLFetch	S7 SQLExtendedFetch
S6 [s or nf]	-- [s or nf]	(S1010)
S11 [x]	S11 [x]	

SQLForeignKeys: see **SQLColumnPrivileges**

SQLFreeConnect

S0 Unallocated	S1 Allocated	S2 – S3 Prepared	S4 Executed	S5 – S7 Cursor	S8 – S10 Need Data	S11 – S12 Async
(S1010)	(S1010)	(S1010)	(S1010)	(S1010)	(S1010)	(S1010)

SQLFreeEnv

S0 Unallocated	S1 Allocated	S2 – S3 Prepared	S4 Executed	S5 – S7 Cursor	S8 – S10 Need Data	S11 – S12 Async
(S1010)	(S1010)	(S1010)	(S1010)	(S1010)	(S1010)	(S1010)

SQLFreeStmt

S0 Unallocated	S1 Allocated	S2 – S3 Prepared	S4 Executed	S5 – S7 Cursor	S8 – S10 Need Data	S11 – S12 Async
(IH) [1]	--	--	S1 ^{np} S2 ^{p}	S1 ^{np} S3 ^{p}	(S1010)	(S1010)
(IH) [2]	S0	S0	S0	S0	(S1010)	(S1010)
(IH) [3]	--	--	--	--	(S1010)	(S1010)

1 This row shows transitions when *fOption* was SQL_CLOSE.

2 This row shows transitions when *fOption* was SQL_DROP.

3 This row shows transitions when *fOption* was SQL_UNBIND or SQL_RESET_PARAMS.

SQLGetConnectOption

S0 Unallocated	S1 Allocated	S2 – S3 Prepared	S4 Executed	S5 – S7 Cursor	S8 – S10 Need Data	S11 – S12 Async
--	--	--	--	--	--	--

SQLGetCursorName

S0 Unallocated	S1 Allocated	S2 – S3 Prepared	S4 Executed	S5 – S7 Cursor	S8 – S10 Need Data	S11 – S12 Async
(IH)	-- [1] (S1015) [2]	-- [1] (S1015) [2]	-- [1] (S1015) [2]	--	(S1010)	(S1010)

1 A cursor name had been set by calling **SQLSetCursorName** or by creating a result set.

2 A cursor name had not been set by calling **SQLSetCursorName** or by creating a result set.

SQLGetData

S0 Unallocated	S1 Allocated	S2 – S3 Prepared	S4 Executed	S5 – S7 Cursor	S8 – S10 Need Data	S11 – S12 Async
(IH)	(S1010)	(S1010)	(24000)	see below	(S1010)	NS [c] (S1010) [o]

SQLGetData (Cursor states)

S5 Opened	S6 SQLFetch	S7 SQLExtendedFetch
(24000)	-- s or nf S11 [x] 24000 [3]	-- s or nf S11 [x] 24000 [b] S1109 [i] S1C00 [v and 1]

1 The rowset size was greater than 1 and the **SQLGetInfo** did not return the SQL_GD_BLOCK bit for the SQL_GETDATA_EXTENSIONS information type.

SQLGetFunctions

S0 Unallocated	S1 Allocated	S2 – S3 Prepared	S4 Executed	S5 – S7 Cursor	S8 – S10 Need Data	S11 – S12 Async
--	--	--	--	--	--	--

SQLGetInfo

S0 Unallocated	S1 Allocated	S2 – S3 Prepared	S4 Executed	S5 – S7 Cursor	S8 – S10 Need Data	S11 – S12 Async
--	--	--	--	--	--	--

SQLGetStmtOption

S0 Unallocated	S1 Allocated	S2 – S3 Prepared	S4 Executed	S5 – S7 Cursor	S8 – S10 Need Data	S11 – S12 Async
(IH)	-- [1] (24000) [2]	-- [1] (24000) [2]	-- [1] (24000) [2]	see below	(S1010)	(S1010)

1 The statement option was not SQL_ROW_NUMBER or SQL_GET_BOOKMARK.

2 The statement option was SQL_ROW_NUMBER or SQL_GET_BOOKMARK.

SQLGetStmtOption (Cursor states)

S5 Opened	S6 SQLFetch	S7 SQLExtendedFetch
-- [1]	-- 1 or (v and 3)	-- 1 or (v and (2 or 3))
(24000) [2 or 3]	24000 [b and 3]	24000 [b and (2 or 3)]
	S1011 [2]	S1109 [i and (2 or 3)]
	S1109 [i and 3]	

1 The *fOption* argument was not SQL_GET_BOOKMARK or SQL_ROW_NUMBER.

2 The *fOption* argument was SQL_GET_BOOKMARK.

3 The *fOption* argument was SQL_ROW_NUMBER.

SQLGetTypeInfo: see **SQLColumnPrivileges**

SQLMoreResults

S0 Unallocated	S1 Allocated	S2 – S3 Prepared	S4 Executed	S5 – S7 Cursor [1]	S8 – S10 Need Data	S11 – S12 Async
(IH)	-- [2]	-- [2]	S1 [nf and np]	-- [s]	(S1010)	NS [c]
			S2 [nf and p]	S1 [nf and np]		(S1010) [o]
			S11 [x]	S3 [nf and p]		
				S11 [x]		

1 For **SQLMoreResults**, the cursor states are somewhat modified. A batch statement, statement submitted with an array of parameters, or procedure can return result sets and **INSERT**, **UPDATE**, or **DELETE** row counts; these are collectively known as results. After the statement is executed, it moves to the S4 state if there are no results and the S5 state if there are results. In the S5 state, **SQLFetch** or **SQLExtendedFetch** returns SQLSTATE 24000 (Invalid cursor state) if the next result is a row count; the application must call **SQLMoreResults** to stop processing the current result and proceed to the next result. After the last result is processed, **SQLMoreResults** returns the statement to the allocated or prepared state.

2 The function always returns SQL_NO_DATA_FOUND in this state.

SQLNativeSql

S0 Unallocated	S1 Allocated	S2 – S3 Prepared	S4 Executed	S5 – S7 Cursor	S8 – S10 Need Data	S11 – S12 Async
--	--	--	--	--	--	--

SQLNumParams

S0 Unallocated	S1 Allocated	S2 – S3 Prepared	S4 Executed	S5 – S7 Cursor	S8 – S10 Need Data	S11 – S12 Async
(IH)	(S1010)	-- [s]	-- [s]	-- [s]	(S1010)	NS [c]
		S11 [x]	S11 [x]	S11 [x]		(S1010) [o]

SQLNumResultCols

S0 Unallocated	S1 Allocated	S2 – S3 Prepared	S4 Executed	S5 – S7 Cursor	S8 – S10 Need Data	S11 – S12 Async
(IH)	(S1010)	-- [s] S11 [x]	-- [s] S11 [x]	-- [s] S11 [x]	(S1010)	NS [c] (S1010) [o]

SQLParamData

S0 Unallocated	S1 Allocated	S2 – S3 Prepared	S4 Executed	S5 – S7 Cursor	S8 – S10 Need Data	S11 – S12 Async
(IH)	(S1010)	(S1010)	(S1010)	(S1010)	see below	NS [c] (S1010) [o]

SQLParamData (Need Data states)

S8 Need Data	S9 Must Put	S10 Can Put
S1 [e and 1] S2 [e, nr, and 2] S3 [e, r, and 2] S7 [e and 3] S9 [s] S11 [x]	S1010	S1 [e and 1] S2 [e, nr, and 2] S3 [e, r, and 2] S4 [s, nr, and (1 or 2)] S5 [s, r, and (1 or 2)] S7 [(s or e) and 3] S9 [d] S11 [x]

1 **SQLExecDirect** returned SQL_NEED_DATA.

2 **SQLExecute** returned SQL_NEED_DATA.

3 **SQLSetPos** returned SQL_NEED_DATA.

SQLParamOptions

S0 Unallocated	S1 Allocated	S2 – S3 Prepared	S4 Executed	S5 – S7 Cursor	S8 – S10 Need Data	S11 – S12 Async
(IH)	--	--	--	--	(S1010)	(S1010)

SQLPrepare

S0 Unallocated	S1 Allocated	S2 – S3 Prepared	S4 Executed	S5 – S7 Cursor	S8 – S10 Need Data	S11 – S12 Async
(IH)	S2 [s and nr] S3 [s and r] S11 [x]	-- [s or (e and 1)] S1 [e and 2] S11 [x]	S1 [e] S2 [s and nr] S3 [s and r] S11 [x]	see below	(S1010)	NS [c] (S1010) [o]

1 The preparation fails for a reason other than validating the statement (in other words, the SQLSTATE was S1009 (Invalid argument value) or S1090 (Invalid string or buffer length)).

2 The preparation fails while validating the statement (in other words, the SQLSTATE was not S1009 (Invalid argument value) or S1090 (Invalid string or buffer length)).

SQLPrepare (Cursor states)

S5 Opened	S6 SQLFetch	S7 SQLExtendedFetch
24000	(24000)	(24000)

SQLPrimaryKeys: see SQLColumnPrivileges

SQLProcedureColumns: see SQLColumnPrivileges

SQLProcedures: see SQLColumnPrivileges

SQLPutData

S0 Unallocated	S1 Allocated	S2 – S3 Prepared	S4 Executed	S5 – S7 Cursor	S8 – S10 Need Data	S11 – S12 Async
(IH)	(S1010)	(S1010)	(S1010)	(S1010)	see below	NS [c] (S1010) [o]

SQLPutData (Need Data states)

S8 Need Data	S9 Must Put	S10 Can Put
S1010	S1 [e and 1] S2 [e, nr, and 2] S3 [e, r, and 2] S7 [e and 3] S10 [s] S11 [x]	-- [s] S1 [e and 1] S2 [e, nr, and 2] S3 [e, r, and 2] S7 [e and 3] S11 [x]

1 **SQLExecDirect** returned SQL_NEED_DATA.

2 **SQLExecute** returned SQL_NEED_DATA.

3 **SQLSetPos** returned SQL_NEED_DATA.

SQLRowCount

S0 Unallocated	S1 Allocated	S2 – S3 Prepared	S4 Executed	S5 – S7 Cursor	S8 – S10 Need Data	S11 – S12 Async
(IH)	(S1010)	(S1010)	--	--	(S1010)	(S1010)

SQLSetConnectOption

S0 Unallocated	S1 Allocated	S2 – S3 Prepared	S4 Executed	S5 – S7 Cursor	S8 – S10 Need Data	S11 – S12 Async
-- [1]	--	--	--	--	(S1010)	(S1010)

1 This row shows transitions when *fOption* was a connection option. For transitions when *fOption* was a statement option, see the statement transition table for **SQLSetStmtOption**.

SQLSetCursorName

S0 Unallocated	S1 Allocated	S2 – S3 Prepared	S4 Executed	S5 – S7 Cursor	S8 – S10 Need Data	S11 – S12 Async
(IH)	--	--	(24000)	(24000)	(S1010)	(S1010)

SQLSetPos

S0 Unallocated	S1 Allocated	S2 – S3 Prepared	S4 Executed	S5 – S7 Cursor	S8 – S10 Need Data	S11 – S12 Async
(IH)	(S1010)	(S1010)	(24000)	see below	(S1010)	NS [c] (S1010) [o]

SQLSetPos (Cursor states)

S5 Opened	S6 SQLFetch	S7 SQLExtendedFetch
(24000)	(S1010)	-- [s] S8 [d] S11 [x] 24000 [b] S1109 [i]

SQLSetScrollOptions

S0 Unallocated	S1 Allocated	S2 – S3 Prepared	S4 Executed	S5 – S7 Cursor	S8 – S10 Need Data	S11 – S12 Async
(IH)	--	(S1010)	(S1010)	(S1010)	(S1010)	(S1010)

SQLSetStmtOption

S0 Unallocated	S1 Allocated	S2 – S3 Prepared	S4 Executed	S5 – S7 Cursor	S8 – S10 Need Data	S11 – S12 Async
(IH)	--	$-- ^1$ $(S1011) ^2$	$-- ^1$ $(24000) ^2$	$-- ^1$ $(24000) ^2$	$(S1010) ^{np \text{ or } 1}$ $(S1011) ^{p \text{ and } 2}$	$(S1010) ^{np \text{ or } 1}$ $(S1011) ^{p \text{ and } 2}$

1 The *fOption* argument was not SQL_CONCURRENCY, SQL_CURSOR_TYPE, SQL_SIMULATE_CURSOR, or SQL_USE_BOOKMARKS.

2 The *fOption* argument was SQL_CONCURRENCY, SQL_CURSOR_TYPE, SQL_SIMULATE_CURSOR, or SQL_USE_BOOKMARKS.

SQLSpecialColumns: see **SQLColumnPrivileges**

SQLStatistics: see **SQLColumnPrivileges**

SQLTablePrivileges: see **SQLColumnPrivileges**

SQLTables: see **SQLColumnPrivileges**

SQLTransact

S0 Unallocated	S1 Allocated	S2 – S3 Prepared	S4 Executed	S5 – S7 Cursor	S8 – S10 Need Data	S11 – S12 Async
--	--	$-- ^{2 \text{ or } 3}$ $S1 ^1$	$-- ^3$ $S1 ^{np \text{ and}(1 \text{ or } 2)}$ $S1 ^{p \text{ and } 1}$ $S2 ^{p \text{ and } 2}$	$-- ^3$ $S1 ^{np \text{ and}(1 \text{ or } 2)}$ $S1 ^{p \text{ and } 1}$ $S3 ^{p \text{ and } 2}$	(S1010)	(S1010)

1 The *fType* argument is SQL_COMMIT and **SQLGetInfo** returns SQL_CB_DELETE for the SQL_CURSOR_COMMIT_BEHAVIOR information type, or the *fType* argument is SQL_ROLLBACK and **SQLGetInfo** returns SQL_CB_DELETE for the SQL_CURSOR_ROLLBACK_BEHAVIOR information type.

2 The *fType* argument is SQL_COMMIT and **SQLGetInfo** returns SQL_CB_CLOSE for the SQL_CURSOR_COMMIT_BEHAVIOR information type, or the *fType* argument is SQL_ROLLBACK and **SQLGetInfo** returns SQL_CB_CLOSE for the SQL_CURSOR_ROLLBACK_BEHAVIOR information type.

3 The *fType* argument is SQL_COMMIT and **SQLGetInfo** returns SQL_CB_PRESERVE for the SQL_CURSOR_COMMIT_BEHAVIOR information type, or the *fType* argument is SQL_ROLLBACK and **SQLGetInfo** returns SQL_CB_PRESERVE for the SQL_CURSOR_ROLLBACK_BEHAVIOR information type.

APPENDIX C

SQL Grammar

The following paragraphs list the recommended constructs to ensure interoperability in calls to **SQLPrepare**, **SQLExecute**, or **SQLExecDirect**. To the right of each construct is an indicator that tells whether the construct is part of the minimum grammar, the core grammar, or the extended grammar. ODBC does not prohibit the use of vendor-specific SQL grammar.

The Integrity Enhancement Facility (IEF) is included in the grammar but is optional. If drivers parse and execute SQL directly and wish to include referential integrity functionality, then we strongly recommend the SQL syntax used for this functionality conform to the grammar used here. The grammar for the IEF is taken directly from the X/Open and SQL Access Group SQL CAE specification (1992) and is a subset of the emerging ISO SQL-92 standard. Elements that are part of the IEF and are optional in the ANSI 1989 standard are presented in the following typeface and font, distinct from the rest of the grammar:

```
table-constraint-definition
```

A given driver and data source do not necessarily support all of the data types defined in this grammar. To determine which data types a driver supports, an application calls **SQLGetInfo** with the SQL_ODBC_SQL_CONFORMANCE flag. Drivers that support every core data type return 1 and drivers that support every core and every extended data type return 2. To determine whether a specific data type is supported, an application calls **SQLGetTypeInfo** with the *fSqlType* argument set to that data type.

If a driver supports data types that map to the ODBC SQL date, time, or timestamp data types, the driver must also support the extended SQL grammar for specifying date, time, or timestamp literals.

Note In **CREATE TABLE** and **ALTER TABLE** statements, applications must use the data type name returned by **SQLGetTypeInfo** in the TYPE_NAME column.

Parameter Data Types

Even though each parameter specified with **SQLBindParameter** is defined using an SQL data type, the parameters in an SQL statement have no intrinsic data type. Therefore, parameter markers can be included in an SQL statement only if their data types can be inferred from another operand in the statement. For example, in an arithmetic expression such as **? + COLUMN1**, the data type of the parameter can be inferred from the data type of the named column represented by COLUMN1. An application cannot use a parameter marker if the data type cannot be determined.

The following table describes how a data type is determined for several types of parameters.

Location of Parameter	Assumed Data Type
One operand of a binary arithmetic or comparison operator	Same as the other operand
The first operand in a **BETWEEN** clause	Same as the other operand
The second or third operand in a **BETWEEN** clause	Same as the first operand
An expression used with **IN**	Same as the first value or the result column of the subquery
A value used with **IN**	Same as the expression
A pattern value used with **LIKE**	VARCHAR
An update value used with **UPDATE**	Same as the update column

Parameter Markers

An application cannot place parameter markers in the following locations:

- In a **SELECT** list.
- As both *expressions* in a *comparison-predicate*.
- As both operands of a binary operator.
- As both the first and second operands of a **BETWEEN** operation.
- As both the first and third operands of a **BETWEEN** operation.
- As both the expression and the first value of an **IN** operation.
- As the operand of a unary + or – operation.
- As the argument of a *set-function-reference*.

For more information, see the ANSI SQL-92 specification.

If an application includes parameter markers in the SQL statement, the application must call **SQLBindParameter** to associate storage locations with parameter markers before it calls **SQLExecute** or **SQLExecDirect**. If the application calls

SQLPrepare, the application can call **SQLBindParameter** before or after it calls **SQLPrepare**.

The application can set parameter markers in any order. The driver buffers argument descriptors and sends the current values referenced by the **SQLBindParameter** argument *rgbValue* for the associated parameter marker when the application calls **SQLExecute** or **SQLExecDirect**. It is the application's responsibility to ensure that all pointer arguments are valid at execution time.

Note The keyword **USER** in the following tables represents a character string containing the *user-name* of the current user.

SQL Statements

The following SQL statements define the base ODBC SQL grammar.

Statement	Mini-mum	Core	Ex-tended
alter-table-statement ::=		■	

    ALTER TABLE *base-table-name*
    {   ADD *column-identifier data-type*
    | ADD (*column-identifier data-type* [, *column-identifier data-type*]...)
    }

Important As a *data-type* in an *alter-table-statement*, applications must use a data type from the TYPE_NAME column of the result set returned by **SQLGetTypeInfo**.

Statement	Mini-mum	Core	Ex-tended
alter-table-statement ::=			■

    ALTER TABLE *base-table-name*
    {   ADD *column-identifier data-type*
    | ADD (*column-identifier data-type* [, *column-identifier data-type*]...)
    | DROP [COLUMN] *column-identifier* [CASCADE | RESTRICT]
    }

Important As a *data-type* in an *alter-table-statement*, applications must use a data type from the TYPE_NAME column of the result set returned by **SQLGetTypeInfo**.

Statement	Mini-mum	Core	Ex-tended
create-index-statement ::=		■	

    CREATE [UNIQUE] INDEX *index-name*
    ON *base-table-name*
    (*column-identifier* [ASC | DESC]
    [, *column-identifier* [ASC | DESC]]...)

Statement	Mini-mum	Core	Ex-tended

create-table-statement ::=
  CREATE TABLE *base-table-name*
  (*column-element* [, *column-element*] ...)
 	
  column-element ::= *column-definition* | *table-constraint-definition*
 	
  column-definition ::=
    column-identifier data-type
    [DEFAULT default-value]
    [*column-constraint-definition*[*column-constraint-definition*]...]
 	
  default-value ::= literal | NULL | USER
 	
  column-constraint-definition ::=
    NOT NULL
    | UNIQUE | PRIMARY KEY
    | REFERENCES ref-table-name referenced-columns
    | CHECK (search-condition)
 	
  table-constraint-definition ::=
    UNIQUE (column-identifier [, column-identifier]...)
    | PRIMARY KEY (column-identifier
      [, column-identifier]...)
    | CHECK (search-condition)
    | FOREIGN KEY referencing-columns REFERENCES
      ref-table-name referenced-columns
	■		

Important   As a *data-type* in a *create-table-statement*, applications must use a data type from the TYPE_NAME column of the result set returned by **SQLGetTypeInfo**.

Statement	Mini-mum	Core	Ex-tended

create-view-statement ::=
  CREATE VIEW *viewed-table-name*
  [(*column-identifier* [, *column-identifier*]...)]
  AS *query-specification*
		■	

delete-statement-positioned ::= DELETE FROM *table-name* WHERE CURRENT OF *cursor-name*		■ ODBC 1.0	■ ODBC 2.0
delete-statement-searched ::= DELETE FROM *table-name* [WHERE *search-condition*]	■		
drop-index-statement ::= DROP INDEX *index-name*		■	

drop-table-statement ::=
  DROP TABLE *base-table-name*
    [CASCADE | RESTRICT]
	■		

Statement	Mini-mum	Core	Ex-tended

drop-view-statement ::=
     DROP VIEW *viewed-table-name*
         [CASCADE ɪ RESTRICT]
		■	

grant-statement ::=
     GRANT {ALL ɪ *grant-privilege* [, *grant-privilege*]... }
     ON *table-name*
     TO {PUBLIC ɪ *user-name* [, *user-name*]... }
 	
     grant-privilege ::=
         DELETE
         ɪ INSERT
         ɪ SELECT
         ɪ UPDATE [(*column-identifier* [, *column-identifier*]...)]
         ɪ REFERENCES [(column-identifier
             [, column-identifier]...)]
		■	

insert-statement ::=
     INSERT INTO *table-name* [(*column-identifier* [, *column-identifier*]...)]
     VALUES (*insert-value*[, *insert-value*]...)
	■		

insert-statement ::=
     INSERT INTO *table-name* [(*column-identifier* [, *column-identifier*]...)]
         { *query-specification* ɪ VALUES (*insert-value* [, *insert-value*]...)}
		■	

ODBC-procedure-extension ::=
     ODBC-std-esc-initiator [?=] call *procedure ODBC-std-esc-terminator*
     ɪ *ODBC-ext-esc-initiator* [?=] call *procedure ODBC-ext-esc-terminator*
			■

revoke-statement ::=
     REVOKE {ALL ɪ *revoke-privilege* [, *revoke-privilege*]... }
     ON *table-name*
     FROM {PUBLIC ɪ *user-name* [, *user-name*]... }
     [CASCADE ɪ RESTRICT]
 	
     revoke-privilege ::=
         DELETE
         ɪ INSERT
         ɪ SELECT
         ɪ UPDATE
         ɪ REFERENCES
		■	

select-statement ::=
     SELECT [ALL ɪ DISTINCT] *select-list*
     FROM *table-reference-list*
     [WHERE *search-condition*]
     [*order-by-clause*]
	■		

Statement	Mini-mum	Core	Ex-tended
select-statement ::= 　　SELECT [ALL | DISTINCT] *select-list* 　　FROM *table-reference-list* 　　[WHERE *search-condition*] 　　[GROUP BY *column-name* [, *column-name*]...] 　　[HAVING *search-condition*] 　　[*order-by-clause*]		■	
select-statement ::= 　　SELECT [ALL | DISTINCT] *select-list* 　　FROM *table-reference-list* 　　[WHERE *search-condition*] 　　[GROUP BY *column-name* [, *column-name*]...] 　　[HAVING *search-condition*] 　　[UNION [ALL] *select-statement*]... 　　[*order-by-clause*] (In ODBC 1.0, the **UNION** clause was in the Core SQL grammar and did not support the **ALL** keyword.)			■
select-for-update-statement ::= 　　SELECT [ALL | DISTINCT] *select-list* 　　FROM *table-reference-list* 　　[WHERE *search-condition*] 　　FOR UPDATE OF [*column-name* [, *column-name*]...]	■ ODBC 1.0		■ ODBC 2.0
statement ::= *create-table-statement* 　　| *delete-statement-searched* 　　| *drop-table-statement* 　　| *insert-statement* 　　| *select-statement* 　　| *update-statement-searched*	■		
statement ::= *alter-table-statement* 　　| *create-index-statement* 　　| *create-table-statement* 　　| *create-view-statement* 　　| *delete-statement-searched* 　　| *drop-index-statement* 　　| *drop-table-statement* 　　| *drop-view-statement* 　　| *grant-statement* 　　| *insert-statement* 　　| *revoke-statement* 　　| *select-statement* 　　| *update-statement-searched*		■	

Statement	Mini-mum	Core	Ex-tended
statement ::= alter-table-statement			■
| *create-index-statement*			
| *create-table-statement*			
| *create-view-statement*			
| *delete-statement-positioned*			
| *delete-statement-searched*			
| *drop-index-statement*			
| *drop-table-statement*			
| *drop-view-statement*			
| *grant-statement*			
| *insert-statement*			
| *ODBC-procedure-extension*			
| *revoke-statement*			
| *select-statement*			
| *select-for-update-statement*			
| *statement-list*			
| *update-statement-positioned*			
| *update-statement-searched*			

(In ODBC 1.0, *select-for-update-statement*, *update-statement-positioned*, and *delete-statement-positioned* were in the Core SQL grammar.)

Statement	Mini-mum	Core	Ex-tended
statement-list ::= statement | statement; statement-list			■
update-statement-positioned ::=		■	■
UPDATE *table-name*		ODBC 1.0	ODBC 2.0
SET *column-identifier* = {*expression* | NULL}			
[, *column-identifier* = {*expression* | NULL}]...			
WHERE CURRENT OF *cursor-name*			
update-statement-searched		■	
UPDATE *table-name*			
SET *column-identifier* = {*expression* | NULL }			
[, *column-identifier* = {*expression* | NULL}]...			
[WHERE *search-condition*]			

Elements Used in SQL Statements

The following elements are used in the SQL statements listed previously .

Element	Mini-mum	Core	Ex-tended
all-function ::= {AVG | MAX | MIN | SUM} (*expression*)		■	
approximate-numeric-literal ::= *mantissa*E*exponent*		■	
approximate-numeric-type ::= {approximate numeric types}		■	
(For example, FLOAT, DOUBLE PRECISION, or REAL. To determine the type name used by a data source, an application calls **SQLGetTypeInfo**.)			
argument-list ::= *expression* | *expression, argument-list*	■		
base-table-identifier ::= *user-defined-name*	■		
base-table-name ::= *base-table-identifier*	■		
base-table-name ::= *base-table-identifier* | *owner-name.base-table-identifier* | *qualifier-name qualifier-separator base-table-identifier* | *qualifier-name qualifier-separator* [*owner-name*].*base-table-identifier*		■	
(The third syntax is valid only if the data source does not support owners.)			
between-predicate ::= *expression* [NOT] BETWEEN *expression* AND *expression*		■	
binary-literal ::= {implementation defined}			■
binary-type ::= {binary types}			■
(For example, BINARY, VARBINARY, or LONG VARBINARY. To determine the type name used by a data source, an application calls **SQLGetTypeInfo**.)			
bit-literal ::= 0 | 1			■
bit-type ::= {bit types}			■
(For example, BIT. To determine the type name used by a data source, an application calls **SQLGetTypeInfo**.)			
boolean-factor ::= [NOT] *boolean-primary*	■		
boolean-primary ::= *predicate* | (*search-condition*)	■		
boolean-term ::= *boolean-factor* [AND *boolean-term*]	■		
character ::= {any character in the implementor's character set}	■		
character-string-literal :: = '{*character*}...'	■		
(To include a single literal quote character (') in a *character-string-literal*, use two literal quote characters ('').)			

Element	Mini-mum	Core	Ex-tended
character-string-type ::= {character types}	■		
(The Minimum SQL conformance level requires at least one character data type. For example, CHAR, VARCHAR, or LONG VARCHAR. To determine the type name used by a data source, an application calls **SQLGetTypeInfo**.)			
column-alias ::= *user-defined-name*		■	
column-identifier ::= *user-defined-name*	■		
column-name ::= [*table-name.*]*column-identifier*	■		
column-name ::= [{*table-name* | *correlation-name*}.]*column-identifier*		■	
comparison-operator ::= < | > | <= | >= | = | <>	■		
comparison-predicate ::= *expression comparison-operator expression*	■		
comparison-predicate ::= *expression comparison-operator* {*expression* | (*sub-query*)}		■	
correlation-name ::= *user-defined-name*		■	
cursor-name ::= *user-defined-name*		■	
data-type ::= *character-string-type*	■		

data-type ::=
    character-string-type
    | *exact-numeric-type*
    | *approximate-numeric-type*
		■	

data-type ::=
    character-string-type
    | *exact-numeric-type*
    | *approximate-numeric-type*
    | *bit-type*
    | *binary-type*
    | *date-type*
    | *time-type*
    | *timestamp-type*
			■

date-separator ::= -			■
date-type ::= {date types}			■
(For example, DATE. To determine the type name used by a data source, an application calls **SQLGetTypeInfo**.)			
date-value ::= *years-value date-separator months-value date-separator days-value*			■
days-value ::= *digit digit*			■
digit ::= 0 | 1 | 2 | 3 | 4 | 5 | 6 | 7 | 8 | 9	■		

Element	Mini-mum	Core	Ex-tended
distinct-function ::= {AVG I COUNT I MAX I MIN I SUM} (DISTINCT *column-name*)		■	
dynamic-parameter ::= ?	■		
empty-string ::=			■
escape-character ::= *character*			■
exact-numeric-literal ::= [+I–] { *unsigned-integer*[.*unsigned-integer*] I *unsigned-integer*. I .*unsigned-integer* }		■	
exact-numeric-type ::= {exact numeric types} (For example, DECIMAL, NUMERIC, SMALLINT, or INTEGER. To determine the type name used by a data source, an application calls **SQLGetTypeInfo**.)		■	
exact-numeric-type ::= {exact numeric types} (For example, DECIMAL, NUMERIC, SMALLINT, INTEGER, and BIGINT. To determine the type name used by a data source, an application calls **SQLGetTypeInfo**.)			■
exists-predicate ::= EXISTS (*sub-query*)		■	
exponent ::= [+I–] *unsigned-integer*		■	
expression ::= *term* I *expression* {+I–} *term*	■		
factor ::= [+I–]*primary*	■		
hours-value ::= *digit digit*			■
index-identifier ::= *user-defined-name*		■	
index-name ::= [*index-qualifier*.]*index-identifier*		■	
index-qualifier ::= *user-defined-name*		■	
in-predicate ::= *expression* [NOT] IN {(*value* {, *value*}...) I (*sub-query*)}		■	
insert-value ::= *dynamic-parameter* I *literal* I NULL I USER	■		
keyword ::= (see list of reserved keywords)	■		
length ::= *unsigned-integer*	■		
letter ::= *lower-case-letter* I *upper-case-letter*	■		
like-predicate ::= *expression* [NOT] LIKE *pattern-value*	■		

Element	Mini-mum	Core	Ex-tended
like-predicate ::= *expression* [NOT] LIKE *pattern-value* [*ODBC-like-escape-clause*]			■
literal ::= *character-string-literal*	■		
literal ::= *character-string-literal* | *numeric-literal*		■	

literal ::= *character-string-literal*
    | *numeric-literal*
    | *bit-literal*
    | *binary-literal*
    | *ODBC-date-time-extension*
			■

lower-case-letter ::= a|b|c|d|e|f|g|h|i|j|k|l|l|m|n|o|p|q|r|s|t|u|v|w|x|y|z	■		
mantissa ::= *exact-numeric-literal*		■	
minutes-value ::= *digit digit*			■
months-value ::= *digit digit*			■
null-predicate ::= *column-name* IS [NOT] NULL	■		
numeric-literal ::= *exact-numeric-literal* | *approximate-numeric-literal*	■		

ODBC-date-literal ::=
    ODBC-std-esc-initiator d '*date-value*' *ODBC-std-esc-terminator*
    | *ODBC-ext-esc-initiator* d '*date-value*' *ODBC-ext-esc-terminator*
			■

ODBC-date-time-extension ::=
    ODBC-date-literal
    | *ODBC-time-literal*
    | *ODBC-timestamp-literal*
			■

ODBC-like-escape-clause ::=
    ODBC-std-esc-initiator escape '*escape-character*'
        ODBC-std-esc-terminator
    | *ODBC-ext-esc-initiator* escape '*escape-character*'
        ODBC-ext-esc-terminator
			■

ODBC-time-literal ::=
    | *ODBC-std-esc-initiator* t '*time-value*' *ODBC-std-esc-terminator*
    | *ODBC-ext-esc-initiator* t '*time-value*' *ODBC-ext-esc-terminator*
			■

ODBC-timestamp-literal ::=
    | *ODBC-std-esc-initiator* ts '*timestamp-value*' *ODBC-std-esc-terminator*
    | *ODBC-ext-esc-initiator* ts '*timestamp-value*' *ODBC-ext-esc-terminator*
			■

ODBC-ext-esc-initiator ::= {			■
ODBC-ext-esc-terminator ::= }			■

Element	Mini-mum	Core	Ex-tended
ODBC-outer-join-extension ::= *ODBC-std-esc-initiator* oj *outer-join ODBC-std-esc-terminator* 	*ODBC-ext-esc-initiator* oj *outer-join ODBC-ext-esc-terminator*			■
ODBC-scalar-function-extension ::= *ODBC-std-esc-initiator* fn *scalar-function ODBC-std-esc-terminator* 	*ODBC-ext-esc-initiator* fn *scalar-function ODBC-ext-esc-terminator*			■
ODBC-std-esc-initiator ::= *ODBC-std-esc-prefix SQL-esc-vendor-clause*			■
ODBC-std-esc-prefix ::= --(*			■
ODBC-std-esc-terminator ::= *)--			■
order-by-clause ::= ORDER BY *sort-specification* [, *sort-specification*]...	■		
outer-join ::= *table-name* [*correlation-name*] LEFT OUTER JOIN {*table-name* [*correlation-name*]	*outer-join*} ON *search-condition* (For outer joins, *search-condition* must contain only the join condition between the specified *table-names*.)			■
owner-name ::= *user-defined-name*		■	
pattern-value ::= *character-string-literal*	*dynamic-parameter* (In a *character-string-literal*, the percent character (%) matches 0 or more of any character; the underscore character (_) matches 1 character.)	■		
pattern-value ::= *character-string-literal*	*dynamic-parameter*	USER (In a *character-string-literal*, the percent character (%) matches 0 or more of any character; the underscore character (_) matches 1 character.)		■	
precision ::= *unsigned-integer*		■	
predicate ::= *comparison-predicate*	*like-predicate*	*null-predicate*	■		
predicate ::= *between-predicate*	*comparison-predicate*	*exists-predicate* 	*in-predicate*	*like-predicate*	*null-predicate*	*quantified-predicate*		■	
primary ::= *column-name* 	*dynamic-parameter* 	*literal* 	(*expression*)	■		
primary ::= *column-name* 	*dynamic-parameter* 	*literal* 	*set-function-reference* 	USER 	(*expression*)		■	

Element	Mini-mum	Core	Ex-tended

primary ::= column-name
   | dynamic-parameter
   | literal
   | ODBC-scalar-function-extension
   | set-function-reference
   | USER
   | (expression)
			■

procedure ::= procedure-name | procedure-name (procedure-parameter-list)			■
procedure-identifier ::= user-defined-name			■

procedure-name ::= procedure-identifier
   | owner-name.procedure-identifier
   | qualifier-name qualifier-separator procedure-identifier
   | qualifier-name qualifier-separator [owner-name].procedure-identifier
 	
(The third syntax is valid only if the data source does not support owners.)
			■

procedure-parameter-list ::= procedure-parameter *| procedure-parameter, procedure-parameter-list*			■
procedure-parameter ::= dynamic-parameter | literal | empty-string (If a procedure parameter is an empty string, the procedure uses the default value for that parameter.)			■
qualifier-name ::= user-defined-name		■	
qualifier-separator ::= {implementation-defined} (The qualifier separator is returned through **SQLGetInfo** with the SQL_QUALIFIER_NAME_SEPARATOR option.)		■	
quantified-predicate ::= expression comparison-operator {ALL | ANY} *(sub-query)*		■	

query-specification ::=
    SELECT [ALL | DISTINCT] *select-list*
    FROM *table-reference-list*
    [WHERE *search-condition*]
    [GROUP BY *column-name*, [*column-name*]...]
    [HAVING *search-condition*]
		■	

ref-table-name ::= base-table-identifier	■		

ref-table-name ::= base-table-identifier
   | owner-name.base-table-identifier
   | qualifier-name qualifier-separator base-table-identifier
   | qualifier-name qualifier-separator [owner-name].base-table-identifier
 	
(The third syntax is valid only if the data source does not support owners.)
		■	

referenced-columns ::= (column-identifier [, *column-identifier*]...)		■	

Element	Mini-mum	Core	Ex-tended
referencing-columns ::= (*column-identifier* [, *column-identifier*]...)		▪	
scalar-function ::= *function-name* (*argument-list*)			▪
(The definitions for the non-terminals *function-name* and *function-name* (*argument-list*) are derived from the list of scalar functions in Appendix F, "Scalar Functions.")			
scale ::= *unsigned-integer*		▪	
search-condition ::= *boolean-term* [OR *search-condition*]	▪		
seconds-fraction ::= *unsigned-integer*			▪
seconds-value ::= *digit digit*			▪
select-list ::= * I *select-sublist* [, *select-sublist*]...	▪		
select-sublist ::= *expression*	▪		
select-sublist ::= *expression* [[AS] *column-alias*] I {*table-name* I *correlation-name*}.*		▪	
set-function-reference ::= COUNT(*) I *distinct-function* I *all-function*		▪	
sort-specification ::= {*unsigned-integer* I *column-name* } [ASC I DESC]	▪		
SQL-esc-vendor-clause ::= VENDOR(Microsoft), PRODUCT(ODBC)			▪
sub-query ::= SELECT [ALL I DISTINCT] *select-list* FROM *table-reference-list* [WHERE *search-condition*] [GROUP BY *column-name* [, *column-name*]...] [HAVING *search-condition*]		▪	
table-identifier ::= *user-defined-name*	▪		
table-name ::= *table-identifier*	▪		
table-name ::= *table-identifier* I *owner-name.table-identifier* I *qualifier-name qualifier-separator table-identifier* I *qualifier-name qualifier-separator* [*owner-name*].*table-identifier* (The third syntax is valid only if the data source does not support owners.)		▪	
table-reference ::= *table-name*	▪		
table-reference ::= *table-name* [*correlation-name*]		▪	
table-reference::= *table-name* [*correlation-name*] I *ODBC-outer-join-extension* (A **SELECT** statement can contain only one *table-reference* that is an *ODBC-outer-join-extension*.)			▪
table-reference-list ::= *table-reference* [,*table-reference*]...		▪	

Element	Mini-mum	Core	Ex-tended
term ::= *factor* | *term* {**\V*} *factor*	▪		
time-separator ::= :			▪
time-type ::= {time types}			▪
(For example, TIME. To determine the type name used by a data source, an application calls **SQLGetTypeInfo**.)			

time-value ::=
    hours-value time-separator minutes-value time-separator
        seconds-value
			▪

timestamp-separator ::=			▪
(The blank character.)			
timestamp-type ::= {timestamp types}			▪
(For example, TIMESTAMP. To determine the type name used by a data source, an application calls **SQLGetTypeInfo**.)			
timestamp-value ::= *date-value timestamp-separator* *time-value*[*.seconds-fraction*]			▪
unsigned-integer ::= {*digit*}...	▪		

upper-case-letter ::=
    A|B|C|D|E|F|G|H|I|J|K|L|M|
    N|O|P|Q|R|S|T|U|V|W|X|Y|Z
	▪		

user-defined-name ::= *letter*[*digit* | *letter* | _]...	▪		
user-name ::= *user-defined-name*		▪	
value ::= *literal* | USER | *dynamic-parameter*		▪	
viewed-table-identifier ::= *user-defined-name*		▪	

viewed-table-name ::= *viewed-table-identifier*
    | *owner-name.viewed-table-identifier*
    | *qualifier-name qualifier-separator viewed-table-identifier*
    | *qualifier-name qualifier-separator* [*owner-name*].*viewed-table-identifier*
		▪	

(The third syntax is valid only if the data source does not support owners.)			
years-value ::= *digit digit digit digit*			▪

List of Reserved Keywords

The following words are reserved for use in ODBC function calls. These words do not constrain the minimum SQL grammar; however, to ensure compatibility with drivers that support the core SQL grammar, applications should avoid using any of these keywords. The **#define** value SQL_ODBC_KEYWORDS contains a comma-separated list of these keywords.

ABSOLUTE	CONNECTION
ADA	CONSTRAINT
ADD	CONSTRAINTS
ALL	CONTINUE
ALLOCATE	CONVERT
ALTER	CORRESPONDING
AND	COUNT
ANY	CREATE
ARE	CURRENT
AS	CURRENT_DATE
ASC	CURRENT_TIME
ASSERTION	CURRENT_TIMESTAMP
AT	CURSOR
AUTHORIZATION	DATE
AVG	DAY
BEGIN	DEALLOCATE
BETWEEN	DEC
BIT	DECIMAL
BIT_LENGTH	DECLARE
BY	DEFERRABLE
CASCADE	DEFERRED
CASCADED	DELETE
CASE	DESC
CAST	DESCRIBE
CATALOG	DESCRIPTOR
CHAR	DIAGNOSTICS
CHAR_LENGTH	DICTIONARY
CHARACTER	DISCONNECT
CHARACTER_LENGTH	DISPLACEMENT
CHECK	DISTINCT
CLOSE	DOMAIN
COALESCE	DOUBLE
COBOL	DROP
COLLATE	ELSE
COLLATION	END
COLUMN	END-EXEC
COMMIT	ESCAPE
CONNECT	EXCEPT

EXCEPTION
EXEC
EXECUTE
EXISTS
EXTERNAL
EXTRACT
FALSE
FETCH
FIRST
FLOAT
FOR
FOREIGN
FORTRAN
FOUND
FROM
FULL
GET
GLOBAL
GO
GOTO
GRANT
GROUP
HAVING
HOUR
IDENTITY
IGNORE
IMMEDIATE
IN
INCLUDE
INDEX
INDICATOR
INITIALLY
INNER
INPUT
INSENSITIVE
INSERT
INTEGER
INTERSECT
INTERVAL
INTO
IS
ISOLATION
JOIN
KEY
LANGUAGE
LAST

LEFT
LEVEL
LIKE
LOCAL
LOWER
MATCH
MAX
MIN
MINUTE
MODULE
MONTH
MUMPS
NAMES
NATIONAL
NCHAR
NEXT
NONE
NOT
NULL
NULLIF
NUMERIC
OCTET_LENGTH
OF
OFF
ON
ONLY
OPEN
OPTION
OR
ORDER
OUTER
OUTPUT
OVERLAPS
PARTIAL
PASCAL
PLI
POSITION
PRECISION
PREPARE
PRESERVE
PRIMARY
PRIOR
PRIVILEGES
PROCEDURE
PUBLIC
RESTRICT

REVOKE
RIGHT
ROLLBACK
ROWS
SCHEMA
SCROLL
SECOND
SECTION
SELECT
SEQUENCE
SET
SIZE
SMALLINT
SOME
SQL
SQLCA
SQLCODE
SQLERROR
SQLSTATE
SQLWARNING
SUBSTRING
SUM
SYSTEM
TABLE
TEMPORARY
THEN
TIME
TIMESTAMP

TIMEZONE_HOUR
TIMEZONE_MINUTE
TO
TRANSACTION
TRANSLATE
TRANSLATION
TRUE
UNION
UNIQUE
UNKNOWN
UPDATE
UPPER
USAGE
USER
USING
VALUE
VALUES
VARCHAR
VARYING
VIEW
WHEN
WHENEVER
WHERE
WITH
WORK
YEAR

APPENDIX D

Data Types

Data stored on a data source has an SQL data type, which may be specific to that data source. A driver maps data source–specific SQL data types to ODBC SQL data types and driver-specific SQL data types. (A driver returns these mappings through **SQLGetTypeInfo**. It also returns the SQL data types when describing the data types of columns and parameters in **SQLColAttributes**, **SQLColumns**, **SQLDescribeCol**, **SQLDescribeParam**, **SQLProcedureColumns**, and **SQLSpecialColumns**.)

Each SQL data type corresponds to an ODBC C data type. By default, the driver assumes that the C data type of a storage location corresponds to the SQL data type of the column or parameter to which the location is bound. If the C data type of a storage location is not the *default* C data type, the application can specify the correct C data type with the *fCType* argument in **SQLBindCol**, **SQLGetData**, or **SQLBindParameter**. Before returning data from the data source, the driver converts it to the specified C data type. Before sending data to the data source, the driver converts it from the specified C data type.

This appendix discusses the following:

- ODBC SQL data types
- ODBC C data types
- Default ODBC C data types
- Transferring data in its binary form
- Precision, scale, length, and display size of SQL data types
- Converting data from SQL to C data types
- Converting data from C to SQL data types

For information about driver-specific SQL data types, see the driver's documentation.

SQL Data Types

The ODBC SQL grammar defines three sets of SQL data types, each of which is a superset of the previous set.

- **Minimum**   SQL data types provide a basic level of ODBC conformance.
- **Core**   SQL data types are the data types in the X/Open and SQL Access Group SQL CAE specification (1992) and are supported by most SQL data sources.
- **Extended**   SQL data types are additional data types supported by some SQL data sources.

A given driver and data source do not necessarily support all of the SQL data types defined in the ODBC grammar. Furthermore, they may support additional, driver-specific SQL data types. To determine which data types a driver supports, an application calls **SQLGetTypeInfo**. For information about driver-specific SQL data types, see the driver's documentation.

Minimum SQL Data Types

The following table lists valid values of *fSqlType* for the minimum SQL data types. These values are defined in SQL.H. The table also lists the name and description of the corresponding data type from the X/Open and SQL Access Group SQL CAE specification (1992).

Note   The minimum SQL grammar requires that a data source support at least one character SQL data type. This table is only a guideline and shows commonly used names and limits of these data types. For a given data source, the characteristics of these data types may differ from those listed below. For information about the data types in a specific data source, see the documentation for that data source.

To determine which data types are supported by a data source and the characteristics of those data types, an application calls **SQLGetTypeInfo**.

---

fSqlType	SQL Data Type	Description
SQL_CHAR	CHAR(n)	Character string of fixed string length n ($1 \leq n \leq 254$).
SQL_VARCHAR	VARCHAR(n)	Variable-length character string with a maximum string length n ($1 \leq n \leq 254$).
SQL_LONGVARCHAR	LONG VARCHAR	Variable length character data. Maximum length is data source–dependent.

Core SQL Data Types

The following table lists valid values of *fSqlType* for the core SQL data types. These values are defined in SQL.H. The table also lists the name and description of the corresponding data type from the X/Open and SQL Access Group SQL CAE specification (1992). In the table, precision refers to the total number of digits and scale refers to the number of digits to the right of the decimal point.

Note This table is only a guideline and shows commonly used names, ranges, and limits of core SQL data types. A given data source may support only some of the listed data types and the characteristics of the supported data types may differ from those listed below. For example, some data sources support unsigned numeric data types. For information about the data types in a specific data source, see the documentation for that data source.

To determine which data types are supported by a data source and the characteristics of those data types, an application calls **SQLGetTypeInfo**.

fSqlType	SQL Data Type	Description
SQL_DECIMAL	DECIMAL(p,s)	Signed, exact, numeric value with a precision p and scale s ($1 \leq p \leq 15; 0 \leq s \leq p$).
SQL_NUMERIC	NUMERIC(p,s)	Signed, exact, numeric value with a precision p and scale s ($1 \leq p \leq 15; 0 \leq s \leq p$).
SQL_SMALLINT	SMALLINT	Exact numeric value with precision 5 and scale 0 (signed: $-32,768 \leq n \leq 32,767$, unsigned: $0 \leq n \leq 65,535$) [a].
SQL_INTEGER	INTEGER	Exact numeric value with precision 10 and scale 0 (signed: $-2^{31} \leq n \leq 2^{31} - 1$, unsigned: $0 \leq n \leq 2^{32} - 1$) [a].
SQL_REAL	REAL	Signed, approximate, numeric value with a mantissa precision 7 (zero or absolute value 10^{-38} to 10^{38}).
SQL_FLOAT	FLOAT	Signed, approximate, numeric value with a mantissa precision 15 (zero or absolute value 10^{-308} to 10^{308}).
SQL_DOUBLE	DOUBLE PRECISION	Signed, approximate, numeric value with a mantissa precision 15 (zero or absolute value 10^{-308} to 10^{308}).

[a] An application uses **SQLGetTypeInfo** or **SQLColAttributes** to determine if a particular data type or a particular column in a result set is unsigned.

Extended SQL Data Types

The following table lists valid values of *fSqlType* for the extended SQL data types. These values are defined in SQLEXT.H. The table also lists the name and description of the corresponding data type. In the table, precision refers to the total number of digits and scale refers to the number of digits to the right of the decimal point.

Note This table is only a guideline and shows commonly used names, ranges, and limits of extended SQL data types. A given data source may support only some of the listed data types and the characteristics of the supported data types may differ from those listed below. For example, some data sources support unsigned numeric data types. For information about the data types in a specific data source, see the documentation for that data source.

To determine which data types are supported by a data source and the characteristics of those data types, an application calls **SQLGetTypeInfo**.

---

fSqlType	Typical SQL Data Type	Description
SQL_BIT	BIT	Single bit binary data.
SQL_TINYINT	TINYINT	Exact numeric value with precision 3 and scale 0 (signed: $-128 \leq n \leq 127$, unsigned: $0 \leq n \leq 255$) [a].
SQL_BIGINT	BIGINT	Exact numeric value with precision 19 (if signed) or 20 (if unsigned) and scale 0 (signed: $-2^{63} \leq n \leq 2^{63} - 1$, unsigned: $0 \leq n \leq 2^{64} - 1$) [a].
SQL_BINARY	BINARY(n)	Binary data of fixed length n ($1 \leq n \leq 255$).
SQL_VARBINARY	VARBINARY(n)	Variable length binary data of maximum length n ($1 \leq n \leq 255$).
SQL_LONGVARBINARY	LONG VARBINARY	Variable length binary data. Maximum length is data source–dependent.
SQL_DATE	DATE	Date data.
SQL_TIME	TIME	Time data.
SQL_TIMESTAMP	TIMESTAMP	Date/time data.

[a] An application uses **SQLGetTypeInfo** or **SQLColAttributes** to determine if a particular data type or a particular column in a result set is unsigned.

C Data Types

Data is stored in the application in ODBC C data types. The core C data types are those that support the minimum and core SQL data types. They also support some extended SQL data types. The extended C data types are those that only support extended SQL data types. The bookmark C data type is used only to retrieve bookmark values and should not be converted to other data types.

Note   Unsigned C data types for integers were added to ODBC 2.0. Drivers must support the integer C data types specified in both ODBC 1.0 and ODBC 2.0; ODBC 2.0 or later applications must use the ODBC 1.0 integer C data types with ODBC 1.0 drivers and the ODBC 2.0 integer C data types with ODBC 2.0 drivers..

The C data type is specified in the **SQLBindCol**, **SQLGetData**, and **SQLBindParameter** functions with the *fCType* argument.

Core C Data Types

The following table lists valid values of *fCType* for the core C data types. These values are defined in SQL.H. The table also lists the ODBC C data type that implements each value of *fCType* and the definition of this data type from SQL.H.

fCType	ODBC C Typedef	C Type
SQL_C_CHAR	UCHAR FAR *	unsigned char FAR *
SQL_C_SSHORT	SWORD	short int
SQL_C_USHORT	UWORD	unsigned short int
SQL_C_SLONG	SDWORD	long int
SQL_C_ULONG	UDWORD	unsigned long int
SQL_C_FLOAT	SFLOAT	float
SQL_C_DOUBLE	SDOUBLE	double

Note   Because objects of the CString class in Microsoft C++ are signed and string arguments in ODBC functions are unsigned, applications that pass CString objects to ODBC functions without casting them will receive compiler warnings.

Extended C Data Types

The following table lists valid values of *fCType* for the extended C data types. These values are defined in SQLEXT.H. The table also lists the ODBC C data type that implements each value of *fCType* and the definition of this data type from SQLEXT.H or SQL.H.

fCType	ODBC C Typedef	C Type
SQL_C_BIT	UCHAR	unsigned char
SQL_C_STINYINT	SCHAR	signed char
SQL_C_UTINYINT	UCHAR	unsigned char
SQL_C_BINARY	UCHAR FAR *	unsigned char FAR *

SQL_C_DATE	DATE_STRUCT	struct tagDATE_STRUCT {
		    SWORD year; [a]
		    UWORD month; [b]
		    UWORD day; [c]
		}

SQL_C_TIME	TIME_STRUCT	struct tagTIME_STRUCT {
		    UWORD hour; [d]
		    UWORD minute; [e]
		    UWORD second; [f]
		}

SQL_C_TIMESTAMP	TIMESTAMP_STRUCT	struct tagTIMESTAMP_STRUCT {
		    SWORD year; [a]
		    UWORD month; [b]
		    UWORD day; [c]
		    UWORD hour; [d]
		    UWORD minute; [e]
		    UWORD second; [f]
		    UDWORD fraction; [g]
		}

[a] The value of the year field must be in the range from 0 to 9,999. Years are measured from 0 A.D. Some data sources do not support the entire range of years.

[b] The value of the month field must be in the range from 1 to 12.

[c] The value of day field must be in the range from 1 to the number of days in the month. The number of days in the month is determined from the values of the year and month fields and is 28, 29, 30, or 31.

[d] The value of the hour field must be in the range from 0 to 23.

[e] The value of the minute field must be in the range from 0 to 59.

[f] The value of the second field must be in the range from 0 to 59.

[g] The value of the fraction field is the number of billionths of a second and ranges from 0 to 999,999,999 (1 less than 1 billion). For example, the value of the fraction field for a half-second is 500,000,000, for a thousandth of a second (one millisecond) is 1,000,000, for a millionth of a second (one microsecond) is 1,000, and for a billionth of a second (one nanosecond) is 1.

Bookmark C Data Type

Bookmarks are 32-bit values used by an application to return to a specific row; an application retrieves a bookmark either from column 0 of the result set with **SQLExtendedFetch** or **SQLGetData** or by calling **SQLGetStmtOption**. For more information, see "Using Bookmarks" in Chapter 7, "Retrieving Results."

The following table lists the value of *fCType* for the bookmark C data type, the ODBC C data type that implements the bookmark C data type, and the definition of this data type from SQL.H.

fCType	ODBC C Typedef	C Type
SQL_C_BOOKMARK	BOOKMARK	unsigned long int

ODBC 1.0 C Data Types

In ODBC 1.0, all integer C data types were signed. The following table lists values of *fCType* for the integer C data types that were valid in ODBC 1.0. To remain compatible with applications that use ODBC 1.0, all drivers must support these values of *fCType*. To remain compatible with drivers that use ODBC 1.0, ODBC 2.0 or later applications must pass these values of *fCType* to ODBC 1.0 drivers. However, ODBC 2.0 or later applications must not pass these values to ODBC 2.0 or later drivers.

fCType	ODBC C Typedef	C Type
SQL_C_TINYINT	SCHAR	signed char
SQL_C_SHORT	SWORD	short int
SQL_C_LONG	SDWORD	long int

Because the ODBC 1.0 integer C data types (SQL_C_TINYINT, SQL_C_SHORT, and SQL_C_LONG) are signed, and because the ODBC integer SQL data types can be signed or unsigned, ODBC 1.0 applications and drivers had to interpret signed integer C data as signed or unsigned.

ODBC 2.0 applications and drivers treat the ODBC 1.0 integer C data types as unsigned only when:

- The column from which data will be retrieved is unsigned, and
- The C data type of the storage location in which the data will be placed is the default C data type for that column. (For a list of default C data types, see "Default C Data Types" later in this chapter.)

In all other cases, these applications and drivers treat the ODBC 1.0 integer C data types as signed.

In other words, for any conversion except the default conversion, ODBC 2.0 drivers check the validity of the conversion based on the numeric data value. For the default conversion, the drivers simply pass the data value without attempting to validate it numerically and applications interpret the data value according to whether the column is signed. (Applications call **SQLGetTypeInfo** to determine whether a column is signed or unsigned.)

For example, the following table shows how an ODBC 2.0 driver interprets ODBC 1.0 integer C data sent to both signed and unsigned SQL_SMALLINT columns.

From C Data Type	To SQL Data Type	C Data Values	SQL Data Values
SQL_C_TINYINT	SQL_SMALLINT (signed)	–128 to 127	–128 to 127
	SQL_SMALLINT (unsigned)	< 0 0 to 127	--- [a] 0 to 127
SQL_C_SHORT (default conversion)	SQL_SMALLINT (signed)	–32,768 to 32,767	–32,768 to 32,767
	SQL_SMALLINT (unsigned)	–32,768 to –1 0 to 32,767	32,768 to 65,535 0 to 32,767
SQL_C_LONG	SQL_SMALLINT (signed)	< –32,768 –32,768 to 32,767 > 32,767	--- [a] –32,768 to 32,767 --- [a]
	SQL_SMALLINT (unsigned)	< 0 0 to 32,767 > 32,767	--- [a] 0 to 32,767 --- [a]

[a] The driver returns SQLSTATE 22003 (Numeric value out of range).

Default C Data Types

If an application specifies SQL_C_DEFAULT for the *fCType* argument in **SQLBindCol**, **SQLGetData**, or **SQLBindParameter**, the driver assumes that the C data type of the output or input buffer corresponds to the SQL data type of the column or parameter to which the buffer is bound. For each ODBC SQL data type, the following table shows the corresponding, or *default*, C data type. For information about driver-specific SQL data types, see the driver's documentation.

Note For maximum interoperability, applications should specify a C data type other than SQL_C_DEFAULT. This allows drivers that promote SQL data types (and therefore cannot always determine default C data types) to return data. It also allows drivers that cannot determine whether an integer column is signed or unsigned to correctly return data.

Note ODBC 2.0 drivers use the ODBC 2.0 default C data types for both ODBC 1.0 and ODBC 2.0 integer C data.

SQL Data Type	Default C Data Type
SQL_CHAR	SQL_C_CHAR
SQL_VARCHAR	SQL_C_CHAR
SQL_LONGVARCHAR	SQL_C_CHAR
SQL_DECIMAL	SQL_C_CHAR
SQL_NUMERIC	SQL_C_CHAR
SQL_BIT	SQL_C_BIT
SQL_TINYINT	SQL_C_STINYINT or SQL_C_UTINYINT [a]
SQL_SMALLINT	SQL_C_SSHORT or SQL_C_USHORT [a]
SQL_INTEGER	SQL_C_SLONG or SQL_C_ULONG [a]
SQL_BIGINT	SQL_C_CHAR
SQL_REAL	SQL_C_FLOAT
SQL_FLOAT	SQL_C_DOUBLE
SQL_DOUBLE	SQL_C_DOUBLE
SQL_BINARY	SQL_C_BINARY
SQL_VARBINARY	SQL_C_BINARY
SQL_LONGVARBINARY	SQL_C_BINARY
SQL_DATE	SQL_C_DATE
SQL_TIME	SQL_C_TIME
SQL_TIMESTAMP	SQL_C_TIMESTAMP

a If the driver can determine whether the column is signed or unsigned, such as when the driver is fetching data from the data source or when the data source supports only a signed type or only an unsigned type, but not both, the driver uses the corresponding signed or unsigned C data type. If the driver cannot determine whether the column is signed or unsigned, it passes the data value without attempting to validate it numerically.

Transferring Data in its Binary Form

Among data sources that use the same DBMS, an application can safely transfer data in the internal form used by that DBMS. For a given piece of data, the SQL data types must be the same in the source and target data sources. The C data type is SQL_C_BINARY.

When the application calls **SQLFetch**, **SQLExtendedFetch**, or **SQLGetData** to retrieve the data from the source data source, the driver retrieves the data from the data source and transfers it, without conversion, to a storage location of type

SQL_C_BINARY. When the application calls **SQLExecute**, **SQLExecDirect**, or **SQLPutData** to send the data to the target data source, the driver retrieves the data from the storage location and transfers it, without conversion, to the target data source.

Note Applications that transfer any data (except binary data) in this manner are not interoperable among DBMS's.

Precision, Scale, Length, and Display Size

SQLColAttributes, **SQLColumns**, and **SQLDescribeCol** return the precision, scale, length, and display size of a column in a table. **SQLProcedureColumns** returns the precision, scale, and length of a column in a procedure. **SQLDescribeParam** returns the precision or scale of a parameter in an SQL statement; **SQLBindParameter** sets the precision or scale of a parameter in an SQL statement. **SQLGetTypeInfo** returns the maximum precision and the minimum and maximum scales of an SQL data type on a data source.

Due to limitations in the size of the arguments these functions use, precision, length, and display size are limited to the size of an SDWORD, or 2,147,483,647.

Precision

The precision of a numeric column or parameter refers to the maximum number of digits used by the data type of the column or parameter. The precision of a nonnumeric column or parameter generally refers to either the maximum length or the defined length of the column or parameter. To determine the maximum precision allowed for a data type, an application calls **SQLGetTypeInfo**. The following table defines the precision for each ODBC SQL data type.

fSqlType	Precision
SQL_CHAR SQL_VARCHAR	The defined length of the column or parameter. For example, the precision of a column defined as CHAR(10) is 10.
SQL_LONGVARCHAR [a, b]	The maximum length of the column or parameter.
SQL_DECIMAL SQL_NUMERIC	The defined number of digits. For example, the precision of a column defined as NUMERIC(10,3) is 10.
SQL_BIT [c]	1
SQL_TINYINT [c]	3
SQL_SMALLINT [c]	5
SQL_INTEGER [c]	10
SQL_BIGINT [c]	19 (if signed) or 20 (if unsigned)

fSqlType	Precision
SQL_REAL [c]	7
SQL_FLOAT [c]	15
SQL_DOUBLE [c]	15
SQL_BINARY SQL_VARBINARY	The defined length of the column or parameter. For example, the precision of a column defined as BINARY(10) is 10.
SQL_LONGVARBINARY [a, b]	The maximum length of the column or parameter.
SQL_DATE [c]	10 (the number of characters in the yyyy-mm-dd format).
SQL_TIME [c]	8 (the number of characters in the hh:mm:ss format).
SQL_TIMESTAMP	The number of characters in the "yyyy-mm-dd hh:mm:ss[.f...]" format used by the TIMESTAMP data type. For example, if a timestamp does not use seconds or fractional seconds, the precision is 16 (the number of characters in the "yyyy-mm-dd hh:mm" format). If a timestamp uses thousandths of a second, the precision is 23 (the number of characters in the "yyyy-mm-dd hh:mm:ss.fff" format).

[a] For an ODBC 1.0 application calling **SQLSetParam** in an ODBC 2.0 driver, and for an ODBC 2.0 application calling **SQLBindParameter** in an ODBC 1.0 driver, when *pcbValue* is SQL_DATA_AT_EXEC, *cbColDef* must be set to the total length of the data to be sent, not the precision as defined in this table.

[b] If the driver cannot determine the column or parameter length, it returns SQL_NO_TOTAL.

[c] The *cbColDef* argument of **SQLBindParameter** is ignored for this data type.

Scale

The scale of a numeric column or parameter refers to the maximum number of digits to the right of the decimal point. For approximate floating point number columns or parameters, the scale is undefined, since the number of digits to the right of the decimal point is not fixed. (For the SQL_DECIMAL and SQL_NUMERIC data types, the maximum scale is generally the same as the maximum precision. However, some data sources impose a separate limit on the maximum scale. To determine the minimum and maximum scales allowed for a data type, an application calls **SQLGetTypeInfo**.) The following table defines the scale for each ODBC SQL data type.

fSqlType	Scale
SQL_CHAR [a] SQL_VARCHAR [a] SQL_LONGVARCHAR [a]	Not applicable.
SQL_DECIMAL SQL_NUMERIC	The defined number of digits to the right of the decimal point. For example, the scale of a column defined as NUMERIC(10,3) is 3.
SQL_BIT [a] SQL_TINYINT [a] SQL_SMALLINT [a] SQL_INTEGER [a] SQL_BIGINT [a]	0
SQL_REAL [a] SQL_FLOAT [a] SQL_DOUBLE [a]	Not applicable.
SQL_BINARY [a] SQL_VARBINARY [a] SQL_LONGVARBINARY [a]	Not applicable.
SQL_DATE [a] SQL_TIME [a]	Not applicable.
SQL_TIMESTAMP	The number of digits to the right of the decimal point in the "yyyy-mm-dd hh:mm:ss[.f...]" format. For example, if the TIMESTAMP data type uses the "yyyy-mm-dd hh:mm:ss.fff" format, the scale is 3.

[a] The *ibScale* argument of **SQLBindParameter** is ignored for this data type.

Length

The length of a column is the maximum number of bytes returned to the application when data is transferred to its default C data type. For character data, the length does not include the null termination byte. Note that the length of a column may be different than the number of bytes required to store the data on the data source. For a list of default C data types, see the "Default C Data Types" earlier in this appendix.

The following table defines the length for each ODBC SQL data type.

fSqlType	Length
SQL_CHAR SQL_VARCHAR	The defined length of the column. For example, the length of a column defined as CHAR(10) is 10.
SQL_LONGVARCHAR [a]	The maximum length of the column.
SQL_DECIMAL SQL_NUMERIC	The maximum number of digits plus 2. Since these data types are returned as character strings, characters are needed for the digits, a sign, and a decimal point. For example, the length of a column defined as NUMERIC(10,3) is 12.
SQL_BIT SQL_TINYINT	1 (one byte).
SQL_SMALLINT	2 (two bytes).
SQL_INTEGER	4 (four bytes).
SQL_BIGINT	20 (since this data type is returned as a character string, characters are needed for 19 digits and a sign, if signed, or 20 digits, if unsigned).
SQL_REAL	4 (four bytes).
SQL_FLOAT	8 (eight bytes).
SQL_DOUBLE	8 (eight bytes).
SQL_BINARY SQL_VARBINARY	The defined length of the column. For example, the length of a column defined as BINARY(10) is 10.
SQL_LONGVARBINARY [a]	The maximum length of the column.
SQL_DATE SQL_TIME	6 (the size of the DATE_STRUCT or TIME_STRUCT structure).
SQL_TIMESTAMP	16 (the size of the TIMESTAMP_STRUCT structure).

[a] If the driver cannot determine the column or parameter length, it returns SQL_NO_TOTAL.

Display Size

The display size of a column is the maximum number of bytes needed to display data in character form. The following table defines the display size for each ODBC SQL data type.

fSqlType	Display Size
SQL_CHAR SQL_VARCHAR	The defined length of the column. For example, the display size of a column defined as CHAR(10) is 10.
SQL_LONGVARCHAR [a]	The maximum length of the column.
SQL_DECIMAL SQL_NUMERIC	The precision of the column plus 2 (a sign, *precision* digits, and a decimal point). For example, the display size of a column defined as NUMERIC(10,3) is 12.
SQL_BIT	1 (1 digit).
SQL_TINYINT	4 if signed (a sign and 3 digits) or 3 if unsigned (3 digits).
SQL_SMALLINT	6 if signed (a sign and 5 digits) or 5 if unsigned (5 digits).
SQL_INTEGER	11 if signed (a sign and 10 digits) or 10 if unsigned (10 digits).
SQL_BIGINT	20 (a sign and 19 digits if signed or 20 digits if unsigned).
SQL_REAL	13 (a sign, 7 digits, a decimal point, the letter E, a sign, and 2 digits).
SQL_FLOAT SQL_DOUBLE	22 (a sign, 15 digits, a decimal point, the letter E, a sign, and 3 digits).
SQL_BINARY SQL_VARBINARY	The defined length of the column times 2 (each binary byte is represented by a 2 digit hexadecimal number). For example, the display size of a column defined as BINARY(10) is 20.
SQL_LONGVARBINARY [a]	The maximum length of the column times 2.
SQL_DATE	10 (a date in the format yyyy-mm-dd).
SQL_TIME	8 (a time in the format hh:mm:ss).
SQL_TIMESTAMP	19 (if the scale of the timestamp is 0) or 20 plus the scale of the timestamp (if the scale is greater than 0). This is the number of characters in the "yyyy-mm-dd hh:mm:ss[.f...]" format. For example, the display size of a column storing thousandths of a second is 23 (the number of characters in "yyyy-mm-dd hh:mm:ss.fff").

[a] If the driver cannot determine the column or parameter length, it returns SQL_NO_TOTAL.

Converting Data from SQL to C Data Types

When an application calls **SQLExtendedFetch**, **SQLFetch**, or **SQLGetData**, the driver retrieves the data from the data source. If necessary, it converts the data from the data type in which the driver retrieved it to the data type specified by the *fCType* argument in **SQLBindCol** or **SQLGetData**. Finally, it stores the data in the location pointed to by the *rgbValue* argument in **SQLBindCol** or **SQLGetData**.

Note The word *convert* is used in this section in a broad sense, and includes the transfer of data, without a conversion in data type, from one storage location to another.

The following table shows the supported conversions from ODBC SQL data types to ODBC C data types. A solid circle indicates the default conversion for an SQL data type (the C data type to which the data will be converted when the value of *fCType* is SQL_C_DEFAULT). A hollow circle indicates a supported conversion.

SQL Data Type	SQL_C_CHAR	SQL_C_BIT	SQL_C_STINYINT	SQL_C_UTINYINT	SQL_C_TINYINT	SQL_C_SSHORT	SQL_C_USHORT	SQL_C_SHORT	SQL_C_SLONG	SQL_C_ULONG	SQL_C_LONG	SQL_C_FLOAT	SQL_C_DOUBLE	SQL_C_BINARY	SQL_C_DATE	SQL_C_TIME	SQL_C_TIMESTAMP
SQL_CHAR	●	○	○	○	○	○	○	○	○	○	○	○	○	○	○	○	○
SQL_VARCHAR	●	○	○	○	○	○	○	○	○	○	○	○	○	○	○	○	○
SQL_LONGVARCHAR	●	○	○	○	○	○	○	○	○	○	○	○	○	○	○	○	○
SQL_DECIMAL	●	○	○	○	○	○	○	○	○	○	○	○	○	○			
SQL_NUMERIC	●	○	○	○	○	○	○	○	○	○	○	○	○	○			
SQL_BIT	○	●	○	○	○	○	○	○	○	○	○	○	○	○			
SQL_TINYINT (signed)	○	○	●	○	○	○	○	○	○	○	○	○	○	○			
SQL_TINYINT (unsigned)	○	○	○	●	○	○	○	○	○	○	○	○	○	○			
SQL_SMALLINT (signed)	○	○	○	○	○	●	○	○	○	○	○	○	○	○			
SQL_SMALLINT (unsigned)	○	○	○	○	○	○	●	○	○	○	○	○	○	○			
SQL_INTEGER (signed)	○	○	○	○	○	○	○	○	●	○	○	○	○	○			
SQL_INTEGER (unsigned)	○	○	○	○	○	○	○	○	○	●	○	○	○	○			
SQL_BIGINT (signed and unsigned)	●	○	○	○	○	○	○	○	○	○	○	○	○	○			
SQL_REAL	○	○	○	○	○	○	○	○	○	○	○	●	○	○			
SQL_FLOAT	○	○	○	○	○	○	○	○	○	○	○	○	●	○			
SQL_DOUBLE	○	○	○	○	○	○	○	○	○	○	○	○	●	○			
SQL_BINARY	○													●			
SQL_VARBINARY	○													●			
SQL_LONGVARBINARY	○													●			
SQL_DATE	○													○	●		○
SQL_TIME	○													○		●	○
SQL_TIMESTAMP	○													○	○	○	●

● Default conversion
○ Supported conversion

The tables in the following sections describe how the driver or data source converts data retrieved from the data source; drivers are required to support conversions to all ODBC C data types from the ODBC SQL data types that they support. For a given ODBC SQL data type, the first column of the table lists the legal input values of the *fCType* argument in **SQLBindCol** and **SQLGetData**. The second column lists the outcomes of a test, often using the *cbValueMax* argument specified in **SQLBindCol** or **SQLGetData**, which the driver performs to determine if it can convert the data. For each outcome, the third and fourth columns list the values of the *rgbValue* and *pcbValue* arguments specified in **SQLBindCol** or **SQLGetData** after the driver has attempted to convert the data.

The last column lists the SQLSTATE returned for each outcome by **SQLExtendedFetch**, **SQLFetch**, or **SQLGetData**.

If the *fCType* argument in **SQLBindCol** or **SQLGetData** contains a value for an ODBC C data type not shown in the table for a given ODBC SQL data type, **SQLExtendedFetch**, **SQLFetch**, or **SQLGetData** returns SQLSTATE 07006 (Restricted data type attribute violation). If the *fCType* argument contains a value that specifies a conversion from a driver-specific SQL data type to an ODBC C data type and this conversion is not supported by the driver, **SQLExtendedFetch**, **SQLFetch**, or **SQLGetData** returns SQLSTATE S1C00 (Driver not capable).

Though it is not shown in the tables, the *pcbValue* argument contains SQL_NULL_DATA when the SQL data value is NULL. For an explanation of the use of *pcbValue* when multiple calls are made to retrieve data, see **SQLGetData**. When SQL data is converted to character C data, the character count returned in *pcbValue* does not include the null termination byte. If *rgbValue* is a null pointer, **SQLBindCol** or **SQLGetData** returns SQLSTATE S1009 (Invalid argument value).

The following terms and conventions are used in the tables:

- **Length of data** is the number of bytes of C data available to return in *rgbValue*, regardless of whether the data will be truncated before it is returned to the application. For string data, this does not include the null termination byte.

- **Display size** is the total number of bytes needed to display the data in character format.

- Words in *italics* represent function arguments or elements of the ODBC SQL grammar. For the syntax of grammar elements, see Appendix C, "SQL Grammar."

SQL to C: Character

The character ODBC SQL data types are:

SQL_CHAR
SQL_VARCHAR
SQL_LONGVARCHAR

The following table shows the ODBC C data types to which character SQL data may be converted. For an explanation of the columns and terms in the table, see the list above.

fCType	Test	rgbValue	pcbValue	SQL-STATE
SQL_C_CHAR	Length of data < *cbValueMax*	Data	Length of data	N/A
	Length of data ≥ *cbValueMax*	Truncated data	Length of data	01004
SQL_C_STINYINT SQL_C_UTINYINT	Data converted without truncation [b]	Data	Size of the C data type	N/A
SQL_C_TINYINT [a] SQL_C_SSHORT SQL_C_USHORT	Data converted with truncation of fractionaldigits [b]	Truncated data	Size of the C data type	01004
SQL_C_SHORT [a] SQL_C_SLONG	Conversion of data would result in loss of whole (as opposed to fractional)digits [b]	Untouched	Untouched	22003
SQL_C_ULONG SQL_C_LONG [a]	Data is not a *numeric-literal* [b]	Untouched	Untouched	22005
SQL_C_FLOAT SQL_C_DOUBLE	Data is within the range of the data type to which the number is being converted [b]	Data	Size of the C data type	N/A
	Data is outside the range of the data type to which the number is being converted [b]	Untouched	Untouched	22003
	Data is not a *numeric-literal* [b]	Untouched	Untouched	22005
SQL_C_BIT	Data is 0 or 1 [a]	Data	1 [c]	N/A
	Data is greater than 0, less than 2, and not equal to 1 [a]	Truncated data	1 [c]	01004
	Data is less than 0 or greater than or equal to 2 [a]	Untouched	Untouched	22003
	Data is not a *numeric-literal* [a]	Untouched	Untouched	22005
SQL_C_BINARY	Length of data ≤ *cbValueMax*	Data	Length of data	N/A
	Length of data > *cbValueMax*	Truncated data	Length of data	01004
SQL_C_DATE	Data value is a valid *date-value* [b]	Data	6 [c]	N/A
	Data value is a valid *timestamp-value*; time portion is zero [b]	Data	6 [c]	N/A
	Data value is a valid *timestamp-value*; time portion is non-zero [b, d]	Truncated data	6 [c]	01004
	Data value is not a valid *date-value* or *timestamp-value* [b]	Untouched	Untouched	22008

fCType	Test	rgbValue	pcbValue	SQL-STATE
SQL_C_TIME	Data value is a valid *time-value* [b]	Data	6 [c]	N/A
	Data value is a valid *timestamp-value*; fractional seconds portion is zero [b, e]	Data	6 [c]	N/A
	Data value is a valid *timestamp-value*; fractional seconds portion is non-zero [b, e, f]	Truncated data	6 [c]	01004
	Data value is not a valid *time-value* or *timestamp-value* [b]	Untouched	Untouched	22008
SQL_C_TIMESTAMP	Data value is a valid *timestamp-value*; fractional seconds portion not truncated [b]	Data	16 [c]	N/A
	Data value is a valid *timestamp-value*; fractional seconds portion truncated [b]	Truncated data	16 [c]	N/A
	Data value is a valid *date-value* [b]	Data [g]	16 [c]	N/A
	Data value is a valid *time-value* [b]	Data [h]	16 [c]	N/A
	Data value is not a valid *date-value, time-value*, or *timestamp-value* [b]	Untouched	Untouched	22008

[a] For more information, see "ODBC 1.0 C Data Types," earlier in this appendix.

[b] The value of *cbValueMax* is ignored for this conversion. The driver assumes that the size of *rgbValue* is the size of the C data type.

[c] This is the size of the corresponding C data type.

[d] The time portion of the *timestamp-value* is truncated.

[e] The date portion of the *timestamp-value* is ignored.

[f] The fractional seconds portion of the timestamp is truncated.

[g] The time fields of the timestamp structure are set to zero.

[h] The date fields of the timestamp structure are set to the current date.

When character SQL data is converted to numeric, date, time, or timestamp C data, leading and trailing spaces are ignored.

All drivers that support date, time, and timestamp data can convert character SQL data to date, time, or timestamp C data as specified in the previous table. Drivers may be able to convert character SQL data from other, driver-specific formats to date, time, or timestamp C data. Such conversions are not interoperable among data sources.

SQL to C: Numeric

The numeric ODBC SQL data types are:

SQL_DECIMAL	SQL_BIGINT
SQL_NUMERIC	SQL_REAL
SQL_TINYINT	SQL_FLOAT

SQL_SMALLINT   SQL_DOUBLE
SQL_INTEGER

The following table shows the ODBC C data types to which numeric SQL data may be converted. For an explanation of the columns and terms in the table, see page 631.

fCType	Test	rgbValue	pcbValue	SQL-STATE
SQL_C_CHAR	Display size < *cbValueMax*	Data	Length of data	N/A
	Number of whole (as opposed to fractional) digits < *cbValueMax*	Truncated data	Length of data	01004
	Number of whole (as opposed to fractional) digits ≥ *cbValueMax*	Untouched	Untouched	22003
SQL_C_STINYINT SQL_C_UTINYINT SQL_C_TINYINT [a] SQL_C_SSHORT SQL_C_USHORT SQL_C_SHORT [a] SQL_C_SLONG SQL_C_ULONG SQL_C_LONG [a]	Data converted without truncation [b]	Data	Size of the C data type	N/A
	Data converted with truncation of fractional digits [b]	Truncated data	Size of the C data type	01004
	Conversion of data would result in loss of whole (as opposed to fractional) digits [b]	Untouched	Untouched	22003
SQL_C_FLOAT SQL_C_DOUBLE	Data is within the range of the data type to which the number is being converted [b]	Data	Size of the C data type	N/A
	Data is outside the range of the data type to which the number is being converted [b]	Untouched	Untouched	22003
SQL_C_BIT	Data is 0 or 1 [b]	Data	1 [c]	N/A
	Data is greater than 0, less than 2, and not equal to 1 [b]	Truncated data	1 [c]	01004
	Data is less than 0 or greater than or equal to 2 [b]	Untouched	Untouched	22003
SQL_C_BINARY	Length of data ≤ *cbValueMax*	Data	Length of data	N/A
	Length of data > *cbValueMax*	Untouched	Untouched	22003

[a] For more information, see "ODBC 1.0 C Data Types," earlier in this appendix.

[b] The value of *cbValueMax* is ignored for this conversion. The driver assumes that the size of *rgbValue* is the size of the C data type.

[c] This is the size of the corresponding C data type.

SQL to C: Bit

The bit ODBC SQL data type is:

SQL_BIT

The following table shows the ODBC C data types to which bit SQL data may be converted. For an explanation of the columns and terms in the table, see page 631.

fCType	Test	rgbValue	pcbValue	SQL-STATE
SQL_C_CHAR	*cbValueMax* > 1	Data	1	N/A
	cbValueMax ≤ 1	Untouched	Untouched	22003
SQL_C_STINYINT SQL_C_UTINYINT SQL_C_TINYINT [a] SQL_C_SSHORT SQL_C_USHORT SQL_C_SHORT [a] SQL_C_SLONG SQL_C_ULONG SQL_C_LONG [a] SQL_C_FLOAT SQL_C_DOUBLE	None [b]	Data	Size of the C data type	N/A
SQL_C_BIT	None [b]	Data	1 [c]	N/A
SQL_C_BINARY	*cbValueMax* ≥ 1	Data	1	N/A
	cbValueMax < 1	Untouched	Untouched	22003

[a] For more information, see "ODBC 1.0 C Data Types," earlier in this appendix.

[b] The value of *cbValueMax* is ignored for this conversion. The driver assumes that the size of *rgbValue* is the size of the C data type.

[c] This is the size of the corresponding C data type.

When bit SQL data is converted to character C data, the possible values are "0" and "1".

SQL to C: Binary

The binary ODBC SQL data types are:

SQL_BINARY
SQL_VARBINARY
SQL_LONGVARBINARY

The following table shows the ODBC C data types to which binary SQL data may be converted. For an explanation of the columns and terms in the table, see page 631.

fCType	Test	rgbValue	pcbValue	SQL-STATE
SQL_C_CHAR	(Length of data) * 2 < *cbValueMax*	Data	Length of data	N/A
	(Length of data) * 2 ≥ *cbValueMax*	Truncated data	Length of data	01004
SQL_C_BINARY	Length of data ≤ *cbValueMax*	Data	Length of data	N/A
	Length of data > *cbValueMax*	Truncated data	Length of data	01004

When binary SQL data is converted to character C data, each byte (8 bits) of source data is represented as two ASCII characters. These characters are the ASCII character representation of the number in its hexadecimal form. For example, a binary 00000001 is converted to "01" and a binary 11111111 is converted to "FF".

The driver always converts individual bytes to pairs of hexadecimal digits and terminates the character string with a null byte. Because of this, if *cbValueMax* is even and is less than the length of the converted data, the last byte of the *rgbValue* buffer is not used. (The converted data requires an even number of bytes, the next-to-last byte is a null byte, and the last byte cannot be used.)

SQL to C: Date

The date ODBC SQL data type is:

SQL_DATE

The following table shows the ODBC C data types to which date SQL data may be converted. For an explanation of the columns and terms in the table, see page 631.

fCType	Test	rgbValue	pcbValue	SQL-STATE
SQL_C_CHAR	$cbValueMax \geq 11$	Data	10	N/A
	$cbValueMax < 11$	Untouched	Untouched	22003
SQL_C_BINARY	Length of data $\leq cbValueMax$	Data	Length of data	N/A
	Length of data $> cbValueMax$	Untouched	Untouched	22003
SQL_C_DATE	None [a]	Data	6 [c]	N/A
SQL_C_TIMESTAMP	None [a]	Data [b]	16 [c]	N/A

[a] The value of *cbValueMax* is ignored for this conversion. The driver assumes that the size of *rgbValue* is the size of the C data type.

[b] The time fields of the timestamp structure are set to zero.

[c] This is the size of the corresponding C data type.

When date SQL data is converted to character C data, the resulting string is in the "yyyy-mm-dd" format.

SQL to C: Time

The time ODBC SQL data type is:

SQL_TIME

The following table shows the ODBC C data types to which time SQL data may be converted. For an explanation of the columns and terms in the table, see page 631.

fCType	Test	rgbValue	pcbValue	SQL-STATE
SQL_C_CHAR	$cbValueMax \geq 9$	Data	8	N/A
	$cbValueMax < 9$	Untouched	Untouched	22003
SQL_C_BINARY	Length of data $\leq cbValueMax$	Data	Length of data	N/A
	Length of data $> cbValueMax$	Untouched	Untouched	22003
SQL_C_TIME	None [a]	Data	6 [c]	N/A
SQL_C_TIMESTAMP	None [a]	Data [b]	16 [c]	N/A

[a] The value of *cbValueMax* is ignored for this conversion. The driver assumes that the size of *rgbValue* is the size of the C data type.

[b] The date fields of the timestamp structure are set to the current date and the fractional seconds field of the timestamp structure is set to zero.

[c] This is the size of the corresponding C data type.

When time SQL data is converted to character C data, the resulting string is in the "hh:mm:ss" format.

SQL to C: Timestamp

The timestamp ODBC SQL data type is:

SQL_TIMESTAMP

The following table shows the ODBC C data types to which timestamp SQL data may be converted. For an explanation of the columns and terms in the table, see page 631.

fCType	Test	rgbValue	pcbValue	SQL-STATE
SQL_C_CHAR	$cbValueMax$ > Display size	Data	Length of data	N/A
	$20 \leq cbValueMax \leq$ Display size	Truncated data [b]	Length of data	01004
	$cbValueMax$ < 20	Untouched	Untouched	22003
SQL_C_BINARY	Length of data $\leq cbValueMax$	Data	Length of data	N/A
	Length of data > $cbValueMax$	Untouched	Untouched	22003
SQL_C_DATE	Time portion of timestamp is zero [a]	Data	6 [f]	N/A
	Time portion of timestamp is non-zero [a]	Truncated data [c]	6 [f]	01004
SQL_C_TIME	Fractional seconds portion of timestamp is zero [a]	Data [d]	6 [f]	N/A
	Fractional seconds portion of timestamp is non-zero [a]	Truncated data [d, e]	6 [f]	01004
SQL_C_TIMESTAMP	Fractional seconds portion of timestamp is not truncated [a]	Data [e]	16 [f]	N/A
	Fractional seconds portion of timestamp is truncated [a]	Truncated data [e]	16 [f]	01004

[a] The value of $cbValueMax$ is ignored for this conversion. The driver assumes that the size of $rgbValue$ is the size of the C data type.

[b] The fractional seconds of the timestamp are truncated.

[c] The time portion of the timestamp is truncated.

[d] The date portion of the timestamp is ignored.

[e] The fractional seconds portion of the timestamp is truncated.

[f] This is the size of the corresponding C data type.

When timestamp SQL data is converted to character C data, the resulting string is in the "yyyy-mm-dd hh:mm:ss[.f...]" format, where up to nine digits may be used for fractional seconds. (Except for the decimal point and fractional seconds, the entire format must be used, regardless of the precision of the timestamp SQL data type.)

SQL to C Data Conversion Examples

The following examples illustrate how the driver converts SQL data to C data:

SQL Data Type	SQL Data Value	C Data Type	cbValueMax	rgbValue	SQL-STATE
SQL_CHAR	abcdef	SQL_C_CHAR	7	abcdef\0 [a]	N/A
SQL_CHAR	abcdef	SQL_C_CHAR	6	abcde\0 [a]	01004
SQL_DECIMAL	1234.56	SQL_C_CHAR	8	1234.56\0 [a]	N/A
SQL_DECIMAL	1234.56	SQL_C_CHAR	5	1234\0 [a]	01004
SQL_DECIMAL	1234.56	SQL_C_CHAR	4	----	22003
SQL_DECIMAL	1234.56	SQL_C_FLOAT	ignored	1234.56	N/A
SQL_DECIMAL	1234.56	SQL_C_SSHORT	ignored	1234	01004
SQL_DECIMAL	1234.56	SQL_C_STINYINT	ignored	----	22003
SQL_DOUBLE	1.2345678	SQL_C_DOUBLE	ignored	1.2345678	N/A
SQL_DOUBLE	1.2345678	SQL_C_FLOAT	ignored	1.234567	N/A
SQL_DOUBLE	1.2345678	SQL_C_STINYINT	ignored	1	N/A
SQL_DATE	1992-12-31	SQL_C_CHAR	11	1992-12-31\0 [a]	N/A
SQL_DATE	1992-12-31	SQL_C_CHAR	10	-----	22003
SQL_DATE	1992-12-31	SQL_C_TIMESTAMP	ignored	1992,12,31, 0,0,0,0 [b]	N/A
SQL_TIMESTAMP	1992-12-31 23:45:55.12	SQL_C_CHAR	23	1992-12-31 23:45:55.12\0 [a]	N/A
SQL_TIMESTAMP	1992-12-31 23:45:55.12	SQL_C_CHAR	22	1992-12-31 23:45:55.1\0 [a]	01004
SQL_TIMESTAMP	1992-12-31 23:45:55.12	SQL_C_CHAR	18	----	22003

[a] "\0" represents a null-termination byte. The driver always null-terminates SQL_C_CHAR data.

[b] The numbers in this list are the numbers stored in the fields of the TIMESTAMP_STRUCT structure.

Converting Data from C to SQL Data Types

When an application calls **SQLExecute** or **SQLExecDirect**, the driver retrieves the data for any parameters bound with **SQLBindParameter** from storage locations in the application. For data-at-execution parameters, the application sends the parameter data with **SQLPutData**. If necessary, the driver converts the data from the data type specified by the *fCType* argument in **SQLBindParameter** to the data type specified by the *fSqlType* argument in **SQLBindParameter**. Finally, the driver sends the data to the data source.

Note The word *convert* is used in this section in a broad sense, and includes the transfer of data, without a conversion in data type, from one storage location to another.

The following table shows the supported conversions from ODBC C data types to ODBC SQL data types. A solid circle indicates the default conversion for an SQL data type (the C data type from which the data will be converted when the value of *fCType* is SQL_C_DEFAULT). A hollow circle indicates a supported conversion.

C Data Type	SQL_CHAR	SQL_VARCHAR	SQL_LONGVARCHAR	SQL_DECIMAL	SQL_NUMERIC	SQL_BIT	SQL_TINYINT (signed)	SQL_TINYINT (unsigned)	SQL_SMALLINT (signed)	SQL_SMALLINT (unsigned)	SQL_INTEGER (signed)	SQL_INTEGER (unsigned)	SQL_BIGINT (signed and unsigned)	SQL_REAL	SQL_FLOAT	SQL_DOUBLE	SQL_BINARY	SQL_VARBINARY	SQL_LONGVARBINARY	SQL_DATE	SQL_TIME	SQL_TIMESTAMP
SQL_C_CHAR	●	●	●	●	●	○	○	○	○	○	○	○	●	○	○	○	○	○	○	○	○	○
SQL_C_BIT	○	○	○	○	○	●	○	○	○	○	○	○	○	○	○	○						
SQL_C_STINYINT	○	○	○	○	○	○	●	○	○	○	○	○	○	○	○	○						
SQL_C_UTINYINT	○	○	○	○	○	○	○	●	○	○	○	○	○	○	○	○						
SQL_C_TINYINT	○	○	○	○	○	○	○	○	○	○	○	○	○	○	○	○						
SQL_C_SSHORT	○	○	○	○	○	○	○	○	●	○	○	○	○	○	○	○						
SQL_C_USHORT	○	○	○	○	○	○	○	○	○	●	○	○	○	○	○	○						
SQL_C_SHORT	○	○	○	○	○	○	○	○	○	○	○	○	○	○	○	○						
SQL_C_SLONG	○	○	○	○	○	○	○	○	○	○	●	○	○	○	○	○						
SQL_C_ULONG	○	○	○	○	○	○	○	○	○	○	○	●	○	○	○	○						
SQL_C_LONG	○	○	○	○	○	○	○	○	○	○	○	○	○	○	○	○						
SQL_C_FLOAT	○	○	○	○	○	○	○	○	○	○	○	○	○	●	○	○						
SQL_C_DOUBLE	○	○	○	○	○	○	○	○	○	○	○	○	○	○	●	●						
SQL_C_BINARY	○	○	○	○	○	○	○	○	○	○	○	○	○	○	○	○	●	●	●	○	○	○
SQL_C_DATE	○	○	○																	●		○
SQL_C_TIME	○	○	○																		●	○
SQL_C_TIMESTAMP	○	○	○																	○	○	●

● Default conversion

○ Supported conversion

The tables in the following sections describe how the driver or data source converts data sent to the data source; drivers are required to support conversions from all ODBC C data types to the ODBC SQL data types that they support. For a given ODBC C data type, the first column of the table lists the legal input values of the *fSqlType* argument in **SQLBindParameter**. The second column lists the outcomes of a test that the driver performs to determine if it can convert the data. The third column lists the SQLSTATE returned for each outcome by **SQLExecDirect**, **SQLExecute**, or **SQLPutData**. Data is sent to the data source only if SQL_SUCCESS is returned.

If the *fSqlType* argument in **SQLBindParameter** contains a value for an ODBC SQL data type that is not shown in the table for a given C data type, **SQLBindParameter** returns SQLSTATE 07006 (Restricted data type attribute violation). If the *fSqlType* argument contains a driver-specific value and the driver does not support the conversion from the specific ODBC C data type to that driver-specific SQL data type, **SQLBindParameter** returns SQLSTATE S1C00 (Driver not capable).

If the *rgbValue* and *pcbValue* arguments specified in **SQLBindParameter** are both null pointers, that function returns SQLSTATE S1009 (Invalid argument value). Though it is not shown in the tables, an application sets the value pointed to by the *pcbValue* argument of **SQLBindParameter** or the value of the *cbValue* argument to SQL_NULL_DATA to specify a NULL SQL data value. The application sets these values to SQL_NTS to specify that the value in *rgbValue* is a null-terminated string.

The following terms are used in the tables:

- **Length of data** is the number of bytes of SQL data available to send to the data source, regardless of whether the data will be truncated before it is sent to the data source. For string data, this does not include the null termination byte.

- **Column length** and **display size** are defined for each SQL data type in the section "Precision, Scale, Length, and Display Size" earlier in this chapter.

- **Number of digits** is the number of characters used to represent a number, including the minus sign, decimal point, and exponent (if needed).

- Words in *italics* represent elements of the ODBC SQL grammar. For the syntax of grammar elements, see Appendix C, "SQL Grammar."

C to SQL: Character

The character ODBC C data type is:

SQL_C_CHAR

The following table shows the ODBC SQL data types to which C character data may be converted. For an explanation of the columns and terms in the table, see page 643.

fSqlType	Test	SQL-STATE
SQL_CHAR SQL_VARCHAR SQL_LONGVARCHAR	Length of data ≤ Column length	N/A
	Length of data > Column length	01004
SQL_DECIMAL SQL_NUMERIC SQL_TINYINT SQL_SMALLINT SQL_INTEGER SQL_BIGINT	Data converted without truncation	N/A
	Data converted with truncation of fractional digits	01004
	Conversion of data would result in loss of whole (as opposed to fractional) digits	22003
	Data value is not a *numeric-literal*	22005
SQL_REAL SQL_FLOAT SQL_DOUBLE	Data is within the range of the data type to which the number is being converted	N/A
	Data is outside the range of the data type to which the number is being converted	22003
	Data value is not a *numeric-literal*	22005
SQL_BIT	Data is 0 or 1	N/A
	Data is greater than 0, less than 2, and not equal to 1	01004
	Data is less than 0 or greater than or equal to 2	22003
	Data is not a *numeric-literal*	22005
SQL_BINARY SQL_VARBINARY SQL_LONGVARBINARY	(Length of data) / 2 ≤ Column length	N/A
	(Length of data) / 2 > Column length	01004
	Data value is not a hexadecimal value	22005
SQL_DATE	Data value is a valid *ODBC-date-literal*	N/A
	Data value is a valid *ODBC-timestamp-literal*; time portion is zero	N/A
	Data value is a valid *ODBC-timestamp-literal*; time portion is non-zero [a]	01004
	Data value is not a valid *ODBC-date-literal* or *ODBC-timestamp-literal*	22008

fSqlType	Test	SQL-STATE
SQL_TIME	Data value is a valid *ODBC-time-literal*	N/A
	Data value is a valid *ODBC-timestamp-literal*; fractional seconds portion is zero [b]	N/A
	Data value is a valid *ODBC-timestamp-literal*; fractional seconds portion is non-zero [b, c]	01004
	Data value is not a valid *ODBC-time-literal* or *ODBC-timestamp-literal*	22008
SQL_TIMESTAMP	Data value is a valid *ODBC-timestamp-literal*; fractional seconds portion not truncated	N/A
	Data value is a valid *ODBC-timestamp-literal*; fractional seconds portion truncated	01004
	Data value is a valid *ODBC-date-literal* [d]	N/A
	Data value is a valid *ODBC-time-literal* [e]	N/A
	Data value is not a valid *ODBC-date-literal*, *ODBC-time-literal*, or *ODBC-timestamp-literal*	22008

[a] The time portion of the timestamp is truncated.
[b] The date portion of the timestamp is ignored.
[c] The fractional seconds portion of the timestamp is truncated.
[d] The time portion of the timestamp is set to zero.
[e] The date portion of the timestamp is set to the current date.

When character C data is converted to numeric, date, time, or timestamp SQL data, leading and trailing blanks are ignored.

When character C data is converted to binary SQL data, each two bytes of character data are converted to a single byte (8 bits) of binary data. Each two bytes of character data represent a number in hexadecimal form. For example, "01" is converted to a binary 00000001 and "FF" is converted to a binary 11111111.

The driver always converts pairs of hexadecimal digits to individual bytes and ignores the null termination byte. Because of this, if the length of the character string is odd, the last byte of the string (excluding the null termination byte, if any) is not converted.

All drivers that support date, time, and timestamp data can convert character C data to date, time, or timestamp SQL data as specified in the previous table. Drivers may be able to convert character C data from other, driver-specific formats to date, time, or timestamp SQL data. Such conversions are not interoperable among data sources.

C to SQL: Numeric

The numeric ODBC C data types are:

SQL_C_STINYINT	SQL_C_SLONG
SQL_C_UTINYINT	SQL_C_ULONG
SQL_C_TINYINT	SQL_C_LONG
SQL_C_SSHORT	SQL_C_FLOAT
SQL_C_USHORT	SQL_C_DOUBLE
SQL_C_SHORT	

For more information about the SQL_C_TINYINT, SQL_C_SHORT, and SQL_C_LONG data types, see "ODBC 1.0 C Data Types," earlier in this appendix. The following table shows the ODBC SQL data types to which numeric C data may be converted. For an explanation of the columns and terms in the table, see page 643.

fSqlType	Test	SQL-STATE
SQL_CHAR SQL_VARCHAR SQL_LONGVARCHAR	Number of digits ≤ Column length	N/A
	Number of whole (as opposed to fractional) digits ≤ Column length	01004
	Number of whole (as opposed to fractional) digits > Column length	22003
SQL_DECIMAL SQL_NUMERIC SQL_TINYINT SQL_SMALLINT SQL_INTEGER SQL_BIGINT	Data converted without truncation	N/A
	Data converted with truncation of fractional digits	01004
	Conversion of data would result in loss of whole (as opposed to fractional) digits	22003
SQL_REAL SQL_FLOAT SQL_DOUBLE	Data is within the range of the data type to which the number is being converted	N/A
	Data is outside the range of the data type to which the number is being converted	22003
SQL_BIT	Data is 0 or 1	N/A
	Data is greater than 0, less than 2, and not equal to 1	01004
	Data is less than 0 or greater than or equal to 2	22003

The value pointed to by the *pcbValue* argument of **SQLBindParameter** and the value of the *cbValue* argument of **SQLPutData** are ignored when data is converted from the numeric C data types. The driver assumes that the size of *rgbValue* is the size of the numeric C data type.

C to SQL: Bit

The bit ODBC C data type is:

SQL_C_BIT

The following table shows the ODBC SQL data types to which bit C data may be converted. For an explanation of the columns and terms in the table, see page 643.

fSqlType	Test	SQL-STATE
SQL_CHAR SQL_VARCHAR SQL_LONGVARCHAR	None	N/A
SQL_DECIMAL SQL_NUMERIC SQL_TINYINT SQL_SMALLINT SQL_INTEGER SQL_BIGINT SQL_REAL SQL_FLOAT SQL_DOUBLE	None	N/A
SQL_BIT	None	N/A

The value pointed to by the *pcbValue* argument of **SQLBindParameter** and the value of the *cbValue* argument of **SQLPutData** are ignored when data is converted from the bit C data type. The driver assumes that the size of *rgbValue* is the size of the bit C data type.

C to SQL: Binary

The binary ODBC C data type is:

SQL_C_BINARY

The following table shows the ODBC SQL data types to which binary C data may be converted. For an explanation of the columns and terms in the table, see page 643.

fSqlType	Test	SQL-STATE
SQL_CHAR SQL_VARCHAR SQL_LONGVARCHAR	Length of data ≤ Column length Length of data > Column length	N/A 01004
SQL_DECIMAL SQL_NUMERIC SQL_TINYINT SQL_SMALLINT SQL_INTEGER SQL_BIGINT SQL_REAL SQL_FLOAT SQL_DOUBLE	Length of data = SQL data length [a] Length of data ≠ SQL data length [a]	N/A 22003
SQL_BIT	Length of data = SQL data length [a] Length of data ≠ SQL data length [a]	N/A 22003
SQL_BINARY SQL_VARBINARY SQL_LONGVARBINARY	Length of data ≤ Column length Length of data > Column length	N/A 01004
SQL_DATE SQL_TIME SQL_TIMESTAMP	Length of data = SQL data length [a] Length of data ≠ SQL data length [a]	N/A 22003

[a] The SQL data length is the number of bytes needed to store the data on the data source. (This may be different than the column length, as defined earlier in this appendix.)

C to SQL: Date

The date ODBC C data type is:

SQL_C_DATE

The following table shows the ODBC SQL data types to which date C data may be converted. For an explanation of the columns and terms in the table, see page 643.

fSqlType	Test	SQL-STATE
SQL_CHAR SQL_VARCHAR SQL_LONGVARCHAR	Column length ≥ 10	N/A
	Column length < 10	22003
	Data value is not a valid date	22008
SQL_DATE	Data value is a valid date	N/A
	Data value is not a valid date	22008
SQL_TIMESTAMP	Data value is a valid date [a]	N/A
	Data value is not a valid date	22008

[a] The time portion of the timestamp is set to zero.

For information about what values are valid in a SQL_C_DATE structure, see "Extended C Data Types," earlier in this appendix.

When date C data is converted to character SQL data, the resulting character data is in the "yyyy-mm-dd" format.

The value pointed to by the *pcbValue* argument of **SQLBindParameter** and the value of the *cbValue* argument of **SQLPutData** are ignored when data is converted from the date C data type. The driver assumes that the size of *rgbValue* is the size of the date C data type.

C to SQL: Time

The time ODBC C data type is:

SQL_C_TIME

The following table shows the ODBC SQL data types to which time C data may be converted. For an explanation of the columns and terms in the table, see page 643.

fSqlType	Test	SQL-STATE
SQL_CHAR SQL_VARCHAR SQL_LONGVARCHAR	Column length ≥ 8	N/A
	Column length < 8	22003
	Data value is not a valid time	22008
SQL_TIME	Data value is a valid time	N/A
	Data value is not a valid time	22008
SQL_TIMESTAMP	Data value is a valid time [a]	N/A
	Data value is not a valid time	22008

[a] The date portion of the timestamp is set to the current date and the fractional seconds portion of the timestamp is set to zero.

For information about what values are valid in a SQL_C_TIME structure, see "Extended C Data Types," earlier in this appendix.

When time C data is converted to character SQL data, the resulting character data is in the "hh:mm:ss" format.

The value pointed to by the *pcbValue* argument of **SQLBindParameter** and the value of the *cbValue* argument of **SQLPutData** are ignored when data is converted from the time C data type. The driver assumes that the size of *rgbValue* is the size of the time C data type.

C to SQL: Timestamp

The timestamp ODBC C data type is:

SQL_C_TIMESTAMP

The following table shows the ODBC SQL data types to which timestamp C data may be converted. For an explanation of the columns and terms in the table, see page 643.

fSqlType	Test	SQL-STATE
SQL_CHAR SQL_VARCHAR SQL_LONGVARCHAR	Column length ≥ Display size	N/A
	19 ≤ Column length < Display size [a]	01004
	Column length < 19	22003
	Data value is not a valid date	22008
SQL_DATE	Time fields are zero	N/A
	Time fields are non-zero [b]	01004
	Data value does not contain a valid date	22008
SQL_TIME	Fractional seconds fields are zero [c]	N/A
	Fractional seconds fields are non-zero [c, d]	01004
	Data value does not contain a valid time	22008
SQL_TIMESTAMP	Fractional seconds fields are not truncated	N/A
	Fractional seconds fields are truncated [d]	01004
	Data value is not a valid timestamp	22008

[a] The fractional seconds of the timestamp are truncated.

[b] The time fields of the timestamp structure are truncated.

[c] The date fields of the timestamp structure are ignored.

[d] The fractional seconds fields of the timestamp structure are truncated.

For information about what values are valid in a SQL_C_TIMESTAMP structure, see "Extended C Data Types," earlier in this appendix.

When timestamp C data is converted to character SQL data, the resulting character data is in the "yyyy-mm-dd hh:mm:ss[.f...]" format.

The value pointed to by the *pcbValue* argument of **SQLBindParameter** and the value of the *cbValue* argument of **SQLPutData** are ignored when data is converted from the timestamp C data type. The driver assumes that the size of *rgbValue* is the size of the timestamp C data type.

C to SQL Data Conversion Examples

The following examples illustrate how the driver converts C data to SQL data:

C DataType	C Data Value	SQL Data Type	Column length	SQL Data Value	SQL-STATE
SQL_C_CHAR	abcdef\0 [a]	SQL_CHAR	6	abcdef	N/A
SQL_C_CHAR	abcdef\0 [a]	SQL_CHAR	5	abcde	01004
SQL_C_CHAR	1234.56\0 [a]	SQL_DECIMAL	8 [b]	1234.56	N/A
SQL_C_CHAR	1234.56\0 [a]	SQL_DECIMAL	7 [b]	1234.5	01004
SQL_C_CHAR	1234.56\0 [a]	SQL_DECIMAL	4	----	22003
SQL_C_FLOAT	1234.56	SQL_FLOAT	not applicable	1234.56	N/A
SQL_C_FLOAT	1234.56	SQL_INTEGER	not applicable	1234	01004
SQL_C_FLOAT	1234.56	SQL_TINYINT	not applicable	----	22003
SQL_C_DATE	1992,12,31 [c]	SQL_CHAR	10	1992-12-31	N/A
SQL_C_DATE	1992,12,31 [c]	SQL_CHAR	9	----	22003
SQL_C_DATE	1992,12,31 [c]	SQL_TIMESTAMP	not applicable	1992-12-31 00:00:00.0	N/A
SQL_C_TIMESTAMP	1992,12,31, 23,45,55, 120000000 [d]	SQL_CHAR	22	1992-12-31 23:45:55.12	N/A
SQL_C_TIMESTAMP	1992,12,31, 23,45,55, 120000000 [d]	SQL_CHAR	21	1992-12-31 23:45:55.1	01004
SQL_C_TIMESTAMP	1992,12,31, 23,45,55, 120000000 [d]	SQL_CHAR	18	----	22003

[a] "\0" represents a null-termination byte. The null-termination byte is required only if the length of the data is SQL_NTS.

[b] In addition to bytes for numbers, one byte is required for a sign and another byte is required for the decimal point.

[c] The numbers in this list are the numbers stored in the fields of the DATE_STRUCT structure.

[d] The numbers in this list are the numbers stored in the fields of the TIMESTAMP_STRUCT structure.

APPENDIX E

Comparison Between Embedded SQL and ODBC

This appendix compares ODBC and embedded SQL.

ODBC to Embedded SQL

The following table compares core ODBC functions to embedded SQL statements. This comparison is based on the X/Open and SQL Access Group SQL CAE specification (1992).

ODBC uses a parameter marker in place of a host variable, wherever a host variable would occur in embedded SQL.

The SQL language is based on the X/Open and SQL Access Group SQL CAE specification (1992).

ODBC Function	Statement	Comments
SQLAllocEnv	none	Driver Manager and driver memory allocation.
SQLAllocConnect	none	Driver Manager and driver memory allocation.
SQLConnect	CONNECT	Association management.
SQLAllocStmt	none	Driver Manager and driver memory allocation.
SQLPrepare	PREPARE	The prepared SQL string can contain any of the valid preparable functions as defined by the X/Open specification, including ALTER, CREATE, *cursor-specification*, searched DELETE, dynamic SQL positioned DELETE, DROP, GRANT, INSERT, REVOKE, searched UPDATE, or dynamic SQL positioned UPDATE.

ODBC Function	Statement	Comments
SQLBindParameter	SET DESCRIPTOR	Dynamic SQL ALLOCATE DESCRIPTOR and dynamic SQL SET DESCRIPTOR. ALLOCATE DESCRIPTOR would normally be issued on the first call to **SQLBindParameter** for an *hstmt*. Alternatively, ALLOCATE DESCRIPTOR can be called during **SQLAllocStmt**, although this call would be unneeded by SQL statements containing no embedded parameters. The descriptor name is generated by the driver.
SQLSetCursorName	none	The specified cursor name is used in the DECLARE CURSOR statement generated by **SQLExecute** or **SQLExecDirect**.
SQLGetCursorName	none	Driver cursor name management.
SQLExecute	EXECUTE or DECLARE CURSOR and OPEN CURSOR	Dynamic SQL EXECUTE. If the SQL statement requires a cursor, then a dynamic SQL DECLARE CURSOR statement and a dynamic SQL OPEN are issued at this time.
SQLExecDirect	EXECUTE IMMEDIATE or DECLARE CURSOR and OPEN CURSOR	The ODBC function call provides for support for a *cursor specification* and statements allowed in an EXECUTE IMMEDIATE dynamic SQL statement. In the case of a *cursor specification*, the call corresponds to static SQL DECLARE CURSOR and OPEN statements.
SQLNumResultCols	GET DESCRIPTOR	COUNT form of dynamic SQL GET DESCRIPTOR.
SQLColAttributes	GET DESCRIPTOR	COUNT form of dynamic SQL GET DESCRIPTOR or VALUE form of dynamic SQL GET DESCRIPTOR with *field-name* in {NAME, TYPE, LENGTH, PRECISION, SCALE, NULLABLE}.
SQLDescribeCol	GET DESCRIPTOR	VALUE form of dynamic SQL GET DESCRIPTOR with *field-name* in {NAME, TYPE, LENGTH, PRECISION, SCALE, NULLABLE}.
SQLBindCol	none	This function establishes output buffers that correspond in usage to host variables for static SQL FETCH, and to an SQL DESCRIPTOR for dynamic SQL FETCH *cursor* USING SQL DESCRIPTOR *descriptor*.
SQLFetch	FETCH	Static or dynamic SQL FETCH. If the call is a dynamic SQL FETCH, then the VALUE form of GET DESCRIPTOR is used, with *field-name* in {DATA, INDICATOR}. DATA and INDICATOR values are placed in output buffers specified in **SQLBindCol**.
SQLRowCount	GET DIAGNOSTICS	Requested field ROW_COUNT.

ODBC Function	Statement	Comments
SQLFreeStmt (SQL_CLOSE option)	CLOSE	Dynamic SQL CLOSE.
SQLFreeStmt (SQL_DROP option)	none	Driver Manager and driver memory deallocation.
SQLTransact	COMMIT WORK or COMMIT ROLLBACK	None.
SQLDisconnect	DISCONNECT	Association management.
SQLFreeConnect	none	Driver Manager and driver memory deallocation.
SQLFreeEnv	none	Driver Manager and driver memory deallocation.
SQLCancel	none	None.
SQLError	GET DIAGNOSTICS	GET DIAGNOSTICS retrieves information from the SQL diagnostics area that pertains to the most recently executed SQL statement. This information can be retrieved following execution and preceding the deallocation of the statement.

Embedded SQL to ODBC

The following tables list the relationship between the X/Open Embedded SQL language and corresponding ODBC functions. The section number shown in the first column of each table refers to the section of the X/Open and SQL Access Group SQL CAE specification (1992).

Declarative Statements

The following table lists declarative statements.

Section	SQL Statement	ODBC Function	Comments
4.3.1	Static SQL DECLARE CURSOR	none	Issued implicitly by the driver if a *cursor specification* is passed to **SQLExecDirect**.
4.3.2	Dynamic SQL DECLARE CURSOR	none	Cursor is generated automatically by the driver. To set a name for the cursor, use **SQLSetCursorName**. To retrieve a cursor name, use **SQLGetCursorName**.

Data Definition Statements

The following table lists data definition statements.

Section	SQL Statement	ODBC Function	Comments
5.1.2	ALTER TABLE	**SQLPrepare**,	None.
5.1.3	CREATE INDEX	**SQLExecute**,	
5.1.4	CREATE TABLE	or **SQLExecDirect**	
5.1.5	CREATE VIEW		
5.1.6	DROP INDEX		
5.1.7	DROP TABLE		
5.1.8	DROP VIEW		
5.1.9	GRANT REVOKE		

Data Manipulation Statements

The following table lists data manipulation statements.

Section	SQL Statement	ODBC Function	Comments
5.2.1	CLOSE	**SQLFreeStmt** (SQL_CLOSE option)	None.
5.2.2	Positioned DELETE	**SQLExecDirect**(...,"DELETE FROM *table-name* WHERE CURRENT OF *cursor-name*")	Driver-generated *cursor-name* can be obtained by calling **SQLGetCursorName**.
5.2.3	Searched DELETE	**SQLExecDirect**(..., "DELETE FROM *table-name* WHERE *search-condition*")	None.
5.2.4	FETCH	**SQLFetch**	None.
5.2.5	INSERT	**SQLExecDirect** (...,"INSERT INTO *table-name* ...")	Can also be invoked by **SQLPrepare** and **SQLExecute**.
5.2.6	OPEN	none	Cursor is OPENed implicitly by **SQLExecute** or **SQLExecDirect** when a SELECT statement is specified.
5.2.7	SELECT ...INTO	none	Not supported.
5.2.8	Positioned UPDATE	**SQLExecDirect**(...,"UPDATE *table-name* SET *column-identifier = expression* ...WHERE CURRENT OF *cursor-name*")	Driver-generated *cursor-name* can be obtained by calling **SQLGetCursorName**.
5.2.9	Searched UPDATE	**SQLExecDirect**(..., "UPDATE *table-name* SET *column-identifier = expression* ...WHERE *search-condition*")	None.

Dynamic SQL Statements

The following table lists dynamic SQL statements.

Section	SQL Statement	ODBC Function	Comments
5.3 (see 5.2.1)	Dynamic SQL **CLOSE**	**SQLFreeStmt** (SQL_CLOSE option)	None.
5.3(see5.2.2)	Dynamic SQL Positioned DELETE	**SQLExecDirect**(..., "DELETE FROM *table-name* WHERE CURRENT OF *cursor-name*")	Can also be invoked by **SQLPrepare** and **SQLExecute**.
5.3(see5.2.8)	Dynamic SQL Positioned UPDATE	**SQLExecDirect**(..., "UPDATE *table-name* SET *column-identifier* = *expression* ...WHERE CURRENT OF *cursor-name*")	Can also be invoked by **SQLPrepare** and **SQLExecute**.
5.3.3	ALLOCATE DESCRIPTOR	None	Descriptor information is implicitly allocated and attached to the *hstmt* by the driver. Allocation occurs at either the first call to **SQLBindParameter** or at **SQLExecute** or **SQLExecDirect** time.
5.3.4	DEALLOCATE DESCRIPTOR	**SQLFreeStmt** (SQL_DROP option)	None.
5.3.5	DESCRIBE	none	None.
5.3.6	EXECUTE	**SQLExecute**	None.
5.3.7	EXECUTE IMMEDIATE	**SQLExecDirect**	None.
5.3.8	Dynamic SQL FETCH	**SQLFetch**	None.
5.3.9	GET DESCRIPTOR	**SQLNumResultCols**	COUNT FORM.
		SQLDescribeCol **SQLColAttributes**	VALUE form with *field-name* in {NAME, TYPE, LENGTH, PRECISION, SCALE, NULLABLE}.
5.3.10	Dynamic SQL OPEN	**SQLExecute**	None.
5.3.11	PREPARE	**SQLPrepare**	None.
5.3.12	SET DESCRIPTOR	**SQLBindParameter**	**SQLBindParameter** is associated with only one *hstmt* where a descriptor is applied to any number of statements with USING SQL DESCRIPTOR.

Transaction Control Statements

The following table lists transaction control statements.

Section	SQL Statement	ODBC Function	Comments
5.4.1	COMMIT WORK	**SQLTransact** (SQL_COMMIT option)	None.
5.4.2	ROLLBACK WORK	**SQLTransact** (SQL_ROLLBACK option)	None.

Association Management Statements

The following table lists association management statements.

Section	SQL Statement	ODBC Function	Comments
5.5.1	CONNECT	**SQLConnect**	None.
5.5.2	DISCONNECT	**SQLDisconnect**	ODBC does not support DISCONNECT ALL.
5.5.3	SET CONNECTION	None	The SQL Access Group (SAG) Call Level Interface allows for multiple simultaneous connections to be established, but only one connection to be active at one time. SAG-compliant drivers track which connection is active, and automatically switch to a different connection if a different connection handle is specified. However, the active connection must be in a state that allows the connection context to be switched, in other words, there must not be a transaction in progress on the current connection.
			Drivers that are not SAG-compliant are not required to support this behavior. That is, drivers that are not SAG-compliant are not required to return an error if the driver and its associated data source can simultaneously support multiple active connections.

Diagnostic Statement

The following table lists the GET DIAGNOSTIC statement.

Section	SQL Statement	ODBC Function	Comments
5.6.1	GET DIAGNOSTICS	**SQLError** **SQLRowCount**	For **SQLError**, the following fields from the diagnostics area are available: RETURNED_SQLSTATE, MESSAGE_TEXT, and MESSAGE_LENGTH. For **SQLRowCount**, the ROW_COUNT field is available.

A P P E N D I X F

Scalar Functions

ODBC specifies five types of scalar functions:

- String functions
- Numeric functions
- Time and date functions
- System functions
- Data type conversion functions

The following sections list functions by function type. Descriptions include associated syntax.

String Functions

The following table lists string manipulation functions.

Character string literals used as arguments to scalar functions must be bounded by single quotes.

Arguments denoted as *string_exp* can be the name of a column, a string literal, or the result of another scalar function, where the underlying data type can be represented as SQL_CHAR, SQL_VARCHAR, or SQL_LONGVARCHAR.

Arguments denoted as *start*, *length* or *count* can be a numeric literal or the result of another scalar function, where the underlying data type can be represented as SQL_TINYINT, SQL_SMALLINT, or SQL_INTEGER.

The string functions listed here are 1-based, that is, the first character in the string is character 1.

Function	Description
ASCII(*string_exp*)	Returns the ASCII code value of the leftmost character of *string_exp* as an integer.
CHAR(*code*)	Returns the character that has the ASCII code value specified by *code*. The value of *code* should be between 0 and 255; otherwise, the return value is data source–dependent.
CONCAT(*string_exp1*, *string_exp2*)	Returns a character string that is the result of concatenating *string_exp2* to *string_exp1*. The resulting string is DBMS dependent. For example, if the column represented by *string_exp1* contained a NULL value, DB2 would return NULL, but SQL Server would return the non-NULL string.
DIFFERENCE(*string_exp1*, *string_exp2*)	Returns an integer value that indicates the difference between the values returned by the SOUNDEX function for *string_exp1* and *string_exp2*.
INSERT(*string_exp1*, *start,length*, *string_exp2*)	Returns a character string where *length* characters have been deleted from *string_exp1* beginning at *start* and where *string_exp2* has been inserted into *string_exp*, beginning at *start*.
LCASE(*string_exp*)	Converts all upper case characters in *string_exp* to lower case.
LEFT(*string_exp*, *count*)	Returns the leftmost *count* of characters of *string_exp*.
LENGTH(*string_exp*)	Returns the number of characters in *string_exp*, excluding trailing blanks and the string termination character.

Function	Description
LOCATE(*string_exp1*, *string_exp2*[, *start*])	Returns the starting position of the first occurrence of *string_exp1* within *string_exp2*. The search for the first occurrence of *string_exp1* begins with the first character position in *string_exp2* unless the optional argument, *start*, is specified. If *start* is specified, the search begins with the character position indicated by the value of *start*. The first character position in *string_exp2* is indicated by the value 1. If *string_exp1* is not found within *string_exp2,* the value 0 is returned.
LTRIM(*string_exp*)	Returns the characters of *string_exp,* with leading blanks removed.
REPEAT(*string_exp*,*count*)	Returns a character string composed of *string_exp* repeated *count* times.
REPLACE(*string_exp1*, *string_exp2*, *string_exp3*)	Replaces all occurrences of *string_exp2* in *string_exp1* with *string_exp3*.
RIGHT(*string_exp*, *count*)	Returns the rightmost *count* of characters of *string_exp*.
RTRIM(*string_exp*)	Returns the characters of *string_exp* with trailing blanks removed.
SOUNDEX(*string_exp*)	Returns a data source–dependent character string representing the sound of the words in *string_exp*. For example, SQL Server returns a four digit SOUNDEX code; Oracle returns a phonetic representation of each word.
SPACE(*count*)	Returns a character string consisting of *count* spaces.
SUBSTRING(*string_exp*, *start*, *length*)	Returns a character string that is derived from *string_exp* beginning at the character position specified by *start* for *length* characters.
UCASE(*string_exp*)	Converts all lower case characters in *string_exp* to upper case.

Numeric Functions

The following table describes numeric functions that are included in the ODBC scalar function set.

Arguments denoted as *numeric_exp* can be the name of a column, the result of another scalar function, or a numeric literal, where the underlying data type could be represented as SQL_NUMERIC, SQL_DECIMAL, SQL_TINYINT, SQL_SMALLINT, SQL_INTEGER, SQL_BIGINT, SQL_FLOAT, SQL_REAL, or SQL_DOUBLE.

Arguments denoted as *float_exp* can be the name of a column, the result of another scalar function, or a numeric literal, where the underlying data type can be represented as SQL_FLOAT.

Arguments denoted as *integer_exp* can be the name of a column, the result of another scalar function, or a numeric literal, where the underlying data type can be represented as SQL_TINYINT, SQL_SMALLINT, SQL_INTEGER, or SQL_BIGINT.

Function	Description
ABS(*numeric_exp*)	Returns the absolute value of *numeric_exp*.
ACOS(*float_exp*)	Returns the arccosine of *float_exp* as an angle, expressed in radians.
ASIN(*float_exp*)	Returns the arcsine of *float_exp* as an angle, expressed in radians.
ATAN(*float_exp*)	Returns the arctangent of *float_exp* as an angle, expressed in radians.
ATAN2(*float_exp1*, *float_exp2*)	Returns the arctangent of the x and y coordinates, specified by *float_exp1* and *float_exp2*, respectively, as an angle, expressed in radians.
CEILING(*numeric_exp*)	Returns the smallest integer greater than or equal to *numeric_exp*.
COS(*float_exp*)	Returns the cosine of *float_exp*, where *float_exp* is an angle expressed in radians.
COT(*float_exp*)	Returns the cotangent of *float_exp*, where *float_exp* is an angle expressed in radians.
DEGREES(*numeric_exp*)	Returns the number of degrees converted from *numeric_exp* radians.
EXP(*float_exp*)	Returns the exponential value of *float_exp*.
FLOOR(*numeric_exp*)	Returns largest integer less than or equal to *numeric_exp*.

Function	Description
LOG(*float_exp*)	Returns the natural logarithm of *float_exp*.
LOG10(*float_exp*)	Returns the base 10 logarithm of *float_exp*.
MOD(*integer_exp1*, *integer_exp2*)	Returns the remainder (modulus) of *integer_exp1* divided by *integer_exp2*.
PI( )	Returns the constant value of pi as a floating point value.
POWER(*numeric_exp*, *integer_exp*)	Returns the value of *numeric_exp* to the power of *integer_exp*.
RADIANS(*numeric_exp*)	Returns the number of radians converted from *numeric_exp* degrees.
RAND([*integer_exp*])	Returns a random floating point value using *integer_exp* as the optional seed value.
ROUND(*numeric_exp*, *integer_exp*)	Returns *numeric_exp* rounded to *integer_exp* places right of the decimal point. If *integer_exp* is negative, *numeric_exp* is rounded to |*integer_exp*| places to the left of the decimal point.
SIGN(*numeric_exp*)	Returns an indicator or the sign of *numeric_exp*. If *numeric_exp* is less than zero, –1 is returned. If *numeric_exp* equals zero, 0 is returned. If *numeric_exp* is greater than zero, 1 is returned.
SIN(*float_exp*)	Returns the sine of *float_exp*, where f*loat_exp* is an angle expressed in radians.
SQRT(*float_exp*)	Returns the square root of *float_exp*.
TAN(*float_exp*)	Returns the tangent of *float_exp*, where *float_exp* is an angle expressed in radians.
TRUNCATE(*numeric_exp*, *integer_exp*)	Returns *numeric_exp* truncated to *integer_exp* places right of the decimal point. If *integer_exp* is negative, *numeric_exp* is truncated to |*integer_exp*| places to the left of the decimal point.

Time and Date Functions

The following table lists time and date functions that are included in the ODBC scalar function set.

Arguments denoted as *timestamp_exp* can be the name of a column, the result of another scalar function, or a time, date, or timestamp literal, where the underlying data type could be represented as SQL_CHAR, SQL_VARCHAR, SQL_TIME, SQL_DATE, or SQL_TIMESTAMP.

Arguments denoted as *date_exp* can be the name of a column, the result of another scalar function, or a date or timestamp literal, where the underlying data type could be represented as SQL_CHAR, SQL_VARCHAR, SQL_DATE, or SQL_TIMESTAMP.

Arguments denoted as *time_exp* can be the name of a column, the result of another scalar function, or a time or timestamp literal, where the underlying data type could be represented as SQL_CHAR, SQL_VARCHAR, SQL_TIME, or SQL_TIMESTAMP.

Values returned are represented as ODBC data types.

Function	Description
CURDATE( )	Returns the current date as a date value.
CURTIME( )	Returns the current local time as a time value.
DAYNAME(*date_exp*)	Returns a character string containing the data source–specific name of the day (for example, Sunday, through Saturday or Sun. through Sat. for a data source that uses English, or Sonntag through Samstag for a data source that uses German) for the day portion of *date_exp*.
DAYOFMONTH(*date_exp*)	Returns the day of the month in *date_exp* as an integer value in the range of 1–31.
DAYOFWEEK(*date_exp*)	Returns the day to the week in *date_exp* as an integer value in the range of 1–7, where 1 represents Sunday.
DAYOFYEAR(*date_exp*)	Returns the day of the year in *date_exp* as an integer value in the range of 1–366.
HOUR(*time_exp*)	Returns the hour in *time_exp* as an integer value in the range of 0–23.
MINUTE(*time_exp*)	Returns the minute in *time_exp* as an integer value in the range of 0–59.
MONTH(*date_exp*)	Returns the month in *date_exp* as an integer value in the range of 1–12.

Function	Description
MONTHNAME(*date_exp*)	Returns a character string containing the data source–specific name of the month (for example, January throughDecember or Jan. through Dec. for a data source that uses English, or Januar through Dezember for a data source that uses German) for the month portion of *date_exp*.
NOW( )	Returns current date and time as a timestamp value.
QUARTER(*date_exp*)	Returns the quarter in *date_exp* as an integer value in the range of 1–4, where 1 represents January 1 through March 31.
SECOND(*time_exp*)	Returns the second in *time_exp* as an integer value in the range of 0–59.
TIMESTAMPADD(*interval*, *integer_exp*, *timestamp_exp*)	Returns the timestamp calculated by adding *integer_exp* intervals of type *interval* to *timestamp_exp*. Valid values of *interval* are the following keywords:

SQL_TSI_FRAC_SECOND
SQL_TSI_SECOND
SQL_TSI_MINUTE
SQL_TSI_HOUR
SQL_TSI_DAY
SQL_TSI_WEEK
SQL_TSI_MONTH
SQL_TSI_QUARTER
SQL_TSI_YEAR

where fractional seconds are expressed in billionths of a second. For example, the following SQL statement returns the name of each employee and their one-year anniversary dates:

```
SELECT NAME,
    {fn TIMESTAMPADD(SQL_TSI_YEAR,
    1, HIRE_DATE)} FROM EMPLOYEES
```

If *timestamp_exp* is a time value and *interval* specifies days, weeks, months, quarters, or years, the date portion of *timestamp_exp* is set to the current date before calculating the resulting timestamp.

If *timestamp_exp* is a date value and *interval* specifies fractional seconds, seconds, minutes, or hours, the time portion of *timestamp_exp* is set to 0 before calculating the resulting timestamp.

An application determines which intervals a data source supports by calling **SQLGetInfo** with the SQL_TIMEDATE_ADD_INTERVALS option.

Function	Description
TIMESTAMPDIFF(*interval*, *timestamp_exp1*, *timestamp_exp2*)	Returns the integer number of intervals of type *interval* by which *timestamp_exp2* is greater than *timestamp_exp1*. Valid values of *interval* are the following keywords:

SQL_TSI_FRAC_SECOND
SQL_TSI_SECOND
SQL_TSI_MINUTE
SQL_TSI_HOUR
SQL_TSI_DAY
SQL_TSI_WEEK
SQL_TSI_MONTH
SQL_TSI_QUARTER
SQL_TSI_YEAR

where fractional seconds are expressed in billionths of a second. For example, the following SQL statement returns the name of each employee and the number of years they have been employed.

```
SELECT NAME,
    {fn TIMESTAMPDIFF('SQL_TSI_YEAR',
    {fn CURDATE()}, HIRE_DATE)}
    FROM EMPLOYEES
```

If either timestamp expression is a time value and *interval* specifies days, weeks, months, quarters, or years, the date portion of that timestamp is set to the current date before calculating the difference between the timestamps.

If either timestamp expression is a date value and *interval* specifies fractional seconds, seconds, minutes, or hours, the time portion of of that timestamp is set to 0 before calculating the difference between the timestamps.

An application determines which intervals a data source supports by calling **SQLGetInfo** with the SQL_TIMEDATE_DIFF_INTERVALS option.

Function	Description
WEEK(*date_exp*)	Returns the week of the year in *date_exp* as an integer value in the range of 1–53.
YEAR(*date_exp*)	Returns the year in *date_exp* as an integer value. The range is data source–dependent.

System Functions

The following table lists system functions that are included in the ODBC scalar function set.

Arguments denoted as *exp* can be the name of a column, the result of another scalar function, or a literal, where the underlying data type could be represented as SQL_NUMERIC, SQL_DECIMAL, SQL_TINYINT, SQL_SMALLINT, SQL_INTEGER, SQL_BIGINT, SQL_FLOAT, SQL_REAL, SQL_DOUBLE, SQL_DATE, SQL_TIME, or SQL_TIMESTAMP.

Arguments denoted as *value* can be a literal constant, where the underlying data type can be represented as SQL_NUMERIC, SQL_DECIMAL, SQL_TINYINT, SQL_SMALLINT, SQL_INTEGER, SQL_BIGINT, SQL_FLOAT, SQL_REAL, SQL_DOUBLE, SQL_DATE, SQL_TIME, or SQL_TIMESTAMP.

Values returned are represented as ODBC data types.

Function	Description
DATABASE( )	Returns the name of the database corresponding to the connection handle (*hdbc*). (The name of the database is also available by calling **SQLGetConnectOption** with the SQL_CURRENT_QUALIFIER connection option.)
IFNULL(*exp*,*value*)	If *exp* is null, *value* is returned. If *exp* is not null, *exp* is returned. The possible data type(s) of *value* must be compatible with the data type of *exp*.
USER( )	Returns the user's authorization name. (The user's authorization name is also available via **SQLGetInfo** by specifying the information type: SQL_USER_NAME.)

Explicit Data Type Conversion

Explicit data type conversion is specified in terms of ODBC SQL data type definitions.

The ODBC syntax for the explicit data type conversion function does not restrict conversions. The validity of specific conversions of one data type to another data type will be determined by each driver-specific implementation. The driver will, as it translates the ODBC syntax into the native syntax, reject those conversions that, although legal in the ODBC syntax, are not supported by the data source. The ODBC function **SQLGetInfo** provides a way to inquire about conversions supported by the data source.

The format of the **CONVERT** function is:

CONVERT(*value_exp*, *data_type*)

The function returns the value specified by *value_exp* converted to the specified *data_type*, where *data_type* is one of the following keywords:

SQL_BIGINT	SQL_LONGVARBINARY
SQL_BINARY	SQL_LONGVARCHAR
SQL_BIT	SQL_REAL
SQL_CHAR	SQL_SMALLINT
SQL_DATE	SQL_TIME
SQL_DECIMAL	SQL_TIMESTAMP
SQL_DOUBLE	SQL_TINYINT
SQL_FLOAT	SQL_VARBINARY
SQL_INTEGER	SQL_VARCHAR

The ODBC syntax for the explicit data type conversion function does not support specification of conversion format. If specification of explicit formats is supported by the underlying data source, a driver must specify a default value or implement format specification.

The argument *value_exp* can be a column name, the result of another scalar function, or a numeric or string literal. For example:

```
{ fn CONVERT( { fn CURDATE() }, SQL_CHAR) }
```

converts the output of the CURDATE scalar function to a character string..

The following two examples illustrate the use of the **CONVERT** function. These examples assume the existence of a table called EMPLOYEES, with an EMPNO column of type SQL_SMALLINT and an EMPNAME column of type SQL_CHAR.

If an application specifies the following:

```
SELECT EMPNO FROM EMPLOYEES WHERE
    --(*vendor(Microsoft),product(ODBC) fn CONVERT(EMPNO,SQL_CHAR)*)--
    LIKE '1%'
```

or its equivalent in shorthand form:

```
SELECT EMPNO FROM EMPLOYEES WHERE
    {fn CONVERT(EMPNO,SQL_CHAR)} LIKE '1%'
```

A driver that supports an ORACLE DBMS would translate the request to:

```
SELECT EMPNO FROM EMPLOYEES WHERE to_char(EMPNO) LIKE '1%'
```

A driver that supports a SQL Server DBMS would translate the request to:

```
SELECT EMPNO FROM EMPLOYEES WHERE convert(char,EMPNO) LIKE '1%'
```

If an application specifies the following:

```
SELECT
--(*vendor(Microsoft),product(ODBC) fn ABS(EMPNO)*)--,
--(*vendor(Microsoft),product(ODBC) fn CONVERT(EMPNAME,SQL_SMALLINT)*)--
    FROM EMPLOYEES WHERE EMPNO <> 0
```

or its equivalent in shorthand form:

```
SELECT {fn ABS(EMPNO)}, {fn CONVERT(EMPNAME,SQL_SMALLINT)}
    FROM EMPLOYEES WHERE EMPNO <> 0
```

A driver that supports an Oracle DBMS would translate the request to:

```
SELECT abs(EMPNO), to_number(EMPNAME) FROM EMPLOYEES WHERE EMPNO <> 0
```

A driver that supports a SQL Server DBMS would translate the request to:

```
SELECT abs(EMPNO), convert(smallint, EMPNAME) FROM EMPLOYEES
    WHERE EMPNO != 0
```

A driver that supports an Ingres DBMS would translate the request to:

```
SELECT abs(EMPNO), int2(EMPNAME) FROM EMPLOYEES WHERE EMPNO <> 0
```

APPENDIX G

ODBC Cursor Library

The ODBC cursor library (ODBCCURS.DLL on Windows 3.1 and ODBCCR32.DLL on Windows NT) supports block scrollable cursors for any driver that complies with the Level 1 API conformance level; it can be redistributed by developers with their applications or drivers. The cursor library also supports positioned update and delete statements for result sets generated by **SELECT** statements. Although it only supports static and forward-only cursors, the cursor library satisfies the needs of many applications. Furthermore, it provides good performance, especially for small- to medium-sized result sets.

The cursor library is a dynamic-link library (DLL) that resides between the Driver Manager and the driver. When an application calls a function, the Driver Manager calls the function in the cursor library, which either executes the function or calls it in the specified driver. For a given connection, an application specifies whether the cursor library is always used, used if the driver does not support scrollable cursors, or never used.

To implement block cursors in **SQLExtendedFetch**, the cursor library repeatedly calls **SQLFetch** in the driver. To implement scrolling, it caches the data it has retrieved in memory and in disk files. When an application requests a new rowset, the cursor library retrieves it as necessary from the driver or the cache.

To implement positioned update and delete statements, the cursor library constructs an **UPDATE** or **DELETE** statement with a **WHERE** clause that specifies the cached value of each bound column in the row. When it executes a positioned update statement, the cursor library updates its cache from the values in the rowset buffers.

Using the ODBC Cursor Library

To use the ODBC cursor library, an application:

1. Calls **SQLSetConnectOption** to specify how the cursor library should be used with a particular connection. The cursor library can be always used, used only if driver does not support scrollable cursors, or never used.

2. Calls **SQLConnect**, **SQLDriverConnect**, or **SQLBrowseConnect** to connect to the data source.

3. Calls **SQLSetStmtOptions** to specify the cursor type, concurrency, and rowset size. The cursor library supports forward-only and static cursors. Forward-only cursors must be read-only, while static cursors may be read-only or use optimistic concurrency control comparing values.

4. Allocates one or more rowset buffers and calls **SQLBindCol** one or more times to bind these buffers to result set columns. For more information, see "Assigning Storage for Rowsets (Binding)" in Chapter 7, "Retrieving Results."

5. Generates a result set by executing a **SELECT** statement or a procedure, or by calling a catalog function. If the application will execute positioned update statements, it should execute a **SELECT FOR UPDATE** statement to generate the result set.

6. Calls **SQLExtendedFetch** one or more times to scroll through the result set.

The application can change data values in the rowset buffers. To refresh the rowset buffers with data from the cursor library's cache, an application calls **SQLExtendedFetch** and with the *fFetchType* argument set to SQL_FETCH_RELATIVE and the *irow* argument set to 0.

To retrieve data from an unbound column, the application calls **SQLSetPos** to position the cursor on the desired row. It then calls **SQLGetData** to retrieve the data.

To determine the number of rows that have been retrieved from the data source, the application calls **SQLRowCount**.

Executing Positioned Update and Delete Statements

After an application has fetched a block of data with **SQLExtendedFetch**, it can update or delete the data in the block. To execute a positioned update or delete, the application:

1. Calls **SQLSetPos** to position the cursor on the row to be updated or deleted.

2. Constructs a positioned update or delete statement with the following syntax:

   UPDATE *table-name*
   SET *column-identifier* = {*expression* I **NULL**}
       [, *column-identifier* = {*expression* I **NULL**}]
   WHERE CURRENT OF *cursor-name*

   DELETE FROM *table-name* **WHERE CURRENT OF** *cursor-name*

The easiest way to construct the **SET** clause in a positioned update statement is to use parameter markers for each column to be updated and use **SQLBindParameter** to bind these to the rowset buffers for the row to be updated.

3. Updates the rowset buffers for the current row if it will execute a positioned update statement. After successfully executing a positioned update statement, the cursor library copies the values from each column in the current row to its cache.

Caution If the application does not correctly update the rowset buffers before executing a positioned update statement, the data in the cache will be incorrect after the statement is executed.

---

4. Executes the positioned update or delete statement using a different *hstmt* than the *hstmt* associated with the cursor.

Caution The **WHERE** clause constructed by the cursor library to identify the current row can fail to identify any rows, identify a different row, or identify more than one row. For more information, see "Constructing Searched Statements" later in this appendix.

All positioned update and delete statements require a cursor name. To specify the cursor name, an application calls **SQLSetCursorName** before the cursor is opened. To use the cursor name generated by the driver, an application calls **SQLGetCursorName** after the cursor is opened.

After the cursor library executes a positioned update or delete statement, the status array, rowset buffers, and cache maintained by the cursor library contain the values shown in the following table.

Statement used	Value in *rgfRowStatus*	Values in rowset buffers	Values in cache buffers
Positioned update	SQL_ROW_UPDATED	New values [1]	New values [1]
Positioned delete	SQL_ROW_DELETED	Old values	Old values

1 The application must update the values in the rowset buffers before executing the positioned update statement; after executing the positioned update statement, the cursor library copies the values in the rowset buffers to its cache.

Code Example

The following example uses the cursor library to retrieve each employee's name, age, and birthday from the EMPLOYEE table. It then displays 20 rows of data. If the user updates this data, the code updates the rowset buffers and executes a positioned update statement. Finally, it prompts the user for the direction to scroll and repeats the process.

```
#define ROWS 20
#define NAME_LEN 30
#define BDAY_LEN 11
#define DONE -1


HENV    henv;
HDBC    hdbc;
HSTMT   hstmt1, hstmt2;
RETCODE retcode;
UCHAR   szName[ROWS][NAME_LEN], szBirthday[ROWS][BDAY_LEN];
UCHAR   szNewName[NAME_LEN], szNewBday[BDAY_LEN];
SWORD   sAge[ROWS], sNewAge[ROWS];
SDWORD  cbName[ROWS], cbAge[ROWS], cbBirthday[ROWS];
UDWORD  fFetchType, crow, irow, irowUpdt;
UWORD   rgfRowStatus[ROWS];

SQLAllocEnv(&henv);
SQLAllocConnect(henv, &hdbc);

/* Specify that the ODBC Cursor Library is always used, then connect. */

SQLSetConnectOption(hdbc, SQL_ODBC_CURSORS, SQL_CUR_USE_ODBC);
SQLConnect(hdbc, "EmpData", SQL_NTS,
                 "JohnS", SQL_NTS,
                 "Sesame", SQL_NTS);

if (retcode == SQL_SUCCESS || retcode == SQL_SUCCESS_WITH_INFO) {

    /* Allocate a statement handle for the result set and a statement */
    /* handle for positioned update statements.                       */

    SQLAllocStmt(hdbc, &hstmt1);
    SQLAllocStmt(hdbc, &hstmt2);

    /* Specify an updateable static cursor with 20 rows of data. Set */
    /* the cursor name, execute the SELECT statement, and bind the   */
    /* rowset buffers to result set columns in column-wise fashion.  */
```

```
SQLSetStmtOption(hstmt1, SQL_CONCURRENCY, SQL_CONCUR_VALUES);
SQLSetStmtOption(hstmt1, SQL_CURSOR_TYPE, SQL_SCROLL_STATIC);
SQLSetStmtOption(hstmt1, SQL_ROWSET_SIZE, ROWS);
SQLSetCursorName(hstmt1, "EMPCURSOR", SQL_NTS);
SQLExecDirect(hstmt1,
              "SELECT NAME, AGE, BIRTHDAY FROM EMPLOYEE\
               FOR UPDATE OF NAME, AGE, BIRTHDAY",
              SQL_NTS);
SQLBindCol(hstmt1, 1, SQL_C_CHAR, szName, NAME_LEN, cbName);
SQLBindCol(hstmt1, 2, SQL_C_SSHORT, sAge, 0, cbAge);
SQLBindCol(hstmt1, 3, SQL_C_CHAR, szBirthday, BDAY_LEN, cbBirthday);

/* Fetch the first block of data and display it. Prompt the user   */
/* for new data values. If the user supplies new values, update    */
/* the rowset buffers, bind them to the parameters in the update   */
/* statement, and execute a positioned update on another hstmt.    */
/* Prompt the user for how to scroll. Fetch and redisplay data as  */
/* needed.                                                         */

fFetchType = SQL_FETCH_FIRST;
irow = 0;
do {

    SQLExtendedFetch(hstmt1, fFetchType, irow, &crow, rgfRowStatus);
    DisplayRows(szName, sAge, szBirthday, rgfStatus);

    if (PromptUpdate(&irowUpdt,szNewName,&sNewAge,szNewBday)==TRUE){
        strcpy(szName[irowUpdt], szNewName);
        cbName[irowUpdt] = SQL_NTS;
        sAge[irowUpdt] = sNewAge;
        cbAge[irowUpdt] = 0;
        strcpy(szBirthday[irowUpdt], szNewBday);
        cbBirthday[irowUpdt] = SQL_NTS;
        SQLBindParameter(hstmt2, 1, SQL_PARAM_INPUT,
              SQL_C_CHAR, SQL_CHAR, NAME_LEN, 0,
              szName[irowUpdt], NAME_LEN, &cbName[irowUpdt]);
        SQLBindParameter(hstmt2, 2, SQL_PARAM_INPUT,
              SQL_C_SSHORT, SQL_SMALLINT, 0, 0,
              &sAge[irowUpdt], 0, &cbAge[irowUpdt]);
        SQLBindParameter(hstmt2, 3, SQL_PARAM_INPUT,
              SQL_C_CHAR, SQL_DATE, 0, 0,
              szBirthday[irowUpdt], BDAY_LEN, &cbBirthday[irowUpdt]);
        SQLExecDirect(hstmt2,
                    "UPDATE EMPLOYEE\
                     SET (NAME = ?, AGE = ?, BIRTHDAY = ?)\
                     WHERE CURRENT OF EMPCURSOR",
                     SQL_NTS);
    }

while (PromptScroll(&fFetchType, &irow) != DONE)
}
```

Implementation Notes

This section describes how the ODBC cursor library is implemented. It describes how the cursor library maintains its cache, executes SQL statements, and implements ODBC functions.

Cursor Library Cache

For each row of data in the result set, the cursor library caches the data for each bound column, the length of the data in each bound column, and the status of the row. The cursor library uses the values in the cache both to return through **SQLExtendedFetch** and to construct searched statements for positioned operations. For more information, see "Constructing Searched Statements" later in this appendix.

Column Data

The cursor library creates a buffer in the cache for each *rgbValue* buffer bound to the result set with **SQLBindCol**. It uses the values in these buffers to construct a **WHERE** clause when it emulates positioned update or delete statement. It updates these buffers from the rowset buffers when it fetches data from the data source and when it executes positioned update statements.

These buffers have the following restrictions:

- On Windows 3.1, the cursor library restricts the size of the buffers bound with **SQLBindCol**; these restrictions do not exist on Windows NT.

  When column-wise binding is used, the size of each *rgbValue* buffer cannot exceed 65,500 bytes, the size of each *pcbValue* buffer cannot exceed 65,500 bytes, and the total size of the data (*rgbValue*) and length-of-data (*pcbValue*) fields for a single row of data cannot exceed 65,500 bytes.

  When row-wise binding is used, the size of the entire rowset buffer, including data and length-of-data fields for each row of each bound column, cannot exceed 65,500 bytes.

- On Windows 3.1, the *rgbValue* and *pcbValue* buffers bound with **SQLBindCol** cannot cross segment boundaries.

- When it updates a column, a data source blank-pads fixed-length character data and zero-pads fixed-length binary data as necessary. For example, a data source stores "Smith" in a CHAR(10) column as "Smith   ". The cursor library does not blank- or zero-pad data in the rowset buffers when it copies this data to its cache after executing a positioned update statement. Therefore, if an application requires that the values in the cursor library's cache are blank- or zero-padded, it must blank- or zero-pad the values in the rowset buffers before executing a positioned update statement.

Length of Column Data

The cursor library creates a buffer in the cache for each *pcbValue* buffer bound to the result set with **SQLBindCol**. It uses the values in these buffers to construct a **WHERE** clause when it emulates positioned update or delete statements. It updates these buffers from the rowset buffers when it fetches data from the data source and when it executes positioned update statements.

Row Status

The cursor library creates a buffer in the cache for the row status. The cursor library retrieves values for the *rgfRowStatus* array in **SQLExtendedFetch** from this buffer. For each row, the cursor library sets this buffer to:

- SQL_ROW_DELETED when it executes a positioned delete statement on the row.
- SQL_ROW_ERROR when it encounters an error retrieving the row from the data source with **SQLFetch**.
- SQL_ROW_SUCCESS when it successfully fetches the row from the data source with **SQLFetch**.
- SQL_ROW_UPDATED when it executes a positioned update statement on the row.

Location of Cache

The cursor library caches data in memory and in Windows temporary files. This limits the size of the result set that the cursor library can handle only by available disk space. If the cursor library terminates abnormally, such as when the power fails, it may leave Windows temporary files on the disk. These are named ~CTT*nnnn*.TMP and are created in the temporary directory (usually the directory specified in the TEMP environment variable).

SQL Statements

The ODBC cursor library passes all SQL statements directly to the driver except the following:

- Positioned update and delete statements.
- **SELECT FOR UPDATE** statements.
- Batched SQL statements.

To execute positioned update and delete statements and to position the cursor on a row to call **SQLGetData** for that row, the cursor library constructs a searched statement that identifies the row.

Positioned Update and Delete Statements

The cursor library supports positioned update and delete statements by replacing the **WHERE CURRENT OF** clause in such statements with a **WHERE** clause that enumerates the values stored in its cache for each bound column. The cursor library passes the newly constructed **UPDATE** and **DELETE** statements to the driver for execution. For positioned update statements, it then updates its cache from the values in the rowset buffers and sets the corresponding value in the *rgfRowStatus* array in **SQLExtendedFetch** to SQL_ROW_UPDATED. For positioned delete statements, it sets the corresponding value in the *rgfRowStatus* array to SQL_ROW_DELETED.

Caution The **WHERE** clause constructed by the cursor library to identify the current row can fail to identify any rows, identify a different row, or identify more than one row. For more information, see "Constructing Searched Statements" later in this appendix.

Positioned update and delete statements are subject to the following restrictions:

- Positioned update and delete statements can only be used when a **SELECT** statement generated the result set, the **SELECT** statement did not contain a join, a **UNION** clause, or a **GROUP BY** clause, and any columns that used an alias or expression in the select list were not bound with **SQLBindCol**.

- If an application prepares a positioned update or delete statement, it must do so after it has called **SQLExtendedFetch**. Although the cursor library submits the statement to the driver for preparation, it closes the statement and executes it directly when the application calls **SQLExecute**.

- If the driver only supports one active *hstmt*, the cursor library fetches the rest of the result set and then refetches the current rowset from its cache before it executing a positioned update or delete statement.

SELECT FOR UPDATE Statements

For maximum interoperability, applications should generate result sets that will be updated with a positioned update statement by executing a **SELECT FOR UPDATE** statement. Although the cursor library does not require this, it is required by most data sources that support positioned update statements.

The cursor library ignores the columns in the **FOR UPDATE** clause of a **SELECT FOR UPDATE** statement; it removes this clause before passing the statement to the driver. In the cursor library, the SQL_CONCURRENCY statement option, along with the restrictions mentioned in the previous section, controls whether the columns in a result set can be updated.

Batched SQL Statements

The cursor library does not support batched SQL statements, including SQL statements for which **SQLParamOptions** has been called with *crow* greater than 1. If an application submits a batched SQL statement to the cursor library, the results are undefined.

Constructing Searched Statements

To support positioned update and delete statements, the cursor library constructs a searched **UPDATE** or **DELETE** statement from the positioned statement. To support calls to **SQLGetData** in a block of data, the cursor library constructs a searched **SELECT** statement to create a result set containing the current row of data. In each of these statements, the **WHERE** clause enumerates the values stored in the cache for each bound column that returns SQL_SEARCHABLE or SQL_ALL_EXCEPT_LIKE for the SQL_COLUMN_SEARCHABLE descriptor type in **SQLColAttributes**.

Caution The **WHERE** clause constructed by the cursor library to identify the current row can fail to identify any rows, identify a different row, or identify more than one row.

If a positioned update or delete statement affects more than one row, the cursor library updates the *rgfRowStatus* array only for the row on which the cursor is positioned and returns SQL_SUCCESS_WITH_INFO and SQLSTATE 01S04 (More than one row updated or deleted). If the statement does not identify any rows, the cursor library does not update the *rgfRowStatusArray* and returns SQL_SUCCESS_WITH_INFO and SQLSTATE 01S03 (No rows updated or deleted). An application can call **SQLRowCount** to determine the number of rows that were updated or deleted.

If the **SELECT** clause used to position the cursor for a call to **SQLGetData** identifies more than one row, **SQLGetData** is not guaranteed to return the correct data. If it does not identify any rows, **SQLGetData** returns SQL_NO_DATA_FOUND.

If an application conforms to the following guidelines, the **WHERE** clause constructed by the cursor library should uniquely identify the current row, except when this is impossible, such as when the data source contains duplicate rows.

- **Bind columns that uniquely identify the row.** If the bound columns do not uniquely identify the row, the **WHERE** clause constructed by the cursor library might identify more than one row. In a positioned update or delete statement, such a clause might cause more than one row to be updated or deleted. In a call to **SQLGetData**, such a clause might cause the driver to return data for the wrong row. Binding all the columns in a unique key guarantees that each row is uniquely identified.

- **Allocate data buffers large enough that no truncation occurs.** The cursor library's cache is a copy of the values in the *rgbValue* buffers bound to the result set with **SQLBindCol**. If data is truncated when it is placed in these buffers, it will also be truncated in the cache. A **WHERE** clause constructed from truncated values might not correctly identify the underlying row in the data source.

- **Specify non-null length buffers for binary C data.** The cursor library allocates length buffers in its cache only if the *pcbValue* argument in **SQLBindCol** is non-null. When the *fCType* argument is SQL_C_BINARY, the cursor library requires the length of the binary data to construct a **WHERE** clause from the data. If there is no length buffer for a SQL_C_BINARY column and the application calls **SQLGetData** or attempts to execute a positioned update or delete statement, the cursor library returns SQL_ERROR and SQLSTATE SL014 (A positioned request was issued and not all column count fields were buffered).

- **Specify non-null length buffers for nullable columns.** The cursor library allocates length buffers in its cache only if the *pcbValue* argument in **SQLBindCol** is non-null. Because SQL_NULL_DATA is stored in the length buffer, the cursor library assumes that any column for which no length buffer is specified is non-nullable. If no length column is specified for a nullable column, the cursor library constructs a **WHERE** clause that uses the data value for the column. This clause will not correctly identify the row.

ODBC Functions

When the ODBC cursor library is enabled for a connection, the Driver Manager calls functions in the cursor library instead of in the driver. The cursor library either executes the function or calls it in the specified driver.

SQLBindCol

An application allocates one or more buffers for the cursor library to return the current rowset in. It calls **SQLBindCol** one or more times to bind these buffers to the result set.

Note On Windows 3.1, the *rgbValue* and *pcbValue* buffers bound with **SQLBindCol** cannot cross segment boundaries and cursor library restricts their size; these restrictions do not exist on Windows NT.

When column-wise binding is used, the size of each *rgbValue* buffer cannot exceed 65,500 bytes, the size of each *pcbValue* buffer cannot exceed 65,500 bytes, and the total size of the data (*rgbValue*) and length-of-data (*pcbValue*) fields for a single row of data cannot exceed 65,500 bytes.

When row-wise binding is used, the size of the entire rowset buffer, including data and length-of-data fields for each row of each bound column, cannot exceed 65,500 bytes.

If the application calls **SQLBindCol** to rebind result set columns after it has called **SQLExtendedFetch**, the cursor library returns an error. Before it can rebind result set columns, the application must close the cursor.

SQLExtendedFetch

The cursor library implements **SQLExtendedFetch** by repeatedly calling **SQLFetch**. It transfers the data it retrieves from the driver to the rowset buffers provided by the application. It also caches the data in memory and disk files. When an application requests a new rowset, the cursor library retrieves it as necessary from the driver or the cache. Finally, the cursor library maintains the status of the cached data and returns this information to the application in the *rgfRowStatus* buffer.

Rowset Buffers

The cursor library optimizes the transfer of data from the driver to the rowset buffer provided by the application if:

- The application uses row-wise binding.

- There are no unused bytes between fields in the structure the application declares to hold a row of data.

- The fields in which **SQLExtendedFetch** returns the number of available bytes for a column follows the buffer for that column and precedes the buffer for the next column. Note that these fields are optional.

When the application requests a new rowset, the cursor library retrieves data from its cache and from the driver as necessary. If the new and old rowsets overlap, the cursor library may optimize its performance by reusing the data from the overlapping sections of the rowset buffers. Thus, unsaved changes to the rowset buffers are lost unless the new and old rowsets overlap and the changes are in the overlapping sections of the rowset buffers. To save the changes, an application submits a positioned update statement.

Note that the cursor library always refreshes the rowset buffers with data from the cache when an application calls **SQLExtendedFetch** with the *fFetchType* argument set to SQL_FETCH_RELATIVE and the *irow* argument set to 0.

Result Set Membership

The cursor library retrieves data from the driver only as the application requests it. Depending on the data source and the setting of the SQL_CONCURRENCY statement option, this has the following consequences:

- The data retrieved by the cursor library may differ from the data that was available at the time the statement was executed. For example, after the cursor was opened, rows inserted at a point beyond the current cursor position can be retrieved by some drivers.

- The data in the result set may be locked by the data source for the cursor library and therefore unavailable to other users.

Once the cursor library has cached a row of data, it cannot detect changes to that row in the underlying data source (except for positioned updates and deletes). This occurs because, for calls to **SQLExtendedFetch**, the cursor library never refetches data from the data source. Instead it refetches data from its cache.

Scrolling

The cursor library supports the following fetch types in **SQLExtendedFetch**:

Cursor Type	Fetch Types
Forward-only	SQL_FETCH_NEXT
Static	SQL_FETCH_NEXT
	SQL_FETCH_PRIOR
	SQL_FETCH_FIRST
	SQL_FETCH_LAST
	SQL_FETCH_RELATIVE
	SQL_FETCH_ABSOLUTE

Errors

If the driver returns SQL_SUCCESS_WITH_INFO to the cursor library from **SQLFetch**, the cursor library ignores the warning. It retrieves the rest of the rowset from the driver and returns SQL_SUCCESS_WITH_INFO for **SQLExtendedFetch**. The application cannot call **SQLError** to retrieve the warning information unless the warning occurred the last time the cursor library called **SQLFetch**.

Interaction with Other Functions

An application must call **SQLExtendedFetch** before it prepares or executes any positioned update or delete statements.

SQLFreeStmt

If an application calls **SQLFreeStmt** with the SQL_UNBIND option after it calls **SQLExtendedFetch**, the cursor library returns an error. Before it can unbind result set columns, an application must call **SQLFreeStmt** with the SQL_CLOSE option.

SQLGetData

The cursor library implements **SQLGetData** by first constructing a **SELECT** statement with a **WHERE** clause that enumerates the values stored in its cache for each bound column in the current row. It then executes the **SELECT** statement to reselect the row and calls **SQLGetData** in the driver to retrieve the data from the data source (as opposed to the cache).

Caution   The **WHERE** clause constructed by the cursor library to identify the current row can fail to identify any rows, identify a different row, or identify more than one row. For more information, see "Constructing Searched Statements" earlier in this appendix.

Calls to **SQLGetData** are subject to the following restrictions:

- **SQLGetData** cannot be called for forward-only cursors.

- **SQLGetData** can only be called when a **SELECT** statement generated the result set, the **SELECT** statement did not contain a join, a **UNION** clause, or a **GROUP BY** clause, and any columns that used an alias or expression in the select list were not bound with **SQLBindCol**.

- If the driver only supports one active *hstmt*, the cursor library fetches the rest of the result set before executing the **SELECT** statement and calling **SQLGetData**.

SQLGetFunctions

The cursor library returns that it supports **SQLExtendedFetch**, **SQLSetPos**, and **SQLSetScrollOptions** in addition to the functions supported by the driver.

SQLGetInfo

The cursor library returns values for the following values of *fInfoType* (| represents a bitwise OR); for all other values of *fInfoType*, it calls **SQLGetInfo** in the driver:

fInfoType	Returned Value
SQL_BOOKMARK_PERSISTENCE	0
SQL_FETCH_DIRECTION	SQL_FD_FETCH_ABSOLUTE | SQL_FD_FETCH_FIRST | SQL_FD_FETCH_LAST | SQL_FD_FETCH_NEXT | SQL_FD_FETCH_PRIOR | SQL_FD_FETCH_RELATIVE
SQL_GETDATA_EXTENSIONS	SQL_GD_BLOCK | any values returned by the driver

Note   When data is retrieved with **SQLExtendedFetch**, **SQLGetData** supports the functionality specified with the SQL_GD_ANY_COLUMN and SQL_GD_BOUND bitmasks.

fInfoType	Returned Value
SQL_LOCK_TYPES	SQL_LCK_NO_CHANGE
SQL_POS_OPERATIONS	SQL_POS_POSITION
SQL_POSITIONED_STATEMENTS	SQL_PS_POSITIONED_DELETE | SQL_PS_POSITIONED_UPDATE | SQL_PS_SELECT_FOR_UPDATE
SQL_ROW_UPDATES	"Y"
SQL_SCROLL_CONCURRENCY	SQL_SCCO_READ_ONLY | SQL_SCCO_OPT_VALUES
SQL_SCROLL_OPTIONS	SQL_SO_FORWARD_ONLY | SQL_SO_STATIC
SQL_STATIC_SENSITIVITY	SQL_SS_UPDATES

Important The cursor library implements the same cursor behavior when transactions are committed or rolled back as the data source. That is, committing or rolling back a transaction, either by calling **SQLTransact** or by using the SQL_AUTOCOMMIT connection option, can cause the data source to delete the access plans and close the cursors for all *hstmts* on an *hdbc*. For more information, see the SQL_CURSOR_COMMIT_BEHAVIOR and SQL_CURSOR_ROLLBACK_BEHAVIOR information types in **SQLGetInfo**.

SQLGetStmtOption

The cursor library supports the following statement options with **SQLGetStmtOption**:

SQL_BIND_TYPE	SQL_ROW_NUMBER
SQL_CONCURRENCY	SQL_ROWSET_SIZE
SQL_CURSOR_TYPE	SQL_SIMULATE_CURSOR

SQLNativeSql

If the driver supports this function, the cursor library calls **SQLNativeSql** in the driver passes the SQL statement. For positioned update, positioned delete, and **SELECT FOR UPDATE** statements, the cursor library modifies the statement before passing it to the driver.

SQLRowCount

When an application calls **SQLRowCount** with the *hstmt* associated with the cursor, the cursor library returns the number of rows of data it has retrieved from the driver.

When an application calls **SQLRowCount** with the *hstmt* associated with a positioned update or delete statement, the cursor library returns the number of rows affected by the statement.

SQLSetConnectOption

An application calls **SQLSetConnectOption** with the SQL_ODBC_CURSORS option to specify whether the cursor library is always used, used if the driver does not support scrollable cursors, or never used. The cursor library assumes that a driver supports scrollable cursors if it returns SQL_FD_FETCH_PRIOR for the SQL_FETCH_DIRECTION option in **SQLGetInfo**.

The application must call **SQLSetConnectOption** to specify the cursor library usage after it calls **SQLAllocConnect** and before it connects to the data source. If an application calls **SQLSetConnectOption** with the SQL_ODBC_CURSORS option while the connection is still active, the cursor library returns an error.

To set a statement option supported by the cursor library for all *hstmts* associated with an *hdbc*, an application must call **SQLSetConnectOption** for that statement option after it connects to the data source and before it opens the cursor. If an application calls **SQLSetConnectOption** with a statement option and a cursor is open on an *hstmt* associated with the *hdbc*, the statement option will not be applied to that *hstmt* until the cursor is closed and reopened.

SQLSetPos

The cursor library only supports the SQL_POSITION operation for the *fOption* argument in **SQLSetPos**. It only supports the SQL_LOCK_NO_CHANGE value for the *fLock* argument.

SQLSetScrollOptions

The cursor library supports **SQLSetScrollOptions** only for backwards compatibility; applications should use the SQL_CONCURRENCY, SQL_CURSOR_TYPE, and SQL_ROWSET_SIZE statement options instead.

SQLSetStmtOption

The cursor library supports the following statement options with **SQLSetStmtOption**:

SQL_BIND_TYPE	SQL_ROWSET_SIZE
SQL_CONCURRENCY	SQL_SIMULATE_CURSOR
SQL_CURSOR_TYPE	

The cursor library supports only the SQL_CURSOR_FORWARD_ONLY and SQL_CURSOR_STATIC values of the SQL_CURSOR_TYPE statement option.

For forward-only cursors, the cursor library supports the SQL_CONCUR_READ_ONLY value of the SQL_CONCURRENCY statement option. For static cursors, the cursor library supports the SQL_CONCUR_READ_ONLY and SQL_CONCUR_VALUES values of the SQL_CONCURRENCY statement option.

The cursor library supports only the SQL_SC_NON_UNIQUE value of the SQL_SIMULATE_CURSOR statement option.

Although the ODBC 2.0 specification supports calls to **SQLSetStmtOption** with the SQL_BIND_TYPE or SQL_ROWSET_SIZE options after **SQLExtendedFetch** has been called, the cursor library does not. Before it can change the binding type or rowset size in the cursor library, the application must close the cursor.

SQLTransact

The cursor library does not support transactions and passes calls to **SQLTransact** directly to the driver. However, the cursor library does support the cursor commit and rollback behaviors as returned by the data source with the SQL_CURSOR_ROLLBACK_BEHAVIOR and SQL_CURSOR_COMMIT_BEHAVIOR information types. Thus:

- For data sources that preserve cursors across transactions, changes that are rolled back in the data source are not rolled back in the cursor library's cache. To make the cache match the data in the data source, the application must close and reopen the cursor.

- For data sources that close cursors at transaction boundaries, the cursor library closes the cursors and deletes the caches for all *hstmts* on the *hdbc*.

- For data sources that delete prepared statements at transaction boundaries, the application must reprepare all prepared *hstmts* on the *hdbc* before reexecuting them.

ODBC Cursor Library Error Codes

The ODBC cursor library returns the following SQLSTATEs in addition to those listed in Chapter 22, "ODBC Function Reference."

SQLSTATE	Description	Can be returned from
01000	Cursor is not updateable	**SQLExtendedFetch**
01000	Cursor library not used. Load failed.	**SQLBrowseConnect** **SQLConnect** **SQLDriverConnect**
01000	Cursor library not used. Insufficient driver support.	**SQLBrowseConnect** **SQLConnect** **SQLDriverConnect**
01000	Cursor library not used. Version mismatch with Driver Manager.	**SQLBrowseConnect** **SQLConnect** **SQLDriverConnect**
01000	Driver returned SQL_SUCCESS_WITH_INFO. The warning message has been lost.	**SQLExtendedFetch**
S1000	General error: Unable to create file buffer	**SQLExtendedFetch** **SQLGetData**
S1000	General error: Unable to read from file buffer	**SQLExtendedFetch** **SQLGetData**
S1000	General error: Unable to write to file buffer	**SQLExtendedFetch** **SQLGetData**
S1000	General error: Unable to close or remove file buffer	**SQLFreeStmt**
SL001	Positioned request cannot be performed because no searchable columns were bound	**SQLExecDirect** **SQLGetData** **SQLPrepare**
SL002	Positioned request could not be performed because result set was created by a join condition	**SQLExecute** **SQLExecDirect** **SQLGetData**
SL003	Bound buffer exceeds maximum segment size	**SQLExtendedFetch**
SL004	Result set was not generated by a SELECT statement	**SQLGetData**
SL005	SELECT statement contains a GROUP BY clause	**SQLGetData**
SL006	Parameter arrays are not supported with positioned requests	**SQLPrepare** **SQLExecDirect**
SL007	Row size exceeds maximum cache buffer size	**SQLExtendedFetch**

SQLSTATE	Description	Can be returned from
SL008	SQLGetData is not allowed on a forward-only (non-buffered) cursor	**SQLGetData**
SL009	No columns were bound prior to calling SQLExtendedFetch	**SQLExtendedFetch**
SL010	SQLBindCol returned SQL_ERROR during an attempt to bind to an internal buffer	**SQLExtendedFetch** **SQLGetData**
SL011	Statement option is only valid after calling SQLExtendedFetch	**SQLGetStmtOption**
SL012	*hstmt* bindings may not be changed while a cursor is open	**SQLBindCol** **SQLFreeStmt** **SQLSetStmtOption**
SL014	A positioned request was issued and not all column count fields were buffered	**SQLExecDirect** **SQLExecute** **SQLPrepare**

Index

M

N

S

SDK Guide

**Microsoft® Open
Database Connectivity™
Software Development Kit**

Version 2.0

For the Microsoft Windows™ and Windows NT™ Operating Systems

Microsoft Corporation

PUBLISHED BY
Microsoft Press
A Division of Microsoft Corporation
One Microsoft Way
Redmond, Washington 98052-6399

Library of Congress Cataloging-in-Publication Data
Microsoft ODBC 2.0 programmer's reference and SDK guide : for
  Microsoft Windows and Windows NT / Microsoft Corporation.
        p.   cm.
    Includes index.
    ISBN 1-55615-658-8
      1. Microsoft Windows (Computer file)   2. Windows NT.   3. ODBC.
  I. Microsoft Corporation.
  QA76.76.W56M56323   1994
  005.75'8--dc20   94-5039
                                                                    CIP

Lucida Typeface Software. © 1985–1988 and 1990 by Bigelow & Holmes.
U.S. Patent Nos. D289420, D289421, D289422, D289773

U. S. Patent No. 4955066

Printed and bound in the United States of America.

  2 3 4 5 6 7 8 9 MLML 9 8 7 6 5 4

For Programmer's Reference: Paradox is a registered trademark of Ansa Software, a Borland Company. Apple is a registered trademark of Apple Computer, Inc. dBASE is a registered trademark of Borland International, Inc. CompuServe is a registered trademark of CompuServe, Inc. DEC is a registered trademark of Digital Equipment Corporation. SQLBase is a registered trademark of Gupta Technologies, Inc. Informix is a registered trademark of Informix Software, Inc. Ingres is a trademark of Ingres Corporation. DB2, IBM, and OS/2 are registered trademarks of International Business Machines Corporation. Microsoft, Microsoft Access, and MS are registered trademarks and Win32, Windows, and Windows NT are trademarks of Microsoft Corporation in the U.S. and other countries. Novell is a registered trademark of Novell, Inc. Oracle is a registered trademark of Oracle Corporation. SYBASE is a registered trademark of Sybase, Inc. NonStop is a trademark of Tandem Computers Inc. UNIX is a registered trademark of UNIX Systems Laboratories. X/Open is a trademark of X/Open Company Limited in the U.K. and other countries.
Document No. DB33920-0494

For SDK Guide: Paradox is a registered trademark of Ansa Software, a Borland Company. dBASE is a registered trademark of Borland International, Inc. CompuServe is a registered trademark of CompuServe, Inc. Intel is a registered trademark of Intel Corporation. CodeView, FoxPro, Microsoft, Microsoft Access, MS, MS-DOS, Visual Basic, and Win32 are registered trademarks and Win32s, Windows, and Windows NT are trademarks of Microsoft Corporation in the U.S. and other countries. Btrieve is a registered tradmark of Novell, Inc.
Document No. DB33919-0494

Contents

CHAPTER 1

Overview of the ODBC SDK

The Microsoft® Open Database Connectivity™ (ODBC) interface is an emerging industry standard and a component of Microsoft's Windows Open Services Architecture (WOSA).

The ODBC interface makes it possible for applications to access data from a variety of database management systems (DBMS's). The ODBC interface permits maximum interoperability—an application can access data in diverse DBMS's through a single interface. Furthermore, that application will be independent of any DBMS from which it accesses data. Users of the application can add software components called *drivers*, which interface between an application and a specific DBMS. For more information on drivers, see the *Microsoft ODBC SDK Programmer's Reference*.

The Microsoft Open Database Connectivity Software Development Kit (ODBC SDK) 2.0 is a set of software components, tools, and documentation designed to help you in developing ODBC drivers and ODBC-enabled applications for the Windows 3.1 and Windows NT operating systems.

Note The Driver Manager and Installer for the ODBC SDK 2.0 do not support Windows 3.0. Drivers developed with the ODBC SDK 2.0 will not work with Windows 3.0.

New with Version 2.0

This version of the ODBC SDK incorporates the following new features:

- 32-bit application development support on Windows 3.1 (Win32s™) and Windows NT (see Appendix A, "Developing 16- and 32-Bit Applications and Drivers")

- Scrollable cursor support through a driver-independent Cursor Library (see the *Microsoft ODBC SDK Programmer's Reference*)

- An improved set of ODBC 1.0 single-tier drivers for several popular data formats (see "Drivers" later in this chapter)

- Sample C++ classes to help developers write C++ classes or applications (see "Samples" later in this chapter)

- Templates that provide a ready-to-use base for writing drivers and auto-test DLLs (see "Samples" later in this chapter)

- Numerous code samples and working tools to help developers write ODBC-enabled applications (see "Samples" later in this chapter)

- Improved and integrated installation procedure for SDK and drivers (see Chapter 2, "Installing the ODBC SDK")

Organization of this Book

The chapters in this book cover the following:

- Chapter 1, "Overview of the ODBC SDK," describes new features, SDK contents (including brief descriptions of the utilities, samples, and drivers), hardware requirements, document conventions, and getting help.

- Chapter 2, "Installing the ODBC SDK," explains how to run the ODBC SDK Setup program for Windows 3.1 and Windows NT.

- Chapter 3, "Managing Data Sources and Drivers," shows you how to use the ODBC Administrator to add and delete drivers and data sources.

- Chapter 4, "Using ODBC Test," covers testing drivers with ODBC Test, creating automated test DLLs, and ODBC Test operating notes and testing tips. (For detailed information on the functions executed by the ODBC Test Menu commands, see the *Microsoft ODBC SDK Programmer's Reference.*)

- Chapter 5, "Using ODBC Spy," describes how to use the ODBC Spy utility to simplify driver development through driver or application emulation, data capture, and breakpoints.

- Chapter 6, "Using the Driver Setup Toolkit," shows you how to customize a setup program to install drivers you develop.

- Appendix A, "Developing 16- and 32-Bit Applications and Drivers," explains architecture and file differences between the Windows 3.1–based and Windows NT–based implementations of the ODBC SDK.

Product Contents

The ODBC SDK contains setup, installation, administration, and ODBC program files. In addition, a set of libraries, include files, help files, utilities, drivers, and sample programs are included. For a complete list of the product components and their filenames, see the file PACKLIST.TXT, which the ODBC SDK Setup program will copy to your \ODBCSDK directory.

Note The 32-bit components included with the ODBC SDK are compatible with Intel-based platforms only.

In addition to the software, the ODBC SDK includes the following three books:

- The *Microsoft ODBC SDK Guide* (this book), which explains how to install the SDK software. It also contains guides to the ODBC Administrator, ODBC Test, ODBC Spy, and Driver Setup Toolkit utilities. Finally, it documents the notable differences in using the ODBC SDK under Windows NT.

- The *ODBC SDK Programmer's Reference*, which introduces the ODBC architecture and explains how to write ODBC drivers and applications that use ODBC. It also explains how to use the ODBC setup, installation, and administration programs in conjunction with your drivers or applications. And, it contains the ODBC API Reference, in which each of the functions in the ODBC API is listed in alphabetic order and described in detail.

- *The ODBC Driver Catalog*, a directory of third-party ODBC driver suppliers.

Samples, Utilities, and Drivers

The ODBC SDK includes several samples, utilities, and drivers to enable you to begin implementing open database connectivity as quickly as possible.

Samples

The ODBC SDK Setup program copies the source code files and makefiles for each of the samples listed below into subdirectories of the \ODBCSDK\SAMPLES directory. Executable sample files are copied to the \ODBCSDK\BIN directory. For more information on each sample, see the samples online Help file.

Note Only the 16-bit versions of the executable files are supplied. However, since the source code and makefiles for all samples are provided, they may be compiled in 32-bit development environments (with the exception of VBDEMO).

Sample Driver (16- and 32-bit versions)

A C-language template provided as an aid for writing drivers. It illustrates how to write an ODBC driver. It also includes a source code template to help you write a driver-specific setup DLL that will work with both the ODBC Administrator and the Driver Setup Toolkit utility (see "Utilities" following).

Sample Auto-Test DLLs for ODBC Test

The Quick Test is a C language DLL written for ODBC Test. It contains a set of test cases which cover basic areas of ODBC driver conformance. Driver writers may use it as a basis for writing automated acceptance tests for ensuring their drivers conform to the ODBC standard. A source code template (CUSTOM.C) is also provided to help you write an auto-test DLL that will work with ODBC Test. For more information on automated test DLLs, see Chapter 4, "Using ODBC Test."

Visual Basic Application

An application written in Visual Basic® which demonstrates how a Visual Basic application could be written using ODBC. It also provides a complete list of function prototypes for the ODBC API.

Cursor Library Sample Application

A C-language program written to show how to take advantage of the block cursor, scrolling, and positioned update and delete capabilities of the ODBC cursor library. For information on the ODBC cursor library, see the *Microsoft ODBC SDK Programmer's Reference*.

ODBC System Administration Tool

A C-language program which uses the ODBC API to execute common administrative requests for a DBMS.

SQL Query Application

A simple C-language program which demonstrates multiple simultaneous connections using ODBC. It enables you to type any SQL query and browse the results.

DLL Viewer/Translation Spy

The DLL Viewer is a configuration utility for the sample translation DLL. It also returns a list of all DLLs currently loaded in memory and allows you to selectively unload them. (This is useful for unloading DLLs that remain in memory after an application or DLL fails.) Translation Spy (the sample translation DLL) allows you to intercept information that is to be translated. (The DLL Viewer does not work under 32-bit environments; Translation Spy works under both 16- and 32-bit environments.) For more information on translation, see the *Microsoft ODBC SDK Programmer's Reference*.

C++ Application

A sample C++ application that demonstrates how the C++ classes might be used to write a simple ODBC application.

Utilities

ODBC Test

An interactive utility which enables you to perform ad hoc and standardized testing on drivers. ODBC Test is covered in detail in Chapter 4, "Using ODBC Test."

ODBC Spy
A debugging tool with which you can capture data source information, emulate drivers, and emulate applications. ODBC Spy is covered in detail in Chapter 5, "Using ODBC Spy."

Driver Setup Toolkit
A set of tools which enables you to customize the driver installation program for your own drivers. The Driver Setup Toolkit is covered in detail in Chapter 6, "Using the Driver Setup Toolkit."

Drivers

The following ODBC 1.0 drivers are shipped with ODBC SDK to help you develop ODBC applications. These are the same drivers included in the Microsoft ODBC Desktop Database Drivers package.

Note Under the terms of the ODBC SDK license agreement, these drivers may not be redistributed. In the U.S., contact Microsoft Sales at (800) 227-4679 for information on purchasing a license to redistribute these drivers. Outside the U.S., contact your local Microsoft subsidiary.

Access
Supports Microsoft Access® version 1.0.

Btrieve
Supports Btrieve® version 5.1. Compatible with both MS-DOS® and Windows-based data formats. The ODBC Btrieve driver requires the stand-alone Btrieve for Windows dynamic-link library (DLL), WBTRCALL.DLL; for more information, see the Btrieve driver Help file.

dBASE
Supports dBASE® versions 3.0 and 4.0.

Excel
Supports Microsoft Excel® versions 3.0 and 4.0.

FoxPro
Supports Microsoft FoxPro® versions 2.0 and 2.5. Compatible with both MS-DOS and Windows-based data formats.

Paradox
Supports Paradox® version 3.5. Compatible with both MS-DOS and Windows-based data formats.

Text
Supports fixed-width or delimited ASCII text files.

For all drivers you have installed, the driver Help files are placed in the \WINDOWS\SYSTEM directory during installation. In addition, for all installed and uninstalled drivers, Help files are placed in the \ODBCSDK\HELP directory. The following table lists the ODBC drivers and their Help files.

ODBC driver	Driver Help file
Btrieve	DRVBTRV.HLP
dBASE	DRVDBASE.HLP
Microsoft Access	DRVACCSS.HLP
Microsoft Excel	DRVEXCEL.HLP
Microsoft FoxPro	DRVFOX.HLP
Paradox	DRVPARDX.HLP
Text	DRVTEXT.HLP

Hardware and Software Requirements

To use the ODBC SDK, you'll need the following minimum hardware configuration:

- A personal computer using the Intel® 80386 (386 DX or 386 SX) or newer processor and a VGA or higher-resolution graphics card
- At least 2 Mb (4 Mb recommended) of random-access memory (RAM)
- At least one 3.5-inch (1.44-Mb) or one 5.25-inch (1.2-Mb) disk drive
- Approximately 10 Mb of hard disk space for the complete installation (including samples) of the SDK (additional disk space for developing ODBC drivers or applications is also required)

Before installing the SDK, make sure that the following software is already installed on your system or available for use:

- MS-DOS version 3.1 or later (MS-DOS 5.0 or later recommended)
- Microsoft Windows 3.1 or Microsoft Windows NT
- Microsoft Windows 3.1 or Win32® Software Development Kit
- A C compiler compatible with Windows dynamic-link libraries and Microsoft C libraries (such as the Microsoft C compiler version 6.0 or later)

Refer to your Microsoft Windows SDK documentation for additional hardware or software requirements.

Document Conventions

This book uses the following typographic conventions.

Format	Used for
WIN.INI	Uppercase letters indicate filenames, SQL statements, macro names, and terms used at the operating-system command level.
RETCODE SQLFetch(hdbc)	This font is used for sample command lines and program code.
argument	Italicized words indicate information that the user or the application must provide, or word emphasis.
SQLTransact	Bold type indicates that syntax must be typed exactly as shown, including function names.
[ ]	Brackets indicate optional items; if in bold text, brackets must be included in the syntax.
|	A vertical bar separates two mutually exclusive choices in a syntax line.
{ }	Braces delimit a set of mutually exclusive choices in a syntax line; if in bold text, braces must be included in the syntax.
...	An ellipsis indicates that arguments can be repeated several times.
. . .	A column of three dots indicates continuation of previous lines of code.

Getting Help

Additional assistance on using the ODBC SDK is provided through the Microsoft Connection on CompuServe® and through various support plans available from Microsoft.

Documentation

The print and online documentation have been extensively reworked for ODBC SDK version 2.0. Many user-suggested corrections and changes have been implemented. Most technical questions can be answered by reading the appropriate sections of the *Microsoft ODBC SDK Programmer's Reference*. For information on specific help documentation, refer to the following table.

For help on	See
ODBC SDK Installation	Chapter 2, "Installing the ODBC SDK"
ODBC Functions	*Microsoft ODBC SDK Programmer's Reference*, ODBC API Help File (\ODBCSDK\HELP\ODBCAPI.HLP)
Sample Programs	ODBC Sample Programs Help File (\ODBCSDK\HELP\ODBCSMPL.HLP)
General ODBC Questions	Knowledge Base Articles Help File (\ODBCSDK\HELP\ODBCKNWL.HLP)
ODBC Test	Chapter 4, "Using ODBC Test"
ODBC Spy	Chapter 5, "Using ODBC Spy"
Driver Setup Toolkit	Chapter 6, "Using the Driver Setup Toolkit"
ODBC Drivers	Chapter 3, "Managing Data Sources and Drivers"
ODBC Administrator	Chapter 3, "Managing Data Sources and Drivers", ODBC Administrator Help (\ODBCSDK\HELP\ODBCINST.HLP)

CompuServe

The Microsoft Connection on CompuServe provides online technical information for Microsoft products, including the ODBC SDK. With the Microsoft Connection, you can exchange messages with Microsoft professionals and experienced Microsoft users, and you can download free software provided by Microsoft and CompuServe members, such as drivers, patches, tools, and add-ons.

By using the Microsoft Connection, you can access the Microsoft Developer Services area. You are encouraged to use this area to communicate directly with Microsoft about developer-related issues. The Microsoft Developer Services area offers the following services:

- **Developer Forums** The ODBC section under the Windows Extension forum provides information about the ODBC API, application development, and driver development. The section leads for these forums are from Microsoft Product Support Services and can help answer your questions about the ODBC API.

- **Confidential Technical Service Requests** Microsoft offers private (fee-based per incident) technical support to help solve your more complex development problems. For more details, see the Microsoft Developer Services area.

- **Developer Knowledge Base** This up-to-date reference tool, compiled by Microsoft Product Support Services, contains developer-specific technical information about Microsoft products.

- **Software Library**   This collection of text and graphics files, sample code, and utilities can be searched by keyword, and the files can be downloaded for local use.

To connect to the Microsoft Connection, type **GO MICROSOFT** at the CompuServe "!" prompt. For information about establishing a CompuServe account, call (800) 848-8199, 8:00 A.M. to 10:00 P.M. EST.

Support Plans

Microsoft also offers a range of comprehensive support plans. For information about Microsoft support offerings, call Microsoft Sales at (800) 227-4679, Monday through Friday, 6:30 A.M. to 5:30 P.M., Pacific time, excluding holidays, or call your local Microsoft subsidiary outside of the U.S.

CHAPTER 2

Installing the ODBC SDK

The ODBC SDK Setup program (SETUP.EXE) is a straightforward installation program. It installs the ODBC SDK in several steps, depending on the operating system with which you plan to use it (Windows 3.1 or Windows NT). Setup automatically detects which operating system is running. During setup, you are prompted for the directory name in which you want the ODBC SDK to reside, as well as for the SDK options you want installed.

Installation Overview

When Setup runs, it identifies the running operating system and then installs the required ODBC SDK files, as well as the libraries, include files, tools, API help file and sample programs that you choose to install.

Note By default, files for Win32 applications are copied into the SDK only on systems running Windows NT. The ODBC thunking components will be installed under Windows 3.1 and Windows for Workgroups to support 32-bit applications. For more information, see Appendix A, "Developing 16- and 32-Bit Applications and Drivers."

The ODBC SDK Setup program continues installation according to the following:

For Windows 3.1 and Windows for Workgroups, Setup will:

- Install and configure 16-bit drivers.
- Install the 16-bit ODBC Administrator control panel device.
- Install the 32-bit thunking layers to the \WINDOWS\SYSTEM directory (for information on the 32-bit thunking layers, see Appendix A, "Developing 16- and 32-Bit Applications and Drivers").
- Create the ODBC SDK 2.0 program group.
- Add icons for 16-bit SDK components to the ODBC SDK 2.0 program group.

- Add an icon for the 16-bit ODBC Administrator to the ODBC SDK 2.0 program group.
- Add icons for the 16-bit sample applications.

For Windows NT, Setup will:

- Install and configure 16-bit drivers.
- Install and configure the available 32-bit drivers.
- Install the 32-bit ODBC Administrator control panel device.
- Create the ODBC SDK 2.0 program group.
- Add icons for 32-bit SDK components to the ODBC SDK 2.0 program group.
- Add icons for the 16- and 32-bit ODBC Administrators to the ODBC SDK 2.0 program group.
- Add icons for the 16-bit sample applications.

Once the ODBC SDK 2.0 program group and ODBC Administrator are installed, Setup will invoke the ODBC Administrator for your system to enable you to load and configure the drivers supplied with the ODBC SDK. For information on using the ODBC Administrator, see Chapter 3, "Managing Data Sources and Drivers."

ODBC SDK Setup Features

The Setup program is designed to be run with minimum input. Some input is required from you, and at various points you will be prompted to select one of five buttons: Continue, Exit, Help, Close, and Back.

Continue Buttons

Choose the Continue button, or press the ALT+C access key sequence to accept the conditions or options of the dialog box and continue installation.

Exit Buttons

If at any time you want to quit Setup, choose an Exit button with the mouse, or press the ALT+X access key sequence. The installation process will halt, and a message box will prompt you to confirm the quit operation or continue the installation.

Note The ODBC SDK will not be properly configured unless the installation procedure finishes. If you quit Setup before the ODBC SDK is completely installed, you will have to run the Setup program again at a later time.

Help Buttons

Many of the dialog boxes have Help buttons. If you want a more detailed explanation of the action that Setup prompts you to do, choose a Help button with the mouse, or press the ALT+H access key sequence.

Close Buttons

The Close button is contained in Setup Help dialog boxes. When you have finished reading the Help dialog box, choose the Close button or press the ALT+L access key sequence to dismiss the Help dialog box and return to the current dialog box.

Back Buttons

Several dialog boxes are configured with the Back button. Choosing the Back button with the mouse, or pressing the ALT+B access key sequence will return to the previous dialog box that prompted you for an installation action.

Running ODBC SDK Setup

▶ **To install the Microsoft ODBC SDK**

1. If Windows 3.1 or Windows NT is not already running,

   - For Windows 3.1, type **win** at the command prompt and then press ENTER.

   - For Windows NT, you need only boot your workstation and log in. If you are running a dual-boot system, then reboot your workstation and choose "Microsoft Windows NT" during the system countdown.

2. Once your Windows operating system is running, close all open applications except the Program Manager.

3. From the Program Manager File menu, run SETUP.EXE.

4. Follow the instructions displayed in the Setup program's dialog boxes.

5. After it has copied files to your system, Setup displays the Install Drivers dialog box in the ODBC Administrator. Select the drivers you want to install; if you only want to install the Driver Manager, do not select any drivers. Choose the OK button.

Note The Driver Manager and drivers are copied to the \ODBCSDK\BIN and \ODBCSDK\BIN32 directories during setup. You must install them to make them available for use by your system. If you do not want to install them at this time, choose the Cancel button.

To install the Driver Manager and drivers at a later time, follow the instructions in "Installing Drivers" in Chapter 3, "Managing Data Sources and Drivers." When the Add Drivers dialog box prompts you for the directory containing the files to install, type **\odbcsdk\bin** or **\odbcsdk\bin32**.

---

6. If you installed any drivers, you may add data sources for them. To add data sources now, follow the instructions in "Adding Data Sources" in Chapter 3, "Managing Data Sources and Drivers." For each driver you install, a data source name is automatically created by Setup. The data source name is similar to the driver's name (for example, Fox_sdk20).To exit the Setup program without adding data sources, choose the Close button.

Note You must add one or more data sources for each ODBC driver before you can access data with that driver. On Windows NT, data sources for 32-bit drivers can be used by both 16-bit and 32-bit applications, but data sources for 16-bit drivers can be used only by 16-bit applications.

7. The setup process is now complete. To exit the Setup program, choose the OK button or press ENTER.

Note On systems running Windows NT, steps 6 and 7 are repeated for the 32-bit ODBC components.

CHAPTER 3

Managing Data Sources and Drivers

This chapter explains how to use the ODBC Administrator to add database drivers and data sources. The ODBC SDK Setup program invokes the ODBC Administrator after it has finished copying the essential SDK program files.

The ODBC Administrator is a Control Panel device on workstations running the Windows operating system version 3.1. In the Windows NT operating system the 16-bit ODBC Administrator is located within the ODBC SDK program group as an executable program item. Also for Windows NT, the 32-bit ODBC Administrator is both a Control Panel device and a program item.

About Drivers and Data Sources

Drivers are the components that process ODBC requests and return data to the application. If necessary, drivers modify an application's request into a form that is understood by the data source. You use the ODBC Administrator to add and delete drivers from your system.

Data sources are the databases or files accessed by a driver. For the drivers shipped with the ODBC SDK, a set of data sources is created upon installation. You use the ODBC Administrator to add, configure, and delete data sources from your system.

Running the ODBC Administrator

You can open the ODBC Administrator in two ways: from the Control Panel, or from the ODBC SDK 2.0 program group, as follows:

- On Windows 3.1 or Windows for Workgroups, use either the Control Panel device or the ODBC SDK 2.0 program group icon.

- On Windows NT use either the Control Panel device or the ODBC SDK 2.0 program group icon (32-bit Administrator) to run ODBC Administrator for 32-bit drivers and data sources.

- For 16-bit drivers and data sources on Windows on Windows (WOW), you can only use the ODBC SDK 2.0 program group icon.

▶ **To open the ODBC Administrator from the Control Panel**

1. Open the Main program group in the Program Manager.

2. Double-click the Control Panel icon in the Main program group. The Control Panel window will open.

3. Double-click the ODBC icon in the Control Panel window. The ODBC Administrator will run.

▶ **To open the ODBC Administrator from the ODBC SDK program group**

1. Open the ODBC SDK 2.0 program group in the Program Manager.

2. Double-click the ODBC icon in the ODBC SDK 2.0 program group. The ODBC Administrator will run.

Once the ODBC Administrator is running, the Data Sources dialog box appears. (See Figure 3.1.)

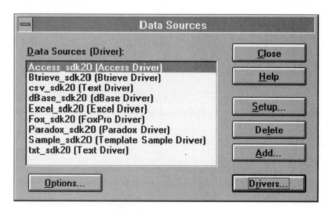

Figure 3.1   Data Sources Dialog Box

Managing Data Sources

After installing an ODBC driver, you can define one or more data sources for it. The data source name should provide a unique description of the data; for example, Payroll or Accounts Payable. The data sources that are defined for all the currently installed drivers are listed in the Data Sources (Driver) list box in the Data Sources dialog box.

A data source associates a particular ODBC driver with the data you want to access through that driver. For example, you might create a data source to use the

ODBC dBASE driver to access one or more dBASE files found in a specific directory on your hard disk or a network drive. With the ODBC Administrator, you can add, delete, and configure the data sources you require.

Note   On Windows NT, data sources for 32-bit drivers can be used by both 16-bit and 32-bit applications, but data sources for 16-bit drivers can be used only by 16-bit applications. If there are two data sources with the same name, one for a 16-bit driver and the other for a 32-bit driver, then the data source for the 32-bit driver is used. This applies to either 16- or 32-bit applications. (The Driver Manager provides thunking layers to allow 16-bit applications to use 32-bit drivers.)

Adding Data Sources

You can add multiple data sources, each one associating a driver with some data you want to access using that driver. You need to give each data source a name that uniquely identifies that data source. For example, if you create a data source for a set of dBASE files that contain customer information, you might name the data source "Customers." Applications typically display data source names for users to choose from.

▶ **To add a data source**

1. Make sure the ODBC Administrator is running. (See "Running the ODBC Administrator" in the previous section.)

2. Choose the Add button. The Add Data Source dialog box appears.

   The Installed ODBC Drivers list box displays the names of installed drivers. If the data source you want to add requires a driver that has not been installed, you will have to install the driver first. (For more information, see "Installing Drivers," later in this chapter.)

3. From the Installed ODBC Drivers list, select the driver for the data source to use.

4. Choose the OK button.

   A driver-specific Setup dialog box for the data source appears.

   Since each driver is different, each data source requires a slightly different configuration. Because of this, each data source has a unique Setup dialog box. For detailed information on the options in a data source Setup dialog box, choose the Help button in the dialog box.

5. Type the required information about the data source, such as its name and file version (for example, dBASE III or dBASE IV).

6. When you have finished configuring the data source, choose the OK button. The driver-specific Setup dialog box disappears.

7. You can repeat steps 2 through 6 if you want to add more data sources.

8. Choose the Close button to close the ODBC Administrator.

Modifying Data Sources

Depending on your requirements, you may find it necessary to reconfigure your data sources. The ODBC Administrator makes it easy.

▶ **To modify a data source**

1. Make sure the ODBC Administrator is running. (See "Running the ODBC Administrator" earlier in this chapter.)

2. Select the data source you want to modify from the Data Sources (Driver) list box. (See Figure 3.1.)

3. Choose the Setup button.

   A driver-specific Setup dialog box appears.

   Since each driver is different, each data source requires a slightly different configuration. Because of this, each data source has a unique Setup dialog box. For detailed information on the options in a data source Setup dialog box, choose the Help button in the dialog box.

4. Modify the data source information, such as its name and file version (for example, dBASE III or dBASE IV).

5. When you have finished configuring the data source, choose the OK button. The driver-specific Setup dialog box disappears.

6. You can repeat steps 2 through 5 if you want to modify more data sources.

7. Choose the Close button to close the ODBC Administrator.

Deleting Data Sources

▶ **To delete a data source**

1. Make sure the ODBC Administrator is running. (See "Running the ODBC Administrator" earlier in this chapter.)

2. Select the data source you want to delete from the Data Sources (Driver) list box. (See Figure 3.1.)

3. Choose the Delete button.

4. A message box appears asking you to confirm removing the data source you have selected:

   - Choose the Yes button to delete the data source.

   - Choose the No button to return to the Data Sources dialog box without deleting the data source.

5. Repeat steps 2 through 4 until you have finished deleting data sources.

6. Choose the Close button to close the ODBC Administrator.

Setting Tracing Options

The ODBC Options dialog box, accessible through the Data Sources dialog box, enables you to configure the way ODBC functions calls are traced. (See Figure 3.2.)

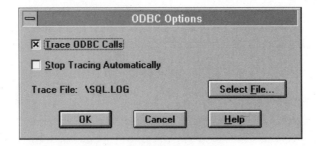

Figure 3.2   ODBC Options Dialog Box

Note   The Trace ODBC Calls box in the ODBC Options dialog box does not take precedence over the ODBC Test Tools menu Trace command. For more information, see Chapter 4, "Using ODBC Test."

How Tracing Works

When you activate tracing from the ODBC Options dialog box, the Driver Manager will log all ODBC function calls for all subsequently run applications. ODBC function calls from applications running before tracing is activated are not logged. Logging is done by writing all ODBC function calls to a log file you specify.

By default, tracing will stop as soon as any application being traced closes. You can choose to have tracing continue after an ODBC application closes. However, keep in mind that while tracing is on, the log file will continue to increase in size, and that the performance of your ODBC applications will be affected.

Enabling and Disabling Tracing

▶ **To enable tracing**

1. Make sure the ODBC Administrator is running. (See "Running the ODBC Administrator" earlier in this chapter.)

2. Choose the Options button. The ODBC Options dialog box appears.

3. Select the Trace ODBC Calls box. The Stop Tracing Automatically box is activated.

4. If you want to disable automatic stopping of ODBC call tracing, clear the Stop Tracing Automatically box. Otherwise, tracing of ODBC calls stops when the first application using tracing terminates.

Note If you disable automatic stopping of ODBC call tracing, the log file will continue to increase in size, and the performance of your ODBC applications will be affected.

When you clear the Stop Tracing Automatically box, the Driver Manager prompts you with a message box for confirmation. Choose the OK button to confirm or Cancel to leave the Stop Tracing Automatically box selected.

5. Choose the Select File Button. Type the name of the log file to which you want the Driver Manager to write the ODBC calls. Or, use the drive and directory boxes to choose an existing log file to which to append new information.

6. Choose the OK button. The ODBC Options dialog box closes. All ODBC applications that you run after you close the Data Sources dialog box will have all ODBC function calls appended to the file you selected.

7. Choose the Close button to close the Data Source dialog box.

Managing Drivers

In order for you to configure data sources, you must have installed at least one driver onto your system. The ODBC SDK comes with a set of drivers you may install during the Setup program. You may install these and additional drivers at any time with the ODBC Administrator. With the ODBC Administrator you may also delete and configure the drivers that are already installed on your system.

Viewing Installed Drivers and Driver Details

▶ **To view installed drivers and driver details**

1. Make sure the ODBC Administrator is running. (See "Running the ODBC Administrator" earlier in this chapter.)

2. Choose the Drivers button. The Drivers dialog box appears. (See Figure 3.3.)

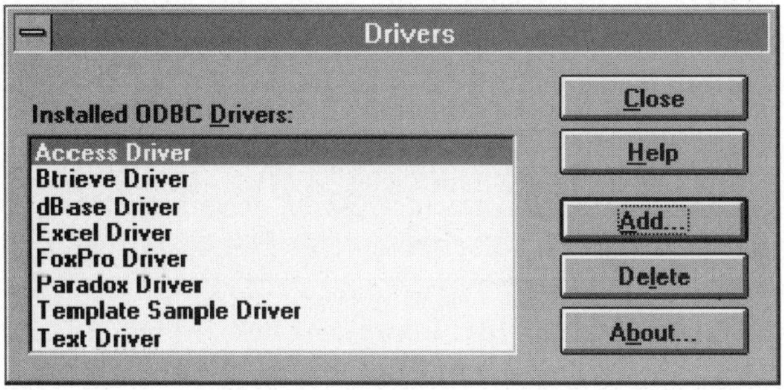

Figure 3.3   Drivers Dialog Box

The Installed ODBC Drivers list box displays the drivers installed on your system.

3. Choose the About button. The About dialog box appears.

   The About dialog box displays file and version information for the selected driver.

4. Choose the OK button. The About dialog box disappears.

5. Repeat steps 2 through 4 until you have finished examining installed driver details.

6. Choose the Close button to close the ODBC Administrator.

Installing Drivers

You install and configure drivers before you can add and configure data sources.

Note If you are running the ODBC SDK Setup program now, then skip to step 6 of this procedure. The Setup program invokes the ODBC Administrator, opening the Install Drivers dialog box directly, so you don't have to do steps 1 through 5.

▶ **To install a driver**

1. Make sure the ODBC Administrator is running. (See "Running the ODBC Administrator" earlier in this chapter.)

2. Choose the Drivers button. The Drivers dialog box appears. (See Figure 3.3.)

3. Choose the Add button. The Add Driver dialog box appears.

4. Type the name of the directory where the driver files are located. (If the driver files are on a floppy disk, make sure the disk is in a disk drive.) If you don't know the name of the directory, choose the Browse button to view drive and directory contents.

5. Once the path is set, choose the OK button. If the ODBC Administrator finds an ODBC.INF file in the directory you specify, the Install Drivers dialog box will display. (If the ODBC Administrator does not find an ODBC.INF file in the directory you specify, you will be prompted to type in a different path.)

Note For the ODBC SDK 2.0, a set of 16-bit drivers is located in the \ODBCSDK\BIN directory; 32-bit drivers are located in the \ODBCSDK\BIN32 directory.

6. The Available ODBC Drivers list box displays all of the drivers you can install. Select any number of drivers to install by pressing SPACEBAR or clicking a driver name with the mouse. You can cancel the selection of a particular driver by selecting it a second time.

7. If you want to set version-dependent installation options for the drivers you selected:

   a. Choose the Advanced button. The Advanced Installation Options dialog box will display. (See Figure 3.4.)

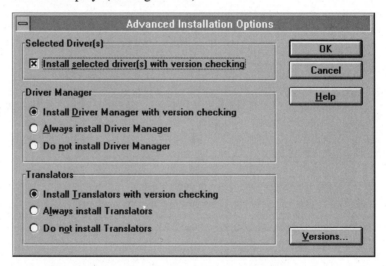

Figure 3.4   Advanced Installation Options Dialog Box

   b. Choose the Drivers, Translators, and Driver Manager options that fit your requirements. You can view the version numbers of the installable drivers by choosing the Versions button.

   For detailed information on the options in the Advanced Installation Options dialog box, choose the Help button.

   c. When you have finished selecting advanced installation options, close the dialog box by choosing the OK button, or choose the Cancel button to dismiss the Advanced Installation Options dialog box with the options unchanged.

Note Usually you won't need to set the advanced installation options. The default for Drivers, Translators, and Driver Manager is to enable version checking. For all files, this means the ODBC Administrator will prompt you for confirmation whenever the version about to be installed is an earlier version than that which already exists on your system.

---

8. Choose the OK button to install the drivers you selected. The ODBC Administrator will copy the necessary files to your \WINDOWS\SYSTEM directory. After the files are copied, the Install Drivers dialog box disappears, and the Drivers dialog box appears.

9. Choose the Close button to close the Drivers dialog box.

10. At this point you may want to configure data sources for your newly installed drivers. For information on adding and modifying data sources, see "Managing Data Sources," earlier in this chapter. Otherwise, choose the Close button to close the ODBC Administrator.

Deleting Drivers

▶ **To delete a driver**

1. Make sure the ODBC Administrator is running. (See "Running the ODBC Administrator" earlier in this chapter.)

2. Choose the Drivers button. The Drivers dialog box appears. (See Figure 3.3.)

3. Select the driver you want to delete from the Installed ODBC Drivers list box.

4. Choose the Delete button.

5. A message box appears asking you to confirm removing the driver you have selected:

   - Choose the Yes button to delete the driver.

   - Choose the No button to return to the Drivers dialog box without deleting the driver.

6. Repeat steps 2 through 5 until you have finished deleting drivers.

7. Choose the Close button to close the Drivers dialog box.

8. Choose the Close button to close the ODBC Administrator.

CHAPTER 4

Using ODBC Test

Microsoft ODBC Test is an ODBC-enabled application that you can use to test ODBC drivers. ODBC Test has four distinct types of menu items that you can use to execute ODBC functions:

- **Functions**   *Functions* are menu items that call ODBC functions. When you select a function from an ODBC Test menu, ODBC Test displays a dialog box that has one control for each argument in the function. When you select the OK button in the dialog box, ODBC Test executes the function using the values specified for each argument.

- **Function Tools**   *Function tools* are menu items that call a group of related ODBC functions or help you use an ODBC function. For example, Full Disconnect calls **SQLDisconnect**, **SQLFreeConnect**, and **SQLFreeEnv**; Fill Param displays a dialog box in which you enter parameter values. Function tools are listed at the bottom of the Connect, Statement, Results, and Misc menus beneath a separator line.

- **Tools**   *Tools* are menu items that help you configure ODBC Test, such as the level of errors to report or whether menu items for functions the driver does not support are disabled.

- **Auto Tests**   Automated tests, or *auto tests*, are dynamic-link libraries (DLLs) that you have written. Each auto test DLL contains one or more test cases. For example, an auto test for **SQLAllocStmt** might contain test cases to call **SQLAllocStmt** with valid and invalid arguments and to call **SQLAllocStmt** until the driver runs out of statement handles. The source code for a sample auto test that tests basic driver functionality (the Quick Test) is shipped with the ODBC SDK in the \ODBCSDK\SAMPLES\QUIKTEST directory.

In order to use ODBC Test, you must understand the ODBC API, the C language, and SQL. For more information on the ODBC API, see the *Microsoft ODBC SDK Programmer's Reference*.

Using the ODBC Test Interface

The ODBC Test interface contains elements that are familiar to programmers. The short tutorial in the next section acquaints you with the interface. If you want to skip the tutorial, the following section discusses the only parts of the interface you may be unfamiliar with: output windows, connection windows, and function dialog boxes.

Tutorial

This tutorial illustrates how to connect to a data source, create a table and insert values into it, retrieve those values, and disconnect from the data source. In so doing, it acquaints you with most of the ODBC Test user interface.

▶ **To connect to a data source**

1. Create a dBASE data source called Test Data using the ODBC Administrator. (For information on creating data sources with the ODBC Administrator, see Chapter 3, "Managing Data Sources and Drivers.")

2. Start ODBC Test. Either double-click the ODBC Test icon in the ODBC SDK 2.0 program group (or the ODBC Test32 icon if you are running Win32s or Windows NT) or choose Run from the File menu in the Program Manager or File Manager and type **\odbcsdk\bin\odbctest.exe** (or **\odbcsdk\bin32\odbcte32.exe** if you are running Win32s or Windows NT).

3. From the Connect menu, choose Full Connect. ODBC Test displays the SQL Data Sources dialog box.

4. Select Test Data from the list of data sources and choose the OK button. ODBC Test connects to the Test Data data source and allocates a statement handle. It displays the connection window and the allocated statement handle in the statement handle list.

▶ **To create a table and insert values into it**

1. Using the connection window from the previous procedure, type the following SQL statement in the input window:

   CREATE TABLE NewTable (City CHAR(10), State CHAR(2))

2. From the Statement menu, choose **SQLExecDirect**. ODBC Test displays the **SQLExecDirect** dialog box. The value of <input window> in the *szSqlStr* argument indicates that ODBC Test will retrieve the SQL statement from the input window.

3. Choose the OK button to execute **SQLExecDirect**. ODBC Test calls **SQLExecDirect** with the specified arguments and displays the function name, input argument values, and return code in the output window.

4. Type the following SQL statements in the input window. You do not need to delete the **CREATE TABLE** statement.

INSERT INTO NewTable VALUES ('Erie', 'PA')
INSERT INTO NewTable VALUES ('Atlanta', 'GA')
INSERT INTO NewTable VALUES ('Cheyenne', 'WY')

5. Using the mouse, select the first **INSERT** statement.

6. From the Statement menu, choose **SQLExecDirect** again, then choose the OK button to execute **SQLExecDirect** with the new arguments. ODBC Test calls the driver to insert the values in the table and displays information about the function call in the output window.

Note If you don't select the line you want to execute, ODBC Test passes all the statements in the input window to the driver. Although some drivers can process multiple statements, the dBASE driver used in this example cannot.

---

7. Repeat steps 5 and 6 for the other two **INSERT** statements.

▶ **To retrieve data from a table**

1. Using the connection window and the table from the previous procedure, type the following SQL statement in the input window and select it with the mouse:

SELECT * FROM NewTable

2. From the Statement menu, choose **SQLExecDirect** again, then choose the OK button to execute **SQLExecDirect** with the new arguments. ODBC Test calls the driver to select the data from the table and displays information about the function call in the output window.

3. From the Results menu, select the Get Data All function tool. The Get Data All function tool retrieves all of the data in the result set created by the **SELECT** statement. It displays the column count, the column names, the data, and the number of rows fetched in the output window:

```
"CITY", "STATE"
"Erie      ", "PA"
"Atlanta   ", "GA"
"Cheyenne  ", "WY"
3 rows fetched from 2 columns.
```

▶ **To disconnect from a data source**

• For the connection window used in the previous procedure, select Full Disconnect from the Connect menu. ODBC Test disconnects from the data source and removes the connection window. It then displays a message that the connection is closed in the general output window.

Using Windows

ODBC Test has three types of windows, a general output window, zero or more connection windows, and zero or more rowset windows. These are illustrated in Figure 4.1.

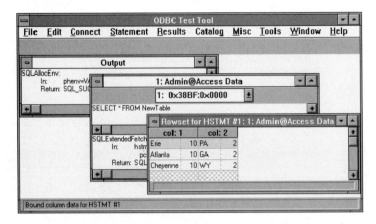

Figure 4.1   ODBC Test Windows

General Output Window

ODBC Test has a single general output window. It uses this window to display information that is not directly related to a connection. For example, ODBC Test displays the output of the **SQLAllocEnv** function in the general output window.

Connection Windows

ODBC Test creates a connection window each time **SQLAllocConnect** is successfully executed; it closes the specified connection window each time **SQLFreeConnect** is successfully executed. To use a specific connection, select the window for that connection.

Each connection window has three parts:

- **Statement Handle List**   At the top of the connection window is a list of allocated statement handles and their values. On Windows, the value is a 16-bit segment address and a 16-bit offset; on Windows NT, the value is a 32-bit address. Each time **SQLAllocStmt** is called, the new statement handle is added to this list; each time **SQLFreeStmt** is called with the SQL_DROP option, the specified statement handle is removed from the list.

  To select a statement handle to use when calling an ODBC function, select the handle from this list. You can also select a null handle.

- **Input Window**   The top half of each connection window is used to enter SQL statements for the **SQLExecDirect**, **SQLNativeSql**, and **SQLPrepare** functions, and data for the **SQLPutData** function. ODBC Test passes the highlighted statements or data to the function. If no statements or data are highlighted, ODBC Test uses all the statements or data in the input window.

To load a text file into the input window, choose Open from the File menu. To save the statements in the input window, choose Save As from the File menu.

- **Output Window**   The bottom half of each connection window is used by ODBC Test to display information about each function that it executes, such as the return code and the input and output argument values. To control what information is displayed, choose User Options from the Tools menu and select the desired level from the Logging Level list. To control whether the output wraps from line to line, choose Word Wrap from the Edit menu.

The input and output windows can each contain up to 60,000 characters. When the number of characters in one of these windows reaches this limit, ODBC Test deletes the first 2000 characters in the window. To clear the input or output window, choose Clear from the Edit menu and specify whether to clear one or both windows.

Rowset Windows

ODBC Test creates a rowset window when **SQLExtendedFetch** is called for the first time on a statement handle. It closes the rowset window when the cursor associated with the statement handle is closed. The rowset window displays the contents of the *rgbValue* and *pcbValue* buffers bound to the result set with **SQLBindCol** and the contents of the *rgfRowStatus* array specified in **SQLExtendedFetch**. You can use the Row Options item on the Tools menu to control whether the *pcbValue* buffers, *rgfRowStatus* array, and column names are displayed.

Note   Rowset windows do not display the results of calls to **SQLGetData**; these are displayed in the output window of the connection window.

To update the value of a cell in a rowset window, highlight the cell and choose the Update Cell function tool from the Results menu or double-click the cell. You can also use the Update Cell function tool to view the value of the *pcbValue* buffer bound to the column with **SQLBindCol**.

Using Function Dialog Boxes

When you choose an ODBC function from a menu, ODBC Test displays a dialog box in which you can specify argument values. The dialog box contains one control for each argument; it may contain additional controls for supplemental information. For example, the **SQLSetStmtOption** dialog box contains a list from which you can select the C data type of the *vParam* argument for a driver-specific statement option. For information about the dialog box for a specific function, see that function in "Function Reference" later in this chapter.

ODBC Test uses text boxes, drop-down combo boxes, and check boxes in function dialog boxes. These are illustrated in Figure 4.2, the dialog box for the **SQLDriverConnect** function.

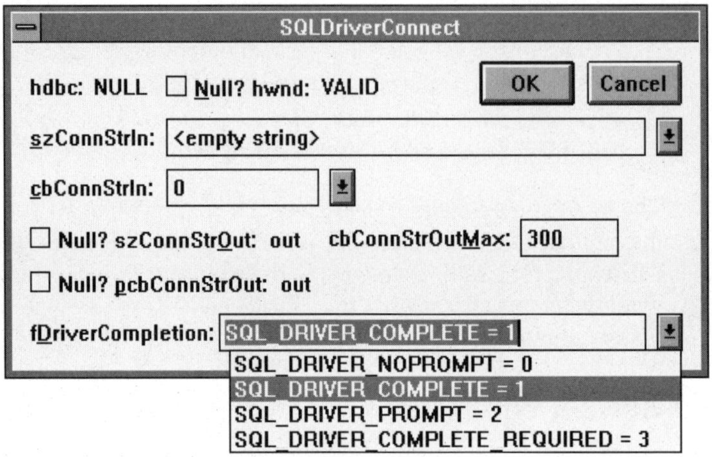

Figure 4.2   SQLDriverConnect Dialog Box

Text Boxes

Text boxes are used to specify values for numeric arguments for which no **#define** values (such as SQL_NTS or SQL_NULL_DATA) apply. For example, text boxes are used to specify values for the *cbConnStrOutMax* argument in **SQLDriverConnect** (shown in Figure 4.2) and the *icol* argument in **SQLBindCol**.

Drop-Down Combo Boxes

Drop-down combo boxes are used to specify values for most arguments. For example, drop-down combo boxes are used to specify values for the *szConnStrIn*, *cbConnStrIn*, and *fDriverCompletion* arguments in **SQLDriverConnect** (shown in Figure 4.2).

For numeric arguments, the list consists of all applicable **#define** names and the numeric value associated with each **#define** name. If Version Numbers in the User Options dialog box is selected, the version of ODBC in which each **#define** name was introduced is also displayed.

For character arguments, the list always contains <empty string> and <null pointer>. It may contain <input window> or <input window selection> (to use the currently selected text in the input window or, if no text is selected, all text in the input window), and any known text values, such as data source names. For character arguments, ODBC Test automatically places the length of the character argument in the corresponding length argument when you move the focus to a different control.

For some arguments, the list may contain <rowset values>. This activates the Rowset hdbc and Rowset hstmt list boxes, which enable you to specify the *hdbc* and *hstmt* of the bound rowset. The Row and Column text boxes allow you specify the row and column number, respectively.

You can either select a value from the list or type a value in the text box. If the argument accepts values for which **#define** names apply, you can type the **#define** name (or any unambiguous portion of it) in the text box. For example, to specify that the driver prompt the user for connection information, select SQL_DRIVER_COMPLETE from the list of values for *fDriverCompletion* or type 1, 0x01, or SQL_DRIVER_COMPLETE (COM would be sufficient).

Check Boxes

Check boxes are used to specify values for input arguments that accept environment, connection, or statement handles; input arguments that accept window handles; and output arguments that accept pointers to handles or pointers to output buffers. For example, check boxes are used to specify values for the *hdbc*, *hwnd*, *szConnStrOut*, and *pcbConnStrOut* arguments in **SQLDriverConnect** (shown in Figure 4.2).

After each check box is the name of the argument and its value:

- For input arguments that accept handles, the value is either the handle value or NULL. ODBC Test retrieves this value from the current environment handle, the connection handle of the current connection window, or the statement handle of the current statement in the current connection window.

- For input arguments that accept window handles and output arguments that accept pointers to handles or pointers to output buffers, the value is either VALID or NULL.

A handle value or VALID indicates that ODBC Test will pass a valid, non-null pointer or handle; NULL indicates that ODBC Test will pass a null pointer or handle. To switch between the two, select or clear the check box.

Data Formats

ODBC Test accepts data in the following formats:

Data Type	Valid Formats
Binary	Hexadecimal. The value must contain an even number of hexadecimal characters. For example, 0x0100 is legal; 0xF is not.
Bit	Decimal (0 to 255).
	Hexadecimal (0x00 to 0xFF).
Character	Character. For example, abc.
	Hexadecimal. The value must contain an even number of hexadecimal characters. For example, 0x 61 62 63 is legal; 0x616 is not.
Date	YYYY-MM-DD. For example, 1993-10-25.
	Hexadecimal. The hexadecimal characters match the DATE_STRUCT structure. You must enter exactly 12 hexadecimal characters. For example, 0x 07C9 000A 0019.
Floating Point	Decimal. For example, 1234.46.
	Scientific notation. For example, 1.23446E3.
	Hexadecimal. The value must contain the exact number of hexadecimal characters required by the floating-point data type. For example, type 0xA64E9A44 for the SFLOAT 1234.46 and type 0x1D5A643BDFD98E40 for the SDOUBLE 987.234.
Integer	Decimal. For example, 255.
	Hexadecimal. The value can contain any number of hexadecimal characters up to the length of the integer. For example, 0xFF or 0xF.
Time	HH:MM:SS. For example, 12:34:56.
	Hexadecimal. The hexadecimal characters match the TIME_STRUCT structure. You must enter exactly 12 hexadecimal characters. For example, 0x 000C 0022 0038.
Timestamp	YYYY-MM-DD (time is set to 0). For example, 1993-10-25.
	HH:MM:SS (date is set to current date). For example, 12:34:56.
	YYYY-MM-DD HH:MM:SS[.F...]. For example, 1993-10-25 12:34:56.
	Hexadecimal. The hexadecimal characters match the TIMESTAMP_STRUCT structure. If you specify the fractional part of a timestamp, you must enter exactly 32 hexadecimal characters. If you do not specify the fractional part of a timestamp, you must enter exactly 24 hexadecimal characters. For example, 0x 07C9 000A 0019 000C 0022 0038 0000 0000 (with the fractional part) or 0x 07C9 000A 0019 000C 0022 0038 (without the fractional part).

Hexadecimal values are subject to the following constraints:

- Values must be in order of most-significant byte to least-significant byte. ODBC Test will convert these values to the byte order of the machine it is running on.

- Letters in hexadecimal values can be upper or lower case. For example, 0xFF, 0xfF, 0xFf, and 0xff are the same.

- Hexadecimal values can contain spaces at any point after the 0x characters; ODBC Test ignores these spaces. For example, 0xFF and 0x FF are the same.

Using Auto Tests

Auto tests are DLLs that you have written to test your driver. An auto test is a self-contained ODBC application, except that it must be run by ODBC Test. It allocates and frees handles, connects and disconnects from data sources, and accesses data in those data sources.

Creating Auto Tests

The following sections describe how to write auto tests, use the Quick Test sample, and build auto tests.

Writing an Auto Test

Writing an auto test is like writing any other ODBC application. You must write code to allocate and free handles, connect to and disconnect from data sources, and access data. As a starting point, you can use CUSTOM.C or QUIKTEST.C in the \ODBCSDK\SAMPLES\QUIKTEST directory.

Note   An auto test does not have to manage handles or connections if it uses the ODBC Test Handles test source. For more information, see the **AutoTestFunc** function description in "Auto Test Function Reference," later in this chapter.

An auto test contains one or more *test cases*, each of which tests some specific functionality. For example, an auto test for **SQLAllocStmt** might contain two test cases, one to call **SQLAllocStmt** with all combinations of valid and invalid arguments and one to call **SQLAllocStmt** repeatedly until the driver runs out of statement handles.

The BUILD program shipped with the ODBC SDK requires specified names for the source files for an auto test DLL. For more information, see "Required Files," later in this section.

The auto test must export the following functions, which are called by ODBC Test:

- **AutoTestName**   This function returns the name of the auto test and the number of test cases it includes. ODBC Test displays the auto test name in the Manage Auto Tests, Manage Groups, and Run Auto Test dialog boxes.

- **AutoTestDesc**   This function returns the name and description of a specific test case. ODBC Test displays the test case name and description in the Run Auto Tests dialog box.

- **AutoTestFunc**   This function invokes the auto test for a specific test source. Information about the test source and a bit array of the test cases to execute are passed to the auto test in a structure created by ODBC Test.

An auto test can call the following two functions in GATORTST.DLL (on Windows 3.1) or GTRTST32.DLL (on Win32s or Windows NT):

- **szLogPrintf**   An auto test calls this function to log test results and other information to the screen and the log file.

- **szMessageBox**   An auto test calls this function to display a message box. This function encapsulates the **MessageBox** function in the Windows API. Unlike the **MessageBox** function, it accepts a format string and a list of arguments with which it constructs a string to pass to **MessageBox**.

For more information about these functions, see "Auto Test Function Reference" and "ODBC Test Function Reference," later in this chapter.

The Quick Test Sample

You can use the Quick Test (\ODBCSDK\SAMPLES\QUIKTEST\QUIKTEST.C) as a starting point for both writing your own auto tests and testing your driver. The Quick Test calls each ODBC function and verifies that it returns the expected code. Next, it calls **SQLError** until that function returns SQL_NO_DATA_FOUND, verifying that the expected SQLSTATEs are returned. Finally, for some functions, it checks if the function returns the expected data.

Note   The Quick Test is *not* an ODBC acceptance or compliance test. It is a starting point for your testing.

Building an Auto Test

To build an auto test DLL from code you have written, change your directory to
\ODBCSDK\SAMPLES\QUIKTEST and use the BUILD.EXE program:

BUILD *tstname* [*options*]

where *tstname* is the base name of your .C file and *options* are one or more of the
following:

Option	Meaning
-16 or -32	Build a 16- or 32-bit DLL. The default is -16.
-a	Build a DLL for each .C file.
-clean	Build all targets, even if the targets are not out of date with respect to their dependents.
-debug or -nodebug	Generate debugging information (-debug) or not (-nodebug). The default is -debug.
-o *filename*	Create a makefile in *filename* that does not reference environment variables. When the -o option is specified, BUILD.EXE does not run the make utility.
-?, -help	Display usage information.

For example, to build all the component files into a 16-bit nodebug version of the
Quick Test, type:

build quiktest -nodebug -clean

Required Files

To build an auto test, BUILD.EXE needs the following files:

File Name	Description
AUTOTEST.H	Include file containing the constants and prototypes required to build an auto test DLL. All auto tests must include this file.
BUILD.INI	Initialization file for BUILD.EXE. For more information, see the "BUILD.INI File" section.
DLLSTUB.C	Source file containing the library entry points for 16- and 32-bit DLLs.
MAKEFILE	Makefile for auto test DLLs.
tstname.C *tstname*1.C *tstname*2.C	Source files. Only *tstname*.C is required. However, if your auto test requires additional source files, the MAKEFILE makefile requires that they are named *tstname*1.C and *tstname*2.C.
tstname.H	Optional include file.
tstname.RC	Optional resource file.

BUILD.INI File

The BUILD.INI file contains a single section, [Build Opts], that contains the following keywords:

Keyword	Value
BLDNAME	Name of the make utility to use. This value cannot include a directory name; the make utility must be in the current path.
CLEANOPT	The flag to pass the make utility specified with the BLDNAME keyword to force a clean compile. For example, this is -a for NMAKE.
DEFAULTS	Default values for the BUILD.EXE command line. For example, to compile a 32-bit nodebug DLL, this would be -32 -nodebug. Values specified on the command line override values specified with this keyword.
INCDIR	The directory containing the *tstname*.H include file.
OBJDIRDBGN	The output directory for a nodebug version of the DLL.
OBJDIRDBGY	The output directory for a debug version of the DLL.
RCDIR	The directory containing the *tstname*.RC resource file.
SRCDIR	The directory containing the *tstname*.C, *tstname*1.C, and *tstname*2.C source files.

Environment Variables

BUILD.EXE creates the following environment variables from the values specified in the BUILD.INI file and the BUILD command line. The MAKEFILE makefile refers to these environment variables.

Note If your make utility cannot use environment variables, run BUILD with the -o option to generate a makefile that does not reference environment variables.

Environment Variable	Description
ADDL1	"Y" if the *tstname*1.C file is found in the SRCDIR directory; otherwise, "N".
ADDL2	"Y" if the *tstname*2.C file is found in the SRCDIR directory; otherwise, "N".
DEBUG	"N" if the -nodebug option was specified; otherwise, "Y".
HFILE	"Y" if the *tstname*.H file is found in the INCDIR directory; otherwise, "N".
INCDIR	The value of the INCDIR keyword in the BUILD.INI file.
OBJDIRDBGN	The value of the OBJDIRDBGN keyword in the BUILD.INI file.
OBJDIRDBGY	The value of the OBJDIRDBGY keyword in the BUILD.INI file.

Environment Variable	Description
RCDIR	The value of the RCDIR keyword in the BUILD.INI file.
RCFILE	"Y" if the *tstname*.RC file is found in the RCDIR directory; otherwise, "N".
SRCDIR	The value of the SRCDIR keyword in the BUILD.INI file.
TSTNM	The value of *tstname* on the BUILD command line.
WIN32	"Y" if the -32 option was specified; otherwise, "N".

Running Auto Tests

In order to run an auto test, you must:

- Create test sources to run the auto test against or plan to run the auto test against the ODBC Test Handles test source, which uses the current connection.
- Install the auto test in ODBC Test.
- Optionally, add the auto test to a test group.

Creating Test Sources

A test source is an ODBC data source and, optionally, all the information necessary to connect silently to that data source. Generally, auto tests are run as a background task—either overnight or on a separate machine—so they should be able to connect to a data source without prompting you for connection information. The ODBC Test Handles test source, which uses the connection and statement handles from the current connection, is always available.

▶ **To create a test source**

1. In ODBC Test, choose Manage Test Sources from the Tools menu. ODBC Test displays the Manage Test Sources dialog box.

2. Choose the New button, type the name of your test source in the Test Source box, and choose the OK button.

3. Select the data source you want to access from the DSN list. If there are no data sources in the list, you can create them with the ODBC Administrator. For more information, see Chapter 3, "Using the ODBC Administrator."

4. If your data source requires a user and password, type the user ID in the UID box and the password in the PWD box.

Caution The password is stored in the \WINDOWS\GATOR.INI file (or the \WINNT\GATOR32.INI file on Windows NT) in unencrypted form. Because of this, you may want to create special data sources and passwords for use with ODBC Test or use only the ODBC Test Handles test source.

---

5. If your auto tests use **SQLDriverConnect** to connect to data sources, and the data source requires any other keywords and attribute values, type these as a connection string in the Keywords box. For example, to specify the Employee database and the DBNMP3.DLL network library, you might type the keywords:

```
DATABASE=Employee;NetLib=DBNMP3
```

6. Choose the Close button.

You can also modify or delete test sources with the Manage Test Sources dialog box.

Installing Auto Tests

ODBC Test cannot automatically recognize which DLLs on your system are auto tests. For this reason, you must install an auto test before you can include it in a test group or run it.

▶ **To install an auto test**

1. In ODBC Test, choose Manage Auto Tests from the Tools menu. ODBC Test displays the Manage Auto Tests dialog box.
2. The Available list lists all DLLs in the \ODBCSDK\BIN directory. To install auto tests from a different directory, choose the From button and select that directory.
3. Select the auto test to install from the Available list and choose the Add button. ODBC Test displays the name of the auto test.
4. Choose the Close button.

Note If you rebuild an auto test, you do not need to reinstall it. Replace the old auto test DLL with the new auto test DLL while ODBC Test is not running.

You can also remove auto tests with the Manage Auto Tests dialog box.

Creating Test Groups

To easily run related auto tests, you can group auto tests together. For example, you might want to create a test group of auto tests for **SQLBindCol**, **SQLGetData**, and **SQLFetch**. An auto test can be included in any number of test groups.

You are not required to create any test groups; all auto tests are automatically included in the All test group.

▶ **To create a test group**

1. In ODBC Test, choose Manage Groups from the Tools menu. ODBC Test displays the Manage Groups dialog box.

2. Choose the New button, type the name of the test group in the Group box, and choose the OK button.

3. The Available list lists all installed auto tests by name. For information about how to install auto tests, see the previous section.

4. Select an auto test to add to the test group from the Available list and choose the Add button. ODBC Test moves the auto test from the Available list to the Installed list. Continue to add auto tests to the group until the group contains all of the auto tests that you want.

5. Choose the Close button.

You can also use the Manage Auto Tests dialog box to add or remove auto tests from an existing test group and delete test groups. Removing an auto test from a test group or deleting a test group that contains an auto test does not affect the auto test; it remains installed in ODBC Test.

Running Auto Tests

After you have created and installed auto tests and created test sources, you can select the test cases you want to run and the test sources you want to run them against.

▶ **To run one or more auto tests**

1. In ODBC Test, choose Run Auto Tests from the Tools menu. ODBC Test displays the Run Auto Tests dialog box.

2. Select the test cases you want to run from the Tests list.

   The Tests list shows the test cases in an heirarchical structure: groups contain auto tests and auto tests contain test cases. To expand or collapse how much of the structure is shown, click on the plus or minus sign beside each group or auto test name. You can select test cases in the following ways:

   - **By Test Group**   Choose the test group name to select all test cases in all auto tests in a group. For example, to select all test cases in all installed auto tests, choose the All group name.

   - **By Auto Test**   Choose the auto test name to select all test cases in an auto test.

   - **By Test Case**   Choose the test case name to select an individual test case.

   To unselect a test case or cases, click on the highlighted test group name, auto test name, or test case name with the mouse or press SPACEBAR.

You can save the list of test cases, or *run list*, you have selected by clicking the Run Lists button and clicking the Save As button. Later, you can select the same test cases by selecting the run list.

3. Select the test sources from the Test Sources dialog box that you want to run the test cases against. When ODBC Test runs the auto tests, it will run each selected test case against each selected test source.

4. Select where you want the auto tests to log output:

- **Log File**   Log output to the file AUTO.LOG in the current directory. To use a different log file, choose the Log File button. In the Log File dialog box, you can also specify whether to append to or replace the log file.

- **Screen**   Log output to the Output window in ODBC Test.

If neither Log File nor Screen is selected, the tests will not log any information. ODBC Test always displays a list in the Output window of which tests were run and how many errors occurred.

5. Select the runtime options you want to use:

- **Debug**   Determines whether the *fDebug* flag in the SERVERINFO structure is set to TRUE or FALSE. What a test does when *fDebug* is TRUE depends on how the test was written.

- **Isolate Tests**   Determines whether **AutoTestFunc** is called once for each selected test case in an auto test (the tests are isolated) or once for the auto test. If **AutoTestFunc** is called once for each test case, only one bit in the *rglMask* bit mask in the SERVERINFO structure is set each time it is called; if it is called once for the auto test, a bit is set in *rglMask* for each selected test case.

- **Cursor Library**   Determines the value of the *vCursorLib* variable in the SERVERINFO structure:

Check Box	*vCursorLib* Value
Cleared	SQL_CUR_USE_DRIVER
Filled	SQL_CUR_USE_IF_NEEDED
Selected	SQL_CUR_USE_ODBC

How *vCursorLib* is used depends on how the test was written; it was intended to be used with the SQL_ODBC_CURSORS option in **SQLSetConnectOption**.

6. Choose the OK button. ODBC Test runs each selected test case against each selected test source.

Auto Test Function Reference

This section describes the three functions that each auto test DLL must contain:

AutoTestName
AutoTestDesc
AutoTestFunc

AutoTestName

Description   **AutoTestName** returns the name of the auto test and the number of test cases it contains.

C Prototype   **BOOL EXTFUN AutoTestName(**
LPSTR   *szName*,   /* Output: Auto test name   */
UINT FAR *   *piTestCases*);   /* Output: Number of test cases   */

Arguments   *szName*
The name of the auto test, such as "SQLAllocStmt Tests," is returned in the *szName* argument. This name must not exceed AUTO_MAX_TEST_NAME characters.

piTestCases
The number of test cases in the auto test is returned in the *piTestCases* argument.

Return Values   TRUE if the auto test name is copied (with or without truncation) to *szName* and the number of test cases in the auto test is copied to *piTestCases*. Otherwise, FALSE.

Comments   ODBC Test calls this function to determine the name of the auto test and the number of test cases it contains.

Code Example   The following code example shows a simple **AutoTestName** function:

```
BOOL EXTFUN AutoTestName(LPSTR szName, UINT FAR * iTestCases);
{
    /* The returned name is shorter than AUTO_MAX_TEST_NAME. */
    lstrcpy(szName, "SQLAllocStmt Tests");
    *iTestCases = 10;
    return TRUE;
}
```

AutoTestDesc

Description   AutoTestDesc returns the name and description of the specified test case.

C Prototype   **BOOL EXTFUN AutoTestDesc(**

UWORD	*iTest,*	/* Input: Test case number	*/
LPSTR	*szName,*	/* Output: Test case name	*/
LPSTR	*szDesc);*	/* Output: Test case description	*/

Arguments   *iTest*
                         The number of the test case. Test cases are numbered sequentially from 1 to
                         the number of test cases in the auto test.

                         szName
                         The name of the test case is returned in the *szName* argument. This name must
                         not exceed AUTO_MAX_TESTCASE_NAME characters.

                         szDesc
                         The description of the test case is returned in the *szDesc* argument. This
                         description must not exceed AUTO_MAX_TESTCASE_DESC characters.

Return Values   TRUE if the test number was valid, the test case name is copied to *szName*, and
                         the test case description is copied to *szDesc*. Otherwise, FALSE.

Comments   ODBC Test calls this function to determine the name and description of a test
                         case. It displays this information when the user is selecting the test cases to run.

Code Example   The following code example shows a simple **AutoTestDesc** function:

```
#define NumCases(s) (sizeof(s) / sizeof(s[0]))

struct {
    LPSTR szName;    /* Test case name        */
    LPSTR szDesc;    /* Test case description */
} TestInfo[] = {
/* szName                       szDesc                                        */
/* -----------------            ----------------------------------------- */
    "Valid connection",         "Call SQLConnect normally.",
    "IM002: No DSN",            "Call SQLConnect with no DSN or default.",
    "IM004: Bad SQLAllocEnv",   "Make driver's SQLAllocEnv fail."
};

BOOL EXTFUN AutoTestDesc(UWORD iTest, LPSTR szName, LPSTR szDesc);
{
    if (iTest >= NumCases(TestInfo))
        return FALSE;
    lstrcpy(szName, TestInfo[iTest-1].szName);
    lstrcpy(szDesc, TestInfo[iTest-1].szDesc);
    return TRUE;
}
```

AutoTestFunc

Description   **AutoTestFunc** runs one or more test cases in an auto test.

C Prototype   **void EXTFUN AutoTestFunc(**
lpSERVERINFO   *lpServer*);   /* Input: Test information   */

Arguments   *lpServer*

The *lpServer* argument is a SERVERINFO structure containing information that includes the test cases to run, the test source to run them against, and how to run them. The SERVERINFO structure is defined in the AUTOTEST.H file. It has the following members:

hwnd

The handle of the window to which **szLogPrintf** and **szMessageBox** write screen output. *hwnd* is not used by **AutoTestFunc**.

szLogFile

The name of the log file to which **szLogPrintf** writes file output. *szLogFile* is not used by **AutoTestFunc**.

henv, hdbc, hstmt

If the test source is not "ODBC Test Handles," these are null and the auto test must allocate its own handles. If the test source is "ODBC Test Handles," these are the currently selected environment, connection, and statement handles; if there are no currently selected environment, connection, and statement handles, these are null.

szSource

The name of the test source.

szValidServer0

The name of the data source associated with the test source. The auto test connects to this data source. *szValidServer0* is a null pointer if the test source is "ODBC Test Handles."

szValidLogin0

The user ID associated with the test source. The auto test uses this to connect to the data source. *szValidLogin0* is a null pointer if the test source is "ODBC Test Handles."

szValidPassword0

The password associated with the test source. The auto test uses this to connect to the data source. *szValidPassword0* is a null pointer if the test source is "ODBC Test Handles."

Caution The password is stored in the \WINDOWS\GATOR.INI file (or the \WINNT\GATOR32.INI file on Windows NT) in unencrypted form. Because of this, you may want to create special data sources and passwords for use with ODBC Test or use only the ODBC Test Handles test source.

---

szKeywords

The keyword-value pairs associated with the test source. The auto test uses these to connect to the data source. *szKeywords* is a null pointer if the test source is "ODBC Test Handles."

rglMask

A bit mask in which each bit represents a test case to be run. The auto test uses the GETBIT macro from the AUTOTEST.H file to determine which bits are set.

failed

Included for backwards compatibility with ODBC Test 1.0.

cErrors

The number of errors that occurred in all test cases run by **AutoTestFunc**. ODBC Test displays this number after it has called **AutoTestFunc**.

fDebug

TRUE if debugging was specified in the Run Auto Tests dialog box; otherwise, FALSE. What **AutoTestFunc** does when *fDebug* is TRUE depends on how it was written.

fScreen

TRUE if the Screen box was selected in the Run Auto Tests dialog box; otherwise, FALSE. *fScreen* is used by the **szLogPrintf** function in ODBC Test to determine whether to log output to the screen; it is not used by **AutoTestFunc**.

fLog

TRUE if the Log File box was selected in the Run Auto Tests dialog box; otherwise, FALSE. *fLog* is used by the **szLogPrintf** function in ODBC Test to determine whether to log output to the log file; it is not used by **AutoTestFunc**.

fIsolate

If the Isolate Tests box was selected in the Run Auto Tests dialog box, this will be TRUE and a single bit will be set in the *rglMask* member. Otherwise, FALSE.

vCursorLib

SQL_CUR_USE_IF_NEEDED, SQL_CUR_USE_ODBC, or SQL_CUR_USE_DRIVER, depending on the setting of the Cursor Library box in the Run Auto Tests dialog box. The auto test can pass this value to **SQLSetConnectOption** for the SQL_ODBC_CURSORS option.

hLoadedInst

The auto test DLL instance handle.

szBuff

Used by **szLogPrintf** to buffer output until it receives the string "\r\n". *szBuff* is not used by **AutoTestFunc**.

cBuff
>Used by **szLogPrintf** to count the output in *szBuff*. *cBuff* is not used by **AutoTestFunc**.

Return Values   None.

Comments   ODBC Test calls this function to run one or more test cases in the auto test. If the *szSource* member of the SERVERINFO structure specified in the *lpServer* argument is ODBC Test Handles, **AutoTestFunc** uses the handles specified in the *henv*, *hdbc*, and *hstmt* members. Otherwise, it connects to the data source specified in the *szValidServer0* member using the information in the *szValidLogin0*, *szValidPassword0*, and *szKeywords* members.

AutoTestFunc runs the test cases specified in the *rglMask* member, using the GETBIT macro to determine which bits are set. It calls **szLogPrintf** to send output to the screen or log file and stores the total number of errors encountered in the *cErrors* member.

Code Example   The following code example shows a simple **AutoTestFunc** function and supporting function:

```
void EXTFUN AutoTestFunc(lpSERVERINFO lpServer)
{
    UINT iCase;

    InitTest(lpServer);

    /* Loop through the rglMask bitmask with the GETBIT macro to      */
    /* determine the test cases to run. NumTests is the count of test */
    /* cases returned by AutoTestName.                                */

    for (iCase = 1; iCase < NumTests; iCase++)
        if (GETBIT(lpServer->rglMask, iCase))
            RunTestCase(lpServer, iCase);

    EndTest(lpServer);
}

void INTFUN RunTestCase(lpSERVERINFO lpServer, UINT iCase);
{
    szLogPrintf(lpServer, FALSE, "Running test case %u.\r\n", iCase);

    /* Run the test case specified by iCase. */

    szLogPrintf(lpServer, FALSE, "Test case %u finished.\r\n", iCase);
}
```

ODBC Test Function Reference

This section describes the functions in ODBC Test (in GATORTST.DLL on Windows 3.1 or GTRTST32.DLL on Win32s or Windows NT) that an auto test calls to log output and display screen messages:

szLogPrintf
szMessageBox

szLogPrintf

Description

szLogPrintf prints output from an auto test on the screen, in a log file, or both.

C Prototype

BOOL szLogPrintf(
lpSERVERINFO	*lpServer,*	/* Input: Test information	*/
BOOL	*fForce,*	/* Input: Force screen output	*/
LPSTR	*szFmt,*	/* Input: Format string	*/
...);		/* Input: Arguments for format string	*/

Arguments

lpServer

The *lpServer* argument is a SERVERINFO structure containing information that includes the output window handle, the log file name, and where to send output. The SERVERINFO structure is defined in the AUTOTEST.H file. For information about the members of the structure, see the *lpServer* argument in **AutoTestFunc**.

When **AutoTestFunc** calls **szLogPrintf**, it should pass the value of *lpServer* that was passed to it by ODBC Test.

fForce

If TRUE, **szLogPrintf** writes the output to the screen regardless of the *fScreen* member of the *lpServer* argument. If FALSE, **szLogPrintf** writes the output to the screen only if the *fScreen* member of the *lpServer* argument is TRUE.

szFmt

A null-terminated format string compatible with the **wsprintf** function.

...

Arguments for the format string specified in the *szFmt* argument.

Return Values

TRUE if the function successfully logged the output; otherwise, FALSE. If FALSE is returned, a message box appears that allows the user to turn off logging.

Comments

Auto tests should call this function to log all output from tests.

Code Example

See **AutoTestFunc**.

szMessageBox

Description   **szMessageBox** formats a string and displays it using the **MessageBox** function in the Windows API.

C Prototype   **int szMessageBox(**

HWND	*hwnd*,	/* Input: Parent window handle	*/
UINT	*style*,	/* Input: Style of message box	*/
LPSTR	*szTitle*,	/* Input: Title of message box	*/
LPSTR	*szFmt*,	/* Input: Format string	*/
...);		/* Input: Arguments for format string	*/

Arguments   *hwnd*

The parent window handle to be passed to **MessageBox**. This should be the *hwnd* member of the *lpServer* structure passed to **AutoTestFunc**.

style

The style of the message box. For more information, see the *fuStyle* argument of the **MessageBox** function in the Windows API.

szTitle

The title of the message box. For more information, see the *lpszTitle* argument of the **MessageBox** function in the Windows API.

szFmt

A null-terminated format string compatible with the **wsprintf** function.

...

Arguments for the format string specified in the *szFmt* argument.

Return Values   **szMessageBox** returns the value returned by **MessageBox**.

Comments   Auto tests can call this function to display a message box. Because most auto tests are designed to be run without user interaction, this function should only be called when user interaction is required. To routinely log output, an auto test should call **szLogPrintf**.

Code Example   The following code example shows how **AutoTestFunc** might use **szMessageBox** to tell the user how to use a dialog box displayed by **SQLDriverConnect**:

```
#define CONN_STR_LEN 100
UCHAR szConnStrIn[CONN_STR_LEN], szConnStrOut[CONN_STR_LEN];
SWORD cbConnStrOut;

/* szTestName is the test name returned by AutoTestName */
szMessageBox(lpServer->hwnd,
             MB_ICONINFORMATION | MB_OK,
             szTestName,
             "Click the Cancel button in the next dialog box.");

lstrcpy(szConnStrIn, "DSN=");
lstrcat(szConnStrIn, lpServer->szValidServer0);
lstrcat(szConnStrIn, "\0");
SQLDriverConnect(hdbc, lpServer->hwnd,
                 szConnStrIn, lstrlen(szConnStrIn),
                 szConnStrOut, CONN_STR_LEN, *cbConnStrOut,
                 SQL_DRIVER_PROMPT);
```

Tool Reference

Tools are menu items that help you configure ODBC Test, such as the level of errors to report or whether menu items for functions the driver does not support are disabled.

User Options

The User Options item on the Tools menu displays the User Options dialog box, which controls the ODBC Test user interface. It also controls how ODBC Test checks the result of function calls. The options in this dialog box do not affect auto tests.

Driver Dependent Menus If selected, ODBC Test disables those menu items not supported by the driver. For example, if the driver does not support **SQLDescribeParam**, ODBC Test disables the SQLDescribeParam menu item.

Automatic Error Checking If selected, ODBC Test calls the Error All function tool after each ODBC function is called. For more information, see "Error All" in the "Function Tool Reference."

Null Terminator Checking If selected, ODBC Test checks to see that the driver null-terminates all returned character values.

Buffer Overwrite Checking   If selected, ODBC Test fills output buffers with the pattern 0xCA before calling a function. After calling the function, it performs the following tests:

- Checks that the driver writes in the buffer when the function returns SQL_SUCCESS or SQL_SUCCESS_WITH_INFO. For example, if **SQLGetInfo** returns SQL_SUCCESS, ODBC Test checks that the driver wrote in the *rgbInfoValue* buffer.

- Checks that the driver does not write in the buffer when the function returns SQL_NO_DATA_FOUND, SQL_ERROR, SQL_INVALID_HANDLE, SQL_STILL_EXECUTING, or SQL_NEED_DATA. For example, if **SQLGetInfo** is called with an invalid *fInfoType*, ODBC Test checks that no data was written in the *rgbValue* buffer.

- Checks that the driver does not write past the end of the buffer. ODBC Test allocates an extra byte at the end of the buffer before calling the function. After calling the function, it checks whether the byte was overwritten. For example, if the *cbInfoValueMax* argument in **SQLGetInfo** is 10 and the data to be returned is 15 bytes long, ODBC Test checks that only 10 bytes were written in the *rgbInfoValue* buffer.

Note   ODBC Test cannot check if the driver writes past the end of an output buffer if that buffer is an array or structure.

Version Numbers   If selected, ODBC Test displays the version number of option values in dialog boxes, such as the values for the *fInfoType* argument in **SQLGetInfo**.

Always Use Cursor Library   If selected, ODBC Test calls **SQLSetConnectOption** with the SQL_ODBC_CURSORS option and the value SQL_CUR_USE_ODBC for each newly allocated connection handle.

Default Buffer Length   Specifies the default length of output buffers, such as *szConnStrOut* in **SQLDriverConnect** or *pvParam* in **SQLGetStmtOption**.

Argument Display Length   Specifies the default length of arguments displayed as output by the W2 logging level.

Max Bind Col All Length   Specifies the maximum length of the *rgbValue* buffer when the Bind Col All function tool is used.

Logging Level   Specifies the level of error output ODBC Test generates. For more information about ODBC Test errors and warnings, see "Error and Warning Messages," later in this chapter.

Error Logging Level	Error Output
W0	Return codes and ODBC Test error messages (TST0*xxx*)
W1	W0 output and ODBC Test warning messages (TST1*xxx*)
W2	W1 output and function name and argument values

Font Button   Displays the Choose Font dialog box in which you can specify the font and point size to be used by all text in the general output, connection, and rowset windows.

Rowset Options

The Rowset Options item on the Tools menu displays the Rowset Options dialog box, which controls the values displayed in rowset windows and how rowset buffers are allocated.

Status Values   If selected, ODBC Test displays the value of the *rgfRowStatus* array specified in **SQLExtendedFetch** at the start of each row in the rowset window.

Length Values   If selected, ODBC Test displays the value of the *pcbValue* buffer bound with **SQLBindCol** at the end of each column in the rowset window.

Column Names   If selected, ODBC Test displays the name of each column in the rowset window.

Reserved Rows   Specifies the number of extra rows to allocate in the rowset buffers used with **SQLExtendedFetch** and **SQLSetPos**. These rows are generally used for add buffers.

Trace

The Trace item on the Tools menu turns tracing on and off. If tracing is currently disabled, choosing this menu item enables tracing. ODBC Test displays a dialog box in which you can specify a trace file and whether the Driver Manager overwrites or appends to that trace file. It is equivalent to calling **SQLSetConnectOption** with the SQL_OPT_TRACE and SQL_OPT_TRACE_FILE options to enable tracing and specify a trace file. While tracing is enabled, ODBC Test places a check mark beside the Trace menu item.

If tracing is currently enabled, this menu item disables tracing. It is equivalent to calling **SQLSetConnectOption** with the SQL_OPT_TRACE option to disable tracing.

Function Tool Reference

Function tools are menu items that call a group of related ODBC functions or help you use an ODBC function. For example, Full Disconnect calls **SQLDisconnect**, **SQLFreeConnect**, and **SQLFreeEnv**; Fill Param displays a dialog box in which you enter parameter values. Function tools are listed at the bottom of the Connect, Statement, Results, and Misc menus beneath a separator line.

Note   To abort those function tools that run in a loop, press the ESC key.

Bind Col All (Results Menu)

The Bind Col All function tool binds all the columns in a result set. It:

1. Calls **SQLFreeStmt** with *fOption* set to SQL_UNBIND to unbind any previously bound columns.
2. Calls **SQLNumResultCols** to determine the number of columns in the result set.
3. Calls **SQLDescribeCol** for each column in the result set to determine the data type and precision of the column. Based on on the precision, it allocates a character buffer of up to the number of bytes specified with the Max Bind All Buffer box in the Rowset Options dialog box.
4. Calls **SQLBindCol** for each column in the result set to bind the column to a SQL_C_CHAR buffer.

Data Sources All (Connect Menu)

The Data Sources All function tool displays a list of all available data sources. It:

1. Calls **SQLDataSources** with *fDirection* set to SQL_FETCH_FIRST.
2. Calls **SQLDataSources** with *fDirection* set to SQL_FETCH_NEXT until it returns SQL_NO_DATA_FOUND.

Describe Col All (Results Menu)

The Describe Col All function tool displays the column name, type, precision, scale, and nullability of each column in the result set on the current *hstmt*. It:

1. Calls **SQLNumResultCols** to determine the number of columns in the result set.
2. Calls **SQLDescribeCol** for each column in the result set.

Drivers All (Connect Menu)

The Drivers All function tool displays a list of all available drivers and their attributes. It:

1. Calls **SQLDrivers** with *fDirection* set to SQL_FETCH_FIRST.

2. Calls **SQLDrivers** with *fDirection* set to SQL_FETCH_NEXT until it returns SQL_NO_DATA_FOUND.

Error All (Misc Menu)

The Error All function tool displays all pending errors. It:

1. Calls **SQLError** with the current *hstmt* until **SQLError** returns SQL_NO_DATA_FOUND.

2. Calls **SQLError** with the current *hdbc* until **SQLError** returns SQL_NO_DATA_FOUND.

3. Calls **SQLError** with the current *henv* until **SQLError** returns SQL_NO_DATA_FOUND.

Fetch All (Results Menu)

The Fetch All function tool fetches all remaining rows in all pending result sets on the current *hstmt*. If any columns were bound, after Fetch All has completed these will contain the values from the last row of the last result set. The Fetch All function tool:

1. Calls **SQLGetFunctions** to determine if the driver supports **SQLMoreResults**.

2. Calls **SQLFetch** until it returns SQL_NO_DATA_FOUND.

3. If the driver supports it, calls **SQLMoreResults**. If **SQLMoreResults** returns SQL_SUCCESS or SQL_SUCCESS_WITH_INFO, the Fetch All function tool returns to step 2. Otherwise, it stops.

Fill Param (Statement Menu)

The Fill Param function tool displays a dialog box in which you can enter the values of the *rgbValue* and *pcbValue* buffers for a parameter specified with **SQLBindParameter**.

If the parameter is a data-at-execution parameter, you can choose the SQL_LEN_DATA_AT_EXEC check box; if this check box is selected, the value of *pcbValue* is used as the *length* parameter of the SQL_LEN_DATA_AT_EXEC macro.

If you have called **SQLParamOptions** with *crow* greater than 1 to specify that you will pass an array of parameters, you can use the Element box to specify which element of the parameter array you are entering a value for. When you change the value in the Row box, ODBC Test stores the current values of *rgbValue* and *pcbValue* boxes in the previously specified element of the parameter arrays.

Full Connect (Connect Menu)

The Full Connect function tool completely connects to a data source. It:

1. Calls **SQLAllocEnv** (if necessary).
2. Calls **SQLAllocConnect**.
3. Calls **SQLSetConnectOption** with the SQL_ODBC_CURSORS option and the value SQL_CUR_USE_ODBC if the Always Use Cursor Library box in the User Options dialog box is selected.
4. Calls **SQLDriverConnect** with the *szConnStrIn* argument set to a null pointer and the *fDriverCompletion* argument set to SQL_DRIVER_COMPLETE. If **SQLDriverConnect** is not supported, it invokes **SQLConnect** with the given connection information.
5. Calls **SQLAllocStmt**.

Full Disconnect (Connect Menu)

The Full Disconnect function tool completely disconnects from the data source on the current *hdbc*. It:

1. Calls **SQLDisconnect**.
2. Calls **SQLFreeConnect**.

Get Data All (Results Menu)

The Get Data All function tool attempts to retrieve and display the data in every row and column in the result set on the current *hstmt*. The Get Data All function tool may not be able to display data for bound columns or columns that occur before the last bound column. It:

1. Calls **SQLGetFunctions** to determine if the driver supports **SQLMoreResults**.
2. Calls **SQLNumResultCols**.
3. Calls **SQLDescribeCol** to retrieve the name and precision of each column in the result set. Based on the precision, it allocates an output buffer of up to 65,535 bytes for each column.
4. Calls **SQLFetch**.

5. Calls **SQLGetData** for each column in the result set with an *fCType* argument of SQL_C_CHAR. The Get Data All function tool only calls **SQLGetData** once for each column. If the data is longer than 65,535 bytes, <trunc> is displayed before the first byte of data in the buffer.

6. Repeats steps 4 and 5 until **SQLFetch** returns SQL_NO_DATA_FOUND.

7. If the driver supports it, calls **SQLMoreResults**. If **SQLMoreResults** returns SQL_SUCCESS or SQL_SUCCESS_WITH_INFO, the Get Data All function tool returns to step 2. Otherwise, it calls **SQLFreeStmt** with *fOption* set to SQL_CLOSE to clear the result set.

Get Data Row (Results Menu)

The Get Data Row function tool retrieves and displays the data for every column in the current row of the result set on the current *hstmt*. You must call **SQLFetch** or **SQLExtendedFetch** before calling the Get Data Row function tool. The Get Data Row function tool:

1. Calls **SQLNumResultCols**.

2. Calls **SQLDescribeCol** to retrieve the name and precision of each column in the result set. Based on the precision, it allocates an output buffer of up to 65,535 bytes for each column.

3. Calls **SQLGetData** for each column in the result set with an *fCType* argument of SQL_C_CHAR. The Get Data Row function tool only calls **SQLGetData** once for each column. If the data is longer that 65,535 bytes, <trunc> is displayed before the first byte of data in the buffer.

Get Functions All (Misc Menu)

The Get Functions All function tool displays whether each ODBC function is supported. It:

• Calls **SQLGetFunctions** for each ODBC function.

Get Info All (Connect Menu)

The Get Info All function tool displays the return value of each information type defined for **SQLGetInfo** in ODBC 2.0. It:

• Calls **SQLGetInfo** for each value of *fInfoType*.

Show Bound Cols (Results Menu)

The Show Bound Cols function tool displays the binding information and the value of each buffer bound to a column with **SQLBindCol**. If the rowset size (specified with the SQL_ROWSET_SIZE statement option) is greater than 1, you must call **SQLExtendedFetch** to view the rest of the rowset. The Show Bound Cols function tool does not call any ODBC functions.

Show Params (Statement Menu)

The Show Params function tool displays the value of each buffer bound to a parameter marker with **SQLBindParameter**. If a successful call to **SQLParamOptions** has been made, it also displays the *pirow* value. It does not call any ODBC functions.

Update Cell (Results Menu)

The Update Cell function tool displays a dialog box in which you can specify the value of the *rgbValue* and *pcbValue* buffers of the current cell in the current rowset window. The dialog box also displays the values of the other arguments from the call to **SQLBindCol** used to bind the column.

Function Reference

Functions are menu items that call ODBC functions. When you select a function from an ODBC Test menu, ODBC Test displays a dialog box that has one control for each argument in the function. When you choose the OK button in the dialog box, ODBC Test executes the function using the values specified for each argument.

This section describes any special characteristics of the dialog boxes that ODBC Test displays for the ODBC functions. The dialog boxes for many functions are straightforward and do not require further explanation. For general information about function dialog boxes, see "Using Function Dialog Boxes," earlier in this chapter. For information about each ODBC function, see the *Microsoft ODBC SDK Programmer's Reference*.

SQLAllocConnect (Connect Menu)

After ODBC Test successfully calls **SQLAllocConnect**, it creates a connection window. If the Always Use Cursor Library box in the User Options dialog box is selected, ODBC Test also calls **SQLSetConnectOption** with the SQL_ODBC_CURSORS option and the value SQL_CUR_USE_ODBC.

SQLAllocEnv (Connect Menu)

You must allocate an *henv* before you can execute any other ODBC functions through the ODBC Test menu. You can allocate an *henv* by executing **SQLAllocEnv** or choosing Full Connect on the Connect menu. If you try to allocate a second *henv* without freeing the first, ODBC Test displays an error message. You do not need to allocate an *henv* before running any auto tests.

SQLAllocStmt (Statement Menu)

After ODBC Test successfully calls **SQLAllocStmt**, it adds the statement handle to the statement handle list of the current connection window.

SQLBindCol (Results Menu)

If the SQL_BIND_TYPE statement option specifies row-wise binding, **SQLBindCol** builds a structure containing elements for the *rgbValue* and *pcbValue* buffers. If you make multiple calls to **SQLBindCol**, each additional pair of elements is added to the end of the structure.

SQLBindParameter (Statement Menu)

Unless you want to specify a null pointer for the *rgbValue* argument, you must enter a value for it. You can change this value later with the Fill Param function tool. If you have data-at-execution parameters, you must enter a valid value for *rgbValue* based on the *fCType* specified.

To bind the parameter to the address of a specific row and column in a bound rowset on another *hstmt*, set the parameter to <rowset values> in the *rgbValue* and *pcbValue* arguments. This activates the Rowset hdbc and Rowset hstmt list boxes, which enable you to specify the *hdbc* and *hstmt* of the bound rowset. The Row and Column text boxes allow you specify the row and column number, respectively.

If you have called **SQLParamOptions** with *crow* greater than 1 to specify that you will pass an array of parameters, ODBC Test places the values you enter for *rgbValue* and *pcbValue* arguments in the first element of the parameter arrays. You can enter values for the other elements of the parameter arrays with the Fill Param function tool.

SQLSetParam has been deprecated for ODBC 2.0. To call **SQLSetParam** in an ODBC 1.0 driver, call **SQLBindParameter**. The Driver Manager ignores the values for *fParamType* and *cbValueMax* and maps the remaining arguments into a call to **SQLSetParam**.

To emulate an ODBC 1.0 application calling **SQLSetParam** in an ODBC 2.0 driver, set *fParamType* to SQL_PARAM_INPUT_OUTPUT and *cbValueMax* to −1 (which is the value of SQL_SETPARAM_VALUE_MAX).

SQLColAttributes (Results Menu)

If you enter an *fDescType* that is not recognized by ODBC Test, it is assumed to be a driver-specific descriptor type. So that ODBC Test can correctly display the value returned for this option, you must specify the value's C data type in the Description Type box. If the description type is SQL_C_ULONG, ODBC Test assumes the value is returned in the *pfDesc* argument; otherwise it assumes the value is returned in the *rgbDesc* argument.

SQLExtendedFetch (Results Menu)

After ODBC Test successfully calls **SQLExtendedFetch** it creates a rowset window.

SQLFreeConnect (Connect Menu)

After ODBC Test successfully calls **SQLFreeConnect**, it closes the current connection window.

SQLFreeStmt (Statement Menu)

After ODBC Test successfully calls **SQLFreeStmt** with the SQL_DROP option, it removes the statement handle from the statement handle list of the current connection window.

SQLGetConnectOption (Connect Menu)

The word "Conn:" prefixes the values in the *fOption* list to signify these are connection options (as opposed to statement options).

If you enter an *fOption* value that is not recognized by ODBC Test, it is assumed to be a driver-specific connection or statement option. So that ODBC Test can correctly display the value returned for this option, you must specify the value's C data type in the Parameter Type box.

SQLGetInfo (Connect Menu)

If you enter an *fInfoType* value that is not recognized by ODBC Test, it is assumed to be a driver-specific information type. So that ODBC Test can correctly display the value returned for this information type, you must specify the value's C data type in the Information Value Type box.

SQLGetStmtOption (Statement Menu)

If you enter an *fOption* value that is not recognized by ODBC Test, it is assumed to be a driver-specific statement option. So that ODBC Test can correctly display the value entered for this option, you must specify the value's C data type in the Parameter Type box.

SQLSetConnectOption (Connect Menu)

The word "Conn:" prefixes values in the *fOption* list that are connection options; the word "Stmt:" prefixes values that are statement options.

If you enter an *fOption* value that is not recognized by ODBC Test, it is assumed to be a driver-specific connection or statement option. So that ODBC Test can correctly display the value entered for this option, you must specify the value's C data type in the Parameter Type box.

SQLSetStmtOption (Statement Menu)

If you enter an *fOption* value that is not recognized by ODBC Test, it is assumed to be a driver-specific statement option. So that ODBC Test can correctly display the value entered for this option, you must specify the value's C data type in the Parameter Type box.

Error and Warning Messages

This section lists error and warning messages generated by ODBC Test. Self-explanatory messages such as "Disk Full" are not listed.

All error and warning messages have the following form:

TST*yxxx* : *message*

where

y

indicates the message level. Zero indicates an error message and 1 indicates a warning message.

xxx

is the message number.

For example:

```
TST0001: The value of cbConnStrLen is less than 0 and not SQL_NTS=-3
```

The following table lists the messages generated by ODBC Test. The values in *italics* are replaced by ODBC Test when it prints the error message. The value *codes* represents a list of return codes.

Message	Level	Description
TST0001	W0	The value of %s is less than 0 and not SQL_NTS=-3.
TST0002	W0	The value returned in %s does not match the length of string returned in %s.
TST0003	W0	The driver returned SQL_SUCCESS or SQL_SUCCESS_WITH_INFO but did not update %s.
TST0004	W0	Invalid return code '%s'.
		Valid return codes are *codes*.
TST0005	W0	Truncation implied but SQL_SUCCESS_WITH_INFO not returned, %s=%d.
		The value returned by the specified *pcb* parameter indicates that truncation occurred. However, SQL_SUCCESS_WITH_INFO was not returned from the driver.

Message	Level	Description
TST0006	W0	The value *%ld* was not a valid named constant for *%s*.
		The value returned for the function named is not one of the legal values as documented in the *Microsoft ODBC SDK Programmer's Reference*. For example, **SQLGetInfo** should return either 0 or 1 for SQL_ODBC_SAG_CLI_COMPLIANCE.
TST0007	W0	The following set bits do not have a corresponding named constant: *0x%08lX*
		A bit in the bitmask returned for the function named is not one of the legal values as documented in the *Microsoft ODBC SDK Programmer's Reference*. For example, **SQLGetInfo** should only set bits for SQL_LCK_NO_CHANGE, SQL_LCK_EXCLUSIVE, and SQL_LCK_UNLOCK for the information type SQL_LOCK_TYPES.
TST0008	W0	Cannot allocate more than *%ld* bytes of memory.
TST0009	W0	Buffer *%s* contained an invalid count byte value.
TST1001	W1	Buffer *%s* was not updated.
		Buffer checking has been enabled, but after the function call the named buffer was not updated.
TST1002	W1	Truncation implied by SQL_SUCCESS_WITH_INFO, *%s=%d*.
		The value returned by the specified *pcb* parameter indicates that a truncation ocurred, and SQL_SUCCESS_WITH_INFO was returned from the driver.
TST1003	W1	The message for SQLState "*%s*" is longer than SQL_MAX_MESSAGE_LENGTH – 1.
		The description of *cbErrorMsgMax* indicates that you should allocate no more than SQL_MAX_MESSAGE_LENGTH for an error returned from **SQLError**. This message indicates that the driver has returned a message which exceeds this limit. Since you should not expect this long of a message, this is a warning to the driver writer that the size of the message should be decreased.
TST1004	W1	Data needed for Parameter #*%u*
		Indicates the parameter that ODBC Test has identified as the next SQL_DATA_AT_EXEC parameter. ODBC Test bases this identification on the value of the *rgbValue* buffer specified in **SQLBindParameter (or SQLBindCol when SQLSetPos is used)** and returned by **SQLParamData**.

Message	Level	Description
TST1005	W1	Highest bound column is %u.
		Returned by the Get Data All function tools when columns are bound. Some drivers cannot return data before this column.
TST1006	W1	A zero was received for %s indicating the driver does not support this function.
		In ODBC 2.0, **SQLGetInfo** returns 0 for integer-valued information types that do not apply to the driver or data source. ODBC Test displays this message when **SQLGetInfo** returns 0 for an information type for which there is no #define with a value of 0.
TST1007	W1	Since prgbValue was NULL, ODBC Test was unable to resolve the data type of the parameter. The data type will be set to SQL_C_CHAR by default.
TST1008	W1	Buffer %s was modified beyond indicated length.
TST1009	W1	Buffer %s was modified and should not have been.
TST1010	W1	Buffer %s contained an invalid count byte value.
TST1011	W1	Buffer %s is not properly null-terminated.
TST1012	W1	Buffer %s contains an embedded NULL.

CHAPTER 5

Using ODBC Spy

ODBC Spy is a utility included with the ODBC SDK with which you can debug your drivers and applications. With ODBC Spy you can:

- Intercept and copy ODBC commands being sent from an application to an ODBC driver (spy on the application-driver connection). This is useful in determining how an ODBC connection fails.

- Emulate the actions of an ODBC driver receiving requests from an application (spy on an application). This is useful for debugging an application.

- Emulate an application and make requests to an ODBC driver (spy on a driver). This is useful for debugging a driver.

ODBC Spy is a low-level debugging tool. While ODBC Test (see Chapter 4, "Using ODBC Test") enables you to test the functionality of your driver, ODBC Spy enables you to determine the specific point at which your driver may be failing.

Both 16- and 32-bit versions of ODBC Spy are available. If you are running the Windows NT operating system, the ODBC SDK Setup program copied both versions to your system. If you are running Windows 3.1, only the 16-bit version was installed.

Note The 16-and 32-bit versions of ODBC Spy may be run simultaneously under Windows NT. However, only one instance of either one may be run at a time.

Spying with ODBC Spy

In order to spy on an application or a driver, you must first spy on an application-driver connection and save the ODBC calls made by the application to a log file. You then use the information in the log file to emulate either a driver or an application. For more information, see "Spying on an Application (Emulating a Driver)," and "Spying on a Driver (Emulating an Application)," later in this section.

Important While in use, ODBC Spy temporarily modifies the ODBC.INI file. In the event of a system failure, the changed information will be retained. You may want to first create a backup copy of your ODBC.INI file before running ODBC Spy.

Spying on an Application-Driver Connection

As stated in the previous section, before you can emulate a driver or an application, you must first record a set of ODBC function calls between an application and its driver, and save it to a log file. You do this with the Capture command. The general procedure is as follows:

▶ **To capture a set of ODBC function calls**

1. From the Spy menu, choose Capture. Select a data source compatible with your driver. If you choose the Log To File box, ODBC Spy prompts you for a log file.

    Note If you will use the information captured here in a driver or application emulation, you must save it to a log file.

2. Start the application that will send commands to the driver.

3. Use the application to access information through your selected data source. This can be done using automated test scripts or user-driven events (by hand). ODBC Spy displays and records all requests to the driver.

    Note If you plan to use ODBC Spy to emulate a driver, and you are not using automated test scripts, write down the sequence of operations you have the application perform. You will need this exact sequence when you use ODBC Spy to emulate a driver.

4. When you have finished recording the set of function calls between the application and its driver, save the log file by choosing Capture Off from the Spy menu. The ODBC Spy workspace clears, and the open log file is closed.

5. Repeat steps 1 through 4 for all the sets of function calls you want to capture. Specify a different log file each time so you can use them later for your emulations.

Once you have finished recording function calls, you can use ODBC Spy to emulate either the driver or the application involved in one of the original recordings.

Understanding Capture Results

The general structure of the information written to the ODBC Spy log file and workspace is:

ODBC Function
  argument value

  .

  .

  .

  RETCODE

You can use ODBC Spy to identify the actual values being passed between the functions called by the application and driver. The left-justified text is the name of the application's function call, and the indented text is the arguments of the call and the driver's response. If you look up the syntax for each captured function in the *Microsoft ODBC SDK Programmer's Reference*, you will find that for each function, the number of indented lines in the captured information matches the total number of arguments (including the return code) specified for the function.

For example, the following results are written to a log file:

```
SQLAllocEnv
    0x00010000
    SQL_SUCCESS
SQLAllocConnect
    0x00010000
    0x00010000
    SQL_SUCCESS
```

In the first statement, the environment handle (*phenv*, 0x00010000) and the return value (SQL_SUCCESS), were generated by the driver. The same process is true for the second statement: the **SQLAllocConnect** statement produced the environment handle (*henv*), the connection handle (*phdbc*), and the return code (RETCODE), in that order.

Note Because ODBC Spy resides between the Driver Manager and a driver, it captures calls to ODBC functions made by the application and calls made solely by the Driver Manager. For example, after the Driver Manager loads the driver, it calls **SQLGetInfo** to determine which version of ODBC the driver supports.

A Capture Example

The following procedure leads you through the capture of the function calls that occur between ODBC Test and an existing driver. The log file produced here will be used as the basis for the emulation examples, later in this chapter.

▶ **To capture function calls between ODBC Test and a driver**

1. From the Spy menu, choose Capture. The Capture dialog box appears.

   Ordinarily, you would choose a data source that uses the driver you would be testing. Because this example uses ODBC Test, you can choose any available data source. (If there is no compatible data source for your application, you have to create one. For information on creating a data source, see Chapter 3, "Managing Data Sources and Drivers.")

   Note You can use only one data source at a time.
   ---

2. Select the Log To File check box. Then choose the OK button. The Log File dialog box appears.

3. Select a directory and type a filename for the log file to which the captured information is to be written. (The data recorded to this file will be the basis for your emulations.) Then choose the OK button. If the filename you select already exists in the directory you propose, ODBC Spy will prompt you to confirm overwriting the old file. Choose the Yes or No button as appropriate. The Log File dialog box disappears.

4. Start ODBC Test. Position it and ODBC Spy for convenient simultaneous viewing in the Windows operating system workspace.

5. From the ODBC Test Connect menu, choose Full Connect. The SQL Data Sources dialog box appears.

6. Select the same data source you selected in step 1. Then choose the OK button.

   The SQL Data Sources dialog box disappears, and ODBC Test sends the functions needed to connect to the data source. It sends **SQLAllocEnv**, **SQLAllocConnect**, **SQLConnect**, six **SQLGetInfo** statements, and one **SQLAllocStmt** request.

   The ODBC Spy workspace displays all ODBC function calls to the data source's driver. Each function is left-justified, with the arguments and return code indented. This information is written to the log file and to the screen simultaneously. (For details on the response information, see the previous section, "Understanding Capture Results.") When the last statement is executed, ODBC Test displays a message in the Output window indicating that it has successfully connected to the data source.

   Note You can disable the ODBC Spy workspace screen refresh by choosing Log on Screen from the ODBC Spy File menu. When the current functions finish, you can choose Log on Screen from the File menu again, and the next function will be highlighted.
   ---

7. From the ODBC Test Connect menu, choose Full Disconnect. The ODBC Spy workspace displays the execution of **SQLDisconnect**, **SQLFreeConnect**, and

SQLFreeEnv. ODBC Test displays a message indicating that the connection has closed.

8. From the ODBC Spy Spy menu, choose Capture Off. The Spy workspace clears, and the open log file is saved and closed.

9. From the ODBC Test File menu, choose Exit. The ODBC Test utility closes.

In this example, the ODBC Test connection was closed first. It is not necessary to close the connection before you quit ODBC Spy; you may close ODBC Spy while a connection is open. This will not affect the communication link between the application and the driver. However, if you close ODBC Spy first, remember that all logging will stop.

Spying on an Application (Emulating a Driver)

To emulate a driver, you need to have already captured a set of function calls between the application with which you want ODBC Spy to interact, and the driver you want ODBC Spy to emulate. (For information on capturing a set of function calls, see the previous section, "Spying on an Application-Driver Connection.")

Note Emulating a driver is particularly useful when the data source connection is expensive (remote), and your main object is to debug an application.

The general procedure for emulating a driver is as follows:

▶ **To emulate a driver**

1. Capture a set of function calls between the application with which you want ODBC Spy to interact, and the driver you want ODBC Spy to emulate. This can be done using automated test scripts or user-driven events (by hand). ODBC Spy displays and records all requests to the driver. If you are running the application by hand, write down the sequence of operations you have the application perform. You will need this exact sequence when you want ODBC Spy to emulate the driver.

2. From the ODBC Spy Spy menu, choose Emulate Driver. The Emulate Driver dialog box appears.

3. Choose the data source compatible with the driver you want ODBC Spy to emulate. Then choose the OK button. The Emulate Driver dialog box disappears, and the Log File dialog box appears.

4. Select the log file that contains the set of function calls you want the driver to use. Then choose the OK button. The Log File dialog box disappears. The contents of the log file are copied into the ODBC Spy workspace. The first function (and its arguments and return values) is highlighted.

5. Run the application that was used to create the current log file.

6. Using the sequence of operations you recorded in step 1 as a reference, have the application call the same ODBC functions as it had originally.

Note The application must call the same functions as when the log file was first created, and it must call them in the same order for a successful test.

As each function is called from the application, it is highlighted in the ODBC Spy workspace. If the application fails during the emulation, the errant function will be highlighted.

7. From the ODBC Spy Spy menu, choose Emulate Driver Off. The ODBC Spy workspace is cleared and the open log file is closed.

Note During driver emulation, ODBC Spy can only handle a single pass of the set of function calls. If you try to use the same log file again without reloading it, ODBC Spy will generate a replay error and close the application (in this case ODBC Test).

If you want to run the emulation sequence again, repeat steps 2 through 7.

Driver Emulation Example

The following procedure leads you through the emulation by ODBC Spy of the driver used in the capture example earlier in this chapter. It uses the log file produced from the brief session between ODBC Spy and ODBC Test (see "A Capture Example" in the previous section).

▶ **To emulate a driver receiving requests from ODBC Test**

1. From the ODBC Spy Spy menu, choose Emulate Driver. The Emulate Driver dialog box appears.

2. Choose the same data source you used during the capture example. Then choose the OK button. The Emulate Driver dialog box disappears, and the Log File dialog box appears.

3. Select the log file that contains the set of ODBC function calls you used for the capture example. Then choose the OK button. The Log File dialog box disappears. The contents of the log file are copied into the ODBC Spy workspace.

4. Run ODBC Test.

5. From the ODBC Test Connect menu, choose Full Connect. This is the first command executed during the capture example. If you don't choose this tool first, an error will occur.

As each request is sent from ODBC Test, the current line in ODBC Spy (highlighted in blue) is advanced. ODBC Spy simply matches the ODBC Test request with that of the current line, sets argument values as specified, and returns the last line of the indented information to ODBC Test. When ODBC

Spy returns the values for the **SQLAllocStmt** statement, ODBC Test displays a message in the Output window indicating a successful connection.

6. From the ODBC Test Connect menu, choose Full Disconnect. This is the second operation done during the capture example. The current line in the ODBC Spy workspace advances as before, and the sequence finishes.

7. From the ODBC Spy Spy menu, choose Emulate Driver Off. The ODBC Spy workspace is cleared and the open log file is closed.

   Once you have reached the end of the log file, you cannot replay the log file a second time. If you want to run the emulation sequence again, repeat the procedure.

Spying on a Driver (Emulating an Application)

To emulate an application, you need to have already captured a set of ODBC function requests between the driver with which you want ODBC Spy to interact, and the application you want ODBC Spy to emulate. (For information on capturing a set of function calls, see "Spying on an Application-Driver Connection" earlier in this chapter.) The general procedure is as follows:

▶ **To emulate an application**

1. Capture a set of function calls from the application you want ODBC Spy to emulate to the driver with which you want ODBC Spy to interact. (You do not need to write down the operations the application performs, because the application itself will not be involved in the playback.)

2. From the ODBC Spy Spy menu, choose Emulate App. The Emulate Application dialog box appears.

3. Choose the data source that uses the driver used by the application you want ODBC Spy to emulate. Then choose the OK button. The Emulate Application dialog box disappears, and the Log File dialog box appears.

4. Select the log file that contains the set of ODBC function calls you want the driver to use. Then choose the OK button. The Log File dialog box disappears. The contents of the log file are copied into the ODBC Spy workspace. The first function (and its return values) is highlighted.

5. If you want to pause while playing back the captured function calls, set the breakpoints now. (For more information, see "Setting and Removing Breakpoints" later in this section.)

6. Start the playback by choosing Go from the Debug menu (or press F5). Playback will stop at the line with the first breakpoint. Or, you can execute the current line by choosing Step from the Debug menu (or press F10).

   ODBC Spy calls the functions in the log file, and compares the arguments and return code returned by the driver to those saved in the log file. Any deviation from the saved values results in an error.

7. If you have run ODBC Spy from within the CodeView® debugger, you can switch back to the debugger while emulating an application by choosing Enter Debugger from the Debug menu, or by pressing CTRL+ALT+SYS RQ. (For more information, see "Using ODBC Spy with the CodeView Debugger" later in this chapter.)

8. Once you have reached the end of the log file, you must restart the log file before you can play ODBC function calls back again. To restart the log file, choose the Go command from the Debug menu and choose the OK button when ODBC Spy prompts you to restart. To play back the function calls again, return to step 6.

9. When you are finished, choose Emulate App Off from the Spy menu. The ODBC Spy workspace clears and the log file is closed.

Setting and Removing Breakpoints

You can set as many breakpoints as you want in the current log file; note that breakpoints are not saved when you close the log file.

▶ **To set a breakpoint**

- Double-click the line in the ODBC Spy workspace on which you want to set a breakpoint. Or, move to the line using the PAGE UP, PAGE DOWN, HOME, END, or arrow keys, and then press F9. The line changes from black to red. When the breakpoint line becomes the current line, its color changes to purple.

▶ **To remove a breakpoint**

- Double-click the line in the ODBC Spy workspace on which you want to clear a breakpoint. Or, move to the line using the PAGE UP, PAGE DOWN, HOME, END, or arrow keys, and then press F9. The line changes from red to black.

▶ **To remove all existing breakpoints**

- From the Debug menu, choose Remove All Breakpoints. All the breakpoints you have set are cleared.

Application Emulation Example

The following procedure leads you through the emulation by ODBC Spy of the application used in the capture example earlier in this chapter. It uses the log file produced from the brief session between ODBC Spy and ODBC Test (see "A Capture Example" earlier in this chapter).

▶ **To emulate ODBC Test making requests to a driver**

1. From the ODBC Spy Spy menu, choose Emulate App. The Emulate Application dialog box appears.

2. Choose the same data source you used during the capture example. Then choose the OK button. The Emulate Application dialog box disappears, and the Log File dialog box appears.

3. Select the log file that contains the set of ODBC function calls you used for the capture example. Then choose the OK button. The Log File dialog box disappears. The contents of the log file are copied into the ODBC Spy workspace.

4. Set a breakpoint on the first **SQLGetInfo** function by double-clicking it with the mouse. ODBC Spy highlights the function in red, marking it as a breakpoint. (If you set the breakpoint on the wrong statement by mistake, just double-click it again with the mouse, and the breakpoint will clear.)

5. From the Debug menu, choose Step, or press F10. ODBC Spy calls the first function in the log file and compares the values returned by the driver to those saved in the log file. Any deviation from the saved values results in an error.

   The current line is advanced to the next command, which becomes highlighted in blue. You can step through as many commands as you want. You do not need to have any breakpoints set to do single-stepping.

6. From the Debug menu, choose Go, or press F5. ODBC Spy executes all the functions from (and including) the current function, to (but not including) the function on which you have set the breakpoint. The breakpoint becomes the current line, and becomes highlighted in purple, indicating that a breakpoint line is now the current line.

7. From the Debug menu, choose Go, or press F5. ODBC Spy calls all remaining functions in the log file to the driver, and compares the returned values to those saved in the log file. Any inconsistencies will cause an error.

8. From the Spy menu, choose Emulate App Off. The ODBC Spy workspace clears, and the open log file is closed.

Using ODBC Spy with the CodeView Debugger

You can use ODBC Spy in conjunction with the Microsoft CodeView debugger when debugging your driver DLL.

Note The ODBC Spy Debug menu Enter Debugger command will work with any debugger that is activated by the **DebugBreak()** function. For more information on the **DebugBreak()** function, see your Windows operating system Software Development Kit documentation.

The general procedure for using ODBC Spy with the CodeView debugger is as follows:

▶ **To use ODBC Spy with CodeView**

1. In ODBC Spy, capture a set of ODBC function calls between an application and your driver (or a driver that will produce a log file that a working version of your driver will be able to use). For more information on capturing a set of function calls, see "Spying on an Application-Driver Connection" earlier in this chapter.

2. Quit ODBC Spy and start Microsoft CodeView on ODBCSPY.EXE.

3. Load your driver DLL with the /L switch. You can set CodeView breakpoints at this time.

4. From within CodeView, switch to ODBCSPY.EXE by typing **Go** in the CodeView command window, or by pressing F5. The system switches to ODBC Spy.

5. From the ODBC Spy Spy menu, choose Emulate App. The Emulate Application dialog box appears.

6. Choose the same data source you used during the capture in step 1. Then choose the OK button. The Emulate Application dialog box disappears, and the Log File dialog box appears.

7. Select the log file that contains the set of ODBC function calls you captured in step 1. Then choose the OK button. The Log File dialog box disappears. The contents of the log file are copied into the ODBC Spy workspace.

8. Set an ODBC Spy breakpoint on or near the point of the log file where you want to invoke the CodeView debugger. ODBC Spy highlights the function in red, marking it as a breakpoint.

9. From the ODBC Spy Debug menu, choose Go. ODBC Spy executes the requests against your driver, and stops at the breakpoint you set in step 8.

10. Now you are ready to enter CodeView. From the ODBC Spy Debug menu, choose Enter Debugger or press CTRL+ALT+SYS RQ. The system switches to the CodeView debugger.

11. Within CodeView, perform debugging operations as needed to debug your driver DLL.

12. When you are ready to switch back to ODBC Spy, type **Go** in the CodeView command window, or press F5. The system switches to ODBC Spy.

13. Repeat steps 8 through 12 as needed to complete the log file, or from the Spy menu, choose Emulate App Off to close the open log file.

Note For more information on using the Microsoft CodeView debugging utility, see your CodeView documentation.

CHAPTER 6

Using the Driver Setup Toolkit

The Driver Setup Toolkit is included with the ODBC SDK to give developers an easy way to include a customized setup program with their deliverable database drivers. The toolkit is located in the \ODBCSDK\DRVSETUP.KIT directory, and is based on the same setup program that installs the drivers included with your ODBC SDK version 2.0 onto your hard disk.

Note The \ODBCSDK\DRVSETUP.KIT\SETUP16 and SETUP32 subdirectories contain platform-specific files.

Help is available during installation by way of Help command buttons installed on the ODBC Administrator dialog boxes. For all dialog boxes with Help command buttons (except driver-specific setup dialog boxes) the file ODBCINST.HLP is called. You must provide the help for the Help command button in the driver-specific setup dialog boxes.

Customizing a Driver Setup Program

The Driver Setup Toolkit is specifically designed to enable you to customize an ODBC-compatible driver setup program. You cannot use it for customizing any other type of installation. Also, you should not modify any of the Driver Setup Toolkit files beyond what is recommended in this chapter. Doing so may produce unexpected results.

You customize your driver setup program by modifying the files in the following procedure. The following sections provide details on these files.

▶ **To build a customized driver setup program**

1. Modify the text captions, labels, and position and size parameters of the dialog boxes in the DRVSETUP.DLG file to suit your requirements. You can modify the DRVSETUP.C source file if you want to change the default functionality.

2. Modify the title and message in the SETUP.LST file. Make sure the value set in the *odbc.inf* entry of the [Files] section is ODBC.INF.

3. Modify the appropriate section entries in your ODBC.INF file.

4. Create a standard .ICO icon file suitable to your installation requirements. (The default is DRVSETUP.ICO.) Make sure your .ICO filename matches the value set in the Images section of the DRVSETUP.RC file.

5. Create a standard .DIB bitmap file for the splash screen that is suitable to your installation requirements. (The default is DRVSETUP.DIB.) Make sure your .DIB filename matches the value set in the Images section of the DRVSETUP.RC file.

6. Modify the DRVSETUP.RC file string table values and version definitions to match your product's needs. Do not change any symbol names. Make sure the values for ICI_ICON and ICI_BITMAP match the names for your .ICO and .DIB files, respectively.

7. Recompile the DRVSETUP.EXE file using the following command:

   build {**setup16** | **setup32**}

   where

   - **setup16** is the option you use to build the 16-bit version in the \ODBCSDK\DRVSETUP.KIT\SETUP16 directory.

   - **setup32** is the option you use to build the 32-bit version in the \ODBCSDK\DRVSETUP.KIT\SETUP32 directory.

   The resource compiler will rebuild the DRVSETUP.EXE file with your new configuration.

8. Place your drivers and customized driver setup program on an installation disk along with the other necessary installation files. (For information on the other necessary files, see "Driver Setup Toolkit Files" later in this chapter.) Make sure the [Source Media Descriptions] section values are correct, and that each driver listed in the [ODBC Drivers] section of the ODBC.INF file is copied to the installation disk.

   If you want to compress the installation files before copying them to the disk, you must use the Microsoft file compression utility (COMPRESS.EXE). (For more information on the COMPRESS.EXE, see your Microsoft Windows Software Development Kit documentation.) Note that the customized driver setup program automatically detects compressed files and attempts to expand them during installation.

Automatic Setup

The driver setup program supports automatic setup. This is useful for multiuser environments, where users can set up your drivers from a network drive; automatic setup provides all users with the same ODBC drivers and data sources. To set up automatically, users run the setup progam with the /AUTO switch.

▶ **To configure a system for automatic setup, the network administrator**

1. Connects to a network directory to which all users have access.

2. Creates a directory from which other users will install the drivers and related ODBC components.

3. Copies all files from your disk to the newly created directory.

4. Installs your drivers on a system that does not have ODBC installed and adds all data sources required by users installing from the network.

5. Copies the ODBC.INI and ODBCINST.INI files from the system used in the previous step to the network directory created in step 2.

6. Adds the following two lines to the [Files] section of the SETUP.LST file on the network directory:

   odbcinst.ini=odbcinst.ini
   odbc.ini=odbc.ini

Note For information about how to use the setup /AUTO switch on Windows NT, double-click the Read Me First icon in the ODBC SDK 2.0 program group.

▶ **To install your drivers automatically, users**

1. Ask the network administrator for the address of the network drive containing your drivers.

2. If Windows is not already running, type **win** at the command prompt.

   If Windows is running, close any open applications.

3. Connect to the newtork drive containing your drivers.

4. From the Program Manager File menu, choose Run.

5. Type the full path of your driver setup program, followed by the **/auto** switch, then press ENTER. For example, if the network drive is O: and the driver setup program is in the \ODBC directory, type **o:\odbc\setup /auto**. After installation, the user is returned to Windows.

Driver Setup Toolkit Files

This section describes the files in the Driver Setup Tookit that you can modify: the files used to create DRVSETUP.EXE and _BOOTSTP.EXE, ODBC.INF, and SETUP.LST.

Files Used to Create DRVSETUP.EXE

DRVSETUP.EXE is the customized driver setup program that you configure by modifying the DRVSETUP.DEF, DRVSETUP.DIB, DRVSETUP.DLG, DRVSETUP.ICO, DRVSETUP.RC, DRVSETUP.C, and DRVSETUP.H files.

Running DRVSETUP.EXE installs your driver's files on a user's system. For information on how to create this file, see "Customizing a Driver Setup Program" in the previous section.

Note You are not required to modify the DRVSETUP.C and DRVSETUP.H files to create a driver setup program; such modifications are not discussed here.

DRVSETUP.DEF

Module definition file for the driver setup program.

DRVSETUP.DIB

This is the splash screen bitmap used as a background for all dialog boxes opened by the customized driver setup program. You can modify this file with a drawing program, such as the Windows operating system utility, Paintbrush (PBRUSH.EXE), or you can substitute your own bitmap file. (If you use your own bitmap file, it must be listed in the DRVSETUP.RC file.)

DRVSETUP.DLG

This is the dialog description file for the setup dialog boxes. You can change the dialog box captions, dialog box positioning, text labels, command button captions, and command button positioning to suit your requirements. You should not change ID numbers or dialog box symbol names, nor should you delete any of the dialog boxes from the DRVSETUP.DLG file. If you do so, you must also make changes in DRVSETUP.C accordingly.

The following dialog boxes are defined in the file:

WELCOME Dialog Box
   This is the first dialog box displayed after the splash screen DRVRSETUP.DIB is displayed.

ASKQUIT Dialog Box
   This dialog box appears whenever a user selects an Exit command button.

EXITSUCCESS Dialog Box
   This dialog box appears if the customized driver setup program completed without failure or interruption.

EXITQUIT Dialog Box
   This dialog box appears if a user selects Exit from the ASKQUIT dialog box.

EXITFAILURE Dialog Box
   This dialog box appears only if a system error prevents continuation of the customized driver setup program.

AWELCOME, AEXITSUCCESS, AEXITFAILURE Dialog Boxes

These three dialog boxes appear only if the customized driver setup program is run with the /AUTO switch to allow automatic setup. For more information on the /AUTO switch, see "Customizing a Driver Setup Program" earlier in this chapter.

For example, the definition for the WELCOME dialog box is as follows:

```
WELCOME DIALOG DISCARDABLE  36, 33, 200, 105
STYLE DS_MODALFRAME | WS_POPUP | WS_VISIBLE | WS_CAPTION | WS_SYSMENU
CAPTION "Microsoft ODBC Setup"
FONT 8, "Helv"
BEGIN
    DEFPUSHBUTTON    "&Continue",IDOK,52,85,40,14,WS_GROUP
    PUSHBUTTON       "E&xit",IDCANCEL,108,85,40,14
    CTEXT            "Welcome to the Microsoft Open Database Connectivity
(ODBC) Setup utility.",
            -1,45,10,140,25,SS_NOPREFIX
    CTEXT            "Setup installs and configures Microsoft Open
Database Connectivity components.  Choose Continue to install or Exit to
leave without installing Microsoft ODBC.",
            -1,10,40,180,35,NOT WS_GROUP
    ICON             IDI_ICON,-1,8,8,18,20
END
```

You might decide to change the size and position of the dialog box, change the CAPTION and CTEXT strings, and even change the command button label, size, and position. As long as the text and size are compatible, your customized driver setup program should run. For more information on working with dialog box definitions, see your Windows operating system Software Development Kit documentation.

DRVSETUP.ICO

This is the icon control displayed on the customized driver setup program dialog boxes. (For more information on the customized driver setup program dialog boxes, see "DRVSETUP.DLG.") You can modify it using an icon editor, or substitute any valid .ICO file. (If you use your own .ICO file, it must be listed in the DRVSETUP.RC file.)

DRVSETUP.RC

This is the resource file containing image, string, and version information. It lists the splash screen bitmap, icon file, and version information for the customized driver setup program. You can change the icon and splash bitmap symbol definitions (but not the symbols), as well as any of the string table or version text.

For example, the Strings section, is shown as following:

```
/* Strings --------------------------------------------------------
 */
STRINGTABLE DISCARDABLE
BEGIN
    IDS_FRAMETITLE  "Microsoft ODBC Sample Driver Setup"
    IDS_BADODBCI"Setup is unable to install ODBC.\n\n%s is either empty
or missing."
    IDS_BADODBC "Setup is unable to create data sources.\n\n%s is either
empty or missing."
    IDS_BADDS   "Setup was unable to create the %s data source."
    IDS_BADINST "Setup was unable to install the ODBC drivers."
END

/* From: Version Information
**
*/
#define VER_COMPANYNAME_STR     "Microsoft Corporation\0"
#define VER_LEGALCOPYRIGHT_STR  "Copyright \251 Microsoft Corporation
1991-1993\0"
#define VER_LEGALTRADEMARKS_STR "ODBC(TM) is a trademark of Microsoft
Corporation.  Microsoft\256 is a registered trademark of Microsoft
Corporation. Windows(TM) is a trademark of Microsoft Corporation.\0"
#define VER_PRODUCTNAME_STR     "Microsoft Open Database Connectivity\0"
#define VER_FILEDESC_STR"Microsoft ODBC Setup\0"
#define VER_FILENAME_STR"ODBCADM.EXE\0"
#define VER_NAME_STR     "ODBCADM\0"
```

For your customized driver setup program, you might decide to change the version definitions.

DRVSETUP.C

Source file for the driver setup program. You can modify this file to change the functionality of the driver setup program.

DRVSETUP.H

Header file referenced by DRVSETUP.RC.

3DCHECK.BMP

File referenced by DRVSETUP.RC for three-dimensional controls. You should not change this file.

Files Used to Create _BOOTSTP.EXE

_BOOTSTP.EXE is a bootstrap program that starts DRVSETUP.EXE. It works under both 16- and 32-bit environments. You can configure _BOOTSTP.EXE by modifying the _BOOTSTP.C and _BOOTSTP.DEF files.

Note   You are not required to modify the _BOOTSTP.C and _BOOTSTP.DEF files to create a driver setup program; such modifications are not discussed here.

_BOOTSTP.C

Source file for _BOOTSTP.EXE. You can modify this file to change the functionality of the bootstrap program.

_BOOTSTP.DEF

Module definition file for _BOOTSTP.EXE.

ODBC.INF

The ODBC.INF file contains information the customized driver setup program uses during installation of your drivers. You can modify the source media descriptions, the default file settings, add drivers to the ODBC Drivers list, and add driver descriptions. For detailed reference information on the structure and content of the ODBC.INF file, see the *Microsoft ODBC SDK Programmer's Reference*.

SETUP.LST

This is the first file read by the customized driver setup program. It contains a list of the files that the customized driver setup program uses while it is installing your drivers. The customized driver setup program copies the files listed in this file to a temporary directory on the user's hard disk and removes them and the directory when it is done. You can modify the message strings and temporary directory settings, but you should not modify any of the other settings.

The SETUP.LST file contains two sections. The following is a copy of the SETUP.LST for the 16-bit Sample Driver. (The 32-bit SETUP.LST file is slightly different.)

```
[Params]
    WndTitle    = Put Your Own Title Here
    WndMess     = Put Your Own Message Here...
    TmpDirSize  = 500
    TmpDirName  = ~smplstp.t
    CmdLine     = _bootstp drvsetup %s %s
    DrvModName  = _BOOTSTP

[Files]
    odbc.inf     = odbc.inf
    _mssetup.ex_ = _mssetup.exe
    _bootstp.exe = _bootstp.exe
    drvsetup.exe = drvsetup.exe
    odbcinst.dl_ = odbcinst.dll
    odbcinst.hl_ = odbcinst.hlp
```

Parameters Section

WndTitle

> This is the title that appears on the initialization dialog box. This dialog box is displayed before the splash screen bitmap. (For information on the splash screen bitmap file, see "DRVSETUP.DIB.") Replace the existing text with any valid string.

WndMess

> This is the title that is displayed within the initialization dialog box. Replace the existing text with any valid string. The customized driver setup program automatically sizes the initialization dialog box to a size that accommodates your message.

TmpDirSize

> Maximum number of files the temporary installation directory may contain. Default is 500.

TmpDirName

> The name of the temporary directory that the customized driver setup program uses to store temporary files. Both the directory and files are removed when the installation has finished. The default is ~SMPLSTP.TMP, and it is placed at the root directory of the hard drive the customized driver setup program uses.

CmdLine

> The customized driver setup program uses this command line to run. Do not change this line. The value is _BOOTSTP DRVSETUP %S %S.

DrvModName

> The customized driver setup program uses this module name to run. Do not change this line. The value is _BOOTSTP.

[Files] Section

The [Files] section contains the files that are used by the customized driver setup program, as described in the following table:

File	Description
ODBC.INF	Installation file (see "ODBC.INF").
_MSSETUP.EXE	MS-DOS utility for updating system files locked by the Windows operating system.
_BOOTSTP.EXE	File that starts DRVSETUP.EXE (see "Files Used to Create _BOOTSTP.EXE").
DRVSETUP.EXE	The customized driver setup program (see "Files Used to Create DRVSETUP.EXE").
ODBCINST.DLL	ODBC Administrator.
ODBCINST.HLP	Help file for the ODBC Administrator.

These files must be included on your driver installation disk. These files are copied to the temporary directory during installation. When the customized driver setup program has finished, they and the temporary directory are removed.

In addition to these files, the SETUP.EXE file must be included on your driver installation disk. This is a shell program which starts _BOOTSTP.EXE, which in turn starts your customized installation program.

A P P E N D I X A

Developing 16- and 32-Bit Applications and Drivers

Using the ODBC SDK, you can develop both 16- and 32-bit applications and drivers. The following table shows the operating systems on which these are supported:

Application	Driver	Operating Systems
16-bit[a]	16-bit	Windows 3.1 [b] Windows NT
16-bit[a]	32-bit	Windows NT
32-bit	16-bit	Win32s [c]
32-bit[a]	32-bit	Windows NT

a On Windows NT, 16-bit applications can use data sources for both 16- and 32-bit drivers, but 32-bit applications can only use data sources for 32-bit drivers.

b In this appendix, Windows 3.1 is used to represent Windows and Windows for Workgroups, versions 3.1.

c Windows NT does not support calling 16-bit DLLs from 32-bit application

Note This release of version 2.0 of the ODBC SDK does not support non-Intel versions of Windows NT.

The ODBC SDK includes the ODBC components necessary to support the configurations listed in the previous table: 16- and 32-bit versions of the Driver Manager and the ODBC Administrator, and "thunking" dynamic-link libraries (DLLs) to convert 16-bit addresses to 32-bit addresses and vice versa. During the setup process, the Setup program determines which operating system you are using and installs ODBC components required by that system. Optionally, you can choose to install the ODBC components used by all systems.

Generally speaking, porting an application or driver from 16- to 32-bits involves five types of changes:

- Changes to message-handling code
- Changes due to integers and handles being 32 bits

- Changes in calls to Windows application programming interfaces (APIs)
- Changes to make the driver thread-safe
- Changes to ODBC components

For information about the first four items, see the Microsoft Win32s and Win32 SDK documentation.

This appendix discusses the differences between 16- and 32-bit ODBC components. From an application or driver programming standpoint, the major difference between 16- and 32-bit ODBC components is that they have different filenames. From a system standpoint, the architecture of each application-driver connection are different and the tools used to manage data sources are different.

Using 16-Bit Applications with 16-Bit Drivers

You can run 16-bit applications with 16-bit drivers on Windows 3.1 and Windows NT. On Windows NT, the Windows on Windows (WOW) subsystem runs the programs in 16-bit mode and resolves 16-bit calls to the operating system. Both 16-bit applications and 16-bit drivers use the Windows API.

Architecture

Figure A.1 shows how 16-bit applications communicate with 16-bit drivers. The application calls the 16-bit Driver Manager, which in turn calls 16-bit drivers.

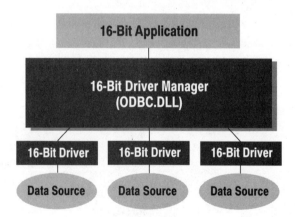

Figure A.1   Using 16-Bit Applications with 16-Bit Drivers

Administration

On Windows 3.1, you can manage data sources for 16-bit drivers through the ODBC Control Panel device or the ODBC Administrator program. The icon for the ODBC Administrator program is in the ODBC SDK 2.0 program group.

On Windows NT, you must manage data sources for 16-bit drivers through the ODBC Administrator program. (The ODBC Control Panel device on Windows NT can only be used to manage data sources for 32-bit drivers.)

Components

The ODBC SDK includes the following components for running 16-bit applications with 16-bit drivers. They are in the \ODBCSDK\REDIST16 directory.

File	Name
ODBC.DLL	16-bit Driver Manager
ODBCINST.DLL	16-bit installer DLL
ODBCADM.EXE	16-bit Administrator program
ODBCINST.HLP	Installer Help file
CTL3DV2.DLL	16-bit three-dimensional window style library

Using 16-Bit Applications with 32-Bit Drivers

You can run 16-bit applications with 32-bit drivers on Windows NT. The Windows on Windows (WOW) subsystem runs the applications in 16-bit mode and resolves 16-bit calls to the operating system. ODBC thunking DLLs resolve 16-bit calls from the application to 32-bit drivers. 16-bit applications use the Windows API and 32-bit drivers use the Win32 API.

Architecture

Figure A.2 shows how 16-bit applications communicate with 32-bit drivers. Between the 16-bit Driver Manager and the 32-bit drivers are generic thunking DLLs that converts 16-bit ODBC calls to 32-bit ODBC calls.

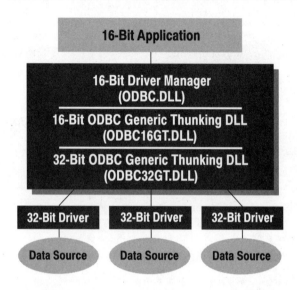

Figure A.2   Using 16-Bit Applications with 32-Bit Drivers

Administration

You can manage data sources for 32-bit drivers through the ODBC Control Panel device, the ODBC Administrator program, or the 32-Bit ODBC Administrator program. The icons for the ODBC Administrator program and the 32-Bit ODBC Administrator program are in the ODBC SDK 2.0 program group.

Figure A.3 shows how a 16-bit application calls a 32-bit driver setup DLL. Between the 16-bit installer DLL and the 32-bit driver setup DLL is a generic thunking DLL that converts 16-bit installer DLL calls to 32-bit installer DLL calls.

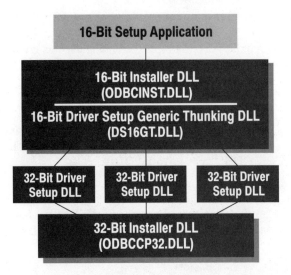

Figure A.3   Using 16-Bit Applications with 32-Bit Driver Setup DLLs

Components

The ODBC SDK includes the following components for running 16-bit applications with 32-bit drivers. The 16-bit components are in the \ODBCSDK\REDIST16 directory and the 32-bit components are in the \ODBCSDK\REDIST32 directory.

File	Name
ODBC.DLL	16-bit Driver Manager
ODBC16GT.DLL	16-bit ODBC generic thunking DLL
ODBC32GT.DLL	32-bit ODBC generic thunking DLL
ODBCINST.DLL	16-bit installer DLL
ODBCCP32.DLL	32-bit installer DLL
ODBCADM.EXE	16-bit Administrator program
ODBCAD32.EXE	32-bit Administrator program
ODBCINST.HLP	Installer Help file
DS16GT.DLL	16-bit driver setup generic thunking DLL
CTL3D32.DLL	32-bit three-dimensional window style library

Using 32-Bit Applications with 16-Bit Drivers

You can run 32-bit applications with 16-bit drivers on Windows 3.1. The Win32s operating system extension runs the applications in 32-bit mode and resolves 32-

bit calls to the operating system. ODBC thunking DLLs resolve 32-bit calls from the application to 16-bit drivers and the 16-bit installer DLL. The application must use the Win32s API and the drivers must use the Windows API.

Architecture

Figure A.4 shows how 32-bit applications communicate with 16-bit drivers. The application calls the 32-bit thunking Driver Manager, which is not a true Driver Manager but a thin layer that calls a universal thunking DLL. The thunking DLL converts 32-bit ODBC calls to 16-bit ODBC calls.

Important Do not use the 32-bit thunking Driver Manager on Windows NT. Although it has the same filename as the 32-bit Driver Manager, it is a different DLL and, if it is used, will return SQL_ERROR for **SQLAllocEnv**.

Figure A.4   Using 32-Bit Applications with 16-Bit Drivers

Administration

You can manage data sources for 16-bit drivers through the ODBC Control Panel device or the ODBC Administrator program. The icon for the ODBC Administrator program is in the ODBC SDK 2.0 program group.

Figure A.5 shows how a 32-bit application calls a 16-bit driver setup DLL. The application calls the 32-bit thunking installer DLL, which is not a true installer DLL but a thin layer that calls a universal thunking DLL. The thunking DLL converts 32-bit installer DLL calls to 16-bit installer DLL calls.

Important Do not use the 32-bit thunking installer DLL on Windows NT. Although it has the same filename as the 32-bit installer DLL, it is a different DLL.

Figure A.5   Using 32-Bit Applications with 16-Bit Driver Setup DLLs

Components

The ODBC SDK includes the following components for running 32-bit applications with 16-bit drivers. They are are in the \ODBCSDK\REDIST16 directory.

File	Name
ODBC32.DLL	32-bit thunking Driver Manager
ODBC.DLL	16-bit Driver Manager
ODBC16UT.DLL	16-bit ODBC universal thunking DLL
ODBCCP32.DLL	32-bit thunking installer DLL
ODBCINST.DLL	16-bit installer DLL
CPN16UT.DLL	16-bit installer universal thunking DLL
ODBCADM.EXE	16-bit Administrator program
ODBCINST.HLP	Installer Help file
CTL3DV2.DLL	32-bit three-dimensional window style library

Using 32-Bit Applications with 32-Bit Drivers

You can run 32-bit applications with 32-bit drivers on Windows NT. Both 32-bit applications and 32-bit drivers use the Win32 API.

Architecture

Figure A.6 shows how 32-bit applications communicate with 32-bit drivers. The application calls the 32-bit Driver Manager, which in turn calls 32-bit drivers.

Important Do not use the 32-bit Driver Manager on Win32s. Although it has the same filename as the 32-bit thunking Driver Manager, it is a different DLL and, if it is used, will return SQL_ERROR for **SQLAllocEnv**.

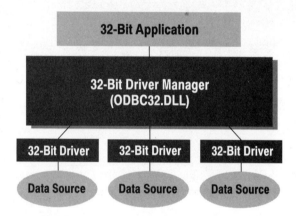

Figure A.6   Using 32-Bit Applications with 32-Bit Drivers

Administration

You can manage data sources for 32-bit drivers through the ODBC Control Panel device or the 32-Bit ODBC Administrator program. The icon for the 32-Bit ODBC Administrator program is in the ODBC SDK 2.0 program group.

Important Do not use the 32-bit installer DLL on Win32s. Although it has the same filename as the thunking 32-bit installer DLL, it is a different DLL.

Components

The ODBC SDK includes the following components for running 32-bit applications with 32-bit drivers. They are in the \ODBCSDK\REDIST32 directory..

File	Name
ODBC32.DLL	32-bit Driver Manager
ODBCCP32.DLL	32-bit installer DLL
ODBCAD32.EXE	32-bit Administrator program
ODBCINST.HLP	Installer Help file
CTL3D32.DLL	32-bit three-dimensional window style library

Upgrading from Win32s to Windows NT

If Windows 3.1 with the Win32s extension is installed on your computer, and you upgrade to Windows NT, you will have to run the ODBC SDK Setup program again to install the ODBC components for Windows NT.

Important If you do not install the ODBC components for Windows NT, your 32-bit applications will attempt to use the 32-bit thunking Driver Manager instead of the 32-bit Driver Manager. The thunking Driver Manager does not run properly on Windows NT. Under these conditions, **SQLAllocEnv** returns SQL_ERROR and all other ODBC function calls return SQL_INVALID_HANDLE.

Dual-Boot Computers

If you have a dual-boot computer that runs both Windows 3.1 and Windows NT, you must run the ODBC SDK Setup program on both Windows 3.1 and Windows NT in order to correctly install the ODBC components required by each operating system. If you do not do this, running 32-bit ODBC applications may result in the errors described in the previous section.

Index

Special Characters

A

B

C

D